If you're wondering why you should buy the new edition of *Understanding Public Policy*, here are six good reasons!

1. Detailed attention is now given to **economic policy and President Obama's *Budget of the United States Government 2010*,** including critical and comprehensive analysis of unprecedented increases in spending and deficit levels. The new material includes coverage of the bank bailouts, stimulus package, TARP program, mortgage modification, the purchase of "toxic assets," and the overall dramatic increases in federal spending. New **tax policies,** including the Obama Administration's promises to raise taxes on capital gains and increase top marginal rates, also receive extensive and refocused attention.

2. **The focus of the defense policy chapter now emphasizes "asymmetrical warfare"** — countering small-scale guerilla operations, ambushes, hidden explosives, suicide bombings, and hostage takings. In addition, three new case studies on the Gulf War, the war in Iraq, and the war in Afghanistan analyze the use of military force. A special section, **"What Went Wrong in Iraq,"** now describes the early mistakes, later stabilization, and phased withdrawal of U.S. forces in that country. The resurrected debate over **comprehensive immigration policy reform and border control i**~~...~~ depth.

3. **New coverage of energy** ~~...~~ incorporated into the envir~~...~~ discussion with treatment ~~...~~ international efforts to redu~~...~~ gas emissions, the "cap and trade" approach favored by the Obama Administration, and the role of the nuclear power industry in the energy sector.

4. **The health policy chapter has been substantially revised to include analysis of President Obama's health care plan.** This chapter explores the conflict between public and private insurance providers, the overall costs of health care in the U.S., the task of providing coverage for the uninsured, and the possibility of a national health insurance program.

5. **Education policy** is reviewed with special attention to controversies over the **No Child Left Behind** Act of 2001. President Obama's plans for teacher accountability, merit pay, and standardized testing are examined, along with coverage of teachers' and unions' concerns.

6. The Thirteenth Edition includes coverage of a number of **new Supreme Court decisions,** including the 2008 hearing of *District of Columbia vs. Heller,* affirming the Second Amendment's right of individuals to possess guns.

Understanding
Public Policy

THIRTEENTH EDITION

Understanding
Public Policy

Thomas R. Dye

McKenzie Professor
of Government, *Emeritus*
Florida State University

Longman

Boston   Columbus   Indianapolis   New York   San Francisco
Upper Saddle River   Amsterdam   Cape Town   Dubai   London   Madrid   Milan
Munich   Paris   Montreal   Toronto Delhi   Mexico City   Sao Paulo   Sydney
Hong Kong   Seoul   Singapore   Taipei   Tokyo

Editor-in-Chief: Eric Stano
Editorial Assistant: Elizabeth Alimena
Marketing Manager: Lindsey Prudhomme
Supplements Editor: Donna Garnier
Production Manager: Stacey Kulig
Project Coordination, Text Design, and Electronic Page Makeup: Pre-PressPMG
Cover Design Manager: John Callahan
Cover Image: © Achim Prill/iStockphoto
Senior Manufacturing Buyer: Dennis J. Para
Printer and Binder: Hamilton Printing Co.
Cover Printer: Lehigh-Phoenix Color

1 2 3 4 5 6 7 8 9 10—HPC—13 12 11 10

Longman
is an imprint of

ISBN-13: 978-0-205-71685-2
ISBN-10:   0-205-71685-7

Contents _____

3 | The Policymaking Process: Decision-Making Activities

4 | Criminal Justice: Rationality and Irrationality in Public Policy

5   Health and Welfare:
The Search for Rational Strategies   88

6   Education:
Group Struggles   116

7 | Economic Policy: Challenging Incrementalism   147

8 | Tax Policy: Battling the Special Interests   169

9 International Trade and Immigration: Elite–Mass Conflict

10 Energy and Environmental Policy: Externalities and Interests

Preface _____

Policy analysis is concerned with "who gets what" in politics and, more important, "why" and "what difference it makes." We are concerned not only with what policies governments pursue, but why governments pursue the policies they do, and what the consequences of these policies are.

Political science, like other scientific disciplines, has developed a number of concepts and models to help describe and explain political life. These models are not really competitive in the sense that any one could be judged as the "best." Each focuses on separate elements of politics, and each helps us understand different things about political life.

We begin with a brief description of eight analytic models in political science and the potential contribution of each to the study of public policy:

Institutional model	Group model
Process model	Elite model
Rational model	Public choice model
Incremental model	Game theory model

Most public policies are a combination of rational planning, incrementalism, competition among groups, elite preferences, public choice, political processes, and institutional influences. Throughout this volume we employ these models, both singly and in combination, to describe and explain public policy. However, certain chapters rely more on one model than another. The policy areas studied are:

Criminal justice	Environmental protection
Health and welfare	Civil rights
Education	State and local spending
Economic policy	National defense
Taxation	Homeland Security
International trade and immigration	

Any of these policy areas might be studied by using more than one model. Frequently our selection of a particular analytic model to study a specific policy area was based as much on pedagogical considerations as on anything else. We simply wanted to demonstrate how political scientists employ analytic models. Once readers are familiar with the nature and uses of analytic models in political science, they may find it interesting to explore the utility of models other than the ones selected by the author in the explanation of particular policy outcomes. For example, we use an elitist model to discuss civil rights policy, but the reader may wish to view civil rights policy from the perspective of group theory. We employ public choice theory to discuss environmental policy, but the reader might prefer studying environmental problems from the perspective of the rational model.

In short, this volume is not only an introduction to the study of public policy but also an introduction to the models political scientists use to describe and explain political life.

The new thirteenth edition of *Understanding Public Policy* focuses on the many policy changes initiated by President Barack Obama. Economic policy receives the most critical attention—the bank bailouts, the stimulus package, the TARP program, mortgage modification, the purchase of "toxic assets," and dramatic increases in federal spending. Indeed, the incremental model previously employed to describe fiscal and monetary policy is no longer descriptive of economic policy changes in Washington. The Obama Administration's *Budget of the United States Government, 2010* sets forth multiple new policy initiatives and unprecedented increases in spending and deficit levels.

Tax policy is recognized as more redistributive than in the past. Increases in top marginal rates combined with tax payments for middle- and low-income workers add to the progressivity of the Tax Code. And the Obama Administration promises to raise taxes on capital gains.

Defense policy now emphasizes "asymmetrical warfare"—countering small-scale guerrilla operations including ambushes, hidden explosives, suicide bombings, and hostage takings. Three case studies of the use of military force are provided: the Gulf War, the war in Iraq, and the war in Afghanistan. A special section, "What Went Wrong in Iraq," describes the early mistakes and later stabilization and phased withdrawal of U.S. forces from that country.

New coverage of energy policy is incorporated into the environmental policy discussion. National and international efforts to reduce greenhouse gas emissions are described, along with the "cap and trade" approach favored by the Obama Administration. Critics of cap and trade view this approach as a new energy tax. The rise and fall, and the possible renaissance, of the nuclear power industry is also reviewed.

Health care is a central focus of Obama's overall policy agenda. The objective of health care reform is to expand coverage to millions of uninsured Americans while at the same time reining in the overall costs of health care to the nation. The Obama plan features a government health insurance program—the "public option"—that would compete with private employer-based plans. It would be open to all Americans with no denials for preexisting conditions and a sliding scale of premiums based on income. Critics worry that the government program will eventually force private insurers out of business creating a single national health insurance program—"socialized medicine." While pledging to make a more efficient health-care system, the Obama plan promises heavy new federal costs to taxpayers.

The Obama Administration has resurrected debate over comprehensive reform of immigration policy. It has proposed to grant legal status and a path to citizenship to 12 to 15 million illegal aliens currently living in the United States. Critics label the proposal "amnesty" and point out that this approach had failed earlier in 1986. No immigration plan can succeed until the United States commits itself to the control of its borders.

Educational policy is reviewed with special attention to controversies over the No Child Left Behind Act of 2001. President Obama has expressed a commitment to "accountability," but teachers unions object to the Act's emphasis on pupil testing. Unions strongly object to proposals to test teachers themselves, as well as proposals to base teacher merit pay on student improvement on standardized tests.

Finally, the thirteenth edition of *Understanding Public Policy* covers a number of new Supreme Court decisions, including *District of Columbia* v. *Heller* (2008) affirming the Second Amendment's right of individuals to possess guns.

I wish to thank the following reviewers for their helpful comments: Michael Bordelon, Houston Baptist University; Euel Elliott, University of Texas at Dallas; Kim Geron, California State University—East Bay; Jon D. Holstine, American Military University; Jesse Horton, San Antonio College; Kathryn Mohrman, Arizona State University; Ira Reed, Trinity University, Washington D.C.; Bruce Rocheleau, Northern Illinois University.

Thomas R. Dye

Policy Analysis

What Governments Do, Why They Do It,
and What Difference It Makes

What is Public Policy?

This book is about public policy. It is concerned with what governments do, why they do it, and what difference it makes. It is also about political science and the ability of this academic discipline to describe, analyze, and explain public policy.

Definition of Policy.   Public policy is whatever governments choose to do or not to do.[1] Governments do many things. They regulate conflict within society; they organize society to carry on conflict with other societies; they distribute a great variety of symbolic rewards and material services to members of the society; and they extract money from society, most often in the form of taxes. Thus public policies may regulate behavior, organize bureaucracies, distribute benefits, or extract taxes—or all these things at once.

Policy Expansion and Government Growth.   Today people expect government to do a great many things for them. Indeed there is hardly any personal or societal problem for which some group will not demand a government solution—that is, a public policy designed to alleviate personal discomfort or societal unease. Over the years, as more and more Americans turned to government to resolve society's problems, government grew in size and public policy expanded in scope to encompass just about every sector of American life.

      Throughout most of the twentieth century, government grew in both absolute size and in relation to the size of the national economy. The size of the economy is usually measured by the gross domestic product (GDP), the sum of all the goods and services produced in the United States in a year (see Figure 1–1). Government spending amounted to only about 8 percent of the GDP at the beginning of the last century, and most governmental activities were carried out by state and local governments. Two world wars, the New Deal programs devised during the Great Depression of the 1930s, and the growth of the Great Society programs of the 1960s and 1970s all greatly expanded the size of government, particularly the

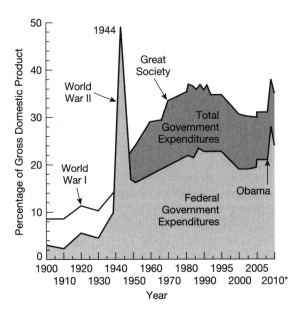

FIGURE 1–1   The Growth of Government   The size of
government can be measured in relation to the size of the
economy. Total federal, state, and local government spending
now exceeds 35 percent of the GDP, the size of the economy.
*Estimate from *Budget of the United States Government 2010.*

federal government. The rise in government growth relative to the economy leveled off during the Reagan presidency (1981–1989). The economy in the 1990s grew faster than government spending, resulting in a decline in the size of government *relative to the economy*. An economic downturn in 2000–2001, together with increased government expenditures for defense and homeland security, caused government to grow relative to the GDP.

The Obama Administration brought about a dramatic increase in federal spending, much of it in response to the recession that began in 2008. Federal spending in 2009 soared to 28 percent of the GDP; this spending included a "stimulus" package designed to jumpstart the economy (see Chapter 7). But it is expected that continued increases in federal spending under President Barack Obama will keep federal spending close to 25 percent of the GDP, the highest figure since World War II. The nation's 50 state governments and 87,000 local governments (cities, counties, towns and townships, school districts, and special districts) combined to account for about 10 percent of the GDP. Total government spending—federal, state, and local—now amounts to about 35 percent of GDP.

Scope of Public Policy.   Not everything that government does is reflected in governmental expenditures. *Regulatory activity*, for example, especially environmental regulations, imposes significant costs on individuals and businesses; these costs are *not* shown in government budgets. Nevertheless, government spending is a common indicator of governmental functions and priorities. For example, Figure 1–2 indicates that the *federal government* spends more on

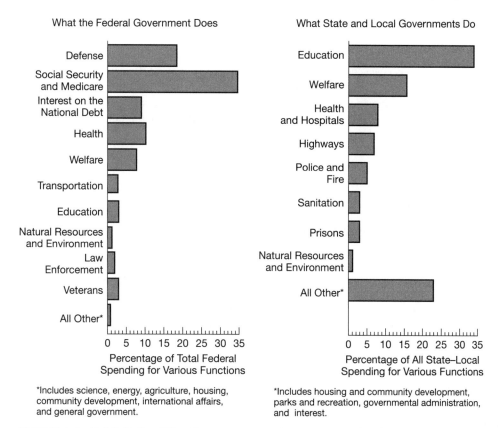

What the Federal Government Does

What State and Local Governments Do

FIGURE 1–2 Public Policy: What Governments Do Government spending figures indicate that Social Security and Medicare consume the largest share of federal spending, while education is the largest item in state and local government spending.
SOURCES: *Budget of the United States Government, 2009; Statistical Abstract of the United States, 2009.*

senior citizens—in Social Security and Medicare outlays—than on any other function, including national defense. Federal welfare and health programs account for substantial budget outlays, but federal financial support of education is very modest. *State and local governments* in the United States bear the major burden of public education. Welfare and health functions consume larger shares of their budgets than highways and law enforcement do.

Why Study Public Policy?

Political science is the study of politics—the study of "who gets what when and how."[2] It is more than the study of governmental institutions, that is, federalism, separation of powers, checks and balances, judicial review, the powers and duties of Congress, the president, and the courts. "Traditional" political science focuses primarily on these institutional arrangements as well as the philosophical justification of government. And political science is more than the study of political processes, that is, campaigns and elections, voting, lobbying, legislating, and adjudicating. Modern "behavioral" political science focuses primarily on these processes.

Political science is also the study of public policy—*the description and explanation of the causes and consequences of government activity*. This focus involves a description of the content of public policy; an analysis of the impact of social, economic, and political forces on the content of public policy; an inquiry into the effect of various institutional arrangements and political processes on public policy; and an evaluation of the consequences of public policies on society, both intended and unintended.

What Can Be Learned from Policy Analysis?

Policy analysis is finding out what governments do, why they do it, and what difference, if any, it makes. What can be learned from policy analysis?

Description.   First, we can describe public policy—we can learn what government is doing (and not doing) in welfare, defense, education, civil rights, health, the environment, taxation, and so on. A factual basis of information about national policy is really an indispensable part of everyone's education. What does the Civil Rights Act of 1964 actually say about discrimination in employment? What did the Supreme Court rule in the *Bakke* case about affirmative action programs? What is the condition of the nation's Social Security program? What do the Medicaid and Medicare programs promise for the poor and the aged? What agreements have been reached between the United States and Russia regarding nuclear weapons? What is being done to fight terrorism at home and abroad? How much money are we paying in taxes? How much money does the federal government spend each year, and what does it spend it on? These are examples of descriptive questions.

Causes.   Second, we can inquire about the causes, or determinants, of public policy. Why is public policy what it is? Why do governments do what they do? We might inquire about the effects of political institutions, processes, and behaviors on public policies (Linkage B in Figure 1–3). For example, does it make any difference in tax and spending levels whether Democrats or Republicans control the presidency and Congress? What is the impact of lobbying by the special interests on efforts to reform the federal tax system? We can also inquire about the effects of social, economic, and cultural forces in shaping public policy (Linkage C in Figure 1–3). For example: What are the effects of changing public attitudes about race on civil rights policy? What are the effects of recessions on government spending? What is the effect of an increasingly older population on the Social Security and Medicare programs? In scientific terms, when we study the *causes* of public policy, policies become the *dependent* variables, and their various political, social, economic, and cultural determinants become the *independent* variables.

Consequences.   Third, we can inquire about the consequences, or impacts, of public policy. Learning about the consequences of public policy is often referred to as *policy evaluation*. What difference, if any, does public policy make in people's lives? We might inquire about the effects of public policy on political institutions and processes (Linkage F in Figure 1–3). For example, what is the effect of the war in Iraq on Republican party fortunes

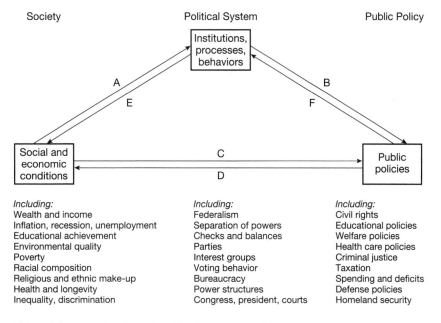

Society   Political System   Public Policy

Linkage A: What are the effects of social and economic conditions on political and governmental institutions, processes, and behaviors?

Linkage B: What are the effects of political and governmental institutions, processes, and behaviors on public policies?

Linkage C: What are the effects of social and economic conditions on public policies?

Linkage D: What are the effects (feedback) of public policies on social and economic conditions?

Linkage E: What are the effects (feedback) of political and governmental institutions, processes, and behaviors on social and economic conditions?

Linkage F: What are the effects (feedback) of public policies on political and governmental institutions, processes, and behaviors?

FIGURE 1–3 **Studying Public Policy, Its Causes and Consequences** This diagram (sometimes referred to as the "systems model") classifies societal conditions, political system characteristics, and public policies, and suggests possible linkages between them.

in Congress? What is the impact of immigration policies on the president's popularity? We also want to examine the impact of public policies on conditions in society (Linkage D in Figure 1–3). For example, does capital punishment help to deter crime? Does cutting cash welfare benefits encourage people to work? Does increased educational spending produce higher student achievement scores? In scientific terms, when we study the *consequences* of public policy, policies become the *independent* variables, and their political, social, economic, and cultural impacts on society become the *dependent* variables.

Policy Analysis and Policy Advocacy

It is important to distinguish policy analysis from policy advocacy. *Explaining* the causes and consequences of various policies is not equivalent to *prescribing* what policies governments ought to pursue. Learning *why* governments do what they do and what the consequences of their actions are is not the same as saying what governments *ought* to do or bringing about changes in what they do. Policy advocacy requires the skills of rhetoric, persuasion, organization, and activism. Policy analysis encourages scholars and students to attack critical policy issues with the tools of systematic inquiry. There is an implied assumption in policy analysis that developing scientific knowledge about the forces shaping public policy and the consequences of public policy is itself a socially relevant activity, and that policy analysis is a *prerequisite to prescription, advocacy, and activism.*

Specifically, policy analysis involves:

1. *A primary concern with explanation rather than prescription.* Policy recommendations— if they are made at all—are subordinate to description and explanation. There is an implicit judgment that understanding is a prerequisite to prescription and that understanding is best achieved through careful analysis rather than rhetoric or polemics.

2. *A rigorous search for the causes and consequences of public policies.* This search involves the use of scientific standards of inference. Sophisticated quantitative techniques may be helpful in establishing valid inferences about causes and consequences, but they are not essential.

3. *An effort to develop and test general propositions about the causes and consequences of public policy and to accumulate reliable research findings of general relevance.* The object is to develop general theories about public policy that are reliable and that apply to different government agencies and different policy areas. Policy analysts clearly prefer to develop explanations that fit more than one policy decision or case study—explanations that stand up over time in a variety of settings.

However, it must be remembered that policy issues are decided not by analysts but by political actors—elected and appointed government officials, interest groups, and occasionally even voters. Social science research often does not fare well in the political arena; it may be interpreted, misinterpreted, ignored, or even used as a weapon by political combatants. Policy analysis sometimes produces unexpected and even politically embarrassing findings. Public policies do not always work as intended. And political interests will accept, reject, or use findings to fit their own purposes.

Policy Analysis and the Quest for Solutions to America's Problems

It is questionable that policy analysis can ever "solve" America's problems. Ignorance, crime, poverty, racial conflict, inequality, poor housing, ill health, pollution, congestion, and unhappy lives have afflicted people and societies for a long time. Of course, this is no excuse for failing to work toward a society free of these maladies. But our striving for a better society should be tempered with the realization that solutions to these problems may be very difficult to find. There are many reasons for qualifying our enthusiasm for policy analysis.

Limits on Government Power. First, it is easy to exaggerate the importance, both for good and for ill, of the policies of governments. It is not clear that government policies, however ingenious, could cure all or even most of society's ills. Governments are constrained by many powerful social forces—patterns of family life, class structure, child-rearing practices, religious beliefs, and so on. These forces are not easily managed by governments, nor could they be controlled even if it seemed desirable to do so. Some of society's problems are very intractable.

Disagreement over the Problem.　Second, policy analysis cannot offer solutions to problems when there is no general agreement on what the problems are. For example, in educational policy some researchers assume that raising achievement levels (measures of verbal and quantitative abilities) is the problem to which our efforts should be directed. But educators often argue that the acquisition of verbal and quantitative skills is not the only, or even the most important, goal of the public schools. They contend that schools must also develop positive self-images among pupils of all races and backgrounds, encourage social awareness and the appreciation of multiple cultures, teach children to respect one another and to resolve their differences peacefully, raise children's awareness of the dangers of drugs and educate them about sex and sexually transmitted diseases, and so on. In other words, many educators define the problems confronting schools more broadly than raising achievement levels.

　　Policy analysis is not capable of resolving value conflicts. If there is little agreement on what values should be emphasized in educational policy, there is not much that policy research can contribute to policymaking. At best it can advise on how to achieve certain results, but it cannot determine what is truly valuable for society.

Subjectivity in Interpretation.　Third, policy analysis deals with very subjective topics and must rely on interpretation of results. Professional researchers frequently interpret the results of their analyses differently. Social science research cannot be value-free. Even the selection of the topic for research is affected by one's values about what is important in society and worthy of attention.

Limitations on Design of Human Research.　Another set of problems in systematic policy analysis centers around inherent limitations in the design of social science research. It is not really possible to conduct some forms of controlled experiments on human beings. For example, researchers cannot order children to go to poor schools for several years just to see if it adversely impacts their achievement levels. Instead, social researchers must find situations in which educational deprivation has been produced "naturally" in order to make the necessary observations about the causes of such deprivation. Because we cannot control all the factors in a real-world situation, it is difficult to pinpoint precisely what causes educational achievement or nonachievement. Moreover, even where some experimentation is permitted, human beings frequently modify their behavior simply because they know that they are being observed in an experimental situation. For example, in educational research it frequently turns out that children perform well under *any* new teaching method or curricular innovation. It is difficult to know whether the improvements observed are a product of the new teaching method or curricular improvement or merely a product of the experimental situation.

Complexity of Human Behavior.　Perhaps the most serious reservation about policy analysis is the fact that social problems are so complex that social scientists are unable to make accurate predictions about the impact of proposed policies. *Social scientists simply do not know enough about individual and group behavior to be able to give reliable advice to policymakers.* Occasionally policymakers turn to social scientists for "solutions," but social scientists do not have any. Most of society's problems are shaped by so many variables that a simple explanation of them, or remedy for them, is rarely possible. The fact that social scientists give so many contradictory recommendations is an indication of the absence of reliable scientific knowledge about social problems. Although some scholars argue that no advice is better than contradictory or inaccurate advice, policymakers still must make decisions, and it is probably better that they act in the light of whatever little knowledge social science can provide than that they act in the absence of any knowledge at all. Even if social scientists cannot predict the impact of future policies, they can at least attempt to measure the impact of current and past public policies and make this knowledge available to decision makers.

Policy Analysis as Art and Craft

Understanding public policy is both an art and a craft. It is an art because it requires insight, creativity, and imagination in identifying societal problems and describing them, in devising public policies that might alleviate them, and then in finding out whether these policies end up making things better or worse. It is a craft because these tasks usually require some knowledge of economics, political science, public administration, sociology, law, and statistics. Policy analysis is really an applied subfield of all of these traditional academic disciplines.

We doubt that there is any "model of choice" in policy analysis—that is, a single model or method that is preferable to all others and that consistently renders the best solutions to public problems. Instead we agree with political scientist Aaron Wildavsky, who wrote:

> Policy analysis is one activity for which there can be no fixed program, for policy analysis is synonymous with creativity, which may be stimulated by theory and sharpened by practice, which can be learned but not taught.[3]

Wildavsky goes on to warn students that solutions to great public questions are not to be expected:

> In large part, it must be admitted, knowledge is negative. It tells us what we cannot do, where we cannot go, wherein we have been wrong, but not necessarily how to correct these errors. After all, if current efforts were judged wholly satisfactory, there would be little need for analysis and less for analysts.

There is no one model of choice to be found in this book, but if anyone wants to begin a debate about different ways of understanding public policy, this book is a good place to begin.

Notes

1. This book discourages elaborate academic discussions of the definition of public policy—we say simply that public policy is whatever governments choose to do or not to do. Even the most elaborate definitions of public policy, on close examination, seem to boil down to the same thing. For example, political scientist

David Easton defines public policy as "the authoritative allocation of values for the whole society"—but it turns out that only the government can "authoritatively" act on the "whole" society, and everything the government chooses to do or not to do results in the "allocation of values."

Political scientist Harold Lasswell and philosopher Abraham Kaplan define policy as a "a projected program of goals, values, and practices," and political scientist Carl Friedrick says, "It is essential for the policy concept that there be a goal, objective, or purpose." These definitions imply a difference between specific government actions and an overall program of action toward a given goal. But the problem raised in insisting that government actions must have goals in order to be labeled "policy" is that we can never be sure whether or not a particular action has a goal, or if it does, what that goal is. Some people may assume that if a government chooses to do something there must be a goal, objective, or purpose, but all we can really observe is what governments choose to do or not to do. Realistically, our notion of public policy must include *all actions* of government, and not what governments or officials say they are going to do. We may wish that governments act in a "purposeful, goal-oriented" fashion, but we know that all too frequently they do not.

Still another approach to defining public policy is to break down this general notion into various component parts. Political scientist Charles O. Jones asks that we consider the distinction among various proposals (specified means for achieving goals), programs (authorized means for achieving goals), decisions (specific actions taken to implement programs), and effects (the measurable impacts of programs). But again we have the problem of assuming that decisions, programs, goals, and effects are linked. Certainly in many policy areas we will see that the decisions of government have little to do with announced "programs," and neither are connected with national "goals." It may be unfortunate that our government does not function neatly to link goals, programs, decisions, and effects, but as a matter of fact it does not.

So we shall stick with our simple definition: *public policy is whatever governments choose to do or not to do.* Note that we are focusing not only on government action but also on government inaction, that is, what government chooses *not* to do. We contend that government *in*action can have just as great an impact on society as government action.

See David Easton, *The Political System* (New York: Knopf, 1953), p. 129; Harold D. Lasswell and Abraham Kaplan, *Power and Society* (New Haven, CT: Yale University Press, 1970), p. 71; Carl J. Friedrich, *Man and His Government* (New York: McGraw-Hill, 1963), p. 70; Charles O. Jones, *An Introduction to the Study of Public Policy* (Boston: Duxbury, 1977), p. 4.

2. Harold Lasswell, *Politics: Who Gets What, When and How* (New York: McGraw Hill, 1936).

3. Aaron Wildavsky, *Speaking Truth to Power* (New York: John Wiley, 1979), p. 3.

Bibliography

ANDERSON, JAMES E. *Public Policymaking*, 6th ed. Boston: Houghton Mifflin, 2006.

COCHRAN, CLARKE E., et al. *American Public Policy: An Introduction*, 8th ed. Belmont, CA: Wadsworth, 2006.

DUNN, WILLIAM N. *Public Policy Analysis*, 3rd ed. Upper Saddle River, NJ: Prentice Hall, 2004.

HEINEMAN, ROBERT A., WILLIAM T. BLUHM, STEVEN A. PETERSON, and EDWARD N. KEARNY. *The World of the Policy Analyst*. New York: Chatham House, 2000.

KRAFT, MICHAEL E., and SCOTT R. FURLONG. *Public Policy: Politics, Analysis and Alternatives,* 2nd ed. Washington, DC: CQ Press, 2008.

PETERS, B. GUY. *American Public Policy: Promise and Performance*, 7th ed. Washington, DC: CQ Press, 2008.

RUSHEFSKY, MARK E. *Public Policy in the United States*, 4th ed. Armonk, NY: M. E. Sharpe, 2008.

WILDAVSKY, AARON. *Speaking Truth to Power*. New York: John Wiley, 1979.

Web Sites

OFFICE OF THE PRESIDENT. White House home page, with president's policy positions, speeches, press releases, etc. *www.whitehouse.gov*

U.S. HOUSE OF REPRESENTATIVES. Official House Web site, with links to individual House members' Web sites. *www.house.gov*

U.S. SENATE. Official Senate Web site, with links to individual senators' Web sites. *www.senate.gov*

U.S. CONGRESS ON THE IINTERNET. Library of Congress Thomas search engine for finding bills and tracing their progress through Congress. *http://thomas.loc.gov*

FEDERAL STATISTICS ONLINE. Links to federal statistical reports, listed by topic A–Z. *www.fedstats.gov*

U.S. CENSUS BUREAU. The official site of the Census Bureau, with access to all current reports—population, income and poverty, government finances, etc. *www.census.gov*

FIRST GOV. U.S. government's official portal to all independent agencies and government corporations. *www.firstgov.gov*

FEDERAL JUDICIARY. U.S. judiciary official site, with links to all federal courts. *www.uscourts.gov*

SUPREME COURT CASES. Compilation of all key U.S. Supreme Court decisions. *www.supct.law.cornell.edu*

LIBRARY OF CONGRESS. Compilation of the laws of the United States. *http://thomas.loc.gov*

<table>
<tr><td><h1>2</h1></td></tr>
</table>

Models of Politics

Some Help in Thinking About Public Policy

Models for Policy Analysis

A model is a simplified representation of some aspect of the real world. It may be an actual physical representation—a model airplane, for example, or the tabletop buildings that planners and architects use to show how things will look when proposed projects are completed. Or a model may be a diagram—a road map, for example, or a flow chart that political scientists use to show how a bill becomes law.

Uses of Models.   The models we shall use in studying policy are *conceptual models*. These are word models that try to

- Simplify and clarify our thinking about politics and public policy.
- Identify important aspects of policy problems.
- Help us to communicate with each other by focusing on essential features of political life.
- Direct our efforts to understand public policy better by suggesting what is important and what is unimportant.
- Suggest explanations for public policy and predict its consequences.

Selected Policy Models.   Over the years, political science, like other scientific disciplines, has developed a number of models to help us understand political life. Throughout this volume we will try to see whether these models have any utility in the study of public policy. Specifically, we want to examine public policy from the perspective of the following models:

- Institutional model
- Process model
- Rational model

- Incremental model
- Group model
- Elite model
- Public choice model
- Game theory model

Each of these terms identifies a major conceptual model that can be found in the literature of political science. None of these models was derived especially to study public policy, yet each offers a separate way of thinking about policy and even suggests some of the general causes and consequences of public policy.

These models are not competitive in the sense that any one of them could be judged "best." Each one provides a separate focus on political life, and each can help us to understand different things about public policy. Although some policies appear at first glance to lend themselves to explanation by one particular model, most policies are a combination of rational planning, incrementalism, interest group activity, elite preferences, game playing, public choice, political processes, and institutional influences. In later chapters these models will be employed, singularly and in combination, to describe and explain specific policies. Following is a brief description of each model, with particular attention to the separate ways in which public policy can be viewed.

Institutionalism: Policy as Institutional Output

Government institutions have long been a central focus of political science. Traditionally, political science was defined as the study of government institutions. Political activities generally center around particular government institutions—Congress, the presidency, courts, bureaucracies, states, municipalities, and so on. Public policy is authoritatively determined, implemented, and enforced by these institutions.

The relationship between public policy and government institutions is very close. Strictly speaking, a policy does not become a *public* policy until it is adopted, implemented, and enforced by some government institution. Government institutions give public policy three distinctive characteristics. First, government lends *legitimacy* to policies. Government policies are generally regarded as legal obligations that command the loyalty of citizens. People may regard the policies of other groups and associations in society—corporations, churches, professional organizations, civic associations, and so forth—as important and even binding. But only government policies involve legal obligations. Second, government policies involve *universality*. Only government policies extend to all people in a society; the policies of other groups or organizations reach only a part of the society. Finally, government monopolizes *coercion* in society—only government can legitimately imprison violators of its policies. The sanctions that can be imposed by other groups or organizations in society are more limited. It is precisely this ability of government to command the loyalty of all its citizens, to enact policies governing the whole society, and to monopolize the legitimate use of force that encourages individuals and groups to work for enactment of their preferences into policy.

Institutionalism: Applying the Model

In Chapter 12, "American Federalism: Institutional Arrangements and Public Policy," we shall examine some of the problems of American federalism—the distribution of money and power among federal, state, and local governments.

The Constitution of the United States establishes the fundamental institutional structure for policymaking. It is "the supreme Law of the Land" (Article VI). Its key structural components—separation of powers and checks and balances among the legislative, executive, and judicial branches of the national government—together with federalism—dividing power between the nation and the states—were designed by the Founders in part "to form a more perfect Union." These institutional arrangements have changed significantly over more than two centuries, yet no other written constitution in the world has remained in place for so long. Throughout this volume we will be concerned with the effect of these institutional arrangements on public policy. And in Chapter 12 we shall explore in some detail the effect of federalism.

Federalism recognizes that both the national government and the state governments derive independent legal authority from their own citizens (Figure 2–1): both can pass their own laws, levy their own taxes, and maintain their own courts. The states also have important roles in the selection of national officeholders—in the apportionment of congressional seats, in the allocation of two U.S. senators to each state, and in the allocation of electoral

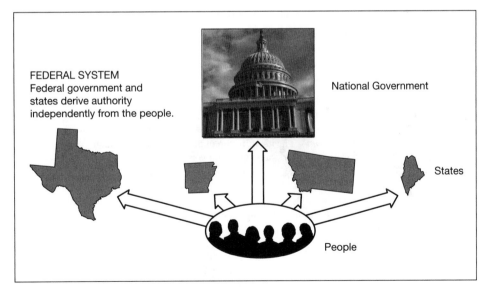

FIGURE 2–1 An Institutional Model: American Federalism Governmental institutional arrangements affect public policy, including federalism—the distribution of money and power among federal, state, and local governments.

votes for president. Most important, perhaps, both the Congress and three-quarters of states must consent to any changes in the Constitution itself.

Process: Policy as Political Activity

Today political processes and behaviors are a central focus of political science. Since World War II, modern "behavioral" political science has studied the activities of voters, interest groups, legislators, presidents, bureaucrats, judges, and other political actors. One of the main purposes has been to discover patterns of activities—or "processes." Political scientists with an interest in policy have grouped various activities according to their relationship with public policy. The result is a set of *policy processes*, which usually follow the general outline in Table 2–1. In short, one can view the policy process as a series of political activities—problem identification, agenda setting, formulation, legitimation, implementation, and evaluation.

  The process model is useful in helping us to understand the various activities involved in policymaking. We want to keep in mind that *policymaking* involves agenda setting (capturing the attention of policymakers), formulating proposals (devising and selecting policy options), legitimating policy (developing political support; winning congressional, presidential, or court approval), implementing policy (creating bureaucracies, spending money, enforcing laws), and evaluating policy (finding out whether policies work, whether they are popular).

Processes: Applying the Model

Political processes and behaviors are considered in each of the policy areas studied in this book. Additional commentary on the impact of political activity on public policy is found in Chapter 3, "The Policymaking Process: Decision-Making Activities."

TABLE 2–1   The Policy Process

- *Problem Identificaton.*   The identificaton of policy problems through demand from individuals and groups for government action.
- *Agenda Setting.*   Focusing the attention of the mass media and public officials on specific public problems to decide what will be decided.
- *Policy Formulation.*   The development of policy proposals by interest groups, White House staff, congressional committees, and think tanks.
- *Policy Legitimation.*   The selection and enactment of policies through actions by Congress, the president, and the courts.
- *Policy Implementation.*   The implementation of policies through government bureaucracies, public expenditures, regulations, and other activities of executive agencies.
- *Policy Evaluation.*   The evaluation of policies by government agencies themselves, outside consultants, the media, and the general public.

Rationalism: Policy as Maximum Social Gain

A rational policy is one that achieves "maximum social gain"; that is, governments should choose policies resulting in gains to society that exceed costs by the greatest amount, and governments should refrain from policies if costs exceed gains.

Note that there are really two important guidelines in this definition of maximum social gain. First, no policy should be adopted if its costs exceed its benefits. Second, among policy alternatives, decision makers should choose the policy that produces the greatest benefit over cost. In other words, a policy is rational when the difference between the values it achieves and the values it sacrifices is positive and greater than any other policy alternative. One should *not* view rationalism in a narrow dollars-and-cents framework, in which basic social values are sacrificed for dollar savings. Rationalism involves the calculation of *all* social, political, and economic values sacrificed or achieved by a public policy, not just those that can be measured in dollars.

To select a rational policy, policymakers must (1) know all the society's value preferences and their relative weights, (2) know all the policy alternatives available, (3) know all the consequences of each policy alternative, (4) calculate the ratio of benefits to costs for each policy alternative, and (5) select the most efficient policy alternative. This rationality assumes that the value preferences of *society as a whole* can be known and weighted. It is not enough to know and weigh the values of some groups and not others. There must be a complete understanding of societal values. Rational policymaking also requires *information* about alternative policies, the *predictive capacity* to foresee accurately the consequences of alternate policies, and the *intelligence* to calculate correctly the ratio of costs to benefits. Finally, rational policymaking requires a *decision-making system* that facilitates rationality in policy formation. A diagram of such a system is shown in Figure 2–2.

However, there are many barriers to rational decision making, so many, in fact, that it rarely takes place at all in government. Yet the model remains important for analytic purposes because it helps to identify barriers to rationality. It assists in posing the question, Why is policymaking *not* a more rational process? At the outset we can hypothesize several important *obstacles to rational policymaking*:

- Many conflicting benefits and costs cannot be compared or weighted; for example, it is difficult to compare or weigh the value of individual life against the costs of regulation.

Rationalism: Applying the Model

Chapter 4, "Criminal Justice: Rationality and Irrationality in Public Policy," shows that rational policies to deter crime—policies ensuring certainty, swiftness, and severity of punishment—have seldom been implemented. The problems of achieving rationality in public policy are also discussed in Chapter 5, "Health and Welfare: The Search for Rational Strategies." We will consider the general design of alternative strategies in dealing with poverty, health, and welfare. We will observe how these strategies are implemented in public policy, and we will analyze some of the obstacles to the achievement of rationality in public policy.

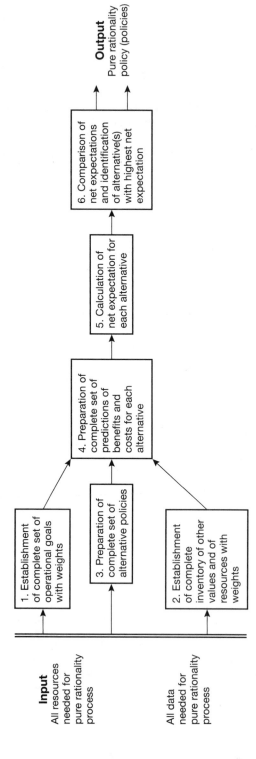

FIGURE 2–2   A Rational Model of a Decision System   The rational model assumes complete agreement on goals, knowledge of alternative policies, and the ability to calculate and select the policies with the greatest benefits and least costs.

- Policymakers may not be motivated to make decisions on the basis of societal goals but instead try to maximize their own rewards—power, status, reelection, and money.

- Policymakers may not be motivated to maximize net social gain but merely to satisfy demands for progress; they do not search until they find "the one best way"; instead they halt their search when they find an alternative that will work.

- Large investments in existing programs and policies (sunk costs) prevent policymakers from reconsidering alternatives foreclosed by previous decisions.

- There are innumerable barriers to collecting all the information required to know all possible policy alternatives and the consequences of each, including the cost of information gathering, the availability of the information, and the time involved in its collection.

- Neither the predictive capacities of the social and behavioral sciences nor those of the physical and biological sciences are sufficiently advanced to enable policymakers to understand the full benefits or costs of each policy alternative.

- Policymakers, even with the most advanced computerized analytical techniques, do not have sufficient intelligence to calculate accurately costs and benefits when a large number of diverse political, social, economic, and cultural values are at stake.

- Uncertainty about the consequences of various policy alternatives compels policymakers to stick as closely as possible to previous policies to reduce the likelihood of unanticipated negative consequences.

- The segmentalized nature of policymaking in large bureaucracies makes it difficult to coordinate decision making so that the input of all the various specialists is brought to bear at the point of decision.

Incrementalism: Policy as Variations on the Past

Incrementalism views public policy as a continuation of past government activities with only incremental modifications. Political scientist Charles E. Lindblom first presented the incremental model in the course of a critique of the rational model of decision making.[1] According to Lindblom, decision makers do *not* annually review the whole range of existing and proposed policies, identify societal goals, research the benefits and costs of alternative policies in achieving these goals, rank order of preferences for each policy alternative in terms of the maximum net benefits, and then make a selection on the basis of all relevant information. On the contrary, constraints of time, information, and cost prevent policymakers from identifying the full range of policy alternatives and their consequences. Constraints of politics prevent the establishment of clear-cut societal goals and the accurate calculation of costs and benefits. The incremental model recognizes the impractical nature of "rational-comprehensive" policy-making, and describes a more conservative process of decision making.

Incrementalism is conservative in that existing programs, policies, and expenditures are considered as a *base*, and attention is concentrated on new programs and policies and on increases, decreases, or modifications of current programs. (For example, budgetary policy for any government activity or program for 2012 might be viewed incrementally, as shown in

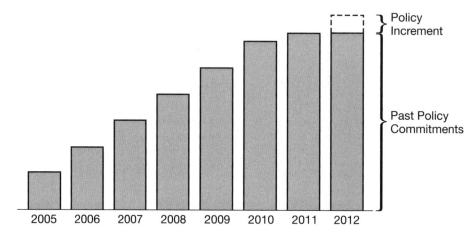

FIGURE 2–3   The Incremental Model The incremental model assumes that policymakers rarely examine past policy commitments, but rather focus their attention on changes in policies and expenditures.

Figure 2–3.) Policymakers generally accept the legitimacy of established programs and tacitly agree to continue previous policies.

They do this because they do not have the time, information, or money to investigate all the alternatives to existing policy. The cost of collecting all this information is too great. Policymakers do not have sufficient predictive capacities to know what all the consequences of each alternative will be. Nor are they able to calculate cost–benefit ratios for alternative policies when many diverse political, social, economic, and cultural values are at stake. Thus completely "rational" policy may turn out to be "inefficient" (despite the contradiction in terms) if the time and cost of developing a rational policy are excessive.

Moreover, incrementalism is politically expedient. Agreement comes easier in policy-making when the items in dispute are only increases or decreases in budgets or modifications to existing programs. Conflict is heightened when decision making focuses on major policy shifts involving great gains or losses, or "all-or-nothing," "yes-or-no" policy decisions. Because the political tension involved in getting new programs or policies passed every year would be very great, past policy victories are continued into future years unless there is a substantial political realignment. Thus, incrementalism is important in reducing conflict, maintaining stability, and preserving the political system itself.

But *the incremental model may fail when policymakers are confronted with crises.* When faced with potential collapse of the nation's financial markets in 2008, the president, Congress, the Treasury Department, and the Federal Reserve Board came together to agree on an

---

Incrementalism: Applying the Model

Special attention to incrementalism is given in the discussion of government budgeting in Chapter 7, "Economic Policy: Incremental and Nonincremental Policymaking."

unprecedented, *nonincremental* expansion of federal power (see Chapter 7, "Economic Policy: Incremental and Nonincremental Policymaking"). Overall, federal spending and deficits increased dramatically, well beyond any levels that might have been predicted by the incremental model. The Treasury Department was given unprecedented authority and $700 billion to "bail out" the nation's major financial institutions. The Federal Reserve Board reduced interest rates to their lowest in history and provided unprecedented amounts of credit to the financial system. Congress itself passed a "stimulus package," the largest single spending bill in the nation's history. Incrementalism was abandoned.

Group Theory: Policy as Equilibrium in the Group Struggle

Group theory begins with the proposition that interaction among groups is the central fact of politics.[2] Individuals with common interests band together formally or informally to press their demands on government. According to political scientist David Truman, an interest group is "a shared-attitude group that makes certain claims upon other groups in the society"; such a group becomes political "if and when it makes a claim through or upon any of the institutions of government."[3] Individuals are important in politics only when they act as part of, or on behalf of, group interests. The group becomes the essential bridge between the individual and the government. Politics is really the struggle among groups to influence public policy. The task of the political system is to *manage group conflict* by (1) establishing rules of the game in the group struggle, (2) arranging compromises and balancing interests, (3) enacting compromises in the form of public policy, and (4) enforcing these compromises.

According to group theorists, public policy at any given time is the equilibrium reached in the group struggle (see Figure 2–4). This equilibrium is determined by the relative influence of various interest groups. Changes in the relative influence of any interest groups

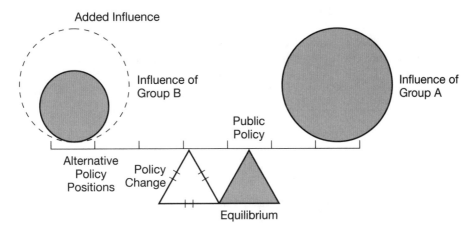

FIGURE 2–4 The Group Model The group model assumes that public policy is a balance of interest group influence; policies change when particular interest groups gain or lose influence.

Group Theory: Applying the Model

Throughout this volume we will describe struggles over public policy. In Chapter 6, "Education: Group Struggles," we will examine group conflict over public policy in the discussions of education and school issues. In Chapter 8, "Tax Policy: Battling the Special Interests," we will observe the power of interest groups in obtaining special treatments in the tax code and obstructing efforts to reform the nation's tax laws.

---

can be expected to result in changes in public policy; policy will move in the direction desired by the groups gaining influence and away from the desires of groups losing influence. The influence of groups is determined by their numbers, wealth, organizational strength, leadership, access to decision makers, and internal cohesion.[4]

The whole interest group system—the political system itself—is held together in equilibrium by several forces. First, there is a large, nearly universal, *latent group* in American society that supports the constitutional system and prevailing rules of the game. This group is not always visible but can be activated to administer overwhelming rebuke to any group that attacks the system and threatens to destroy the equilibrium.

Second, *overlapping group membership* helps to maintain the equilibrium by preventing any one group from moving too far from prevailing values. Individuals who belong to any one group also belong to other groups, and this fact moderates the demands of groups who must avoid offending their members who have other group affiliations.

Finally, the *checking and balancing resulting from group competition* also helps to maintain equilibrium in the system. No single group constitutes a majority in American society. The power of each group is checked by the power of competing groups. "Countervailing" centers of power function to check the influence of any single group and protect the individual from exploitation.

Elite Theory: Policy as Elite Preference

Public policy may also be viewed as the preferences and values of a governing elite.[5] Although it is often asserted that public policy reflects the demands of "the people," this may express the myth rather than the reality of American democracy. Elite theory suggests that the people are apathetic and ill informed about public policy, that elites actually shape mass opinion on policy questions more than masses shape elite opinion. Thus, public policy really turns out to be the preferences of elites. Public officials and administrators merely carry out the policies decided on by the elite. Policies flow downward from elites to masses; they do not arise from mass demands (see Figure 2–5).

Elite theory can be summarized briefly as follows:

- Society is divided into the few who have power and the many who do not. Only a small number of persons allocate values for society; the masses do not decide public policy.

- The few who govern are not typical of the masses who are governed. Elites are drawn disproportionately from the upper socioeconomic strata of society.

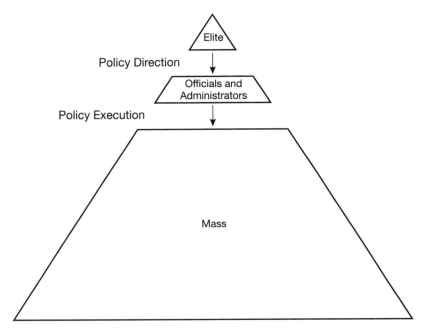

FIGURE 2–5   The Elite Model The elite model implies that public policy does not flow upward from demands by the people, but rather downward from the interests, values, and preferences of elites.

- The movement of nonelites to elite positions must be slow and continuous to maintain stability and avoid revolution. Only nonelites who have accepted the basic elite consensus can be admitted to governing circles.
- Elites share consensus in behalf of the basic values of the social system and the preservation of the system. In America, the bases of elite consensus are the sanctity of private property, limited government, and individual liberty.
- Public policy does not reflect the demands of masses but rather the prevailing values of the elite. Changes in public policy will be incremental rather than revolutionary.
- Active elites are subject to relatively little direct influence from apathetic masses. Elites influence masses more than masses influence elites.

Elite Theory: Applying the Model

Chapter 9, "International Trade and Immigration: Elite-Mass Conflict," expands on the elite model by arguing that when elite preferences differ from those of the masses, the preferences of elites prevail. Chapter 11, "Civil Rights: Elite and Mass Interaction," portrays the civil rights movement as an effort by established national elites to extend equality of opportunity to blacks. Opposition to civil rights policies is found among white masses in the states.

What are the implications of elite theory for policy analysis? Elitism implies that public policy does not reflect the demands of the people so much as it does the interests, values, and preferences of elites. Therefore, change and innovations in public policy come about as a result of redefinitions by elites of their own values. Because of the general conservatism of elites—that is, their interest in preserving the system—change in public policy will be incremental rather than revolutionary. Changes in the political system occur when events threaten the system, and elites, acting on the basis of enlightened self-interest, institute reforms to preserve the system and their place in it. The values of elites may be very "public regarding." A sense of *noblesse oblige* may permeate elite values, and the welfare of the masses may be an important element in elite decision making. Elitism does not necessarily mean that public policy will be hostile toward mass welfare but only that the responsibility for mass welfare rests on the shoulders of elites, not masses.

Public Choice Theory: Policy as Collective Decision Making by Self-Interested Individuals

Public choice is the economic study of nonmarket decision making, especially the application of economic analyses to public policymaking. Traditionally, economics studied behavior in the marketplace and assumed that individuals pursued their private interests; political science studied behavior in the public arena and assumed that individuals pursued their own notion of the public interest. Thus, separate versions of human motivation developed in economics and political science: the idea of *homo economicus* assumed a self-interested actor seeking to maximize personal benefits; that of *homo politicus* assumed a public-spirited actor seeking to maximize societal welfare.

But public choice theory challenges the notion that individuals act differently in politics than they do in the marketplace. This theory assumes that all political actors—voters, taxpayers, candidates, legislators, bureaucrats, interest groups, parties, and governments—*seek to maximize their personal benefits in politics as well as in the marketplace.* James Buchanan, the Nobel Prize–winning economist and leading scholar in modern public choice theory, argues that individuals come together in politics for their own mutual benefit, just as they come together in the marketplace; and by agreement (contract) among themselves they can enhance their own well-being, in the same way as by trading in the marketplace.[6] In short, people pursue their self-interest in both politics and the marketplace, but even with selfish motives they can mutually benefit through collective decision making.

Government itself arises from a *social contract* among individuals who agree for their mutual benefit to obey laws and support the government in exchange for protection of their own lives, liberties, and property. Thus, public choice theorists claim to be intellectual heirs to the English political philosopher John Locke, as well as to Thomas Jefferson, who incorporated this social contract notion into the American Declaration of Independence. Enlightened self-interest leads individuals to a constitutional contract establishing a government to protect life, liberty, and property.

Public choice theory recognizes that government must perform certain functions that the marketplace is unable to handle, that is, it must remedy certain "market failures." First, government must provide *public goods*—goods and services that must be supplied to everyone if they are supplied to anyone. The market cannot provide public goods because their costs

---

Public Choice: Applying the Model

The public choice theory is employed in Chapter 10, "Energy and Environmental Policy: Externalities and Interests," to aid in recognizing environmental pollution as a problem in the control of externalities in human activity. Public choice theory also helps us to understand the behavior of environmental interest groups in dramatizing and publicizing their cause.

---

exceed their value to any single buyer, and a single buyer would not be in a position to keep nonbuyers from using it. National defense is the most common example: protection from foreign invasion is too expensive for a single person to buy, and once it is provided no one can be excluded from its benefits. So people must act collectively through government to provide for the common defense. Second, *externalities* are another recognized market failure and justification for government intervention. An externality occurs when an activity of one individual, firm, or local government imposes uncompensated costs on others. The most common examples are air and water pollution: the discharge of air and water pollutants imposes costs on others. Governments respond by either regulating the activities that produce externalities or imposing penalties (fines) on these activities to compensate for their costs to society.

Public choice theory helps to explain why political parties and candidates generally fail to offer clear policy alternatives in election campaigns. Parties and candidates are not interested in advancing principles but rather in winning elections. They formulate their policy positions to win elections; they do not win elections to formulate policy. Thus each party and candidate seeks policy positions that will attract the greatest number of voters.[7] *Given a unimodal distribution of opinion on any policy question* (see Figure 2–6), *parties and candidates*

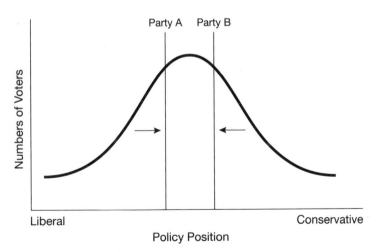

FIGURE 2–6 Public Choice: A Vote-Maximizing Model of Party Competition Public choice theory assumes that individuals and organizations seek to maximize their own benefits in politics; for example, parties and candidates whose policy views may be distinctly liberal or conservative move to the center at election time to win the most votes.

will move toward the center to maximize votes. Only "ideologues" (irrational, ideologically motivated people) ignore the vote-maximizing centrist strategy.

Game Theory: Policy as Rational Choice in Competitive Situations

Game theory is the study of decisions in situations in which two or more *rational* participants have choices to make and the outcome depends on the choices made by each. It is applied to areas in policymaking in which there is no independently "best" choice that one can make—in which the "best" outcomes depend upon what others do.

The idea of "game" is that rational decision makers are involved in choices that are interdependent. "Players" must adjust their conduct to reflect not only their own desires and abilities but also their expectations about what others will do. Perhaps the connotation of a "game" is unfortunate, suggesting that game theory is not really appropriate for serious conflict situations. But just the opposite is true: game theory can be applied to decisions about war and peace, the use of nuclear weapons, international diplomacy, bargaining and coalition building in Congress or the United Nations, and a variety of other important political situations. A "player" may be an individual, a group, or a national government—indeed, anybody with well-defined goals who is capable of rational action.

Consider the game of "chicken." Two adolescents drive their cars toward each other at a high speed, each with one set of wheels on the center line of the highway. If neither veers off course they will crash. Whoever veers is "chicken." Both drivers prefer to avoid death, but they also want to avoid the "dishonor" of being "chicken." The outcome depends on what both drivers do, and each driver must try to predict how the other will behave. This form of "brinkmanship" is common in international relations (see Figure 2–7). Inspection

The game theorist himself or herself supplies the numerical values to the payoffs. If Driver A chooses to stay on course and Driver B chooses to stay on course also, the result might be scored as –10 for both players, who wreck their cars. But if Driver A chooses to stay on course and Driver B veers, then Driver A might get +5 ("courage") and Driver B –5 ("dishonor"). If Driver A veers but Driver B stays on course, the results would be reversed. If both veer, each is dishonored slightly (–1), but not as much as when one or the other stayed on course.

		DRIVER A'S CHOICES	
		Stay on Course	Veer
DRIVER B'S CHOICES	Stay on course	A: –10 B: –10	A: –5 B: +5
	Veer	A: +5 B: –5	A: –1 B: –1

FIGURE 2–7 A Game-Theoretic Matrix for the Game of Chicken   Game theory suggests that policymakers, or "players," adjust their conduct to reflect not only their own preferences but also the likely choices of opponents.

Game Theory: Applying the Model

Game theory is frequently applied in international conflicts. We will explore the utility of game theory, especially the notion of deterrence, in Chapter 13, "Defense Policy: Strategies for Serious Games." We will also explore the weakness of deterrence in defending against terrorism in Chapter 14, "Homeland Security: Terrorism and Nondeterrable Threats."

---

of the payoff matrix suggests that it would be better for both drivers to veer in order to minimize the possibility of a great loss (−10). But the matrix is too simple. One or both players may place a different value on the outcomes than is suggested by the numbers. For example, one player may prefer death to dishonor in the game. Each player must try to calculate the values of the other, and neither has complete information about the values of the opponent. Moreover, bluffing or the deliberate misrepresentation of one's values or resources to an opponent is always a possibility. For example, a possible strategy in the game of chicken is to allow your opponent to see you drink heavily before the game, stumble drunkenly toward your car, and mumble something about having lived long enough in this rotten world. The effect of this communication on your opponent may increase his or her estimate of your likelihood of staying on course, and hence provide incentive for your opponent to veer and allow you to win.

An important component of game theory is the notion of *deterrence*. Deterrence is the effort to prevent an opponent from undertaking an action by inspiring fear of the consequences of the action. Players engage in deterrence when they threaten their opponents with retaliatory actions that promise to impose costs on their opponents that are far in excess of any benefits their opponents might envision by taking these actions. *Deterrence is really a psychological defense: it tries to prevent opponents from undertaking a particular action by creating in their minds the fear of costly retaliation.*

The success of deterrence depends on the credibility of the retaliatory threat and on the rationality of the opponent. Opponents must truly believe that their actions will result in retaliatory responses that inflict unacceptable costs on themselves, their people, or their nation. Opponents who do not really believe a retaliatory attack will occur are not deterred. Moreover, opponents must be *rational*—opponents must weigh the potential costs and benefits of their actions and choose a course of action that does not result in costs that exceed gains. Opponents who are irrational—who do not consider the costs of their actions to themselves, or their people, or their nation—are not deterred.

Models: How to Tell if They Are Helping or Not

A model is merely an abstraction or representation of political life. When we think of political systems or elites or groups or rational decision making or incrementalism or games, we are abstracting from the real world in an attempt to simplify, clarify, and understand what is really important about politics. Before we begin our study of public policy, let us set forth some general criteria for evaluating the usefulness of concepts and models.

Order and Simplify Reality.   Certainly the utility of a model lies in its ability to order and simplify political life so that we can think about it more clearly and understand the relationships we find in the real world. Yet too much simplification can lead to inaccuracies in our thinking about reality. On the one hand, if a concept is too narrow or identifies only superficial phenomena, we may not be able to use it to explain public policy. On the other hand, if a concept is too broad and suggests overly complex relationships, it may become so complicated and unmanageable that it is not really an aid to understanding. In other words, some theories of politics may be too complex to be helpful, while others may be too simplistic.

Identify What Is Significant.   A model should also identify the really significant aspects of public policy. It should direct attention away from irrelevant variables or circumstances and focus on the real causes and significant consequences of public policy. Of course, what is "real," "relevant," or "significant" is to some extent a function of an individual's personal values. But we can all agree that the utility of a concept is related to its ability to identify what it is that is really important about politics.

Be Congruent with Reality.   Generally, a model should be congruent with reality—that is, it ought to have real empirical referents. We would expect to have difficulty with a concept that identifies a process that does not really occur or symbolizes phenomena that do not exist in the real world. However, we must not be too quick to dismiss unrealistic concepts *if* they succeed in directing our attention to why they are unrealistic. For example, no one contends that government decision making is completely rational—public officials do not always act to maximize societal values and minimize societal costs. Yet the concept of rational decision making may still be useful, albeit unrealistic, if it makes us realize how irrational government decision making really is and prompts us to inquire why.

Provide Meaningful Communication.   A concept or model should also communicate something meaningful. If too many people disagree over the meaning of a concept, its utility in communication is diminished. For example, if no one really agrees on what constitutes an elite, the concept of an elite does not mean the same thing to everyone. If one defines an elite as a group of democratically elected public officials who are representative of the general public, one is communicating a different idea in using the term than one who defines an elite as an unrepresentative minority that makes decisions for society based on its own interests.

Direct Inquiry and Research.   A model should help to direct inquiry and research into public policy. A concept should be operational—that is, it should refer directly to real-world phenomena that can be observed, measured, and verified. A concept, or a series of interrelated concepts (which we refer to as a model), should suggest relationships in the real world that can be tested and verified. If there is no way to prove or disprove the ideas suggested by a concept, the concept is not really useful in developing a science of politics.

Suggest Explanations.   Finally, a model should suggest an explanation of public policy. It should suggest hypotheses about the causes and consequences of public policy—hypotheses that can be tested against real-world data. A model that merely describes public policy is not as useful as one that explains public policy, or at least suggests some possible explanations.

Notes

1. See Charles E. Lindblom, "The Science of Muddling Through," *Public Administration Review,* 19 (Spring 1959), 79–88; Aaron Wildavsky, *The Politics of the Budgetary Process* (Boston: Little, Brown, 1964).
2. The classic statement on group theory is David B. Truman, *The Governmental Process* (New York: Knopf, 1951).
3. Ibid., p. 37.
4. Earl Latham, "The Group Basis of Politics," *in Political Behavior,* ed. Heinz Eulau, Samuel J. Eldersveld, and Morris Janowitz (New York: Free Press, 1956), p. 239.
5. Elite theory is explained at length in Thomas R. Dye and Harmon Zeigler, *The Irony of Democracy,* 14th ed. (Belmont, CA: Wadsworth, 2009).
6. James M. Buchanan and Gordon Tullock, *The Calculus of Consent* (Ann Arbor: University of Michigan Press, 1962).
7. Anthony Downs, *An Economic Theory of Democracy* (New York: Harper & Row, 1957).

Bibliography

BICKERS, KENNETH N., and JOHN T. WILLIAMS. *Public Policy Analysis: A Political Economy Approach.* Boston: Houghton Mifflin, 2001.

BUCHANAN, JAMES M., and GORDON TULLOCK. *The Calculus of Consent.* Ann Arbor: University of Michigan Press, 1962.

DAHL, ROBERT A., and BRUCE STINEBRICKNER. *Modern Political Analysis,* 6th ed. New York: Longman 2003.

DOWNS, ANTHONY. *An Economic Theory of Democracy.* New York: Harper & Row, 1957.

DYE, THOMAS R. *Top Down Policymaking.* Washington, DC: CQ Press, 2000.

LINDBLOM, CHARLES E., and EDWARD J. WOODHOUSE. *The Policy-Making Process,* 3rd ed. New York: Longman, 1993.

TRUMAN, DAVID B. *The Government Process.* New York: Knopf, 1954.

WATSON, JOEL. *Strategy: An Introduction to Game Theory.* New York: W. W. Norton, 2001.

WILDAVSKY, AARON. *The New Politics of the Budgetary Process,* 2nd ed. New York: HarperCollins, 1992.

Web Sites

AMERICAN POLITICAL SCIENCE ASSOCIATION. Home page of academic political scientists' professional organization. *www.apsanet.org*

PUBLIC AGENDA ONLINE. Brief guide to a variety of policy issues, including public opinion surveys on these issues. *www.publicagenda.org*

ALMANAC OF POLICY ISSUES. Background information on a variety of issues with links to sources. *www.policy-almanac.org*

PUBLIC OPINION ONLINE. Compilation of recent public opinion polls on policy issues, political actors, government institutions, etc. *www.pollingreport.com*

THE GALLUP ORGANIZATION. Home page of the Gallup public opinion organization. *www.gallup.com*

NATIONAL CENTER FOR POLICY RESEARCH. Conservative policy research organization, with studies on a variety of policy issues. *www.nationalcenter.org*

PROGRESSIVE POLICY INSTITUTE. Liberal policy research organization, with policy briefs on a variety of issues. *www.ppionline.org*

NATIONAL ISSUES. Collection of current articles on a variety of policy issues. *www.nationalissues.com*

3

The Policymaking Process

Decision-Making Activities

The Policy Process: How Policies Are Made

Policy studies often focus on *how policies are made* rather than on their content or their causes and consequences. The study of how policies are made generally considers a series of activities, or *processes,* that occur within the political system. These processes, together with the activities involved and likely participants, may be portrayed as in Table 3–1.

Although it may be helpful to think about policymaking as a series of processes, in the real world these activities seldom occur in a neat, step-by-step sequence. Rather these processes often occur simultaneously, each one collapsing into the others. Different political actors and institutions—politicians, interest groups, lobbyists and legislators, executives and bureaucrats, reporters and commentators, think tanks, lawyers and judges—may be engaged in different processes at the same time, even in the same policy area. Policymaking is seldom as neat as the process model. Nonetheless, it is often useful for analytical purposes to break policymaking into component units in order to understand better how policies are made.

Problem Identification and Agenda Setting

Who decides what will be decided? The power to decide what will be a policy issue is crucial to the policymaking process. Deciding what will be the problems is even more important than deciding what will be the solutions. Many civics textbooks imply that agenda setting just "happens." It is sometimes argued that in an open plural society such as ours, channels of access and communication to government are always open, so that any problem can be discussed and placed on the agenda of national decision making. Individuals and groups, it is said, can organize themselves to assume the tasks of defining problems and suggesting solutions. People can define their own interests, organize themselves, persuade others to support their cause, gain access to government officials, influence decision making, and watch over the implementation of government policies and programs. Indeed, it is sometimes argued that the absence of political activity such as this is an indicator of satisfaction.

TABLE 3–1 Policymaking as a Process Policymaking can be seen as a process—*how* policies are made—in a step-by-step sequence; but in reality these processes overlap and intertwine.

Process	Activity	Participants
Problem Identification	Publicizing societal problems Expressing demands for government action	Mass media Interest groups Citizen initiatives Public opinion
⇩	⇩	⇩

Agenda Setting	Deciding what issues will be
	    decided, what problems will be
	    addressed by government
		Elites, including president,
		    Congress
		
		Candidates for elective office
		Mass media

⇩	⇩	⇩

Policy Formulation	Developing policy proposals to
	    resolve issues and ameliorate
	    problems
		Think tanks
		President and executive office
		Congressional committees
		Interest groups

⇩	⇩	⇩
Policy Legitimation	Selecting a proposal Developing political support for it Enacting it into law Deciding on its constitutionality	Interest groups President Congress Courts
⇩	⇩	⇩
Policy Implementation	Organizing departments and agencies Providing payments or services Levying taxes	President and White House staff Executive departments and agencies
⇩	⇩	⇩

Policy Evaluation	Reporting outputs of government
	    programs
	Evaluating impacts of policies on
	    target and nontarget groups
	Proposing changes and "reforms"
		Executive departments and
		    agencies
		Congressional oversight
		    committees
		Mass media
		Think tanks

But, in reality, policy issues do not just "happen." Creating an issue, dramatizing it, calling attention to it, and pressuring government to do something about it are important political tactics. These tactics are employed by influential individuals, organized interest groups, policy-planning organizations, political candidates and office-holders, and perhaps most important, the mass media. These are the tactics of "agenda setting."

Agenda Setting from the Bottom Up

The prevailing model of policymaking in American political science is a popularly driven, "bottom-up" portrait of decision making. This "democratic-pluralist" model assumes that any problem can be identified by individuals or groups, by candidates seeking election, by political leaders seeking to enhance their reputation and prospects for reelection, by political parties seeking to define their principles and/or create favorable popular images of themselves, by the mass media seeking to "create" news, and even by protest groups deliberately seeking to call attention to their problems. And, of course, various crises and disasters—from natural disasters such as hurricanes and droughts to man-made tragedies such as school shootings and airplane crashes—attract public attention and compel public officials to respond.

Public Opinion and Agenda Setting.   Events, and the media's reporting of them, can focus public attention on issues, problems, and "crises." Concern over terrorism dominated the public's mind following the horrific televised attacks on the World Trade Center and the Pentagon on September 11, 2001. Later the war in Iraq became "the most important problem facing the country" according to opinion polls. Iraq appeared to be the nation's top policy issue during the congressional elections of 2006 in which opposition Democrats captured control of both houses of Congress.

But the threat of financial collapse and deep recession soon replaced all other issues on the public's agenda. The nation's "top priority" for President Barack Obama became jobs and the economy (see Table 3–2). Defending against future terrorist attacks fell to second place in the policy priorities of most Americans. Other issues—Social Security, education, healthcare, budget deficits, the poor, crime, defense, taxes—followed behind. A minority of Americans listed the environment, immigration, lobbying, and international trade as top priority issues. Global warming was last on the nation's list.

TABLE 3–2   Policy Priorities of the American Public I'd like to ask you some questions about priorities for President Obama and Congress this year. As I read from a list, tell me if you think the item should be a top priority, important but lower priority, not too important, or should it not be done?

	Percent Saying Top Priority
Strengthening the nation's economy	85
Improving the job situation	82
Defending the country from future terrorist attacks	76
Taking steps to make Social Security financially sound	63
Improving the educational system	61
Dealing with the nation's energy problem	60
Taking steps to make Medicare financially sound	60
Reducing healthcare costs	59
Reducing the budget deficit	53
Providing health insurance to the uninsured	52
Dealing with the problems of poor and needy people	50
Reducing crime	46
Dealing with the moral breakdown of the country	45
Strengthening the U.S. military	44
Reducing federal income taxes for the middle class	43
Protecting the environment	41
Dealing with the issue of illegal immigration	41
Reducing the influence of lobbyists in Washington	36
Dealing with global trade issues	31
Dealing with global warming	30

SOURCE: *Pew Research Center Survey,* January 2009, *www.pollingreport.com.*

Agenda Setting from the Top Down

When V. O. Key wrestled with the same problem confronting us—namely, the determination of the impact of popular preferences on public policy—he concluded that "the missing piece of the puzzle" was "that thin stratum of persons referred to variously as the political elite, the political activists, the leadership echelons, or the influentials."

> The longer one frets with the puzzle of how democratic regimes manage to function, the more plausible it appears that a substantial part of the explanation is to be found in the motives that activate the *leadership echelon,* the values that it holds, the rules of the political game to which it adheres, in the expectations which it entertains about its own status in society, and perhaps in some of the objective circumstances, both material and institutional, in which it functions.[1]

Popular Perceptions of Policymaking. It is interesting to note that most Americans believe that the government pays very little attention to their views on public policy and that people in government have little understanding of what people think (see Table 3–3). An overwhelming majority of Americans believe that their government is "run by a few big

TABLE 3–3 Popular Attitudes Toward Government Policymaking The American public is highly skeptical of politicians and people in government, believing that they should pay more attention to the public's views.

How much say do you think people like yourself have about what the government does—a good deal, some, or not much?

A good deal	10%
Some	25
Not much	64

Would you say the government is pretty much run by a few big interests looking out for themselves or that it is run for the benefit of all the people?

A few big interests	64%
All of the people	28

Do you think that quite a few of the people running the government are crooked, not very many are, or do you think hardly any of the them are crooked?

Quite a few	52%
Not very many	28
Hardly any	10
All (volunteered)	5

If the leaders of the nation followed the views of the public more closely, do you think that the nation would be better off or worse off than it is today?

Better	81%
Worse	10%

Please tell me which statement you agree with most: (A) When members of Congress are thinking about how to vote on an issue, they should read up on the polls, as this can help them get a sense of the public's view on the issue. (B) When members of Congress are thinking about how to vote on an issue, they should not read the polls, because this will distract them from thinking about what is right.

Should read the polls	67%
Should not read the polls	26%

SOURCE: *The Polling Report* (2008), *www.pollingreport.com.*

interests looking out for themselves" rather than "for the benefit of all of the people." And an overwhelming majority believe that the nation would be better off if public policy followed the views of citizens more closely. While policymakers often publicly expressed disdain for opinion polls, most Americans believe that they should pay *more* attention to them. In short, most Americans believe that policy is made from the top down.

Elite Agenda Setting.   The elitist model of agenda setting focuses on the role of leaders in business, finance, and the media, as well as in government. These leaders may observe societal developments they perceive as threatening to their own values or interests; or they may perceive opportunities to advance their own values and interests or their own careers.

According to sociologist G. William Domhoff, agenda setting "begins informally in corporate boardrooms, social clubs, and discussion groups, where problems are identified as 'issues' to be solved by new policies. It ends in government, where policies are enacted and implemented."[2] This model suggests that the initial impetus for policy change and initial resources for research, planning, and formulation of national policy are derived from corporate and personal wealth. This wealth is channeled into foundations, universities, and policy-oriented think tanks in the form of endowments, grants, and contracts. Moreover, corporate presidents, directors, and top wealth-holders also sit on the governing boards of these institutions and oversee the general direction of their work.

Political Entrepreneurship.   Candidates for public office at all levels must keep their names and faces before the voters—in public appearances, interviews, speeches, and press releases. In order to do so, they must say something, that is, deliver a message or theme that creates a favorable image of themselves. Most of these campaign messages, themes, and images are largely devoid of any specific policy content, except in very general terms, for example, "stands up against the special interests," "fights for the taxpayer," or "change you can believe in." But occasionally candidates focus their campaigns on what they perceive to be issues that will motivate voters. Political challengers as well as officials seeking reelection may seize upon particular problems, publicize them, and even propose solutions. If they win the election, they may even claim a "mandate" from the people to pursue the policy direction emphasized in their campaign. Whether or not their success was in fact a product of their policy position, they may believe that they have a responsibility to put forth policy proposals consistent with their campaign messages and themes.

Opinion–Policy Linkage.   The problem in assessing the independent effect of mass opinion on the actions of decision makers is that their actions help to mold mass opinion. Even when public policy is in accord with mass opinion, we can never be sure whether mass opinion shaped public policy or public policy shaped mass opinion. The distinguished American political scientist V. O. Key, Jr., wrote, "Government, as we have seen, attempts to mold public opinion toward support of the programs and policies it espouses. Given that endeavor, perfect congruence between public policy and public opinion could be government of public opinion rather than government *by* public opinion."[3]

Policy Effects.   Public policy shapes public opinion more often than opinion shapes policy, for several reasons. First, few people have opinions on the great bulk of policy questions confronting the nation's decision makers. Second, public opinion is very unstable. It can change in a matter of days in response to news events precipitated by leaders. Third, leaders do not have a clear perception of mass opinion. Most communications received by decision makers are from other elites—newspersons, interest group leaders, and other influential persons—and not from ordinary citizens.

Media Effects. We must not assume that the opinions expressed in the news media are public opinion. Frequently, this is a source of confusion. Newspersons believe *they* are the public, often confusing their own opinions with public opinion. They even tell the mass public what its opinion is, thus actually helping to mold it to conform to their own beliefs. Decision makers, then, may act in response to news stories or the opinions of influential newspersons in the belief that they are responding to public opinion.

Communicating with Policymakers. Decision makers can easily misinterpret public opinion because the communications they receive have an elite bias. Members of the mass public seldom call or write their senators or representatives, much less converse with them at dinners, cocktail parties, or other social occasions. Most of the communications received by decision makers are *intraelite*, from newspersons, organized group leaders, influential constituents, wealthy political contributors, and personal friends—people who, for the most part, share the same views. It is not surprising, therefore, that members of Congress say that most of their mail is in agreement with their own position; their world of public opinion is self-reinforcing. Moreover, persons who initiate communication with decision makers, by writing or calling or visiting their representatives, are decidedly more educated and affluent than the average citizen.

The President and White House Staff. The president and the executive branch are generally expected to be the "initiators" of policy proposals, with members of Congress in the role of "arbiters" of policy alternatives. (The same division of labor is usually found at the state and local levels, with governors, mayors, and even city managers expected to formulate policy proposals and state legislators and city councils to approve, amend, or reject them.) The Constitution of the United States appears to endorse this arrangement in Article II, Section 3: "[The president] shall from time to time give to Congress information of the State of the Union, and recommend to their consideration such measures as he shall judge necessary and expedient." Each year the principal policy statements of the president come in the State of the Union message, and more importantly, in the Budget of the United States Government, prepared by the Office of Management and Budget (see Chapter 7). Many other policy proposals are developed by executive departments in their specialized areas; these proposals are usually transmitted to the White House for the president's approval before being sent to Congress.

Presidents have many motivations to seize the initiative in policymaking. First-term presidents must build a record of success that later can be used in their reelection campaign. They must show that they can "get things done in Washington." They must build and maintain their electoral coalition. They must show that they are capable of following through on at least some of their campaign promises. Second-term presidents are often motivated by a concern for their "place in history." They seek policy achievements that will contribute to their presidential "greatness" in history.

Congress and Legislative Staff. While Congress is generally portrayed as the "arbiter" of policy proposals initiated by others, occasionally leaders in the Congress will try to set forth their own agendas. Perhaps the most well-publicized effort in the Congress to seize the initiative in policymaking was the 1994 "Contract with America" led by then Speaker of the House Newt Gingrich. Republican House candidates across the country united behind a comprehensive set of proposals, including a balanced budget constitutional amendment, term limits for Congress, welfare reform, and so on. But despite a stunning GOP victory in 1994 congressional elections, enthusiasm for the Contract with America quickly dissipated, and President Bill Clinton soon regained policy leadership.

Nonetheless, members of Congress sometimes serve as agenda setters. They may do so to challenge a president of the opposing party, to gain a reputation as a power broker themselves, or indeed to place on the national agenda an issue they feel requires attention. Committee chairs enjoy a special advantage in congressional agenda setting; they control the agenda of their committees' hearings. And these hearings offer the best opportunity for congressional involvement in agenda setting. Congressional staffs—committee staffs, staffs of the legislative leadership, and aides to individual legislators—often play an important role in bringing issues to the attention of their bosses.

Interest Groups. Interest groups may initiate their own policy proposals, perhaps in association with members of Congress or their staffs who share the same interest. Interest group staffs often bring valuable technical knowledge to policy formation, as well as political information about their group's position on the issues. Because Congress members and their staffs value both kinds of information, interest groups can often provide the precise language they desire in proposed bills and amendments. Thus, interest group staffs often augment the work of congressional staffs. Interest groups also provide testimony at congressional hearings as well as technical reports and analyses used by congressional staffs.

Agenda Setting: The Mass Media

Television is the major source of information for the vast majority of Americans. More than two-thirds report that they receive all or most of their news from television. Television is really the first form of *mass* communication, that is, communication that reaches nearly everyone, including children. More important, television presents a visual image, not merely a printed word. The visual quality of television—the emotional impact that is conveyed by pictures—enables the TV networks to convey emotions as well as information.

Media Power. The media are both players and referees in the game of politics. They not only report to the people on the struggles for power in society, but they also participate in those struggles themselves. They are an elite group, competing for power alongside the more traditional leadership groups from business, labor, government, and other sectors of society. As political journalist Theodore White once observed, "The power of the press in America is a primordial one. It sets the agenda of public discussion; and this sweeping power is unrestrained by any law. It determines what people will talk about and think about—an authority that in other nations is reserved for tyrants, priests, parties, and mandarins."[4]

Media power is concentrated in the hands of a relatively small number of people: the editors, producers, anchors, reporters, and columnists of the leading television networks (ABC, CBS, NBC, FOX, and CNN) and the prestigious press (*New York Times, Washington Post, Wall Street Journal, Newsweek, Time,* and *U.S. News and World Report*). Producers and editors generally work behind the scenes, and many influential print journalists are known only by their bylines. But most Americans have come to recognize the faces of the television network anchors and leading reporters. These media people are courted by politicians, treated as celebrities, studied by scholars, and known to millions of Americans by their television images.

Newsmaking.   Newsmaking involves all-important decisions about what is "news" and who is "newsworthy." Television executives and producers and newspaper and magazine editors must decide what people, organizations, and events will be given attention—attention that makes these topics matters of general public concern and political action. Without media coverage the general public would not know about these personalities, organizations, or events. They would not become objects of political discussion, nor would they be likely to be considered important by government officials.

Media attention can create issues and personalities. Media inattention can doom issues and personalities to obscurity. The TV camera cannot be "a picture of the world" because the whole world cannot squeeze into the picture. News executives must sort through a tremendous surplus of information and decide what is to be "news."

In addition to deciding what is and what is not news, news executives provide cues to mass audiences about the importance of an issue, personality, or event. Some matters are covered prominently by the media, with early placement on a newscast and several minutes of time, or with front-page newspaper coverage, including big headlines and pictures. The amount of coverage tells us what is important and what is not.

Of course, politicians, professional public relations people, interest group spokespersons, and various aspiring celebrities all know that the decisions of the media are vital to the success of their issue, their organization, and themselves. So they try to attract media attention by deliberately engaging in behavior or manufacturing situations that are likely to win coverage. The result is the "media event"—an activity arranged primarily to stimulate coverage and thereby attract public attention to an issue or individual. Generally, the more bizarre, dramatic, and sensational it is, the more likely it is to attract coverage. A media event may be a press conference to which reporters from the television stations and newspapers are invited by public figures—even when there is really no news to announce. Or it may be a staged debate, confrontation, or illustration of injustice. Political candidates may visit coal mines, ghetto neighborhoods, and sites of fires or other disasters. Sometimes protests, demonstrations, and even violence have been staged primarily as media events to dramatize and communicate grievances.

Media Bias.   In exercising their judgment regarding which stories should be given television time or newspaper space, media executives must rely on their own political values and economic interests as guidelines. In general, these executives are more liberal in their views than other segments of the nation's leadership. Topics selected weeks in advance for coverage reflect, or often create, current liberal issues: concern for problems affecting the poor and minorities, women's issues, opposition to defense spending, environmental concerns, and so forth. But liberalism is not the major source of bias in the news.

The principal source of distortion in the news is caused by the need for drama, action, and confrontation to hold audience attention. Television must entertain. To capture the attention of jaded audiences, news must be selected on the basis of emotional rhetoric, shocking incidents, dramatic conflict, overdrawn stereotypes. Race, sex, violence, and corruption in government are favorite topics because of popular interest. More complex problems such as inflation, government spending, and foreign policy must either be simplified and dramatized or ignored. To dramatize an issue news executives must find or create a dramatic incident; tape it; transport, process, and edit the tape; and write a script for the introduction, the "voice-over," and the "recapitulation." All this means that most "news" must be created well in advance of scheduled broadcasting.

Media Effects.   Media effects can be categorized as (1) identifying issues and setting the agenda for policymakers, (2) influencing attitudes and values toward policy issues, and (3) changing the behavior of voters and decision makers. These categories are ranked by the degree of influence the media are likely to have over their audiences. The power of television does not really lie in persuading viewers to take one side of an issue or another. Instead, *the power of television lies in setting the agenda for decision making*—deciding what issues will be given attention and what issues will be ignored.

The media can create new opinions more easily than they can change existing ones. They can often suggest how we feel about new events or issues—those for which we have no prior feelings or experiences. And the media can reinforce values and attitudes that we already hold. But there is very little evidence that the media can change existing values.

The viewer's psychological mechanism of *selective perception* helps to defend against bias in news and entertainment programming. Selective perception means mentally screening out information or images with which one disagrees. It causes people to tend to see and hear only what they want to see and hear. It reduces the impact of television bias on viewers' attitudes and behavior.

Formulating Policy

Policy formulation is the development of policy alternatives for dealing with problems on the public agenda. Policy formulation occurs in government bureaucracies; interest group offices; legislative committee rooms; meetings of special commissions; and policy-planning organizations, otherwise known as think tanks. The details of policy proposals are usually formulated by staff members rather than by their bosses, but staffs are guided by what they know their leaders want.

Think Tanks.   Policy-planning organizations are central coordinating points in the policy-making process. Certain policy-planning groups—for example, the Council on Foreign Relations, the American Enterprise Institute, the Heritage Foundation, Center for American Progress, and the Brookings Institution—are influential in a wide range of key policy areas. Other policy-planning groups—the Urban Institute, Resources for the Future, the Population Council, for example—specialize in a particular policy field.

These organizations bring together the leadership of corporate and financial institutions, the foundations, the mass media, the leading intellectuals, and influential figures in the government. They review the relevant university and foundation-supported research on topics of interest, and more important, they try to reach a consensus about what action should be taken on national problems under study. Their goal is to develop action recommendations—explicit policies or programs designed to resolve national problems. These policy recommendations of the key policy-planning groups are distributed to the mass media, federal executive agencies, and Congress. The purpose is to lay the groundwork for making policy into law.

The following are among the more influential think tanks:

The Brookings Institution. The Brookings Institution has long been the dominant policy-planning group for American domestic policy, despite the growing influence of competing think tanks over the years. Brookings staffers dislike its reputation as a liberal think tank, and they deny that Brookings tries to set national priorities. Yet the Brookings Institution has been very influential in planning the War on Poverty, welfare reform, national defense, and taxing and spending policies. The *New York Times* columnist and Harvard historian writing team, Leonard Silk and Mark Silk, describe Brookings as the central locus of the Washington "policy network," where it does "its communicating: over lunch, whether informally in the Brookings cafeteria or at the regular Friday lunch around a great oval table at which the staff and their guests keen over the events of the week like the chorus of an ancient Greek tragedy; through consulting, paid or unpaid, for government or business at conferences, in the advanced studies program; and, over time, by means of the revolving door of government employment."[5]

The American Enterprise Institute. For many years Republicans dreamed of a "Brookings Institution for Republicans" that would help offset the liberal bias of Brookings itself. In the late 1970s, that role was assumed by the American Enterprise Institute (AEI). The AEI appeals to both Democrats and Republicans who have doubts about big government. President William Baroody, Jr., distinguished the AEI from Brookings: "In confronting societal problems those who tend to gravitate to the AEI orbit would be inclined to look first for a market solution . . . while the other orbit people have a tendency to look for a government solution."[6]

The Heritage Foundation. Conservative ideologues have never been welcome in the Washington establishment. Yet influential conservative businesspersons gradually came to understand that without an institutional base in Washington they could never establish a strong and continuing influence in the policy network. So they set about the task of "building a solid institutional base" and "establishing a reputation for reliable scholarship and creative problem solving."[7] The result of their efforts was the Heritage Foundation.

Center for American Progress. On the left of the political spectrum is the newly influential Center for American Progress (CAP), the intellectual source of policy "change" in the Obama Administration. CAP is funded largely by George Soros, the billionaire sponsor of MoveOn.org and other flourishing left-liberal outlets. It was founded in 2003 by John Podesta, former chief of staff to President Bill Clinton, and designed to give the "progressive" movement the same ideological influence in the Obama Administration as the Heritage

Foundation exercised in the Reagan Administration[8] CAP promises to "engage in a war of ideas with conservatives," and to be more active on behalf of progressive policies than the more scholarly Brookings Institution.

The Council on Foreign Relations.   Political scientist Lester Milbraith observes that the influence of the Council Foreign Relations (CFR) throughout government is so pervasive that it is difficult to distinguish the CFR from government programs: "The Council on Foreign Relations, while not financed by government, works so closely with it that it is difficult to distinguish Council actions stimulated by government from autonomous actions."[9] The CFR itself, of course, denies that it exercises any control over U.S. foreign policy. Indeed, its bylaws declare, "The Council shall not take any position on questions of foreign policy and no person is authorized to speak or purport to speak for the Council on such matters."[10] But policy initiation and consensus building do not require the CFR to officially adopt policy positions. Many foreign policy decisions are first aired in the CFR's prestigious publication, *Foreign Affairs.*[11]

Interest Groups and Policymaking

Washington is awash in special interest groups, lawyers and law firms, lobbyists, and influence peddlers. Interest groups are active in both policy formulation and policy legitimating. Organized interests frequently develop policy proposals of their own and forward them to the White House or to members of Congress or the mass media to place on the agenda of decision making. And they are even more active in policy legitimating. Indeed, political life in Washington is a blur of "lobbying," "fund-raising," "opening doors," "mobilizing grassroots support," "rubbing elbows," and "schmoozing."

Interest groups influence government policy in a variety of ways. It is possible to categorize efforts to influence government policy as follows:

1. Direct lobbying, including testifying at committee hearings, contacting government offices directly, presenting research results, and assisting in the writing of legislation

2. Campaign contributions made through political action committees (PACs)

3. Interpersonal contacts, including travel, recreation, entertainment, and general "schmoozing," as well as the "revolving door" exchange of personnel between government offices and the industries and organizations representing them

4. Litigation designed to force changes in policies through the court system, wherein interest groups and their lawyers bring class-action suits on behalf of their clients or file *amicus curiae* (friend of the court) arguments in cases in which they are interested

5. Grassroots mobilization efforts to influence Congress and the White House by encouraging letters, calls, and visits by individual constituents and campaign contributors.

Lobbying.   Washington's influence industry is a billion-dollar business. Each year lobbyists spend almost $3 billion dollars trying to influence policy—more than $5 million for each member of Congress![12]

At the industry group level, pharmaceutical and health product manufacturers spend the most on lobbying. The insurance industry ranks second in direct lobbying expenditures, followed by telephone utilities, the oil and gas industry, and electric utilities (see Table 3–4). Of the top twenty-five groups spending money on lobbying, only three might be considered noneconomic groups. These include governments and public employee unions, educational groups including the National Education Association, and the miscellaneous grouping of single-issue organizations (e.g., AARP, National Rifle Association, Christian Coalition).

It is important to note that direct lobbying expenditures provide only one indicator of an industry's or corporation's clout in Washington. Effective lobbying also requires backup by campaign contributions and in-kind services, election endorsements, and grassroots political support. For example, a survey of Washington insiders conducted by *Fortune* ranked the AARP, the American Israel Public Affairs Committee, and the AFL-CIO as the three most powerful lobbies in Congress.[13] Indeed, only about one-half of the magazine's designated "Power Twenty-Five" were industry lobbies; others included the National Rifle Association, the Christian Coalition, the National Right to Life Committee, independent unions (NEA, AFSCME, Teamsters), and veterans' groups.

Occasionally, when Congress is embarrassed by media reports on extravagant lobbyist-paid travel, vacations, dinners, parties, and other perks, cries are heard for new restrictions on lobbying expenditures. Another reform frequently advocated is the elimination of "earmarking"

TABLE 3–4 Washington's Top Lobbying Spenders* Lobbying is a $1 billion business in Washington, with big corporations and trade associations regularly spending the most.

Rank*	Organization
1	US Chamber of Commerce
2	American Medical Assn
3	General Electric
4	American Hospital Assn
5	Pharmaceutical Rsrch & Mfrs of America
6	AARP
7	Edison Electric Institute
8	Business Roundtable
9	Northrop Grumman
10	National Assn of Realtors
11	Blue Cross/Blue Shield
12	Freddie Mac
13	Boeing Co
14	General Motors
15	Exxon Mobil
16	Southern Co
17	SBC Communications
18	Lockheed Martin
19	Ford Motor Co
20	Verizon Communications

SOURCE: Center for Responsive Politics, accessed April 1, 2008, *www.crp.org.*
*Rankings are for 1998 through 2008.

of particular spending items in larger appropriations bills—items that are heavily lobbied for, yet often are overlooked by most members of Congress when voting on appropriations bills.

PACs.   Contributions virtually ensure access to government decision makers. It is highly unlikely that any member of Congress will fail to meet with representatives of groups that helped to fund his or her election. And top White House staff and cabinet officials, if not the president, are almost always prepared to meet with interests that have made significant contributions to the presidential campaign. Contributions do not guarantee a favorable decision, but they can be counted on to guarantee a hearing.

Political action committees (PACs) solicit and receive contributions from members of organizations—unions, corporations, professional and trade associations, as well as ideological, environmental, and issue-oriented groups—and then distribute these funds to political candidates. PACs are regulated by the Federal Elections Commission, which requires them to register their finances and political contributions, and limits their contributions to $5,000 to any candidate per election.

PAC contributions are heavily weighted toward incumbents running for reelection. Usually two-thirds of all PAC contributions go to incumbents; this is true for corporate as well as union and other PACs. PACs are well aware that more than 90 percent of incumbent members of Congress seeking reelection win. Labor unions make heavy use of PACs; union PAC money is heavily weighted toward Democrats (see Table 3–5).

TABLE 3–5   Top PAC Spenders* In addition to lobbying spending, businesses, trade associations, and labor unions contribute billions to political campaigns through political action committees (PACs).

		Percentage Given to:	
Rank	PAC Name	Democrats	Republicans
1	Operating Engineers Union	86	14
2	Intl Brotherhood of Electrical Workers	98	2
3	National Assn of Realtors	61	39
4	AT&T Inc	38	62
5	American Assn for Justice	97	3
6	American Bankers Assn	39	61
7	Machinists/Aerospace Workers Union	97	3
8	Laborers Union	92	8
9	National Beer Wholesalers Assn	52	48
10	Sheet Metal Workers Union	96	4
11	International Assn of Fire Fighters	75	25
12	United Parcel Service	44	56
13	Credit Union National Assn	58	42
14	National Air Traffic Controllers Assn	76	24
15	Air Line Pilots Assn	85	15
16	National Auto Dealers Assn	37	63
17	Plumbers/Pipefitters Union	93	7
18	American Fedn of St/Cnty/Munic Employees	99	1
19	National Assn of Home Builders	45	55
20	American Crystal Sugar	65	35

SOURCE: Center for Responsive Politics, accessed April 1, 2008, *www.crp.org.*
*Rankings are for 2007–2008.

Assessing Interest Group Influence. Most Americans believe that interest group PACs, as well as big corporations, the news media, and lobbyists, "have too much power and influence on Washington."[14] But it is difficult to assess exactly how much power interest groups actually wield in the nation's capital. First of all, the views of members of Congress may coincide with the positions of interest groups independently of any direct lobbying efforts or campaign contributions. Second, the most important effects of interest group efforts may not be found on roll call votes but rather on various earlier stages of the legislative process, including behind-the-scenes negotiations over specific provisions, the drafting of amendments, and the markup of bills in committees and subcommittees. Third, interest group lobbying may have its greatest effect on the details of specific legislation rather than on overall policy directions. Finally, party leadership, constituency influence, and the personal views of the members of Congress all combine to modify the independent effect of interest group activities.

Policy Legitimation: The Proximate Policymakers

What is the role of the "proximate policymakers"? The activities of these policymakers—the president, Congress, courts, federal agencies, congressional committees, White House staff, and interest groups—have traditionally been the central focus of political science and are usually portrayed as the whole of the policymaking process. But the activities of the proximate policymakers are only the final phase of a much more complex process. This final stage is the open, public stage of the policymaking process, and it attracts the attention of the mass media and most political scientists. The activities of the proximate policymakers are much easier to study than the private actions of corporations, foundations, the mass media, and the policy-planning organizations.

Formal Lawmaking Process. Congress is designated in the U.S. Constitution as the principal instrument of policy legitimation. Article I describes the national government's powers (for example, "to lay and collect Taxes Duties Imposts and Excises") as powers of *Congress.* It is important to note, however, that Congress is not the exclusive repository of policy legitimacy. Courts also bear a heavy responsibility to maintain the legitimacy of governmental authority, and to a somewhat lesser extent, so do administrative bureaucracies. By focusing attention on the Congress in the policy legitimation process, we do not mean to detract from the importance of other governmental institutions in maintaining legitimacy.

Congress has developed highly institutionalized rules and procedures to help legitimate its actions. Indeed, its rules and procedures have become so elaborate that proposed policy changes are extremely difficult. Very few of the bills introduced in Congress are passed; in a typical two-year session more than 10,000 bills will be introduced, but fewer than 800 (less than 10 percent) will be enacted in any form. Congress is accurately perceived more as an obstacle to than a facilitator of policy change.

The formal process of lawmaking is outlined in Figure 3–1. The familiar path is taught in virtually every high school and college government class in America. But this outline of the formal lawmaking process fails to describe the role of parties and leadership in guiding

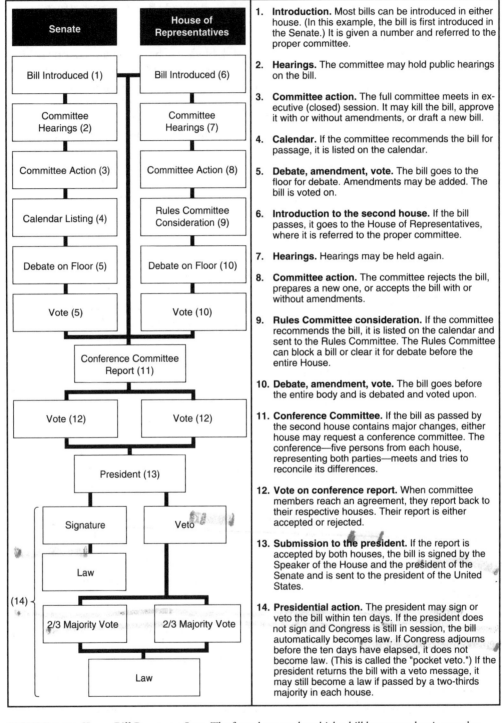

Senate	House of Representatives
Bill Introduced (1)	Bill Introduced (6)
Committee Hearings (2)	Committee Hearings (7)
Committee Action (3)	Committee Action (8)
Calendar Listing (4)	Rules Committee Consideration (9)
Debate on Floor (5)	Debate on Floor (10)
Vote (5)	Vote (10)

Conference Committee Report (11)

Vote (12)	Vote (12)

President (13)

Signature	Veto
Law	

(14)

2/3 Majority Vote	2/3 Majority Vote

Law

1. **Introduction.** Most bills can be introduced in either house. (In this example, the bill is first introduced in the Senate.) It is given a number and referred to the proper committee.

2. **Hearings.** The committee may hold public hearings on the bill.

3. **Committee action.** The full committee meets in executive (closed) session. It may kill the bill, approve it with or without amendments, or draft a new bill.

4. **Calendar.** If the committee recommends the bill for passage, it is listed on the calendar.

5. **Debate, amendment, vote.** The bill goes to the floor for debate. Amendments may be added. The bill is voted on.

6. **Introduction to the second house.** If the bill passes, it goes to the House of Representatives, where it is referred to the proper committee.

7. **Hearings.** Hearings may be held again.

8. **Committee action.** The committee rejects the bill, prepares a new one, or accepts the bill with or without amendments.

9. **Rules Committee consideration.** If the committee recommends the bill, it is listed on the calendar and sent to the Rules Committee. The Rules Committee can block a bill or clear it for debate before the entire House.

10. **Debate, amendment, vote.** The bill goes before the entire body and is debated and voted upon.

11. **Conference Committee.** If the bill as passed by the second house contains major changes, either house may request a conference committee. The conference—five persons from each house, representing both parties—meets and tries to reconcile its differences.

12. **Vote on conference report.** When committee members reach an agreement, they report back to their respective houses. Their report is either accepted or rejected.

13. **Submission to the president.** If the report is accepted by both houses, the bill is signed by the Speaker of the House and the president of the Senate and is sent to the president of the United States.

14. **Presidential action.** The president may sign or veto the bill within ten days. If the president does not sign and Congress is still in session, the bill automatically becomes law. If Congress adjourns before the ten days have elapsed, it does not become law. (This is called the "pocket veto.") If the president returns the bill with a veto message, it may still become a law if passed by a two-thirds majority in each house.

FIGURE 3–1 How a Bill Becomes a Law The formal process by which a bill becomes a law is complex, making it easier a defeat a bill than to pass a bill.

legislation in the House and Senate, the influence of constituents and interest groups, the influence of the president and White House staff, and, above all, the continuing pressing need of members of Congress to raise money for their reelection campaigns.

Party Influence.   Party loyalty is stronger among members of Congress and other political activists than it is among voters. Party votes—roll call votes in the House and Senate on which a majority of Democrats vote in opposition to a majority of Republicans—occur on more than half the roll call votes in Congress. Indeed, party votes appear to have risen in recent years, indicating an increase in partisanship in Washington. Party unity in Congress—the average percentage of support among members of each party for their party's position on party votes—is also fairly high. On average, both the Democratic and Republican parties can expect more than 80 percent of their members to support their party on a party line vote.

It is true, of course, that party loyalty and party line voting in the Congress may not necessarily be a product of party loyalty or discipline. They may result more from ideological or issue agreement among members of each party.

The social bases in the electorate of the Democratic and Republican parties are slightly different. Both parties draw support from all social groups in America, but the Democrats draw disproportionately from labor, big-city residents, ethnic voters, blacks, Jews, and Catholics; Republicans draw disproportionately from rural, small-town, and suburban Protestants, businesspeople, and professionals. To the extent that the policy orientations of these two broad groups differ, the thrust of party ideology also differs.

What are the issues that cause conflict between the Democratic and Republican parties? In general, Democrats have favored federal action to assist low-income groups through public assistance, housing, and antipoverty programs, and generally a larger role for the federal government in launching new projects to remedy domestic problems. Republicans, in contrast, have favored less government involvement in domestic affairs, lower taxes, and greater reliance on private action.

Presidential Influence.   Presidents are expected to set forth policy initiatives in speeches, in messages to the Congress (including the annual State of the Union message), and in the annual Budget of the United States Government. Presidents and their chief advisers regularly sift through policies formulated in think tanks and policy-planning organizations, developed in the offices of interest groups, law firms, and lobbyists, and suggested by heavy campaign contributors in the course of preparing a White House legislative agenda.

But a president's success in getting legislation enacted into law is closely tied to party control of the Congress. Presidents are far more successful when they can work with a Congress controlled by their own party. Presidential "box scores"—the percentage of policy initiatives on which the president took a clear-cut position that is enacted into law by the Congress—depend primarily on whether or not the president's party controls one or both houses of Congress (see Figure 3–2). Ronald Reagan benefited from having a Republican majority in the Senate in his first term, but suffered when Democrats gained control of the Senate in his second term. Bill Clinton was very successful in his first two years in office when the Democrats controlled Congress. But his box scores plummeted following the capture of the Congress by Republicans in 1994. President George H. W. Bush faced a

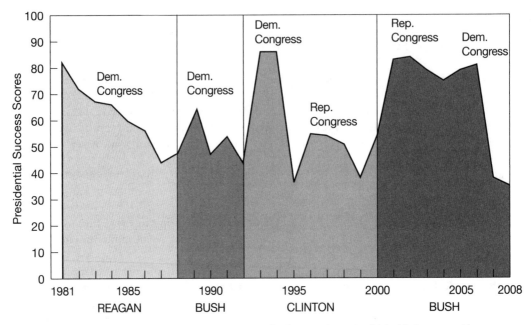

FIGURE 3–2   Presidential Support in Congress A president's success in getting his legislation enacted by Congress is most heavily influenced by whether or not his party controls the House or Senate or both bodies.
SOURCE: *Congressional Quarterly*, various issues.

Democratic Congress and managed to get only about half of his proposed legislation passed. Republican President George W. Bush enjoyed the support of a Republican Congress through 2006, but the election of a Democratic Congress that year led to "a marked" decline in his legislative success. President Barack Obama's success in Congress is closely tied to the large Democratic majorities in both the House and Senate.

Presidents are more successful in stopping legislation they oppose than in getting legislation they support passed by the Congress. The veto is the president's most important weapon in dealing with Congress. Even the threat of the veto greatly enhances the president's legislative power. A bill vetoed by the president can be passed into law only by the two-thirds vote of both houses of Congress. Seldom is a president so weak that he cannot hold the loyalty of at least one-third of either the House or the Senate. From George Washington to Barack Obama, more than 96 percent of all presidential vetoes have been sustained.

Constituency Influence.   Members of Congress like to think of themselves as independent-minded, public-spirited "trustees" rather then merely message-carrying "delegates" sent to Washington by their districts' voters. The philosophical justification for this notion was offered by the English parliamentarian Edmund Burke more than 200 years ago in a speech to his constituents: "Your representative owes you, not his industry only, but his judgment; and betrays, instead of serving you, if he sacrifices it to your opinion."[15]

But the rationale for Congress members' independence from constituency influence may not be so noble as that implied by Burke. Members know that their constituents are largely unaware of their voting records in Congress. Only occasionally, on a highly publicized vote, where home state or district feelings are intense, will a member defer to constituents' views over those of their party's leadership and campaign-cash-contributing interest groups. On most issues, members are free to ignore their constituents: "They don't know much about my votes. Most of what they know is what I tell them. They know more of what kind of a guy I am. It comes through in my letters: 'You care about the little guy.'"[16] A long record of "home-style" politics—doing casework for constituents, performing favors, winning pork-barrel projects for the district, making frequent visits back home to "press the flesh"—can protect members from any opposition that might be generated by their voting records.

Contributor Influence. The cost of running for Congress today virtually guarantees the dependency of its members on heavy campaign contributors. The average incumbent House member now spends nearly $1 million running for office *every two years.* The average incumbent U.S. senator spends more than $5 million to maintain his or her seat, and the price tag in some big states can run $25 million or more.

Corporations, interest group PACs, and individual "fat cats" have become the real constituents of Congress (see Table 3–6). Large corporate and individual donors, together with interest group PACs, constitute more than two-thirds of the campaign cash flowing into congressional elections. Small individual donors ($500 or less) provide less than one-third of campaign funds. Most members of Congress spend hours each day making fund-raising calls from their offices on Capitol Hill. "Making your calls" is a basic responsibility of the job.

Throughout the lawmaking process, big campaign contributors expect to be able to call or visit and present their views directly to the officeholders they supported. At the pres-idential level, major contributors expect to get a meeting with the president or at least with high-level White House staff or cabinet members. At the congressional level, major contrib-utors usually expect to meet directly with representatives and senators. Members of Con-gress frequently boast of responding to letters, calls, or visits by any constituent. But big contributors expect "face time" with the political leaders who they help keep in office.

Campaign contributions are rarely made on a direct quid pro quo basis—that is, direct dollar payments in exchange for sponsoring a bill in Congress or for voting for or against a bill in committee or on the floor. Such direct trade-offs risk exposure as bribery and may be prosecuted under law. Bribery, where it occurs, is probably limited to very narrow and spe-cific policy actions: payments to intervene in a particular case before an administrative agency, payments to insert a very specific break in a tax law or a specific exemption in a trade bill, payments to obtain a specific contract with the government. Bribery on major issues is very unlikely; there is simply too much publicity and too much risk of exposure. But Con-gress members are smart enough to know what issues concern the contributors and how to vote in order to keep the contributions coming in the future.

Policy Implementation: The Bureaucracy

"Implementation is the continuation of politics by other means."[17] Policymaking does not end with the passage of a law by Congress and its signing by the president. Rather, it shifts

TABLE 3–6   All-Time Big-Money Contributors   The cost of running for Congress has skyrocketed, making Congress members ever more dependent on contributions from big corporations and labor unions.

		1989–2008					1989–2008	
Rank	Organization Name	Dems	Repubs		Rank	Organization Name	Dems	Repubs
1.	American Fedn of State, County & Municipal Employees	98%	1%		25.	EMILY's List	99%	0%
2.	AT&T Inc	44%	55%		26	National Assn of Letter Carriers	87%	12%
3.	National Assn of Realtors	47%	52%		27.	National Beer Wholesalers Assn	28%	71%
4.	American Assn for Justice (trail lawyers)	90%	9%		28.	JPMorgan Chase & Co	50%	48%
5.	Goldman Sachs	62%	37%		29.	Time Warner	69%	30%
6.	Intl Brotherhood of Electrical Workers	97%	2%		30.	AFL-CIO	95%	3%
7.	National Education Assn	93%	6%		31.	Microsoft Corp	49%	49%
8.	Laborers Union	91%	7%		32.	National Rifle Assn	16%	83%
9.	Service Employees International Union	95%	3%		33.	Morgan Stanley	45%	54%
10.	Carpenters & Joiners Union	89%	9%		34.	Verizon Communications	38%	60%
11.	Communications Workers of America	99%	0%		35.	Ernst & Young	44%	55%
12.	Teamsters Union	92%	7%		36.	Sheet Metal Workers Union	97%	2%
13.	Citigroup Inc	49%	50%		37.	Lockheed Martin	41%	58%
14.	American Medical Assn	38%	61%		38.	General Electric	48%	51%
15.	United Auto Workers	98%	0%		39.	Credit Union National Assn	47%	52%
16.	American Federation of Teachers	98%	1%		40.	Bank of America	46%	53%
17.	Altria Group	27%	72%		41.	American Hospital Assn	51%	48%
18.	Machinists & Aerospace Workers Union	98%	0%		42.	American Dental Assn	44%	55%
19.	United Food & Commercial Workers Union	98%	1%		43.	BellSouth Corp	45%	54%
20.	United Parcel Service	35%	63%		44.	Plumbers & Pipefitters Union	94%	5%
21.	National Auto Dealers Assn	31%	68%		45.	Blue Cross/Blue Shield	38%	61%
22.	FedEx Corp	44%	55%		46.	United Steelworkers	99%	0%
23.	National Assn of Home Builders	35%	64%		47.	Natl Assn/Insurance & Financial Advisors	42%	57%
24.	American Bankers Assn	40%	59%		48.	Operating Engineers Union	84%	14%
					49.	Deloitte Touche Tohmatsu	32%	67%
					50.	Air Line Pilots Assn	83%	16%

SOURCE: Center for Responsve Politics, "Top All-Time Donor Profiles," *www.opensecrets.org*.

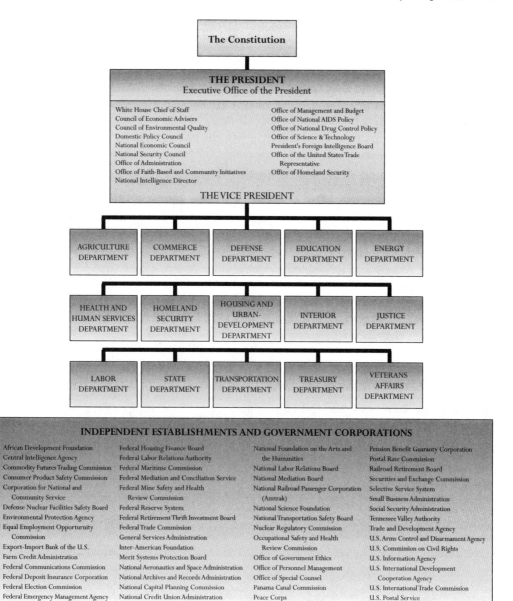

FIGURE 3–3 The Federal Bureaucracy Policymaking continues in the vast federal bureaucracy even after the passage of a law by Congress and its signing by the president.

from Capitol Hill and the White House to the bureaucracy—to the departments, agencies, and commissions of the executive branch (see Figure 3–3). The bureaucracy is not constitutionally empowered to decide policy questions, but it does so, nonetheless, as it performs its task of implementation.

Implementation and Policymaking.   Implementation involves all of the activities designed to carry out the policies enacted by the legislative branch. These activities include the creation of new organizations—departments, agencies, bureaus, and so on—or the assignment of new responsibilities to existing organizations. These organizations must translate laws into operational rules and regulations. They must hire personnel, draw up contracts, spend money, and perform tasks. All of these activities involve decisions by bureaucrats—decisions that determine policy.

As society has grown in size and complexity, the bureaucracy has increased its role in the policymaking process. The standard explanation for the growth of bureaucratic power is that Congress and the president do not have the time, energy, or technical expertise to look after the details of environmental protection or occupational safety or equal employment opportunity or transportation safety or hundreds of other aspects of governance in a modern society. Bureaucratic agencies receive only broad and general policy directions in the laws of Congress. They must decide themselves on important details of policy. This means that much of the actual policymaking process takes place *within* the Environmental Protection Agency (EPA), the Occupational Safety and Health Administration (OSHA), the Equal Employment Opportunity Commission (EEOC), the National Transportation Safety Board, and hundreds of other bureaucratic agencies.

Bureaucratic power in policymaking is also explained by political decisions in Congress and the White House to shift responsibility for many policies to the bureaucracy. Congress and the president can take political credit for laws promising "safe and effective" drugs, "equal opportunity" employment, the elimination of "unfair" labor practices, and other equally lofty, yet vague and ambiguous, goals. It then becomes the responsibility of bureaucratic agencies, for example, the Food and Drug Administration (FDA), the EEOC, and the National Labor Relations Board (NLRB), to give practical meaning to these symbolic measures. Indeed, if the policies developed by these agencies turn out to be unpopular, Congress and the president can blame the bureaucrats.

Regulation and Policymaking.   Policy implementation often requires the development of formal rules and regulations by bureaucracies. Federal executive agencies publish about 60,000 pages of rules in the *Federal Register* each year. The rule-making process for federal agencies is prescribed by the Administrative Procedures Act, which requires agencies to

- Announce in the *Federal Register* that a new rule or regulation is being proposed.
- Hold hearings to allow interest groups to present evidence and assignments regarding the proposed rule.
- Conduct research on the proposed rule's economic impact, environmental impact, and so on.
- Solicit "public comments" (usually the arguments of interest groups).
- Consult with higher officials, including the Office of Management and Budget.
- Publish the new rule or regulation in the *Federal Register.*

Rule making by the bureaucracy is central to the policymaking process. Formal rules that appear in the *Federal Register* have the force of law. Bureaucratic agencies may levy fines and penalties for violations of these regulations, and these fines and penalties are enforceable in the courts. Congress itself can only amend or repeal a formal regulation by passing a new law and obtaining the president's signature. Controversial bureaucratic regulations (policies) may remain in effect when Congress is slow to act, when legislation is blocked by key congressional committee members, or when the president supports the bureaucracy and refuses to sign bills overturning regulations. The courts usually do not overturn bureaucratic regulations unless they exceed the authority granted to the agency by law or unless the agency has not followed the proper procedure in adopting them.

Adjudication and Policymaking. Policy implementation by bureaucracies often involves adjudication of individual cases. (While rule making resembles the legislative process, adjudication resembles the judicial process.) In adjudication, bureaucrats must decide whether a person, firm, corporation, and so on has complied with laws and regulations and, if not, what penalties or corrective actions are to be applied. Federal regulatory agencies—for example, the EPA, the EEOC, the Internal Revenue Service (IRS), the Federal Trade Commission (FTC), the Securities and Exchange Commission (SEC)—are heavily engaged in adjudication. They have established procedures for investigation, notification, hearing, decision, and appeal; individuals and firms involved in these proceedings often hire lawyers specializing in the field of regulation. Administrative hearings are somewhat less formal than a court trial, and the "judges" are employees of the agency itself. Losers may appeal to the federal courts, but the history of agency successes in the courts discourages many appeals. The record of agency decisions in individual cases is a form of public policy. Just as previous court decisions reflect judicial policy, previous administrative decisions reflect bureaucratic policy.

Bureaucratic Discretion and Policymaking. It is true that much of the work of bureaucrats is administrative routine—issuing Social Security checks, collecting and filing income tax returns, delivering the mail. But bureaucrats almost always have some discretion in performing even routine tasks. Often individual cases do not exactly fit established rules; often more than one rule might be applied to the same case, resulting in different outcomes. For example, the IRS administers the U.S. tax code, but each auditing agent has considerable discretion in deciding which rules to apply to a taxpayer's income, deductions, business expenses, and so on. Indeed, identical tax information submitted to different IRS offices almost always results in different estimates of tax liability. But even in more routine tasks, from processing Medicare applications to forwarding mail, individual bureaucrats can be friendly and helpful, or hostile and obstructive.[18]

Policy Bias of Bureaucrats. Generally bureaucrats believe strongly in the value of their programs and the importance of their tasks. EPA officials are strongly committed to the environmental movement; officials in the Central Intelligence Agency (CIA) believe strongly in the importance of good intelligence to the nation's security; officials in the Social Security Administration are strongly committed to maintaining the benefits of the retirement system. But in addition to these professional motives, bureaucrats, like everyone else, seek higher pay, greater job security, and added power and prestige for themselves.

Professional and personal motives converge to inspire bureaucrats to expand the powers, functions, and budgets of their agencies. (Conversely bureaucrats try to protect their "turf" against reductions in functions, authority, and budgets.) "Budget maximization"—expanding the agency's budget as much as possible—is a driving force in government bureaucracies.[19] This is especially true regarding discretionary funds in an agency's budget—funds that bureaucrats have flexibility in deciding how to spend, rather than funds committed by law to specific purposes. The bureaucratic bias toward new functions and added authority and increases in personnel and budgets helps explain the growth of government over time.

Policy Evaluation: Impressionistic versus Systematic

The policy process model implies that evaluation is the final step in policymaking. It implies that policymakers—Congress, the president, interest groups, bureaucrats, the media, think tanks, and so on—seek to learn whether or not policies are achieving their stated goals; at what costs; and with what effects, intended and unintended, on society. Sophisticated versions of the model portray a "feedback" linkage—evaluations of current policy identify new problems and set in motion the policymaking process once again.

However, most policy evaluations in Washington, state capitols, and city halls are unsystematic and impressionistic. They came in the form of interest group complaints about the inadequacies of laws or budgets in protecting or advancing their concerns; in media stories exposing waste or fraud or mismanagement in a program or decrying the inadequacies of government policies in dealing with one crisis or another; in legislative hearings in which executive officials are questioned and occasionally badgered by committee members or their staffs about policies or programs; and sometimes even in citizens' complaints to members of Congress, the White House, or the media. Yet these "evaluations" often succeed in stimulating reform—policy changes designed to remedy perceived mistakes, inadequacies, wasteful expenditures, and other flaws in existing policy.

But as we shall observe in Chapter 15 ("Policy Evaluation: Finding Out What Happens after a Law Is Passed") *systematic policy evaluation* is relatively rare in government. We define systematic evaluation to mean careful, objective, scientific assessment of the current and long-term effects of policies on both target and nontarget situations or groups, as well as an assessment of the ratio of current and long-term costs to whatever benefits are identified.

SUMMARY

The policy process model focuses on *how* policies are made, rather than on the substance or content of policies. The model identifies a variety of activities that occur within the political system, including identification of problems and agenda setting, formulating policy proposals, legitimating policies, implementing policies, and evaluating their effectiveness.

1. Agenda setting is deciding what will be decided; that is, what issues will be covered by the media, brought to the attention of decision makers, and identified as problems requiring government solutions.

2. A "bottom-up" portrayal of policymaking emphasizes the role of public opinion in setting the agenda for policymakers. Events, and media reporting of them, can focus public opinion on issues, problems, and "crises." But it is not always clear whether opinion molds policy or policy creates opinion.

3. A "top-down" model of policymaking emphasizes the role of national leadership in creating issues and formulating policy. The general public does not have opinions on many specific policy questions. In opinion polls, Americans express doubt about whether the government understands their thinking or acts for the benefit of all.

4. The mass media, particularly the television networks, play a major role in agenda setting. By deciding what will be news, the media set the agenda for political discussion. The continuing focus on the dramatic, violent, and negative aspects of American life may unintentionally create apathy and alienation—television malaise.

5. A great deal of policy formulation occurs outside the formal governmental process. Prestigious, private, policy-planning organizations—such as the Council on Foreign Relations—explore policy alternatives, advise governments, develop policy consensus, and even supply top governmental leaders. The policy-planning organizations bring together the leadership of the corporate and financial worlds, the mass media, the foundations, the leading intellectuals, and top government officials.

6. The activities of the proximate policymakers—the president, Congress, executive agencies, and so forth—attract the attention of most commentators and political scientists. But nongovernmental leaders, in business and finance, foundations, policy-planning organizations, the mass media, and other interest groups, may have already set the policy agenda and selected major policy goals. The activities of the proximate policymakers tend to center around the means, rather than the ends, of public policy.

7. Congress is designated in the Constitution as the principal instrument of policy legitimation. Congress members are influenced by the views of their cash constituents as much or more than by the views of their voting constituents back home. Big-money campaign contributors usually enjoy direct access to members of Congress during the lawmaking process.

8. Partisanship is on the rise in Congress. Party line voting now occurs on more than half of all roll call votes in Congress. Party divisions have occurred on many key votes in Congress in recent years.

9. Presidents are expected to provide the initiative for congressional lawmaking. Presidential initiatives are usually outlined in the annual State of the Union message and followed up in the presidential Budget of the United States Government. Presidents are more successful in getting their legislative proposals enacted when their own party controls Congress.

10. Policy implementation is an important component of the policymaking process. Bureaucrats make policy as they engage in the tasks of implementation—making regulations, adjudicating cases, and exercising their discretion. Professional and personal motives combine to bias bureaucrats toward expanding the powers and functions of their agencies and increasing their budgets, especially their discretionary funds.

Notes

1. V. O. Key, Jr., *Public Opinion and American Democracy* (New York: Knopf, 1967), p. 537.
2. G. William Domhoff, *Who Rules America? Power and Politics in the Year 2000* (Mountain View, CA: Mayfield, 1998), p. 127.
3. V. O. Key, Jr., *Public Opinion and American Democracy* (New York: Knopf, 1967), pp. 422–423.
4. Theodore White, *The Making of the President, 1972* (New York: Bantam, 1973), p. 7.
5. Leonard Silk and Mark Silk, *The American Establishment* (New York: Basic Books, 1980), p. 160.
6. Ibid., p. 179.
7. *Heritage Foundation Annual Report 1985* (Washington, DC: Heritage Foundation, 1985).
8. See Mark Green and Michele Jolin, eds., *Change for America: A Progressive Blueprint for the 44th President* (New York: Basic Books, 2009).
9. Lester Milbraith, "Interest Groups in Foreign Policy," in *Domestic Sources of Foreign Policy,* ed. James Rosenau (New York: Free Press, 1967), p. 247.
10. Council on Foreign Relations, *Annual Report,* 1988, p. 160.
11. Serious students of public policy are advised to read the books and journals published by these leading policy-planning organizations, especially *The Brookings Review* (published quarterly by the Brookings Institution, 1775 Massachusetts Avenue NW, Washington, DC 20036); *The American Enterprise* (published bimonthly by the American Enterprise Institute, 1150 17th Street NW, Washington, DC 20036); *Policy Review* (published quarterly by the Heritage Foundation, 214 Massachusetts Avenue NE, Washington, DC 20002); *Foreign Affairs* (published five times annually by the Council on Foreign Relations, 58 East 68th Street, New York, NY 10021).
12. Center for Responsive Politics (2009) *www.crp.org*
13. *Fortune,* December 1997.
14. *Polling Report,* March 1999.
15. "Speech to the Electors of Bristol," November 3, 1774.
16. Richard F. Fenno, Home Style (Boston: Little, Brown, 1978); also quoted in Roger H. Davidson and Walter T. Oleszek, *Congress and Its Members* (Washington, DC: CQ Press, 2000), p. 149.
17. Donald S. Van Meter and Carl E. Vanltorn, "The Policy Implementation Process," *Administration and Society,* 6 (February 1975), p. 447.
18. See James Q. Wilson, *Bureaucracy: What Governments Do and Why They Do It* (New York: Basic Books, 1989).
19. William Niskanen, *Bureaucracy and Representative Government* (Chicago: Aldine, 1971).

Bibliography

ANDERSON, JAMES E. *Public Policymaking: Introduction,* 6th ed. Boston: Houghton Mifflin, 2007.

CAMPBELL, COLTON C., and PAUL S. HERRNSON. *War Stories on Capitol Hill.* Upper Saddle River, NJ: Prentice Hall, 2004.

CIGLAR, ALLAN J., and BURDETT A. LOUIS. *Interest Group Politics,* 7th ed. Washington, DC: CQ Press, 2006.

DAVIDSON, ROGER H., WALTER J. OLESZEK, and FRANCES E. LEE. *Congress and Its Members,* 11th ed. Washington, DC: CQ Press, 2007.

GORMLEY, WILLIAM T., and STEVEN T. BALA. *Bureaucracy and Democracy: Accountability and Performance,* 2nd ed. Washington, DC: CQ Press, 2007.

GRABER, DORIS A. *Mass Media and American Politics,* 7th ed. Washington, DC: CQ Press, 2005.

HETHERINGTON, MARK T., and WILLIAM O. KEEFE. *Parties, Politics, and Public Policy in America,* 10th ed. Washington, DC: CQ Press, 2006.

KERWIN, CORNELIUS, M. *Rulemaking: How Government Agencies Write Law and Make Policy*, 3rd ed. Washington, DC: CQ Press, 2003.

KINGDON, JOHN W. *Agendas, Alternatives, and Public Policies.* Boston: Little, Brown, 1984.

SMITH, JAMES A. *The Idea Brokers: Think Tanks and the Rise of the New Policy Elite.* New York: Macmillan, 1991.

Web Sites

CENTER FOR RESPONSIVE POLITICS. Source of information on campaign finances—contributions, recipients, PACs, lobbyists, etc. *www.opensecrets.org*

FEDERAL ELECTIONS COMMISSION. Official government site for campaign finance reports. *www.fec.gov*

REPUBLICAN NATIONAL COMMITTEE. Official site of the RNC, including GOP policy positions, press releases, news, etc. *www.rnc.org*

DEMOCRATIC NATIONAL COMMITTEE. Official site of the DNC, including Democratic Party policy positions, press releases, news, etc. *www.democrat.org*

THE BROOKINGS INSTITUTION. Liberal think tank for policy research, with policy studies, press briefings, etc. *www.brookings.org*

AMERICAN ENTERPRISE INSTITUTE. Moderate think tank for policy research, with policy studies, press briefings, etc. *www.aei.org*

HERITAGE FOUNDATION. Conservative think tank for policy research, with policy briefs, news about issues currently being debated in Congress, press releases, etc. *www.heritage.org*

COUNCIL ON FOREIGN RELATIONS. Leading foreign relations think tank, with task force reports and access to its journal, *Foreign Affairs. www.cfr.org*

CATO INSTITUTE. Libertarian (minimal government) think tank, with policy studies, press releases, etc. *www.cato.org*

CENTER FOR POLICY ALTERNATIVES. Think tank focusing on problems confronting state legislatures. *www.cfpa.org*

Criminal Justice

Rationality and Irrationality in Public Policy

Crime in America

Crime is a central problem confronting any society. The rational strategy of crime fighting is known as *deterrence*. The goal of deterrence is to make the costs of committing crimes far greater than any benefits potential criminals might derive from their acts. With advanced knowledge of these costs, rational individuals should be deterred from committing crimes. But before we describe the deterrence model and assess its effectiveness, let us examine the nature and extent of crime in America.

Measuring Crime. It is not easy to learn exactly how much crime occurs in society. The official crime rates are based on the Federal Bureau of Investigation's Uniform Crime Reporting Program, but the FBI reports are based on figures supplied by state and local police agencies (see Table 4–1). The FBI has established a uniform classification of the number of serious crimes per 100,000 people that are reported to the police: *violent crimes* (crimes against persons)—murder and nonnegligent manslaughter, forcible rape, robbery, aggravated assault; and *property crimes* (crimes committed against property only)—burglary, larceny, arson, and theft, including auto theft. But one should be cautious in interpreting official crime rates. They are really a function of several factors: (1) the willingness of people to report crimes to the police, (2) the adequacy of the reporting system that tabulates crime, and (3) the amount of crime itself.

Trends in Crime Rates. Crime is no longer at the top of the nation's policy agenda. Since peaking in the early 1990s, crime rates have actually declined (see Figure 4–1). Law enforcement officials attribute successes in crime fighting to police "crackdowns," more aggressive "community policing," and longer prison sentences for repeat offenders, including "three strikes you're out" laws. (All are discussed later in this chapter.) In support of this claim, they observe that the greatest reductions in crime occurred in the nation's largest cities, especially those such as New York that adopted tougher law enforcement practices.

TABLE 4–1   Crime Rates in the United States Official crime rates (offenses reported to police) are compiled and published each year by the FBI, enabling us to follow the rise and fall of various types of crimes.

	Offenses Reported to Police per 100,000 Population								
	1960	**1970**	**1980**	**1985**	**1990**	**1995**	**2000**	**2004**	**2008**
Violent Crimes	160	360	597	557	730	685	507	463	467
Murder	5	8	10	8	9	8	6	6	6
Forcible Rape	9	18	37	37	41	37	32	32	30
Robbery	60	172	251	209	256	221	145	137	148
Assault	85	162	298	303	423	418	324	289	284
Property Crimes	1,716	3,599	5,353	4,666	5,073	4,591	3,618	3,514	3,264

SOURCE: Federal Bureau of Investigation, *Crime in the United States* (annual).

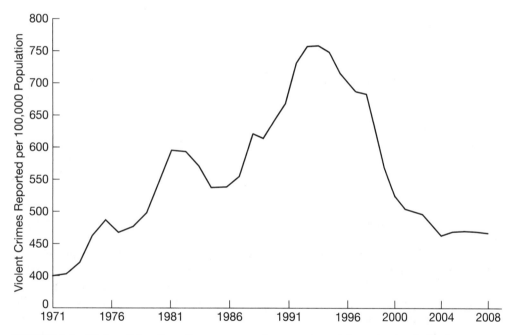

FIGURE 4–1   Violent Crime Rate Contrary to popular perceptions, violent crime has declined dramatically over the past fifteen years.
SOURCES: U.S. Department of Justice, Bureau of Justice Statistics, *Sourcebook of Criminal Justice Statistics, 1999;* Federal Bureau of Investigation, *Crime in the United States, 2008.*

Violence attributed to terrorism is now separately reported by the FBI. (Thus, the murder rate reported for 2001 in the FBI's Uniform Crime Reporting Program does *not* include the deaths that resulted from the terrorist attacks on America on September 11, 2001.) In all, there were 3,047 deaths from the 9/11 terrorist attack on New York's World Trade Center, the Pentagon in Washington, and the airliner crash in Somerset County, Pennsylvania (see Chapter 14).

Victimization. FBI official crime rates understate the real amount of crime. Many crimes are not reported to the police and therefore cannot be counted in the official rate. In an effort to learn the real amount of crime in the nation, the U.S. Justice Department regularly surveys a national sample, asking people whether they have been a victim of a crime during the past year.[1] These surveys reveal that the victimization rate is much higher than the official crime rate. The number of forcible rapes, as well as burglaries, assaults, and robberies, is twice the number reported to police. And property crimes are three times higher. Only auto theft and murder statistics are reasonably accurate, indicating that most people call the police when their car is stolen or someone is murdered.

The victimization rate for violent crime, although over twice as high as the reported crime rate, has generally risen and fallen over the years in the same fashion as the crime rate. That is, the victimization rate for violent crime peaked in the early 1990s, and then fell dramatically during the remainder of the decade. Why do people fail to report crime to the police? The most common reason given by interviewees is the belief that the police cannot be effective in dealing with the crime. Other reasons include the feeling that the crime is "a private matter" or that the victim does not want to harm the offender. Fear of reprisal is mentioned much less frequently, usually in cases of assault and family crimes.

Juvenile Crime. The juvenile system is not designed for deterrence. Children are not held fully responsible for their actions, in the belief that they do not possess the ability to understand the nature or consequences of their behavior or its rightness or wrongness. Yet juvenile crime, most of which is committed by 15- to 17-year-olds, accounts for about 20 percent of the nation's overall crime rate. Offenders under 18 years of age are usually processed in a separate juvenile court.

Juvenile courts rarely impose serious punishment. Available data suggest that about 13 percent of juveniles charged with *violent* crimes are sent to adult court; 16 percent are sent to juvenile detention centers; and the remaining 71 percent are either dismissed, placed on probation, given suspended sentences, or sent home under supervision of a parent.[2] Very few juveniles who are sentenced to detention facilities stay there very long. Even those convicted of murder cannot be kept in detention facilities beyond the age of 21. Moreover, the names of juveniles arrested, charged, or convicted are withheld from publication or broadcast, eliminating whatever social stigma might be associated with their crimes. Their juvenile criminal records are expunged when they become adults, so that they can begin adulthood with "clean" records. Whatever the merits of the juvenile system in the treatment of young children, it is clear that the absence of deterrence contributes to criminal behavior among older youths—15-, 16-, and 17-year-olds. Indeed these years are among the most crime-prone ages.

Only in the last few years have states begun to change their juvenile systems to incorporate the notion of deterrence. All 50 states now try some juvenile offenders age 14 and over in the adult system for serious crimes. In most states decisions to transfer juveniles to the adult court system are made by either judges or prosecutors. However, relatively few juveniles are tried as adults.

"Nonserious" and "Victimless" Crimes. The FBI's Uniform Crime Reporting Program does not count so-called nonserious or victimless crimes, including drug violations, prostitution and sex crimes, gambling, driving while intoxicated, and liquor law violations. These crimes vastly outnumber the FBI's indexed serious crimes. There are five times as many arrests for non-serious as for serious crimes.

Some crimes are labeled "victimless" because participation by all parties to the crime is presumed to be voluntary. For example, prostitution is considered a victimless crime because both the buyer and seller voluntarily engage in it. Most drug crimes—the sale and use of modest amounts of drugs—are voluntary and considered victimless. Nonetheless, there is a close relationship between these nonserious crimes and more serious FBI index crimes. Prostitutes are vulnerable to violence and theft because perpetrators know that they are unlikely to report crime to the police for fear of prosecution themselves. Drug dealers have no way to enforce agreements by going to the courts. They must resort to violence or intimidation to conclude deals, and they too are unlikely to report crimes to the police. It is sometimes argued that if drugs and prostitution were legalized, their association with serious crime would diminish, just as the end of prohibition largely ended crime associated with the sale of alcohol.

White-Collar Crime. Most white-collar crime does not appear in the FBI's index of crimes. Nonetheless, white-collar crime is estimated to cost the American public more in lost dollars than all of the "serious" index crimes put together. Fraud (the perversion of the truth in order to cause others to part with their money), as well as forgery, perjury (lying under oath), tax evasion, and conspiring with others to commit these crimes, are all part of white-collar crime. Perhaps the most well-publicized white-collar crimes occurred in Enron Corporation, once the seventh-largest corporation in America. The fraud involved upper management and their accountants hiding billions of dollars in corporate losses in covert "partnerships" in order to make Enron appear profitable and its stock valuable. Top Enron executives invested employee retirement savings in the company's stock. These same executives then sold their own stock at inflated prices, pocketing millions for themselves. When the fraud was unraveled in 2001, Enron went bankrupt, and the stock became worthless. Investors, employees, retirees, and others were defrauded.

Corruption in Government. It is widely believed that "politics is corrupt," but it is difficult to measure the full extent of corruption in government. Part of the problem is in defining terms: what is "corrupt" to one observer may be "just politics" to another. The line between unethical behavior and criminal activity is a fuzzy one. Unethical behavior may include favoritism toward relatives, friends, and constituents, or conflicts of interest, in which public officials decide issues in which they have a personal financial interest. Not all unethical behavior is criminal conduct. But *bribery* is a criminal offense—soliciting or receiving anything of value in exchange for the performance of a governmental duty. And *perjury* is lying under oath.

The U.S. Justice Department reports on *federal* prosecutions of public officials for violations of federal criminal statutes. These reports do not include state prosecutions, so they do not cover all of the criminal indictments brought against public officials each year. Nonetheless, these figures indicate that over 1,100 public officials are indicted by the Justice Department each year.[3]

It is not uncommon for special interests to contribute to the campaign chests of elected officeholders from whom they are seeking favorable governmental actions. Indeed, public officials may come to expect contributions from contractors, developers, unions, and others doing business with government. A "pay to play" culture develops in many cities and states. But the key difference between merely rewarding supporters and engaging in bribery is the *quid pro quo*: if a payment or contribution is made for a specific governmental action, it risks criminal prosecution as bribery. So prudent interests to ensure that their contributions are made well in advance of the governmental actions they seek. Prudent politicians avoid any communications that suggest that a particular official action was made in exchange for a payment or contribution.

Hate Crimes.   Hate crimes are offenses motivated by hatred against a victim or a group based upon race, religion, sexual orientation, ethnicity or national origin, or disability. A hate crime is bias-motivated criminal *conduct*; it is not the mere *expression* of bias or hatred.

Since the official reporting of hate crimes began in the 1990s, roughly 8,000 incidents of hate crimes have been reported annually to the FBI. This is a small proportion of the more than 12 million crimes reported each year. A majority of reported hate crimes are motivated by race, with most of these crimes directed at African Americans (see Figure 4–2). Of religious hate crimes, most are anti-Jewish. Of ethnicity-motivated crimes, most are anti-Hispanic. And of sexual orientation hate crimes, most are anti-male homosexual.

Bias-motivated crimes cause greater harm to society than crimes committed with other motivations, for example, greed, passion, etc. The U.S. Supreme Court in upholding a Wisconsin law that increased the penalty for crimes intentionally inflicted upon victims based upon their race, religion, sexual orientation, national origin or disability, observed that "bias-motivated crimes are more likely to provoke retaliatory crimes, inflict distinct emotional harms on their victims, and incite community unrest . . . the State's desire to

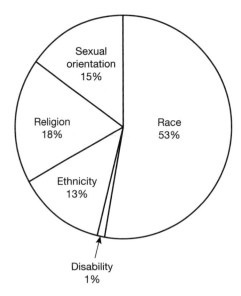

FIGURE 4–2   Bias Motivation in Hate Crimes Bias-motivated crimes are a small proportion of total crimes committed each year, not they are considered to be especially harmful to society.
SOURCE: Data from *Statistical Abstract of the United States 2008*, p. 198.

redress these perceived wrongs provides an adequate explanation for its penalty enhancement provision over and above mere disagreement with offenders' beliefs or biases.[4] Motivation has always been an element in criminal cases. It does not violate the First Amendment freedom of expression to consider motivation in a criminal case, but there must be a crime committed, independent of the defendant's beliefs or biases.

Historically the Supreme Court viewed prohibitions on offensive speech as unconstitutional infringements of First Amendment freedoms. "The remedy to be applied is more speech, not enforced silence." The Supreme Court was called upon to review prohibitions on hate speech in 1992 when the city of Saint Paul, Minnesota, enacted an ordinance prohibiting any communication that "arouses anger, alarm, or resentment among others on the basis of race, color, creed, religion, or gender." But the Supreme Court, in a unanimous decision, struck down the city's effort to prohibit expressions only because they "hurt feelings."[5] Speech expressing racial, gender, or religious intolerance is still speech and is protected by the First Amendment.

While upholding enhanced penalties for bias-motivated crimes, the Supreme Court has held that a criminal defendant's "abstract beliefs, however obnoxious to most people, may not be taken into consideration by a sentencing judge."[6] But the defendants motive for committing a particular criminal act has traditionally been a factor in sentencing, and a defendant's verbal statements can be used to determine motive.

Crime and Deterrence

The deterrence strategy in criminal justice policy focuses on punishment—its certainty, swiftness, and severity. The effectiveness of deterrence depends on:

- The *certainty* that a crime will be followed by costly punishment. Justice must be sure.
- The *swiftness* of the punishment following the crime. Long delays between crime and punishment break the link in the mind of the criminal between the criminal act and its consequences. And a potential wrongdoer must believe that the costs of a crime will occur within a meaningful time frame, not in a distant, unknowable future. Justice must be swift.
- The *severity* of the punishment. Punishment that is perceived as no more costly than the ordinary hazards of life on the streets, which the potential criminal faces anyhow, will not deter. Punishment must clearly outweigh whatever benefits might be derived from a life of crime in the minds of potential criminals. Punishment must be severe.

These criteria for an effective deterrent policy are ranked in the order of their probable importance. That is, it is most important that punishment for crime be certain. The severity of punishment is probably less important than its swiftness or certainty.

Social Heterogeneity. Of course, there are many other conflicting theories of crime in America. For example, it is sometimes argued that this nation's crime rate is a product of its social heterogeneity—the multiethnic, multiracial character of the American population. Low levels of crime in European countries, Japan, and China are often attributed to their

TABLE 4–2   Federal and State Prisoners by Race Blacks and Hispanics comprise a majority of federal and state prisoners; these groups are also far more likely than whites to be victims of crime.

Race	Percent
White	34.3
Black	40.7
Hispanic	19.2
Other races	2.9
Two or more races	2.9

SOURCE: Bureau of Justice Statistics, 2008.

TABLE 4–3   Murder: Victims and Weapons Black males are almost eight times more likely to be murdered than white males; most murders are committed with guns.

	Victims (Murder Rate, 2005)	Weapons (Percent, 2005)	
Total	5.9	Guns, total	68
		Handguns	50
		Stabbing	13
White			
Male	5.3	Blunt object	4
Female	1.9	Strangulation	1
Black		Beating	6
Male	37.1	Arson	1
Female	6.4	Other	7

SOURCE: *Statistical Abstract of the United States 2008*, pp. 195–196.

homogeneous populations and shared cultures. African Americans in the United States are both victims and perpetrators of crime far more frequently than whites. Whereas African Americans constitute only 12.7 percent of the population, they account for nearly 40 percent of all persons in federal and state prisons (see Table 4–2).

African Americans are also much more likely to be victims of crime; the murder victimization rate for African American males is almost ten times greater than for white males (see Table 4–3).

Socialization and Control.   Yet another explanation of crime focuses on the erosion of social institutions—families, schools, churches, communities—that help to control behavior. These are the institutions that transmit values to children and socially censure impermissible behavior among adults. When ties to family, church, and community are loosened or nonexistent, individuals are less constrained by social mores. Older juveniles turn to peer groups, including gangs, for status and recognition. Defiance of authority, including arrest and detention, and other "macho" behaviors become a source of pride among young males. The deterrent effect of the criminal justice system is minimized. In contrast, when family oversight of behavior is close or when young people find status and recognition in school activities, sports or recreation, or church affairs, social mores are reinforced.

Irrational Crime. It is also argued that crime is irrational—that the criminal does not weigh benefits against potential costs before committing the act. Many acts of violence are committed by persons acting in blind rage—murders and aggravated assaults among family members, for example. Many rapes are acts of violence, inspired by hatred of women, rather than efforts to obtain sexual pleasure. More murders occur in the heat of argument than in the commission of other felonies. These are crimes of passion rather than calculated acts. Thus, it is argued, *no* rational policies can be devised to deter these irrational acts.

Deterrence versus Liberty. Finally, we must recognize that the reduction of crime is not the overriding value of American society. Americans cherish individual liberty. Freedom from repression—from unlawful arrests, forced confessions, restrictions on movement, curfews, arbitrary police actions, unlimited searches of homes or seizures of property, punishment without trial, trials without juries, unfair procedures, brutal punishments, and so on—is more important to Americans than freedom from crime. Many authoritarian governments boast of low crime rates and criminal justice systems that ensure certain, swift, and severe punishment, but these governments fail to protect the personal liberties of their citizens. Indeed, given the choice of punishing all of the guilty, even if some innocents are also punished by mistake, or taking care that innocent persons not be punished, even if some guilty people escape, most Americans would choose the second alternative—protecting the innocent.

Does Crime Pay?

While we acknowledge that there are multiple explanations for crime, we shall argue that the frequency of crime in America is affected by rational criminal justice policy: *crime is more frequent when deterrence is lax, and crime declines with the movement toward stricter deterrence policy.*

Lack of Certainty. The best available estimates of the certainty of punishment for serious crime suggests that very few crimes actually result in jail sentences for the perpetrators. Yearly 12 million serious crimes are reported to the police annually, but only 1 million persons are arrested for these crimes (see Figure 4–3). Some of those arrested are charged with committing more than one crime, but it is estimated that the police "clear" less than 20 percent of reported crimes by arresting the offender. Some offenders are handled as juveniles; some are permitted to plead guilty to minor offenses; others are released because witnesses fail to appear or evidence is weak or inadmissible in court. Convicted felons are three times more likely to receive probation than a prison sentence. Thus, even if punishment could deter crime, our current criminal justice system does *not* ensure punishment for crime.

Lack of Swiftness. The deterrent effect of a criminal justice system is lost when punishment is so long delayed that it has little relationship to the crime. The bail system, together with trial delays, allow criminal defendants to escape the consequences of their acts for long, indefinite periods of time. Most criminal defendants are free on bail shortly after their arrest;

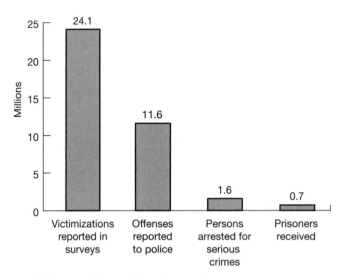

FIGURE 4–3   Crime and Punishment Many crimes are not reported to police, many crimes do not result in arrests, and relatively few criminals are imprisoned; this lack of certainty of punishment for crime undermines deterrence.
SOURCE: Data from *Statistical Abstract of the United States*, 2008.

only those accused of the most serious crimes, or adjudged to be likely to flee before trial, are held in jail without bond. In preliminary hearings held shortly after arrest, judges release most defendants pending trial; even after a trial and a guilty verdict, many defendants are free on bail pending the outcome of lengthy appeals. The Constitution guarantees persons accused of crimes freedom from "excessive bail" (Eighth Amendment), and judges may not hold defendants in jail simply because they think the defendants might commit additional crimes while out on bail.

The court system works very slowly, and delays favor the criminal defendant. Defendants request delays in court proceedings to remain free as long as possible. Moreover, they know that witnesses against them will lose interest, move away, grow tired of the hassle, and even forget key facts, if only the case can be postponed long enough.

Justice delayed destroys the deterrent effect, especially in the minds of youthful offenders, who may be "present oriented" rather than "future oriented." They may consider the benefits of their criminal acts to be immediate, while the costs are so far in the future that they have no real meaning. Or the costs may be estimated to be only the arrest itself and a night in jail before release on bail. For deterrence to work, the perceived costs of crime must be greater than the perceived benefits in *the minds of potential wrongdoers.*

The Question of Severity.   More people are imprisoned today in America than at any previous time. State and federal prisons currently hold over 1,400,000 prisoners, up from 320,000 in 1980. Not only are there more inmates in the nation's prisons, but also the percentage of the nation's population behind bars, the incarceration rate, is the highest in recent history.[7]

In recent years, prison sentences have lengthened dramatically. Prison-building programs, begun in the states in the 1980s, expanded the nation's prison capacity and resulted in fewer early releases of prisoners. Many state legislatures enacted mandatory minimum prison terms for repeat offenders (including popular "three strikes you're out" laws mandating life sentences for third violent felonies). And many states enacted determinant sentencing or sentencing guidelines (legally prescribed specific prison terms for specified offenses) limiting judicial discretion in sentencing.

The result of these changes in judicial policy has been a dramatic increase in the time served for violent offenses. The average time served for such offenses has doubled since 1990, and the average percentage of sentences served has risen from less than 50 percent to more than 80 percent.

Deterrence or Incapacitation?   Even if stricter criminal justice policies are partly or primarily responsible for declining crime rates, it is not clear whether these policies are creating a deterrent effect or simply incapacitating wrongdoers and thereby preventing them from committing crimes outside prison walls.

But there is a close correlation between *rising* incarceration rates and *declining* rates of violent crime (see Figure 4–4). Perhaps the nation is succeeding in getting more violent

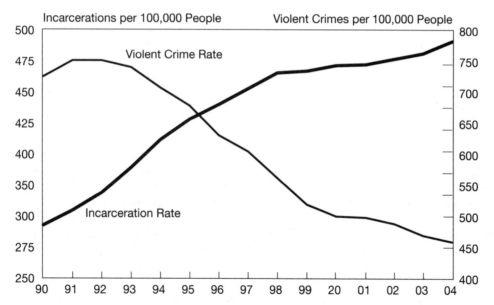

FIGURE 4–4   As Incarceration Rate Rises, Violent Crime Declines The incarceration rate (the number of prisoners in relation to the nation's population) has risen dramatically, while the violent crime rate has declined dramatically, suggesting that imprisoning criminals reduces crime.
Note: Violent Crime Rate Scale on right axis, ranging from 732 in 1990 to 465 in 2004.
    Incarcerations Rate Scale on left axis, ranging from 297 in 1990 to 495 in 2004.
*Includes prisoners in federal and state prisons at year's end.
SOURCE: Bureau of Justice Statistics, 2006.

criminals off the streets (incapacitation). Or perhaps the increased severity of punishment is having a deterrent effect.

Police and Law Enforcement

The principal responsibility for law enforcement in America continues to rest with state and local governments. The major *federal* law enforcement agencies—the FBI and the Drug Enforcement Administration (DEA) in the Department of Justice, and the Bureau of Alcohol, Tobacco, and Firearms (ATF) in the Treasury Department—are charged with enforcing federal laws. Although the role of the federal government in law enforcement is growing, state and local governments continue to carry the major burdens of police protection, judicial systems, and prison and parole programs. The federal Department of Justice employs about 175,000 people in all law enforcement activities, compared with about 1.7 million state and local government law enforcement and corrections personnel.[8] Federal prisons contain about 175,000 inmates, compared with over 1.3 million in state prisons.[9]

Police Functions.   At least three important functions in society are performed by police: enforcing laws, keeping the peace, and furnishing services. Actually, law enforcement may take up only a small portion of a police officer's daily activity. The service function is far more common—attending accidents, directing traffic, escorting crowds, assisting stranded motorists, and so on. The function of peacekeeping is also very common—breaking up fights, quieting noisy parties, handling domestic or neighborhood quarrels, and the like. It is in this function that police exercise the greatest discretion in the application of the law. In most of these incidents, it is difficult to determine blame, and the police must use personal discretion in handling each case.

The police are on the front line of society's efforts to resolve conflict. Indeed, instead of a legal or law enforcement role, the police are more likely to adopt a peace-keeping role. They are generally lenient in their arrest practices, that is, they use their arrest powers less often than the law allows. Rather than arresting people, the police prefer first to reestablish order. Of course, the decision to be more or less lenient in enforcing the law gives the police a great deal of discretion—they exercise decision-making powers on the streets.

Police Discretion.   What factors influence police decision making? Probably the first factor is the attitude of the other people involved in police encounters. If a person adopts an acquiescent role, displays deference and respect for the police, and conforms to police expectations, he or she is much less likely to be arrested than a person who shows disrespect or uses abusive language.[10] This is not just an arbitrary response. The police learn through training and experience the importance of establishing their authority on the streets.

Community Policing.   Most police activity is "reactive": typically two officers in a patrol car responding to a radio dispatcher who is forwarding reports of incidents. Police agencies frequently evaluate themselves in terms of the number and frequency of patrols, the number of calls responded to, and the elapsed time between the call and the arrival of officers on the scene. But there is little evidence that any of these measures affect crime rates or even citizens' fear of crime or satisfaction with the police.[11]

An alternative strategy is for police to become more "proactive": typically by becoming more visible in the community by walking or bicycling the sidewalks of high crime areas; learning to recognize individuals on the streets and winning their confidence and respect; deterring or scaring away drug dealers, prostitutes, and their customers by a police presence. But this "community policing" is often expensive.

Police Crackdowns.   Police crackdowns—beefed-up police actions against juvenile gangs, prostitutes, and drug traffickers; the frisking of likely suspects on the street for guns and drugs; and arrests for (often ignored) public drinking, graffiti, and vandalism—can reduce crime only if supported by the community as well as prosecutors and judges. Crime rates, even murder rates, have been significantly reduced during periods of police crackdowns in major cities.[12] But these efforts are often sporadic; enthusiasm ebbs as jails fill up and the workload of prosecutors and courts multiplies.

Broken Windows.   New York City's experience suggests what can be accomplished by stepped-up police activity. In 1993 the city's newly elected mayor Rudolph Giuliani began to implement what became known as the "broken windows" strategy in law enforcement. The strategy is based on the notion that one neglected broken window in a building will soon lead to many other broken windows. In crime fighting, this theory translates into more arrests for petty offenses (for example, subway turnstile jumping, graffiti, vandalism, and aggressive panhandling, including unwanted automobile window washing) in order not only to improve the quality of life in the city but also to lead to the capture of suspects wanted for more serious crimes. This strategy was coupled with the use of the latest computer mapping technology to track crime statistics and pinpoint unusual activity in specific neighborhoods. Each police precinct was regularly evaluated on the number and types of crimes occurring in it.

The introduction of these hard-line tactics created more than a little controversy. Civil libertarians, as well as many minority-group leaders, complained that these police tactics fall disproportionately on minorities and the poor. It was alleged that Mayor Giuliani's hard-nosed attitude toward crime created an atmosphere that led to increased police brutality.

But the "broken windows" strategy appears to have made New York City, once among the highest crime rate cities in the nation, now the safest large city in America. Over a five-year period following the introduction of Mayor Giuliani's tough policies, the city's overall crime rate fell by an unprecedented 50 percent, and murders fell by 70 percent.[13]

Federalizing Crime

Politicians in Washington are continually pressured to make "a federal crime" out of virtually every offense in society. Neither Democrats nor Republicans, liberals nor conservatives, are willing to risk their political futures by telling their constituents that crime fighting is a state and local responsibility. So Washington lawmakers continue to add common offenses to the ever lengthening list of federal crimes.

The Federal Role in Law Enforcement.   Traditionally, the federal government's responsibilities were limited to the enforcement of a relatively narrow range of federal criminal laws, including laws dealing with counterfeiting and currency violations; tax evasion, including alcohol, tobacco, and firearm taxes; fraud and embezzlement; robbery or theft of federally insured funds, including banks; interstate criminal activity; murder or assault of a federal official; and federal drug laws. While some federal criminal laws overlapped state laws, most criminal activity—murder, rape, robbery, assault, burglary, theft, auto theft, gambling, sex offenses, and so on—fell under state jurisdiction. Indeed, the *police power* was believed to be one of the "reserved" powers states referred to in the Tenth Amendment.

But over time Congress has made more and more offenses *federal* crimes. Today federal crimes range from drive-by shootings to obstructing sidewalks in front of abortion clinics. Any violent offense motivated by racial, religious, or ethnic animosity is a "hate crime" subject to federal investigation and prosecution. "Racketeering" and "conspiracy" (organizing and communicating with others about the intent to commit a crime) is a federal crime. The greatest impact of federal involvement in law enforcement is found in drug-related crime. Drug offenders may be tried in either federal or state courts or both. Federal drug laws, including those prohibiting possession, carry heavier penalties than those of most states.

Constitutional Constraints.   Only recently has the U.S. Supreme Court recognized that federalizing crime may impinge upon the reserved powers of states. In 1994 Congress passed a popular Violence Against Women Act that allowed victims of gender-motivated violence, including rape, to sue their attackers for monetary damages in federal court. Congress defended its constitutional authority to involve itself in crimes against women by citing the Commerce Clause, arguing that crimes against women interfered with interstate commerce, the power over which is given to the national government in Article 1 of the Constitution. But in 2000 the Supreme Court said, "If accepted, this reasoning would allow Congress to regulate any crime whose nationwide, aggregate impact has substantial effects on employment, production, transit, or consumption. Moreover, such reasoning will not limit Congress to regulating violence, but may be applied equally as well, to family law and other areas of state regulation since the aggregate effect of marriage, divorce, and childbearing on the national economy is undoubtedly significant. The Constitution requires a distinction between what is truly national and what is truly local, and there's no better example of the police power, which the Founders undeniably left reposed in the states and denied the central government, than the suppression of violent crime in vindication of its victims."[14] In Justice Scalia's opinion, allowing Congress to claim that violence against women interfered with interstate commerce would open the door to federalizing *all* crime: this "would allow general federal criminal laws, because all crime affects interstate commerce."

Multiple Federal Agencies.   The U.S. Department of Justice, headed by the attorney general, handles all criminal prosecutions for violation of federal laws. The Justice Department succeeds in convicting nearly 75,000 offenders in federal district courts, about one-third of these convictions are for drug offenses. The federal government's principal investigative agencies are the Federal Bureau of Investigation (FBI) and the Drug Enforcement Administration (DEA), both units of the Department of Justice, and the Bureau of Alcohol, Tobacco, and Firearms (ATF) in the Treasury Department.

Efforts to combine these federal law enforcement agencies have consistently foundered in bureaucratic turf battles. (The Central Intelligence Agency (CIA) is an independent agency, which, prior to the passage of the USA Patriot Act in 2001, was constrained in sharing intelligence information with domestic law enforcement agencies.) The Department of Homeland Security includes the Transportation Security Administration; Immigration and Customs Enforcement (ICE), formerly the Immigration and Naturalization Service (INS); the Border Patrol; the Secret Service; and the U.S. Coast Guard, all of which exercise some law enforcement responsibilities (see Chapter 14). This proliferation of federal law enforcement organizations does little to help fight crime.

Crime and Guns

Gun control legislation is a common policy initiative following highly publicized murders or assassination attempts on prominent figures. The federal Gun Control Act of 1968 was a response to the assassinations of Senator Robert F. Kennedy and Martin Luther King, Jr., in that year, and efforts to legislate additional restrictions occurred after attempts to assassinate Presidents Gerald Ford and Ronald Reagan. The rationale for restricting gun purchases, licensing gun owners, or banning guns altogether is that fewer crimes would be committed with guns if guns were less readily available. Murders, especially crimes of passion among family members or neighbors, would be reduced, if for no other reason than that it is physically more difficult to kill someone with only a knife, a club, or one's bare hands. Most murders are committed with guns (see Table 4–3).

Federal Gun Laws.   Various federal gun control acts[15] include the following:

- A ban on interstate and mail-order sales of handguns
- Prohibition of the sale of any firearms to convicted felons, fugitives, illegal aliens, drug users, or adjudicated mental defectives
- A requirement that all firearms dealers must be licensed by the federal Bureau of Alcohol, Tobacco, and Firearms
- A requirement that manufacturers record by serial number all firearms, and dealers record all sales. (Dealers must require proof of identity and residence of buyers, and buyers must sign a statement certifying their eligibility to purchase.)
- Continued restrictions of private ownership of automatic weapons, military weapons, and other heavy ordinance

Federal regulations also ban the importation of "assault weapons," which are generally defined as automatic weapons.

The Brady Law.   The federal Brady Law of 1993 requires a five-day waiting period for the purchase of a handgun. The national law is named for James S. Brady, former press secretary to President Ronald Reagan, who was severely wounded in the 1981 attempted assassination of the president. Brady and his wife, Sarah, championed the bill for many years before its adoption. Under the law's provisions, handgun dealers must send police agencies a form completed by the buyer (which is also required in most states); police agencies have five days to make certain the purchaser is not a convicted felon, fugitive, drug addict, or mentally ill person. Supporters believe the law is a modest step in keeping handguns from dangerous people. Opponents, including the National Rifle Association lobby, believe that the law is an empty political gesture at fighting crime that erodes the Second Amendment right to bear arms.

The rejection rate of Brady gun applications is less than 2 percent.

Gun Ownership.   Gun ownership is widespread in the United States. Estimates vary, but there are probably 200 million firearms in the hands of the nation's 300 million people. In public opinion surveys half of all American families admit to owning guns. A majority of gun owners say their guns are for hunting and sports; about one-third say the purpose of their gun ownership is self-defense. Interestingly, both those who favor a ban on handguns and those who oppose such a ban cite crime as the reason for their position. Those who want to ban guns say they contribute to crime and violence. Those who oppose a ban feel they need guns for protection against crime and violence.

There are about 30,000 gun-related deaths in the United States each year. A majority of these deaths (58 percent) are suicides; over one-third (38 percent) are homicides; and the remaining (4 percent) are accidental. It is relatively easy to count gun-related deaths, but it is very difficult to estimate the number of deaths, injuries, or crimes that are prevented by citizens using guns. *Protective* uses of guns against murder, burglary, assault, and robbery have been estimated to be as high as 2 million per year.[16] If this estimate is correct, then guns are used more for self-protection than for crime.

State Laws.   State laws, and many local ordinances, also govern gun ownership. Handgun laws are common. Most states require that a record of sale be submitted to state or local government agencies; some states require an application and a waiting period before the purchase of a handgun; a few states require a license or a permit to purchase one; most states require a license to carry a "concealed weapon" (hidden gun). Private gun sales are largely unregulated. Until recently, most states allowed unregulated private sales at "gun shows." Private sales are not covered by the Brady Act.

Gun Laws and Crime.   There is no systematic evidence that gun control laws reduce violent crime. If we compare violent crime rates in jurisdictions with very restrictive gun laws (for example, New York, Massachusetts, New Jersey, Illinois, and the District of Columbia) to those in jurisdictions with very loose controls, we find no differences in rates of violent crime that cannot be attributed to social conditions. Gun laws, including purchase permits, waiting periods, carrying permits, and even complete prohibitions, seem to have no effect on violent crime, or even crimes committed with guns.[17] Indeed, gun laws do not even appear to have any effect on gun ownership. Even the Massachusetts ban on handguns, which calls for a mandatory prison sentence for unlicensed citizens found carrying a firearm, did not reduce gun-related crime.[18] The total number of persons imprisoned for gun crimes was essentially unchanged; however, more persons without criminal records were arrested and charged with gun law violations. To date we must conclude that "there is little evidence to show that gun ownership among the population as a whole is, per se, an important cause of criminal violence."[19]

Indeed, some criminologists argue that guns in the hands of law-abiding citizens may reduce violent crime.[20] It is difficult to obtain evidence of "nonevents," in this case crimes averted by citizens with weapons, or crimes *un*committed by potential offenders fearing confrontation with armed citizens. Proponents of gun control have ready access to data on the number of murders committed with handguns. But there is also some evidence that as many or more crimes against both persons and property are foiled or deterred by gun ownership.[21]

The Right to Bear Arms.   The gun control debate also involves constitutional issues. The Second Amendment to the U.S. Constitution states, "A well regulated militia, being necessary to the security of a free state, the right of the people to keep and bear arms, shall not be infringed." For many years arguments over gun control centered on whether "the right to bear arms" was an individual right like the First Amendment freedom of speech, or whether the prefatory clause referring to "a well regulated milita" meant that the Second Amendment protected only the collective right of the states to form militias, that is, the right of states to maintain National Guard units.

Proponents of gun control often cited a Supreme Court decision, *United States* v. *Miller* (1939).[22] In this case, the Court considered the constitutionality of the federal National Firearms Act of 1934, which among other things prohibited the transportation of sawed-off shotguns in interstate commerce. The defendant claimed that Congress could not infringe on his right to keep and bear arms. But the Court responded that a sawed-off shotgun had no "relationship to the preservation or efficiency of a well-regulated militia." The clear implication of this decision is that the right to bear arms refers only to a state's right to maintain a militia.

Opponents of gun control argued that the rights set forth in the Bill of Rights ought to be interpreted as individual rights. The history surrounding the adoption of the Second Amendment reveals the concern of citizens with the attempt by a despotic government to confiscate their arms and render them helpless to resist tyranny. James Madison writes in *The Federalist,* No. 46, that "the advantage of being armed which the Americans posses over the people of almost every other nation . . . forms a barrier against the enterprise of [tyrannical] ambition." Early American political rhetoric is filled with praise for an armed citizenry able to protect its freedoms with force if necessary. And the "militia" was defined as every adult free male able to carry a weapon. Even early English common law recognized the right of individuals "to have and use arms for self-protection and defense."[23]

The Supreme Court finally resolved the underlying issue in *District of Columbia* v. *Heller* (2008) by holding that "The Second Amendment protects an individual right to possess a firearm unconnected with service in a militia, and to use that arm for traditionally lawful purposes, such as self-defense within the home."[24] The Court held that the District of Columbia's complete ban on handguns in the home violated the individual's right under the Second Amendment "to keep and bear arms." The Court observed that many bills of rights in state constitutions at the time of the Second Amendment's ratification contained an individual right to bear arms. And it noted that the earlier case, *United States* v. *Miller,* applied only to a type of weapon not commonly used for lawful purposes. The Court also held that the District's requirement that all guns in the home be either disassembled or guarded with a trigger lock violated the right of self-defense by rendering guns nonfunctional.

But the Supreme Court went on to observe that "Like most rights, the Second Amendment right is not unlimited. It is not a right to keep and carry any weapon whatsoever in any manner whatsoever and for whatever purpose." Justice Scalia, writing for a 5–4 majority, wrote that various government restrictions on guns may be constitutional, including restrictions on carrying concealed weapons, prohibitions on the possession of firearms by felons and the mentally ill, or laws forbidding the carrying of firearms in sensitive places, such as schools and government buildings. Thus, the Supreme Court left open the issue of exactly which gun controls are constitutional and which are not. It is likely that arguments over the constitutionality of various gun-control measures will occupy the courts for some time to come.

The Drug War

Americans have long harbored ambivalent attitudes toward drug use. Alcohol and tobacco are legal products. The manufacture, sale, or possession of heroin and cocaine are criminal offenses under both state and federal laws. Marijuana has been "decriminalized" in several states, making its use or possession a misdemeanor comparable to a traffic offense; a majority of states, however, retain criminal sanctions against the possession of marijuana, and its manufacture and sale are still prohibited by federal law. However, popular referenda votes in several states, including California, indicate that voters approve of the use of marijuana for medical purposes.

Drug Use. Overall drug use in the United States today appears to be below levels of two or three decades ago. However, since the mid-1990s, drug use has crept upward. These conclusions are drawn from national surveys on drug use regularly undertaken by the federal government (see Figure 4–5).

Marijuana is the most commonly used drug in the United States. Roughly 8 percent of the population over 12 years old report that they have used marijuana in the past month. There is conflicting evidence as to whether or not marijuana is more or less dangerous to health than alcohol or tobacco. The White House Office of National Drug Control Policy contends that the effects of marijuana include frequent respiratory infections, impaired memory and learning, and increased heart rate. It defines marijuana as an addictive drug because it causes physical dependence, and some people report withdrawal symptoms. In contrast, the National Organization for the Reform of Marijuana Laws (NORML) argues that marijuana is nontoxic; it cannot cause death by overdose; and its "responsible use" is "far less dangerous than alcohol or tobacco." The real problem, it contends, is that marijuana's prohibition creates an environment for criminal activity, wastes criminal justice resources, and invites government to invade our private lives.

Cocaine use is much more limited than marijuana use. About 1 percent of the population over 12 years of age report using cocaine in the past month. Cocaine is not regarded as physically addictive, although the psychological urge to continue its use is strong. It is made from coca leaves and imported into the United States. Originally, its high cost and celebrity

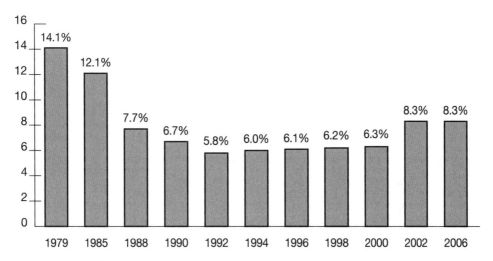

FIGURE 4–5 Drug Use in America* Drug use has declined significantly since the 1970s, although there has been a slight rise in recent years.
SOURCE: Substance Abuse and Mental Health Services (SAMHSA), National Survey of Drug Use and Health. *www.samhsa.gov*
*Current (past-month) use of any illicit drug.

use made it favored in upper-class circles. However, cocaine spread rapidly in the streets with the introduction of "crack" in the 1980s. Crack cocaine can be smoked and a single "hit" purchased for a few dollars. The health problems associated with cocaine use are fairly serious, as reported by the National Institute on Drug Abuse. Death, although rare, can occur from a single ingestion. The power of the coca leaf has been known for hundreds of years; Coca-Cola originally contained cocaine, though the drug was removed from the popular drink in 1903.

Heroin use is relatively rare. The Harrison Narcotic Act of 1916 made the manufacture, sale, or possession of heroin in the United States a federal crime. Various "designer" drugs, for example, "ecstasy," occasionally appear in clubs and on the streets. Some are prepared in underground laboratories where hallucinogens, stimulants, and tranquilizers are mixed in various combinations. Drugs that are injected intravenously, rather than inhaled, pose additional health dangers. Intravenous injections with contaminated needles are a major contributor to the spread of the HIV-AIDS virus.

Prescription Drugs.   Prescription drug abuse is now perceived as a major concern in the war on drugs. Past month use of prescription drugs for nonmedical purposes is currently estimated to exceed the use of marijuana. This use appears to be especially prevalent among young people, who often obtain these drugs from their parents' medicine cabinets. A number of factors may contribute to the increased use of prescription drugs: the belief that they are safer than illicit street drugs; the relative ease with which they can be obtained from family and friends; and a lack of awareness of potentially serious consequences of their nonmedical use, especially when mixed with alcohol.

TABLE 4–4   Drug Use by Age Young Americans are much more likely to use illicit drugs and to binge drink than older Americans.

	18–25	26–34	35 and Over
Any illicit[a]	19.4%	11.1%	4.2%
marijuana	16.1	8.3	3.1
cocaine	2.1	1.4	0.5
Alcohol[a]	60.5	53.0	50.3
binge use[b]	41.2	21.1	22.8
Cigarettes[a]	39.5	24.1	24.9

[a] Current (within the past month) use
[b] Five or more drinks on the same occasion
SOURCE: National survey of Drug Use and Health, *Statistical Abstract of the United States, 2007*, p. 126.

Drugs and Youth.   Drug use varies considerably by age group. Younger people are much more likely to use illicit drugs than older people, and young people are more likely to "binge" drink (see Table 4–4).

Drug Trafficking.   It is very difficult to estimate the total size of the drug market. The U.S. Office of Drug Control Policy estimates that Americans spend about $65 billion on illicit drugs each year. This would suggest that the drug business is comparable in size to one of the ten largest U.S. industrial corporations. More important, perhaps, drugs produce huge profit margin. Huge profits in turn allow drug traffickers to corrupt police and government officials as well as private citizens in the United States and other nations.

Drug Policy Options

Antidrug efforts can be categorized as (a) interdiction, including international attacks on the supply of drugs; (b) domestic law enforcement, including federal and state incarceration for the possession and sale of drugs; (c) treatment, including rehabilitation centers, drug courts, and methadone; (d) prevention, including school-based, community, and media-centered antidrug education. The bulk of federal antidrug spending is concentrating on interdiction and law enforcement (see Figure 4–6).

Interdiction.   Efforts to seal U.S. borders against the importation of drugs have been frustrated by the sheer volume of smuggling. Each year increasingly large drug shipments are intercepted by the U.S. Drug Enforcement Administration, the U.S. Customs Service, the U.S. Coast Guard, and state and local agencies. Yet each year the volume of drugs entering the country seems to increase. Drug "busts" are considered just another cost of business to the traffickers.

Federal drug policy also includes efforts to destroy the sources of drugs. U.S. military as well as drug enforcement officers are sent abroad to assist foreign governments (Colombia, for example) in destroying coca crops and combating drug cartels. But these activities often result in strained relationships with foreign countries. Our neighbors wonder why the U.S.

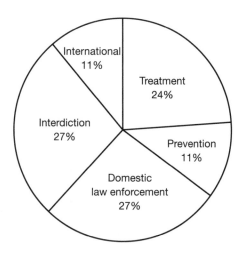

FIGURE 4–6   Federal Antidrug Spending About two-thirds of federal antidrug spending is directed at interdiction and law enforcement; only about one-third at treatment and prevention.
SOURCE: Office of National Drug Control Policy, 2008.

government directs its efforts at the suppliers, when the demand for drugs arises within the United States itself. The continued availability of drugs on the nation's streets—drugs at lower prices and higher purities—suggests that interdiction has largely failed.

Education.   Efforts aimed at educating the public about the dangers of drugs have inspired many public and private campaigns over the years, from the Advertising Council's TV ads "This is your brain on drugs" to local police–sponsored DARE (drug abuse resistance education) programs.

The decline in overall drug use over several decades is often overlooked in political debates over drug policy. Culturally, drug use went from being stylish and liberating to being unfashionable, unwise, and unhealthy. Perhaps educational campaigns contributed to drug use decline, as well as the onset of HIV-AIDS, and the well-publicized drug-related deaths of celebrity athletes and entertainers. Recent fluctuations in reported drug use, however, suggest that educational campaigns may grow stale over time.

Enforcement.   The FBI and state and local law enforcement agencies already devote a major portion of their efforts toward combating drugs. Over 1.5 *million* persons are arrested for drug violations each year (see Figure 4–7). Federal and state prisons now hold a larger percentage of the nation's population than ever before. Sentences have been lengthened for drug trafficking.

Federal law calls for a mandatory minimum sentence of five years for the possession or sale of various amounts of heroin, cocaine, or marijuana. Drug offenders account for 59 percent of the federal prison population and 21 percent of state prison populations. It costs about $25,000 per year to house a federal prison inmate.

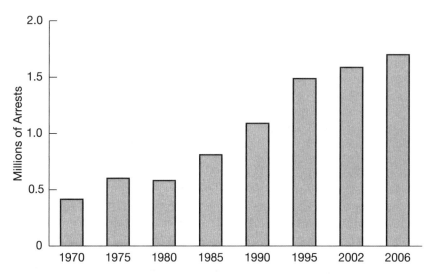

FIGURE 4–7   Drug Arrests Drug arrests, relatively low in the 1970s, have more than tripled in recent years. Arrests for drug offenses exceed those for any other crime. SOURCE: Federal Bureau of Investigation, *Uniform Crime Reports, 2006.*

The U.S. Drug Enforcement Administration (DEA) in the Department of Justice was created by Congress in 1973. Because it has the authority to enforce federal drug laws both in the United States and abroad, DEA officers may go abroad to collect international intelligence and to cooperate with foreign authorities. The U.S. Customs Service has responsibility for stopping the entry of narcotics at U.S. borders. The U.S. Coast Guard cooperates in drug interception. The FBI monitors drug trafficking that contributes to other federal crimes. Surveillance of low-level buying and selling of drugs is usually left to state and local authorities.

Congress created a "drug czar" position in 1988 (officially the National Drug Control Policy Director) to develop and coordinate antidrug policy in the United States. The national "war on drugs" has included federal funds for prison construction, state and local drug law enforcement activity, and state and local drug treatment programs. Each year, the federal government allocates about $14 billion to the war on drugs.

Treatment.   Special "drug courts" and diversion programs developed in the states often give nonviolent drug users a choice between entering treatment programs or going to jail. While some users benefit from treatment, the overall success of treatment programs is very poor; most heavy drug users have been through treatment programs more than once. An estimated 60 to 80 percent of heavy cocaine users return to heavy use after treatment.[25]

Legalization?   The failure of antidrug policies to significantly reduce the drug supply or demand, coupled with the high costs of enforcement and the loss of civil liberties, has caused some observers to propose the legalization of drugs and government control of their production and sale. Prohibition failed earlier in the twentieth century to end alcohol consumption, and crime, official corruption, and the enormous cost of futile efforts to stop individuals from drinking eventually forced the nation to end Prohibition. It is similarly argued that the legalization of drugs would end organized crime's profit monopoly over the drug trade; raise billions of dollars by legally taxing drugs; end the strain on relations with Latin American nations caused by efforts to eradicate drugs; and save additional billions in enforcement costs, which could be used for education and drug treatment.[26] If drugs were legally obtainable under government supervision, it is argued that many of society's current problems would be alleviated: the crime and violence associated with the drug trade, the corruption of public officials, the spread of diseases associated with drug use, and the many infringements of personal liberty associated with antidrug wars.

But even the suggestion of drug legalization offends Americans who believe that it would greatly expand drug use in the country. Cheap, available drugs may greatly increase the numbers of addicted persons, creating a "society of zombies" that would destroy the social fabric of the nation. Cocaine and heroin are far more habit forming than alcohol, and legalization may encourage the development of newer and even more potent and addictive synthetic drugs. Whatever the health costs of drug abuse today, it is argued that legalization would produce public health problems of enormous magnitude.[27] Cocaine is very cheap to produce; the current five- to ten-dollar cost of a "hit" is mostly profit for the dealer; legalization, even with taxation, might produce a fifty-cent "hit." Whatever the damages to society from drug-related crime and efforts to prohibit drugs, the damages from cheap, available drug use may be far greater.

Crime and the Courts

The development of rational policies in criminal justice is complicated by conflicting values—our commitment to due process of law and our determination to fight crime. Public opinion has long held that the court system is overly concerned with the rights of accused criminals. A majority of Americans believe that the Supreme Court has gone too far in protecting the rights of defendants in criminal cases and that the courts are more concerned with protecting these rights than the rights of victims.[28]

Yet although society needs the protection of the police, it is equally important to protect society *from* the police. Arbitrary searches, seizures, and arrests; imprisonment without hearing or trial; forced confessions; beatings and torture; tainted witnesses; excessive punishments; and other human rights violations are all too common throughout the world. The courts function to protect citizens accused of crime as well as to mete out punishment for criminal behavior.

Insufficient Evidence and Dismissal. About half of all felony arrests result in dismissal of the charges against the defendant. This decision is usually made by the prosecutor (the state's attorney, district attorney, or county prosecutor, as the office is variously designated in the states; or a prosecuting attorney in the U.S. Department of Justice in a federal criminal case). The prosecutor may determine that the offense is not serious or that the offender is not a danger to society or that the resources of the office would be better spent pursuing other cases. But the most common reason for dismissal of the charges is insufficient evidence.

Unreasonable Searches and Seizures.   Individuals are protected by the Fourth Amendment from "unreasonable searches and seizures" of their private "persons, houses, papers, and effects." The amendment lays out specific rules for searches and seizures of evidence: "No warrants shall issue but upon probable cause, supported by Oath or affirmation, and particularly describing the place to be searched, and the persons or things to be seized." Judges cannot issue a warrant just to let the police see if an individual has committed a crime; there must be "probable cause" for such issuance. The indiscriminate searching of whole neighborhoods or groups of people is unconstitutional and is prevented by the Fourth Amendment's requirement that the place to be searched must be specifically described in the warrant. This requirement is meant to prevent "fishing expeditions" into an individual's home and personal effects on the possibility that some evidence of unknown illegal activity might crop up. The only exception is if police officers, in the course of a valid search for a specified item, find other items whose very possession is a crime, for example, illicit drugs.

However, the courts permit the police to undertake many other "reasonable" searches *without* a warrant: searches in connection with a valid arrest, searches to protect the safety of police officers, searches to obtain evidence in the immediate vicinity and in the suspect's control, searches to preserve evidence in danger of being immediately destroyed, and searches with the consent of a suspect. Indeed, most police searches today take place without a warrant under one or another of these conditions. The Supreme Court has also allowed automobile searches and searches of open fields without warrants in many cases. The requirement of "probable cause" has been very loosely defined; even a "partially corroborated anonymous informant's tip" qualifies as probable cause to make a search, seizure, or arrest.[29] And if the police, while making a warranted search or otherwise lawfully on the premises, see evidence of a crime "in plain view," they may seize such evidence without further authorization.[30]

Self-Incrimination and Right to Counsel.   Freedom from self-incrimination originated in English common law; it was originally designed to prevent persons from being tortured into confessions of guilt. It is also a logical extension of the notion that individuals should not be forced to contribute to their own prosecution, that the burden of proof rests upon the state. The Fifth Amendment protects people from both physical and psychological coercion.[31] It protects not only accused persons at their own trial but also witnesses testifying in trials of others, civil suits, congressional hearings, and so on. Thus, "taking the Fifth" has become a standard phrase in our culture: "I refuse to answer that question on the grounds that it might tend to incriminate me." The protection also means that judges, prosecutors, and juries cannot use the refusal of people to take the stand at their own trial as evidence of guilt. Indeed, a judge or attorney is not even permitted to imply this to a jury, and a judge is obligated to instruct a jury *not* to infer guilt from a defendant's refusal to testify.

The Supreme Court under Justice Earl Warren greatly strengthened the Fifth Amendment protection against self-incrimination and the right to counsel in a series of rulings in the 1960s:

> *Gideon* v. *Wainwright* (1963)—Equal protection under the Fourteenth Amendment requires that free legal counsel be appointed for all indigent defendants in all criminal cases.
>
> *Escobedo* v. *Illinois* (1964)—Suspects are entitled to confer with counsel as soon as a police investigation focuses on them or once "the process shifts from investigatory to accusatory."

METROPOLITAN POLICE DEPARTMENT Warning as to Your Rights	WAIVER
You are under arrest. Before we ask you any questions you must understand what your rights are. You have the right to remain silent. You are not required to say anything to us at any time or to answer any questions. Anything you say can be used against you in court. You have the right to talk to a lawyer for advice before we question you and to have him with you during questioning. If you cannot afford a lawyer and want one, a lawyer will be provided for you. If you want to answer questions now without a lawyer present, you will still have the right to stop answering at any time. You also have the right to stop answering at any time until you talk to a lawyer.	1. Have you read or had read to you the warning as to your rights?_____ 2. Do you understand these rights? _____ 3. Do you wish to answer any questions? _____ 4. Are you willing to answer questions without having an attorney present? _____ 5. Signature of defendant on line below. _____ 6. Time _____ Date _____ 7. Signature of officer _____ 8. Signature of witness _____

FIGURE 4–8 The Miranda Warning The Supreme Court, in its 1966 Miranda decision, ruled that police must inform suspects of their constitutional rights before questioning them.

Miranda v. *Arizona* (1966)—Before questioning suspects, a police officer must inform them of all their constitutional rights, including the right to counsel (appointed at no cost to the suspect, if necessary) and the right to remain silent. Although suspects may knowingly waive these rights, the police cannot question anyone who at any point asks for a lawyer or declines "in any manner" to be questioned. The Supreme Court reaffirmed in 2000 that "*Miranda* has become embedded in routine police practice to the point where the warnings have become part of our national culture."[32] (See Figure 4–8.)

The Exclusionary Rule. Illegally obtained evidence and confessions may not be used in criminal trials. If police find evidence of a crime in an illegal search, or if they elicit statements from suspects without informing them of their rights to remain silent or to have counsel, the evidence or statements produced are not admissible in a trial. This exclusionary rule is one of the more controversial procedural rights that the Supreme Court has extended to criminal defendants. The rule is also unique to the United States: in Great Britain evidence obtained illegally may be used against the accused, although the accused may bring charges against the police for damages.

The rule provides enforcement for the Fourth Amendment guarantee against unreasonable searches and seizures, as well as the Fifth Amendment guarantee against compulsory self-incrimination and the guarantee of counsel. Initially applied only in federal cases, in *Mapp* v. *Ohio* (1961),[33] the Supreme Court extended the exclusionary rule to *all* criminal cases in the United States. A "good faith exception" is made "when law enforcement officers have acted in objective good faith or their transgressions have been minor."[34]

The exclusionary rule is a controversial court policy. Many trial proceedings today are not concerned with the guilt or innocence of the accused but instead focus on possible procedural errors by police or prosecutors. If the defendant's attorney can show that an error was committed, the defendant goes free, regardless of his or her guilt or innocence.

Plea Bargaining.   Most convictions are obtained by guilty pleas. Indeed, about 90 percent of the criminal cases brought to trial are disposed of by guilty pleas before a judge, not trial by jury. The Constitution guarantees defendants a trial by jury (Sixth Amendment), but guilty pleas outnumber jury trials by ten to one.[35]

Plea bargaining, in which the prosecution either reduces the seriousness of the charges, drops some but not all charges, or agrees to recommend lighter penalties in exchange for a guilty plea by the defendant, is very common. Some critics of plea bargaining view it as another form of leniency in the criminal justice system that reduces its deterrent effects. Other critics view plea bargaining as a violation of the Constitution's protection against self-incrimination and guarantee of a fair jury trial. Prosecutors, they say, threaten defendants with serious charges and stiff penalties to force a guilty plea. Still other critics see plea bargaining as an under-the-table process that undermines respect for the criminal justice system.

While the decision to plead guilty or go to trial rests with the defendant, this decision is strongly influenced by the policies of the prosecutor's office. A defendant may plead guilty and accept the certainty of conviction with whatever reduced charges the prosecutor offers and/or accept the prosecutor's pledge to recommend a lighter penalty. Or the defendant may go to trial, confronting serious charges with stiffer penalties, with the hope of being found innocent. However, the possibility of an innocent verdict in a jury trial is only one in six. This apparently strong record of conviction occurs because prosecutors have already dismissed charges in cases in which the evidence is weak or illegally obtained. Thus, most defendants confronting strong cases against them decide to "cop a plea."

It is very fortunate for the nation's court system that most defendants plead guilty. The court system would quickly break down from overload if any substantial proportion of defendants insisted on jury trials.

RICO versus Liberty

Many authoritarian governments throughout the world boast of low crime rates and criminal justice systems that mete out swift and severe punishments. How far do we wish to go in restricting individual liberty to fight crime?

Congress passed the Racketeer Influenced and Corrupt Practices (RICO) Act in 1970, following a 1968 presidential campaign in which President Richard Nixon and Independent candidate George C. Wallace made "getting tough on crime" a key issue. RICO was designed to combat organized crime and drug trafficking. Among other provisions, it allows the U.S. Department of Justice to seize the money and property of people suspected of crimes. The popular slogan was "Take the profit out of crime!"

Criminal Forfeiture. Under RICO, federal authorities may seize cash, bank accounts, homes, cars, boats, businesses, and other assets that they *believe* were used in criminal activity or were obtained with profits from criminal activity. People may be stopped in an airport terminal, bus station, or street on suspicion of drug trafficking, and have their cash and cars seized by law enforcement agents.

Assets forfeited to federal law enforcement agencies—FBI, DEA, Customs Service, Treasury and Justice Departments—are usually retained by these agencies (or the profits of selling these assets at auction) and often shared with state and local law enforcement agencies that cooperated in the investigation. Thus, there is a strong bureaucratic incentive for agencies to go after "the profits of crime" and to concentrate on cases likely to result in forfeiture of these assets—primarily drug cases. There is increasing evidence that this incentive has placed drug enforcement ahead of other law enforcement activities in federal, state, and local agencies.

Cause and Burden of Proof in Seizures. RICO permits the government to seize property before any adjudication of guilt. Indeed, a subsequent guilty verdict in a criminal trial is not necessary for the government to retain possession of the property seized. Originally, the only requirement was that law enforcement agents have "probable cause" to believe a crime had been committed and that the property seized was used in the crime or purchased with the profits of crime. "Probable cause" was a very loose standard; it included anonymous tips, "suspicious" behavior, and persons fitting descriptions ("profiles") of classes of criminals. In 2000, Congress raised the standard for seizures from "probable cause" to "a preponderance of evidence."

People whose property is seized under RICO have the burden of appealing to the Justice Department and proving that they are innocent of any crime and, more important, that officers had no cause to seize their property. The burden of litigation, including hiring an attorney to institute proceedings for the return of the property, falls on the citizen, not on the government. The proceedings are considered a civil suit by an individual against the government, not a criminal case by the government against the individual.[36] Thus, the government need not prove "beyond a reasonable doubt" that the person was involved in criminal activity or the property was used in a crime. Rather the person must prove his or her own innocence and the government's lack of "a preponderance of evidence" to seize the property.

The USA Patriot Act of 2001, a key component of the nation's "War on Terrorism" (see Chapter 14), applies the same type of forfeiture provisions against suspected terrorists.

Reform. Efforts in Congress to reform RICO's forfeiture and seizure provisions met with strong opposition by the U.S. Department of Justice, the National Association of Attorneys General, the National District Attorney Association, and many state and local law enforcement officials. But in 2000, after years of horror stories by innocent parties regarding unjust seizures, Congress passed the Civil Asset Forfeiture Reform Act that made some modest changes. In addition to raising the seizure standard to "a preponderance of evidence," the act now requires the government to prove in the civil case that the property had a "substantial connection" to a criminal act, and prohibits the government from seizing the property of "innocent owners"—those who had no knowledge of its use in criminal activities. But seizures will continue to occur *before* and even *without* criminal convictions.

Prisons and Correctional Policies

At least four separate theories of crime and punishment compete for preeminence in guiding correctional policies. *Justice*: First, there is the ancient Judeo-Christian idea of holding individuals responsible for their guilty acts and compelling them to pay a debt to society. Retribution is an expression of society's moral outrage, and it lessens the impulse of victims and their families to seek revenge. *Deterrence*: Another philosophy argues that punishment should be sure, speedy, commensurate with the crime, and sufficiently conspicuous to deter others from committing crimes. *Incapacitation*: Still another philosophy in correctional policy is that of protecting the public from lawbreakers or habitual criminals by segregating them behind prison walls. *Rehabilitation*: Finally, there is the theory that criminals are partly or entirely victims of social circumstances beyond their control and that society owes them comprehensive treatment in the form of rehabilitation.

Rising Prison Populations.   More than 10 million Americans are brought to a jail, police station, juvenile home, or prison each year. The vast majority are released within hours or days. There are, however, about 1.4 million inmates in state and federal prisons in the United States. These prisoners are serving time for serious offenses; almost all had a record of crime before they committed the act that led to their current imprisonment. These are persons serving at least one year of prison time; an additional 700,000 persons are held in local jails, serving less than one year of imprisonment. In all, over 2 million Americans are currently in prisons or jails.

Failure of Rehabilitation.   If correctional systems could be made to work—that is, actually to rehabilitate prisoners as useful, law-abiding citizens—the benefits to the nation would be enormous. Eighty percent of all felonies are committed by repeat offenders—individuals who have had prior contact with the criminal justice system and were not corrected by it. Reformers generally recommend more education and job training, more and better facilities, smaller prisons, halfway houses where offenders can adjust to civilian life before parole, more parole officers, and greater contact between prisoners and their families and friends. But there is no convincing evidence that these reforms reduce what criminologists call "recidivism," the offenders' return to crime.[37] In short, there is no evidence that people can be rehabilitated, no matter what is done. But prison policies now combine conflicting philosophies in a way that accomplishes none of society's goals. They do not effectively punish or deter individuals from crime. They do not succeed in rehabilitating the criminal. Even the maintenance of order within prisons and the protection of the lives of guards and inmates are serious problems.

Prison life does little to encourage good behavior, as noted by policy analyst John DiIulio, Jr.: "For the most part, the nation's adult and juvenile inmates spend their days in idleness punctuated by meals, violence, and weight lifting. Meaningful educational, vocational, and counseling programs are rare. Strong inmates are permitted to pressure weaker prisoners for sex, drugs, and money. Gangs organized along racial and ethnic lines are often the real 'sovereigns of the cellblock.'"[38]

TABLE 4–5 Jail, Prison, Probation, and Parole Population
Almost 7 million people in the United States are serving on
probation or parole, or have been sentenced to jail or prison.

Total	6,996,500
Prison	1,421,911
Jail	713,990
Probation	4,151,125
Parole	765,355

SOURCE: *Statistical Abstract of the United States, 2007,* p. 209.

Failure of Probation.   In addition to the nation's prison population of 1.4 million, there are about 4 million people currently on probation for serious crimes (see Table 4–5). But probation has been just as ineffective as prison in reducing crime. Even though people placed on probation are considered less dangerous to society than those imprisoned, studies indicate that nearly two-thirds of probationers will be arrested and over one-half will be convicted for a crime committed *while on probation.*

Failure of Parole.   Over two-thirds of all prisoner releases come about by means of parole. Modern penology, with its concern for reform and rehabilitation, appears to favor parole over unconditional releases. The function of parole and postrelease supervision is to procure information on the parolees' postprison conduct and to facilitate the transition between prison and complete freedom. These functions are presumably oriented toward protecting the public and rehabilitating the offender. However, studies of recidivism indicate that up to three-fourths of the persons paroled from prison will be rearrested for serious crimes. There is no difference in this high rate of recidivism between those released under supervised parole and those released unconditionally. Thus, it does not appear that parole succeeds in its objectives.

Capital Punishment

Capital punishment has been the topic of a long and heated national debate. Opponents of the death penalty argue that it is cruel and unusual punishment, in violation of the Eighth Amendment of the Constitution. They also argue that the death penalty is applied unequally. A large proportion of those executed have been poor, uneducated, and non-white. In contrast, a sense of justice among many Americans demands retribution for heinous crimes—a life for a life. A mere jail sentence for a multiple murderer or rapist-murderer seems unjust compared with the damage inflicted on society and the victims. In most cases, a life sentence means less than ten years in prison under the current parole and probation policies of many states. Convicted murderers have been set free, and some have killed again.

Prohibition on Unfair Application.   Prior to 1972, the death penalty was officially sanctioned by about half of the states as well as by federal law. However, no one had actually suffered the death penalty since 1967 because of numerous legal tangles and direct challenges to the constitutionality of capital punishment.

In *Furman* v. *Georgia* (1972), the Supreme Court ruled that capital punishment as then imposed violated the Eighth Amendment and Fourteenth Amendment prohibitions against cruel and unusual punishment and due process of law.[39] The reasoning in the case is very complex. Only two justices declared that capital punishment itself is cruel and unusual. The other justices in the majority felt that death sentences had been applied unfairly: a few individuals were receiving the death penalty for crimes for which many others were receiving much lighter sentences. These justices left open the possibility that capital punishment would be constitutional if it were specified for certain kinds of crime and applied uniformly.

After this decision, a majority of states rewrote their death penalty laws to try to ensure fairness and uniformity of application. Generally, these laws mandate the death penalty for murders committed during rape, robbery, hijacking, or kidnapping; murders of prison guards; murder with torture; and multiple murders. Two trials would be held—one to determine guilt or innocence and another to determine the penalty. At the second trial, evidence of "aggravating" and "mitigating" factors would be presented; if there were aggravating factors but no mitigating factors, the death penalty would be mandatory.

Death Penalty Reinstated.   In a series of cases in 1976 (*Gregg* v. *Georgia, Profitt* v. *Florida, Jurek* v. *Texas*)[40] the Supreme Court finally held that "the punishment of death does not invariably violate the Constitution." The Court upheld the death penalty, employing the following rationale: the men who drafted the Bill of Rights accepted death as a common sanction for crime. It is true that the Eighth Amendment prohibition against cruel and unusual punishment must be interpreted in a dynamic fashion, reflecting changing moral values. But the decisions of more than half of the nation's state legislatures to reenact the death penalty since 1972 and the decision of juries to impose the death penalty on hundreds of people under these new laws are evidence that "a large proportion of American society continues to regard it as an appropriate and necessary criminal sanction." Moreover, said the Court, the social purposes of retribution and deterrence justify the use of the death penalty. This ultimate sanction is "an expression of society's moral outrage at particularly offensive conduct." The Court affirmed that *Furman* v. *Georgia* struck down the death penalty only where it was inflicted in "an arbitrary and capricious manner." The Court upheld the death penalty in states where the trial was a two-part proceeding and where, during the second part, the judge or jury was provided with relevant information and standards. The Court upheld the consideration of "aggravating and mitigating circumstances." It also upheld automatic review of all death sentences by state supreme courts to ensure that these sentences were not imposed under the influence of passion or prejudice, that aggravating factors were supported by the evidence, and that the sentence was not disproportionate to the crime. However, the Court disapproved of state laws *mandating* the death penalty in first degree murder cases, holding that such laws were "unduly harsh and unworkably rigid."[41]

The Supreme Court has also held that executions of the mentally retarded are "cruel and unusual punishments" prohibited by the Eighth Amendment.[42] In 2005 the Court held that the Eighth Amendment prohibited executions of offenders who were under age 18 when they committed their crimes.[43] And in 2008 the court held that the death penalty for the rape of a child violated the Eighth Amendment; the implication of the decision is that the death penalty can only be imposed for "crimes that take a victim's life."[44]

Racial Bias.   The death penalty has also been challenged as a violation of the Equal Protection Clause of the Fourteenth Amendment because of a racial bias in the application of the punishment. White murderers are just as likely to receive the death penalty as black murderers. However, some statistics show that if the *victim* is white, there is a greater chance that the killer will be sentenced to death than if the victim is black. Nonetheless the Supreme Court has ruled that statistical disparities in the race of victims by itself does not bar the death penalty in all cases. There must be evidence of racial bias against a particular defendant for the Court to reverse a death sentence.[45]

Executions.   Today, there are about 3,200 prisoners nationwide on death row, that is, persons convicted and sentenced to death. But only about fifty executions are actually carried out each year. The strategy of death row prisoners and their lawyers, of course, is to delay indefinitely the imposition of the death penalty with endless stays and appeals. So far the strategy has been successful for all but a few luckless murderers. As trial judges and juries continue to impose the death penalty and appellate courts continue to grant stays of execution, the number of prisoners on death row grows. The few who have been executed have averaged ten years of delay between trial and execution.

The writ of habeas corpus is guaranteed in the U.S. Constitution, but how many habeas corpus petitions should a condemned prisoner be allowed to submit? The death penalty, of course, is irreversible, and it must not be imposed if there is any doubt whatsoever about the defendant's guilt. But how many opportunities and resulting delays should death row inmates have to challenge their convictions and sentences? In recent years the Supreme Court has limited habeas corpus petitions in federal courts by prisoners who have already filed claims and lost and who have failed to follow rules of appeal. If new evidence is uncovered after all court appeals have been exhausted, the Supreme Court has indicated that appeal lies with governors' powers of pardon.

The potential for wrongful executions has always worried Americans. The development of DNA evidence in recent years has made it possible to review and appeal some death penalty sentences. And indeed, DNA evidence has resulted in the release of a few death row prisoners. Other prisoners have been removed from death row because of trial errors, attorney incompetence, evidence withheld by the prosecution, and other procedural errors.

Deterrent Value.   The death penalty as it is employed today—inflicted on so few after so many years following the crime—has little deterrent effect. Nonetheless, it serves several purposes. It gives prosecutors some leverage in plea bargaining with murder defendants. The defendants may choose to plead guilty in exchange for a life sentence when confronted with the possibility that the prosecutor may win a conviction and the death penalty in a jury trial. More important, perhaps, the death penalty is symbolic of the value society places on the lives of innocent victims. It dramatically signifies that society does not excuse or condone the taking of innocent lives. It symbolizes the potential for society's retribution against heinous crime.

SUMMARY

Crime is a central problem in our society. We face a conflict between our desire to retain individual freedoms and our desire to ensure the safety of our people.

1. After dramatic increases in crime rates over many years, crime rates have been falling since 1993. Law enforcement officials frequently attribute this decline to the adoption of public policies designed to deter crime and incapacitate criminals.

2. A rational policy toward crime would endeavor to make its costs far outweigh its benefits and in theory deter potential wrongdoers. Effective deterrence requires that punishment be certain, swift, and severe. However, certainty and swiftness are probably of more importance to deterrence than is severity.

3. But punishment for crime in the United States today is neither certain nor swift. The likelihood of going to jail for any particular crime is probably less than one in a hundred. Speedy trial and punishment are rare; criminal defendants usually succeed in obtaining long delays between arrest and trial, when most remain free on bail prior to trial.

4. However, incapacitation (placing more criminals in prison for longer terms) appears to be related to lower crime rates. Prison building in the 1980s, together with mandatory sentencing laws and sentencing guidelines in the states, has resulted in higher incarceration rates (numbers of prisoners per 100,000 population).

5. The police provide many services to society in addition to law enforcement. Indeed, only a small proportion of their time is spent in fighting crime. It is difficult to demonstrate conclusively that increased police protection reduces the actual amount of crime.

6. Guns are used in a large number of violent crimes. Public policy on gun control varies throughout the nation. However, states with strict gun control laws do not have lower rates of violent crime, or even of gun-related crime, than states without such laws. The Supreme Court has declared that gun ownership is an individual right guaranteed by the Second Amendment.

7. Public policies toward alcohol and drug use are ambivalent. Although the health dangers of cigarettes, alcohol, marijuana, cocaine, and heroin are widely known, the manufacture, sale, and use of each of these substances are treated differently in law enforcement.

8. Court congestion, increased litigation, excessive delays, endless appeals, variation in sentencing, and excessive plea bargaining all combine to detract from deterrence. The exclusionary rule, which prohibits the use of illegally obtained evidence in court, has generated controversy since it was first announced by the Supreme Court in *Mapp* v. *Ohio* in 1961.

9. About half of all serious charges are dismissed by prosecutors before trial. But most convictions are obtained by guilty pleas without jury trials. Plea bargaining is the most common means of resolving criminal cases. Without plea bargaining, the court system would break down from overload.

10. Prison and parole policies have failed to rehabilitate prisoners. Prisons can reduce crime only by incapacitating criminals for periods of time. Most prisoners are recidivists—persons who previously served a sentence of incarceration before being sentenced again. Parolees—persons released by officials for good behavior—are just as likely to commit new crimes as those released after serving full sentences.

11. Capital punishment as currently imposed—on very few persons and after very long delays—is not an effective deterrent.

Notes

1. U.S. Department of Justice, *Criminal Victimization in the United States*, published annually (Washington, DC: Bureau of Justice Statistics).
2. U.S. General Accounting Office, *Juvenile Justice* (Washington, DC: Government Printing Office, 1995), p. 2.
3. Statistical Abstract of the United States, 2008, p. 206.
4. *Wisconsin* v. *Mitchell*, 508 U.S. 476 (1993).
5. *R.A.V.* v. *City of St. Paul*, 505 U.S. 377 (1992).
6. *Whitney* v. *California*, 274 U.S. 357 (1927).
7. Bureau of Justice Statistics, *www.ojp.usdoj.gov/bjs*.
8. *Statistical Abstract of the United States, 2008*, p. 298.
9. Ibid., p. 262.
10. Stuart A. Sheingold, "Cultural Cleavage and Criminal Justice," *Journal of Politics*, 40 (November 1978), 865–897.
11. See Stuart Sheingold, *The Politics of Law and Order* (New York: Layman, 1984).
12. For a summary, see John J. DiIulio, Jr., "Arresting Ideas: Tougher Law Enforcement Is Driving Down Crime," *Policy Review* (Fall 1995), 12–16.
13. William S. Bratlon, "The New City Police Department's Civil Enforcement of Quality of Life Crimes," *Journal of Law and Policy 1995*, pp. 447–464; also cited by William J. Bennett, John J. DiIulio, Jr., and John P. Walters, *Body Count* (New York: Simon & Schuster, 1996).
14. *United States* v. *Morrison,* 529 U.S. 598 (2000).
15. Gun Control Act of 1968; Firearms Owners' Protection Act of 1986; Brady Handgun Violence Protection Act of 1993; Omnibus Crime Control Act of 1994.
16. See Gary Kleck and Marc Gertz, "Armed Resistance to Crime: The Prevalence and Nature of Self-Defense with Guns," *Journal of Criminal Law and Criminology*, 86 (Fall 1996), 150–187; Gary Kleck, *Targeting Guns* (New York: Aldine de Gruyter, 1997).
17. Douglas R. Murray, "Handguns, Gun Control Laws and Firearm Violence," *Social Problems*, 23 (1975); James D. Wright and Peter H. Rossi, *Weapons, Crime, and Violence in America* (Washington, DC: U.S. Department of Justice, National Institute of Justice, 1981).
18. David Rossman, *The Impact of the Mandatory Gun Law in Massachusetts* (Boston: Boston University School of Law, 1979).
19. Wright and Rossi, *Weapons, Crime, and Violence*, p. 540.
20. Gary Kleck, *Point Blank: Guns and Violence in America* (New York: Aldine de Gruyter, 1991); Gary Kleck, "The Impact of Gun Control and Gun Ownership Levels on Violence Rates," *Journal of Quantitative Criminology* (1993), 249–287; John R. Lott, *More Guns, Less Crime*, 2nd ed. Chicago: University of Chicago Press, 2000.
21. Gary Kleck and Mark Gertz, "Carrying Guns for Protection," *Journal of Research on Crime and Delinquency*, 35 (May 1998), 190–198.
22. *United States* v. *Miller*, 307 U.S. 174 (1939).
23. William Blackstone, *Commentaries of the Laws of England*, Vol. 1, p. 144.
24. *District of Columbia* v. *Heller* (June 26, 2008).
25. Various studies cited by William J. Bennett, et al., *Body Count*, pp. 172–180.
26. Ethan A. Nadelmann, "The Case for Legalization," *The Public Interest* (Summer 1988), 3–31.
27. John Kaplan, "Taking Drugs Seriously," *The Public Interest* (Summer 1988), 32–50.
28. Public Agenda Online, September 2002.

29. *Illinois* v. *Gates*, 462 U.S. 213 (1983).
30. *Arizona* v. *Hicks*, 480 U.S. 321 (1987).
31. *Spano* v. *New York*, 360 U.S. 315 (1959).
29. *Dickerson* v. *U.S.*, 530 U.S. 428 (2000).
33. *Mapp* v. *Ohio*, 367 U.S. 643 (1961).
34. *United States* v. *Leon*, 468 U.S. 897 (1984).
35. U.S. Department of Justice, Bureau of Justice Statistics, *The Prevalence of Guilty Pleas*, December 1984.
36. *Toledo* v. *Pearson Yacht Leasing*, 416 U.S. 663 (1974); *Caplin & Drysdale* v. *U.S.*, 491 U.S. 617 (1989).
37. Daniel Glaser, *Effectiveness of a Prison and Parole System* (New York: Bobbs-Merrill, 1969), p. 4.
38. John J. DiIulio, Jr., "Punishing Smarter," *Brookings Review* (Summer 1989), 8.
39. *Furman* v. *Georgia*, 408 U.S. 238 (1972).
40. *Gregg* v. *Georgia, Profitt* v. *Florida, Jurek* v. *Texas*, 428 U.S. 153 (1976).
41. *Summer* v. *Schman*, 107 S. Ct. 2716 (1987).
42. *Atkins* v. *Virginia*, 536 U.S. 304 (2002).
43. *Roper* v. *Simmons*, March 1, 2005.
44. *Kennedy* v. *Louisiana*, June 25, 2008.
45. *McCluskey* v. *Kemp*, 481 U.S. 279 (1987).

Bibliography

Bennett, William J., John J. DiIulio, Jr., and John P. Walters. *Body Count*. New York: Simon & Schuster, 1996.

Cole, George F., and Christopher E. Smith. *The American System of Criminal Justice*, 10th ed. Belmont, CA: Wadsworth, 2004.

Hagan, John, and Bill McCarthy. *Mean Streets*. New York: Cambridge University Press, 1998.

Kleck, Gary. *Point Blank: Guns and Violence in America*. New York: Aldine de Gruyter, 1991.

Schmalleger, Frank. *Criminal Justice Today*, 9th ed. Upper Saddle River, NJ: Prentice Hall, 2007.

Spitzer, Robert J. *The Politics of Gun Control*, 4th ed. Washington DC: CQ Press, 2007.

Vizzard, William J. *Shots in the Dark: The Policy and Politics of Gun Control*. Latham, MD: Rowman and Littlefield, 2000.

Wilson, James Q. *Thinking about Crime*, 2nd ed. New York: Basic Books, 1984.

Wilson, James Q., and Richard J. Herrnstein. *Crime and Human Nature*. New York: Simon & Schuster, 1985.

Wright, Richard A. *In Defense of Prisons*. Westport, CT: Greenwood Press, 1994.

Web Sites

Federal Bureau of Investigation. Official Web site of the FBI, including uniform crime reports, "ten most wanted," etc. *www.fbi.gov*

Bureau of Justice Statistics, U.S. Department of Justice. Statistics on crime rates, victimization, sentencing, corrections, etc. *www.ojp.usdoj.gov/bjs*

Death Penalty Information Center. Advocacy group opposing death penalty, with information on executions. *www.deathpenalty.org*

NATIONAL RIFLE ASSOCIATION. Advocacy organization defending Second Amendment right to bear arms. *www.nra.org*

AMERICAN CIVIL LIBERTIES UNION. Advocacy organization for civil liberties. *www.aclu.org*

U.S. DRUG ENFORCEMENT ADMINISTRATION. Official DEA Web site, with information on drug laws and enforcement. *www.usdoj.gov/dea*

NATIONAL INSTITUTE ON DRUG ABUSE. Government information about drugs and their effects, including trends and statistics on drug use. *www.nida.nih.gov*

NATIONAL ORGANIZATION FOR THE REFORM OF MARIJUANA LAWS. Advocacy organization supporting the legalization of marijuana. *www.norml.org*

OFFICE OF NATIONAL DRUG CONTROL POLICY. Official site of the government's "Drug Czar," with information on national drug control strategy, etc. *www.whitehousedrugpolicy.gov*

DRUG POLICY ALLIANCE. Advocacy organization opposed to the war on drugs. *www.drugpolicy.org*

5

Health and Welfare

The Search for Rational Strategies

Rationality and Irrationality in the Welfare State

Why does poverty persist in a nation where total social welfare spending is many times the amount needed to eliminate poverty? The answer is that the poor are *not* the principal beneficiaries of social welfare spending. Most of it, including the largest programs—Social Security and Medicare—goes to the *non*poor. Only about one-sixth of federal social welfare spending is "means-tested" (see Figure 5–1), that is, distributed to recipients based on their low-income or poverty status. The middle class, not the poor, is the major beneficiary of the nation's social welfare spending.

"Entitlements."   Entitlements are government benefits for which Congress has set eligibility criteria—age, income, retirement, disability, unemployment, and so forth. Everyone who meets the criteria is "entitled" by law to the benefit.

   Most of the nation's major entitlement programs were launched either in the New Deal years of the 1930s under President Franklin D. Roosevelt (Social Security, Unemployment Compensation; Aid to Families with Dependent Children [AFDC], now called Temporary Assistance to Needy Families [TANF], and Aid to Aged, Blind, and Disabled, now called Supplemental Security Income or SSI); or the Great Society years of the 1960s under President Lyndon B. Johnson (food stamps, Medicare, Medicaid).

   Today nearly one-third of the population of the United States is "entitled" to some form of government benefit. *Social insurance* entitlements may be claimed by persons regardless of their income or wealth. Entitlement to Social Security and Medicare is determined by *age*, not income or poverty. Entitlement to unemployment compensation benefits is determined by employment status. Federal employee and veterans' retirement benefits are based on previous government or military service. These *non*–means-tested programs account for the largest number of recipients of government benefits. In contrast, *public assistance*

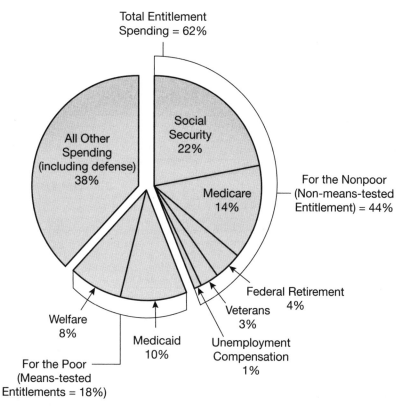

FIGURE 5–1   Federal Entitlement Spending for the Poor and Nonpoor
Entitlement spending exceeds 60 percent of the federal budget, but most entitlement
spending goes to the nonpoor.
SOURCE: *Budget of the United States Government*, 2009.

programs (including cash welfare assistance, Medicaid, food stamps, and so forth) are
means-tested: benefits are limited to low-income recipients (see Table 5–1). Because many
programs overlap, with individuals receiving more than one type of entitlement benefit, it is
not really possible to know exactly the total number of people receiving government assistance. But it is estimated that *over half of all families in the nation include someone who receives
a government check.*

Rational Strategies, Irrational Results.   It is not possible in this chapter to describe all
the problems of the poor in America or all the difficulties in developing rational social
welfare policies. But it is possible to describe the general design of alternative strategies to
deal with welfare and health in America, to observe how these strategies have been
implemented in public policy, and to outline some of the obstacles to a rational approach
to social welfare problems.

TABLE 5–1   Major Federal Entitlement Program Nearly one-third of the nation's population receives some kind of direct government entitlement.

Social Insurance Programs (No Means Test for Entitlement to Benefits)	Beneficiaries (Millions)
Social Security	47.3
Medicare	39.6
Government Retirement	2.4
Veterans' Benefits	3.5
Unemployment Compensation	7.9

Public Assistance Programs (Means-Tested Entitlement)	Beneficiaries (Millions)
Cash Aid	
Temporary Assistance for Needy Families (formerly AFDC)	4.5
SSI	7.0
Earned income tax credit	19.1
Medical Care	
Medicaid	37.5
Veterans	1.6
Food Benefits	
Food stamps	25.7
School lunches	29.6
School breakfasts	3.1
Women, infants, children (WIC)	8.0
Housing Benefits	
Total	3.3
Education Aid	
Stafford loans	5.6
Pell Grants	5.2
Head Start	0.8
Job Training	
Total	0.8
Energy Assistance	
Total	4.6

SOURCE: *Statistical Abstract of the United States*, 2008.

Defining the Problem: Poverty in America

A rational approach to policymaking requires a clear definition of the problem. But political conflict over the nature and extent of poverty in America is a major obstacle to a rational approach to social welfare policy.

Proponents of programs for the poor frequently make high estimates of that population. They view the problem of poverty as persistent, even in an affluent society; they contend that many millions of people suffer from hunger, exposure, and remedial illness. Their definition of the problem virtually mandates immediate and massive public welfare programs.

TABLE 5–2 **Poverty in America** In recent years, approximately 12 to 13 percent of the population has lived below the poverty line; poverty is most prevalent among female-headed households; blacks and Hispanics experience more poverty than whites.

Poverty definition for family of four	$21,834
Number of poor	37 million
Poverty percentage of total population	12.3
Race (% poor)	
White	10.3
Black	24.2
Hispanic	20.6
Age (% poor)	
Under 18	17.4
Over 65	9.9
Family (% poor)	
Married couple	6.4
Female householder, no husband	30.5

SOURCE: U.S. Bureau of the Census (2008), *www.census.gov.*

In contrast, others minimize the number of poor in America. They believe that the poor are considerably better off than the middle class of fifty years ago and even wealthy by the standards of most other societies in the world. They believe government welfare programs cause poverty, destroy family life, and rob the poor of incentives to work, save, and assume responsibility for their own well-being. They deny that anyone needs to suffer from hunger, exposure, or remedial illness if they use the services and facilities available to them.

How Many Poor? How much poverty really exists in America? According to the U.S. Bureau of the Census, there were between 35 and 40 million poor people in the United States in recent years (see Table 5–2), or approximately 12 to 13 percent of the population.[1] This official estimate of poverty includes all those Americans whose annual cash income falls below that which is required to maintain a decent standard of living. (The dollar amount of the "poverty line" is flexible to take into account the effect of inflation; the amount rises each year with the rate of inflation. In 2008 the poverty line for a family of four was approximately $21,834 per year.)

Liberal Criticism. This official definition of poverty has many critics. Some liberal critics believe that poverty is underestimated because (1) the official definition includes cash income from welfare and Social Security, and without this government assistance, the number of poor would be much higher, perhaps 20 percent of the total population; (2) the official definition does not count the many "near poor"; there are 50 million Americans, or about 17 percent of the population, who live below 125 percent of the poverty level; (3) the official definition does not take into account regional differences in the cost of living, climate, or accepted styles of living; and (4) the official definition does not consider what people *think* they need to live adequately.

Conservative Criticism. Some conservative critics also challenge the official definition of poverty: (1) it does not consider the value of family assets; people (usually older) who own their own mortgage-free homes, furniture, and automobiles may have current incomes below the poverty line yet not suffer hardship; (2) there are many families and individuals who are officially counted as poor but who do not think of themselves as such—students, for example, who deliberately postpone earning an income to secure an education; (3) many persons (poor and nonpoor) underreport their real income, which leads to overestimates of the number of poor; and (4) more importantly, the official definition of poverty excludes "in-kind" (noncash) benefits given to the poor by governments, for example, food stamps, free medical care, public housing, and school lunches. If these benefits were costed out (calculated as cash income), there may be only half as many poor people as shown in official statistics. This figure might be thought of as the "net poverty" rate, which refers to people who remain poor even after counting their in-kind government benefits. The net poverty rate is only about 8 percent, compared to over 12 percent for the official poverty rate.

Latent Poverty.   How many people would be poor if we did *not* have government Social Security and welfare programs? What percentage of the population can be thought of as "latent poor," that is, persons who would be poor without the assistance they receive from federal programs? Latent poverty is well above the official poverty line. It has ranged from about 19 to 22 percent in recent years. So, in the absence of federal social welfare programs, about one-fifth of the nation's population would be poor.

Who Are the Poor?

Poverty occurs in many kinds of families and all races and ethnic groups. However, some groups experience poverty in proportions greater than the national average.

Family Structure.   Poverty is most common among female-headed families. The incidence of poverty among these families has ranged between 25 and 30 percent in recent years, compared to only 5 to 7 percent for married couples (see Table 5–2). Nearly half of all female-headed families with children under 18 live in poverty. These women and their children make up more than two-thirds of all the persons living in poverty in the United States. These figures describe "the feminization of poverty" in America. Clearly, poverty is closely related to family structure. Today the disintegration of the traditional husband–wife family is the single most influential factor contributing to poverty.

Race.   Blacks experience poverty in much greater proportions than whites. Over the years the poverty rate among blacks in the United States has been over twice as high as that among whites. Poverty among Hispanics is also significantly greater than among whites.
    The relationship between race and family structure is a controversial topic. About 50 percent of all black families in the United States in 2008 were headed by females, compared with about 18 percent of all white families.[2]

Age.   The aged in the United States experience *less* poverty than the nonaged. The aged are not poor, despite the popularity of the phrase "the poor and the aged." The poverty rate for persons over sixty-five years of age is well below the national average. Moreover, the aged are much wealthier than the nonaged. They are more likely than younger people to own homes with paid-up mortgages. A large portion of their medical expenses are paid by Medicare. With fewer expenses, the aged, even with relatively smaller cash incomes, experience poverty in a different fashion than a young mother with children.

Temporary versus Persistent Poverty.   Most poverty is temporary, and most welfare dependency is relatively brief, lasting less than two years. Tracing poor families over time presents a different picture of the nature of poverty and welfare from the "snapshot" view taken in any one year. For example, we know that over recent decades 11 to 15 percent of the nation's population had been officially classified as poor in any one year (see Figure 5–2). However, over a decade as many as 25 percent of the nation's population may have fallen below the poverty line at one time or another.[3] Only some poverty is persistent: about 6 percent of the population remains in poverty for more than five years. This means that most of the people who experience poverty in their lives do so for only a short period of time.

However, the *persistently poor* place a disproportionate burden on welfare resources. Less than half of the people on welfare rolls at any one time are persistently poor, that is,

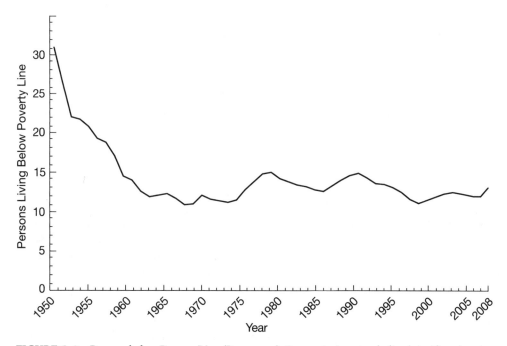

FIGURE 5–2   Persons below Poverty Line (Percentage) Poverty in America declined significantly prior to the 1960s. The enactment of many Great Society programs may have encouraged the continuation of poverty by promoting social dependency. Poverty has varied between 12 and 15 percent of the population since 1970.

SOURCE: U.S. Census Bureau, *Poverty in the United States: 2003* (Washington, DC: Government Printing Office, 2004), pp. 40–45; and *www.census.gov.*

likely to remain poor for five or more years. Thus, for most welfare recipients, welfare payments are a relatively short-term aid that helps them over life's difficult times. But for some, welfare is a more permanent part of their lives.

Why Are the Poor Poor?

Inasmuch as policymakers cannot even agree on the definition of poverty, it comes as no surprise that they cannot agree on its causes. Yet rationality in public policymaking requires some agreement on the causes of social problems.

Low Productivity.   Many economists explain poverty in terms of *human capital theory.* The poor are poor because their economic productivity is low. They do not have the human capital—the knowledge, skills, training, work habits, abilities—to sell to employers in a free market. Absence from the labor force is the largest single source of poverty. Over two-thirds of the poor are children, mothers of small children, or aged or disabled people, all of whom cannot reasonably be expected to find employment. No improvement in the general economy is likely to affect these people directly. Since the private economy has no role for them, they are largely the responsibility of government. The poorly educated and unskilled are also at a disadvantage in a free labor market. The demand for their labor is low, employment is often temporary, and wage rates are low.

Economic Stagnation.   Economists also recognize that some poverty results from inadequate aggregate demand. Serious recessions with increases in unemployment raise the proportion of the population living below the poverty line. According to this view, the most effective antipoverty policy is to assure continued economic growth and employment opportunity. Historically, the greatest reductions in poverty have occurred during prosperous times.

Discrimination.   Discrimination plays a role in poverty that is largely unaccounted for by economic theory. We have already observed that blacks are more likely to experience poverty than whites. It is true that some of the income differences between blacks and whites are a product of educational differences. However, *blacks earn less than whites even at the same educational level.* If the free market operated without interference by discrimination, we would expect little or no difference in income between blacks and whites with the same education.

Culture of Poverty.   Yet another explanation focuses on a "culture of poverty." According to this notion, poverty is a "way of life," which is learned by the poor. The culture of poverty involves not just a low income but also indifference, alienation, apathy, and irresponsibility. This culture fosters a lack of self-discipline to work hard, to plan and save for the future, and to get ahead. It also encourages family instability, immediate gratification, and "present-orientedness" instead of "future-orientedness." All of these attitudes prevent the poor from taking advantage of the opportunities available to them. Even cash payments do not change the way of life of these hard-core poor very much. According to this theory, additional money will be spent quickly for nonessential or frivolous items.

Opponents of this idea argue that it diverts attention from the conditions of poverty that *foster* family instability, present-orientedness, and other ways of life of the poor. The question is really whether a lack of money creates a culture of poverty, or vice versa. Reformers are likely to focus on the condition of poverty as the fundamental cause of the social pathologies that afflict the poor.

Disintegrating Family Structure.   Poverty is closely associated with family structure. As we have seen, poverty is greatest among female-headed households and least among husband–wife households. It may be fashionable in some circles to view husband–wife families as traditional or even antiquated and to redefine *family* as any household with more than one person. But no worse advice could be given to the poor.

Of all age groups, children are most likely to be poor; about 20 percent of America's children live in poverty. Disintegrating family structure explains most of this: only about 10 percent of children living with married parents currently live in poverty, whereas over 40 percent of those living with single mothers do so.[4] Major increases up through 1995 in births to unmarried women occurred among both blacks and whites, but rates among blacks were especially high (see Figure 5–3). This upward trend may now have leveled off.

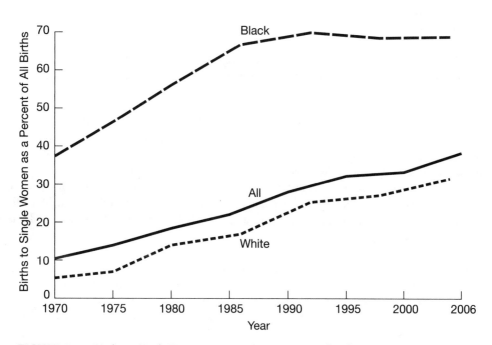

FIGURE 5–3   Births to Single Women Poverty is greatest among female-headed households; births to single women leveled off in recent years, perhaps as a result of welfare reform.
SOURCE: National Center for Health Statistics, 2008.

The Preventive Strategy: Social Security

The administration of President Franklin D. Roosevelt brought conscious attempts by the federal government to develop rational programs to achieve societal goals. In the most important piece of legislation of the New Deal, the Social Security Act of 1935, the federal government undertook to establish the basic framework for welfare policies at the federal, state, and local levels and, more important, to set forth a strategy for dealing with poverty. The Great Depression of that era convinced the nation's leadership that poverty could result from forces over which the individual had no control—loss of job, old age, death of the family breadwinner, or physical disability. One solution was to require individuals to purchase insurance against their own indigency resulting from any of these misfortunes.

Social Insurance.   The social insurance concept devised by the New Deal planners was designed to *prevent* poverty resulting from uncontrollable forces. Social insurance was based on the same notion as private insurance—sharing risks and setting aside money for a rainy day. Social insurance was not to be charity or public assistance; it was to be preventive. It relied on the individual's compulsory contribution to his or her own protection. In contrast, public assistance is only alleviative and relies on general tax revenues from all taxpayers. Indeed, when the Roosevelt administration presented the social insurance plan to Congress in the Social Security Act of 1935, it contended that it would eventually abolish the need for any public assistance program because individuals would be compelled to protect themselves against poverty.

OASDI.   The key feature of the Social Security Act of 1935 is the Old Age Survivor's and Disability Insurance (OASDI) program, generally known as Social Security.* This is a compulsory social insurance program financed by regular deductions from earnings, which gives individuals a legal right to benefits in the event of certain occurrences that cause a reduction of their income: old age, death of the head of household, or permanent disability. OASDI now covers about nine out of every ten workers in the United States, including the self-employed. The only large group outside its coverage are federal employees, who have their own retirement system. Both employees (through payroll deductions) and employers pay equal amounts into the Federal Insurance Contributions Act (FICA) toward the employees' insurance. The total FICA tax on wages, including Medicare, is 15.3 percent of earnings up to a specified amount ($102,000 in 2008) that increases each year.

Retirement Benefits.   Upon retirement, an insured worker is entitled to monthly benefit payments based on age at retirement and the amount earned during his or her working years. Retirees may choose reduced benefits at age 63 or full benefits at age 65. In 1972 Congress ordered automatic cost-of-living adjustments (COLAs) indexed to inflation. The formula for calculating COLAs increases benefits faster than actual cost of living for the elderly.

---

*The original Social Security Act of 1935 did not include disability insurance; this was added by amendment in 1950. Health insurance for the aged—Medicare—was added by amendment in 1965; this is discussed later in the chapter.

Survivor and Disability Benefits. OASDI also provides benefit payments to survivors of an insured worker, including a spouse if there are dependent children. But if there are no dependent children, benefits will not begin until the spouse reaches retirement age. OASDI provides benefit payments to persons who suffer permanent and total disabilities that prevent them from working for more than one year.

Unemployment Compensation. A second important feature of the Social Security Act of 1935 was that it induced states to enact unemployment compensation programs through the imposition of the payroll tax on all employers. A federal unemployment tax is levied on the payroll of employers of four or more workers, but employers paying into state insurance programs that meet federal standards may use these state payments to offset most of their federal unemployment tax. In other words, the federal government threatens to undertake an unemployment compensation program and tax if the states do not do so themselves. This federal program succeeded in inducing all fifty states to establish such programs. However, the federal standards are flexible and the states have considerable freedom in shaping their own programs. In all cases, unemployed workers must report in person and show that they are willing and able to work in order to receive unemployment compensation benefits. In practice, this means that unemployed workers must register with the U.S. Employment Service (usually located in the same building as the state unemployment compensation office) as a condition of receiving their unemployment checks. States cannot deny workers benefits for refusing to work as strikebreakers or for rates lower than prevailing rates. But basic decisions concerning the amount of benefits, eligibility, and the length of time that benefits can be drawn are largely left to the states.

Intended and Unintended Consequences of Social Security

The framers of the Social Security Act of 1935 created a "trust fund" with the expectation that a reserve would be built up from social insurance premiums from working people. The reserve would earn interest, and the interest and principal would be used in later years to pay benefits. Benefits for an individual would be in proportion to his or her contributions. General tax revenues would not be used at all. It was intended that the system would resemble the financing of private insurance, but it turned out not to work that way at all.

The "Trust Fund." The social insurance system is now financed on a pay-as-you-go, rather than a reserve system. Today, the income from all social insurance premiums (taxes) pays for current Social Security benefits. Today, this generation of workers is paying for the benefits of the last generation, and it is hoped that this generation's benefits will be financed by the next generation of workers. Social Security "trust fund" revenues are now lumped together with general tax revenues in the federal budget. Indeed, Social Security payments now comprise over 40 percent of total federal revenues.

Social Security taxes are shown in the federal budget as current revenues (see Chapter 8). Today, Social Security taxes continue to *exceed* the payments made to beneficiaries. This Social

Security "surplus" helps to hide deficits in overall federal spending. The "trust fund" is merely an accounting gimmick; current Social Security taxes are being used to finance current government spending, and future retirement benefits will have to be paid from future government revenues.

The Generational Compact.   Taxing current workers to pay benefits to current retirees may be viewed as a compact between generations. Each generation of workers in effect agrees to pay benefits to an earlier generation of retirees, in the hope that the next generation will pay for their own retirement. But low birth rates (reducing the number of workers), longer life spans (increasing the number of retirees), and generous benefits are straining workers' ability to pay. The generational compact is likely to break sometime in the future. Currently, Social Security trust fund income from workers' taxes exceeds benefit payments to retirees and other eligible recipients. Federal deficits are reduced by these surplus Social Security tax receipts. But it is estimated that around 2016, payments to retirees and others will exceed income from Social Security taxes (see Figure 5–4). The Social Security trust fund (actually general revenues of federal government) will be obliged to make up the difference. By 2040, the trust fund will be exhausted.

The Dependency Ratio.   Since current workers must pay for the benefits of current retirees and other beneficiaries, the dependency ratio becomes an important component of evaluating the future of Social Security. The dependency ratio for Social Security is the number of recipients as a percentage of the number of contributing workers. Americans are living longer, thereby increasing the dependency ratio. A child born in 1935, when the Social Security system was created, could expect to live only to age 61, four years *less* than the retirement age of 65. The life expectancy of a child born in 2005 is 78 years, 13 years *beyond* the retirement age.[5] In the early years of Social Security, there were ten workers supporting each retiree—a dependency ratio of 10 to 1. But today, as the U.S. population

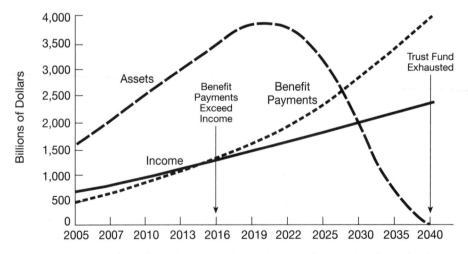

FIGURE 5–4   The Future of Social Security The Social Security fund may be exhausted as the "baby-boom" generation ages; Social Security reform has been put off again and again by Congress. SOURCE: *Social Security Administration Trustee Report, 2005.*

grows older—because of lower birth rates and longer life spans—there are only three workers for each retiree, and by 2030 the dependency ratio will rise to two workers for each retiree.

Tax Burdens. Congress has gradually increased the Social Security payroll tax from 3 percent combined employee and employer contributions to 15.3 percent combined contribution today. The maximum contribution has grown from $30 to over $15,600 (in 2008) since the beginning of the program. The Social Security tax is now *the second-largest source of federal revenue*. Today most workers pay more in Social Security taxes than in federal income taxes.

Generous COLAs. Currently Social Security annual COLAs (cost-of-living adjustments) are based on the consumer price index (CPI), which estimates the cost of all consumer items each year. There are serious problems with the use of the CPI to provide annual values in Social Security benefits. First of all, cost estimates in the CPI include home buying, mortgage interest, child rearing, and other costs that many retirees do not confront. Most *workers* do not have the same protection against inflation as retirees, that is, average wage rates do not always match the increases in cost of living. Over the years, the COLAs have improved the economic well-being of Social Security recipients relative to American workers. Second, the CPI has been shown to *over*estimate rises in the real cost of living. (It does so by ignoring quality improvements in goods as well as shifts of consumers to cheaper products and discount stores when prices rise.) Overestimates in the CPI result in more generous COLAs each year.

Wealthy Retirees. Social Security benefits are paid to all eligible retirees, regardless of whatever other income they may receive. There is no means test for benefits. The result is that large numbers of affluent Americans receive government checks each month. Of course, they paid into Social Security during their working years and they can claim these checks as a legal "entitlement" under the insurance principle. But currently their benefits far exceed their previous payments.

Since the aged experience *less* poverty than today's workers (see Table 5–2) and possess considerably more wealth, Social Security benefits constitute a "negative" redistribution of income, that is, a transfer of income from poorer to richer people. The elderly are generally better off than the people supporting them.

Social Security Reform?

Without significant reform, Social Security will become increasingly burdensome to working taxpayers in the next century. The "baby boom" from 1945 to 1960 produced a large generation of people who crowded schools and colleges in the 1960s and 1970s and who will be retiring beginning in 2010. Changes in lifestyle—less smoking, more exercise, better weight control—as well as medical advances, may increase the aged population even more.

"Saving" Social Security. "Saving" Social Security is a popular political slogan in Washington. But agreement on exactly how to reform the system continues to evade lawmakers.

Social Security is such a politically volatile topic that presidents have resorted to independent and nonpartisan commissions to recommend reform, rather than undertake to initiate reforms themselves. In 1983 a National Commission on Social Security Reform, appointed by President Ronald Reagan and made up of equal numbers of Democrats and Republicans, recommended increases in Social Security taxes to build a reserve for the large number of baby-boom generation retirees expected after the year 2010. The commission also recommended, and Congress enacted, a gradual increase in the full retirement age from 65 to 67, beginning in 2000. The Social Security tax was also increased to its current combined employer and employee 15.3 percent. However, no real "reserve" was ever created, other than as an accounting gimmick.

Reform Options.   There is no lack of reform proposals for Social Security.[6] The problem is that no particular proposal enjoys widespread popular support. In theory, Congress could limit benefits in several ways, for example, by raising the eligibility age for full retirement to 68 or 70, by limiting COLAs to the true increases in the cost of living for retirees, or by reducing benefits for high-income retirees. Or, Congress could increase Social Security revenues by raising the payroll tax rate, or by eliminating the cap on earnings that are taxed. But politically, such reforms are very controversial.

Various proposals to "privatize" all or part of Social Security represent yet another approach to reform. One idea was to allow the Social Security trust fund to invest in the private stock market with the expectation that stock values will increase over time. But if stock market investment decisions were made by the government itself, presumably the Social Security Administration, controversies would be bound to arise over these decisions. Critics object to the idea of government making private investment decisions for Americans. A related idea is that American workers be allowed to deposit part of their Social Security payroll tax into individual retirement accounts to buy securities of their own choosing. Of course, such a plan would expose workers to the risk of bad investment decisions. None of these reforms appear to be very popular with the American people.

The "Third Rail" of American Politics.   Social Security is the most expensive program in the federal budget but also the most politically sacrosanct. Politicians regularly call it the "third rail" of American politics—touch it and die.

Senior citizens are the most politically powerful age group in the population. They constitute 28 percent of the voting-age population, but more important, because of their high turnout rates, they constitute nearly one-third of the voters on election day. Moreover, seniors are well represented in Washington; the American Association of Retired Persons (AARP) is the nation's single largest organized interest group, with heavy 80 million members. Most seniors, and their lobbyists in Washington, adamantly oppose any Social Security reforms that might reduce benefits.

The Alleviative Strategy: Public Assistance

The Social Security and unemployment compensation programs were based on the insurance strategy to *prevent* poverty, but in the Social Security Act of 1935 the federal government also undertook to help the states provide public assistance to certain needy people.

This strategy was designed to *alleviate* the conditions of poverty. The original idea was to provide a minimum level of subsistence to certain categories of needy adults—the aged, blind, and disabled—and to provide for the care of dependent children.

Supplemental Security Income. Supplemental Security Income (SSI) is a means-tested, federally administered income assistance program that provides monthly cash payments to needy elderly (65 or older), blind, and disabled people. A loose definition of "disability"—including alcoholism, drug abuse, and attention deficiency among children—has led to a rapid growth in the number of SSI beneficiaries.

Medicaid. Medicaid is a joint federal–state program that provides health services to low-income Americans. Women and children receiving public assistance benefits qualify for Medicaid, as does anyone who gets cash assistance under SSI. States can also offer Medicaid to the "medically needy"—those who face crushing medical costs but whose income or assets are too high to qualify for SSI or Temporary Assistance for Needy Families, including pregnant women and young children not receiving other aid. Medicaid also pays for long-term nursing home care, but only after beneficiaries have used up virtually all of their savings and income.

Food Stamps. The food stamp program provides low-income households with coupons that they can redeem for enough food to provide a minimal, nutritious diet. The program is overseen by the federal government, but is administered by the states.

Temporary Assistance for Needy Families. Today the largest cash assistance program is a federal block grant to the states for needy families with dependent children. A result of welfare reform legislation passed by a Republican-controlled Congress in 1996 and signed by President Bill Clinton, this program replaces Aid to Families with Dependent Children (AFDC). Its major provisions include the following:

> *Work requirements.* Adults receiving welfare benefits are required to begin working within two years of receiving aid. States may exempt from this work requirement a parent of a child 12 months of age or younger. States were required to have at least 50 percent of their welfare caseload engaged in work by 2002.
>
> *Restrictions on aid.* Federal funds cannot be used for adults who have *received welfare for more than five years,* although state and local funds could be used. States can exempt up to 20 percent of their caseload from this time limit. States can also opt to impose a shorter time limit on benefits. None of the funds can be used for adults who do not work *after receiving welfare for two years.* In addition, states have the option to deny welfare to unwed parents under age 18 unless they live with an adult and attend school.

Welfare Reform

Developing a rational strategy to assist the poor is hampered by the clash of values over individual responsibility and social compassion. As Harvard sociologist David Ellwood explains,

> Welfare brings some of our most precious values—involving autonomy, responsibility, work, family, community and compassion—into conflict. We want to help those who are not making it but in so doing, we seem to cheapen the efforts of those who are struggling hard just to get by. We want to offer financial support to those with low incomes, but if we do we reduce the pressure on them and their incentive to work. We want to help people who are not able to help themselves but then we worry that people will not bother to help themselves. We recognize the insecurity of single-parent families but, in helping them, we appear to be promoting or supporting their formation.[7]

The social insurance programs that largely serve the middle class (Social Security, Medicare, unemployment compensation) are politically popular and enjoy the support of large numbers of politically active beneficiaries. But public assistance programs that largely serve the poor (cash aid, SSI, food stamps, Medicaid) are far less popular and are surrounded by many controversies.

Public Policy as a Cause of Poverty?   Can the government itself encourage poverty by fashioning social welfare programs and policies that destroy incentives to work, encourage families to break up, and condemn the poor to social dependency?

Poverty in America steadily declined from 1950, when about 30 percent of the population was officially poor, to 1970, when about 12 percent of the population was poor. During this period of progress toward the elimination of poverty, government welfare programs were minimal. But the downward trend in poverty ended in the 1970s and early 1980s (see Figure 5–2). This was a period in which AFDC payments were significantly increased and eligibility rules were relaxed. The food stamp program was initiated in 1965 and became a major new welfare benefit. Medicaid was initiated in the same year and by the late 1970s became the costliest of all welfare programs. Federal aid to the aged, blind, and disabled were merged into a new SSI program (Supplement Security Income), which quadrupled in numbers of recipients. The greatest increases in poverty occurred in families headed by *working-age* persons. Policymakers became obliged to consider the possibility that policy changes—new welfare programs, expanded benefits, and relaxed eligibility requirements—contributed to increased poverty.[8]

Welfare Reform Politics.   A consensus grew over the years that long-term social dependency had to be addressed in welfare policy. The fact that most *non*poor mothers work convinced many liberals that welfare mothers had no special claim to stay at home with their children. And many conservatives acknowledged that some transitional assistance—education, job training, continued health care, and day care for children—might be necessary to move welfare mothers into the work force.

Although President Bill Clinton had promised "to end welfare as we know it," it was the Republican-controlled Congress elected in 1994 that proceeded to do so. The Republican-sponsored welfare reform bill ended the 60-year-old federal "entitlement" for low-income families with children—the venerable AFDC program. In its place the Republicans devised a "devolution" of responsibility to the states through federal block grants—Temporary Assistance to Needy Families—lump sum allocations to the states for cash welfare payments with benefits and eligibility requirements decided by the states. Conservatives in Congress imposed

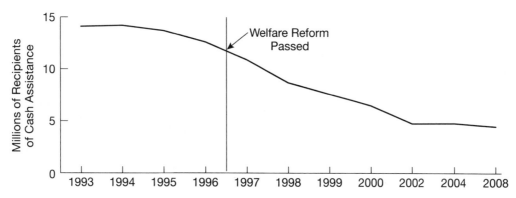

FIGURE 5–5 Evaluating Welfare Reform Since the passage of welfare reform in 1996, the percentage of the population receiving cash benefits has declined dramatically.
SOURCE: U.S. Department of Health and Human Services.

tough-minded "strings" to state aid, including a two-year limit on continuing cash benefits and a five-year lifetime limit; a "family cap" that would deny additional cash benefits to women already on welfare who bear more children; the denial of cash welfare to unwed parents under 18 years of age unless they live with an adult and attend school. President Clinton vetoed the first welfare reform bill passed by Congress in early 1996, but as the presidential election neared, he reversed himself and signed the welfare reform act establishing the Temporary Assistance to Needy Families program (described earlier). Food stamps, SSI, and Medicaid were continued as federal "entitlements."

Evaluation: Is Welfare Reform Working?   If welfare reform is evaluated in terms of the numbers of people receiving cash welfare payments, then TANF has been a stunning success. Welfare recipients dropped by two-thirds in the years following welfare reform (see Figure 5–5). Yet during this same period recipients of food stamps, SSI, and Medicaid increased.

Continuing Welfare Needs.   While nearly everyone agrees that getting people off of welfare rolls and onto payrolls is the main goal of reform, there are major obstacles to the achievement of this goal. First of all, a substantial portion (perhaps 25 to 40 percent) of long-term welfare recipients have handicaps—physical disabilities, chronic illnesses, learning disabilities, alcohol or drug abuse problems—that prevent them from holding a full-time job. Many long-term recipients have no work experience (perhaps 40 percent) and two-thirds of them did not graduate from high school. Almost half have three or more children, making day-care arrangements a major obstacle. It is unlikely that any counseling, education, job training, or job placement programs advocated by liberals could ever succeed in getting these people into productive employment. Policymakers argue whether there are 4 million jobs available to unskilled mothers, but even if there are such jobs available, they would be low-paying, minimum-wage jobs that would not lift them out of poverty.

The Working Poor

Significant numbers of people who work part-time or even full-time still fall below the poverty line. These "working poor" constitute about 10 percent of the nation's work force.

The Minimum Wage.   The Fair Labor Standards Act of 1937, an important part of President Franklin D. Roosevelt's New Deal, set a standard 40-hour workweek and minimum hourly wage for American workers. Congress periodically raises the minimum wage. (For 2009 the federal minimum wage is set at $7.15 per hour.) Over time, however, larger numbers of workers have become independent "contractors" or "managers" or other classifications of employees that fall outside the protection of federal wage and hour laws.

The Earned Income Tax Credit.   Low-income workers in America currently benefit more from the Earned Income Tax Credit (EITC) than the minimum wage. The EITC was enacted in 1975 to provide an incentive to work. The credit does more than eliminate the burden of the federal income tax for low-income people; rather, it results in a "refund" check for those who claim and qualify for the credit. (In 2008 families with two or more children and incomes below $40,000 qualified for the credit and received a check from the government.) The maximum check in 2008 was $4,700. The EITC may be thought of as a "negative income tax." It results in government payments to low-income workers.

The EITC is now the largest means-tested program other than Medicaid. Over 20 million families receive EITC checks. Nonetheless, it is estimated that about one-third of qualifying families fail to take advantage of their EITC benefits.

Homelessness and Public Policy

Homeless "street people" may be the most visible social welfare problem confronting the nation. The homeless suffer exposure, alcoholism, drug abuse, and chronic mental illness while wandering the streets of the nation's larger cities. No one really knows the true number of homeless.[9] The issue has become so politicized that an accurate assessment of the problem and a rational strategy for dealing with it have become virtually impossible.[10] The term *homeless* is used to describe many different situations. There are the street people who sleep in subways, bus stations, parks, or the streets. Some of them are temporarily traveling in search of work; some have left home for a few days or are youthful runaways; others have roamed the streets for months or years. There are the *sheltered homeless* who obtain housing in shelters operated by local governments or private charities. As the number of shelters has grown in recent years, the number of sheltered homeless has also grown. But most of the sheltered homeless come from other housing, not the streets. These are people who have been recently evicted from rental units or have previously lived with family or friends. They often include families with children; the street homeless are virtually all single persons.

Who Are the Homeless?   Among all homeless, both street people and sheltered homeless, single men make up 41 percent, families with children 44 percent, single women 13 percent, and unaccompanied youth 5 percent.[11] Among single people living on the streets, close to half are chronic alcohol and/or drug abusers, and an additional one-fourth to one-third are mentally ill. Families with children were found among the sheltered homeless, and many of the sheltered homeless are employed. The sheltered homeless remain for an average of six months. Single street people may remain homeless for years.

Public Policy as a Cause of Homelessness.   The current plight of many of the street home- less is a result of various "reforms" in public policy, notably the "deinstitutionalization" of care for the mentally ill, the "decriminalization" of vagrancy and public intoxication, newly recognized rights to refuse treatment, and the renewal of central cities and the elimination of low-rent apartments and cheap hotels.

Deinstitutionalization.   Deinstitutionalization was a reform advanced by mental health care professionals and social welfare activists in the 1960s and 1970s to release chronic men- tal patients from state-run mental hospitals. It was widely recognized that aside from drugs, no psychiatric therapies have much success among the long-term mentally ill. Drug therapies can be administered on an outpatient basis; they usually do not require hospitalization. So it was argued that no one could be rightfully kept in a mental institution against his or her will; people who had committed no crimes and who posed no danger to others should be released. Federal and state monies for mental health were to be directed toward community mental health facilities that would treat the mentally ill on a voluntary outpatient basis. The nation's mental hospitals were emptied of all but the most dangerous patients.

Decriminalization.   "Vagrancy" and public intoxication are no longer crimes. Involuntary confinement has been abolished for the mentally ill and for substance abusers, unless a per- son is adjudged in court to be "a danger to himself or others," which means a person must commit a serious act of violence before the courts will intervene. For many homeless this means the freedom to "die with their rights on." The homeless are victimized by cold, expo- sure, hunger, the availability of alcohol and illegal drugs, and violent street crimes perpe- trated against them, in addition to the ravages of their illness itself.

The Failure of Community Care.   Community-based care is largely irrelevant to the plight of the chronic mentally ill and alcohol and drug abusers in the streets. Many are "uncooperative"; they are isolated from society; they have no family members or doctors or counselors to turn to for help. For them, community care is a Salvation Army meal and cot; a night in a city-run refuge for the homeless; or a ride to the city hospital psychiatric ward for a brief period of "obser- vation," after which they must be released again to the streets. The nation's vast social welfare sys- tem provides little help. They lose their Social Security, welfare, and disability checks because they have no permanent address. They cannot handle forms, appointments, or interviews; the welfare bureaucracy is intimidating.

Health Care in America

There is no better illustration of the dilemmas of rational policymaking in America than in the field of health. Again, the first obstacle to rationalism is in defining the problem. Is our goal to have *good health*—that is, whether we live at all (infant mortality), how well we live (days lost to sickness), and how long we live (life spans and adult mortality)? Or is our goal to have *good medical care*—frequent visits to the doctor, well-equipped and accessible hospitals, and equal access to medical care by rich and poor alike?

Perhaps the first lesson in health policy is understanding that good medical care does not necessarily mean good health. Good health correlates best with factors over which doctors and hospitals have no control: heredity, lifestyle (smoking, obesity, drinking, exercise, worry), and the physical environment (sewage disposal, water quality, conditions of work, and so forth). Most of the bad things that happen to people's health are beyond the reach of doctors and hospitals. In the long run, infant mortality, sickness and disease, and life span are affected very little by the quality of medical care. If you want a long, healthy life, choose parents who have lived a long, healthy life, and then do all the things your mother always told you to do: don't smoke, don't drink, get lots of exercise and rest, don't overeat, relax, and don't worry.

Leading Causes of Death. Historically, most of the reductions in infant and adult death rates have resulted from public health and sanitation, including immunization against small-pox, clean public water supply, sanitary sewage disposal, improved diets, and increased standards of living. Many of the leading causes of death today (see Table 5–3), including heart disease, stroke, cirrhosis of the liver, accidents, and suicides, are closely linked to personal habits and lifestyles and are beyond the reach of medicine.

Access to Medical Care. Americans now generally view access to medical care as a right. No one should be denied medical care or suffer pain or remedial illness for lack of financial resources. There is widespread agreement on this ethical principle. The tough questions arise when we seek rational strategies to implement it.

Medicare: Health Care as Government Insurance. Medicare, was enacted in 1965 as an amendment to the nation's basic Social Security Act. Medicare provides prepaid hospital insurance and low-cost voluntary medical insurance for the aged, directly under federal

TABLE 5–3 Leading Causes of Death[a] Many of the leading causes of death today are closely linked to personal habits and life styles; the overall death rate has declined significantly since 1960.

	1960	1970	1980	1990	2000	2007
Heart disease	369.0	362.0	334.3	289.0	257.5	272.2
Stroke (cerebrovascular)	108.0	101.9	80.5	57.9	60.2	51.1
Cancer	149.2	162.8	181.9	201.7	200.5	188.6
Accidents	52.3	56.4	48.4	37.3	33.9	38.1
Pneumonia	37.3	30.9	26.7	31.3	24.3	20.3
Diabetes	16.7	18.9	15.5	19.5	24.9	24.9
Suicide	10.6	11.6	12.5	12.3	10.3	10.4
Homicide	4.7	8.3	9.4	10.2	5.8	5.6
AIDS/HIV	—	—	—	9.6	5.4	4.5
Alzheimer's disease	—	—	—	—	21.8	22.5

[a]Deaths per 100,000 population per year.

SOURCE: *Statistical Abstract of the United States, 2008*, p. 83. Center for Disease Control, *www.cdc.gov/nchs.*

administration. Medicare includes HI—a compulsory basic health insurance plan covering hospital costs for the aged, which is financed out of payroll taxes collected under the Social Security system—and SMI—a voluntary, supplemental medical insurance program that will pay 80 percent of "allowable" charges for physicians' services and other medical expenses, financed in part by contributions from the aged and in part by general tax revenues.

Only *aged* persons are covered by Medicare provisions. Eligibility is not dependent on income; all aged persons eligible for Social Security are also eligible for Medicare. No physical examination is required and preexisting conditions are covered. The costs of SMI are so low to the beneficiaries that participation by the elderly is almost universal.

Medicare requires patients to pay small initial charges or "deductibles." The purpose is to discourage unnecessary hospital or physician care. HI generally pays the full charges for the first 60 days of hospitalization each year after a deductible charge equivalent to one day's stay; but many doctors charge higher rates than allowable under SMI. Indeed, it is estimated that only about half of the doctors in the nation accept SMI allowable payments as payment in full. Many doctors bill Medicare patients for charges above the allowable SMI payments. Medicare does not pay for eyeglasses, dental expenses, hearing aids, or routine physical examinations.

Medicaid: Health Care as Welfare. Medicaid is the federal government's largest single welfare program for the poor. Its costs now exceed the costs of all other public assistance programs—including family assistance, SSI, and the food stamp program. Medicaid was begun in 1965 and grew quickly.

Medicaid is a combined federal and state program. The states exercise fairly broad administrative powers and carry almost half of the financial burden. Medicaid is a welfare program designed for needy persons: no prior contributions are required, monies come from general tax revenues, and most recipients are already on welfare rolls. Although states differ in their eligibility requirements, they must cover all people receiving federally funded public assistance payments. Most states also extend coverage to other "medically needy"— individuals who do not qualify for public assistance but whose incomes are low enough to qualify as needy.

States also help set benefits. All states are required by the federal government to provide inpatient and outpatient hospital care, physicians' services, family planning, laboratory services and X-rays, and nursing and home health care. They must also develop an early and periodic screening, diagnosis, and treatment program for all children under Medicaid. However, states themselves generally decide on the rate of reimbursement to hospitals and physicians. Low rates can discourage hospitals and physicians from providing good care. To make up for low payments, they may schedule too many patients in too short a time, prescribe unnecessary tests and procedures designed to make treatment more expensive, or shift costs incurred in treating Medicaid patients to more affluent patients with private insurance.

SCHIP: Health Care for Children. Under the State Children's Health Insurance Program (SCHIP) the federal government provides grants to states to extend health insurance to children who would not otherwise qualify for Medicaid. The program is generally targeted toward families with incomes below 200 percent of the poverty level. But each state may set its own eligibility limits and each state has flexibility in the administration of the program. States may expand their Medicaid programs to include children or develop separate child health programs.

The Uninsured.   Approximately 85 percent of the population of the United States is covered by either private or government health insurance. But about 15 percent of the population (about 45 million people) has no medical insurance. Most of the uninsured are working Americans and their families—people who are not poor enough to qualify for Medicaid nor old enough to qualify for Medicare. Young adults are the least insured age group.

Health Care Access and Costs

The United States spends more of its resources on health care than any other advanced industrialized nation, yet it ranks below other nations in many key measures of the health of its people (see Figure 5–6). Life expectancy in the United States is lower, and the infant death rate is higher, than in many of these nations. The United States offers the most advanced and sophisticated medical care in the world, attracting patients from countries that rank ahead of us in these common health measures. The United States is the locus of the most advanced

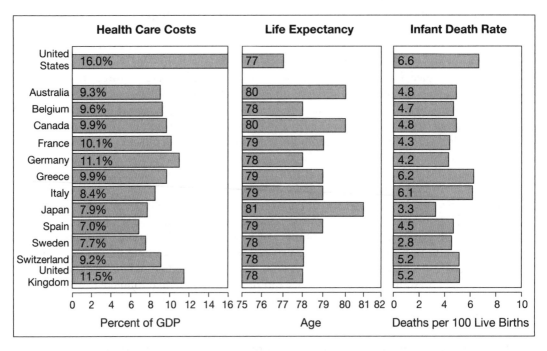

FIGURE 5–6   Health Care Costs and Benefits: A Cross-National Comparison   The United States spends a larger proportion of its GDP on health care than any other nation, yet many other nations enjoy better overall health than Americans.
SOURCE: *Statistical Abstract of the United States, 2008,* pp. 831, 834.

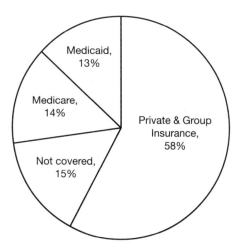

FIGURE 5–7 **Health Care Coverage and the Uninsured**
SOURCE: Statistical Abstract of the United States. 2008, p. 107.

medical research in the world, drawing researchers from all over the world. This apparent paradox—the highest quality medical care, combined with poor health statistics for the general public—suggests that our nation's health care problems center more on access to care, education, and prevention of health problems than on the quality of care available.

Access to Health Care. While Medicare covers the aged and Medicaid covers the poor, many working Americans and their dependents have no health insurance. These people may postpone or go without needed medical care or be denied medical care by hospitals and physicians except in emergencies. Confronted with serious illness they may be obliged to impoverish themselves to become eligible for Medicaid. Their unpaid medical bills must be absorbed by hospitals or shifted to paying patients and their insurance companies. Many uninsured people work for small businesses or are self-employed or unemployed (see Figure 5–7).

Nursing-Home Care. As the number and proportion of the elderly population grow in the United States (80 years and over is the fastest-growing age group in the nation), the need for long-term nursing-home care grows. Medicare does not pay for long-term care or catastrophic illness. It covers only the first 60 days of hospitalization and nursing-home care for 100 days only if the patient is sent there from a hospital. Medicaid assistance to the needy is paid to nursing-home patients, but middle-class people cannot qualify for Medicaid without first "spending down" their savings. Long-term nursing-home care threatens their assets and their children's inheritance. Private insurance policies covering long-term care are said to be too expensive. So senior citizen groups have lobbied heavily for long-term nursing-home care to be paid for by taxpayers under Medicare.

Health Care Costs. The United States spends over $2 trillion on health care each year—almost $8,000 per person. These costs represent approximately 16 percent of the GDP and they are growing rapidly. It is estimated that by 2017 almost 20 percent of the GDP—more than $4 trillion—will be spent on health care. The enactment of the Medicare and Medicaid programs in 1965 and their growth throughout the 1970s contributed to this inflation of health care costs. But there were many other causes as well. Advances in medical technology have produced elaborate and expensive equipment. Hospitals that have made heavy financial investment in this equipment must use it as often as possible. Physicians trained in highly specialized techniques and procedures wish to use them. The threat of malpractice suits forces doctors to practice "defensive medicine"—to order multiple tests and consultations to guard against even the most remote medical possibilities. Pharmaceutical companies have driven up spending for drugs by advertising expensive brand-name prescription drugs on television, encouraging patients to ask their doctors for these drugs. (Prior to 1997 direct advertising for prescription drugs was not permitted.) Cheaper generic versions of the same drugs receive no such publicity.

The Aging Population.   In the not-too-distant future, an aging population will drive up medical care costs to near astronomical figures. Currently, one-third of all health care expenditures benefit the aged. When the baby-boom generation reaches 65 and over (see Figure 5–8), neither the current Medicare or Medicaid programs will be able to provide them adequate medical care. The fastest-growing cost now in the Medicaid program is nursing-home care. Medicare does not pay nursing-home costs, but Medicaid does. But to qualify for Medicaid nursing-home assistance, the elderly must first exhaust all of their financial resources— improverishing themselves to be eligible for assistance.

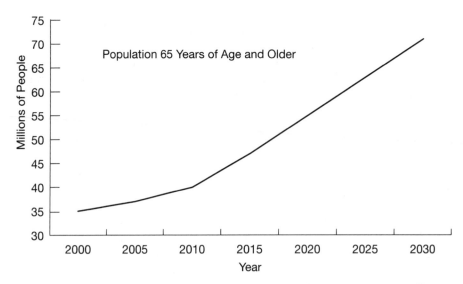

FIGURE 5–8   The Aging of America Increases in the nation's aged population increase health care costs and threaten to exhaust Medicare funds.
SOURCE: U.S. Census Bureau Projections of the Population by Selected Age Groups. *www.census.gov.*

Managed Care Programs.   Skyrocketing costs have caused both governments and private insurance companies to promote various types of "managed care" programs. Both Medicare and Medicaid have shifted many of their beneficiaries to managed care programs.

Health maintenance organizations (HMOs) are the most common type of managed care program. They try to control costs by requiring patients to use a network of approved doctors and hospitals, and by reviewing what these "preferred" caregivers do. For example, a managed care organization might insist that doctors prescribe cheaper generic drugs in place of brand-name products. In many cases, patients must get the organization's approval before undergoing operations or other treatments. And patients have to pay more to visit a doctor who is not in the network. In contrast, under traditional "fee-for-service" health insurance plans, the patient chooses a doctor, gets treated, and the bill is sent to the insurance company. The patient may have to pay a deductible for a percentage of the total bill—a "co-pay."

Controversies over Managed Care.   But efforts of both private insurers and government to control costs have created new political controversies. Many of the cost-control regulations and restrictions instituted by insurance companies and HMOs frustrate both patients and physicians. For example, both doctors and patients complain that preapproval of treatment by insurance companies removes medical decisions from the physician and patient and places them in hands of insurance company administrators. And patients complain that HMOs refuse to allow them to see specialists, limit the number and variety of tests, and even encourage doctors to minimize treatment.

Health Care Reform Strategies

Health care reform centers on two central problems: controlling costs and expanding access and benefits. These problems are related: expanding access to Americans who are currently uninsured and closing gaps in coverage require increases in costs, even while the other thrust of reform is to slow the growth of overall health care costs.

Single-Payer Plans.   Liberals have pressed for a Canadian-style health care system in which the government would provide health insurance for all Americans in a single national plan paid for by increases in taxes. In effect, a single-payer plan would expand Medicare, now available to only the aged, to everyone. The plan boasts of simplicity, savings in administrative costs over multiple insurers, and direct federal control over prices to be paid for hospital and physician services and drugs. Single-payer universal coverage would require major new taxes.

Obama Healthcare Transformation.   President Obama has proposed a major overhaul of the nation's health care system, a project attempted unsuccessfully by past presidents including Franklin Delanor Roosevelt, Harry Truman and Bill Clinton. In the president's words, "moving to provide all Americans with health insurance is not only a moral imperative, but it is also essential to a more effective and efficient health-care system."[12] Among the many health-care proposals on the Obama agenda: expanding SCHIP program for children, computerizing the nation's health records, and expanding COBRA health insurance to unemployed workers. Obama promises that in this healthcare transformation the Medicare, Medicaid, and Veterans Administration healthcare programs will remain unchanged. The transformed system will continue to rely primarily on private health insurance companies. However private insurers will no longer be permitted to deny insurance for pre-existing conditions, or to drop coverage when patients get stick, and they will be required to provide for routine checkups and preventative care. These particular reforms face no serious opposition.

- National Health Insurance Exchange. The president also has proposed a National Health Insurance Exchange that will bring together individuals and small businesses as a group to better negotiate with insurance companies in a competitive marketplace. Individuals and small businesses will be able to bargain for affordable insurance in the fashion of large businesses and government employees.
- "The Public Option". The central reform in the Obama health care agenda is the creation of a government-run "public option" as part of the national health insurance exchange. This public not-for-profit health insurance program would function side-by-side with private health insurance. Premiums are likely to be based on a sliding scale according to income. This public plan would not put private insurers out of business, but according to the president "keep them honest" by offering reasonable coverage at affordable prices.
- Critics view the public option as a "government takeover" of the nation's health care system. As a not-for-profit government-run agency, the public plan would enjoy a competitive advantage over private insurers. Gradually private insurance companies would lose out to this public program, over time creating a single national health insurance system or "socialized medicine". (Indeed, some critics believe this is the true intent of President Obama.)
- Cost. President Obama asserts that the costs of health care reform can be found in savings to be made in the existing health-care system—"a system that is currently full of waste and abuse". The President claims that eliminating waste and inefficiency in Medicare and Medicaid will pay for most of his plan. But critics doubt that such savings exist. Indeed, the proposal to cut waste and abuse in Medicare has inspired critics to claim that health-care reform is going to come at the expense of the elderly. The Congressional Budget Office estimates the cost of Obama's health care reform proposals at one trillion dollars.

The Interest Group Challenges.   Rational reform strategies confront the reality of interest group politics, and interest group battles over the details of health care reform have been intense. Virtually everyone has a financial stake in the nation's health care system.

- Employers, especially small businesses, are fearful of added costs of government-mandated insurance.
- Physicians strongly oppose price controls and treatment guidelines, as well as programs that take away a patient's choice of physician.
- Drug companies want to see prescription drugs paid for, but they vigorously oppose price controls on drugs.
- Hospitals want all patients to be insured but oppose government payment schedules.

- Insurance companies, oppose a government-run "public election" that would compete with private insurers.

- The powerful senior citizens lobby wants added benefits, including coverage for drugs, eyeglasses, dental care, and nursing homes, but it fears folding Medicare into a large health care system.

- Veterans groups want to retain separate Veterans Administration (VA) hospitals and medical services.

- Opponents of abortion rights are prepared to do battle to keep national coverage from including such procedures, whereas supporters of abortion rights argue that abortion must be included.

- Trial lawyers oppose any limits on patients' rights to sue doctors, hospitals, HMOs, or anyone else, and they oppose any limits on monetary awards from these suits.

SUMMARY

A rational approach to social welfare policy requires a clear definition of objectives, the development of alternative strategies for achieving them, and a careful comparison and weighing of the costs and benefits of each. But there are seemingly insurmountable problems in developing a completely rational policy:

1. Contrasting definitions of poverty constitute one obstacle to rational policymaking. Official government sources define poverty in terms of minimum dollar amounts required for subsistence. In recent years about 12 to 15 percent of the population has fallen below the official poverty line. Latent poverty refers to people who would fall below the poverty line in the absence of government assistance; about 20 percent of the population falls within this definition of poverty. Net poverty refers to people who remain poor even after receiving government assistance; about 8 percent of the population falls within this definition.

2. Contrasting explanations of poverty also make it difficult to formulate a rational policy. Is poverty a product of a lack of knowledge, skills, and training? Or recession and unemployment? Or a culture of poverty? Certainly the disintegration of the traditional husband–wife family is closely associated with poverty. How can the government devise a rational policy to keep families together, or at least not encourage them to dissolve?

3. Government welfare policies themselves may be a significant cause of poverty. Poverty in America had steadily declined before the development of Great Society programs, the relaxation of eligibility requirements for welfare assistance, and the rapid increase of welfare expenditures in the 1970s. To what extent do government programs themselves encourage social dependency and harm the long-term prospects of the poor?

4. The social insurance concept was designed as a preventive strategy to insure people against indigence arising from old age, death of a family breadwinner, or physical disability. But the Social Security "trust fund" idea remains in name only. Today each generation of workers is expected to pay the benefits for each generation of retirees. Sometime after the year 2020 the dependency ratio will rise to a point where it will

become increasingly difficult for workers to support the large number of Social Security recipients.

5. The federal government also pursues an alleviative strategy in assisting the poor with a variety of direct cash and in-kind benefit programs. The SSI program provides direct federal cash payments to the aged, blind, and disabled. As a welfare program, SSI is paid from general tax revenues, and recipients must prove their need. The largest in-kind welfare programs are the federal food stamp and Medicaid programs.

6. Welfare reform in 1996, including a two-year limit on cash assistance and work and/or school requirements, appears to have reduced welfare rolls substantially. But some people are not capable of moving from welfare to work; further cuts in welfare rolls may create real hardship.

7. "Rational" strategies sometimes produce unintended consequences. Deinstitutionalization of the mentally ill and decriminalization of public intoxication produced many homeless people. It is often difficult to reach these people through conventional welfare programs.

8. The paramount objective in national health policy has never been clearly defined. Is it *good health*, as defined by lower death rates, less illness, and longer life? Or is it *access to good medical care?* If good health is the objective, preventive efforts to change people's personal habits and lifestyles are more likely to improve health than anything else.

9. Medicare for the aged and Medicaid for the poor, together with private and employer-provided insurance, guarantee access to health care for about 85 percent of the population. But about 15 percent, including many workers and their families, have no health insurance; many other Americans worry about loss of insurance with unemployment or job changes.

10. Health care reform centers on two conflicting goals—expanding access to all Americans while containing costs. Comprehensive, rational reform is threatened by the multiple demands of interest groups.

Notes

1. U.S. Bureau of the Census, *Statistical Abstract of the United States, 2008*, p. 471.
2. *Statistical Abstract of the United States, 2008*, p. 54.
3. Greg J. Duncan, *Years of Poverty, Years of Plenty* (Ann Arbor, MI: Institute of Social Research, 1984).
4. *Statistical Abstract of the United States, 2008*, p. 459.
5. Ibid, p. 76.
6. See Henry J. Aaron and Robert D. Reichaucer, *Countdown to Reform: The Great Social Security Debate* (Washington, DC: Brookings Institution, 2001).
7. David Ellwood, *Poor Support: Poverty in the American Family* (New York: Basic Books, 1988), p. 6.
8. Charles Murray, *Losing Ground* (New York: Basic Books, 1984).
9. Peter H. Rossi, *Down and Out in America* (Chicago: University of Chicago Press, 1989).
10. Robert C. Ellickson, "The Homelessness Muddle," *The Public Interest*, Spring 1990, pp. 45–60.
11. U.S. Conference of Mayors, *Report of the Taskforce on Hunger and Homelessness*, December 2002.
12. *Budget of the United States Government 2010*, p. 26.

Bibliography

AARON, HENRY J. *Saving Social Security: Which Way to Reform?* Washington, DC: Brookings Institution Press, 2006.

BETTELHEIN, ADRIEL. *Aging in America.* Washington, DC: CQ Press, 2001.

DIAMOND, PETER and PETER R. ORSZAG. *Saving Social Security,* rev. ed. Washington, DC: Brookings Institution Press, 2005.

DINITTO, DIANA M., and LINDA K. CUMMINS. *Social Welfare: Politics and Policy,* 6th ed. New York: Allyn & Bacon, 2007.

GRAIG, LAURENE. *Health of Nations: An International Perspective on U.S. Health Care.* Washington, DC: CQ Press, 1999.

JENCKS, CHRISTOPHER, and PAUL E. PETERSON. *The Urban Underclass.* Washington, DC: Brookings Institution Press, 1991.

MACMANUS, SUSAN. *Young versus Old.* Boulder, CO: Westview Press, 1996.

MURRAY, CHARLES. *Losing Ground.* New York: Basic Books, 1984.

PATEL, KANT, and MARK E. RUSHEFSKY. *Health Care in America: Seperate and Unequal.* New York: M.E. Sharpe, 2008.

ROGERS, HAROLD R., Jr. *American Poverty in a New Age of Reform.* New York: M. E. Sharpe, 2nd ed. 2006.

SHILLER, BRADLEY R. *The Economics of Poverty and Discrimination,* 9th ed. Upper Saddle River, NJ: Prentice Hall, 2004.

WILSON, WILLIAM J. *The Truly Disadvantaged.* Chicago: University of Chicago Press, 1987.

Web Sites

CHILDREN'S DEFENSE FUND. Advocacy organization for welfare programs, with special emphasis on aid for children. *www.childrensdefense.org*

URBAN INSTITUTE. Think tank with emphasis on welfare issues. *www.urban.org*

AMERICAN ASSOCIATION OF RETIRED PERSONS (AARP). Home page of the leading advocacy group for seniors. *www.aarp.org*

CATO INSTITUTE (SOCIAL SECURITY). Libertarian think tank's special site advocating privatizing Social Security. *www.socialsecurity.org*

NATIONAL COMMITTEE TO PRESERVE SOCIAL SECURITY AND MEDICARE. Advocacy organization for expansion of benefits under Social Security and Medicare. *www.ncpssm.org*

THIRD MILLENNIUM. Advocacy organization for young adults concerned with deficit spending, Social Security reform, etc. *www.millennium.org*

U.S. SOCIAL SECURITY ADMINISTRATION. Official site with information on Social Security—history, statistics, projections for the future, etc. *www.ssa.gov*

U.S. CENTERS FOR DISEASE CONTROL AND PREVENTION. Official site with data on health topics A–Z. *www.cdc.gov*

U.S. CENTER FOR MEDICARE AND MEDICAID SERVICES. Official site for Medicare and Medicaid programs, with laws, regulations, press releases, etc. *www.cms.hhs.gov*

ROBERT WOOD JOHNSON FOUNDATION. Leading research foundation on health care issues. *www.rwjf.org*

WELFARE INFORMATION NETWORK. Information, analysis, and sources relating to welfare and community services. *www.financeprojectinfo.org*

KAISER NETWORK. Up-to-date information on health-care legislation in Congress. *www.kaisernetwork.org*

6

Education

Group Struggles

Multiple Goals in Educational Policy

Perhaps the most widely recommended "solution" to the problems that confront American society is more and better schooling. If there ever was a time when schools were expected only to combat ignorance and illiteracy, that time is far behind us. Today, schools are expected to do many things: resolve racial conflict and inspire respect for "diversity"; provide values, aspirations, and a sense of identity to disadvantaged children; offer various forms of recreation and mass entertainment (football games, bands, choruses, cheerleading, and the like); reduce conflict in society by teaching children to get along well with others and to adjust to group living; reduce the highway accident toll by teaching students to be good drivers; fight disease and poor health through physical education, health training, and even medical treatment; eliminate unemployment and poverty by teaching job skills; end malnutrition and hunger through school lunch and milk programs; fight drug abuse and educate children about sex; and act as custodians for teenagers who have no interest in education but whom we do not permit either to work or to roam the streets unsupervised. In other words, nearly all the nation's problems are reflected in demands placed on the nation's schools. And, of course, these demands are frequently conflicting.

Educational policy affects a wide variety of interests and stimulates a great deal of interest group activity. We will describe the major interests involved in federal educational policy and examine the constitutional provisions and court policies dealing with religion in the public schools. We will observe how both racial and religious group interests are mobilized in educational policymaking, and we will see the importance of resolving group conflict in the development of educational policy. We will also describe the structure of educational decision making and the resulting multiple points of group access in a fragmented federal-state-local educational system. We will examine the broad categories of group interests—teachers and teacher unions, professional educators and school administrators, school board members, parents and taxpayers—involved in educational policy. Finally, we will discuss the governing and financing of public higher education—the nation's investment in state colleges and universities.

116

Today about 55 million pupils attend preschool, grade school, and high school in America, about 49 million of whom attend public schools and about 6 million attend private schools. About 17 million students are enrolled in institutions of higher education—community colleges, colleges, and universities.[1]

Educational Attainment

Educational attainment is measured by the years of schools completed, rather than by student knowledge. In educational attainment, the nation has an enviable record, with 85 percent of the overall population now graduating from high school and 28 percent graduating from college. Discrepancies between white and black educational attainment have diminished (see Figure 6–1). High school graduation rates of blacks and whites are nearing parity. Only Hispanic educational levels still appear to lag.

A college education is now fairly common. The white college graduation rate has reached 28 percent and the black college graduation rate over 18 percent. Again, the Hispanic

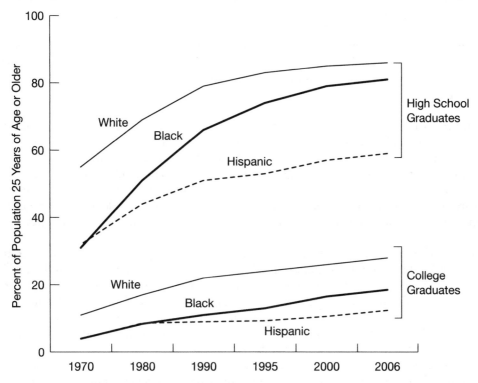

FIGURE 6–1 Educational Attainments by Race Educational attainment has risen for all races in the past three decades, with 85 percent of the overall population now graduating from high school and 28 percent graduating from college.
SOURCE: *Statistical Abstract of the United States, 2008,* p. 145.

rate seems to lag. As late as 2000, women's educational attainment rates were below those of men. But that condition has changed; today, women of all races have *higher* educational attainment rates than men.

The Educational Groups

Interest group activity in education involves a wide array of racial, religious, labor, and civil rights organizations, as well as parents', citizens', and educational groups.

Parents and Citizens versus Professionals.   Many disputes over education pit parents' and citizens' groups against professional educators. Citizens' groups assert that schools are public institutions that should be governed by the local citizenry through their elected representatives. This was the original concept in American public education developed in the nineteenth century. But as school issues became more complex, the knowledge of citizen school boards seemed insufficient to cope with the many problems confronting the schools—teaching innovations, curricular changes, multimillion-dollar building programs, special education programs, and so forth. In the twentieth century, the school superintendent and his or her administrative assistants came to exercise more and more control over day-to-day operations of the schools. Theoretically, the superintendent only implements the policies of the board, but in practice he or she has assumed much of the policymaking in education. The superintendent is a full-time administrator, receiving direct advice from attorneys, architects, accountants, and educational consultants, and generally setting the agenda for school board meetings.

Professional Educators.   Professional educators can be divided into at least three distinct groups. Numerically, the largest group (2.5 million) is composed of schoolteachers. But perhaps the most powerful group is that of professional school administrators, particularly the superintendents of schools. A third group consists of the faculties of teachers' colleges and departments of education at universities. This last group often interacts with the state departments of education, diffuses educational innovations and ideologies to each generation of teachers, and influences requirements for teacher certification within the states.

Teachers' Unions.   Most of the nation's teachers are organized into either the older and larger National Education Association (NEA), with about 2 million members, or the smaller but more militant American Federation of Teachers (AFT). The NEA maintains a large Washington office and makes substantial campaign contributions to political candidates. The AFT has a smaller membership, concentrated in big-city school districts, but as an affiliate of the AFL-CIO it can call on assistance from organized labor. State and district chapters of both unions have achieved collective bargaining status in most states and large urban school districts. The chapters have shut down schools to force concessions by superintendents, board members, and taxpayers not only in salaries and benefits but also in classroom conditions, school discipline, and other educational matters. Both educational groups lobby Congress as well as the White House and other parts of the executive branch, particularly the

Department of Education (DOE). Indeed, the DOE was created in 1979 largely because of President Carter's campaign pledge to educational groups to create a separate education department.

Voters and Taxpayers.   School politics at the community level differ from one community to another, but it is possible to identify a number of political groups that appear on the scene almost everywhere. There is, first, the small band of voters who turn out for school elections. On the average, only about 25 to 35 percent of eligible voters bother to cast ballots in school elections. Voter turnout at school bond and tax elections also demonstrates no groundswell of public interest in school affairs. Perhaps even more interesting is the finding that the larger the voter turnout in a school referendum, the more likely the *defeat* of educational proposals. In general, the best way to defeat a school bond referendum is to have a large turnout. Proponents of educational expenditures are better advised *not* to work for a large turnout but rather for a better-informed and more educationally oriented electorate.

Parents.   Parents of schoolchildren are somewhat more likely to vote in school board elections. A few active parents even attend school board meetings and voice their opinions. However, Parent–Teacher Associations (PTAs) in most local communities are dominated by teachers and school administrators. Only occasionally are local PTAs "captured" by disgruntled parents and turned into groups opposed to administrative or school board policies.

Parents are generally more supportive of taxing and spending for schools than nonparents, including older voters who have already raised their children. Indeed, in many communities parents of school-age children are pitted against older taxpayers in battles over school spending.

School Boards.   School board members constitute another important group of actors in local school politics. They are selected largely from among parents (often with ties to schoolteachers or administrators), as well as among local civic leaders. There is some evidence that people who are interested in education and have some knowledge of what the schools are doing tend to support education more than do the less informed citizens.

Racial and Religious Groups.   Because of the frequent involvement of racial and religious issues in education, such groups as the National Association for the Advancement of Colored People (NAACP), the National Catholic Education Conference, the American Jewish Congress, Americans United for the Separation of Church and State, and the American Civil Liberties Union all become involved in educational policy. These well-established national organizations have long led the battles in federal courts over segregation and other racial issues in the schools, prayer and Bible reading in the schools, and public financing of religious schools.

Community-based religious groups are often active on behalf of the restoration of traditional moral values in local schools. Among the well-publicized issues of concern in these community battles are sex education courses that imply approval of premarital sex, the distribution of contraceptives in schools, and the teaching of evolution and the exclusion of creationism.

Battling over the Basics

Citizens' groups with an interest in education—parents, taxpayers, and employers—have confronted professional educators—school administrators, state education officials, and teachers' unions—over the vital question of what should be taught in public schools. Public sentiment is strongly in favor of teaching the basic "three Rs" ("reading, 'riting, and 'rithmetic"), enforcing minimum standards with tests, and even testing teachers themselves for their mastery of the basics. Parents are less enthusiastic than professional educators about emotional growth, "getting along with others," self-expression and self-image, cultural enrichment, and various "innovative" programs of education.

The SAT Score Controversy.   For many years critics of modern public education cited declining scores on standardized tests, particularly the Scholastic Assessment Test (SAT), required by many colleges and universities, as evidence of the failure of the schools to teach basic reading and mathematics skills. The SAT scores declined significantly during the 1960s and 1970s, even as per pupil educational spending was rising and federal aid to education was initiated (see Figure 6–2). Critics charged that the nation was pouring money into a failed educational system; they pressed their case for a return to the basics. (In 1996, the Scholastic Aptitude Test was replaced by the Scholastic Assessment Test. Scores prior to 1996 were converted to reflect the change. The maximum score in each section is 800.)

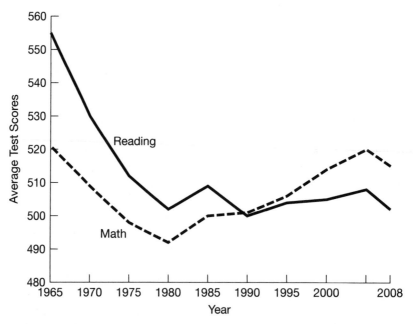

FIGURE 6–2   Average SAT Score Trends Average SAT scores declined dramatically prior to the 1980s, then began a slow recovery.
SOURCE: The College Board, Princeton, N.J., *www.collegeboard.com*

However, professional educators argued that declining SAT scores were really a function of how many students took the test. During the years of declining scores, increasing numbers and proportions of students were taking the test—students who never aspired to college in the past whose test scores did not match those of the earlier, smaller group of college-bound test-takers.

A Nation at Risk. The decline in SAT scores ended in the 1980s. A "back to basics" citizens' reform movement in education was given impetus by an influential 1983 report by the National Commission on Excellence in Education entitled "A Nation at Risk."[2]

> Our nation is at risk. . . .If an unfriendly foreign power had attempted to impose on America the mediocre educational performance that exists today, we might well have viewed it as an act of war.

The commission's recommendations set the agenda for educational policy for many years. Among the recommendations were these:

- A minimum high school curriculum of four years of English, three years of mathematics, three years of social science, and one-half year of computer science
- Four to six years of foreign language study beginning in the elementary grades
- Standardized tests for achievement for all of these subjects
- More homework, a seven-hour school day, and a 200- to 220-day school year
- Reliable grades and standardized tests for promotion and graduation
- "Performance-based" salaries for teachers and rewards for "superior" teaching

Improved Performance and Testing. In recent years SAT scores have improved somewhat. Improvement has been greater in mathematics than in reading. (In 2006 a writing test was added to the SAT.) Improvement is likely a result of the movement toward greater emphasis on basic skills and minimum competence testing in the schools. Tests may be used as diagnostic tools to determine the need for remedial education, or minimum scores may be required for promotion or graduation.

Professional educators have been less enthusiastic about testing than citizen groups and state legislators. Educators contend that testing leads to narrow "test-taking" education rather than broad preparation for life. That is, it requires teachers to devote more time to coaching students on how to pass an exam rather than preparing them for productive lives after graduation.

Racial Conflict. But the most serious opposition to testing has come from minority group leaders, who charge that the tests are racially biased. Average scores of black students are frequently lower than those of white students on standardized tests, including the SAT (see Figure 6–3). Larger percentages of black students are held back from promotion and graduation by testing than are white students. Some black leaders charge that racial bias in the examination itself, as well as racial isolation in the school, contribute to black–white differences in exam scores. Denying a disproportionate number of black students a diploma because of the schools' failure to teach basics may be viewed as a form of discrimination. However, to date, federal courts have declined to rule that testing requirements for

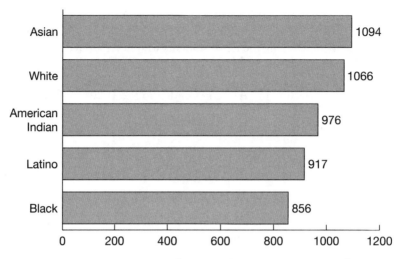

FIGURE 6–3 Average SAT Scores by Race, Ethnicity* SAT scores vary by race and ethnicity.
*Figures for 2008. Combined reading and math scores.
SOURCE: The College Board, Princeton, N.J., *www.collegeboard.com.*

promotion or graduation are discriminatory, as long as sufficient time and opportunity have been provided for all students to prepare for the examinations.

Dropout Rates. Another indicator of educational performance is the dropout rate. Yet school administrators differ with most taxpayers on how to measure it. School administrators, seeking to minimize this embarrassing statistic, count only those students who are officially recorded as having stopped attending school during the tenth, eleventh, or twelfth grade, as a percentage of total attendance in these grades. This measure is very low, nationally between 4 and 5 percent. But the U.S. Census Bureau measures the dropout rate as *persons age 18 to 24 who are not attending school and have not graduated, as a percentage of all 18- to 24-year-olds* (see Figure 6–4). This is a much higher figure, nationally about 13 percent. However measured, national dropout rates are declining very slowly.

Cross-National Comparisons. It is also possible to measure educational performance by comparing scores of American students with those of students of other nations on common school subjects, notably math and science. The results of one such study, published by the U.S. National Center for Educational Statistics, are shown in Figure 6–5. The performance of the U.S. students can only be described as mediocre. In the countries with top-performing students, education appears to have a higher cultural priority; that is, education is highly valued in the family and society generally. Moreover, in all of the top-performing nations, educational standards and testing are determined at the national level rather than by states and school districts as in the United States. These international comparisons appear to support efforts in the United States to develop national standards and national testing. But

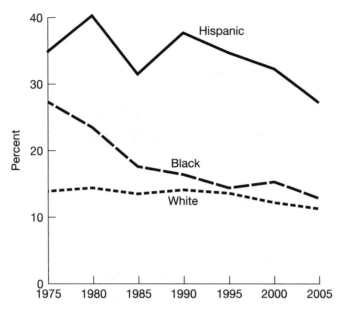

FIGURE 6–4   National Dropout Rates*
*Percentage of persons age 18–24 who are not attending school and
have not graduated from high school.
SOURCE: *Statistical Abstract of the United States, 2008,* p. 171.

educational groups in the states, as well as conservative groups fearing a "federal takeover" of
American education, generally resist the imposition of national standards.

The Federal Government's Role in Education

Traditionally, education in the United States was a community responsibility. But over the
years, state governments have assumed major responsibility for public education. The federal
government remains largely an interested spectator in the area of educational policy. While the
U.S. Supreme Court has taken the lead in guaranteeing racial equality in education and separating religion from public schools, the U.S. Congress has never assumed any significant share
of the costs of education. State and local taxpayers have always borne over 90 percent of the
costs of public elementary and secondary education; the federal share has never exceeded
10 percent. Similarly, federal expenditures for higher education have never exceeded 15 percent
of the total costs.

Nonetheless the federal government's interest in education is a long-standing one. In the
famous Northwest Ordinance of 1787, Congress offered land grants for public schools in the
new territories and gave succeeding generations words to be forever etched on grammar school
cornerstones: "Religion, morality, and knowledge, being necessary to good government and the
happiness of mankind, schools and the means for education should ever be encouraged." The
earliest democrats believed that the safest repository of the ultimate powers of society was
the people themselves. If the people made mistakes, the remedy was not to remove power from

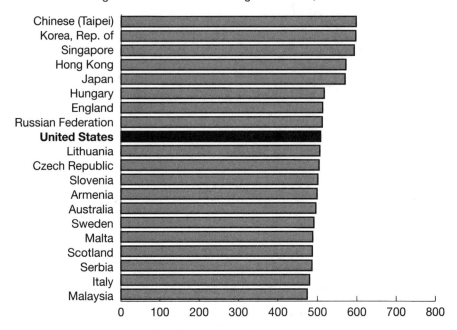

International Math Scores
Average Mathematics Score of Eighth Graders, 2007

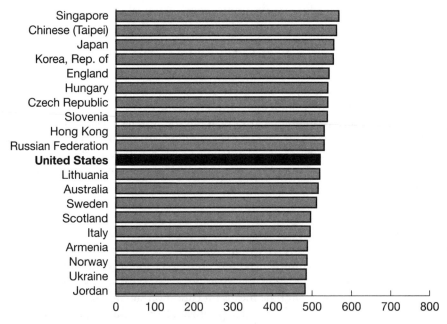

International Science Scores
Average Science Score of Eighth Graders, 2007

FIGURE 6–5 Educational Achievement: Cross-National Comparisons Amercians students are only mediocre compared to students of other nations in math and science.
SOURCE: National Center for Education Statistics. "Trends in International Mathematics and Science Study," December, 2008.

their hands but to help them in forming their judgment through education. If the common people were to be granted the right to vote, they must be educated for the task. This meant that public education had to be universal, free, and compulsory. Compulsory education began in Massachusetts in 1852 and was eventually adopted by Mississippi in 1918.

Early Federal Aid.   In 1862, the Morrill Land Grant Act provided grants of federal land to each state for the establishment of colleges specializing in agricultural and mechanical arts. These became known as land-grant colleges. In 1867, Congress established a U.S. Office of Education; in 1979, a separate, cabinet-level Department of Education was created. The Smith-Hughes Act of 1917 set up the first program of federal grants-in-aid to promote vocational education, enabling schools to provide training in agriculture, home economics, trades, and industries. In the National School Lunch and Milk programs, begun in 1946, federal grants and commodity donations were made for nonprofit lunches and milk served in public and private schools. In the Federal Impacted Areas Aid program, begun in 1950, federal aid was authorized for "federally impacted" areas of the nation. These are areas in which federal activities create a substantial increase in school enrollments or a reduction in taxable resources because of a federally owned property. In response to the Soviet Union's success in launching the first satellite into space in 1957, Congress became concerned that the American educational system might not be keeping abreast of advances being made in other nations, particularly in science and technology. In the National Defense Education Act of 1958, Congress provided financial aid to states and public school districts to improve instruction in science, mathematics, and foreign languages. Congress also established a system of loans to undergraduates, fellowships to graduate students, and funds to colleges—all in an effort to improve the training of teachers in America.

ESEA.   The Elementary and Secondary Education Act (ESEA) of 1965 established the single largest federal aid to education programs. "Poverty-impacted" schools were the principal beneficiaries of ESEA, receiving instructional materials and educational research and training. Title I of ESEA provided federal financial assistance to "local educational agencies serving areas with concentrations of children from low-income families" for programs "which contribute particularly to meeting the special needs of educationally deprived children."

Educational Block Grants.   Early in the Reagan administration, the Education Consolidation and Improvement Act of 1981 consolidated ESEA and other federal educational grant programs into single block grants for states and communities. The purpose was to give states and local school districts greater discretion over the use of federal educational aid. Title I educational aid was retained, but greater flexibility in its use was given to local school officials.

Head Start.   The most popular federal educational aid program is Head Start, which emerged from President Lyndon B. Johnson's "War on Poverty" in the 1960s to provide special preschool preparation to disadvantaged children before they enter kindergarten or first grade. Over the years it has enjoyed great popularity among parents, members of Congress, and both Republican and Democratic presidents. However, despite an avalanche of research by professional educators seeking to prove the value of the program, the results can only be described as mixed at best. Much of the value of Head Start preparation disappears after a

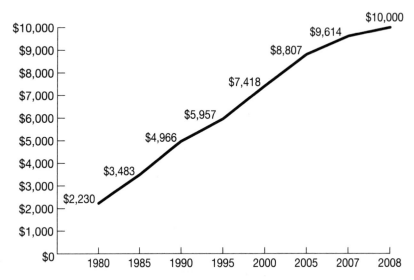

FIGURE 6–6   Public School Spending per Pupil Average spending in public
schools has risen dramatically to nearly $10,000 per pupil, suggesting that money
alone cannot raise student performance.
SOURCE: *Digest of Education Statistics*, National Center for Education Statistics, 2008.

few years of schooling; disadvantaged pupils who attended Head Start do not perform much
better in middle school than disadvantaged pupils who did not attend. Nevertheless, Head
Start remains politically very popular.

Educational Spending and Student Achievement.   There is no reliable evidence that
increased spending for public education improves student achievement. Public elementary and
secondary school spending per pupil has risen dramatically over the years (see Figure 6–6).
Yet SAT scores and other test measures of learning have failed to improve significantly (see
Figure 6–2). The apparent failure of money alone, including federal aid, has directed the focus
of educational improvement to new and sometimes controversial reforms.

No Child Left Behind

At the urging of newly elected President George W. Bush, Congress passed comprehensive
educational reform in the No Child Left Behind Act of 2001. While this act is officially only
an amendment to Title I of the Elementary and Secondary Education Act of 1965, it really
redefined the federal role in public education.

Testing.   The No Child Left Behind Act (NCLB) relies primarily on testing as a means to
improve performance of America's elementary and secondary schools. The preferred phrase-
ology is "accountability"—requiring states to establish standards in reading and mathematics
and undertaking to annually test all students in grades 3–8. (Testing under this act is in addition to the U.S. Department of Education's National Assessment of Educational Progress

tests given each year to a sample of public and private school students in the fourth, eighth, and twelfth grades; results of these NAEP tests are frequently cited as indicators of educational achievement for the nation.) Among the goals of testing is to ensure that every child can read by the end of third grade.

Test results and school progress toward proficiency goals are published, including results broken out by poverty, race, ethnicity, disability, and limited-English proficiency, in order to ensure that no group is "left behind." School districts and individual schools that fail to make adequate yearly progress (AYP) toward statewide proficiency goals are to face "corrective action" and "restructuring measures" designed to improve their performance. Student achievement and progress are measured according to tests that are given to every child. Annual report cards on school performance give parents information about their child's school and all other schools in their district.

Parental Choice. Parents whose children attend schools that fail to make adequate yearly progress are given the opportunity to send their children to another public school or a public charter school within the school district. The school district is required to use its own money for transportation to the new school and to use Title I federal funds to implement school choice and supplemental educational services to the students. The objective is to ensure that no pupil is "trapped" in a failing school, and in addition to provide an incentive for low-performing schools to improve. Schools that wish to avoid losing students, along with a portion of their annual budgets typically associated with these students, are required to make AYP. Schools that fail to make AYP for five years run the risk of "restructuring."

Flexibility. NCLB promises the states "flexibility in accountability." It allows the states themselves to design and administer the tests and decide what constitutes low performance and adequate yearly progress. The Act does *not* impose national achievement standards; standards are set by each state.

Racial Bias? Opposition to testing has also arisen from minority group leaders who charge that the tests are racially biased. Average black student scores are frequently lower than average white student scores, and a larger percentage of black students than white students are held back from promotion by testing. Some black leaders charge that racial bias exists in the examination itself. Denying a disproportionate number of black students a diploma because of the school's failure to teach basics may be viewed as a form of discrimination. However, to date, federal courts have declined to rule that testing itself is discriminatory, as long as sufficient time and opportunity have been provided to all students to prepare for the examination.

High-Stakes Testing. A number of states, including Texas and Florida, require all high school students, even after passing their courses, to pass a standardized statewide test to receive their diplomas. Supporters argue that such high-stakes testing guarantees that high school graduates have at least mastered basic skills, that they can read and do mathematics, and that they are reasonably well prepared to enter the work force or continue on to higher education. Opponents contend that it is unfair to students who have already earned all of their high school credits to subject them to the added pressure of a single test in order to obtain their diplomas. They also argue that with so much riding on the test results for both teachers and students, there is a tendency in the classroom to focus narrowly on basic drills rather than broader and more useful knowledge. And again minority group leaders argue that low-income and minority students fail these tests at disproportionate rates and are denied their diplomas.

Controversies Over "No Child"

Professional educators and teachers unions have been vocal critics of No Child Left Behind. The federal drive for achievement testing may be popular among reformers, legislators, and parents, but it is decidedly unpopular in educational circles.

Teaching to the Test.   Critics of NCLB contend that an emphasis on testing leads to "test-taking" education rather than broad preparation for life. Testing requires teachers to devote more time to coaching students on how to pass an exam than on preparing them for productive lives after graduation. Many teachers and school administrators have called for "multiple indicators" in lieu of test scores—allowing schools to evaluate student progress through alternative means, such as graduation rates, student "portfolios," and subjective evaluations. Another common recommendation is to expand testing to other subjects besides reading and mathematics—history and civics, for example.

Testing Teachers and Merit Pay.   But while professional educators seek to modify the test-taking provisions of NCLB, others seek to strengthen these provisions, including controversial proposals to test teachers themselves and to base teachers merit pay on student improvement on standardized tests. If students are to be tested, why not test teachers as well? Professional education groups strongly oppose teacher competency tests on the grounds that standardized tests cannot really measure performance in the classroom. The National Education Association and the American Federation of Teachers oppose both testing teachers and merit pay. While most states test teachers prior to certification, only a few states require all teachers to be tested. But where they have done so, the results have been disquieting. Large numbers of veteran classroom teachers have failed the tests.

Punishing Poor Performing Schools.   Many educators object to punishing schools that fail to meet annual yearly progress (AYP) for two or more years running. (Pupils in these schools must be given the opportunity to transfer to higher-performing schools.) Rather, many educators would prefer an approach that emphasizes additional aid to low-performing schools. But additional aid may be seen as a "reward" for poor performance.

Funding.   Some supporters of NCLB complain that it is not adequately funded by either the federal government or the states. The costs of implementation have not been fully funded by the federal government, creating an "unfunded mandate" for states and school districts.

The Future of Educational Reform.   Interest group conflict is likely to slow educational reform in the coming years. Teachers' unions—the National Education Association and the

American Federation of Teachers—exercise considerable influence in the Obama Administration, as well as within Democratic majorities in the House and Senate. These unions have been highly critical of No Child Left Behind reforms. They generally oppose educational evaluations based upon test results, teacher testing, merit pay for teachers based on student performance, and school choice for parents whose children attend low-performing schools. The thrust of reform in the Obama Administration appears to be toward assistance for low-performing schools and schools that serve low-income students. While this has been the federal approach ever since the enactment of the ESEA of 1965, "presidential leadership in promoting fundamental fairness in the distribution of federal [ESEA] funds could have an enormously positive effect."[3]

Obama Education Agenda

The Obama Administration laid out an ambitious agenda for education—an agenda that envisions spending additional billions of dollars of federal monies for a wide variety of programs. The bulk of this new spending is to go to poorer inter-city schools. Overseeing this new spending is President Obama's Secretary of Education, Arne Duncan, a longtime friend and adviser to the president and a former chief executive of the Chicago Public Schools.

Teacher Performance.   Among the many recommendations are several dealing with incentives to recruit teachers and reward their performance. These proposals include the recruitment of new teachers through alternative certification programs and nontraditional channels. State education officials, colleges of education, and teacher's unions have traditionally been reluctant to certify as teachers people who have not acquired a formal accreditation through colleges of education. Less controversial are proposals to provide pay incentives to teachers who work in economically disadvantaged schools and to those who teach math and science.

President Obama has also voiced support for tying teacher compensation to measures of student performance. But education unions that supported Obama's election will vigorously oppose any compensation schemes that are tied to student test results.

Standards and Assessments.   Requiring states to develop and implement standards of student achievement—the idea behind the No Child Left Behind Act—remains on the Obama agenda. It is likely, however, that additional measures of student performance will be added to the assessment of school success, including problem-solving and critical thinking skills. Additional funds are to be provided for the prevention of dropouts.

National Standards?   Under the current NCLB Act each state sets its own performance standards. States are required to set "proficiency" standards in reading and mathematics, but each state defines for itself what "proficiency" means. Comparisons among schools within each state are possible, as well as comparisons among racial and ethnic groups within states; yearly progress of pupils in schools within states can also be assessed. But a *national* system of standards and testing is required if we are to really evaluate state efforts in education. President Obama's Secretary of Education Arne Duncan has expressed support for national standards. But states themselves, including many state education officials and state legislators, have been cool to the notion of national testing. And teachers' unions and professional educators have been cool to testing itself. So this combination of interests is likely to subvert efforts to reform education through the adoption of national standards and testing.

Assisting Higher Education.   Spending for higher education is scheduled to increase in the Obama Administration. The maximum Pell Grant will rise to $5,550 in 2010 and be indexed to inflation in the future. Hope Scholarships—$2,500 tax credits—will be extended from two to four years. Low-interest loans to students are to be expanded.

Parental Choice in Education

Social science research suggests that educational performance is enhanced when the schools are perceived by children to be extensions or substitutes for their family.[4] Academic achievement and graduation rates improve for all students, but especially for students from disadvantaged backgrounds, in schools where there is a high expectation of achievement, an orderly and disciplined environment for learning, an emphasis on basic skills, frequent monitoring of students' progress, and teacher–parent interaction and agreement on values and norms. When parents choose schools for their children, as in the case of private and Catholic schools, these values are strengthened.[5]

Parental Choice.   "Choice" is a key word in the movement to reform American education. Parental choice among schools and the resulting competition among schools for enrollment is said to improve academic achievement and graduation rates as well as increase parental satisfaction and teachers' morale. Principals and teachers are encouraged to work directly with parents to set clear goals, develop specialized curricula, impose discipline, and demand more from the students. Choice plans are said to do more than just benefit the parents who have the knowledge to choose schools wisely for their children. They also send a message to educators to structure their schools to give parents what they want for their children or risk losing enrollment and funding.[6]

Charter Schools.   One way to implement parental choice is the charter school. Community educational groups sign a "charter" with their school district or state educational authority to establish their own school. They receive waivers from most state and school district regulations to enable them to be more innovative; in exchange for this flexibility they promise to show specific student achievement.

Magnet Schools.   Another common reform proposal is the magnet school. High schools might choose to specialize, some emphasizing math and science, others the fine arts, others business, and still others vocational training. Some schools might be "adopted" by business, professional organizations, or universities. Magnet schools, with reputations for quality and specialized instruction, are frequently recommended for inner-city areas in order to attract white pupils and reduce racial isolation.

Educational Vouchers.   A more controversial version of parental choice involves educational vouchers that would be given to parents to spend at any school they choose, public or private. State governments would redeem the vouchers submitted by schools by paying specified amounts—perhaps the equivalent of the state's per pupil educational spending. All public and private schools would compete equally for students, and state education funds would flow to those schools that enrolled more students. Competition would encourage all schools to satisfy parental demands for excellence. Racial or religious or ethnic discrimination would be strictly prohibited in any private or public school receiving vouchers. Providing vouchers for private school education would be most effective for children from poor or disadvantaged homes. These children currently do not have the same options as children from more affluent homes of fleeing the public schools and enrolling in private academies.

Yet there is strong opposition to the voucher idea, especially from professional school administrators and state educational agencies. They argue that giving parents the right to move their children from school to school disrupts educational planning and threatens the viability of schools that are perceived as inferior. It may lead to a stratification of schools into popular schools that would attract the best students and less popular schools that would be left with the task of educating students whose parents were unaware or uninterested in their children's education. Other opponents of choice plans fear that public education might be undermined if the choice available to parents includes the option of sending their children to private, church-related schools. Public education groups are fearful that vouchers will divert public money from public to private schools. And, finally, there is the constitutional issue of whether vouchers—notably those given to parents who send their children to religiously affiliated schools—violate the First Amendment's prohibition against an "establishment of religion." We will return to this topic later in the chapter.

Vouchers Have *Not* Been Popular with Voters.   The voucher movement was dealt a major setback in 1993 when California voters soundly defeated a citizens' initiative that promised to "empower parents" by granting each schoolchild a "scholarship" (voucher) equal to about one-half of the average amount of state and local government aid per pupil in California. The money was to be paid directly to the schools in which parents chose to enroll their children. Either public or private schools could qualify as "independently scholarship-redeeming schools."

Opposition groups, including the powerful California Teachers Association, argued that the proposal would create "a two-tier system of schools, one for the haves, one for the have-nots." They portrayed vouchers as "an entitlement program offering wealthy families a private-school subsidy for their children, paid for by the taxpayers," noting that there was no means test for the vouchers. Opponents warned that public education would suffer grievously if both money and gifted students were removed from public schools. The effect of the California anti-voucher campaign appeared to impact public opinion nationwide. Prior to 1993, polls regularly reported that 65 to 75 percent of Americans supported vouchers ("allowing students and parents to choose a private school to attend at public expense"), but today Americans appeared to be evenly divided over the issue.[7] Moreover, most Americans say they would prefer "improving existing schools," rather than "providing vouchers."[8]

Battles over School Finances

Spending for education varies enormously across the United States. Nationwide nearly $10,000 per year is spent on the public education of each child. Yet national averages can obscure as much as they reveal about the record of the states in public education. In 2007, for example, public school expenditures for each pupil ranged from nearly $15,000 in New Jersey to less than $6,000 in North Dakota and Utah.[9] (See Table 12–2 in Chapter 12 for a ranking of the states in educational spending per pupil.) Why is it that some states spend more than twice as much on the education of each child as other states? Economic resources are an important determinant of a state's willingness and ability to provide educational services. Most of the variation among states in educational spending can be explained by differences among them in economic resources (see Chapter 12).

Inequalities among School Districts.   Another issue in the struggle over public education is that of distributing the benefits and costs of education equitably. Most school revenues are derived from *local* property taxes. In every state except Hawaii, local school boards must raise money from property taxes to finance their schools. This means that communities that do *not* have much taxable property cannot finance their schools as well as communities that are blessed with great wealth.

School Inequalities as a Constitutional Issue.   Do disparities among school districts within a state deny "equal protection of laws" guaranteed by the Fourteenth Amendment of the U.S. Constitution and similar guarantees found in most state constitutions? The U.S. Supreme Court ruled that disparities in financial resources among school districts in a state, and resulting inequalities in educational spending per pupil across a state, do *not* violate the Equal Protection Clause of the Fourteenth Amendment. There is no duty under the U.S. Constitution for a state to equalize educational resources within the state.[10]

However, in recent years *state courts* have increasingly intervened in school financing to ensure equality among school districts based on their own interpretation of *state* constitutional provisions. Beginning with an early California state supreme court decision requiring that state funds be used to help equalize resources among the state's school districts,[11] many state courts have pressured their legislatures to come up with equalization plans in state school grants to overcome disparities in property tax revenues among school districts. State court equalization orders are generally based on *state* constitutional provisions guaranteeing equality. To achieve equity in school funding among communities, an increasing number of state courts are ordering their legislatures to substitute state general revenues for local property taxes.

Public Policy and Higher Education

State governments have been involved in higher education since the colonial era. State governments in the Northeast frequently made contributions to private colleges in their states, a practice that continues today. The first state university to be chartered by a state legislature was the University of Georgia in 1794. Before the Civil War, northeastern states relied exclusively on private colleges, and the southern-states assumed the leadership in public higher education. The antebellum curricula at southern state universities, however, resembled the rigid classical studies of the early private colleges—Greek and Latin, history, philosophy, and literature.

Growth of Public Universities.   It was not until the Morrill Land Grant Act of 1862 that public higher education began to make major strides in the states. Interestingly, the eastern states were slow to respond to the opportunity afforded by the Morrill Act to develop public universities. The southern states were economically depressed in the post–Civil War period, and leadership in public higher education passed to the midwestern states. The philosophy of the Morrill Act emphasized agricultural and mechanical studies rather than the classical curricula of eastern colleges, and the movement for "A and M" education spread rapidly in the agricultural states. The early groups of midwestern state universities were closely tied to agricultural education, including agricultural extension services. State universities also took the responsibility for the training of public school teachers in colleges of education. The state universities introduced a broad range of modern subjects in the university curricula—business administration, agriculture, home economics, education, engineering. It was not until the 1960s that the eastern states began to emphasize public higher education, as evidenced by the development of the huge, multicampus State University of New York.

About 17 million students are currently enrolled in institutions of higher education. About two-thirds of high school graduates enroll in college—universities, public and private; four-year colleges; and two-year community colleges. Public higher education enrolls three-fourths of these college and university students (see Table 6–1). Women outnumber men— 57 to 43 percent—on college campuses nationwide.[12]

Funding Higher Education   Tuition and fees paid by students and their families cover only a small portion of the total cost of public higher education. The major sources of income for

TABLE 6–1   Higher Education in America Almost 17 million people are enrolled in more than 4,000 institutions of higher education.

Institutions	
Four-year colleges and universities	2,582
Two-year colleges	1,699
Faculty (thousands)	1,290
Percent full-time	52
Enrollment (thousands)	
Total	17,487
Four-year colleges and universities	10,999
Two-year colleges	6,488
Public	13,022
Private	6,456
Graduate	2,186
Undergraduate	14,964
Men	7,456
Women	10,032

SOURCE: *Statistical Abstract of the United States, 2008* p. 174.

1

TABLE 6–2 Funding Public Higher Education State and local governments provide the largest share of the income of public colleges and universities.

Sources of income for public institutions[1]	
Tuition and fees from students	16.5%
Federal government	15.8
State and local governments	37.2
Endowment/private gift income	1.8
Sales and other services	20.7
Other sources[2]	8.0

[1] Not including capital improvement revenue.
[2] Including investment income, auxiliary services, and independent operations.
SOURCE: American Council on Education, *A Brief Guide to U.S. Higher Education,* Washington, DC: ACE, 2007.

state colleges and universities and community colleges are state and local government appropriations (see Table 6–2). The federal government provides only about 16 percent of the costs of public higher education.

Traditionally state appropriations made up the bulk of institutional revenue at public colleges and universities, but these appropriations are diminishing as a share of institutional revenue. The result has been increased tuitions and increased efforts by public institutions to solicit private donations from individuals and corporations.

Federal Aid. Although the federal government generally does not provide direct operational support to colleges and universities, federal funding for research contracts and grants is an important source of revenue for some institutions. And of course federal revenue comes with strings attached. In order for colleges and universities to participate in federally financed programs, they must comply with a wide range of requirements, including, for example, the Americans with Disabilities Act, laws governing the responsible experimental use of both animals and people, and Title IX regulations to ensure gender equity in intercollegiate athletics. Federal contracts and grants are closely monitored by the various federal agencies that fund them.

Historically, the Morrill Act of 1862 provided the groundwork for federal assistance to higher education. In 1890 Congress activated several federal grants to support the operations of the land-grant colleges, and this aid, although very modest, continues today. The GI bills following World War II and the Korean War (enacted in 1944 and 1952, respectively) were not, strictly speaking, aid-to-education bills but rather a form of assistance to veterans to help them adjust to civilian life. Nevertheless, these bills had a great impact on higher education because of the millions of veterans who were able to enroll in college. Congress continues to provide educational benefits to veterans but at reduced levels from the wartime GI bills. The National Defense Education Act of 1958 also affected higher education by assisting students, particularly in science, mathematics, and modern foreign languages.

Today, the federal government directly assists many colleges and universities through grants and loans for construction and improvement of facilities; and it supports the U.S.

Military Academy (West Point), U.S. Naval Academy (Annapolis), U.S. Air Force Academy (Colorado Springs), U.S. Coast Guard Academy, U.S. Merchant Marine Academy, Gallaudet College, and Howard University.

Student Assistance.   A major source of federal aid for higher education comes to colleges and universities from various forms of student assistance. Basic Educational Opportunity Grants (commonly called Pell Grants for their original sponsor, U.S. Senator Claiborne Pell) provide college students in good standing with grants based on what their families could be expected to pay. In addition, the federal government now makes loans directly to students (Federal Direct Student Loan program) and to families (Federal Family Education Loans). Repayment usually does not begin until after the student graduates or leaves college. A Perkins Loan program extends this guarantee to students from very low-income families. A Supplemental Educational Opportunity Grant program allows students to borrow from the financial aid offices of their own universities. Finally, the College Work-Study program uses federal funds to allow colleges and universities to employ students part time while they go to school.

The Federal Swing toward Loans over Grants.   The federal government is placing greater emphasis on loans over grants each year. Loans burden students after graduation, but allow the federal government to retrieve most of its money over time. The average student loan is $4,500. The federal government has been deemphasizing grants, perhaps as a cost-saving measure. Only about half as many grants are made as loans. Moreover, the average grant is only $2,500.

Federal Research Support.   Federal support for scientific research has also had an important impact on higher education. In 1950 Congress established the National Science Foundation (NSF) to promote scientific research and education. The NSF has provided fellowships for graduate education in the sciences, supported many specific scientific research projects, and supported the construction and maintenance of scientific centers. In 1965 Congress established a National Endowment for the Arts and a National Endowment for the Humanities but funded these fields at only a tiny fraction of the amount given to NSF. In addition to NSF, many other federal agencies have granted research contracts to universities for specific projects. Thus, with federal support, research has become a very big item in university life.[13]

"Diversity" in Higher Education

Most colleges and universities in the United States—public as well as private—identify "diversity" as a goal, a term that refers to racial and ethnic representation in the student body and faculty.

Arguments over Diversity.   University administrators as well as civil rights groups across the nation argue that students benefit when they interact with others from different cultural heritages. There is some evidence that students admitted under policies designed to increase diversity do well in their postcollege careers.[14] And there are claims that racial and ethnic diversity on the campus improves students' "self-evaluation," "social historical thinking," and "intellectual engagement."

But despite numerous efforts to develop scientific evidence that racial or ethnic diversity on the campus improves learning, no definitive conclusions have emerged. Educational research on this topic is rife with political and ideological conflict. There is very little evidence that racial diversity does in fact promote the expression of ideas on the campus or change perspectives or viewpoints of students.

Diversity and Affirmative Action.   Even if diversity provides any educational benefits, the question arises as to how to achieve it. Diversity is closely linked to affirmative action programs on campuses throughout the nation. When affirmative action programs are designed as special efforts to recruit and encourage qualified minority students, they enjoy widespread public support. (See "Mass Opinion and Affirmative Action" in Chapter 11.) But when affirmative action programs include preferences or quotas for racial minority applicants over equally or better-qualified nonminorities, public support disappears. Respondents in national polls, both faculty and students, oppose "relaxing standards" in order to add more minority students or faculty.[15]

Diversity as a Constitutional Question.   The use of racial or ethnic classifications of applicants to colleges and universities in order to achieve "diversity" raises serious constitutional questions. The Fourteenth Amendment to the U.S. Constitution provides that "No State shall . . . deny to any person the equal protection of the laws." The Civil Rights Act of 1964, Title VI, prohibits discrimination based on race, color, or national origin by recipients of federal financial assistance (see Chapter 11).

The U.S. Supreme Court has held that the Fourteenth Amendment requires that racial classifications be subject to "strict scrutiny."[16] This means that race-based actions by governments—and any disparate treatment of racial or ethnic groups by federal, state, or local public agencies, including colleges and universities—must be found necessary to advance a "compelling government interest" and must be "narrowly tailored" to further that interest.

The U.S. Supreme Court held in 2003 that diversity may be a compelling government interest because it "promotes cross-racial understanding, helps to break down racial stereotypes, and enables [students] to better understand persons of different races." This opinion was written by Justice Sandra Day O'Connor in a case involving the University of Michigan's Law School's affirmative action program. In the 5–4 decision, Justice O'Connor, writing for the majority, said the Constitution "does not prohibit the law school's narrowly tailored use of race in admissions decisions to further a compelling interest in obtaining the educational benefits of flow from a diverse student body."[17]

However, in a companion case involving the University of Michigan's affirmative action program for undergraduate admissions, the Supreme Court held that the admissions policy was "not narrowly tailored to achieve respondents' asserted interest in diversity" and therefore violated the Equal Protection Clause of the Fourteenth Amendment. The Court again recognized that diversity may be a compelling interest, but rejected an affirmative action plan that made race the decisive factor for every minimally qualified minority applicant. "The University's current policy, which automatically distributes 20 points, or one-fifth of the points needed to guarantee admission, to every single underrepresented minority applicant solely because of race, is not narrowly tailored to achieve the interest in educational diversity that the respondents claim justifies their program."[18]

The Supreme Court restated its support for limited affirmative action programs that use race as a "plus" factor, a position the court has held since the *Bakke* case in 1978 (see Chapter 11 "The Supreme Court and Affirmative Action"). But the Court has consistently rejected numerical plans or quotas that automatically reject white applicants.

Race-Neutral Approaches to Diversity.   There are a variety of ways of achieving diversity without using racial preferences in the admission of students. The U.S. Department of Education in the administration of President George W. Bush cited (1) preferences based on socioeconomic status; (2) recruitment and outreach efforts targeted at students from traditionally low-performing schools; and (3) admission plans for students who finish at the top of their high school classes without regard to their SAT or ACT scores.[19] Three states—Texas, California, and Florida—ended racial preferences in college and university admissions and substituted admission plans based on students' standings among graduates of their high schools. (Texas was ordered to end racial preferences by federal courts; California voters passed a constitutional initiative, Proposition 209, requiring the state to end racial preferences (see Chapter 11 "Mass Initiatives against Racial Preferences"); and Florida ended race-based admissions by order of Governor Jeb Bush.) The Texas Top-10 Percent Plan not only admits any student who graduates in the top 10 percent of their high school class but also considers hardships or obstacles that an applicant may have been obliged to overcome (employment during school, raising children, etc.). Florida's Talented Twenty Plan admits students to the state's higher education system who graduate in the top 20 percent of their high school class. In both Texas and Florida these plans have resulted in racial and ethnic diversity on their campuses; and in addition, these plans have resulted in greater regional and socioeconomic diversity. California has adopted an admissions system that purports to recognize a variety of race-neutral attributes of candidates.

Groups in Higher Education

There are many influential groups in public higher education—aside from the governors and legislators who must vote the funds each year.

Trustees.   First, there are the boards of trustees (often called regents) that govern public colleges and universities. Their authority varies from state to state, but in nearly every state they are expected not only to set broad policy directions in higher education but also to insulate higher education from direct political involvement of governors and legislators. Prominent citizens who are appointed to these boards are expected to champion higher education with the public and the legislature.

Presidents.   Another key group in higher education is made up of university and college presidents and their top administrative assistants. Generally, university presidents are the chief spokespersons for higher education, and they must convince the public, the regents, the governor, and the legislature of the value of state colleges and universities. The president's crucial role is to maintain support for higher education in the state; he or she frequently delegates administrative responsibilities for the internal operation of the university to the vice presidents and deans. Support for higher education among the public and its representatives can be affected by a broad spectrum of university activities, some of which are not directly related to the pursuit of knowledge. A winning football team can stimulate legislative enthusiasm and gain appropriations for a new classroom building. University service-oriented research—developing new crops or feeds, assessing the state's mineral resources, advising state and local government agencies on administrative problems, analyzing the state economy, advising local school authorities, and so forth—may help to convince the public of the practical benefits of knowledge. University faculties may be interested in advanced research and the education of future Ph.D.s, but legislators and their constituents are more interested in the quality and effectiveness of undergraduate teaching.

Faculty. The faculties of the nation's 4,000 colleges and universities traditionally identified themselves as professionals with strong attachments to their institutions. The historic pattern of college and university governance included faculty participation in policymaking—not only academic requirements but also budgeting, personnel, building programs, and so forth. But governance by faculty committee has proven cumbersome, unwieldy, and time-consuming in an era of large-scale enrollments, multimillion-dollar budgets, and increases in the size and complexity of academic administration. Increasingly, concepts of public accountability, academic management, cost control, and centralized budgeting and purchasing have transferred power in colleges and universities from faculties to professional academic administrators.

Full-time faculty are gradually being replaced by part-time "adjunct" faculty as a cost-cutting measure in colleges and universities throughout the nation. To date, *about half of all classes taught nationwide are taught by adjunct faculty or graduate students, rather than full-time faculty members.* Traditionally, college and university faculty aspired to "tenure"—protection against dismissal except for "cause," a serious infraction of established rules or dereliction of duty, shown in quasi-judicial administrative proceedings. Tenure was usually granted after five to seven years of satisfactory performance. Part-time adjunct faculty and graduate students cannot acquire tenure, nor do they usually receive medical, retirement, or other benefits.

Unions. The traditional organization of faculties has been the American Association of University Professors (AAUP); historically, this group confined itself to publishing data on salaries and officially censuring colleges or universities that violate long-standing notions of academic freedom or tenure. In recent years, the American Federation of Teachers (AFT) succeeded in convincing some faculty members that traditional patterns of individual bargaining over salaries, teaching load, and working conditions in colleges and universities should be replaced by collective bargaining in the manner of unionized labor. The growth of the AFT has spurred the AAUP on many campuses to assume a more militant attitude on behalf of faculty interests. The AAUP remains the largest faculty organization in the nation, but most of the nation's faculties are not affiliated with either the AAUP or the AFT.

Students. The nation's 17 million students are the most numerous yet least influential of the groups directly involved in higher education. Students can be compared to other consumer groups in society, which are generally less well organized than the groups that provide goods and services. American student political activism has been sporadic and generally directed toward broad national issues. Most students view their condition in life as a short-term one; organizing for effective group action requires a commitment of time and energy that most students are unwilling to subtract from their studies and social life. Nonetheless, students' complaints are often filtered through parents to state legislators or university officials.

Students and their parents appear to be most concerned about rapidly rising tuitions at both private and public institutions. The average tuition at private four-year universities rose from $7,000 in 1985 to over $24,000 in 2005; the average tuition at public four-year universities rose from $1,400 to $6,000 in that same period. Average tution at public two-year colleges is about $1,850.[20] State government support for higher education has not kept up with increased enrollments and universities offer this explanation for their increases in tuition. Public universities now compete vigorously with private colleges for the financial support of alumni and philanthropic foundations.

Higher education in the United States is now open to virtually every high school graduate. Today about 64 percent of recent U.S. graduates enroll in a two-year or four-year college or university.

Reading, Writing, and Religion

The First Amendment of the Constitution of the United States contains *two* important guarantees of religious freedom: (1) "Congress shall make no law respecting an establishment of religion . . ." and (2) "or prohibiting the free exercise thereof." The due process clause of the Fourteenth Amendment made these guarantees of religious liberty applicable to the states and their subdivisions (including school districts) as well as to Congress.

"Free Exercise."   Most of the debate over religion in the public schools centers on the "no establishment" clause of the First Amendment rather than the "free exercise" clause. However, it was respect for the "free exercise" clause that caused the Supreme Court in 1925 to declare unconstitutional an attempt by a state to prohibit private and parochial schools and to force all children to attend public schools. In the words of the Supreme Court, "The fundamental theory of liberty upon which all governments in this Union repose excludes any general power of the state to standardize its children by forcing them to accept instruction from public teachers only. The child is not the mere creature of the state."[21] It is this decision that protects the entire structure of private religious schools in this nation.

"No Establishment."   A great deal of religious conflict in America has centered on the meaning of the "no establishment" clause, and the public schools have been the principal scene of this conflict. One interpretation of the clause holds that it does not prevent the government from aiding religious schools or encouraging religious beliefs in the public schools as long as it does not discriminate against any particular religion. Another interpretation is that the clause creates a "wall of separation" between church and state in America to prevent the government from directly aiding religious schools or encouraging religious beliefs in any way.

Government Aid to Church-Related Schools.   The question of how much government aid can go to church schools and for what purposes is still largely unresolved. Proponents of public aid for church schools argue that these schools render a valuable public service by instructing millions of children who would have to be instructed by the state, at great expense, if the church schools were to close. There seem to be many precedents for public support of religious institutions: church property has always been exempt from taxation, church contributions are deductible from federal income taxes, federal funds have been appropriated for the construction of hospitals operated by religious organizations, chaplains are provided in the armed forces as well as in Congress, veterans' programs permit veterans to use their educational subsidies to finance college educations at church-related universities, and so on.

Opponents of aid to church schools argue that free public schools are available to the parents of all children regardless of religious denomination. If religious parents are not content with the type of school that the state provides, they should expect to pay for the operation of religious schools. The state is under no obligation to finance their religious preferences. Opponents also argue that it is unfair to compel taxpayers to support religion directly or indirectly. The diversion of any substantial amount of public funds to church schools would weaken the public school system. The public schools bring together children of different religious backgrounds and by so doing supposedly encourage tolerance and understanding. In contrast, church-related schools segregate children of different backgrounds, and it is not in the public interest to encourage such segregation. And so the dispute continues.

The "Wall of Separation."   Those favoring government aid to church-related schools frequently refer to the language found in several cases decided by the Supreme Court, which appears to support the idea that government can, *in a limited fashion,* support the activities of church-related schools. In *Everson* v. *Board of Education* (1947), the Supreme Court upheld bus transportation for parochial school children at public expense on the grounds that the "wall of separation between church and state does not prohibit the state from adopting a general program which helps *all* children." Interestingly in this case, even though the Court permitted the expenditure of public funds to assist children going to and from parochial schools, it voiced the opinion that the "no establishment" clause of the First Amendment should constitute a "wall of separation" between church and state. In the words of the Court,

> Neither a state nor the federal government can set up a church. Neither can pass laws which aid one religion, aid all religions, or prefer one religion over another. Neither can force nor influence a person to go to or to remain away from church against his will, or force him to profess a belief or disbelief in any religion. No person can be punished for entertaining or professing religious beliefs or disbeliefs, for church attendance or nonattendance. No tax in any amount, large or small, can be levied to support any religious activities or institutions, whatever they may be called, or whatever form they may adopt to teach or practice religion. Neither a state nor the federal government can, openly or secretly, participate in the affairs of any religious organizations or groups, and vice versa.[22]

So the *Everson* case can be cited by those interests that support the allocation of public funds for assistance to children in parochial schools, as well as those interests that oppose any public support, direct or indirect, of religion.

Avoiding "Excessive Entanglement." One of the more important Supreme Court decisions in the history of church-state relations in America came in 1971 in the case of *Lemon* v. *Kurtzman*.[23] The Supreme Court set forth a three-part *Lemon test* for determining whether a particular state law constitutes "establishment" of religion and thus violates the First Amendment. To be constitutional, a law affecting religious activity:

1. Must have a secular purpose.
2. As its primary effect, must neither advance nor inhibit religion.
3. Must not foster "an excessive government entanglement with religion."

Using this three-part test the Supreme Court held that it was unconstitutional for a state to pay the costs of teachers' salaries or instructional materials in parochial schools. The justices argued that this practice would require excessive government controls and surveillance to ensure that funds were used only for secular instruction and thus would create an "excessive entanglement between government and religion."

However, the Supreme Court has upheld the use of tax funds to provide students attending church-related schools with nonreligious textbooks, lunches, transportation, sign-language interpreting, and special education teachers. And the Court has upheld a state's granting of tax credits to parents whose children attend private schools, including religious schools.[24] The Court has also upheld government grants of money to church-related colleges and universities for secular purposes.[25] The Court has ruled that if school buildings are open to use for secular organizations, they must also be open to use by religious organizations.[26] And the Court has held that a state institution (the University of Virginia) not only can but must grant student activity fees to religious organizations on the same basis as it grants these fees to secular organizations.[27] But the Court held that a Louisiana law requiring the teaching of creationism along with evolution in the public schools was an unconstitutional establishment of a religious belief.[28]

Vouchers. Educational vouchers given to parents by governments to use as tuition at either public or private religiously affiliated schools raise the question of whether they violate the No Establishment Clause of the First Amendment. In 2002 the Supreme Court, in a 5–4 decision, held that an Ohio program designed for needy students attending poor Cleveland schools did *not* violate the No Establishment Clause, even though parents could use the vouchers for tuition at religiously affiliated schools.[29] Indeed, over 90 percent of the parents receiving vouchers chose to use them at religious schools. Nonetheless, the Supreme Court held that the program did not violate the No Establishment Clause because (1) it had a valid secular purpose, (2) it was neutral with respect to religion (parents could send their children to nonreligious schools), and (3) the aid went to parents, who then directed it to religious schools "as a result of their own genuine and independent private choice." The vouchers were only an "incidental advancement of religion . . . attributable to individual aid recipients, not the government whose role ends with the distribution of the vouchers."

Prayer in Public Schools. Religious conflict also focuses on the question of prayer and Bible-reading ceremonies in public schools. A few years ago the practice of opening the school day with such ceremonies was widespread in American public schools. Usually the prayer was a Protestant rendition of the Lord's Prayer and the reading was from the King James version of the Bible. To avoid the denominational aspects of the ceremonies, the New York State Board of Regents substituted a nondenominational prayer, which it required to be said aloud in each class in the presence of a teacher at the beginning of each school day: "Almighty God, we acknowledge our dependence upon Thee, and we beg Thy blessings upon us, our parents, our teachers, and our country."

New York argued that this prayer did not violate the "no establishment" clause because it was denominationally neutral and because students' participation was voluntary. However, in *Engle* v. *Vitale* (1962), the Supreme Court stated that "the constitutional prohibition against laws respecting an establishment of a religion must at least mean in this country it is no part of the business of government to compose official prayers for any group of the American people to recite as part of a religious program carried on by government." The Court pointed out that making prayer voluntary did not free it from the prohibitions of the "no establishment" clause; that clause prevented the establishment of a religious ceremony by a government agency, regardless of whether the ceremony was voluntary or not:

> Neither the fact that the prayer may be denominationally neutral, nor the fact that its observance on the part of the students is voluntary can serve to free it from the limitations of the establishment clause, as it might from the free exercise clause, of the First Amendment, both of which are operative against the states by virtue of the Fourteenth Amendment. . . . The establishment clause, unlike the free exercise clause, does not depend on any showing of direct governmental compulsion and is violated by the enactment of laws which establish an official religion whether those laws operate directly to coerce nonobserving individuals or not.[30]

One year later, in the case of *Abbington Township* v. *Schempp,* the Court considered the constitutionality of Bible-reading ceremonies in the public schools.[31] Here again, even though the children were not required to participate, the Court found that Bible reading as an opening exercise in the schools was a religious ceremony. The Court went to some trouble in its opinion to point out that it was not "throwing the Bible out of the schools," for it specifically stated that the study of the Bible or of religion, when presented as part of a secular program of education, did not violate the First Amendment, but religious *ceremonies* involving Bible reading or prayer, established by a state or school district, did so.

State efforts to encourage "voluntary prayer" in public schools have also been struck down by the Supreme Court as unconstitutional. When the state of Alabama authorized a period of silence for "meditation or voluntary prayer" in public schools, the Court ruled that this was an "establishment of religion." The Court said that the law had no secular purpose, that it conveyed "a message of state endorsement and promotion of prayer," and that its real intent was to encourage prayer in public schools.[32] In a stinging dissenting opinion, Warren Burger, chief justice at the time, noted that the Supreme Court itself opened its session with a prayer, that both houses of Congress opened every session with prayers led by official chaplains paid by the government. "To suggest that a moment of silence statute that includes the word *prayer* unconstitutionally endorses religion, manifests not neutrality but hostility toward religion." But Burger's view remains a minority view. The Court has gone on to hold that invocations and benedictions at public high school graduation ceremonies are an unconstitutional establishment of religion.[33] And it has held that a student-led prayer at a football game is unconstitutional because it was carried over the school's public address system at a school-sponsored event.[34]

SUMMARY

Let us summarize educational policy issues with particular reference to group conflicts involved:

1. American education reflects all of the conflicting demands of society. Schools are expected to address themselves to virtually all of the nation's problems, from racial conflict to drug abuse to highway accidents. They are also supposed to raise the verbal and mathematical performance levels of students to better equip the nation's work force in a competitive global economy. Various interests give different priorities to these diverse and sometimes conflicting goals.

2. In recent years, citizen groups, parents, taxpayers, and employers have inspired a back-to-basics movement in the schools, emphasizing reading, writing, and mathematical performance and calling for frequent testing of students' skills and the improvement of teachers' competency. Professional educators—school administrators, state education officials, and teachers' unions—have tended to resist test-oriented reforms, emphasizing instead the education of the whole child.

3. Conflict between citizens and professional educators is reflected in arguments over "professionalism" versus "responsiveness" in public schools. Parents, taxpayers, and locally elected school board members tend to emphasize responsiveness to citizens' demands; school superintendents and state education agencies tend to emphasize professional administration of the schools. Teachers' unions, notably state and local chapters of the NEA and AFT, represent still another group interest in education—organized teachers.

4. Professional educational groups and teachers' unions have long lobbied in Washington for increased federal financing of education. Federal aid to education grew with the Elementary and Secondary Education Act of 1965, but the federal share of educational spending never exceeded 10 percent. State and local governments continue to bear the major burden of educational finance. The creation of a cabinet-level Department of Education in 1979 also reflected the influence of professional educators.

5. There is little direct evidence that increased funding for schools improves the educational performance of students. Citizen groups and independent study commissions emphasized reforms in education rather than increased federal spending. The No Child Left Behind Act of 2001 relies heavily on testing to improve learning. Public school pupils are tested each year and schools must show adequate yearly progress in average test scores or face the prospect of their students transferring to another school at the school district's expense.

6. Parental choice in education would empower parents and end the monopoly of public school administrators. But plans that allow parents to choose private over public schools threaten America's traditional reliance on public education. Choice *within*

public school systems is somewhat less controversial, and various states have established charter and magnet schools.

7. Public higher education in the states involves many groups—governors, legislators, regents, college and university presidents, and faculties. State governments, through their support of state colleges and universities, bear the major burden of higher education in the United States. Federal support for research, plus various student loan programs, are an important contribution to higher education. Yet federal support amounts to less than 15 percent of total higher education spending.

8. A central issue in higher education today is achieving "diversity" on campus—the reference to racial and ethnic representation in the student body and faculty. The U.S. Supreme Court has recognized that diversity may be a "compelling government interest" that allows race to be considered in university admissions without violating the Fourteenth Amendment to the U.S. Constitution. However, the Court also held that race cannot be the sole or decisive factor in admissions.

9. Religious groups, private school interests, and public school defenders frequently battle over the place of religion in education. The U.S. Supreme Court has become the referee in the group struggle over religion and education. The Court must interpret the meaning of the "no establishment" clause of the First Amendment of the Constitution as it affects government aid to church-related schools and prayer in the public schools.

Notes

1. *Statistical Abstract of the United States, 2008*, p. 178.
2. National Commission on Excellence in Education, *A Nation at Risk* (Washington, DC: U.S. Government Printing Office, 1983).
3. Mark Green and Michelle Jolin, eds., *Change for America, a Progressive Blueprint for the 44th President* (New York: Basic Books, 2009), p. 141.
4. See James S. Coleman, Thomas Hoffer, and Sally Kilgore, *High School Achievement* (New York: Basic Books, 1982); John E. Chubb and Terry M. Moe, *Politics, Markets, and America's Schools* (Washington, DC: Brookings Institution Press, 1990); Chester E. Finn, Jr., *We Must Take Charge: Our Schools and Our Future* (New York: Free Press, 1991).
5. James S. Coleman and Thomas Hoffer, *Public and Private High Schools* (New York: Basic Books, 1987).
6. See John E. Chubb and Terry M. Moe, "Politics, Markets, and the Organization of Schools," *American Political Science Review* 82 (December 1988), 1065–1087.
7. Gallup Opinion polls, 1993, 2003.
8. Gallup Opinion poll, June, 2002.
9. *National Center for Education Statistics, http://nces.ed.gov.*
10. *Rodriguez* v. *San Antonio Independent School District,* 411 U.S. 1 (1973).
11. *Serrano* v. *Priest,* 5 Cal. 584 (1971).
12. *Statistical Abstract of the United States, 2007*, p. 171.
13. *Statistical Abstract of the United States, 2007*, p. 519.
14. William G. Bowen and Derek Bok, *The Shape of the River* (Princeton, NJ: Princeton University Press, 2000).
15. Gallup poll, as reported in *USA Today,* June 24, 2003.
16. *Adarand* v. *Peña,* 515 U.S. 200 (1995).

17. *Grudder* v. *Bollinger*, 539 U.S. 306 (2003).
18. *Gratz* v. *Bollinger*, 539 U.S. 244 (2003).
19. U.S. Department of Education, Office for Civil Rights, "Race-Neutral Alternatives in Post Secondary Education," March, 2003.
20. Data in this paragraph from *Statistical Abstract of the United States, 2007,* p.181.
21. *Pierce* v. *The Society of Sisters,* 268 U.S. 510 (1925).
22. *Everson* v. *Board of Education,* 330 U.S. 1 (1947).
23. *Lemon* v. *Kurtzman,* 403 U.S. 602 (1971).
24. *Muebler* v. *Adams,* 463 U.S. 602 (1983).
25. *Tilton* v. *Richardson,* 403 U.S. 602 (1971).
26. *Lambs Chapel* v. *Center Moriches Union Free School District,* 508 U.S. 384 (1993).
27. *Rosenberger* v. *University of Virginia,* 515 U.S. 819 (1995).
28. *Edwards* v. *Aguillard,* 482 U.S. 578 (1987).
29. *Zelman, Superintendent of Public Instruction of Ohio* v. *Simmons-Harris,* 536 U.S. 639 (2002).
30. *Engle* v. *Vitale,* 370 U.S. 421 (1962).
31. *Abbington Township* v. *Schempp,* 374 U.S. 203 (1963).
32. *Wallace* v. *Jaffree,* June 4, 1985.
33. *Lee* v. *Weisman,* 505 U.S. 577 (1992).
34. *Santa Fe Independent School District* v. *Doe,* 530 U.S. 290 (2000).

Bibliography

BLOOM, ALLAN D. *The Closing of the American Mind.* New York: Simon & Schuster, 1987.

CHUBB, JOHN E., and TERRY M. MOE. *Politics, Markets, and America's Schools.* Washington, DC: Brookings Institution Press, 1990.

COLEMAN, JAMES S., and THOMAS HOFFER. *Public and Private High Schools.* New York: Basic Books, 1987.

HOWELL, WILLIAM G., and PAUL E. PETERSON. *The Education Gap: Vouchers and Urban Schools.* Washington, DC: Brookings Institution, 2005.

MOE, TERRY M. *School Vouchers and the American Public.* Washington, DC: Brookings Institution, 2002.

NATIONAL COMMISSION ON EXCELLENCE IN EDUCATION. *A Nation at Risk.* Washington, DC: U.S. Government Printing Office, 1983.

THERNSTROM, STEPHEN AND ABIGALE. *America in Black and White.* New York: Simon & Schuster, 1997.

Web Sites

AMERICAN FEDERATION OF TEACHERS. The home page of the teachers' union, with information on a range of education issues. *www.aft.org*

CENTER FOR EDUCATION REFORM. Advocacy organization for school choice—vouchers, charter schools, etc. *www.edreform.org*

FIRE. The Foundation for Individual Rights in Education defends free speech on campus against "political correctness." *www.thefire.org*

NATIONAL CENTER FOR EDUCATION STATISTICS. Official site for all government statistics relating to education. *http://nces.ed.gov*

NATIONAL EDUCATION ASSOCIATION. Home page of the largest teachers' organization, with information on a variety of education issues. *www.nea.org*

U.S. DEPARTMENT OF EDUCATION. Official site of the Education Department, with information on laws, policies, and issues. *www.ed.gov*

AMERICAN COUNCIL ON EDUCATION. Organization representing major universities; includes policy positions on higher education. *www.acenet.org*

AMERICAN ASSOCIATION OF UNIVERSITY PROFESSORS. Organization representing university professors, with information on issues in higher education including salaries of faculty. *www.aaup.org*

NATIONAL ASSOCIATION OF SCHOLARS. Academic organization devoted to restoring individual merit and academic freedom in higher education. *www.nas.org*

Economic Policy

Challenging Incrementalism

Incremental and Nonincremental Policymaking

Traditionally, fiscal and monetary policies were made *incrementally*; that is, decision makers concentrated their attention on modest changes—increases or decreases—in existing taxing, spending, and deficit levels, as well as the money supply and interest rates. Incrementalism was especially pervasive in annual federal budget making. The president and Congress did not reconsider the value of all existing programs each year, or pay much attention to previously established expenditure levels. Rather last year's expenditures were considered as a base of spending for each program, attractive consideration of the budget proposals focused on new items or increases over last year's base.

But crises often force policymakers to abandon incrementalism and reach out in *nonincremental* directions. In economic policy, the president and Congress and the Fed are pressured to "do something" in the face of a perceived economic crisis, even if there is little consensus on what should be done, or even whether there is anything the federal government can do to resolve the crisis. As we shall see later in this chapter, the recession that began in 2008 caused policymakers to search for new policies and make dramatic changes in spending and deficit levels and to undertake unprecedented measures to prevent the collapse of financial markets and avoid a deep recession.

Fiscal and Monetary Policy

Economic policy is exercised primarily through the federal government's *fiscal policies*—decisions about taxing, spending, and deficit levels—and its *monetary policies*—decisions about the money supply and interest rates.

Fiscal policy is made in the annual preparation of the federal budget by the president and the Office of Management and Budget, and subsequently considered by Congress in its annual appropriations bills and revisions of the tax laws. These decisions determine overall federal spending levels, as well as spending priorities among federal programs. Together with tax policy decisions (see Chapter 8), these spending decisions determine the size of the federal government's annual deficits or surpluses.

Monetary policy is the principal responsibility of the powerful and independent Federal Reserve Board—"the Fed"—which can expand or contract the money supply through its oversight of the nation's banking system (see "The Fed at Work" later in this chapter). Congress established the Federal Reserve System and its governing Board in 1913 and Congress could, if it wished, reduce its power or even abolish the Fed altogether. But no serious effort has ever been undertaken to do so.

Economic Theories As Policy Guides

The goals of economic policy are widely shared: growth in economic output and standards of living, full and productive employment of the nation's work force, and stable prices with low inflation. But a variety of economic theories compete for preeminence as ways of achieving these goals. From time to time, economic policy has been guided by different theories; or worse, it has been guided by conflicting theories simultaneously.

Classical Theory.   Classical economists generally view a market economy as a self-adjusting mechanism that will achieve an equilibrium of full employment, maximum productivity, and stable prices if left alone by the government. The price mechanism will adjust the decisions of millions of Americans to bring into balance the supply and demand of goods and labor. Regarding recessions, if workers are temporarily unemployed because the supply for workers exceeds the demand, wages (the price of labor) will fall; eventually it will again become profitable for businesses to have more workers at lower wages and thus end unemployment. Similarly, if the demand for goods (automobiles, houses, clothing, kitchenware, and so forth) falls, business inventories will rise and businesspeople will reduce prices (often through rebates, sales, etc.) until demand picks up again. Regarding inflation, general increases in prices will reduce demand and automatically bring it back into line with supply unless the government interferes. In short, classical economic theory relies on the free movement of prices to counter both recession and inflation.

Keynesian Theory.   But the Great Depression of the 1930s shattered popular confidence in classical economics. During that decade, the average unemployment rate was 18 percent, rising to 25 percent in the worst year, 1933. But even in 1936, seven years after the great stock market crash in 1929, unemployment was still 18 percent of the work force, raising questions about the ability of the market to stabilize itself and ensure high employment and productivity.

According to the British economist John Maynard Keynes, economic instability was a product of fluctuations in demand. Both unemployment and lower wages reduced the demand for goods; businesses cut production and laid off more workers to adjust for lower demand for their goods, but cuts and layoffs further reduced demand and accelerated the downward spiral. Keynesian theory suggested that the economy could fall into a recession and stay there. Only government could take the necessary countercyclical steps to expand demand by spending more money itself and lowering taxes. Of course, the government cannot add to aggregate demand if it balances the budget. Rather, during a recession it must incur deficits to add to total demand, spending more than it receives in revenues. Government borrowing—and the national debt—would grow during recessions. Borrowed money would make up the difference (the deficit) between lowered revenues and higher spending. To counter inflationary trends, the government should take just the opposite steps. Thus government would "counter" economic cycles, that is, engage in "countercyclical" fiscal policies.

Supply-Side Economics.   Supply-side economists argue that attention to long-term economic growth is more important than short-term manipulation of demand. Economic growth, which requires an expansion in the productive capacity of society, increases the overall supply of goods and services and thereby holds down prices. Inflation is reduced or ended altogether. More important, everyone's standard of living is improved with the availability of more goods and services at stable prices. Economic growth even increases government revenues over the long run.

Most supply-side economists believe that the free market is better equipped than government to bring about lower prices and more supplies of what people need and want. Government, they argue, is the problem, not the solution. Government taxing, spending, and monetary policies have promoted immediate consumption instead of investment in the future. High taxes penalize hard work, creativity, investment, and savings. The government should provide tax incentives to encourage investment and savings; tax rates should be lowered to encourage work and enterprise. Overall government spending should be held in check. Government regulations should be minimized to increase productivity and growth. Overall, the government should act to stimulate production and supply rather than demand and consumption.

Measuring the Performance of the American Economy

Measures of the actual performance of the American economy include the gross domestic product (GDP), the unemployment rate, and the rate of inflation.

Economic Growth.   The GDP is the nation's total production of goods and services for a single year valued in terms of market prices. It is the sum of all of the goods and services that people purchase, from wheat and corn to bicycles, from machine tools to maid service, from aircraft manufacturing to bus rides, from automobiles to chewing gum. GDP counts only final purchases of goods and services (that is, it ignores the purchase of steel by carmakers until it is sold as a car) to avoid double counting in the production process. GDP also excludes financial transactions (such as the sale of bonds and stocks) and income transfers (such as Social Security, welfare, and pension payments) that do not add to the production of goods and services. Although GDP is expressed in current dollar prices, it is often recalculated in constant dollar terms to reflect real values over time, adjusting for the effect of inflation. GDP estimates are prepared each quarter by the U.S. Department of Commerce; these figures are widely reported and closely watched by the business and financial community.

Economic recessions and recoveries are measured as fluctuations or swings in the growth of GDP (see Figure 7–1). Historical data reveal that periods of economic growth

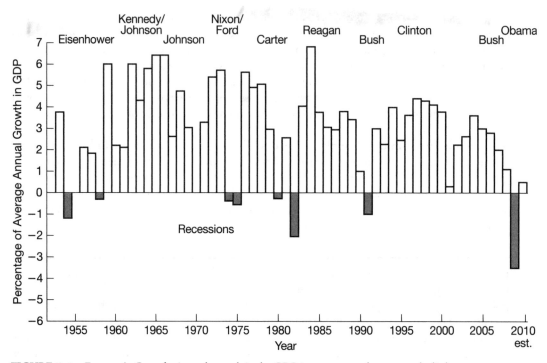

FIGURE 7–1   Economic Growth Annual growth in the GDP in recent years has averaged a little over
3 percent; recessions (when the economy actually contracts) have occurred periodically.
SOURCES: U.S. Bureau of Economic Analysis, *www.bea.gov; Budget of the United States Government, 2010.*

have traditionally been followed by periods of contraction, giving rise to the notion of economic cycles. The average annual GDP growth over the last half-century has been about
3 percent. But recessions (shown in Figure 7–1 as negative annual growth) have occurred
periodically. The GDP in current dollars in 2009 was about $14 trillion.

Unemployment.   The unemployment rate is the percentage of the civilian labor force who
are looking for work or waiting to return to or begin a job. Unemployment is different from
not working; people who have retired or who attend school and people who do not work
because of sickness, disability, or unwillingness are not considered part of the labor force and
so are not counted as unemployed. People who are so discouraged about finding a job that
they have quit looking for work are also not counted in the official unemployment rate.
Only people who are currently out of work and seeking a job are counted as unemployed.
The unemployment rate fluctuates with the business cycle, reflecting recessions and recoveries (see Figure 7–2). Generally, unemployment lags behind GDP growth, often going down
only after the recovery has begun. Following years of economic growth in the 1990s, the
nation's unemployment rate fell to near record lows, below 5 percent. With the economic
recession in 2008, unemployment rose again.

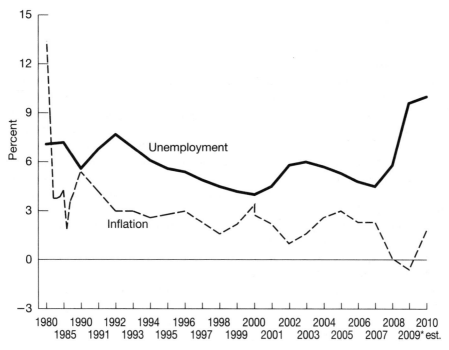

FIGURE 7–2 Unemployment and Inflation Unemployment rises with recessions; inflation is a problem during growth periods.
*Negative inflation—"deflation"—occured in 2009."

Inflation. Inflation erodes the value of the dollar because higher prices mean that the same dollars can now purchase fewer goods and services. Thus inflation erodes the value of savings, reduces the incentive to save, and hurts people who are living on fixed incomes. When banks and investors anticipate inflation, they raise interest rates on loans in order to cover the anticipated lower value of repayment dollars. Higher interest rates, in turn, make it more difficult for new or expanding businesses to borrow money, for home buyers to acquire mortgages, and for consumers to make purchases on credit. Thus inflation and high interest rates slow economic growth.

Recession. Economists define a recession as two or more quarters of negative economic growth, that is, declines in the gross domestic product (In politics, a recession is often proclaimed when the economy only slows its growth rate or when unemployment rises.) Recessions also entail a rise in unemployment and declines in consumer spending and capital investment. In some recessions, prices decline as well—"deflation." During the Great Depression of the 1930s the GDP fell by over 33 percent and the unemployment rate spiraled upward to a peak of 25 percent. The unemployment rate remained above 10 percent for nearly ten years, from 1930 to 1940. Compared to the Great Depression, the recession that began in 2008 appears relatively mild.

Financial Crisis and Nonincremental Policy Change

For years Americans lived on easy credit. Families ran up credit card debt and borrowed heavily for cars, tuition, and especially home buying. Mortgage lenders approved loans for borrowers without fully examining their ability to pay. Loans were often made with little or no down payment. Some mortgages were "predatory," with the initial low payments followed by steep upward adjustable rates. Federally sponsored corporations, Fannie Mae and Freddie Mac, encouraged mortgage loans to low income and minority homebuyers. A nationwide market in "subprime mortgages" attracted financial institutions seeking quick profits. To make matters worse, banks and financial institutions bundled mortgages together and sold these mortgage-backed securities as "derivatives." Risks were frequently overlooked. Banks, insurers, and lenders all assumed that housing prices would inevitably rise. Housing construction boomed.[1]

Eventually the bubble burst. Housing prices fell dramatically. The number of houses for sale greatly exceeded the number of people willing to buy them. Homeowners found themselves holding "upside down" mortgages—mortgages that exceeded the value of their homes. Many were unable or unwilling to meet their mortgage payments. Foreclosures and delinquencies spiraled upward. Investors who held mortgage-backed securities began to incur heavy losses. Investment banks, such as Bear Stearns, and mortgage insurers, including Fannie Mae and Freddie Mac, found themselves in serious financial trouble. Bankruptcies and federal bailouts multiplied. The stock market plummeted.

Wall Street Bailout.   In 2008 the credit crunch ballooned into Wall Street's biggest crisis since the Great Depression. Hundreds of billions of dollars in mortgage-related investments went bad, and the nation's leading investment banks and insurance companies sought the assistance of the Treasury Department and Federal Reserve System. The Fed acted to stave off the bankruptcy of Bear Stearns and the Treasury Department took over Fannie Mae and Freddie Mac. The nation's largest insurance company, American International Group (AIG), was bailed out by the Fed. But the hemorrhaging continued and it was soon clear that the nation was tumbling into a deep recession.

In September, President Bush sent Secretary of the Treasury Henry Paulson, accompanied by Federal Reserve Chairman Ben Bernanke, to Congress to plead for a massive $700 billion bailout of banks, insurance companies, and investment firms that held mortgage-backed "illiquid assets." They argued that their proposal was absolutely essential to safeguard the financial security of the nation. A full-blown depression might result if the federal government failed to purchase these troubled assets.

The nation's top leadership—President Bush, the Treasury secretary and Fed chairman, House and Senate Democratic and Republican leaders, and even the presidential candidates, Barack Obama and John McCain—all supported the bill. But polls show that most Americans opposed a "Wall Street bailout." Congress members were asked by their leaders to ignore the folks back home. The initial House vote stunned Washington and Wall Street: "nay" votes prevailed. The stock market plunged.

Predictions of economic catastrophe inspired a renewed effort to pass the bill. The Senate responded by passing it with a comfortable margin, while adding various sweeteners, mostly tax benefits to gain House support. Tensions were high when the House voted on the

Senate version of the bill. In a sharp reversal of its earlier action, the House approved the Emergency Economic Stabilization Act of 2008. President Bush promptly signed it into law.

Treasury's TARP. The Treasury Department was given unprecedented power to bail out the nation's financial institutions. Secretary Paulson initially proposed to use the $700 billion appropriation by Congress to buy up "toxic assets"—mortgage-backed securities whose value had dropped sharply. The program was named the Troubled Asset Relief Program (TARP). But shortly afterward, Paulson reversed course and decided to use the TARP money to inject cash directly into banks by purchasing preferred shares of their stock. The nation's largest bank, Citigroup, was first in line, and other major banks and investment firms followed (see Table 7–1).

Critics of the program noted that by accepting ownership shares in the nation's leading banks and investment houses, the government was tilting toward "socialism." Government ownership of the financial industry, that is, "nationalization" of the banks, would have been considered unthinkable before the crisis. The financial crisis had inspired a decidedly nonincremental policy change.

Mortgage Modification. Later, under President Obama's new Treasury Secretary, Timothy Geithner, banks receiving TARP assistance were obliged to adopt mortgage loan modification procedures to prevent foreclosures. This foreclosure modification program provided financial assistance to mortgage lenders as an incentive for them to modify home mortgages that were in danger of default. (To be eligible, borrowers had to show "hardship.") The intention was to help as many as 5 million mortgage borrowers refinance their loans at lower interest rates. Critics of the program expressed the fear of rising resentment among the millions of Americans who sacrificed to keep up with their mortgage payments.

Public–Private Investment Program. The key to loosening credit and jump starting the economy appeared to be relieving the nation's banks of their "toxic" assets—securities backed by mortgages that were in foreclosure or default. President Obama's Secretary of the Treasury developed a Public-Private Investment Program that uses TARP money to leverage private purchases of toxic assets. The Federal Deposit Insurance Corp. and the Federal Reserve are to facilitate private purchases by providing low-interest loans to buyers of these assets. By

TABLE 7–1 Top Federal Bailout Recipients

American International Group
Citigroup
JPMorgan Chase
Wells Fargo
Bank of America
Goldman Sachs
Merrill Lynch
Morgan Stanley
PNC Financial Services
U.S. Bankcorp

relieving banks of these "nonperforming" loans, banks should be prepared to make new loans and thereby stimulate the economy. In effect, the government is creating a "yard sale" for junk securities at a cost of $500 billion to $1 trillion.

GM Bankruptcy.   General Motors is an American institution, the biggest of the big three domestic automobile manufacturers—GM, Chrysler, and Ford. With federal supervision, GM and Chrysler sought bankruptcy protection in 2009; Ford managed to stay afloat by itself. Even before declaring bankruptcy, General Motors had received billions of federal dollars in loans and loan guarantees. Federal involvement forced out GM's chief executive officer. In bankruptcy the federal government took majority ownership of GM. President Obama declared that the federal government had no interest in the day-to-day operations of General Motors. Yet the White House issued guidelines for limiting the salaries of top executives of GM and of other institutions receiving TARP funds.

Fed Reponses.   In addition to the TARP bailouts, the Federal Reserve Board made a dramatic decision to pump over $1.5 *trillion* into the nation's financial system in order to unlock mortgage, credit card, college and auto lending. The Fed lowered its discount rate to less than 1 percent, and then later to zero percent, to encourage banks to make loans. But most of the Fed's efforts came in the form of loan guarantees to banks, credit unions, mortgage lenders, and automakers' financial arms. The objective was to lower interest rates on all forms of credit and thereby inspire consumers to borrow and lenders to lend, jumpstarting the economy. But low-interest rates and easy credit do not guarantee that banks will lend money or that businesses and individuals will borrow money. As the recession deepened in early 2009, the president and Congress sought to provide additional economic "stimulus."

The Economic Stimulus Package

A massive economic stimulus plan, officially called the American Recovery and Reinvestment Act of 2009, was the centerpiece of President Barack Obama's early policy agenda. Its combination of spending increases and tax cuts totaled $757 billion—the largest single fiscal policy measure in American history. It was written in record time by a Democratic-controlled Congress; House Republicans were unanimous in opposition, and only three Republican senators supported the bill.

Spending Priorities.   The stimulus package consisted of roughly two-thirds spending and one-third tax rebates. Democrats in the Congress used the package to increase spending in a wide variety of domestic programs—in education, Medicaid, unemployment compensation, food stamps, health technology, child tax credits, disability payments, higher education grants, renewable energy subsidies, and rail and transit transportation—as well as traditional spending for highways and bridge building (see Table 7–2). Republicans complained that much of the spending had little to do with stimulating the economy but rather increased government involvement in domestic policy areas favored by Democrats. Republicans had traditionally relied upon tax cuts to stimulate the economy.

TABLE 7–2 The Stimulus Package Major categories of items in the American Recovery and Reinvestment Act of 2009

- Tax payments: $400 to individuals with incomes under $75,000, and $800 to couples with incomes under $150,000
- State Medicaid assistance
- Education and job training aid to school districts
- Unemployment compensation: increase payments and extend to thirty-three weeks
- Highways and bridges: money to states for "shovel ready" projects
- Healthcare for unemployed: health insurance for unemployed for nine months
- Food stamp program increases
- Index the Alternative Minimum Tax for inflation
- Health technology grants and subsidies
- Renewable energy grants and subsidies
- Child care tax credits
- Pell Grant increases
- Health science research
- Extend Hope Scholarships from two year to four years
- Increase Title I education monies
- Increase aid for special education
- Rail transportation and public transit

Total $787 Billion

Tax "Cuts."   The stimulus package also included a version of Obama's campaign promise of a middle-class tax cut. The tax "cuts" in the package, labeled "Making Work Pay," were actually payments of $400 to individuals with incomes under $75,000 and payments of $800 to couples with incomes under $150,000. These payments were to be made to anyone who paid Social Security taxes. It was not necessary to have paid any income taxes in order to receive these tax "cuts." Critics labeled these payments "welfare checks."

Also included in the package was a provision to index the Alternative Minimum Tax (AMT) to inflation and thereby protect millions of middle-class Americans from having to pay a tax designed for high-income taxpayers (see Chapter 8).

Making "Recovery" Permanent.   The stimulus package was initially presented to Congress as an emergency measure requiring quick passage in order to deal with a deepening recession. But many of its provisions were recommended to Congress as permanent measures by President Barack Obama in his very first budget message. The Making Work Pay tax payments were repackaged as "the first stage" of a middle-class tax cut promised by Obama during the presidential campaign. These payments are designed to offset the Social Security payroll tax (FICA) (see Chapter 8). Also to be made permanent were the child tax credits, increases in food stamp benefits, increases in disability payments, and increases in unemployment compensation benefits. Moreover, a whole host of new programs in energy, education, and health care, given initial impetus in the stimulus package, were to become major policy initiatives in the Obama Administration.

Financial Regulation.   The Obama Administration also sought authority from Congress to exercise broad regulatory oversight of the financial industry, including insurance and investment firms as well as banks. This authority would enable the government to use a range of actions to prevent the collapse of financial institutions whose failure could disrupt the broader economy. These actions guaranteeing losses, buying assets, taking partial federal ownership stakes, or even seizing firms.

"Cash for Clunkers." Separate from the stimulus bill, Congress also enacted a Car Allowance Rebate System (CARS), also known as "cash for clunkers." CARS offers vouchers up to $4500 for trade-ins of old gas-guzzling cars and trucks in exchange for new models that get better gas mileage. The program turned out to be very popular with auto owners, car manufacturers, the United Automobile Workers Union, and car dealers. Some environmental groups criticized the program for not having high enough mile-per-gallon standards for new vehicles.

The Fed at Work

Most economically advanced democracies have central banks whose principal responsibility is to regulate the supply of money, both currency in circulation and bank deposits. And most of these democracies have found it best to remove this responsibility from the direct control of elected politicians. Politicians everywhere are sorely tempted to inflate the supply of money in order to fund projects and programs with newly created money instead of new taxes. The result is a general rise in prices and a reduction in goods and services available to private firms and individuals—inflation.

The Federal Reserve System. The task of the Fed is to regulate the money supply and by so doing to help avoid both inflation and recession. The Fed oversees the operation of the nation's twelve Federal Reserve Banks, which actually issue the nation's currency, called "Federal Reserve Notes." The Federal Reserve Banks are banker's banks; they do not directly serve private citizens or firms. They hold the deposits, or "reserves," of banks; lend money to banks at "discount rates" that the Fed determines; buy and sell U.S. Government Treasury bonds; and assure regulatory compliance by private banks and protection of depositors against fraud. The Fed determines the reserve requirements of banks and otherwise monitors the health of the banking industry. The Fed also plays an important role in clearing checks throughout the banking system.

Understanding Monetary Policy. Banks create money—"demand deposits"—when they make loans. Currency (cash) in circulation, together with demand deposits, constitute the nation's money supply—"M-1." But demand deposits far exceed currency; only about 5 percent of the money supply is in the form of currency. So banks really determine the money supply in their creation of demand deposits. However, the Fed requires that all banks maintain a reserve in deposits with a Federal Reserve Bank. If the Fed decides that there is too much money in the economy (inflation), it can raise the reserve requirement, reducing what a bank can create in demand deposits. Changing the "reserve ratio" is one way that the Fed can expand or contract the money supply.

The Fed can also expand or contract the money supply by changing the interest rate it charges member banks to borrow reserve. A bank can expand its demand deposits by borrowing reserve from the Fed, but it must pay the Fed an interest rate, called the "discount rate," in order to do so. By raising the discount rate, the Fed can discourage banks from borrowing reserve and thereby contract the money supply; lowering the discount rate encourages banks to expand the money supply. Interest rates generally—on loans to businesses, mortgages, car loans, and the like—rise and fall with rises and falls in the Fed's discount rate. Lowering rates encourages economic expansion; raising rates dampens inflation when it threatens the economy.

Finally, the Fed can also buy and sell U.S. Treasury bonds and notes in what is called "open market operations." The reserve of the Federal Reserve System consists of U.S. bonds and notes. If it sells more than it buys, it reduces its own reserve, and hence its ability to lend reserve to banks; this contracts the money supply. If it buys more than it sells, it adds to its own reserve, enabling it to lend reserve to banks and thereby expand the money supply.

Fed Independence. The decisions of the Federal Reserve Board are made independently. They need not be ratified by the president, Congress, the courts, or any other governmental institution. Indeed, the Fed does not even depend on annual federal appropriations, but instead finances itself. This means that Congress does not even exercise its "power of the purse" over the Fed. Theoretically, Congress could amend or repeal the Federal Reserve Act of 1913, but to do so would be politically unthinkable. The only changes to the act have been to *add to* the powers of the Fed. The Fed chairman often appears before committees of Congress and is given far more respect by committee members than other executive officials.

Fed Responses to Recession. In previous recessions, the monetary policies of the Federal Reserve Board succeeded fairly well in easing credit and encouraging recovery. But in the recession that began in 2008, Fed policies appeared to be insufficient by themselves in stimulating the economy. The Fed lowered the discount rate first to one percent and then later to zero. This unprecedented action was designed to encourage banks to borrow reserve and extend loans, thereby expanding the money supply. Later the Fed joined with the Treasury Departments TARP to help bail out the nation's financial institutions (see Table 7–1). And the Fed pumped over $1.5 trillion into the money supply in order to encourage lending, especially mortgage lending.

But *monetary policy* used to offset recession is often characterized as "trying to push with a string." Making available money at low interest rates does not guarantee that banks will lend more or that businesses and individuals will borrow more. Credit may remain "frozen" if banks and other lenders have lost confidence in the ability of businesses and individuals to repay loans. It is then advised that only *fiscal policy*—government increases in spending, reductions in taxes, and increases in deficits—can counter an especially deep recession.

The Growth of Government Spending

Government spending grows in all presidential administrations, regardless of promises to "cut government spending." Total federal spending grew from $480 billion in 1959 to $3.5 trillion in 2010 (see Table 7–3). At this level, federal government spending amounts to about 24 percent of the nation's gross domestic product.

TABLE 7–3   The Growth of Federal Government Spending
Federal government spending of more than $3.5 trillion represents over 24 percent of the GDP.

	GDP (Billions)	Federal Government Spending (Billions)	Percentage of GDP
1959	480.2	92.1	19.2
1965	671.0	118.2	17.6
1970	985.4	195.6	19.8
1975	1,509.8	332.3	22.0
1980	2,644.1	590.9	22.3
1985	3,967.7	946.4	23.8
1992	5,868.6	1,381.8	23.5
1995	7,269.6	1,538.9	22.5
2000	9,872.9	1,789.2	18.4
2005	12,487.1	2,972.2	20.2
2008	14,181.0	2,983.0	21.0
2009	14,270.0*	3,998.0*	28.0*
2010	14,729*	3,591.0*	24.4*

SOURCES: *Statistical Abstract of the United States, 2008; Budget of the United States Government, 2010.* May, 2009 update.
*Estimates.

Challenging Incrementalism.   For years federal government spending rose more or less incrementally, remaining close to 20 percent of the GDP. But the recession beginning in 2008 drove Congress and the president to increase spending to dramatically higher levels. In 2009 federal spending rose by almost $1 trillion from the previous year, the single largest year-to-year increase in history. Federal spending in that year rose to almost 28 percent of the GDP. Federal revenues declined that year; the extra spending was financed through a $1.7 trillion deficit, the largest annual deficit in history. The bulk of this increase in spending and deficits levels can be attributed to the stimulus package designed to jump-start the sagging economy. But high levels of federal spending and deficits continued in 2010 (see Figure 7–3).

"Entitlement" Spending.   The largest share of the federal government budget is devoted to "entitlements." These are spending items determined by past policies of Congress and represent commitments in future federal budgets. Entitlements provide classes of people with legally enforceable rights to benefits, and they account for about 60 percent of all federal spending, including Social Security, Medicare and Medicaid, welfare and food stamps, federal employees' retirement, and veterans benefits. In addition to entitlements, other "mandatory" spending includes interest payments on the national debt. Only about 20 percent of the budget remains for "nondefense discretionary" spending (see Figure 7–4).

Incrementalism in Entitlements.   Each year as more people become entitled to Social Security benefits and Medicare—the two largest entitlement programs—government spending rises accordingly. It is true that, in theory, Congress could change the basic laws establishing these programs and thereby avoid annual increases in entitlement spending. But politically such a course of action is virtually unthinkable. Reducing long-promised benefits would be regarded by voters as a failure of trust.

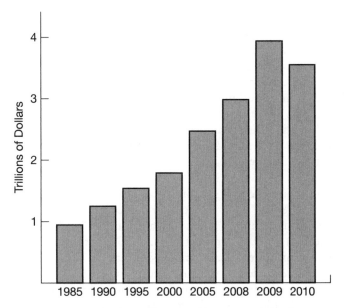

FIGURE 7–3   Federal Spending in Trillions Federal spending grew incrementally until 2009 when countercyclical "stimulus" efforts sent spending to unprecedented levles.
SOURCE: *Budget of the United States Government, 2010.*

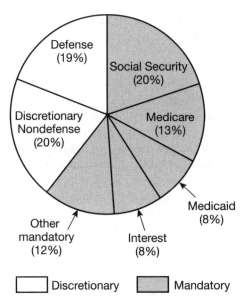

FIGURE 7–4   The Federal Budget Most federal spending is considered "mandatory," that is, required by past commitments.
SOURCE: *Budget of the United States Government, 2010.*

Indexing of Benefits.   Another reason that spending increases each year is that Congress has authorized automatic increases in benefits tied to increases in prices. Benefits are "indexed" to the Consumer Price Index under Social Security, SSI, food stamps, and veterans' pensions. This indexing pushes up the cost of entitlement programs each year. Indexing, of course, runs counter to federal efforts to restrain inflation. Moreover, the Consumer Price Index generally overestimates real increases in the cost of living.

Increasing Costs of In-Kind Benefits.   Rises in the cost of major in-kind (noncash) benefits, particularly medical costs of Medicaid and Medicare, also guarantee growth in federal spending. These in-kind benefit programs have risen faster in cost than cash benefit programs.

Backdoor Spending.   Some federal spending does not appear on the budget. For example, spending by the postal service is not included in the federal budget. No clear rule explains why some agencies are in the budget and others are not. But "off-budget" agencies have the same economic effects as other government agencies. Another form of backdoor spending is found in government-guaranteed loans. Initially government guarantees for loans—FHA housing, guaranteed student loans, veterans' loans, and so forth—do not require federal money. The government merely promises to repay the loan if the borrower fails to do so. Yet these loans create an obligation against the government.

Government Deficits and the National Debt

The federal government regularly spends more than it receives in revenues (see Figure 7–5). These annual deficits have driven up the accumulated debt of the United States government to over $12 trillion. The national debt now exceeds $40,000 for every man, woman, and child in the nation!

The national debt is owed mostly to American banks and financial institutions and private citizens who buy U.S. Treasury bonds. But an increasing share of the debt is held by foreign investors, notably China, who also buy U.S. Treasury bonds. As old debt comes due, the Treasury Department sells new bonds to pay off the old; that is, it continues to "roll over" or "float" the debt. The debt today is smaller as a percentage of the GDP than at some periods in U.S. history. Indeed, in order to pay the costs of fighting World War II, the U.S. government ran up a debt of 110 percent of GDP; the current debt is the highest in history in dollar terms but only about 80 percent of the GDP.

The ability to float such a huge debt depends on public confidence in the U.S. government—confidence that it will continue to pay interest on its debt, that it will pay off the principal of bond issues when they come due, and that the value of the bonds will not decline over time because of inflation.

Politics, Surpluses, and Deficits.   Economic growth increases tax revenues. The nation's economic performance in the 1990s was much better than either politicians or economists expected. Tax revenues grew faster than government spending, and the federal government's annual deficits began to decline. President Clinton and a Democratic-controlled Congress passed a major tax increase in 1993 (see Chapter 8). After 1994, a Republican-controlled

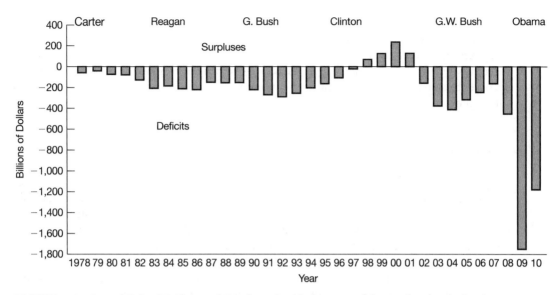

FIGURE 7–5 **Annual Federal Deficits and Surpluses** In only four years of the past four decades has the federal government enjoyed a surplus of revenues over expenditures; annual deficits have accumulated, creating a national debt of over $12 trillion dollars.
SOURCES: *Statistical Abstract of the United States, 2008 Budget of the United States Government, 2010.*

Congress slowed the growth of federal spending. Not surprisingly, both Democrats and Republicans claimed credit for ending forty years of deficits in 1998. For four years the federal government actually enjoyed surpluses of revenues over expenditures.

However, deficits returned in 2002 when economic growth slowed. Federal spending for national defense and homeland security increased after the terrorist attacks of September 11, 2001. And President Bush was committed to lowering federal income taxes. In his first year in office President Bush pushed Congress to enact a major tax reduction (see Chapter 8). Democrats argued that this tax reduction contributed to the return to deficit spending. Republicans argued that tax reductions stimulate the economy and that economic growth would eventually increase revenues and reduce deficits. Again in 2003 President Bush succeeded in getting Congress to enact further tax reductions. But large annual federal deficits continued through the end of the Bush Administration.

Deficits exploded under President Barack Obama. In his first budget message to Congress, he stated that the stimulus package would push the annual deficit for 2009 to $1.7 trillion, an amount over four times greater than any previous budget deficit. The budget for 2010 envisions a deficit of over $1 trillion. Assuming the nation emerges from the recession, President Obama estimates that deficits will be only a half-trillion dollars by 2012. But annual deficits are predicted far into the future.

The Burdens of Government Debt. Even if the federal government managed to balance its annual budgets, the accumulated national debt, and the interest payments that must be made on it, would remain obligations of current and future taxpayers. Interest payments on the national debt come from current taxes; interest payments soon will amount to about 10 percent of the federal government's budget. This means that for every dollar paid in federal taxes, taxpayers currently receive only 90 cents in government goods and services. Interest payments might otherwise be used for government programs in health, education, research, and so on. The burden of future interest payments is shifted to young people and future generations.

The Formal Budgetary Process

The president, through the Office of Management and Budget (OMB), located in the Executive Office, has the key responsibility for budget preparation. In addition to this major task, the OMB has related responsibilities for improving the organization and management of the executive agencies, for coordinating the extensive statistical services of the federal government, and for analyzing and reviewing proposed legislation to determine its effect on administration and finance.

The Constitution gives the president no formal powers over taxing and spending. Constitutionally all the president can do is "make recommendations" to Congress. It is difficult to imagine that prior to 1921 the president played no direct role in the budget process. The secretary of the Treasury compiled the estimates of the individual agencies, and these were sent, without revision, to Congress for its consideration. It was not until the Budget and Accounting Act of 1921 that the president acquired responsibility for budget formulation and thus developed a means of directly influencing spending policy.

OMB—Preparing the Presidential Budget.　Preparation of the fiscal budget starts more than a year before the beginning of the fiscal year for which it is intended. After preliminary consultation with the executive agencies and in accord with presidential policy, the OMB develops targets or ceilings within which the agencies are encouraged to build their requests. This work begins a full sixteen to eighteen months before the beginning of the fiscal year for which the budget is being prepared. (In other words, work would begin in January 2009 on the budget for the fiscal year beginning October 1, 2010, and ending September 30, 2011.) Budgets are named for the fiscal year in which they end, so this example describes the work on the *Budget of the United States Government, 2011* or more simply, "FY11."

Budget materials and instructions go to the agencies with the request that the forms be completed and returned to the OMB. This request is followed by about three month of arduous work by agency-employed budget officers, department heads, and the grass-roots bureaucracy in Washington and out in the field. Budget officials at the bureau level check requests from the smaller units, compare them with the previous years' estimates, hold conferences, and make adjustments. The process of checking, reviewing, modifying, and discussing is repeated on a larger scale at the department level.

The heads of agencies are expected to submit their completed requests to the OMB by mid-September or early October. Occasionally a schedule of "over ceiling" items (requests above the suggested ceilings) will be included.

With the requests of the spending agencies at hand, the OMB begins its own budget review. Hearings are given to each agency. Top agency officials support their requests as convincingly as possible. On rare occasions dissatisfied agencies may ask the budget director to take their cases to the president.

In December, the president and the OMB director will devote time to the document, which by now is approaching its final stages of assembly. They and their staffs will "blue-pencil," revise, and make last-minute changes as well as prepare the president's message, which accompanies the budget to Congress. After the budget is in legislative hands, the president may recommend further alterations as needs dictate.

Although the completed document includes a revenue plan with general estimates for taxes and other income, it is primarily an expenditure budget. Revenue and tax policy staff work centers in the Treasury Department and not in the OMB. In late January the president presents the *Budget of the United States Government* for the fiscal year beginning October 1 to Congress (see Figure 7–6).

House and Senate Budget Committees.   In an effort to consider the budget as a whole, Congress has established House and Senate budget committees and a Congressional Budget Office (CBO) to review the president's budget after its submission to Congress. These committees draft a first budget resolution (due May 15) setting forth target goals to guide committee actions on specific appropriation and revenue measures. If appropriations measures exceed the targets in the budget resolution, it comes back to the floor in a reconciliation measure. A second budget resolution (due September 15) sets binding budget figures for committees and subcommittees considering appropriations. In practice, however, these two budget resolutions have been folded into a single measure because Congress does not want to reargue the same issues.

Appropriations Acts.   Congressional approval of each year's spending is usually divided into thirteen separate appropriations bills, each covering separate broad categories of spending. These appropriations bills are drawn up by the House and Senate appropriations committees and their specialized subcommittees. Indeed, House appropriations subcommittees function as overseers of the agencies included in their appropriations bill. The appropriations committees must stay within the overall totals set forth in the budget resolutions adopted by Congress.

An *appropriations* act provides money for spending, and no funds can be spent without it. An *authorization* is an act of Congress establishing a government program and defining the amount of money that it may spend. Authorizations may be for several years. However, the authorization does not actually provide the money that has been authorized; only an appropriations act can do that. Appropriations acts are almost always for a single fiscal year. Congress has its own rule that does not allow appropriations for programs that have not been authorized. However, appropriations frequently provide less money for programs than earlier authorizations.

Appropriations acts include both obligational *authority* and *outlays*. An obligation of authority permits a government agency to enter into contracts calling for payments into future years (new obligated authority). Outlays are to be spent in the fiscal year for which they are appropriated.

Appropriations Committees.   Considerations of specific appropriations measures are functions of the appropriations committees in both houses. Committee work in the House of Representatives is usually more thorough than it is in the Senate; the committee in the

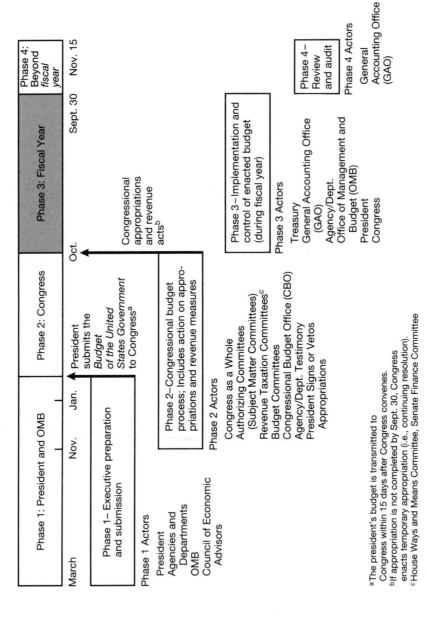

FIGURE 7–6 Major Steps in the Budget Process The president and the OMB begin the preparation of the executive budget almost a year before it is sent to Congress; the new fiscal year begins October 1, but Congress rarely has passed all of the appropriations measures required by that date.

Phase 1: President and OMB	Phase 2: Congress	Phase 3: Fiscal Year	Phase 4: Beyond *fiscal year*

March   Nov.   Jan.   Oct.   Sept. 30   Nov. 15

Phase 1– Executive preparation and submission

Phase 1 Actors

President
Agencies and
  Departments
OMB
Council of Economic
  Advisors

President submits the *Budget of the United States Government* to Congress[a]

Phase 2–Congressional budget process; Includes action on appropriations and revenue measures

Phase 2 Actors

Congress as a Whole
Authorizing Committees
  (Subject Matter Committees)
Revenue Taxation Committees[c]
Budget Committees
Congressional Budget Office (CBO)
Agency/Dept. Testimony
President Signs or Vetos
Appropriations

Congressional appropriations and revenue acts[b]

Phase 3– Implementation and control of enacted budget (during fiscal year)

Phase 3 Actors

Treasury
General Accounting Office (GAO)
Agency/Dept.
Office of Management and Budget (OMB)
President
Congress

Phase 4 – Review and audit

Phase 4 Actors

General Accounting Office (GAO)

[a] The president's budget is transmitted to Congress within 15 days after Congress convenes.
[b] If appropriation is not completed by Sept. 30, Congress enacts temporary appropriation (i.e., continuing resolution).
[c] House Ways and Means Committee, Senate Finance Committee

Senate tends to be a "court of appeal" for agencies opposed to House action. Each committee, moreover, has about ten largely independent subcommittees to review the requests of a
particular agency or a group of related functions. Specific appropriations bills are taken up
by the subcommittees in hearings. Departmental officers answer questions on the conduct of
their programs and defend their requests for the next fiscal year; lobbyists and other witnesses testify.

Supplemental Appropriations. The appropriations acts often fail to anticipate events that
require additional federal spending during the fiscal year. For example, the Iraq War and
Hurricane Katrina both incurred government spending well above the original appropriations acts for defense and homeland security. It is common for the president to request Congress to appropriate additional funds in such cases—funds not in the original budget for the
fiscal year or in the original congressional appropriations acts.

Revenue Acts. The House Committee on Ways and Means and the Senate Finance Committee are the major instruments of Congress for consideration of taxing measures. Through
long history and jealous pride they have maintained formal independence of the appropriations committees, further fragmenting legislative consideration of the budget.

Presidential Veto. In terms of aggregate amounts, Congress does not regularly make great
changes in the executive budget. It is more likely to shift money among programs and
projects. The budget is approved by Congress in the form of appropriations bills, usually
thirteen of them, each ordinarily providing for several departments and agencies. The number of revenue measures is smaller. As with other bills that are passed by Congress, the president has ten days to approve or veto appropriations legislation.

Although Congress authorized the president to exercise a "line-item veto" in 1996, the
U.S. Supreme Court declared it to be an unconstitutional violation of the separation of powers. The line-item veto would have given the president the authority to "cancel" specific
spending items and specific limited tax benefits in an overall appropriations act. But the
Court held that this procedure would transfer legislative power—granted by the Constitution only to Congress—to the president.

Continuing Resolutions and "Shutdowns." All appropriations acts *should* be passed by
both houses and signed by the president into law before October 1, the date of the start of
the fiscal year. However, it is rare for Congress to meet this deadline, so the government usually finds itself beginning a new fiscal year without a budget. Constitutionally, any U.S. government agency for which Congress does not pass an appropriations act may not draw
money from the Treasury and thus is obliged to shut down. To get around this problem,
Congress adopts a "continuing resolution" that authorizes government agencies to keep
spending money for a specified period, usually at the same level as in the previous fiscal year.

A continuing resolution is supposed to grant additional time for Congress to pass, and
the president to sign, appropriations acts. But occasionally this process has broken down in
the heat of political combat over the budget. The time period specified in a continuing resolution has expired without agreement on appropriations acts or even on a new continuing
resolution. In theory, the absence of either appropriations acts or a continuing resolution

should cause the entire federal government to "shut down," that is, to cease all operations and expenditures for lack of funds. (Shutdowns occurred during the bitter battle between President Bill Clinton and the Republican-controlled Congress over the Fiscal Year 1996 budget.) But in practice, shutdowns have been only partial, affecting only "nonessential" government employees and causing relatively little disruption.

SUMMARY

Government influences the economy through fiscal policies—decisions about taxing, spending, and deficit levels—and monetary policy—decisions about the money supply interest rates. Traditionally fiscal and monetary policy decisions were made incrementally. But incrementalism fails to describe or explain policymaking during the economic crisis confronting the nation beginning in 2008.

1. Keynesian theory recommends government manipulation of aggregate demand to counter economic cycles—raising spending, lowering taxes, and incurring debt during recessions and pursuing the opposite policies during inflation. Supply-side economists argue that high government taxing and spending levels promote immediate consumption instead of investment in the future and penalize hard work, creativity, and savings.

2. Fiscal policymaking rests with the president, primarily in his preparation of the annual *Budget of the United States Government*, and with Congress, which actually appropriates all the funds to be spent by the federal government each year.

3. Monetary policy rests with the Federal Reserve Board—the "Fed"—which influences the supply of money in a variety of ways. It determines how much reserve banks must maintain and what interest rates banks must pay to borrow additional reserves. Through these decisions, the Fed can expand or contract the money supply to help counter recessions and inflation.

4. But traditional *monetary* policies appeared inadequate in coping with the recession that began in 2008. The Fed dramatically increased the money supply in an effort to encourage banks and other lenders to make loans and jump-start the economy. The Fed also undertook to rescue many of the nation's leading financial institutions. But deepening recession caused the president and Congress to look to *fiscal* policy to stimulate the economy.

5. The economic "stimulus" package passed by Congress and signed by the president in early 2009 was a decidedly nonincremental response to perceived economic crisis. It was the largest single fiscal policy measure in history—a combination of tax payments and spending increases that raised government deficits to unprecedented levels.

6. Entitlement spending accounts for about 60 percent of all federal government spending. These are spending items determined by past policies of Congress and represent commitments in future federal budgets. They provide classes of people with legally enforceable rights to benefits, including Social Security, Medicare, Medicaid, welfare and food stamps, federal employees' retirement, and veterans' benefits. Entitlement spending rises incrementally each year.

7. The accumulated annual federal deficits have resulted in a total national debt of over 12 *trillion* dollars. This debt is owed to banks and financial institutions and private citizens who buy U.S. Treasury bonds, including foreign governments, notably China. The Treasury Department continually "floats" the debt by issuing new bonds to pay off old bonds when they become due. Interest paid on the national debt will soon account for about 10 percent of total federal spending.

8. The budget process itself remains largely incremental. Policymakers generally consider last year's expenditure as a base and focus their attention on proposed increases. Evaluating the desirability of every public program every year might create politically insoluble conflict as well as exhausting energies of budget makers. The Office of Management and Budget in the Executive Office of the President recommends taxing spending and deficit levels to Congress in the annual *Budget of the United States Government*. But only Congress can appropriate monies for government spending or decide upon tax laws.

Notes

1. See Michael Comiskey and Pawan Madhorgarthia, "Unraveling the Financial Crisis of 2008," *PS: Political Science & Politics*, vol. 42 (April, 2009), pp. 271–275.
2. William A. Niskanen, *Bureaucracy and Representative Government* (Chicago: Aldine, 1971).

Bibliography

GREIDER, WILLIAM. *Secrets of the Temple: How the Federal Reserve Runs the Country.* New York: Simon & Schuster, 1987.

MIKESELL, JOHN. *Fiscal Administration*, 7th ed. Belmont, CA: Wadsworth, 2007.

RAHM, DIANNE. *United States Public Policy: A Budgetary Approach.* Belmont, CA: Wadsworth, 2004.

SCHICK, ALLEN. *The Federal Budget*, 3rd ed. Washington, DC: Brookings Institution, 2007.

WILDAVSKY, AARON, and NAOMI CAIDEN. *The New Politics of the Budgetary Process*, 5th ed. New York: Longman, 2004.

SMITH, ROBERT W., and THOMAS D. LYNCH. *Public Budgeting in America,* 5th ed. Upper Saddle River, NJ: Prentice Hall, 2004.

KETTL, DONALD F. *Deficit Politics.* New York: Longman, 2003.

NEIMAN, MAX. *Defending Government: Why Big Government Works.* Upper Saddle River, NJ.: Prentice Hall, 2000.

Web Sites

FEDERAL RESERVE SYSTEM. Official site of the FRB, with information about the money supply, inflation, interest rates, etc. *www.federalreserve.gov*

U.S. OFFICE OF MANAGEMENT AND BUDGET. Official site of OMB, with the current Budget of the United States. *www.whitehouse.gov/omb*

U.S. CONGRESSIONAL BUDGET OFFICE.   Official site of CBO, with reports on economic and budget issues. *www.cbo.gov*

U.S. DEPARTMENT OF TREASURY.   Official Treasury site, with information on taxes, revenues, and debt. *www.treas.gov*

AFL-CIO.   Home page of the AFL-CIO; includes information on unemployment, wages, strikes, and management salaries. *www.aflcio.org*

AMERICAN ENTERPRISE INSTITUTE.   Moderate think tank, with reports on government taxing, spending, and deficits. *www.aei.org*

CONCORD COALITION.   Organization devoted to balanced federal budgets. *www.concordcoalition.org*

INSTITUTE FOR POLICY INNOVATION.   Organization advocating less government spending, lower taxes, and fewer regulations, with studies of policy options. *www.ipi.org*

8

Tax Policy

Battling the Special Interests

Interest Groups and Tax Policy

The interplay of interest groups in policymaking is often praised as "pluralism."[1] Public policy is portrayed by interest group theory as the equilibrium in the struggle between interest groups (see Chapter 2). While this equilibrium is not the same as majority preference, it is considered by pluralists to be the best possible approximation of the public interest in a large and diverse society.

But what if only a small proportion of the American people are organized into politically effective interest groups? What if the interest group system represents well-organized, economically powerful producer groups who actively seek immediate tangible benefits from the government? What if the interest group system leaves out a majority of Americans, particularly the less organized, economically dispersed consumers and taxpayers, who wish for broad policy goals such as fairness, simplicity, and general economic well-being?

There is no better illustration of the influence of organized interest groups in policymaking than national tax policy. Every economics textbook tells us that the public interest is best served by a tax system that is universal, simple, and fair and that promotes economic growth and well-being. But the federal tax system is very nearly the opposite: it is complex, unfair, and nonuniversal. Over *one-half* of all personal income in the United States escapes taxation through various exemptions, deductions, and special treatments in tax laws. Tax laws treat different types of income differently. They penalize work, savings, and investment and divert capital investment into nonproductive tax shelters and an illegal underground economy. The unfairness, complexity, and inefficiency of the tax laws can be attributed largely to organized interest groups.

In this chapter we will first outline the current federal tax system, then review some of the underlying issues that drive tax politics, and finally examine the influence of the special interests in shaping tax policy.

The Federal Tax System

The federal government derives its revenues from a variety of sources—the individual income tax; Social Security and Medicare are payroll deductions; the corporate income tax; excise taxes on gasoline, liquor, tobacco, telephones, air travel, and other consumer items; estate and gift taxes; custom duties, and a wide variety of charges and fees (see Figure 8–1).

Individual Income Taxes.   More than 100 years ago, Supreme Court Justice Stephen J. Field, in striking down as unconstitutional a progressive income tax enacted by Congress, predicted that such a tax would lead to class wars: "Our political contests will become a war of the poor against the rich, a war constantly growing in intensity and bitterness."[2] But populist sentiment in the early twentieth century—the anger of midwestern farmers toward eastern railroad tycoons and the beliefs of impoverished southerners that they would never have incomes high enough to pay an income tax—helped secure the passage of the Sixteenth Amendment to the U.S. Constitution. The federal income tax that was passed by Congress in 1914 had a top rate of 7 percent; less than 1 percent of the population had incomes high enough to be taxed. After 2010 the top rate becomes 39.6 percent and about half of the population pays income taxes.

The personal income tax is the federal government's largest single source of revenue. After 2010 personal income will be taxed at seven separate rates—10, 15, 25, 28, 33, 35, and

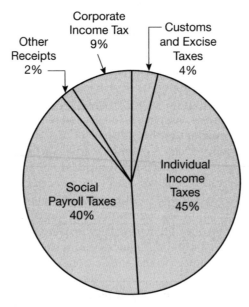

FIGURE 8–1   Sources of Federal Revenue The individual income tax provides the largest share of federal revenue, with Social Security payroll taxes close behind.
SOURCE: *Budget of the United States Government, 2010.*

39.6 percent.* These rates apply progressively to levels of income, or "brackets," that are indexed annually to reflect inflation.

The federal income tax is automatically deducted from the paychecks of all employees except farm and domestic workers. This withholding system is the backbone of the income tax. There is no withholding of nonwage income, but taxpayers with such income must file a Declaration of Estimated Taxes and pay this estimate in quarterly installments. Before April 15 of each year, all income-earning Americans must report their taxable income to the Internal Revenue Service on its Form 1040.

Americans are usually surprised to learn that half of all personal income is *not* taxed. To understand why, we must know how the tax laws distinguish between *adjusted gross income* (which is an individual's total money income minus expenses incurred in earning it) and *taxable income* (that part of adjusted gross income subject to taxation). Federal tax rates apply only to taxable income. Federal tax laws allow many reductions in adjusted gross income in the calculation of taxable income.

Tax expenditures is a term meant to identify tax revenues that are lost to the federal government because of exemptions, deductions, and special treatments in tax laws. Table 8–1 lists the major tax expenditures in federal tax law. There is a continual struggle between proponents of special tax exemptions to achieve social goals and those who believe that the tax laws should be simplified and social goals met by direct expenditures.

Most working families pay no personal income taxes, although Social Security taxes are deducted from their paychecks. (A combination of the personal deduction and the standard deduction ensures that families of four with incomes under $30,000 pay no income taxes.)

TABLE 8–1 Major "Tax Expenditures" in Federal Tax Policy Exemptions, deductions, exclusions, and credits in tax laws are often referred to as "tax expenditures."

Personal exemptions and deduction for dependents
Deductibility of mortgage interest on owner-occupied homes
Deductibility of property taxes on first and second homes
Deferral of capital gains on home sales
Deductibility of charitable contributions
Credit for child-care expenses
Exclusion of employer contributions to pension plans and medical insurance
Partial exclusion of Social Security benefits
Exclusion of interest on public-purpose state and local bonds
Deductibility of state and local income and sales taxes
Exclusion of income earned abroad
Accelerated depreciation of machinery, equipment, and structures
Medical expenses over 7.5 percent of income
Tax credits for children
Tax credits for two years of college
Deductible contributions to IRAs and 401(k) retirement plans
Deductible contributions for education accounts
Deductions for health savings accounts
Deductions for hurricane losses

*A health care reform package may add a tax "surcharge" on high incomes bringing the top marginal rate to 45 percent.

Moreover, most of these families are also entitled to an earned income tax credit (EITC)—a direct payment to low-income taxpayers who file for it (see "The Working Poor" in Chapter 5).

Upper-income taxpayers usually itemize their deductions, but about 75 percent of all taxpayers take the standardized deduction; the 25 percent who itemize are middle- and upper-income taxpayers who have deductions exceeding the standardized amount.

To further complicate tax laws, an Alternative Minimum Tax requires taxpayers to compute a separate AMT tax in addition to their "regular" income tax. Taxpayers are required to pay whichever tax is higher. The AMT has a broader definition of taxable income and disallows many standard deductions. It was designed to ensure that higher income taxpayers with many exclusions and deductions pay a minimum tax. It was originally passed by Congress in 1969, but it was not indexed to inflation. This means that increasing numbers of middle-class taxpayers are finding themselves subject to the AMT. In recent years Congress has acted annually to protect many middle-class taxpayers from the AMT.

In addition to multiple means of tax *avoidance* (legal means), an "underground economy" that facilitates tax *evasion* (illegal means of dodging taxes) costs the federal government many billions of dollars. Independent estimates of the size of the underground economy place the loss at 15 percent of all taxes due.[3] Many citizens receive direct cash payments for goods and services, and it simply does not occur to them to report these amounts as income in addition to the wage statements they receive from their employer. Many others receive all or most of their income from cash transactions; they have a strong incentive to underreport their income. And, of course, illegal criminal transactions such as drug dealing are seldom reported on personal income tax forms. Hiding income becomes more profitable as tax rates rise.

Who Pays the Federal Income Tax?   The federal personal income tax is highly progressive. Its seven tax brackets, together with personal and standard exemptions for families and earned income tax credits for low-income earners, combine to remove most of the tax burden from middle- and low-income Americans. Indeed, the lower 50 percent of income earners in America pay only 3 percent of all federal income taxes (see Figure 8–2). (However, the burden of Social Security payroll taxes falls mostly on these low- and middle-income workers.) The top 10 percent of income earners pay 70 percent of all personal income taxes, and the top 1 percent pay 39 percent.

Social Security Taxes.   The second-largest source of federal revenue is social insurance payroll taxes. Social insurance payroll taxes include Social Security (OASDI, or Old Age Survivors and Disability Insurance) and Medicare (HI, or Health Insurance). Employers pay half of these taxes directly and withhold half from employees' wages. Over the years Social Security taxes rose incrementally in two ways: a gradual increase in the combined employer–employee tax rate (percent) and a gradual increase in the maximum earnings base of the tax (see Table 8–2). Today the OASDI tax (12.4 percent) and the HI tax (2.90 percent) are differentiated (total payroll tax–15.3 percent), with proceeds going to separate OASDI and HI "trust funds" in the federal treasury. The OASDI tax is limited to the first $102,000 (in 2008) in wage income; wages above that amount as well as nonwage income (profits, interest, dividends, rents, and so forth) are not subject to this tax. Thus, the OASDI tax is "regressive"—that is, it captures a larger share of the income of lower-income Americans than of higher-income Americans.

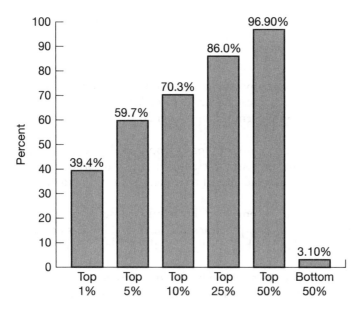

FIGURE 8–2   Who pays the Federal Income Tax? The federal income tax is steeply progressive in its effect. Almost all of is paid by the upper half of income earners. Over two-thirds of it is paid by the top 10 percent of income earners.
SOURCE: National Taxpayers Union analysis of Internal Revenue Service data for tax year 2005.

TABLE 8–2   Social Security Taxes The combined employee–employer Social Security tax rate is currently 15.3 percent of wages up to $102,000 (in 2008, a figure that increases each year with inflation).

	Combined Employee–Employer Tax Rate OASDI and HI	Maximum Wage Base OASDI
1937	2.0%	$ 3,000
1950	3.0	3,000
1960	6.0	4,800
1970	9.6	7,800
1980	12.26	25,900
1985	14.10	39,600
1990	15.3	67,600
2000	15.3	76,200
2006	15.3	94,200
2008	15.3	102,000

SOURCE: Social Security Administration, 2009.

The taxes collected under Social Security are earmarked (by Social Security number) for the account of each taxpayer. Workers, therefore, feel that they are receiving benefits as a right rather than as a gift of the government. However, benefits are only slightly related to the earning record of the individual worker; there are both minimum and maximum benefit levels, which prevent benefits from corresponding to payments. Indeed, for current recipients of

Social Security, less than 15 percent of the benefits can be attributed to their prior contributions. Current taxpayers are paying more than 85 percent of the benefits being received by current retirees.

Corporate Income Taxes. The corporate income tax provides only less than 10 percent of the federal government's total income. The Tax Reform Act of 1986 reduced the top corporate income tax from 46 to 34 percent; Congress raised the corporate income tax rate to 35 percent in 1993.

The corporate income tax is notorious for its loopholes. Indeed, interest groups representing specific industries, and lobbyists representing individual corporations, have inserted so many exemptions, deductions, and special treatments into corporate tax laws that most corporate profits go untaxed.

Who pays the corporate income tax? Economists differ over whether this tax is "shifted" to consumers or whether corporations and their stockholders bear its burden. The evidence on the *incidence*—that is, who actually bears the burden—of the corporate income tax is inconclusive.[4]

Religious, charitable, and educational organizations, as well as labor unions, are exempt from corporate income taxes, except for income they may derive from "unrelated business activity."

Estate and Gift Taxes. Taxes on property left to heirs is one of the oldest forms of taxation in the world. Federal estate taxes now begin on estates of $1 million and levy a tax of 46 percent on amounts above this level. Because taxes at death could be easily avoided by simply giving estates to heirs while still alive, a federal gift tax is also levied. There is an annual exclusion of $12,000 in gifts per donee.

Critics of the estate tax refer to it as "the death tax" and ridicule the federal government for "taxing people to die." Only a tiny proportion of all estates are subject to the tax. However, as the large baby-boom generation of voters reaches the age when their parents are passing away and leaving them estates, political pressure is building against the estate tax.

Excise Taxes and Custom Duties. Federal excise taxes on liquor, tobacco, gasoline, telephones, air travel, and other so-called luxury items account for only 3 percent of total federal revenue. Customs taxes on imports provide another 1 percent of total federal revenue.

Taxation, Fairness, and Growth

The goal of any tax system is not only to raise sufficient revenue for the government to perform its assigned tasks, but also to do so simply, efficiently, and fairly, and in a way that does not impair economic growth. The argument on behalf of tax reform is that the federal tax system fails to meet *any* of these criteria:

- Tax forms are so complex that a majority of taxpayers hire professional tax preparers; an army of accountants and lawyers make their living from the tax code.

- Tax laws are unfair in treating various sources of income differently; the many exemptions, deductions, and special treatments are perceived as loopholes that allow the privileged to escape fair taxation.

- Tax laws encourage tax avoidance, directing investment away from productive uses and into inefficient tax shelters; whenever people make decisions about savings and investment based on tax laws instead of most productive use, the whole economy suffers.

- Tax laws encourage cheating and reduce trust in government; they encourage the growth of an underground economy, transactions that are never reported on tax forms.

- High marginal tax rates discourage work and investment; economic growth is diminished when individuals face tax rates of 50 percent or more (combined federal, state, and local taxes) on additional income they receive from additional work, savings, or investments.

But the goals of fairness, simplicity, and economic growth are frequently lost in the clash of special interests. Various interests define "fairness" differently; they demand special treatment rather than universality in tax laws; and produce a U.S. Tax Code of several thousand pages of provisions, definitions, and interpretations.

Deciding What's Fair. A central issue in tax politics is the question of who actually bears the heaviest burden of a tax—that is, which income groups must devote the largest proportion of their income to the payment of taxes. Taxes that require high-income groups to pay a larger percentage of their incomes in taxes than low-income groups are said to be *progressive,* and taxes that take a larger share of the income of low-income groups are called *regressive.* Taxes that require all income groups to pay the same percentage of their income in taxes are said to be *proportional.* Note that the *percentage of income* paid in taxes is the determining factor. Most taxes take more money from the rich than the poor, but a progressive or regressive tax is distinguished by the percentages of income taken from various income groups.

The federal income tax has a progressive rate structure. In 2008 tax rates rose from 10 to 35 percent through six brackets of increasingly taxable income. Rates apply to income in each bracket or for all taxpayers. For example, in 2008 a married taxpayer filing jointly with $400,000 in taxable income paid the 35 percent rate only on the amount over $357,700; that same taxpayer pfid only 10 percent on the first $16,050, 15 percent on income between $16,050 and $65,100, and so on up through each bracket. (These are bracket figures for 2008, bracket figures change each year to reflect inflation. See Table 8–3.) A taxpayer with $400,000 in taxable income did not pay 35 percent of his or her total income in taxes; rather, this taxpayer paid approximately $119,000 in taxes, or about 30 percent of his or her total taxable income.

The Argument for Progressivity. Progressive taxation is generally defended on the principle of ability to pay; the assumption is that high-income groups can afford to pay a larger *percentage* of their incomes into taxes at no more of a sacrifice than that required of low-income groups to devote a smaller percentage of their income to taxation. This assumption is

TABLE 8–3   Federal Income Tax Rates 2008

Taxable Income Over	But not over	Tax Rate
0	$16,050	10%
$16,050	$65,100	15%
$65,100	$131,450	25%
$131,450	$200,300	28%
$200,300	$357,700	33%
$357,700	—	35%

Note: Top tax rate scheduled to rise to 39.6% in 2010.

based on what economists call *marginal utility theory* as it applies to money: each additional dollar of income is slightly less valuable to an individual than preceding dollars. For example, a $10,000 increase in the income of an individual already earning $400,000 is much less valuable than a $10,000 increase to an individual earning only $20,000 or to an individual with no income. Hence, *added* dollars of income can be taxed at higher *rates* without violating equitable principles.

The Argument for Proportionality.   Opponents of progressive taxation generally assert that equity can be achieved only by taxing everyone at the *same percentage of his or her income*, regardless of its size. A tax that requires all income groups to pay the same percentage of their income is called a *proportional* or *flat tax*. These critics believe that progressivity penalizes initiative, enterprise, and risk and reduces incentives to expand and develop the nation's economy. Moreover, by taking incomes of high-income groups, governments are taking money that would otherwise go into business investments and stimulate economic growth. Highly progressive taxes curtail growth and make everyone poorer.

Universality.   Another general issue in tax policy is universality, which means that all types of income should be subject to the same tax rates. This implies that income earned from investments should be taxed at the same rate as income earned from wages. But traditionally federal tax laws have distinguished between "ordinary income" and *capital gains*—profits from the buying and selling of property, including stocks, bonds, and real estate. The top marginal rate on capital gains is only 15 percent. The argument by investors, as well as the real estate and securities industries, is that a lower rate of taxation on capital gains encourages investment and economic growth. But it is difficult to convince many Americans that income earned by *working* should be taxed at higher rates than income earned by *investing*. If it is true that high tax rates discourage investing, they must also discourage work, and both capital and labor are required for economic productivity and growth.

The principle of universality is also violated by the thousands of exemptions, deductions, and special treatments in the tax laws. It is true that most people wish to retain many widely used tax breaks—charitable deductions, child-care deductions, and home mortgage deductions. Proponents of these popular tax treatments argue that they serve valuable social purposes—encouraging charitable contributions, helping with child care, and encouraging home ownership. But reformers argue that tax laws should not be used to promote social policy objectives by granting a wide array of tax preferences.

Economic Growth.   High tax rates discourage economic growth. Excessively high rates cause investors to seek "tax shelters"—to use their money not to produce more business and employment but rather to produce tax breaks for themselves. High tax rates discourage work, savings, and productive investment; they also encourage costly "tax avoidance" (legal methods of reducing or eliminating taxes) as well as "tax evasion" (illegal means of reducing or eliminating taxes).

According to supply-side economists (see "Economic Theories as Policy Guides" in Chapter 7), tax cuts do not necessarily create government deficits. Rather, they argue that if tax rates are reduced, the result may be to *increase* government revenue because more people would work harder and start new businesses, knowing they could keep a larger share of their earnings. This increased economic activity would produce more government revenue even though tax rates were lower.

Economist Arthur Laffer developed the diagram shown in Figure 8–3. If the government imposed a zero tax rate, of course, it would receive no revenue (point A). Initially, government revenues rise with increases in the tax rate. However, when tax rates become too high (beyond point C), they discourage workers and businesses from producing and investing. When this discouragement occurs, the economy declines and government revenues fall. Indeed, if the government imposed a 100 percent tax rate (if the government confiscated everything anyone produced), everyone would quit working and government revenues would fall to zero (point B). Laffer does not claim to know exactly what the optimum rate of taxation should be, but he (and the Reagan administration) clearly believed that the United States had been in the "prohibitive range" prior to the 1980s.

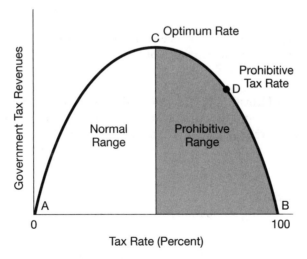

FIGURE 8–3   The Laffer Curve The "Laffer Curve" argues that when tax rates become too high, federal revenue actually declines because economic activity is discouraged.

Tax Reform and the Special Interests Case Study

Nothing arouses interest groups more than the prospects of tax "reform," with its implied threats to their special exemptions, deductions, and treatments. The Tax Reform Act of 1986 was one of the most heavily lobbied pieces of legislation in the history of the Congress of the United States.[5] President Reagan offered this reform bill as a trade-off—a reduction in tax *rates* in exchange for the elimination of many tax *breaks*. The rate structure was reduced from 14 brackets, ranging from 11 to 50 percent, to two brackets of 15 and 28 percent. To make up for lost revenue, many exemptions, deductions, and special treatments were to be reduced or eliminated. But powerful special interest groups fought hard against giving up their tax breaks in order to lower rates.

Industry. Opponents of tax reform were led by the U.S. Chamber of Commerce, the National Association of Manufacturers, and the Business Roundtable. Manufacturing businesses strongly opposed the elimination of the investment tax credit, accelerated depreciation, and foreign tax credit provisions in existing tax laws. The lowering of the corporation tax rate did not really appeal to large manufacturers because few of them paid significant taxes anyway due to generous loopholes in the law.

Real Estate and Housing. The National Association of Home Builders strongly opposed the elimination of mortgage interest deductions for second and vacation homes as well as the elimination of real estate tax shelters, which encouraged investors to put money into real estate projects that earned little or no income. The real estate industry also wanted to preserve deductions for property taxes.

Oil and Gas. The American Petroleum Institute, representing the powerful oil companies, fought bitterly against any reductions in their depletion allowance or deductions for intangible costs. Their familiar argument was that any change in their privileged status in the tax code would inhibit capital investment in energy and reduce production. But as an old Washington hand observed, "There are three reasons for keeping the oil depletion allowance—Texas, Oklahoma, and Louisiana."

Wall Street Investment Firms. The Securities Industries Association, the American Council for Capital Formation, and the nation's large investment firms lobbied heavily to keep preferential treatment of capital gains—profits from the sales of stocks and bonds. And the investment firms joined with banks in arguing for the retention of tax-free Individual Retirement Accounts (IRAs).

Charities and Foundations. Even before President Reagan sent his tax reform proposals to Congress, the nation's leading foundations had petitioned the president to retain deductions for charitable contributions.

Restaurants and Entertainment. The president proposed to limit business deductions for restaurant meals and to eliminate entertainment deductions—nightclubs, concerts, sport tickets, and so forth. The National Restaurant Association, representing high-priced restaurants, convinced Congress that business would falter without $100 meals and three-martini lunches; even the restaurant workers' union appeared to plead the same case. The National Football League, the National Basketball Association, and the National Hockey League all reported that businesses purchased most of their season tickets as tax deductions.

Labor Unions. The AFL-CIO was unimpressed with the notion of reducing and simplifying tax rates. Instead, it focused its opposition on the proposal to tax fringe benefits, including employer-paid health insurance and group life insurance. Unions also wanted to keep the deduction for union dues.

Banks. Banking interests, led by the American Bankers Association, wished to continue unlimited deductions for all interest payments. This makes borrowing easier by shifting part of the costs of borrowing from the debtor to the government and the taxpayers who must make up the lost revenue. Interest deductions make more customers for banks.

Auto Industry. The auto industry fought hard to keep deductions for interest paid on auto loans.

Government Lobbies. Lobbyists from state, county, and city governments, particularly those with high taxes, convened in Washington to lobby against tax reform. The leading state and local government lobbying organizations were the National Governors' Association, the National League of Cities, the National Conference of State Legislatures, the U.S. Conference of Mayors, the Council of State Governments, and the International City Managers Association. They were joined by labor unions representing public employees, notably the American Federation of State, County, and Municipal Employees.

These lobbies understood that federal deductibility of state and local income, sales, and property taxes reduced the direct costs of their own taxing decisions. In other words, when these state and local officials voted for higher taxes in their states, they knew that their taxpayers could deduct these taxes from their federal income tax liability, in effect shifting part of the cost to the federal government.

A Mixed Outcome. President Reagan succeeded in pushing Congress to lower rates to two simplified brackets—15 and 28 percent. Nevertheless, the special interests succeeded in keeping many of their favorite exemptions, deductions, and special treatments. The real estate industry—builders, developers, mortgage lenders—succeeded in restoring deductions for vacation homes. Tax shelters of many kinds were eliminated; the act prevented taxpayers from using "passive" losses generated from investments to reduce other income for tax purposes. The oil and gas industry, however, succeeded in retaining most of their special preferences in the tax code, including "depletion allowances" and "intangible" drilling costs. But the banking and automotive industries lost their fight to retain interest deductions on auto and consumer loans. The AFL-CIO knocked out the proposal to tax employer-paid fringe benefits but lost its fight to keep union dues deductible. The restaurant and entertainment industries restored 80 percent of their favorite deductions. State and local governments were successful in retaining the exemption from taxation of interest received from state and local government bonds, and they also succeeded in keeping the deductions for state and local government income and property taxes.

Politics and Tax Rates

Breaking Promises. George H. W. Bush campaigned for the presidency in 1988 with an emphatic promise to veto any attempt to raise taxes—"Read my lips! No new taxes!" But the president's pledge did not last through his second year in office. In a budget summit with leaders of the Democratic-controlled Congress, President Bush announced his willingness to support a tax increase as part of a deficit reduction agreement. Once the Democratic leaders in Congress detected the irresolution of the Republican president, they proceeded to enact their own taxing and spending program, while placing the political blame on Bush. The resulting budget plan made deep cuts in defense spending and token cuts in domestic spending, together with major tax increases.

Reversing the downward trend in top marginal tax rates, the Bush 1990 budget package raised the top rate from 28 to 31 percent (see Figure 8–4). The resulting rate structure became three-tiered—15, 28, and 31 percent. Democrats cheered the return to a more progressive rate structure. They ridiculed as "trickle-down economics" the arguments by supply-side theorists that high marginal tax rates would slow economic growth.

Raising Top Marginal Rates Again. President Bill Clinton's plan to reduce deficits centered on major tax increases on upper-income Americans. Specifically, Clinton succeeded in getting a Democratic-controlled Congress to add two new top marginal rates—36 and 39.6 percent. The corporate income tax was raised from 34 to 35 percent. But the special interests retained virtually all of their deductions, exemptions, and special treatments.

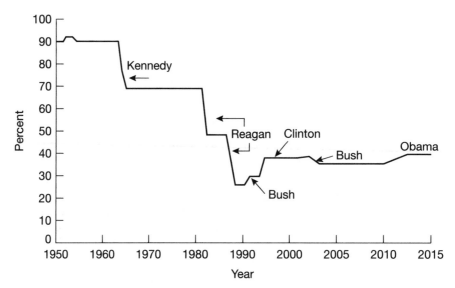

FIGURE 8–4   Maximum Income Tax Rates President Kennedy reduced the top income tax rate to 70 percent; President Reagan reduced it in two steps to 28 percent; Presidents Bush (the elder) and Clinton raised it to 39.6 percent; and President George W. Bush reduced it to 35 percent. Under President Barack Obama the top rate returns to 39.6 percent.

Indeed, so-called targeted tax exemptions and deductions remain very popular in Washington. Targeted breaks—whether for the elderly, for education, for child care, for home buying, for investment income, or for a wide variety of particular industries—have strong, concentrated interest group support. In contrast, broad-based "across-the-board" tax reductions do not inspire the same kind of interest group enthusiasm or campaign contributions to Congress members. Indeed, cynics might argue that politicians deliberately enact high tax rates in order to inspire interest groups to seek special protections by making campaign contributions and otherwise providing for the comfort of lawmakers.

Lower Rates, Continued Breaks.   George W. Bush came into office vowing *not* to make the same mistake as his father, raising tax rates to fight deficit spending. On the contrary, Bush was strongly committed to lowering taxes, arguing that doing so would revive the economy. He believed that federal deficits were the result of slow economic growth; tax reductions might temporarily add to deficits but eventually the economic growth inspired by lower taxes would increase revenues and eliminate deficits.

In two separate tax reduction ("economic stimulus") packages in 2001 and 2003, Bush moved the Republican-controlled Congress to lower the top marginal rate from 39.6 to 35 percent. The Bush 2003 tax package also contained a variety of new targeted credits and special treatments:

> *Dividends.* Corporate stock dividends are to be taxed at a low 15 percent rather than at the same rate as earned income. Bush and the Republicans in Congress initially proposed eliminating all taxes on dividends. They argued that corporations already paid taxes on corporate profits, and inasmuch as dividends come out of profits, taxing them as personal income amounted to "double taxation." They also recognized that nearly one-half of all American families now own stock or mutual funds, and they hoped that this new tax break would be politically popular. The 15 percent tax rate on dividends is less than half of the top marginal rate of 35 percent on earned income.

> *"Marriage penalty."* For married couples the new law made the standard personal deduction twice that of a single person. This change corrected a flaw in the tax law that had long plagued married persons filing joint returns.

> *Child's tax credit.* The per child tax credit was raised to $1,000 (from $600). This was a politically popular change supported by many Democrats as well as Republicans.

> *Capital gains.* Finally, the Bush tax package chipped away again at the tax on capital gains— profits from the sale of investments held at least one year. The capital gains tax was reduced from 20 to 15 percent, a rate less than half of the top marginal rate on earned income of 35 percent.

The Bush tax package was approved in the Republican-controlled House and Senate on largely party line votes. Most Democrats opposed the package, arguing that it primarily benefited the rich, that it would do little to help the economy, and that it would add to the already growing annual federal deficits. Republicans argued that the package benefited all taxpayers, and inasmuch as the rich pay most of the taxes it is only fair that they should benefit from tax reductions.

Redistributing Income via the Tax Code

President Barack Obama campaigned on a promise to lower taxes on the middle class, which he defined as 95 percent of taxpayers. He also pledged to raise taxes on upper-income Americans, which he later defined as families earning $250,000 a year or more. This combination of changes in taxation make the Tax Code more progressive.

Middle-Class Tax "Cut."   A central item in the stimulus package of 2009 was "Making Work Pay"—tax payments of $400 to individuals with incomes under $75,000 and $800 to families with incomes under $150,000. These payments were made to anyone who paid the Social Security payroll tax, whether or not they paid income taxes. Indeed, President Obama argued that these payments would offset in part the Social Security payroll tax. Later Congress made these tax payments permanent.

Raising Taxes on the "Rich."   The Bush tax cuts had been scheduled to expire at the end of 2010. (Republicans in Congress had agreed to this expiration date, believing that these tax cuts would eventually be made permanent; however, when Democrats captured control of Congress in 2006, Republicans were unable to do so.) Republicans argued that the failure to make the tax cuts permanent would result in a "tax increase"; Democrats argued that expiration of the cuts would simply return tax rates to their previous levels.

President Obama urged Congress to allow the Bush tax cuts to expire, thus raising the top marginal tax rate from 35 to 39.6 percent. Obama also recommended a phaseout of deductions, including charitable contributions and mortgage payments, for families making over $250,000. Congress appeared less enthusiastic about the phaseout of these deductions.

The combination of these changes in the Tax Code—tax payments to families making less than $150,000 and an increase in the top marginal tax rate to 39.6 percent—has the effect of redistributing after-tax income among Americans. Critics charge that redistributing income is "socialism," that it penalizes work, initiative, and talent. Americans generally believe in tax progressivity—higher-income people can afford to be taxed larger percentages of their added income than lower-income people. But deliberate attempts by government to use the Tax Code to equalize income violates traditional American notions of fairness. It is also argued that income redistribution fosters class conflict; when a majority of Americans no longer have to pay taxes, the incentive exists to raise taxes to prohibitive levels.

The Capital Gains Controversy

A capital gain is the profit made from buying and selling any asset—real estate, bonds, stocks, etc. Preferential tax treatment for capital gains appeals to a wide variety of interests, especially Wall Street brokerage houses and investment firms in the real estate industry. And, of course, it significantly reduces the tax burden on high income taxpayers—those most likely to have income from the sale of these assets (see Figure 8–5).

Preferential Treatment for Capital Gains.   Why should income derived from investment be taxed at a lower rate than income made from work? A central reform in the Reagan Tax

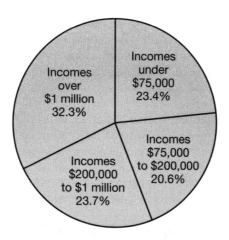

FIGURE 8–5 Who Benefits from Capital Gains? Capital gains, from buying and selling stocks, bonds, real estate, etc., go mainly to upper-income groups; these groups gain the most from reductions in capital gains taxes. SOURCE: Congressional Budget Office.

Reform Act of 1986 was the elimination of preferential treatment for income from capital gains. But when President George H. W. Bush and Congress agreed to increase the top marginal rate to 31 percent in 1990 they quietly made this increase applicable only to *earned* income; income from capital gains continued to be taxed at a top rate of 28 percent. This ploy succeeded in restoring preferential treatment to capital gains. The same tactic was employed again in 1993 when President Bill Clinton won congressional approval for an additional increase in the top marginal rate to 39.6 percent on earned income; the tax on income from capital gains remained at 28 percent.

Republicans continued to urge reductions in capital gains taxation. Following their congressional victory in the 1994 midterm elections, Republicans pushed through a 20 percent top rate on capital gains, about one half of the then-existing top rate on earned income. Again in 2003 Republicans in Congress, following President George W. Bush's lead, succeeded in lowering the capital gains tax rate again, this time to 15 percent.

Continuing Preferential Treatment.   President Barack Obama recommended an increase in the capital gains tax rate from 15 to 20 percent. This still leaves a significant tax preference for capital gains income. Capital gains are to be taxed at a rate roughly one-half of the top marginal rate on earned income.

Replacing the Income Tax?

Special interest politics make comprehensive tax reform an unlikely prospect for America. Nonetheless, serious proposals have been offered in recent years to reform the nation's tax laws.

The Flat Tax.   A "flat tax" has been recommended by economists over the years. It would eliminate all exemptions, exclusions, deductions, and special treatments, and replace the current progressive tax rates with a flat 19 percent tax on all forms of income.[6] This low rate would produce just as much revenue as the current complicated system, even excluding family incomes under $40,000. It would sweep away the nation's army of tax accountants and lawyers and lobbyists, and increase national productivity by relieving taxpayers of millions of hours of record keeping and tax preparation. A flat tax could be filed on a postcard form (see Figure 8–6). Removing progressive rates would create incentives to work, save, and invest in America. It would lead to more rapid economic growth and improve efficiency by directing investments to their most productive uses rather than to tax avoidance. It would eliminate current incentives to underreport income, overstate exemptions, and avoid and evade taxation. Finally, by including a generous personal and family allowance, the flat tax would be made fair.

However, many Americans support deductions for home mortgages and charitable contributions. This suggests a major political weakness in the flat tax idea: even if enacted,

Your first name and initial (if joint return, also give spouse's name and initial)	Last name	Your Social Security number
Home address (number and street, including apartment number or rural route)		Spouse's Social Security number
City, town, or post office, state, and ZIP code		Your occupation
		Spouse's occupation
1 Wages and salary		1
2 Pension and retirement benefits		2
3 Total compensation *(line 1 plus line 2)*		3
4 Personal allowance		
(a) 0 $16,500 for married filing jointly		4a
(b) 0 $9,500 for single		4b
(c) 0 $14,000 for single head of household		4c
5 Number of dependents, not including spouse		5
6 Personal allowances for dependents *(line 5 multiplied by $4,500)*		6
7 Total personal allowances *(line 4 plus line 6)*		7
8 Taxable compensation *(line 3 less line 7, if positive; otherwise zero)*		8
9 Tax *(19% of line 8)*		9
10 Tax withheld by employer		10
11 Tax due *(line 9 less line 10, if positive)*		11
12 Refund due *(line 10 less line 9, if positive)*		12

FIGURE 8–6   Armey-Shelby Flat Tax Postcard Return   Hypothetically, a simple "flat tax" with no exemptions, deductions, or special treatments (except for a personal allowance for dependents) would result in a one-page "postcard" tax return.

politicians would gradually erode the uniformity, fairness, and simplicity of a flat tax by introducing popular deductions. Lobbyists for special tax treatments would continue to pressure Congress, and, over time, deductions, exemptions, and exclusions would creep back into the tax laws.

Moreover, the flat tax violates the principle of progressivity described earlier. If it is true that added (marginal) income of higher-income recipients is less valuable to them than the income of lower-income recipients, then a flat tax appears unfair. A flat tax is also opposed by those who believe that government should undertake to reduce income differences among people.

The National Sales Tax. A national retail sales tax, similar to sales taxes currently levied by many states, could replace the federal income tax and "get the IRS completely out of our lives."[7] By taxing sales rather than income, it would penalize consumption rather than production. (A value-added tax or "VAT" is comparable in effect to a sales tax, but taxes are levied on each stage of a product's development rather than on retail sales.) By eliminating taxes on income, Americans would be encouraged to engage in all of the activities that produce income—working, investing, inventing, starting businesses, and so on. It would encourage people to save money by levying taxes on their *spending* rather than their savings. It would discourage people from borrowing to purchase goods. Increased savings and reduced borrowing would bring about lower interest rates, making it easier for people to buy homes and automobiles. A sales tax would also get at the underground economy; drug dealers who do not report their income would pay a sales tax on their purchases of expensive homes, cars, and jewelry. It could be made more progressive (less regressive) by reducing or eliminating sales taxes on food, rent, medical care, or other necessities. Finally, collection costs, both in dollar terms and in lost freedom and privacy, would be greatly reduced by administering a sales tax rather than the income tax.

But a national sales tax is likely to be regressive, even if food, rent, and other basic necessities are excluded. Low-income groups spend almost all of their income, saving very little. This means that virtually all of their income would be subject to sales taxation. In contrast, higher-income groups save larger shares of their income, thereby avoiding sales taxation on the proportion saved. A single national sales tax rate on all goods and services would violate the principle of progressivity. It would not satisfy liberals who believe that government tax policy should be shaped to serve social objectives, including the reduction of income inequality. And conservatives worry that such a tax might be adopted to supplement rather than replace an income tax. Finally, if different types of goods and services were taxed at different rates, interest groups would engage in a continuing frenzy of legislative activity seeking to lower the rate on their particular products.

Encouraging Savings. Various provisions in the tax laws currently encourage savings. Taxpayers can use Roth IRAs, traditional IRAs, 401k retirement plans, and 529 college plans, to exclude limited amounts of savings from current taxation. Despite these plans, the percentage of personal income that Americans devote to savings has declined dramatically in recent years. To encourage savings, the tax code could be changed to tax people only on the money they *spend*, that is, to exempt *all* savings from taxation. (This can be done incrementally by increasing amounts that could be contributed tax-free to IRA-type accounts.) Tax rates would rise on the money people spend. But again, excluding savings from taxation raises the issue of regressivity—wealthy taxpayers save a larger proportion of their income than less wealthy taxpayers.

Reining in the IRS.   The Internal Revenue Service (IRS) is the most intrusive of all government agencies, overseeing the finances of every taxpaying citizen and corporation in America. It maintains personal records on more than 130 million Americans and requires them to submit more than a billion forms each year. It may levy fines and penalties and collect taxes on its own initiative; in disputes with the IRS, the burden of proof falls on the taxpayer, not the agency. Americans pay over $30 billion for the services of tax accountants and preparers, and they waste some $200 billion in hours of record keeping and computing their taxes.

The Internal Revenue Code (the tax law) contains about 10,000 pages, and the IRS has promulgated over 100,000 additional pages of rules and regulations. The result is a quagmire of confusion over compliance. The IRS itself is unable to provide accurate, consistent answers to tax questions. The U.S. General Accountability Office cites an "appallingly high error rate" in IRS handling of individual taxpayer questions. Submitting the exact same information to multiple tax experts almost always results in different computations of taxes owed. In 1998, Congress passed a "Taxpayers' Bill of Rights" that made it illegal for the IRS to establish quota systems for tax collections for its agents, and sought to limit harassment of taxpayers and overly aggressive property seizures.

Simplifying the Tax Code.   The dream of a simplified tax code remains just that, a dream. Tax reformers have dreamed for decades of tax filing on a postcard or through a simple Web site. But despite the lure of simplification, tax laws will remain complex. Powerful interests have a stake in maintaining the thousands of exemptions, deductions, exclusions, and special treatments that have accumulated in the tax code over decades. Accountants and tax lawyers live off the complexity of the tax code.

And Congress members themselves benefit directly from tax complexity. Complexity keeps the special interests coming to Capitol Hill and seeking to gain or maintain narrow targeted tax provisions. They open their pocketbooks for campaign contributions to Congress members who assist them in their quests for preferential treatments. Members can boast to special interests in their states and district—farmers, ranchers, oil and gas producers, real estate investors, bankers, small business owners, and a host of others—that they have protected their existing tax breaks or have sponsored new ones. And every tax break necessitates greater complexity in the tax code. Even if some simplification could be achieved, as it was in 1986, interest group theory tells us that complexity would return over time.

SUMMARY

Modern pluralism praises the virtues of an interest group system in which public policy represents the equilibrium in the group struggle and the best approximation of the public interest. Yet it is clear that the interest group system puts broad segments of the American public at a disadvantage.

1. Tax reform to achieve fairness, simplicity, and economic growth is an elusive goal. The interest group system, designed to protect special privileges and treatments, especially in the tax code, frustrates efforts to achieve true tax reform.

2. Special interests can take advantage of the difficulties in defining fairness. Is fairness proportionality, with everyone paying the same percentage of income in taxes? Or is fairness progressivity, with the percentage of income paid in taxes increasing with increases in income?

3. Over half of the nation's total personal income escapes income taxation through exemptions, deductions, and special treatments.

4. The corporate income tax currently provides only 13 percent of total federal revenues. The individual income tax (47 percent) and Social Security payroll tax (35 percent) provide most of the federal government's revenue.

5. Supply-side economists are concerned about the impact of high marginal tax rates on economic behavior, including disincentives to work, save, and invest, and on inefficiencies created by tax avoidance activity. According to the Laffer curve, reducing high marginal tax rates increases government revenues by encouraging productivity.

6. The Tax Reform Act of 1986 was one of the most heavily lobbied pieces of legislation in the history of Congress. Powerful interests opposing significant tax reform included the nation's largest manufacturers, the real estate and housing industries, multinational corporations, timber, oil, and gas companies, labor unions, banks, the restaurant and entertainment industries, and even many state and local governments. Although these special interests won some important battles, on balance they lost the war over tax reform.

7. But the special interests never abandoned the battlefield. They won an important victory in 1990 when President George H.W. Bush agreed with the Democratic Congress to raise the top marginal rate on earned income to 31 percent, but to keep the tax on capital gains at 28 percent. President Clinton and Congress continued this preferential treatment for capital gains. Clinton's 1993 deficit reduction plan centered on major tax increases, including raising the top marginal income tax rate to 39.6 percent.

8. President George W. Bush inspired a Republican-controlled Congress to reduce taxes as an "economic stimulant." The top marginal rate was lowered from 39.6 to 35 percent, the marriage penalty was ended, and the child tax credit increased. Investors won a special low tax rate of 15 percent on dividends and capital gains. But the Bush tax cuts are scheduled to expire in 2010, promising new battles between the parties and among the special interests.

9. Major tax reform is regularly thwarted by special interest politics. Replacing the current federal income tax with a flat tax or a national sales tax is unlikely in the foreseeable future.

Notes

1. Robert A. Dahl, *A Preface to Democratic Theory* (Chicago: University of Chicago Press, 1956), p. 124.
2. *Pollock* v. *Farmer's Loan,* 158 U.S. 601 (1895).
3. "The Underground Economy," National Center for Policy Analysis, 1998.

4. Joseph A. Pechman, *Federal Tax Policy,* 5th ed. (Washington, DC: Brookings Institution, 1987), Chap. 5.
5. For accounts of the politics surrounding the Tax Reform Act of 1986, see David A. Stockman, *The Triumph of Politics* (New York: Harper & Row, 1986), and Jeffrey H. Birnbaum and Alan S. Murray, *Showdown at Gucci Gulch* (New York: Random House, 1987).
6. See Dick Armey, *The Flat Tax* (New York: Fawcett, 1996).
7. Congressman Bill Archer, "Tear the Income Tax Out by Its Roots," *Madison Review* 1 (Spring 1996), 17–21.

Bibliography

ARMEY, DICK. *The Flat Tax.* New York: Ballantine Books, 1996.

BIRNBAUM, JEFFREY H., and ALAN S. MURRAY. *Showdown at Gucci Gulch.* New York: Random House, 1987.

GALE, WILLIAM G. *Rethinking Estate and Gift Taxation.* Washington, DC: Brookings Institution, 2001.

HALL, ROBERT E., and ALVIN RABUSHKA. *The Flat Tax.* Stanford, CA: Hoover Institution Press, 1985.

HOWARD, CHRISTOPHER. *The Hidden Welfare State: Tax Expenditures and Social Policies.* Princeton, NJ: Princeton University Press, 1997.

ORSZAG, PETER R. *Taxing the Future.* Washington DC: Brookings Institution, 2006.

KENNEDY, DIANE. *Loopholes for the Rich.* New York: Warner Books, 2001.

STEURLE, C. EUGENE. *Contemporary U.S. Tax Policy.* Washington, DC: Urban Institute Press, 2004.

STOCKMAN, DAVID A. *The Triumph of Politics.* New York: Harper & Row, 1986.

Web Sites

TAX FOUNDATION. Information on taxes and tax burdens, including an explanation of "Tax Freedom Day." *www.taxfoundation.org*

NATIONAL TAXPAYERS UNION. Organization devoted to minimizing taxes, with information on tax policies and issues. *www.ntu.org*

NATIONAL CENTER FOR POLICY ANALYSIS. Conservative think tank, with information on tax and spending issues. *www.ncpa.org*

CITIZENS FOR TAX JUSTICE. Liberal organization favoring progressive income taxation and opposing tax cuts for the rich. *www.ctj.org*

AMERICANS FOR FAIR TAXATION. Organization opposed to federal income tax and supportive of national sales tax. *www.fairtax.org*

CITIZENS FOR AN ALTERNATIVE TAX SYSTEM. Organization devoted to eliminating Internal Revenue Service. *www.cats.org*

HOOVER INSTITUTION. Think tank devoted to issues of economic growth and free markets. *www.hoover.stanford.edu*

U.S. INTERNAL REVENUE SERVICE. Official site of IRS, with information on federal tax collections. *www.irs.gov*

U.S. DEPARTMENT OF TREASURY, OFFICE OF TAX POLICY. Presidential tax policy proposals; documents and studies of tax policy. *www.ustreas.gov/offices/tax-policy*

International Trade and Immigration

Elite–Mass Conflict

The elite model portrays public policy as a reflection of the interests and values of elites. The model does not necessarily require that elites and masses be locked in conflict—conflict in which elites inevitably prevail at the expense of masses. Rather, the model envisions elites determining the direction of public policy, with the masses largely apathetic and poorly informed and/or heavily influenced by elite views. The model also acknowledges that elites may choose to pursue "public regarding" policies that benefit masses. Nonetheless, critics of the elite model often demand proof of elite–mass conflict over public policy and the subsequent shaping of policy to reflect elite preferences over mass well-being. Indeed, critics often demand proof that elites knowingly pursue policies that benefit themselves while hurting a majority of Americans. While this is not a fair test of elite theory, there is ample evidence that on occasion elites do pursue narrow self-serving interests.

In describing immigration and international trade policy, we rely on the elite model. Arguably, U.S. policy, especially in international trade, serves the interests of the nation's largest multinational corporations at the expense of average American workers. We will argue that global trade policies have lowered average earnings *and* increased inequality in America. We will also argue that masses and elites have very different policy preferences regarding immigration.

The Global Economy

International trade—the buying and selling of goods and services between individuals and firms located in different countries—has expanded very rapidly in recent decades. Today, almost one-quarter of the *world's* total output is sold in a country other than the one in which it was produced. Today the United States exports about 12 percent of the value of its gross domestic product (GDP) and imports about 17 percent.[1] Exports and imports were

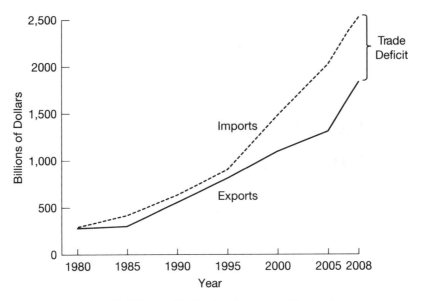

FIGURE 9–1   U.S. World Trade The "trade deficit"—the difference between what Americans import from abroad and what they export—has become wider over the years. SOURCE: Bureau of Economic Analysis, *www.bea.gov.*

only about 10 percent of GDP in 1980 (see Figure 9–1). Global competition heavily impacts the American economy.

Currently, America's leading trading partners are Canada, Mexico, China, Japan, Germany, Taiwan, Great Britain, South Korea, France, and Italy (see Figure 9–2). Note that some of these nations (Canada, Japan, Germany, for example) are advanced industrialized economies not unlike our own. But trade with developing countries (Mexico, China, Taiwan, South Korea, for example) is growing rapidly. And, as we shall see, it is trade with these nations that raises the most serious problems for America's labor force.

Years ago America's principal imports were oil and agricultural products not grown in the United States, for example, coffee. Today, however, our largest dollar-value imported products are automobiles, followed by office machinery, television sets, clothing, shoes, and toys. Our largest dollar-value exports are aircraft, computers, power generators, and scientific instruments. The United States also exports wheat and corn, which can be harvested with high-tech machinery; it imports fruits, vegetables, and other agricultural products that require harvest by hand.

Changing Elite Preferences for World Trade

Historically, American business supported high tariffs, but as the U.S. economy matured and the costs of global transportation and communication declined, America's largest corporations began to look beyond the nation's borders.

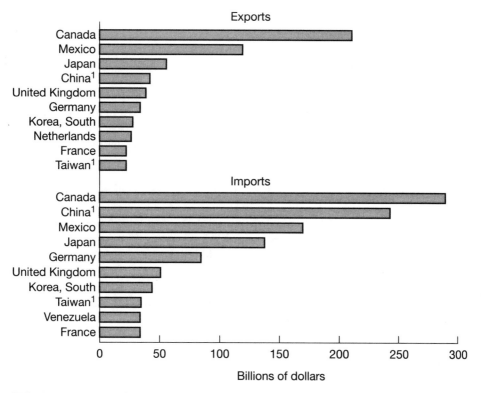

FIGURE 9–2 America's Leading Trading Partners Canada is our largest trading partner, but goods imported from China and Mexico are growing rapidly; the U.S. has a trade deficit with all of its major trading partners.
SOURCE: *Statistical Abstract of the United States, 2008,* p. 797.

Tariffs. Tariffs are simply taxes on foreign imports. Prior to World War II, U.S. tariffs on all imported goods averaged 30 to 50 percent in various decades. This suited U.S. manufacturers very well, eliminating most foreign competition from the U.S. market. U.S. firms enjoyed sheltered markets; they could raise prices to levels just below the price of imported goods with their high tariffs attached. Not only did this improve U.S. profit margins, but it also allowed U.S. firms that were less efficient than foreign producers to survive and prosper under the protection of tariffs. The pressure to cut wages and downsize work forces was less that it would be if U.S. firms had to face foreign corporations directly. American consumers, of course, paid higher prices than they otherwise would if foreign goods could enter the country without tariffs. But the U.S. steel, automobile, and electrical appliance industries grew powerful economically and politically.

Quotas. Trade quotas, in which foreign producers are prohibited from selling more than a specified number of units in the United States, also protect domestic manufacturers. To implement quotas, permits are granted by the U.S. State Department to favored firms in favored nations to sell specified amounts in the U.S. market. Note that quotas do not bring any revenue to the U.S. government as tariffs do; quotas allow the foreign firms exercising them to reap all of the benefits.

Protectionism.   Today supporters of open global markets refer to tariffs, quotas, and other barriers to free trade as "protectionism." Protectionism, they argue, is inefficient: it not only raises prices for American consumers, but it also directs American capital and labor away from their best uses into aging, inefficient industries. This reduces a nation's overall productivity and ultimately its standard of living. Moreover, they argue that protectionist policies initiated by the United States invite retaliatory actions by other nations. U.S. exporting industries may be adversely affected by the resulting trade wars.

Enter the Multinationals.   After World War II, the American economy was the most powerful in the world. American manufacturing corporations had few international competitors in most industries. Given their dominant position in world trade, American corporations sought to lower trade barriers around the world. America's top exporting corporations dictated U.S. trade policy. The Council on Foreign Relations (see Chapter 3) and America's largest corporations lobbied Congress for reductions in U.S. tariffs in order to encourage other nations to reduce their own tariffs. The result was a rapid decline in average U.S. tariffs (see Figure 9–3). In effect, the United States became an open market. Inasmuch as U.S. firms largely dominated their domestic markets in the 1950s and 1960s (steel, automobiles,

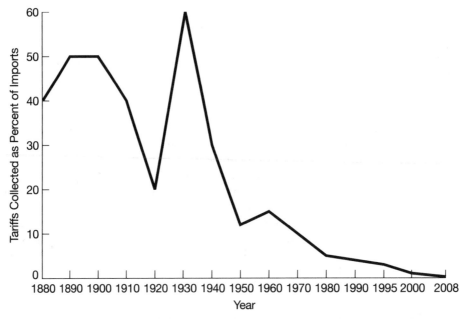

FIGURE 9–3   U.S. Tariff Policy over Time The U.S. followed a "protectionist" policy with high tariff duties until the late 1940s when it gradually reduced tariffs, creating a virtually free market in the U.S. for foreign goods.
SOURCE: U.S. Department of Commerce.

aircraft, computers, drugs, electronics, appliances, agriculture, and so forth), they had little fear of foreign competition. On the contrary, they expanded their own international sales, becoming multinational corporations.

Prior to 1980 the United States incurred a *positive* trade balance, that is, exporting more goods and services than it imported. But since 1980 the United States has incurred balance of trade *deficits* every year. Nonetheless, today U.S. multinational corporations receive substantial revenues from their exports. Moreover, most have manufacturing facilities as well as sales and distribution staffs worldwide. They stand to gain much more from the globalization of trade than they might lose from domestic competition from foreign firms.

Elite Gains from Trade

The classic argument for free trade is based on the principle of "comparative advantage." If nations devote more of their resources to the production of those goods that they produce most efficiently, and trade for those goods that other nations produce more efficiently, then all trading nations benefit.

The "Comparative Advantage" Argument. Trade between two nations can improve efficiency even when one nation is much better at producing aircraft and somewhat better at producing clothing than its trading partner. Comparative advantage focuses on what each nation does *relatively* better than the other. Trade shifts resources (investment capital, jobs, technology, raw materials, etc.) in each nation toward what each does best. (Imagine a lawyer who is also a faster typist than her secretary. Even though the lawyer is better than her secretary at both law and typing, it makes more sense for her to concentrate on law and leave the typing to her secretary. Their combined output of lawyering *and* typing will be greater than if each did some of the other's work.) Over time our nation will shift its resources to its aircraft industry and will import clothing from the other nation, and vice versa. Each nation will benefit more from trading than from trying to produce both airplanes and clothing.

Benefits from Trade. The efficiencies achieved by trading are said to directly benefit consumers by making available cheaper imported goods. Export industries also benefit when world markets are opened to their products. American exporters benefit directly from sales abroad and they also benefit indirectly when foreign firms are allowed to sell in the American market. This is because sales of foreign goods in America provide foreigners with U.S. dollars which they can use to purchase the goods of America's exporting industries.

It is also argued that the pressure of competition from foreign-made goods in the American marketplace forces our domestic industries to become more efficient—cutting their costs and improving the quality of their own goods. Trade also quickens the flow of ideas and technology, allowing nations to learn from each other. Finally, trade expands the menu of goods and services available to trading countries. American consumers gain access to everything from exotic foods and foreign-language movies to Porsches, BMWs, and Jaguars.

The World Trade Organization. A multinational General Agreement on Tariffs and Trade (GATT) organization was created following World War II for the purpose of regulating international trade. Over the years GATT has been dominated by banking, business, and commercial interests in Western nations seeking multilateral tariff reductions and the relaxation of quotas. They have been especially successful over the years in opening the giant U.S. market to foreign goods. Indeed, average U.S. tariffs fell from more than 30 percent in 1947 to less than 1 percent today.

Through a series of GATT negotiations, known as rounds, a number of rules and regulations were developed that today run to some 30,000 pages. The first rounds dealt with tariffs and rules for trading in goods; later rounds dealt with services, including banking, insurance, telecommunications, hotels and transportation, and finally with the protection of intellectual property—copyrights, patents, and trademarks.

The "Uruguay Round" in 1993 resulted in the creation of the World Trade Organization (WTO). The WTO was given power to adjudicate trading disputes among countries and monitor and enforce the trade agreements under GATT. Countries bring disputes to the WTO if they think their rights under the agreements are being infringed. Judgments by specially appointed independent experts are based on their interpretations of the agreements.

A "Doha Round" of WTO multinational trade negotiations (2001–2008) failed to produce a workable agreement on trade in agricultural and food products.

The WTO describes itself as a "democratic" organization that seeks to "improve the welfare of peoples of member countries" through trade liberalization. But the WTO's highest decision-making body is its Ministerial Conference, which includes member nations' trade representatives.

Anti-globalization groups—a mix of labor, environmental, and human rights groups—have mounted demonstrations at various WTO meetings. They charge that the WTO has failed to enforce labor rights or correct labor abuses, that it has failed to protect the environment, and that it disadvantages poorer, less-developed countries.

International Monetary Fund and World Bank. The IMF's purpose is to facilitate international trade, allowing nations to borrow to stabilize their balance of trade payments. However, when economically weak nations incur chronic balance of trade deficits and perhaps face deferral or default on international debts, the IMF may condition its loans on changes in a nation's economic policies. It may require a reduction in a nation's government deficits by reduced public spending and/or higher taxes, or require a devaluation of its currency, making its exports cheaper and imports more expensive. It may also require the adoption of noninflationary monetary policies. Currently, the IMF as well as the World Bank are actively involved in assisting Russia and other states of the former Soviet Union to convert to free market economies.

The World Bank makes long-term loans, mostly to developing nations, to assist in economic development. It works closely with the IMF in investigating the economic conditions of nations applying for loans and generally imposes IMF requirements on these nations as conditions for loans.

NAFTA. In 1993 the United States, Canada, and Mexico signed the North American Free Trade Agreement. Objections by labor unions in the United States (and 1992 and 1996 Reform Party presidential candidate Ross Perot) were drowned out in a torrent of support by the American corporate community, Democrats and Republicans in Congress, President Bill Clinton, and former President George H. W. Bush. NAFTA envisions the removal of tariffs on virtually all products by all three nations over a period of 10 to 15 years. It also allows banking, insurance, and other financial services to cross these borders (see Table 9–1). NAFTA has succeeded in increasing trade between all three nations. The jobs lost by the United States to Mexico have been in lower-paying industries, while the jobs gained have been in higher-paying industries.

Free Trade Area of the Americas.   Currently the United States and the nations of North, Central, and South America are engaged in negotiations designed to create a free trade area

---

TABLE 9–1   Major Provisions of NAFTA NAFTA is the model of U.S.-backed free trade agreements.

Market Access

1. Within fifteen years after its implementation in 1994, all tariffs will be eliminated on North American products traded among Canada, Mexico, and the United States.
2. Within five years after its implementation, 65 percent of all U.S. exports of industrial goods to Mexico will enter tariff-free.
3. Mexico, immediately upon implementation of the treaty, eliminated tariffs on nearly 50 percent of all industrial goods imported from the United States.
4. Government procurement is to be opened up over ten years, with firms of the three countries able to bid on government contracts.
5. Tariffs are to be removed on car imports over a period of ten years. Mexico's import quota on cars is also to be lifted during the same period.
6. Most tariffs between the United States and Mexico on agricultural products were eliminated immediately after implementation of the agreement in 1994.

Investment

1. NAFTA gives U.S. companies the right to establish firms in Mexico and Canada or acquire existing firms.
2. Investors have the right to repatriate profits and capital; the right to fair compensation in the event of expropriation; and the right to international arbitration in disputes between investors and government that involve monetary damage.
3. NAFTA broadens investments to cover such areas as banking, real estate, legal services, consulting, publishing, and tourism.
4. Certain types of investments are restricted. Mexico prohibits foreign investment in petroleum and railroads; Canada prohibits investment in its cultural media; and the United States excludes investments in aviation transport, maritime, and telecommunication.

Intellectual Property Rights

1. NAFTA requires each country to provide for the enforcement of the rights of authors, artists, and inventors against infringement and piracy.
2. It ensures protection for North American producers of computer programs, sound recordings, motion pictures, encrypted satellite signals, and other creations.
3. It locks in the availability of patent protection for most technologies in Mexico, allowing U.S. firms to patent a broad range of inventions in Mexico.

SOURCE: Robert Langran and Martin Schnitzer, *Government, Business, and the American Economy* (Upper Saddle River, NJ: Prentice Hall, 2001), p. 285.

throughout most of the Western Hemisphere. The Free Trade Area of the Americas (FTAA) is to resemble NAFTA. Barriers to trade and investment are to be progressively eliminated. The rules of the WTO will constitute a base for the FTAA agreements.

FTAA was supposed to be completed by 2005. But the agreement met with serious opposition with the election of an anti-American government in Venezuela, as well as opposition from other South American countries. Opponents argue that FTAA will drive down wages, erode labor union protections, destroy the environment, and increase poverty and inequality. These conditions will result from multinational corporations choosing to move their operations to countries with the lowest wages, fewest regulations, weakest unions, and lowest environmental standards—"a race to the bottom."

Anti-Dumping Policy.   Dumping—the sale of foreign goods in the U.S. market at prices below those charged in the producing nation—presents a special trade problem. Dumping is often undertaken by foreign firms to introduce new products in the U.S. market; once Americans have accepted the product, prices go up. This pattern has been regularly followed by Japanese automobile manufacturers. Dumping is also undertaken in order to destroy U.S. firms by underselling their products and forcing them out of business. Once foreign producers have driven out U.S. manufacturers, they raise their own prices. Dumping provides only temporary advantages to American consumers.

Dumping is officially illegal. The Trade Agreements Act of 1979 provides that special anti-dumping tariffs may be imposed when it is proven that a product is being sold in the United States at a price lower than that in the domestic market of a foreign producing nation. But it is a difficult and lengthy process for U.S. domestic firms to bring formal complaints to the U.S. government and obtain relief.

Trade Deficits.   For many years the United States has imported a higher dollar value of goods than it has exported. The difference is referred to as a trade deficit (the area in Figure 9–1 between the exports and imports lines). The trade deficit is made up by the transfer of American dollars, government bonds, corporate securities, and so on, to foreign firms. U.S. banks as well as the U.S. Treasury actually benefit from the deficit because it means that foreigners are accepting U.S. paper—currency, bonds, and securities—in exchange for their products. This makes it easier for the U.S. government to fund its own huge debt—selling bonds to foreign investors. U.S. interest payments on this part of the national debt flow out of the country.

Retreat from Free Trade?   The Obama Administration voices its general support for free trade and open markets. Yet its support for trade agreements appears to be contingent upon the inclusion of worker protections and environmental safeguards in future trade agreements with foreign countries. Obama advisors recommend a "major review of trade policies" to ensure that trade agreements "include enforceable labor and environmental standards ... and a new focus on ensuring that trade rules help combat climate change and do not impede the essential global energy transformation."[2] They also warn against unfair trade practices and currency manipulation, especially with regard to China. These concerns promise to complicate future trade negotiations with other countries.

"Fast Track" Authority.   Like his predecessors, President Obama seeks "fast track" authority from Congress in negotiating trade agreements—a commitment from Congress to vote on negotiated trade agreements without amendments. It is argued that U.S. trade negotiators will not be taken seriously by other nations at the bargaining table unless Congress agrees to "fast track" agreements.

Mass Losses from Trade

The global economy has produced growth and profit for America's largest corporations and amply rewarded the nation's highest skilled workers. Indeed, global trade has *raised aggregate income* for the nation. But at the same time, it has *worsened inequality* in America. Elite gains have been accompanied by mass losses.

Stagnating Worker Earnings.   Average hourly and weekly earnings of American workers are no higher today than 30 years ago. In real dollars (controlling for the effects of inflation), average hourly earnings declined from $8.55 in 1973 to $7.40 in 1995 (see Figure 9–4). The economic expansion of the 1990s partially restored real wages. But wages today are only now approaching levels of the 1970s.

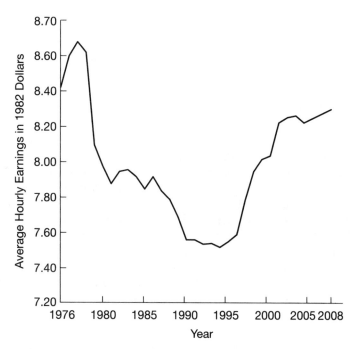

FIGURE 9–4   Real Earnings of American Workers Real (inflation-adjusted) hourly wages for American workers declined in the 1980s and 1990s, and have yet to return to the levels of the 1970s.
SOURCE: Bureau of Labor Statistics, *www.bls.gov.*

Is the huge supply of unskilled labor in the global economy holding down the wages of American workers? Increased trade, especially with less developed economies such as Mexico, China, and India, with their huge numbers of low-wage workers, creates competition for American workers. It is difficult to raise the wage levels of American jobs, especially in labor intensive industries, in the face of such competition. American corporations may initially respond by increasing their investment in capital and technology, making American workers more productive and hence capable of maintaining their high wages. But over time developing nations are acquiring more capital and technology themselves. And U.S. corporations can move their manufacturing plants to low-wage countries, especially to northern Mexico where the transportation costs of moving finished products back to the U.S. market are minimal.

Worsening Inequality. U.S. export industries have thrived on international trade expansion, adding jobs to the American economy and raising the incomes of their executives and their most highly skilled workers. But the combination of effects of international trade on the American economy—*lower* wages for less skilled workers and *higher* wages for executives and highly skilled workers—worsens inequality in the nation. Inequality can worsen even though the aggregate income of the nation rises.

Inequality in America is worsening. The percentage of the nation's total family income received by the poorest quintile (the lowest 20 percent of income earners) declined from 4.3 percent to 3.4 percent between 1975 and 2005. Meanwhile the percentage of total family income of the highest income earners increased from 43.6 percent of total income to 50.1 percent. Figure 9–5 shows the percentage of losses and gains since 1980 of families in each income class. Lowest income families have lost nearly 25 percent of their share of income over these years, while the highest income families have gained 16 percent of their share. The top 5 percent of families have gained 43 percent.

Policy Options. Both Democratic and Republican presidents over the past half-century have supported expanded world trade. The U.S. market is the largest in the world and the most open to foreign-made goods. Our policy has been to maintain an open American market while encouraging other nations to do the same. Indeed, the United States has led international efforts to liberalize world trade and investment and to eliminate foreign market barriers to American exports. The efforts include support for the WTO multinational trade agreement; NAFTA, the Canada, Mexico, and U.S. agreement; and a number of bilateral agreements with Japan and other Asian trading partners.

The elite response to declining real wages and worsening inequality is to stress the need for American workers to improve their productivity through better education and increased training. The "solution" found in the *Economic Report of the President* reads as follows:

> Ultimately, the only lasting solution to the increase in wage inequality that results from increased trade is the same as that for wage inequality arising from any other source: better education and increased training, to allow low-income workers to take advantage of the technological changes that raise productivity.[3]

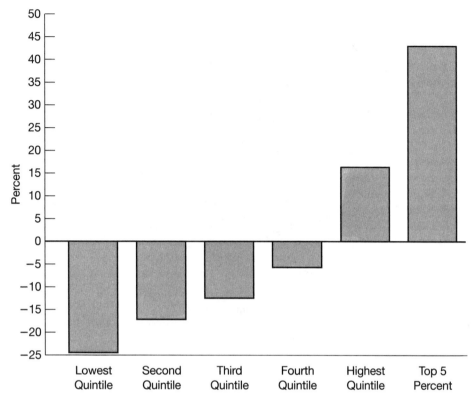

FIGURE 9–5 Worsening Inequality Change in Percent Distribution of Family Income by Quintile, 1980–2004. Inequality in income has risen in the U.S.; the highest income groups have increased their share of total family income, while lower income groups lost shares.
SOURCE: *Statistical Abstract of the United States, 2007,* p. 450; *www.bls.gov.*

Elite–Mass Differences over Immigration

The United States accepts more immigrants than all other nations of the world combined. Officially about 1 million legal immigrants come to the United States each year. These are people who are granted permanent residence or "green cards." Unofficially, perhaps as many as 4 million legal and illegal immigrants cross the nation's borders each year.[4] Some cross the Mexican or Canadian borders surreptitiously or with false documentation. Others simply overstay their tourist or student visas. Immigration and Customs Enforcement (ICE) acknowledges about 33 million admissions to the United States each year. Most of these admissions are for tourists, businesspeople, and students. The government does *not* track visitors, nor does it systematically proceed against individuals who overstay their visas. Estimates of the number of illegal immigrants living in the United States range up to 15 million.

Most immigrants come to the United States for economic opportunity. Currently, the vast majority come from the less developed nations of Asia and Latin America (see Figure 9–6).

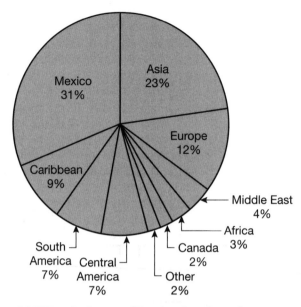

FIGURE 9–6   Sources of Immigration   Currently most
immigrants are coming to the United States from Mexico and
other Latin American countries as well as from Asia.
SOURCE: Data from the Center for Immigration Studies from the
US-Bureau of the Census, *Current Population Survey*, 2007.

Most personify the traits we typically think of as American: ambition, perseverance, initiative,
and a willingness to work hard. As immigrants have always done, they frequently take dirty,
low-paying, thankless jobs that other Americans shun. When they open their own businesses,
they often do so in blighted, crime-ridden neighborhoods long since abandoned by other
entrepreneurs.

The Immigration Surge.   The nation's foreign-born or immigrant population (legal and
illegal) reached a record high of over 38 million people in 2008 (see Figure 9–7). Immigrants
now account for over 12 percent of the population. Earlier in the twentieth century, at the
peak of the last great surge in immigration, there were fewer immigrants, although they
accounted for almost 15 percent of the population.

The recession beginning in 2008 appears to have reduced the flow of immigration
somewhat. A weak job market discourages immigration. It has also increased the numbers of
immigrants returning to their home countries.

Cultural Conflict.   The politics of immigration center on both cultural and economic
issues. Elites, notably the nation's business and corporate leaders, tend to view immigration
in economic terms, principally as an increase in the supply of low-wage workers in the
United States. Most middle-class Americans view immigration in cultural terms, principally
its impact on the ethnic composition of their communities.

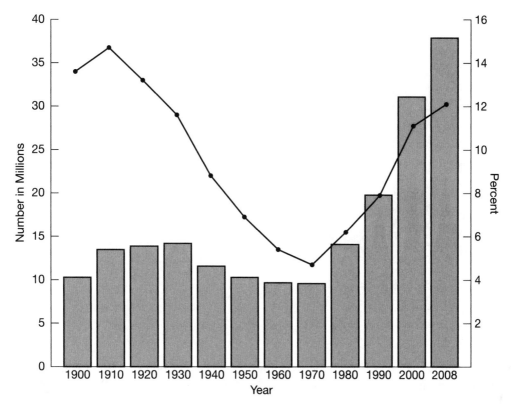

FIGURE 9–7 **Immigrants in the U.S., Number and Percent 1900–2008** Immigration has surged
since 2000; currently 12.6 percent of the U.S. population is foreign born, almost as high a population of
Americans as at the beginning of the century.
* Bars represent *numbers* of immigrants in millions; the line represents the immigrant *percentage* of the U.S. population.
SOURCE: Center for Immigration Studies, *www.cis.org*.

While most Americans are themselves the descendants of immigrants (Native Americans
constitute about 1 percent of the population), most believe that today's immigrants are different from earlier waves. Population projections based on current immigration and fertility
(birth) rates suggest that the ethnic character of the nation will shift dramatically over time (see
Figure 9–8).

America has always been an ethnically pluralist society, but all were expected to adopt
American political culture—including individual liberty, economic freedom, political equality, and equality of opportunity—and to learn American history and traditions, as well as the
English language. The nation's motto is "E Pluribus Unum" (from many, one), but opponents of large-scale immigration fear that it currently represents a threat to cultural and
political unity.[5] There were always Italian, Irish, Polish, Chinese, and other ethnic neighborhoods in big cities. But the children of immigrants, if not immigrants themselves, quickly
became "Americanized." In contrast, today policymakers are divided over whether to protect
and preserve language and cultural differences, for example through bilingual education,

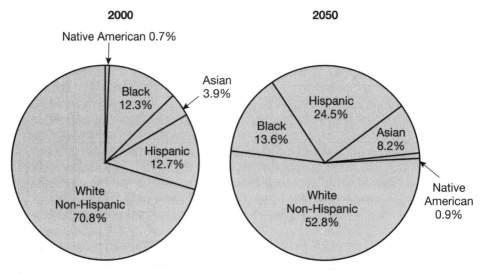

FIGURE 9–8 Projected Ethnic Changes in the United States over Time As a result of both immigration and differences in birthrates, the ethnic composition of the United States will change dramatically by 2050.
SOURCE: U.S. Census Bureau, 2008.

bilingual language ballots, and "language minority" voting districts (all currently required by amendments and interpretations of the Civil Rights Act of 1964 and the Voting Rights Act of 1965).

Elite Support of Immigration.   Powerful industry groups that benefit from the availability of legal and illegal immigrants have led the fight in Washington to keep America's doors open. They have fought not only to expand legal immigration but also to weaken enforcement of laws against illegal immigration.

   Current U.S. immigration policy—the admission of more than 1 million *legal* immigrants per year and weak enforcement of laws against *illegal* immigration—is largely driven by industry groups seeking to lower their labor costs. Agriculture, construction, restaurants, clothing, and hospitals, for example, all lobby heavily in Washington to weaken immigration laws and their enforcement. Large agribusinesses benefit from a heavy flow of unskilled immigrants who harvest their crops at very low wages. Clothing, textile, and shoe companies that have not already moved their manufacturing overseas are anxious to hire low-paid immigrants for their assembly lines. Even high-tech companies have found that they can recruit skilled computer analysts and data processors from English-speaking developing nations (India, for example) for wages well below those paid to American citizens with similar skills. These business interests frequently operate behind the scenes in Washington, allowing pro-immigration ethnic and religious groups to capture media attention. And indeed, large numbers of Americans identify with the aspirations of people striving to come to the United States, whether legally or illegally. Many Americans still have family and relatives living abroad who may wish to immigrate. Hispanic groups have been especially concerned about immigration enforcement efforts that may lead to discrimination against all Hispanic Americans. Foreign governments, especially Mexico, have also protested U.S. enforcement policies.

National Immigration Policy

America is a nation of immigrants, from the first "boat people," the Pilgrims, to the later Cuban "balseros" (rafters). Americans are proud of their immigrant heritage and the freedom and opportunity the nation has extended to generations of "huddled masses yearning to be free"—the words emblazoned upon the Statue of Liberty in New York's harbor. Today about 38 million people, or over 12 percent, of the U.S. population is foreign born.

Legal Immigration.   Immigration policy is a responsibility of the national government. It was not until 1882 that Congress passed the first legislation restricting entry into the United States of persons alleged to be "undesirable" as well as virtually all Asians. Following the end of World War I, Congress passed a comprehensive Immigration Act of 1921 that established maximum numbers of new immigrants each year and set a quota for each foreign country at 3 percent (later reduced to 2 percent) of the number of that nation's foreign born living in the United States in 1890. These restrictions reflected anti-immigration feelings that were generally directed at the large wave of southern and eastern European, Catholic, and Jewish immigrants (Poland, Russia, Hungary, Italy, Greece) that had entered the United States prior to World War I. It was not until the Immigration Act of 1965 that national-origin quotas were abolished, replaced by preference categories for relatives and family members and pro-fessional and skilled persons.

Immigration "Reform."   Immigration "reform" was the announced goal of Congress in the Immigration Reform and Control Act of 1986, also known as the Simpson-Mazzoli Act. It sought to control immigration by placing principal responsibility on employers; it set fines for knowingly hiring an illegal alien. However, it allowed employers to accept many different forms of easily forged documentation and subjected them to penalties for discriminating against legal foreign-born residents. To win political support, the act granted *amnesty* to ille-gal aliens who had lived in the United States since 1982. Predictably, the act failed to reduce the flow of either legal or illegal immigrants.

Current Immigration Policy.   Today, roughly 1 million people per year are admitted *legally* to the United States as "lawful permanent residents" (persons who have relatives who are U.S. citizens or lawful permanent residents, or who have needed job skills); or as "refugees," or "asylees" (persons with "a well-founded fear of persecution" in their country of origin). In addition, more than 33 million people are awarded visas each year to enter the United States for study, pleasure, or business. Federal law recognizes the following categories of noncitizens admitted into the United States:

- *Legal immigrants* (also "lawful permanent residents" or "permanent resident aliens"). These immigrants are admitted to the United States under a ceiling of 675,000 per year, with some admitted on the basis of job skills but most coming as family members of persons legally residing in the United States. Legal immigrants may work in the United States and apply for citizenship after five years of continuous residence.

- *Refugees and asylees.* These are persons admitted to the United States because of "a well-founded fear of persecution because of race, religion, nationality, political opinion, or membership in a social group." (Refugees are persons not yet in the United States; asylees are persons who have already arrived and apply for refugee protection.) They may work in the United States and are eligible for all federal assistance programs.

- *Parolees* (or persons enjoying "temporary protected status"). These are persons admitted to the United States for humanitarian or medical reasons or whose countries are faced with natural or man-made disasters.

- *Legalized aliens* (also called "amnesty aliens"). These formerly illegal aliens were given legal status (amnesty) under the Immigration Reform and Control Act of 1986. To qualify, they must show some evidence of having resided in the United States since 1982. They may work in the United States and are eligible for all federal assistance programs after five years.

- *Nonimmigrants* (also "nonresident legal aliens"). Over 33 million people are awarded visas to enter the United States for pleasure and business. Time limits are placed on these visas, usually by stamping a passport. Additionally, students, temporary workers and trainees, transient aliens, and foreign officials are eligible for temporary visas.

Illegal Immigration.   The United States is a free and prosperous society with more than 5,000 miles of borders (2,000 with Mexico) and hundreds of international air- and seaports. In theory, a sovereign nation should be able to maintain secure borders, but in practice the United States has been unwilling and unable to do so. Estimates of illegal immigration vary wildly, from the official U.S. government estimate of 400,000 per year (about 45 percent of the legal immigration), to unofficial estimates ranging up to 4 million per year. The government estimates that about 4 million illegal immigrants currently reside in the United States; unofficial estimates range up to 15 million or more. Many illegal immigrants slip across U.S. borders or enter ports with false documentation, while many more overstay tourist or student visas.

As a free society, the United States is not prepared to undertake massive roundups and summary deportations of millions of illegal residents. The Fifth and Fourteenth Amendments to the U.S. Constitution require that every *person* (not just *citizen*) be afforded "due process of law." ICE may turn back persons at the border or even hold them in detention camps. The Coast Guard may intercept boats at sea and return persons to their country of origin.[6] Aliens have no constitutional right to come to the United States. However, *once in the United States, whether legally or illegally, every person is entitled to due process of law and equal protection of the laws.* Once immigrants set foot on U.S. soil, they are entitled to a fair hearing prior to any government attempt to deport them. Aliens are entitled to apply for asylum and present evidence at a hearing of their "well-founded fear of persecution" if returned to their country. Localized experiments in border enforcement have indicated that illegal immigration can be reduced by half or more with significant increases in Border Patrol personnel and technology.

Immigration and Federalism. Although the federal government has exclusive power over immigration policy, its decisions have very significant effects on states and communities—on their governmental budgets, on the use of their public services, and even on their social character. Immigration is by no means uniform across the states. On the contrary, legal and illegal immigration are concentrated in a relatively few states. California, Hawaii, New York, Florida, and Texas have the highest proportions of legal immigrants among their populations. And these states, together with Arizona, New Mexico, Colorado, Illinois, and New Jersey, probably have the highest numbers of illegal immigrants as well. Moreover, the populations of particular cities—such as Los Angeles, Miami, El Paso, and San Antonio—may be one-third to one-half foreign born.

The U.S. Supreme Court has mandated that state and local governments may not exclude either legal or *illegal* immigrants from public education, and—perhaps by implication—from any other benefits or services available to citizens.[7] Thus, federal immigration policy heavily impacts state and local budgets, especially in states with disproportionate numbers of immigrants. (Although family "sponsors" may have pledged support of immigrants, and immigrants who become a "public charge" may be deported legally, these provisions of the law are almost never enforced.) Indeed, some states have tried unsuccessfully to sue the federal government to recover the costs of providing services to immigrants.

Welfare Benefits for Immigrants. California's Proposition 187 in 1994 set off renewed national debate over immigration. Placed on the ballot by citizen initiative, Proposition 187 denied public education, nonemergency health care, and social service benefits to illegal aliens in that state. Following a highly spirited and well-publicized contest over the initiative, California voters approved it by a solid 59 to 41 percent. However, the Fourteenth Amendment declares that no state shall "deny to any *person* within its jurisdiction the equal protection of the laws." Federal courts quickly overturned most of the provisions of Proposition 187.

The Fence. The United States has attempted to stem the tide of illegal immigration by building a 700-mile security fence along portions of its border with Mexico. U.S.–Mexican border extends approximately 2,000 miles, so a 700-miles fence leaves open most of the border area. The fence, however, is directed at sectors of frequent crossing. The fence is controversial: Americans are equally divided over it (favor 49 percent, oppose 48 percent).[8]

Comprehensive Immigration Reform. Conflict in Washington over immigration policy is intense. To date, conflicting interests have prevented any effective action to halt illegal immigration, or to determine the status of millions of illegal immigrants already living in the United States, or to decide how many immigrants should be admitted each year and what the criteria for their admission should be. Among the diverse interests with a stake in immigration policy are employers seeking to keep immigration as open as possible, millions of illegal immigrants seeking a legal path to citizenship, and citizens seeking border security and opposed to "amnesty" for illegal aliens.

"Comprehensive" immigration reform implies compromises among these interests. In 2007 Congress considered a comprehensive 789-page bill, cosponsored by Senators Edward

M. Kennedy and John McCain, that included the following major provisions: strengthening border enforcement, including funding of 700 miles of fencing; granting legal status to millions of undocumented immigrants currently living in the country; providing a path to citizenship that includs criminal background checks, paying fines and fees, and acquiring English proficiency; establishing a temporary (two-year) guest worker program; shifting the criteria for legal immigration from family-based preferences to a greater emphasis on skills and education. But opponents of one or another of these various provisions, both Democrats and Republicans, united to defeat the bill in the U.S. Senate.

It is argued that *no* program of immigration reform can be successful without first securing America's borders. Yet doing so involves some controversial measures. The U.S. Border Patrol must be increased in numbers and given improved technology. The current policy of "catch and release"—releasing illegal immigrants into the general population to await a court hearing—must be replaced by expanding the capacity to detain them until their hearings are held and expediting their judicial proceedings—a policy of "catch and return." Illegal immigrants convicted of a crime must be deported immediately after serving their prison sentences. Finally, cities that offer "sanctuary"—cities that prohibit police from informing U.S. immigration officials of the arrest of illegal immigrants—must be dissuaded from doing so.

Beyond these border enforcement efforts, additional measures could be put into place to deter businesses from hiring illegal immigrants. Social Security numbers could be checked through a national database. Social Security cards must be made more difficult to counterfeit. States could deny drivers' licenses to illegal immigrants and make licenses more difficult to counterfeit.

But immigration reform must also deal with the millions of undocumented immigrants already in the country. And it must recognize the fact that immigrant labor plays an important role in our economy. Some legal channel must be devised for persons currently living illegally in United States to win permanent residency and perhaps even the opportunity for citizenship after living and working in the country for a specified number of years. (The word *amnesty* is now politically unacceptable; some other term must be used to describe how current illegals can gain legitimate status.) And some sort of highly controlled temporary worker program must be devised to provide the labor that the nation seems to need. But again, these reforms cannot be put in place until the nation's borders are controlled.

Mass Opinion.   Americans are more concerned that steps be taken to halt the flow of immigrants slipping in at the border than they are about the government developing a plan for dealing with the illegal immigrants already living here. Americans also believe that illegal immigration can be reduced by instituting tough penalties for businesses that hire illegal immigrants. But Americans also believe that undocumented immigrants currently living here should be given a path to citizenship (63 percent) as opposed to the more drastic action of deporting them (18 percent). Among those who support a path to citizenship, the most common requirements mentioned are: have a job (89 percent), learn to speak English (84 percent), pass a health screening test (83 percent), pay all taxes owed on past income earned in the United States (81 percent), and have lived in United States for at least five years (67 percent).[9]

SUMMARY

The elite model portrays public policy as the preferences of elites. While the model does not assert that these preferences necessarily conflict with the welfare of the masses, it does imply that the elite preferences will prevail in public policy even when opposed by the masses in a democratic society.

1. The principal beneficiaries of the emergence of a global economy and the expansion of U.S. trade have been America's large multinational corporations.

2. Historically, American business supported high tariffs in order to disadvantage foreign competition in the U.S. market. But after World War II, American industry gained worldwide dominance and changed their policy preference. The United States led the worldwide effort to establish a global marketplace.

3. The principal instruments used to open world markets to U.S. goods were the General Agreement on Tariffs and Trade (GATT) later becoming the World Trade Organization (WTO), the International Monetary Fund (IMF), and the World Bank.

4. In 1993, elite support for the North American Free Trade Agreement (NAFTA) envisioning the removal of tariffs on virtually all goods traded between the United States, Canada, and Mexico, prevailed over the opposition of American labor unions.

5. The benefits of international trade are unevenly distributed between elites and masses in America. Average real hourly wages of American workers have stagnated since 1970.

6. Global trade appears to have worsened inequality in the United States in recent years. Today, greater differences exist between well-educated and less-educated workers and high-skilled and low-skilled workers than 20 years ago. America's less-educated, low-skilled workers must now compete against low-wage workers in less developed countries around the world.

7. The United States accepts more immigrants than all other nations of the world combined. More than 1 million legal immigrants enter the United States each year, as well as 3 to 4 million illegal immigrants.

8. Immigration today is higher than at any period in United States history. Most immigration today is from the less developed nations of Asia and Central and South America.

9. Powerful industry groups that benefit from the availability of low-wage workers lobby in Washington to maintain high levels of legal immigration and weaken efforts to reduce illegal immigration.

10. Immigration impacts the states differently, with California, Hawaii, New York, Florida, and Texas reporting the largest numbers of legal immigrants.

Notes

1. *Statistical Abstract of the United States, 2007,* p. 434, 805.
2. Mark Green and Michelle Jolin, eds. *Change for America* (New York: Basic Books, 2009), p. 148.

3. *Economic Report of the President 1995,* p. 232.
4. Center for Immigration Studies, 2008, *www.cis.org.*
5. See Peter Brimelow, *Alien Nation* (New York: Random House, 1995); Samuel P. Huntington, *Who Are We? The Challenge to America's National Identity* (NewYork: Simon & Schuster, 2004).
6. *Sale* v. *Haitian Centers Council,* 125 L. Ed. 2d 128 (1993).
7. *Plyler* v. *Doe,* 457 U.S. 202 (1982).
8. AP Poll, March 3–5, 2008, *www.pollingreport.com.*
9. Gallup opinion poll, April 7–9, 2006, *www.pollingreport.com.*

Bibliography

ALBA, RICHARD, and VICTOR NEE. *Remaking the American Mainstream: Assimilation and Contemporary Immigration.* Cambridge, MA: Harvard University Press, 2003.

BRIMELOW, PETER. *Alien Nation.* New York: Random House, 1995.

BURTLESS, GARY. *Globaphobia: Confronting Fears About Open Trade.* Washington, DC: Brookings Institution, 1998.

DREZNER, DANIEL W. *U.S. Trade Policy.* New York: Council on Foreign Relations Press, 2005.

GILPIN, ROBERT, and JEAN M. GILPIN. *Global Political Economy.* Princeton, NJ: Princeton University Press, 2001.

HUNTINGTON, SAMUEL P. *Who Are We? The Challenges to America's National Identity.* New York: Simon & Schuster, 2004.

HUSTED, STEVEN and MICHAEL MELVIN. *International Economics,* 7th ed. New York: Addison-Wesley, 2007.

STIGLITZ, JOSEPH E. *Globalization and Its Discontents.* New York: W. W. Norton, 2002.

TONELSON, ALAN. *The Race to the Bottom: Why a Worldwide Worker Surplus and Uncontrolled Free Trade Are Sinking American Living Standards.* New York: Westview Press, 2002.

Web Sites

U.S. DEPARTMENT OF STATE. Official Web site of the State Department, with policies, press releases, speeches, news, etc. *www.state.gov*

U.S. TRADE AND DEVELOPMENT AGENCY. Official Web site of U.S. agency responsible for promoting international trade, with policies, press releases, etc. *www.tda.gov*

UNITED NATIONS. Official Web site of the U.N., with links to all U.N. agencies, member nations, etc. *www.un.org*

WORLD TRADE ORGANIZATION. Official Web site of the WTO, with information on membership, trade agreements, and statistics on trade. *www.wto.org*

WORLD BANK. Official Web site of the World Bank, with information on policies, loans to various nations, etc. *www.worldbank.org*

INTERNATIONAL MONETARY FUND. The official Web site of the IMF, with information on currency transactions, national deficits, etc. *www.imf.org*

ORGANIZATION FOR ECONOMIC COOPERATION DEVELOPMENT. Official Web site of the OECD, with statistics on national GDP, imports and exports, etc. *www.oecdwash.org*

CENTER FOR IMMIGRATION STUDIES. Organization advocating control of U.S. borders, with policy studies, data on immigration, etc. *www.cis.org*

COUNCIL ON FOREIGN RELATIONS. Leading think tank supporting expansion of world trade. *www.foreignrelations.org*

OFFICE OF THE UNITED STATES TRADE REPRESENTATIVE. List of U.S trade agreements; current issues in trade policy. *www.ustr.gov*

U.S. CITIZENSHIP AND IMMIGRATION SERVICES (ICE). Formerly the Immigration and Naturalization Service (INS); carries information on obtaining visas to the U.S., applying for asylum and refugee status, and applying for naturalization. *www.uscis.gov*

10

Energy and Environmental Policy

Externalities and Interests

Public Choice and the Environment

All human activity produces waste. We can no more "stop polluting" than we can halt our natural body functions. As soon as we come to understand that we cannot outlaw pollution and come to see pollution as a cost of human activity, we can begin to devise creative environmental policies.

Environmental Externalities. Public choice theory views pollution as a "problem" when it is not a cost to its producer—that is, when producers can ignore the costs of their pollution and shift them onto others or society in general. An "externality" occurs when one individual, firm, or government undertakes an activity that imposes unwanted costs on others. A manufacturing firm or local government that discharges waste into a river shifts its own costs to individuals, firms, or local governments downstream, who must forgo using the river for recreation and water supply or else undertake the costs of cleaning it up themselves. A coal-burning electricity-generating plant that discharges waste into the air shifts its costs to others, who must endure irritating smog. By shifting these costs to others, polluting firms lower their production costs, which allows them to lower their prices to customers and/or increase their own profits. Polluting governments have lower costs of disposing their community's waste, which allows them to lower taxes for their own citizens. As long as these costs of production can be shifted to others, polluting individuals, firms, and governments have no incentive to minimize waste or develop alternative techniques of production.

Costs of Regulation. Environmental policies are costly. These costs are often ignored when environmental regulations are considered. Direct spending by business and government for pollution abatement and control has grown rapidly over recent years. Yet governments themselves—federal, state, and local governments combined—pay less than one-quarter of the environmental bill. Businesses and consumers pay over three-quarters of the environmental bill. Governments can shift the costs of their policies onto private individuals and

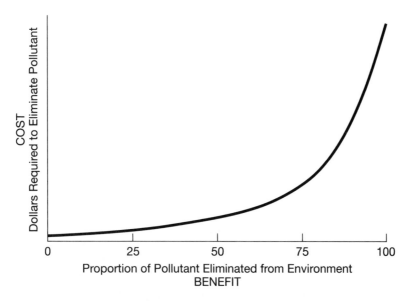

FIGURE 10–1   Cost Benefit Ratio in Environmental Protection Costs rise exponentially as society tries to eliminate the last measure of pollution.

firms by enacting *regulations* requiring pollution control. A government's own budget is unaffected by these regulations, but the costs are paid by society.

Benefits in Relation to Costs.   Public choice theory requires that environmental policies be evaluated in terms of their net benefits to society; that is, the costs of environmental policies should not exceed their benefits to society. It is much less costly to reduce the first 50 to 75 percent of any environmental pollutant or hazard than to eliminate all (100 percent) of it (see Figure 10–1). As any pollutant or hazard is reduced, the cost of further reductions rises and the net benefits to society of additional reductions decline. As the limit of zero pollution or zero environmental risk is approached, additional benefits are minuscule but additional costs are astronomical. Ignoring these economic realities simply wastes the resources of society, lowers our standard of living, and in the long run impairs our ability to deal effectively with any societal problem, including environmental protection.

Environmental Externalities

The air and water in the United States are far cleaner today than in previous decades. This is true despite growth in population and even greater growth in waste products. Nonetheless, genuine concern for environmental externalities centers on the disposal of solid waste (especially hazardous wastes), water pollution, and air pollution.

Solid Waste Disposal.   Every American produces about 4.5 pounds of solid waste per day (see Table 10–1). The annual load of waste dumped on the environment includes 82 million

TABLE 10–1   Growth in Solid Wastes   Each day the average American produces more than four pounds of waste; about 30 percent of waste can be recycled.

	1960	1970	1980	1990	2000	2005
Gross waste (millions of tons)	87.50	120.50	151.2	205.2	231.9	245.7
Waste per person per day (lb)	2.65	3.22	3.7	4.5	4.5	4.5
Percent recycled	NA	NA	9.6	16.4	30.1	32.1

SOURCE: *Statistical Abstract of the United States, 2008*, p. 229.

tons of paper, 48 billion cans, 26 billion bottles and jars, 2 billion disposable razors, 16 billion disposable diapers, and 4 million automobiles and trucks. The nation spends billions of dollars annually on hauling all this away from homes and businesses.

There are three methods of disposing of solid wastes—landfills, incineration, and recycling. Modern landfills have nearly everywhere replaced town dumps. Landfills are usually lined with clay so that potentially toxic wastes do not seep into the water system. Even so, hazardous wastes are separated from those that are not hazardous and handled separately. Given a reasonable site, there is nothing especially wrong with a landfill that contains no hazardous wastes. However, landfill sites need to meet strict standards and people do not want landfills near their residences. These conditions combine to make it difficult to develop new landfills.

Contrary to popular rhetoric, there is no "landfill crisis"; the nation is not "running out of land." However, both government agencies and private waste disposal firms are frequently stymied by the powerful, organized NIMBYs ("not in my back yard"). Landfill sites are plentiful but local opposition is always strong. Timid politicians cannot confront the NIMBYs, so they end up overusing old landfills or trying to ship their garbage elsewhere.

Another alternative is to burn the garbage. Modern incinerators are special plants, usually equipped with machinery to separate the garbage into different types, with scrubbers to reduce air pollution from the burning and often with electrical generators powered by heat from the garbage fire. Garbage is put through a shredder to promote even burning; metal is separated out by magnets, and the garbage is passed over screens that separate it further. At this point about half the garbage has been removed and hauled to a landfill. The remaining garbage is shredded still further into what is called fluff, or perhaps it is compressed into pellets or briquets. This material is then burned, usually at another site and perhaps together with coal, to produce electricity. The ash is handled by the public utility as it would handle any other ash, which often means selling it to towns to use on roads. One problem with this method is the substances emitted from the chimney of the incinerator or the utility that is burning the garbage. Another problem: because the garbage separated during the screening phase still has to be disposed of, the need for landfill sites is only reduced, not eliminated.

A third method of reducing the amount of solid waste is recycling. Recycling is the conversion of wastes into useful products. Most of the time, waste cannot be recycled into the same product it was originally but rather into some other form. Newspapers are recycled into cardboard, insulation, animal bedding, and cat litter, but in an exception to the general rule, some are recycled into newsprint.

Overall, about 30 percent of all solid waste in the United States is recovered for reuse.[1] This is a notable improvement over the mere 10 percent that was recycled 30 years ago. Some materials lend themselves fairly well to recycling (e.g., aluminum cans, paper products), but other materials do not (e.g., plastics). At present there is more material available for recycling than plants can effectively use; millions of tons of recycled newspapers are either piled up as excess inventory in paper mills or dumped or burned. Nonetheless, recycling does have an effect in reducing the load on incinerators and landfills.

Hazardous Waste.   Hazardous (toxic) wastes are those that pose a significant threat to public health or the environment because of their "quantity, concentration, or physical, chemical, or infectious characteristics."[2] The Resource Conservation and Recovery Act of 1976 gave the Environmental Protection Agency (EPA) the authority to determine which substances are toxic and the EPA has so classified several hundred substances. Releases of more than a specified amount must be reported to the National Response Center. Substances are considered hazardous if they easily catch fire, are corrosive, or react easily with other chemicals. Many substances are declared toxic by the EPA because massive daily doses administered to laboratory animals cause cancers to develop. Toxic chemical releases must also be reported annually. These reports show that toxic releases have been reduced by more than half over the last decade.[3] Thus far, the United States has avoided any toxic releases comparable to the accident in Bhopal, India, in 1984, which killed almost 3,000 people.

Nuclear wastes create special problems. These are the wastes from nuclear fission reactors and nuclear weapons plants. Some have been in existence for 50 years. Because the waste is radioactive and some of it stays radioactive for thousands of years, it has proven very difficult to dispose of. Current plans to store some wastes in deep, stable, underground sites have run into local opposition. Most nuclear waste in the United States is stored at the site where it was generated, pending some long-term plan for handling it.

Hazardous wastes from old sites also constitute an environmental problem. These wastes need to be moved to more secure landfills. Otherwise, they can affect the health of people living near the waste site, often by seeping into the water supply. The EPA is committed to cleaning up such sites under the Superfund laws of 1980 and 1986. As a first step, it developed a National Priority List of sites that needs attention, based on a hazard ranking system. The EPA listed about 1,300 hazardous waste sites. Cleanups have been done by the EPA itself, other federal state or local government agencies, or the company or party responsible for the contamination.

Water Pollution.   Debris and sludge, organic wastes, and chemical effluents are the three major types of water pollutants. These pollutants come from (1) domestic sewage, (2) industrial waste, (3) agricultural runoff of fertilizers and pesticides, and (4) "natural" processes, including silt deposits and sedimentation, which may be increased by nearby construction. A common standard for measuring water pollution is biochemical oxygen demand (BOD), which identifies the amount of oxygen consumed by wastes. This measure, however, does not consider chemical substances that may be toxic to humans or fish. It is estimated that domestic sewage accounts for 30 percent of BOD, and industrial and agricultural wastes for 70 percent.

Primary sewage treatment—which uses screens and settling chambers, where filth falls out of the water as sludge—is fairly common. Secondary sewage treatment is designed to remove organic wastes, usually by trickling water through a bed of rocks 3 to 10 feet deep, where bacteria consume the organic matter. Remaining germs are killed by chlorination. Tertiary sewage treatment uses mechanical and chemical filtration processes to remove almost all contaminants from water. Some cities dump sewage sludge into the ocean after only primary treatment or no treatment at all. Although federal law prohibits dumping raw sewage into the ocean, it has proven difficult to secure compliance from coastal cities. Federal water pollution abatement goals call for the establishment of secondary treatment in all American communities. In most industrial plants, tertiary treatment ultimately will be required to deal with the flow of chemical pollutants. But tertiary treatment is expensive; it costs two or three times as much to build and operate a tertiary sewage treatment plant as it does a secondary plant.

Phosphates are major water pollutants that overstimulate plant life in water, which in turn kills fish. Phosphates run off from fertilized farm land. Farming is the major source of water pollution in the United States.

Waterfronts and seashores are natural resources. The growing numbers of waterfront homes, amusement centers, marinas, and pleasure boats are altering the environment of the nation's coastal areas. Marshes and estuaries at the water's edge are essential to the production of seafood and shellfish, yet they are steadily shrinking with the growth of residential-commercial-industrial development. Oil spills are unsightly. Although pollution is much greater in Europe than in America, America's coastal areas still require protection. Federal law makes petroleum companies liable for the cleanup costs of oil spills and outlaws flushing of raw sewage from boat toilets. The *EXXON Valdez* oil spill in Alaska in 1989 focused attention on the environmental risks of transporting billions of barrels of foreign and domestic oil each year in the United States.

The federal government has provided financial assistance to states and cities to build sewage treatment plants ever since the 1930s. Efforts to establish national standards for water quality began in the 1960s and culminated in the Water Pollution Control Act of 1972. This "Clean Water Act" set "national goals" for elimination of all discharges of *all* pollutants into navigable waters; it required industries and municipalities to install "the best available technology"; it gave the EPA authority to initiate legal actions against pollution caused by firms and governments; it increased federal funds available to municipalities for the construction of sewage treatment plants.

The EPA is authorized by the Safe Drinking Water Act of 1974 to set minimum standards for water quality throughout the nation. The EPA does not set a zero standard for fecal bacteria or phosphate or other pollutants; to do so would commit the nation to astronomical cost projections for "clean" water and would never be possible to attain anyway. The EPA has considerable power to raise or lower standards, and hence to increase or reduce costs.

Water quality in the United States has improved significantly over the years (see Table 10–2). The problem, of course, is that removing *all* pollutants is neither cost-effective nor possible.

Air Pollution. The air we breathe is about one-fifth oxygen and a little less than four-fifths nitrogen, with traces of other gases, water vapor, and the waste products we put into it. Air pollution is caused, first of all, by the gasoline-powered internal combustion engines of cars, trucks, and buses. The largest industrial polluters are petroleum refineries, smelters (aluminum, copper, lead, and zinc), and iron foundries. Electrical power plants also contribute

TABLE 10–2   Improvements in Water Quality Water quality has improved dramatically over the last three decades.

Pollutant (Standard)	1975	1980	1985	1990	1995	2000
Fecal coliform bacteria (above 200 cells per 100 mL)	36	31	28	26	28	26
Dissolved oxygen (allow 5 mg per liter)	5	5	3	2	1	1
Phosphorus (above 1 mg per liter)	5	4	3	3	4	4
Lead (above 50 micrograms per liter)	NA	5	0	0	0	0

NOTE: Figures are violations rates—the proportion of measures that violate the EPA standards.

SOURCE: Environmental Protection Agency, *National Water Quality Inventory,* 2002.

to total air pollutants by burning coal or oil for electric power. Heating is also a major source of pollution; homes, apartments, and offices use coal, gas, and oil for heat. Another source of pollution is the incineration of garbage, trash, metal, glass, and other refuse by both governments and industries.

   Air pollutants fall into two major types: particles and gases. The particles include ashes, soot, and lead, the unburnable additive in gasoline. Often the brilliant red sunsets we admire are caused by large particles in the air. Less obvious but more damaging are the gases: (1) sulfur dioxide, which in combination with moisture can form sulfuric acid; (2) hydrocarbons—any combination of hydrogen and carbon; (3) nitrogen oxide, which can combine with hydrocarbons and the sun's ultraviolet rays to form smog; and (4) carbon monoxide, which is produced when gasoline is burned.

   The EPA sets limits on fine particulate matter (soot, dust) in the air. But many large cities, for example New York, Los Angeles, Chicago, and Washington, DC, exceed these limits. A recent federally financed study reported that "the risk of dying from lung cancer as well as heart disease in the most polluted cities was comparable to the risk associated with nonsmokers being exposed to second-hand smoke over a long period of time."[4]

   The air we breathe is significantly cleaner today than thirty years ago (see Figure 10–2). Federal clean air legislation (described later in this chapter) is generally credited with causing

	Millions of Tons Per Year							
	1980	1985	1990	1995	2000	2005	2006	Percent Change 1980–2006
Carbon Monoxide (CO)	178	170	144	120	102	91	88	−50
Lead	0.074	0.023	0.005	0.004	0.002	0.003	0.002	−97
Nitrogen Oxides (NO$_x$)	27	26	25	25	22	19	18	−33
Volatile Organic Compounds (VOC)	30	27	23	22	17	15	15	−50
Particulate Matter (PM$_{10}$)	6.2	3.6	3.2	3.1	2.3	2.6	2.6	−58
Sulfur Dioxide (SO$_2$)	26	23	23	19	16	15	14	−47
Totals	267	249	218	189	159	142	137	−49

SOURCE: *www.epa.gov/air/airtrends.*

FIGURE 10–2   Improvements in Air Quality Contrary to much popular opinion, the air is much cleaner today than in prior years.

these improvements. The Environmental Protection Agency claims that the Clean Air Act of 1970 and subsequent amendments to it have resulted in an overall reduction in principal pollutants since 1970 of 57 percent. This improvement in air quality has come about despite increases in the gross domestic product (207 percent), vehicle miles traveled (179 percent), energy consumption (49 percent), and population growth (47 percent). (See Figure 10–3.)

Interest Group Effects

Americans live longer and healthier lives today than at any time in their country's history. Life expectancy at birth is now 78.5 years (75.6 for males; 81.4 for females), up eight full years since 1970. Cancer deaths are up slightly but not because of environmental hazards. The primary causes of premature death are what they have always been: smoking, diets rich in fat and lean in fiber, lack of exercise, and alcohol abuse. Yet public opinion generally perceives the environment as increasingly contaminated and dangerous, and this perception drives public policy.

Interest Group Economics.   Organized environmental interests must recruit memberships and contributions (see Table 10–3). They must justify their activities by publicizing and dramatizing environmental threats. When Greenpeace boats disrupt a U.S. Navy exercise, they are attracting the publicity required for a successful direct-mail fund-raising drive. The mass media, especially the television networks, welcome stories that capture and hold audiences' attention. Stories are chosen for their emotional impact, and threats to personal life and safety satisfy the need for drama in the news. Statistics that indicate negligible risks or scientific testimony that minimizes threats or presents ambiguous findings do not make good news stories. Politicians wish to be perceived as acting aggressively to protect citizens from any risk, however minor. Politicians want to be seen as "clean" defenders of the pristine wilderness. And government bureaucrats understand that the greater the public fear of environmental threat, the easier it is to justify expanded powers and budgets.

Shaping Public Opinion.   Interest group activity and media coverage of environmental threats have succeeded in convincing most Americans that environmental pollution is getting worse. Evidence that the nation's air and water are measurably cleaner today than in the 1970s is ignored. Opinion polls report that 57 percent of Americans agree with this statement: "Protecting the environment is so important that requirements and standards cannot be too high and continued environmental improvements must be made *regardless of cost.*"[5] If

TABLE 10–3   Leading Environmental Organizations Environmental politics in Washington are heavily influenced by environmental interest groups.

National Wildlife Federation	Natural Resources Defense Council
Greenpeace	Environmental Defense Fund
National Audubon Society	Defenders of Wildlife
Sierra Club	Friends of the Earth
Wilderness Society	Union of Concerned Scientists

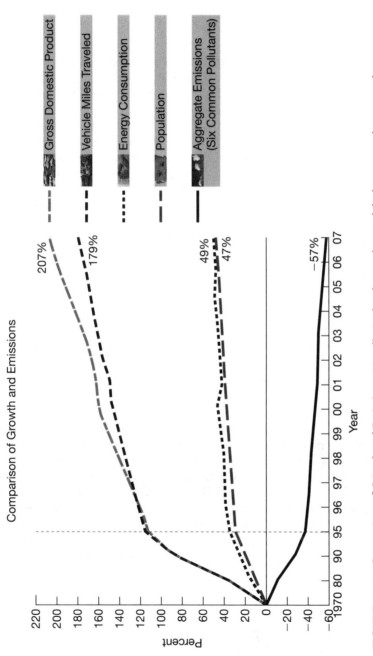

FIGURE 10–3 Comparison of Growth and Emissions Air pollution has decreased even while the economy has grown, the population has grown, more miles are traveled, and more energy is consumed.
SORUCE: Environmental Protection Agency, "Six Common Air Pollutants," *www.epa.gov.*

taken seriously, such an attitude would prevent either scientific or economic considerations from guiding policy. Environmentalism threatens to become a moral crusade that dismisses science and economics as irrelevant or even wicked. In such a climate of opinion, moral absolutism replaces rational public policy.

Interest Group Politics.   Everyone is opposed to pollution. It is difficult publicly to oppose clean air or clean water laws—who wants to stand up for dirt? Thus the environmentalists begin with a psychological and political advantage: they are "clean" and their opponents are "dirty." The news media, Congress, and executive agencies can be moved to support environmental protection measures with little consideration of their costs—in job loss, price increases, unmet consumer demands, increased dependence on foreign sources of energy. Industry—notably the electric power companies, oil and gas companies, chemical companies, automakers, and coal companies—must fight a rearguard action, continually seeking delays, amendments, and adjustments in federal standards. They must endeavor to point out the increased costs to society of unreasonably high standards in environmental protection legislation. But industry is suspect; the environmentalists can charge that industry opposition to environmental protection is motivated by greed for higher profits. And the charge is partially true, although most of the cost of antipollution efforts is passed on to the consumer in the form of higher prices.

The environmentalists are generally upper-middle-class or upper-class individuals whose income and wealth are secure. Their aesthetic preferences for a no-growth, clean, unpolluted environment take precedence over jobs and income, which new industries can produce. Workers and small business people whose jobs or income depend on energy production, oil refining, forestry, mining, smelting, or manufacturing are unlikely to be ardent environmentalists. But there is a psychological impulse in all of us to preserve scenic beauty, protect wildlife, and conserve natural resources. It is easy to perceive industry and technology as the villain, and "man against technology" has a humanistic appeal.

NIMBY Power.   Environmental groups have powerful allies in the nation's NIMBYs—local residents who feel inconvenienced or threatened by specific projects. Even people who otherwise recognize the general need for new commercial or industrial developments, highways, airports, power plants, pipelines, or waste disposal sites, nonetheless voice the protest "not in my back yard," earning them the NIMBY label. Although they may constitute only a small group in a community, they become very active participants in policymaking—meeting, organizing, petitioning, parading, and demonstrating. NIMBYs are frequently the most powerful interests opposing specific developmental projects and are found nearly everywhere. They frequently take up environmental interests, using environmental arguments to protect their own property investments.

Radical Environmentalism.   At the extreme fringe of the environmental movement one finds strong opposition to economic development, to scientific advancement, and even to humanity. According to the Club of Rome (a radical environmental organization), "The real enemy, then, is humanity itself."[6] The "green" movement is international, with well-organized interest groups and even political parties in Western European nations. Its program to "Save the Planet" includes the deindustrialization of Western nations; reduction of the human population; elimination of all uses of fossil fuels, including automobiles; the elimination of nuclear power; an end to cattle raising, logging, land clearance, and so on; and the transfer of existing wealth from the industrialized nations to underdeveloped countries.[7]

Global Warming/Climate Change

Gloomy predictions about catastrophic warming of the Earth's surface have been issued by the media and environmental interest groups in support of massive new regulatory efforts. Global warming is theorized to be a result of emissions of carbon dioxide and other gases that trap the sun's heat in the atmosphere. As carbon dioxide increases in the atmosphere as a result of increased human activity, more heat is trapped. Deforestation contributes to increased carbon dioxide by removing trees, which absorb carbon dioxide and produce oxygen. The dire predictions of greenhouse effects include droughts and crop destruction, melting of the polar ice caps, and ocean flooding.

Climate Change.   It is true that the Earth's atmosphere creates a greenhouse effect; if not, temperatures on the Earth's surface would be like those on the moon—unbearably cold (–270°F) at night and unbearably hot (+212°F) during the day. The greenhouse gases, including carbon dioxide, moderate the Earth's surface temperature. And it is true that carbon dioxide is increasing in the atmosphere, an increase of about 25 percent since the beginning of the Industrial Revolution in 1850, and 13 percent since 1970 (see Figure 10–4).

It is also true that the Earth has been warming over the past century, since the beginning of the Industrial Revolution. Global average temperatures have risen about 1.4°F. Average sea levels have risen and the northern hemispheric snow cover has diminished. Various computer simulations of the effect of increased dioxides in the atmosphere have predicted future increases in temperature ranging from 1° (not significant) to 8° (significant if it occurs rapidly).[8]

Global climate change is caused by a variety of factors: slight changes in the Earth's orbit, causing ice ages over millennia (the last ice age, when average temperatures were 9° cooler, ended 15,000 years ago.); solar activity including sun flares (a "little" ice age between 1500–1850 is estimated to have cooled the Earth by about 2°F); and volcanic activity, which tends to block sunlight and contribute to short-term cooling (a volcano in Indonesia in 1815 lowered global temperatures by 5°F and historical accounts in New England described 1816 as "the year without a summer").

Is human activity contributing to global warming? Fossil fuels emit carbon dioxide (CO_2) into the atmosphere. Since the beginning of the Industrial Revolution atmospheric carbon dioxide concentrations have increased by about 25 percent. This increase corresponds to an increase in average global temperature (see Figure 10–4). This correspondence does not prove causation, but it underlies the fundamental argument of global warming theory.

International Panel on Climate Change.   A UN-sponsored International Panel on Climate Change (IPCC) reported with "very high confidence" that human activity since the Industrial Revolution has contributed to increases in atmospheric concentrations of carbon dioxide, methane, and nitrous oxide.[9] The IPCC does not do its own research but rather

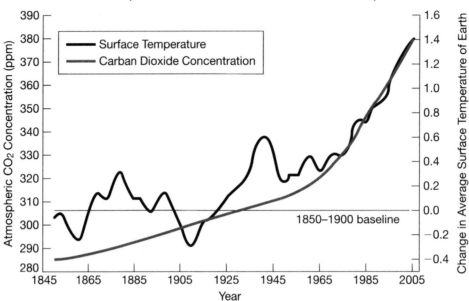

FIGURE 10–4 **Trends in Atmospheric Carbon Dioxide and Global Surface Temperature**
Recent increases in atmospheric concentrations of carbon dioxide (CO_2) have corresponded
with increases in average surface temperatures on Earth. The sharpest rises in CO_2 and
temperatures have occurred since 1970.
SOURCE: Pew Center on Global Climate Change, *www.pewclimate.org.*

assesses scientific reports from other bodies. Its *Fourth Assessment Report: Climate Change 2007* is widely cited by environmentalists: "Most of the observed increase in global average temperatures since the mid-20th century is very likely due to the observed increase in anthropogenic [caused by human activity] greenhouse gas concentrations." The popularity of the report was reflected in the awarding of a Nobel Prize to the IPCC and to its principal publicist, Al Gore. Gore's movie, *An Inconvenient Truth* dramatizes the effects of global warming.

Greenhouse Gases. Carbon dioxide (CO_2) contributes about three-quarters of total greenhouse gas emissions; methane and nitrous oxide are also classified as greenhouse gases. The principal source of CO_2 emissions are power plants (30 percent), industrial processes (21 percent), transportation (19 percent), residential (13 percent), land use (9 percent), and other fossil fuel uses (8 percent). Any serious effort to reduce overall greenhouse gas emissions must deal with electric utilities, waste disposal facilities, natural gas producers, petroleum refineries, smelters, and motor vehicle emissions, among other sources.

Recently China surpassed the United States as the largest single national contributor of atmospheric pollutants. Both nations together currently produce about 50 percent of the world's output of greenhouse gases. But China, together with India and Indonesia, contributes to the largest annual *increases* in greenhouse emissions. Whatever policies the

United States adopts to limit its own emissions, the Earth's atmosphere will continue to be polluted by other nations. Environmentalists argue that the United States must act first in order to set an example for the world.

The Rio Treaty. Environmentalists argue that "drastic action" is required now to avert "catastrophic" global warming. Former Vice President Al Gore is a leading exponent of the view that governments cannot afford to wait until the scientific evidence demonstrates conclusively that human activity contributes to global warming. Rather, governments must immediately impose a system of "global environmental regulations" in order to "save the planet."[10] Inasmuch as Third World nations are just beginning to industrialize, they pose the greatest threat of new sources of global pollution. But the industrialized nations are responsible for "undermining the Earth's life support system" (the United States is usually singled out as the primary culprit), and therefore they must compensate poorer nations in exchange for their pledge not to add to global pollution. The international environmental agenda includes massive transfers of wealth from industrialized nations to less developed countries.

The Rio Treaty incorporates these ideas. It is a product of the "Earth Summit," officially the United Nations Conference on Environment and Development held in Rio de Janeiro, Brazil, in 1992. It was attended by 178 nations as well as hundreds of environmental interest groups, officially sanctioned as "nongovernmental organizations" or "NGOs." The conference produced a Global Climate Change Treaty, signed by President George H.W. Bush, but not ratified by the U.S. Senate, which declares, among other things, that "lack of scientific certainty shall not be used as a reason for postponing cost-effective measures to prevent environmental degradation"! The statement is, of course, a contradiction: without scientific information, it is impossible to determine cost-effectiveness.[12]

Copenhagen Conference. Governments and non-governmental organizations have been meeting in Copenhagen Denmark with the goal of developing a legally binding treaty to reduce world-wide carbon emissions. The negotiations are sponsored by the UN Framework Convention on Climate Change. The United States is among the 192 countries participating in the Conference; the United States favors the development of nonbinding pledges regarding carbon emissions, rather than legally binding emissions cuts. Less developed nations have demanded compensation from the developed nations in exchange for limiting growth in their emissions. At present the prospects for agreement appear dim.

The Kyoto Protocol. In 1997, a far-reaching amendment to the Rio Treaty, known as the Kyoto Protocol, was negotiated under the United Nations Convention on Global Climate Change. Whereas the Rio Treaty set voluntary national goals for reducing greenhouse gases, the Kyoto agreement required the United States and other developed nations to reduce their emissions below 1990 levels sometime between 2008 and 2012. Reductions by developed nations were designed to offset expected increases in emissions by developing nations. The reduction mandated for the United States was 7 percent below its 1990 level—a reduction that would entail approximately a 40 percent reduction in fossil fuel use. The Clinton administration supported the Kyoto Protocol, but declined to submit it for ratification to the U.S. Senate in view of its likely defeat in that body. The Bush administration opposed the Protocol.

Energy Policy

Environmental policy and energy policy are closely intertwined. Currently America gets most of its energy from fossil fuels—oil, natural gas, and coal (see Figure 10–5). These sources produce pollutants, including carbon dioxide emissions that appear related to global climate change. Despite heavy subsidization by the federal government, "renewable" energy sources—hydroelectric, geothermal, solar, wind, and biomass—account for only about 7 percent of the energy used in the United States.

Energy Consumption.   Electric power plants account for the greatest share of energy produced in the United States (see Figure 10–5). About half of all electric generating plants are powered by coal; almost 20 percent are nuclear powered; most of the remainder are powered from oil or natural gas; less than 10 percent of electric power is derived from renewable energy sources. Transportation accounts for nearly 30 percent of total energy use in America, almost all of it from oil.

Energy consumption *per person* in United States has stabilized over the last thirty years. Growth in overall energy consumption has matched population growth. Energy consumption has actually *declined* relative to the gross national product, suggesting that America is becoming more efficient over time in energy use. And energy expenditures have declined as a share of the GDP. This good news is not widely reported in the mass media.

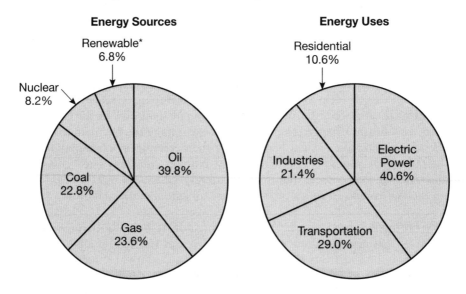

*Hydroelectric, geothermal, solar, wind, biomass.

FIGURE 10–5   Energy Sources and Uses   The U.S. gets most of its energy from oil, gas, and coal, all of which produce greenhouse gases. Clean nuclear and renewable sources provide relatively little energy for the country. Electric power plants and motor vehicles together use nearly 70 percent of the energy generated.

SOURCE: Data from Energy Information Administration, U.S. Department of Energy, *www.eia.doe.gov.*

Energy Supply. Supply-side energy policies emphasize the search for more sources of energy. Domestic oil production can be increased through exploration and drilling in public lands and offshore waters. ("Drill, baby, drill" became a popular slogan at Republican campaign stops in 2008.) Drilling in the Alaska National Wildlife Refuge (ANWR) in Alaska is an especially controversial option. Natural gas is more plentiful than petroleum, but its widespread use would require a complete overhaul of the nation's automobile and truck fleets to run on natural gas rather than gasoline. Nuclear power promises a clean source of energy for electrical power plants, but to date political struggles have effectively foreclosed the nuclear option (see "Nuclear Industry Meltdown" later in this chapter). The federal government heavily subsidizes research and development into "renewable" energy sources—land, solar, geothermal, and biomass (including ethanol production from corn). But none of these sources appear to be commercially feasible on any significant scale. Nevertheless the call for greater reliance on these sources of energy remains politically very popular.

Fuel Efficiency. The federal government requires automobile manufacturers to maintain corporate average fuel efficiency (CAFE) standards in the production of automobiles and light trucks. These averages are calculated from highway miles-per-gallon figures for all models of cars and light trucks produced by each manufacturer. (In recent years, the CAFE standards for cars has been 27.5 miles per gallon, and for light trucks, vans, and sports utility vehicles, 22.2 miles per gallon.) Determining CAFE standards engenders near constant political conflict in Washington, pitting auto manufacturers and auto workers' unions against environmental and consumer groups. The popularity of pickup trucks, minivans, and sports utility vehicles means that overall fuel efficiency on the roads is difficult to improve. Alternative fuel vehicles and hybrids—cars powered entirely or in part by electricity, natural gas, hydrogen, ethanol, etc.—constitute less than 5 percent of new vehicle sales.

Projections. The U.S. Department of Energy annually produces an "Energy Outlook" that projects energy use in greenhouse gas emissions to 2030. Among its current projections:[11]

- Growth in energy consumption in greenhouse gas emissions is likely to moderate as a result of government policies and high energy prices.
- Fossil fuels will continue to provide nearly 80 percent of total energy use.
- Energy efficiencies will cause declines in per capita energy use and declines in energy use per dollar of GDP.
- Hybrid motor vehicles—partly powered by electricity—are projected to increase significantly in numbers.
- Growth in electrical use will moderate with improved efficiency in homes and industry.
- Nonrenewable energy sources will increase, but remain less than 10 percent of total energy supply.
- Growth in energy-related carbon dioxide emissions will slow along with slowing growth in energy use.

Cap and Trade

In his first budget message to Congress, President Barack Obama recommended an innovative approach to energy policy. In addition to pledging federal subsidies for research and development in "clean energy technologies," he proposed a new carbon emissions trading program known as "cap and trade."

A Ceiling on Carbon Emissions.   The cap and trade program envisions the federal government setting overall national ceilings on carbon emissions. The government would then hold a national auction in which polluting industries and firms could purchase tradable emission allowances. The total amount of emission allowances auctioned off would not exceed the cap. In effect, industries would be purchasing allowances to pollute. These allowances could be traded on an open market, allowing polluting industries to keep polluting but at a price, and at the same time, encouraging industries to invest dollars in reducing carbon emissions. An industry that succeeded in reducing emissions below its allowance could then sell its allowance to other industries.

Relying in Part on the Market Mechanism.   The cap and trade approach to reducing carbon emissions is recommended over direct regulatory control. Because it relies in part on a market mechanism, it is sometimes labeled free-market environmentalism. Setting the overall cap is a regulatory measure, but individual firms are free to choose how or if they will reduce their emissions. The system encourages innovation by individual firms. If they are successful in reducing their emissions, they can sell their allowances to other firms.

Costs to Consumers.   The cost of the cap and trade program would be borne by all energy users. The federal government would actually make money from auction revenues. The costs to energy consumers would be largely invisible, passed on by industries in the form of price increases. Everything from gasoline prices to electric bills would incorporate the prices industries paid for emission allowances at auction or in trades.

Enforcement.   The federal government would put in place a vast new bureaucracy to oversee the carbon emissions of individual industries and firms. It will be necessary to measure the "carbon footprint" of industries and firms to ensure that they are operating within the emission allowances purchased at auction or in trade.

The Nuclear Industry Meltdown

Nuclear power is the cleanest and safest form of energy available. But the political struggle over nuclear power has all but destroyed early hopes that nuclear power could reduce U.S. dependence on fossil fuels. Nuclear power once provided about 20 percent of the nation's total energy. Many early studies recommended that the United States strive for 50 percent nuclear electric generation. But under current policies it is unlikely that nuclear power will ever be able to supply any more energy than it does today—less than ten percent (see Figure 10–5). The nuclear industry itself has been in a state of "meltdown," and the cause of the meltdown is political, not technological.

History of Regulation. In its developmental stages, nuclear power was a government monopoly. The Atomic Energy Act of 1946 created the Atomic Energy Commission (AEC), which established civilian rather than military control over nuclear energy. The AEC was responsible for the research, development, and production of nuclear weapons, as well as the development of the peaceful uses of nuclear energy. The AEC contracted with the Westinghouse Corporation to build a reactor and with the Duquesne Light Company to operate the world's first nuclear power plant at Shippingport, Pennsylvania, in 1957. Under the Atomic Energy Act of 1954 the AEC granted permits to build, and licenses to operate, nuclear plants; the AEC also retained control over nuclear fuel.

The AEC promoted the growth of the nuclear industry for over 20 years. But opponents of nuclear power succeeded in the Energy Reorganization Act of 1974 in separating the nuclear regulatory function from the research and development function. Today a separate agency, the Nuclear Regulatory Commission (NRC), regulates all aspects of nuclear power. Only 104 nuclear power plants are currently in the United States today.

"No-nukes." Nuclear power has long been under attack by a wide assortment of "no-nuke" groups. The core opposition is found among environmental activist groups. But fear plays the most important role in nuclear politics. The mushroom cloud image of the devastation of Japanese cities at the end of World War II is still with us. The mass media cannot resist dramatic accounts of nuclear accidents. The public is captivated by the "China syndrome" story—an overheated nuclear core melts down the containing vessels and the plant itself and releases radioactivity that kills millions.

Nuclear power offers a means of generating electricity without discharging any pollutants into the air or water. It is the cleanest form of energy production. It does not diminish the world's supply of oil, gas, or coal. However, used reactor fuel remains radioactive for hundreds of years and there are potential problems in burying this radioactive waste. Spent fuel is now piling up in storage areas in specially designed pools of water at nuclear power sites. When these existing storage places are filled to capacity, spent fuel will have to be transported somewhere else, adding to new complaints about the dangers of radioactive waste. There are many technical alternatives in dealing with waste, but there is no political consensus about which alternative to choose.

Safety. The nuclear power industry in the United States has a 60-year record of safety. No one has ever died or been seriously harmed by radioactivity from a nuclear power plant in the United States. This record includes more than 100 nuclear power plants operated in the United States and hundreds of nuclear-powered surface and submarine ships operated by the U.S. Navy. Despite sensational media coverage, the failure of the nuclear reactor at Three Mile Island, Pennsylvania, in 1979 did not result in injury to anyone or cause damage beyond the plant. There are about 450 nuclear power plants operating outside of the United States. France generates 76 percent of its electricity by nuclear means. The worst nuclear accident in history occurred at Chernobyl in the Ukraine in 1986; it resulted in 31 immediate-term deaths from radiation.

Zero risk is an impossible standard, and the costs of efforts to approach zero risk are astronomical. Under popular pressure to achieve near-zero risk, the NRC has imposed licensing requirements that now make nuclear plants the most expensive means of generating electricity. No new nuclear plants have been built in over two decades, and private utilities have canceled dozens of planned nuclear plants.

The stated policy of the national government may be to keep open the nuclear power option, but the actual effect of nuclear regulatory policy has been to foreclose that option.

The Future of Nuclear Power.   What are the prospects for a "nuclear renaissance"? A variety of factors suggest a reexamination of the utility of nuclear power: the U.S. Department of Energy projects that electricity demand will rise 25 percent by 2030, requiring the construction of hundreds of new power plants; oil price increases make nuclear power generation more competitive; concerns over global warming and pollution from fossil fuel use drive a new interest in nuclear power; and national security concerns regarding U.S. dependence on foreign oil suggests the need to develop reliable domestic power sources.

But reviving the nuclear energy industry will require, first of all, a streamlined and cost-conscious regulatory environment, one that encourages private companies to make the long-term capital investments required to bring new nuclear plants into operation. Secondly, the federal government must decide on, finance, and implement a nuclear waste management program, one that includes spent nuclear materials from both military and private power uses. Finally, nuclear power cannot be revived without federal subsidies and loan guarantees for private power companies to encourage them to move forward building new nuclear plants. Yet even if Washington responded favorably to nuclear industry requirements, new plants are not likely to begin producing power in the United States for another ten years.

Politicians and Bureaucrats: Regulating the Environment

Federal environmental policymaking began in earnest in the 1970s with the creation of the Environmental Protection Agency (EPA) and the passage of clean air and water acts. Potentially, the EPA is the most powerful and far-reaching bureaucracy in Washington today, with legal authority over any activity in the nation that affects the air, water, or ground.

The Environmental Protection Agency.   The EPA was created in an executive order by President Richard Nixon in 1970 to reorganize the federal bureaucracy to consolidate responsibility for (1) water pollution, (2) air pollution, (3) solid waste management, (4) radiation control, and (5) hazardous and toxic substance control. The EPA is a regulatory agency with power to establish and enforce policy.

The National Environmental Protection Act.   In 1970 Congress created the Council on Environmental Quality (CEQ) to advise the president and Congress on environmental matters. The CEQ is an advisory agency. However, the act requires all federal agencies as well as state, local, and private organizations receiving federal monies to file lengthy "environmental impact statements." If the CEQ wants to delay or obstruct a project, it can ask for endless revisions, changes, or additions in the statement. The CEQ cannot by itself halt a project, but it can conduct public hearings for the press, pressure other governmental agencies, and make recommendations to the president. The courts have ruled that the requirement for an environmental impact statement is judicially enforceable.

The Clean Air Act of 1970.   The Clean Air Act of 1970 authorized the EPA to identify air pollutants that cause a health threat and to establish and enforce standards of emission. The EPA began by focusing on automobile emissions, requiring the installation of pollution equipment on all new cars. The EPA ordered lead removed from auto fuel and engines redesigned for lead-free gasoline. It also ordered the installation of emission controls in automobiles. More radical solutions advanced by the EPA (for example, to halt driving in certain cities) were blocked by courts and Congress. The EPA was even more aggressive in pursuing stationary sources of air pollution with requirements for "smokestack scrubbers," low-sulfur coal, and other costly devices.

The Water Pollution Control Act of 1972.   This act stiffened early antipollution laws, but set an unrealistic goal: "that the discharge of pollutants into the navigable waters be eliminated by 1985." After a flood of lawsuits the EPA was forced to abandon the zero-discharge standard. Forcing municipal governments to clean up their discharges proved more difficult than forcing industry to do so. Many municipalities remain in violation of federal water quality standards.

Endangered Species Act of 1973.   This legislation authorizes the U.S. Fish and Wildlife Service to designate endangered species for federal protection and to regulate activities in their "critical habitat." Initially the law was widely praised as at least partially responsible for the survival of nationally symbolic species such as the bald eagle; but increasingly the law has been used to prevent landowners from using their property in order to protect obscure varieties of rodents, birds, and insects. Today more than 1,000 species are on the endangered species list, and there is virtually no land in the United States on which an endangered species does *not* live. The U.S. Fish and Wildlife Service has the potential to control any land in the nation under the Endangered Species Act.

Wetlands.   In 1975 a federal court ruled that the Clean Water Act of 1972 also applied to "wetlands" adjacent to navigable waters. This gave the EPA control over millions of acres of land, estimated to be the equivalent of Ohio, Indiana, and Illinois combined. The result has been a bureaucratic nightmare for owners of land that is classified as wetlands.

Resource Conservation and Recovery Act of 1976.   The act authorizes EPA to oversee the nation's solid waste removal and disposal, including the regulation of landfills, incinerators, industrial waste, hazardous waste, and recycling programs.

Toxic Substances Control Act of 1976.   The Toxic Substances Control Act authorized the EPA to designate hazardous and toxic substances and to establish standards for their release into the environment.

The Comprehensive Environmental Response Act of 1980.   The Comprehensive Environmental Response Act established a "Superfund" for cleaning up old toxic and hazardous waste sites. Out of 20,000 potential sites, the EPA has placed more than 1,200 on its National Priority List. The act specifies that EPA oversee the cleanup of these sites, assessing costs to the parties responsible for the pollution. If these parties cannot be found or have no money, then the government's Superfund is to be used. But over the years, cleanup efforts have been seriously hampered by EPA's overly rigid site orders (for example, dirt must be cleaned to the point where it can be safely eaten daily by small children), lengthy lawsuits against previous owners and users (including Little League teams) that divert funds to legal fees, and complicated negotiations with local government over the cleanup of old landfill sites. EPA also enforces "retroactive liability," holding owners liable for waste dumped legally before the law was enacted in 1980. Under current EPA policies, full cleanup of all hazardous waste sites on the National Priority List would cost many billions of dollars, far more than presidents or Congresses are likely to appropriate.

Clean Air Act of 1990.   The Clean Air Act Amendments of 1990 enacted many new regulations aimed at a variety of perceived threats to the environment:

> *Acid rain.* Sulfur dioxide emissions must be cut from 20 to 10 million tons annually, and nitrogen oxide emissions must be cut by 2 million tons. Midwestern coal-burning utilities must burn low-sulphur coal and install added smoke-scrubbing equipment at increased costs to their consumers.
>
> *Ozone hole.* Production of chlorofluorocarbons and hydrochlorofluorocarbons (aerosol sprays, insulating materials) is outlawed, and new regulations are placed on chemicals used in air conditioners and refrigerators.
>
> *Urban smog.* Additional mandated pollution control equipment is required on new automobiles. Oil companies must produce cleaner-burning fuel. There is also a special requirement that automobile companies produce an experimental fleet of cars to be sold in southern California.
>
> *Toxic air pollutants.* New definitions and regulations govern more than 200 substances as "toxic air pollutants" released into the air from a wide variety of sources, from gas stations to dry cleaners. The EPA is given authority to require all of these sources to install "the best available control technology" and to provide "an ample margin of safety" for nearby residents.

EPA Regulation of Carbon Dioxide, 2009.   The Environmental Protection Agency issued an official finding in 2009 that carbon dioxide is a danger to human health and the environment and therefore subject to EPA regulation under the Clean Air Act. This "endangerment finding" potentially allows the EPA to draw up regulations governing greenhouse gas emissions from electric power plants, refineries, chemical plants, motor vehicles and other sources of emissions, including schools, hospitals, homes and apartment buildings.

Encouraged by the Obama Administration, and relying heavily on studies cited by the International Panel on Climate Change (see above), the EPA issued its finding. Earlier in 2007 the US Supreme Court had held that the Clean Air Act "expressly authorized" the EPA to regulate air "pollutants" and that the EPA itself did not challenge the contention that carbon dioxide was a pollutant.[12]

The threat of EPA regulation of all carbon emissions provides an incentive for Congress itself to act on "cap and trade." The EPA is busy constructing a comprehensive system for reporting emissions of carbon dioxide and other greenhouse gases produced by major sources in the United States. This reporting system may provide the data for comprehensive regulation envisioned by cap and trade.

SUMMARY

Public choice theory views environmental pollution as an externality of human activity. Individuals, firms, and governments frequently impose unwanted costs on others. The environment, especially air and water, is a common-pool resource: access is unrestricted; there are no clearly defined property rights to it; no one has the individual responsibility of caring for it; individuals, firms, and governments tend to use it to carry off waste materials, thus generating unwanted costs or externalities on everyone else. The government has a legitimate interest in managing environmental externalities. Public choice theory offers valuable guidelines in dealing with them.

1. Economic growth is not incompatible with environmental protection. On the contrary, increases in wealth and advances in technology provide the best hope for a cleaner environment.

2. Effective pollution control and risk reduction must be balanced against its costs. Environmental policies whose costs exceed benefits will impair society's ability to deal effectively with environmental problems.

3. The costs of removing additional environmental pollutants and risks rise as we approach zero tolerance. Total elimination of pollutants from air, water, or ground involves astronomical costs and wastes the resources of society.

4. Rational determination of benefits and costs requires scientific evidence. The deliberate rejection of scientific evidence on environmental issues, and the ideological or emotional inspiration to act even in the absence of scientific information, renders cost-effective policymaking impossible.

5. Traditional command and control approaches to environmental protection are less effective than market incentives. Legislatures and bureaucrats that endeavor to devise laws and regulations to reduce pollution are less effective than individuals, firms, and local governments with strong market incentives to reduce pollution in a cost-effective manner.

6. The air and water in the United States are significantly cleaner today than in 1970, when the first major environmental policies were enacted. Improvements in air and water quality have occurred despite growth in the population and growth in waste products.

7. Nonetheless, most Americans believe that pollution is growing worse. Interest group activity and media coverage of environmental "crises," have pushed environmental issues to the forefront of American politics. Predictions of global doom create a climate of opinion that precludes rational analyses of the benefits and costs of environmental policies.

8. Current policy initiatives focus on sulfur dioxide and nitrogen oxide from coal-burning utilities, emissions of ozone and carbon monoxide from automobiles and stationary sources, and toxic air pollutants released from a wide variety of sources.

9. If firms were taxed on the basis of the pollutants they emit, a strong market incentive would be created for a reduction in pollution. A pollution tax would capture the externalities and force producers and consumers to incorporate the full environmental costs of products in the price. It would encourage polluters to find ways themselves to reduce pollution rather than simply comply with government regulations. Waste charges would encourage consumers to reduce their use of waste-producing goods.

Notes

1. *Statistical Abstract of the United States, 2008*, p. 224.
2. Resource Conservation and Recovery Act, PL 94–580, Section 4001 (1976).
3. *Statistical Abstract of the United States, 2008*, p. 225.
4. National Institute of Environmental Health Sciences, March 5, 2002.
5. CBS News/*New York Times* Survey, November 2002, As reported at *www.publicagenda.org*.
6. Club of Rome, *The First Global Revolution* (New York: Pantheon Books, 1991), p. 115.
7. Christopher Manes, *Green Rage* (Boston: Little, Brown, 1990).
8. Hugh W. Ellsaesser et al., "Global Climate Trends as Revealed by Recorded Data," *Review of Geophysics* 24 (November 1986), 745–792; Patrick J. Michaels and David E. Stooksbury, "Global Warming: A Reduced Threat?" *Bulletin of the American Meteorological Society* 23 (October 1992), 1563–1577; Roy W. Spence and John R. Christy, "Precise Monitoring of Global Temperature Trends from Satellites," *Science* 247 (March 1990), 1558–1562.
9. International Panel on Climate Change, *Fourth Assessment Report: Climate Change 2007*, *www.ipcc.ch*.
10. Al Gore, *Earth in the Balance* (Boston: Houghton Mifflin, 1992).
11. U.S. Department of Energy, *Annual Energy Review 2008*, *www.eia.doe.gov*.
12. *Massachusetts v. EPA*, April 2, 2007.

Bibliography

BLOCK, BEN, and HAROLD LYONS. *Apocalypse Not: Science, Economics, and Environmentalism.* Washington, DC: CATO Institute, 1993.

GORE, AL. *Earth in the Balance.* Boston: Houghton Mifflin, 1992.

KRAFT, MICHAEL E. *Environmental Policy and Politics*, 4th ed. New York: Longman, 2007.

LIPSCHUTZ, RONNIE D. *Global Environmental Politics.* Washington, DC: CQ Press, 2003.

ROSENBAUM, WALTER A. *Environmental Politics and Policy*, 7th ed. Washington, DC: CQ Press, 2007.

VIG, NORMAN J., and MICHAEL E. KRAFT. *Environmental Policy*, 6th ed. Washington, DC: CQ Press, 2005.

Web Sites

U.S. ENVIRONMENTAL PROTECTION AGENCY. Official Web site of the EPA, with laws, regulations, key issues, press releases, etc. *www.epa.gov*

U.S. NATIONAL OCEANIC AND ATMOSPHERIC ADMINISTRATION. Official Web site of NOAA, with information on weather, climate, atmospheric research, etc., as well as real-time satellite imagery. *www.noaa.gov*

ENVIRONMENTAL DEFENSE FUND. Advocacy organization for environmental programs and spending. *www.environmentaldefense.org*

GREENPEACE. Home page of militant environmental organization opposed to world trade, whaling, fishing, deforestation, etc. *www.greenpeace.org*

NATIONAL WILDLIFE FEDERATION. Home page of moderate organization supporting wildlife conservation and environmental education. *www.nwf.org*

SIERRA CLUB. Advocacy organization for environmental protection, with information on issues, press releases, and voting records of Congress members. *www.sierraclub.org*

NATURAL RESOURCE DEFENSE COUNCIL. Advocacy organization that relies mainly on lawsuits to advance goals in clean air, clean water, nuclear waste, etc. *www.nrdc.org*

COMPETITIVE ENTERPRISE INSTITUTE. Advocacy organization opposed to centralize command approaches to environmental protection and favoring competitive free enterprise approaches. *www.cei.org*

INTERNATIONAL PANEL ON CLIMATE CHANGE, *UN-Spanned organization given responsibility for assessing global warming. www.ipcc.ch.*

NUCLEAR ENERGY INSTITUTE. News and information from the nuclear power industry, *www.nei.org.*

11

Civil Rights

Elite and Mass Interaction

Elite and Mass Opinions and Race

Race has been the central domestic issue of American politics over the long history of the nation. In describing this issue we have relied heavily on the elite model—because elite and mass attitudes toward civil rights differ, and public policy appears to reflect the attitudes of elites rather than masses. Civil rights policy is a response of a national elite to conditions affecting a minority of Americans rather than a response of national leaders to majority sentiments. Policies of the national elite in civil rights have met with varying degrees of mass resistance at the state and local levels. We will contend that national policy has shaped mass opinion more than mass opinion has shaped national policy.

Black–White Opinion Differences. The attitudes of white masses toward African Americans are ambivalent. Relatively few whites believe that there is much discrimination in society, or that discrimination is a very serious problem (see Table 11–1). In contrast, most blacks believe that discrimination is a very serious problem. However, whites and blacks agree that the election of Barak Obama as president will improve race relations.

Whites constitute a large majority of the nation's population (see Figure 11–1). If public policy reflected the views of this *majority*, there would be very little civil rights legislation. Civil rights policy is *not* a response of the government to the demands of the white majority.

Mass Opinion Lags behind Policy. White majority opinion has *followed* civil rights policy rather than inspired it. That is, public policy has shaped white opinion rather than white opinion shaping public policy. Consider the changes in opinion among whites toward school integration over the years. Between 1942 and 1985, samples of white Americans were asked this question: "Do you think white and black students should go to the same schools or separate schools?" (See Table 11–2.) In 1942, not one white American in three approved of integrated schools. In 1956, two years *after* the historic *Brown* v. *Topeka* court decision, white attitudes began to shift, although about half of all whites still favored segregation. By 1964,

TABLE 11–1   White and Black Opinion about Discrimination White and black opinion differs on whether or not discrimination is a serious problem in America.

Q. How serious do you think racial discrimination against blacks is in this country: a very serious problem, a somewhat serious problem, not too serious, or not at all serious?

	Very Serious	Somewhat Serious	Not Too Serious	Not at All Serious
Whites	12%	45%	33%	9%
Blacks	56%	34%	9%	1%

Q. As a result of Barack Obama's election, do you think race relations in this country will get a lot better, get a little better, not change, get a little worse, or get a lot worse?

Get a Lot Better	Get a Little Better	Not Change	Get a Little Worse	Get a Lot Worse
28%	42%	17%	7%	3%

SOURCE: Various polls, 2008, reported in *www.pollingreport.com.*

two out of every three whites supported integrated schools. As public school integration proceeded in America, white parents became more accepting of sending their children to schools with substantial black enrollments. But, again, white opinion generally *follows* public policy rather than leads it.

Elite–Mass Differences.   There is a wide gap between the attitudes of masses and elites on the subject of civil rights. The least favorable attitudes toward blacks are found among the less privileged, less educated whites. Whites of lower socioeconomic status are much less

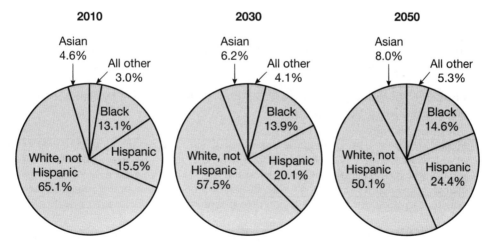

FIGURE 11–1   Racial Composition of the United States Hispanics are now the largest minority in the nation and their proportion of the population is projected to continue to grow.
SOURCE: U.S. Census of the Population, *www.census.gov.*

TABLE 11–2   Changing White Attitudes toward School Integration   Over time, white opinion regarding school integration changed from strong opposition to strong support.

Q. "Do you think white students and black students should go to the same school or to separate schools?"

Same Schools

	Brown v. *Topeka (1954)*			**Civil Rights Act (1964)**			
	1942	**1956**	**1964**	**1970**	**1972**	**1980**	**1985**
Percent	30	48	62	74	80	86	92

SOURCE: General Social Survey, reported in Harold W. Stanley and Richard G. Niemi, *Vital Statistics on American Politics, 2007–2008* (Washington, DC: CQ Press, 2008), p. 161.

willing to have contact with blacks than those with higher socioeconomic status, whether it is a matter of using the same public restrooms, going to a movie or restaurant, or living next door. It is the affluent, well-educated white who is most concerned with discrimination and who is most willing to have contact with blacks. The political implication of this finding is obvious: opposition to civil rights legislation and to black advancement in education, jobs, income, housing, and so on, is likely to be strongest among less educated and less affluent whites. Within the white community support for civil rights will continue to come from the educated and affluent.

The Development of Civil Rights Policy

The initial goal in the struggle for equality in America was the elimination of discrimination and segregation practiced by governments, particularly in voting and public education. Later, discrimination in both public and private life—in transportation, theaters, parks, stores, restaurants, businesses, employment, and housing—came under legal attack.

The Fourteenth Amendment.   The Fourteenth Amendment, passed by Congress after the Civil War and ratified in 1868, declares,

> All persons born or naturalized in the United States, and subject to the Jurisdiction thereof, are citizens of the United States and of the State wherein they reside. No State shall make or enforce any law which shall abridge the privileges or immunities of citizens of the United States; nor shall any State deprive any person of life, liberty, or property, without due process of law; nor deny to any person within its jurisdiction the equal protection of the laws.

The language of the Fourteenth Amendment and its historical context leave little doubt that its original purpose was to achieve the full measure of citizenship and equality for African Americans. During Reconstruction and the military occupation of the Southern states, some radical Republicans were prepared to carry out in Southern society the revolution this amendment implied. The early success of Reconstruction was evident in widespread black voting throughout the South and the election of blacks to federal and state offices. Congress even tried to legislate equal treatment in theaters, restaurants, hotels, and public transportation in the Civil Rights Act of 1875, only to have the Supreme Court declare the effort unconstitutional in 1883.[1]

Eventually Reconstruction was abandoned; the national government was not prepared to carry out the long and difficult task of really reconstructing society in the eleven states of the former Confederacy. In the Compromise of 1877, the national government agreed to end military occupation of the South, gave up its efforts to rearrange Southern society, and lent tacit approval to white supremacy in that region. In return, the Southern states pledged their support of the Union; accepted national supremacy; and agreed to permit the Republican candidate, Rutherford B. Hayes, to assume the presidency, even though his Democratic opponent, Samuel J. Tilden, had won more popular votes in the disputed election of 1876.

Segregation.   The Supreme Court agreed to the terms of the compromise. The result was a complete inversion of the meaning of the Fourteenth Amendment so that it became a bulwark of segregation. State laws segregating the races were upheld. The constitutional argument on behalf of segregation under the Fourteenth Amendment was that the phrase "equal protection of the laws" did not prevent state-enforced *separation* of the races. Schools and other public facilities that were "separate but equal" won constitutional approval. This separate but equal doctrine became the Supreme Court's interpretation of the Equal Protection Clause of the Fourteenth Amendment in *Plessy* v. *Ferguson* in 1896.[2]

However, segregated facilities, including public schools, were seldom if ever equal, even in physical conditions. In practice, the doctrine of segregation was separate and *un*equal. The Supreme Court began to take notice of this after World War II. Although it declined to overrule the segregationist interpretation of the Fourteenth Amendment, it began to order the admission of individual blacks to white public universities when evidence indicated that separate black institutions were inferior or nonexistent.[3]

NAACP.   Leaders of the newly emerging civil rights movement in the 1940s and 1950s were not satisfied with court decisions that examined the circumstances in each case to determine if separate school facilities were really equal. Led by Roy Wilkins, executive director of the National Association for the Advancement of Colored People (NAACP), and Thurgood Marshall, chief counsel for the NAACP, the civil rights movement pressed for a court decision that segregation *itself* meant inequality within the meaning of the Fourteenth Amendment, whether or not facilities were equal in all tangible respects. In short, they wanted a complete reversal of the separate but equal interpretation of the Fourteenth Amendment and a ruling that laws separating the races were unconstitutional.

The civil rights groups chose to bring suit for desegregation to Topeka, Kansas, where segregated black and white schools were equal in buildings, curricula, qualifications, and salaries of teachers, and other tangible factors. The object was to prevent the Court from ordering the admission of blacks because tangible facilities were not equal and to force the Court to review the doctrine of segregation itself.

Brown v. Topeka.   The Court rendered its historic decision in *Brown v. Board of Education of Topeka, Kansas,* on May 17, 1954:

> Segregation of white and colored children in public schools has a detrimental effect upon the colored children. The impact is greater when it has the sanction of law, for the policy of separating the races is usually interpreted as denoting the inferiority of the Negro group.[4]

Note that this first great step toward racial justice in the twentieth century was taken by the *nonelective* branch of the federal government. Nine men, secure in their positions with lifetime appointments, responded to the legal arguments of highly educated black leaders, one of whom—Thurgood Marshall—would later become a Supreme Court justice himself. The decision was made by a judicial elite, not by the people or their elected representatives.

Mass Resistance to Desegregation

Although the Supreme Court had spoken forcefully in the *Brown* case in declaring segregation unconstitutional, from a political viewpoint the battle over segregation was just beginning. Segregation would remain a part of American life, regardless of its constitutionality, until effective elite power was brought to bear to end it. The Supreme Court, by virtue of the American system of federalism and separation of powers, has little direct force at its disposal. Congress, the president, state governors and legislatures, and even mobs of people can act more forcefully than the federal judiciary. The Supreme Court must rely largely on the other branches of the federal government and on the states to enforce the law of the land.

Segregationist States   In 1954 the practice of segregation was widespread and deeply ingrained in American life (see Figure 11–2). Seventeen states *required* the segregation of the races in public schools:

Alabama	Mississippi	Texas	Maryland
Arkansas	North Carolina	Virginia	Missouri
Florida	South Carolina	Delaware	Oklahoma
Georgia	Tennessee	Kentucky	West Virginia
Louisiana			

The Congress of the United States required the segregation of the races in the public schools of the District of Columbia. Four additional states—Arizona, Kansas, New Mexico, and Wyoming—authorized segregation on the option of local school boards.

Thus, in deciding *Brown v. Topeka,* the Supreme Court struck down the laws of twenty-one states and the District of Columbia in a single opinion. Such a far-reaching decision was bound to meet with difficulties in implementation. In an opinion delivered the following year, the Supreme Court declined to order immediate nationwide desegregation but instead turned over the responsibility for desegregation to state and local authorities under the supervision of federal district courts. The way was open for extensive litigation, obstruction, and delay by states that chose to resist.

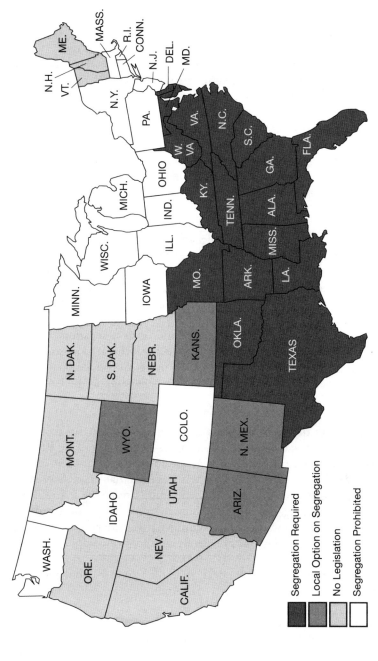

FIGURE 11–2 Segregation Laws in the United States in 1954 Prior to *Brown v. Topeka* in 1954 segregation was required in twenty-one states and the District of Columbia; four additional states gave local school districts the option of segregation.

The six border states with segregated school systems—Delaware, Kentucky, Maryland, Missouri, Oklahoma, West Virginia—together with the school districts in Kansas, Arizona, and New Mexico that had operated segregated schools chose not to resist desegregation formally. The District of Columbia also desegregated its public schools the year following the Supreme Court's decision.

State Resistance.   However, resistance to school integration was the policy choice of the eleven states of the Old Confederacy. Refusal of a school district to desegregate until it was faced with a federal court injunction was the most common form of delay. State laws that were obviously designed to evade constitutional responsibilities to end segregation were struck down in federal courts; but court suits and delays slowed progress toward integration. On the whole, those states that chose to resist desegregation were quite successful in doing so from 1954 to 1964. In late 1964, ten years after the *Brown* decision, only about 2 percent of the black schoolchildren in the eleven southern states were attending integrated schools.

Presidential Use of Force.   The historic *Brown* decision might have been rendered meaningless had President Dwight Eisenhower not decided to use military force in 1957 to secure the enforcement of a federal court order to desegregate Little Rock's Central High School. Governor Orval Faubus had posted state units of the Arkansas National Guard at the high school to prevent federal marshals from carrying out federal court orders to admit black students. President Eisenhower officially called the Arkansas National Guard units into federal service, ordered them to leave the high school, and replaced them with units of the U.S. Eighty-Second Airborne Division under orders to enforce desegregation. Eisenhower had not publicly spoken on behalf of desegregation, but the direct threat to national power posed by a state governor caused the president to assert the power of the national elite. President John F. Kennedy also used federal troops to enforce desegregation at the University of Mississippi in 1962.

Congress and the Power of the Purse.   Congress entered the civil rights field in support of court efforts to achieve desegregation in the Civil Rights Act of 1964. Title VI provided that every federal department and agency must take action to end segregation in all programs or activities receiving federal financial assistance. It was specified that this action was to include termination of financial assistance if states and communities receiving federal funds refused to comply with federal desegregation orders. Thus, in addition to court orders requiring desegregation, states and communities faced administrative orders, or "guidelines," from federal executive agencies threatening loss of federal funds for noncompliance.

Unitary Schools.   The last legal excuse for delay in implementing school desegregation collapsed in 1969 when the Supreme Court rejected a request by Mississippi school officials for a delay in implementing school desegregation in that state. The Court declared that every school district was obligated to end dual school systems "at once" and "now and hereafter" to operate only unitary schools.[5] The effect of the decision, fifteen years after the original *Brown* case, was to eliminate any further legal justification for the continuation of segregation in public schools.

Racial Balancing in Public Schools

After over a half century of efforts at desegregation by law, de facto segregation—black children attending public schools in which more than half the pupils are black—continues to characterize American education. Indeed, nationwide, roughly two-thirds of all black public school pupils attend schools with a black majority. One-third of black pupils attend schools with 90 to 100 percent minority enrollment.[6] Years ago, the U.S. Civil Rights Commission reported that even when segregation was de facto—that is, a product of segregated housing patterns and neighborhood school attendance—the adverse effects on black students were still significant.[7]

Ending racial isolation in the public schools often involves busing schoolchildren into and out of segregated neighborhoods. The objective is to achieve a racial balance in each public school, so that each has roughly the same percentage of blacks and whites as are found in the total population of the entire school district. Indeed, in some large cities where blacks make up the overwhelming majority of public school students, ending racial isolation may require city students to be bused to the suburbs and suburban students to be bused to the core city.

Federal Court Intervention.   Federal district judges enjoy wide freedom in fashioning remedies for past or present discriminatory practices by governments. If a federal district court anywhere in the United States finds that any actions by governments or school officials have contributed to racial imbalances (e.g., by drawing school district attendance lines), the judge may order the adoption of a desegregation plan to overcome racial imbalances produced by official action.

In the important case of *Swann* v. *Charlotte-Mecklenburg County Board of Education* (1971), the Supreme Court upheld (1) the use of racial balance requirements in schools and the assignment of pupils to schools based on race, (2) "close scrutiny" by judges of schools that are predominantly of one race, (3) gerrymandering of school attendance zones as well as "clustering" or "grouping" of schools to achieve equal balance, and (4) court-ordered busing of pupils to achieve racial balance.[8] The Court was careful to note, however, that racial imbalance in schools is not itself grounds for ordering these remedies, unless it is also shown that some present or past government action contributed to the imbalance.

In the absence of any government actions contributing to racial imbalance, states and school districts are *not* required by the Fourteenth Amendment to integrate their schools. For example, where central-city schools are predominantly black and suburban schools are predominantly white because of residential patterns, cross-district busing is not required unless some official action brought about these racial imbalances. Thus, in 1974, the Supreme Court threw out a lower federal court order for massive busing of students between Detroit and fifty-two suburban school districts. Although Detroit city schools were 70 percent black, none of the Detroit-area school districts segregated students within their own boundaries. Chief Justice Burger, writing for the majority, said, "Unless [Detroit officials] drew the district lines in a discriminatory fashion, or arranged for the white students residing in the Detroit district to attend schools in Oakland or Macomb counties, they were under no constitutional duty to make provision for Negro students to do so."[9] In a strong dissent, Justice Thurgood Marshall wrote, "In the short run it may seem to be the easiest course to allow our great metropolitan areas to be divided up each into cities—one white, the other black—but it is a course, I predict, our people will ultimately regret." This important decision means that the largely black central cities, surrounded by largely white suburbs, will remain segregated in practice.

Racial isolation continues to characterize public schools in many of the nation's largest cities; racial isolation is especially prevalent in cities with majority African American populations, for example, Atlanta, Baltimore, Cleveland, Detroit, Memphis, New Orleans, Newark, St. Louis, and Washington, DC.[10]

An End to Racial Balancing?   Recent Supreme Court decisions suggest that racial balancing in public elementary and secondary schools may be nearing an end. With regard to schools with a history of segregation (Southern schools), the Supreme Court has begun to address the question of when desegregation has been achieved and therefore when racial balancing plans can be abandoned. In the 1990s the Court began to free school districts from direct federal court supervision and court-ordered racial balancing. When the last vestiges of state-sanctioned discrimination have been removed "as far as practicable," the Supreme Court has allowed lower federal courts to dissolve racial balancing plans even though imbalances due to residential patterns continue to exist.[11]

The Supreme Court has also held that all racial classifications by governments for whatever purpose are subject to "strict scrutiny" by the courts.[12] This means that racial classifications must be "narrowly tailored" to achieve a "compelling government interest." When a Seattle, Washington, school district voluntarily adopted student assignment plans that relied on race to determine which schools certain children would attend, the Supreme Court held that the district had violated the Fourteenth Amendment's guarantee of equal protection of the laws.[13] In as much as the Seattle district had no history of segregation, its racial balancing was subject to the strict scrutiny test. The Court went on to reason that achieving "diversity" in the student body was not proven to be a compelling interest in public elementary and secondary schools. Moreover, the Seattle district's racial balancing plan was not narrowly tailored; the district had failed to consider race-neutral assignment plans that might achieve the same outcome as racial classifications. The Court noted that the Seattle plan considered race exclusively and not in a broader definition of "diversity." The effect of the decision is to force school districts across the country to reconsider voluntary racial balancing plans.

The Civil Rights Movement

The early goal of the civil rights movement in America was to prevent discrimination and segregation by *governments,* particularly states, municipalities, and school districts. But even while important victories for the civil rights movement were being recorded in the prevention of discrimination by governments, particularly in the *Brown* case, the movement began to broaden its objectives to include the elimination of discrimination in *all* segments of American life, private as well as public. Governments should not only cease discriminatory practices of their own, they should also act to halt discrimination by private firms and individuals.

The goal of eliminating discrimination in private life creates a positive obligation of government to act forcefully in public accommodations, employment, housing, and many other sectors of society. When the civil rights movement turned to combating private discrimination, it had to carry its fight into the legislative branch of government. The federal courts could help end discrimination by state and local governments and school authorities, but only Congress, state legislatures, and city councils could end discrimination practiced by private owners of restaurants, hotels, and motels, private employers, landlords, real estate agents, and other individuals who were not government officials.

The Montgomery Bus Boycott.   The leadership in the struggle to eliminate discrimination and segregation from private life was provided by a young African American minister, Martin Luther King, Jr. His father was the pastor of one of the South's largest and most influential congregations, the Ebenezer Baptist Church in Atlanta, Georgia. Martin Luther King, Jr., received his doctorate from Boston University and began his ministry in Montgomery, Alabama. In 1955 the African American community of Montgomery began a year-long boycott, with frequent demonstrations against the Montgomery city buses over segregated seating. The dramatic appeal and the eventual success of the boycott in Montgomery brought nationwide attention to its leader and led to the creation in 1957 of the Southern Christian Leadership Conference.

Nonviolent Direct Action.   Under King's leadership the civil rights movement developed and refined political techniques for minorities in American politics, including nonviolent direct action, a form of protest that involves breaking "unjust" laws in an open, "loving," nonviolent fashion. The general notion of civil disobedience is not new; it has played an important role in American history, from the Boston Tea Party to the abolitionists who illegally hid runaway slaves, to the suffragettes who demonstrated for women's voting rights, to the labor organizers who formed the nation's major industrial unions, to the civil rights workers of the early 1960s who deliberately violated segregation laws. The purpose of the nonviolent direct action is to call attention, or to "bear witness," to the existence of injustice. In the words of King, civil disobedience "seeks to dramatize the issue so that it can no longer be ignored."[14]

There should be no violence in true civil disobedience, and only "unjust" laws are broken. Moreover, the law is broken "openly, lovingly" and with a willingness to accept the penalty. Punishment is actively sought rather than avoided since it will help to emphasize the injustice of the law. The object is to stir the conscience of an elite and win support for measures that will eliminate the injustices. By willingly accepting punishment for the violation of an unjust law, one demonstrates the strength of one's convictions. The dramatization of injustice makes news, the public's sympathy is won when injustices are spotlighted, and the willingness of demonstrators to accept punishment is visible evidence of their sincerity. Cruelty or violence directed against the demonstrators by police or others plays into the hands of the protesters by further emphasizing the injustices they are experiencing.

Martin Luther King, Jr.   In 1963 a group of Alabama clergymen petitioned Martin Luther King, Jr., to call off mass demonstrations in Birmingham. King, who had been arrested in the demonstrations, replied in his famous "Letter from Birmingham City Jail":

> In no sense do I advocate evading or defying the law as the rabid segregationist would do. This would lead to anarchy. One who breaks an unjust law must do it *openly, lovingly* (not hatefully as the white mothers did in New Orleans when they were seen on television screaming "nigger,

nigger, nigger") and with a willingness to accept the penalty. I submit that an individual who breaks a law that conscience tells him is unjust, and willingly accepts the penalty by staying in jail to arouse the conscience of the community over its injustice, is in reality expressing the very highest respect for law.[15]

It is important to note that King's tactics relied primarily on an appeal to the conscience of white elites. The purpose of demonstrations was to call attention to injustice and stimulate established elites to remedy the injustice by lawful means. The purpose of civil disobedience was to dramatize injustice; only *unjust* laws were to be broken "openly and lovingly," and punishment was accepted to demonstrate sincerity. King did *not* urge black masses to remedy injustice themselves by any means necessary; and he did *not* urge the overthrow of established elites.

In 1964, Martin Luther King, Jr., received the Nobel Peace Prize in recognition of his unique contributions to the development of nonviolent methods of social change.

"I Have a Dream."　The culmination of the nonviolent philosophy was a giant, yet orderly, march on Washington, held on August 28, 1963. More than 200,000 blacks and whites participated in the march, which was endorsed by many labor leaders, religious groups, and political figures. The march ended at the Lincoln Memorial where King delivered his most eloquent appeal, entitled "I Have a Dream": "I have a dream. It is a dream deeply rooted in the American dream. I have a dream that one day this nation will rise up and live out the true meaning of its creed: 'We hold these truths to be self-evident, that all men are created equal.' " In response President Kennedy sent a strong civil rights bill to Congress, which was passed after his death—the famous Civil Rights Act of 1964.

The Civil Rights Act of 1964.　The Civil Rights Act of 1964 passed both houses of Congress by better than a two-thirds favorable vote; it won the overwhelming support of both Republican and Democratic members of Congress. It was signed into law by President Lyndon Johnson on July 4, 1964. It ranks with the Emancipation Proclamation, the Fourteenth Amendment, and *Brown* v. *Topeka* as one of the most important steps toward full equality for blacks in America. Among its most important provisions are the following:

> *Title II:*　It is unlawful to discriminate or segregate persons on the grounds of race, color, religion, or national origin in any public accommodation, including hotels, motels, restaurants, movies, theaters, sports arenas, entertainment houses, and other places that offer to serve the public. This prohibition extends to all establishments whose operations affect interstate commerce or whose discriminatory practices are supported by state action.

> *Title VI:*　Each federal department and agency shall take action to end discrimination in all programs or activities receiving federal financial assistance in any form. This action shall include termination of financial assistance.

> *Title VII:*　It shall be unlawful for any employer or labor union to discriminate against any individual in any fashion in employment because of his race, color, religion, sex, or national origin, and that an Equal Employment Opportunity Commission shall be established to enforce this provision by investigation, conference, conciliation, persuasion, and if need be, civil action in federal court.

The Civil Rights Act of 1968.   For many years fair housing had been considered the most sensitive area of civil rights legislation. Discrimination in the sale and rental of housing was the last major civil rights problem on which Congress took action. Discrimination in housing had not been mentioned in any previous legislation—not even in the comprehensive Civil Rights Act of 1964. Prohibiting discrimination in the sale or rental of housing affected the constituencies of northern members of Congress more than any of the earlier, southern-oriented legislation.

The prospects for a fair housing law were not very good at the beginning of 1968. However, when Martin Luther King, Jr., was assassinated on April 4, the mood of Congress and the nation changed dramatically. Congress passed a fair housing law as tribute to the slain civil rights leader.

The Civil Rights Act of 1968 prohibited the following forms of discrimination:

Refusal to sell or rent a dwelling to any person because of his race, color, religion, or national origin.

Discrimination against a person in the terms, conditions, or privileges of the sale or rental of a dwelling.

Advertising the sale or rental of a dwelling indicating a preference or discrimination based on race, color, religion, or national origin.

Public Policy and Affirmative Action

The gains of the early civil rights movement were primarily gains in *opportunity* rather than in *results.* Racial politics today center on the actual inequalities between whites and minorities in incomes, jobs, housing, health, education, and other conditions of life.

Continuing Inequalities.   The problem of inequality is often posed as differences in the "life chances" of whites and minorities (see Table 11–3). The average income of a black household is only 68 percent of the average white household income. More than 24 percent of all black families are below the recognized poverty line, while only about 10 percent of white families live in poverty. The black unemployment rate is more than twice as high as the white unemployment rate. The civil rights movement of the 1960s opened up new opportunities for black Americans. But equality of opportunity is not the same as equality of results.

Opportunity versus Results.   Most Americans are concerned more with equality of opportunity than equality of results. *Equality of opportunity* refers to the ability to make of oneself what one can; to develop one's talents and abilities; and to be rewarded for work, initiative, and achievement. It means that everyone comes to the same starting line with the same chance of success, that whatever differences develop over time do so as a result of abilities, talents, initiative, hard work, and perhaps good luck. *Equality of results* refers to the equal sharing of income, jobs, contracts, and material rewards regardless of one's condition in life. It means that everyone starts and finishes the race together, regardless of ability, talent, initiative, or work.

TABLE 11–3 Minority Life Chances Continuing inequalities between races are revealed in income, poverty, education, and unemployment.

Median Income of Families				
Race	**1980**	**1990**	**2000**	**2006**
White	38,621	41,668	45,860	48,554
Black	22,250	24,917	30,980	30,858
Hispanic	28,218	29,792	34,636	35,967

Persons below Poverty Level				
Race	**1980 (%)**	**1990 (%)**	**2000 (%)**	**2006 (%)**
White	10.2	10.7	9.5	10.6
Black	32.5	31.9	22.5	24.9
Hispanic	25.7	28.1	21.5	21.8

Persons over 25 Completing		
Race	**High School (%)**	**Bachelor's Degree (%)**
White	85.8	28.2
Black	80.6	17.6
Hispanic	58.4	12.1

Unemployment Rate			
Race	**1992**	**2000**	**2006**
White	5.5	2.6	9.0
Black	11.0	5.4	8.9
Hispanic	9.8	4.4	5.2

SOURCE: *Statistical Abstract of the United States, 2008.*

Equal Opportunity versus Affirmative Action.   The earlier emphasis of government policy, of course, was nondiscrimination, or equal employment opportunity. "It was not a program to offer special privilege to any one group of persons because of their particular race, religion, sex, or national origin."[16] This appeared to conform to the original nondiscrimination approach, beginning with President Harry Truman's decision to desegregate the armed forces in 1946 and carrying through Title VI and Title VII of the Civil Rights Act of 1964 to eliminate discrimination in federally aided projects and private employment.

Gradually, however, the goal of the civil rights movement shifted from the traditional aim of *equality of opportunity* through nondiscrimination alone to affirmative action to establish "goals and timetables" to achieve *equality of results* between blacks and whites. While avoiding the term *quota,* the notion of affirmative action tests the success of equal employment opportunity by observing whether blacks achieve admissions, jobs, and promotions in proportion to their numbers in the population.

Affirmative action programs were initially products of the federal bureaucracy. They were not begun by Congress. Instead, they were developed by the federal executive agencies that were authorized by the Civil Rights Act of 1964 to develop "rules and regulations" for desegregating activities receiving federal funds (Title VI) and private employment (Title VII). President Lyndon B. Johnson gave impetus to affirmative action with Executive Order No. 11246 in 1965, which covered employment and promotion in federal agencies and businesses contracting with the federal government. In 1972 the U.S. Office of Education issued guidelines that mandated "goals" for university admissions and faculty hiring of minorities and women. The Equal Employment Opportunity Commission, established by the Civil Rights Act of 1964 (Title VII) to eliminate discrimination in private employment, has carried the notion of affirmative action beyond federal contractors and recipients of federal aid into all sectors of private employment.

The Supreme Court and Affirmative Action

Affirmative action programs pose some important constitutional questions. Do these programs discriminate against whites in violation of the Equal Protection Clause of the Fourteenth Amendment? Do these programs discriminate against whites in violation of the Civil Rights Act of 1964, which prohibits discrimination "on account of race," not just discrimination against African Americans?

The Bakke Case. In an early, controversial case, *Regents of the University of California* v. *Bakke* (1978), the Supreme Court struck down a special admissions program for minorities at a state medical school on the grounds that it excluded a white applicant because of his race and violated his rights under the equal protection clause.[17] Allan Bakke applied to the University of California Davis Medical School two consecutive years and was rejected; in both years black applicants with significantly lower grade point averages and medical aptitude test scores were accepted through a special admissions program that reserved sixteen minority places in a class of one hundred.* The University of California did not deny that its admissions decisions were based on race. Instead, it argued that its racial classification was "benign," that is, designed to assist minorities, not to hinder them. The special admissions program was designed (1) to "reduce the historical deficit of traditionally disfavored minorities in medical schools and the medical profession," (2) to "counter the effects of societal discrimination," (3) to "increase the number of physicians who will practice in communities currently underserved," and (4) to "obtain the educational benefits that flow from an ethnically diverse student body."

The Court held that these objectives were legitimate and that race and ethnic origin may be considered in reviewing applications to a state school without violating the Equal Protection Clause. However, the Court also held that a separate admissions program for minorities with a specified quota of openings that were unavailable to white applicants did

---

*Bakke's grade point average was 3.51; his MCAT scores were verbal 96, quantitative 94, science 97, general information 72. The *average* for the special admissions students were grade point average 2.62, MCAT verbal 34, quantitative 30, science 37, general information 18.

violate the Equal Protection Clause. The Court ordered Bakke admitted to medical school and the elimination of the special admissions program. It recommended that California consider developing an admissions program that considered disadvantaged racial or ethnic background as a "plus" in an overall evaluation of an application, but did not set numerical quotas or exclude any persons from competing for all positions.

Affirmative Action as a Remedy for Past Discrimination.   However, the Supreme Court has approved affirmative action programs where there is evidence of past discriminatory actions. In *United Steelworkers of America* v. *Weber* (1979), the Court approved a plan developed by a private employer and a union to reserve 50 percent of higher-paying, skilled jobs for minorities. Kaiser Aluminum Corporation and the United Steelworkers Union, under federal government pressure, had established a program to get more African Americans into skilled technical jobs. When Weber was excluded from the training program and African Americans with less seniority and fewer qualifications were accepted, he filed suit in federal court claiming that he had been discriminated against because of his race in violation of Title VII of the Civil Rights Act of 1964. But the Supreme Court held that Title VII of the Civil Rights Act of 1964 "left employers and unions in the private sector free to take such race-conscious steps to eliminate manifest racial imbalances in traditionally segregated job categories. We hold that Title VII does not prohibit such . . . affirmative action plans." Weber's reliance on the clear language of Title VII was "misplaced." According to the Court, it would be "ironic indeed" if the Civil Rights Act were used to prohibit voluntary, private race-conscious efforts to overcome the past effects of discrimination.[18]

Despite changing membership over time, the Supreme Court has not altered its policy regarding affirmative action as a remedy for past discrimination. In *United States* v. *Paradise* (1987), the Court upheld a rigid 50 percent African American quota system for promotions in the Alabama Department of Safety, which had excluded blacks from the ranks of state troopers before 1972 and had not promoted any blacks higher than corporal before 1984. In a 5-to-4 decision, the majority stressed the long history of discrimination in the agency as a reason for upholding the quota system. Whatever burdens were imposed on innocent parties were outweighed by the need to correct the effects of past discrimination.[19]

Cases Questioning Affirmative Action.   Yet in the absence of past discrimination, the Supreme Court has expressed concern about whites who are directly and adversely affected by government action solely because of their race. In *Firefighters Local Union* v. *Stotts* (1984), the Court ruled that a city could not lay off white firefighters in favor of black firefighters with less seniority.[20] In *Richmond* v. *Crosen* (1989), the Court held that a minority set-aside program in Richmond, Virginia, which mandates that 30 percent of all city construction contracts must go to "blacks, Spanish-speaking, Orientals, Indians, Eskimos, or Aleuts," violated the Equal Protection Clause of the Fourteenth Amendment.[21]

However, the Supreme Court has never adopted the *color-blind doctrine* first espoused by Justice John Harlan in his dissent from *Plessy* v. *Ferguson*—that "our constitution is color-blind and neither knows nor tolerates classes among citizens."[22] If the Equal Protection Clause required that the laws of the United States and the states be truly color-blind, then *no* racial preferences, goals, or quotas would be tolerated. This view has occasionally been expressed in minority dissents and concurring opinions.[23]

Proving Discrimination.   The Civil Rights Act of 1964, Title VII, bars racial or sexual discrimination in employment. But how can persons who feel that they have been passed over for jobs or promotions go about the task of proving that discrimination was involved? Evidence of direct discrimination is often difficult to obtain. Can underrepresentation of minorities or women in a work force be used as evidence of discrimination, in the absence of any evidence of direct discriminatory practice? If an employer uses a requirement or test that has a "disparate effect" on minorities or women, who has the burden of proof that the requirement or test is relevant to effective job performance?

The Supreme Court responded to both of these questions in its interpretation of the Civil Rights Act in *Wards Cove Packing Co., Inc. v. Atonio* (1989).[24] In a controversial 5-to-4 decision, the Court held that statistical imbalances in race or gender in the workplace were *not* sufficient evidence by themselves to prove discrimination. The Court also ruled that it was up to the plaintiffs to prove that an employer had no business reason for requirements or tests that had an adverse impact on minorities or women. This decision clearly made it more difficult to prove job discrimination.

Civil rights groups were highly critical of what they regarded as the Supreme Court's "narrowing" of the Civil Rights Act protections in employment. They turned to Congress to rewrite portions of the Civil Rights Act to restore these protections. Business lobbies, however, believed that accepting statistical imbalances as evidence of discrimination or shifting the burden of proof to employers would result in hiring by "quotas" simply to avoid lawsuits. After nearly two years of negotiations on Capitol Hill and a reversal of President George H.W. Bush's initial opposition, Congress crafted a policy in its Civil Rights and Women's Equity Act of 1991. Among the more important provisions of the act are the following:

Statistical imbalances: The mere existence of statistical imbalance in an employer's work force is not, by itself, sufficient evidence to prove discrimination. However, statistical imbalances may be evidence of employment practices (rules, requirements, academic qualifications, tests) that have a "disparate impact" on minorities or women.

Disparate employment practices: Employers bear the burden of proof that any practice that has a "disparate impact" is necessary and has "a significant and manifest relationship to the requirements for effective job performance."

"Strict Scrutiny."   In 1995, the Supreme Court held that racial classifications in law must be subject to "strict scrutiny." This means that race-based actions by government—any disparate treatment of the races by federal, state, or local public agencies—must be found necessary to remedy past proven discrimination, or to further clearly identified legitimate and "compelling" government objectives. Moreover, it must be "narrowly tailored" so as not to adversely affect the rights of individuals. In striking down a federal construction contract set-aside program for small businesses owned by racial minorities, the Court expressed skepticism about governmental racial classifications: "There is simply no way of determining what classifications are 'benign' and 'remedial' and what classifications are in fact motivated by illegitimate notions of racial inferiority or simple racial politics."[25]

Affirmative Action in Higher Education.   College and university efforts to achieve "diversity" in higher education, that is, efforts to recruit more minority students and faculty are also subject to "strict scrutiny". In practice, diversity is another term for affirmative action. (See "'Diversity in Higher Education" in Chapter 6.) The U.S. Supreme Court ruled in 2003 that diversity may be "a compelling government interest."[26] However, programs to achieve diversity must be "narrowly tailored" to that purpose. They must not establish race as the "decisive factor" in university admissions.[27]

Mass Opinion and Affirmative Action

Americans are divided over the issue of affirmative action. Polls reveal that whites are almost equally divided when the question is posed as general support for "affirmative action." In contrast, blacks and Hispanics are strongly supportive of affirmative action programs for racial minorities.[28]

Q. "Do you generally favor or oppose affirmative action programs for racial minorities?"

	Favor	Oppose	Unsure
All	49%	43%	8%
Whites	44%	49%	7%
Blacks	70%	21%	9%
Hispanics	83%	28%	9%

But when the question is phrased in a way that implies minority preference over merit for admission to colleges and universities, then a strong majority of whites favor admission "solely on the basis of merit." Hispanics also favor merit over racial preference, but blacks appeared to be split on the issue.

Q. "Which comes closer to your view about evaluating students toward admission into a college or university?

Applicants should be admitted solely on the basis of merit, even if that results in few minority students being admitted. Or, an applicant's race and ethnic background should be considered to help promote diversity on college campuses, even if that means admitting some minority students who otherwise would not be admitted."

	Solely Merit	Race/Ethnicity	Unsure
All	69%	27%	4%
Whites	75%	22%	3%
Blacks	44%	49%	7%
Hispanics	59%	36%	5%

Most Americans agree that discrimination still exists in American society. Many supporters of affirmative action would ideally prefer a society in which "our children will one day live in a nation where they will not be judged by the color of their skin but by the content of their character." Martin Luther King, Jr.'s dream remains the ultimate goal for the nation. Elites are more likely to see race-conscious policies as a continuing necessity to remedy current discrimination and the effects of past discrimination. Elites perceive affirmative action as a necessary tool in achieving equality of opportunity.

Mass Initiatives against Racial Preferences. "Direct democracy," in which the people themselves initiate and decide on policy questions, has always been viewed with skepticism by America's elite. James Madison believed that "such democracies have ever been spectacles of turbulence and contention." Policy should be made "through the medium of a chosen body of citizens, whose wisdom may best discern the true interests of their country."[29] There is no provision in the U.S. Constitution for national referenda. But the Progressive Era of the late nineteenth and early twentieth centuries brought with it many popular reforms, including the initiative and referendum. Currently, eighteen states provide for state constitutional initiatives—allowing citizens to place amendments on the ballot by petition—followed by a referendum vote—allowing citizens to adopt or reject the amendment.[30]

Mass opposition to affirmative action has been expressed in several states through the popular initiative device. California voters led the way in 1996 with a citizens' initiative (Proposition 209) that added the following phrase to that state's constitution:

> Neither the state of California nor any of its political subdivisions or agents shall use race, sex, color, ethnicity or national origin as a criterion for either discriminating against, or granting preferential treatment to, any individual or group in the operation of the State's system of public employment, public education or public contracting.

Supporters of the "California Civil Rights Initiative" argued that this initiative leaves all existing federal and state civil rights protections intact. It simply extends the rights of specially protected groups to all of the state's citizens. Opponents argued that it sets back the civil rights movement, that it will end the progress of minorities in education and employment, and that it denies minorities the opportunity to seek assistance and protection from government. The initiative was approved by 54 percent of California's voters.

Following the adoption of the California initiative, opponents filed suit in federal court arguing that it violated the Equal Protection Clause of the U.S. Constitution because it denied minorities and women an opportunity to seek preferential treatment by governments. But a federal Circuit Court of Appeals upheld the constitutionality of the initiative: "Impediments to preferential treatment do not deny equal protection."[31] The court reasoned that the Constitution allows some race-based preferences to correct past discrimination, but it does not prevent states from banning racial preferences altogether.

The success of the California Civil Rights Initiative inspired similar mass movements in other states: Washington adopted a similarly worded stare constitutional amendment in 1998, and Michigan approved a statewide ban on racial preferences in public education, employment, and state contracts in 2006. In Michigan this initiative was opposed by elites in the political, business, and academic worlds, including both Democratic and Republican gubernatorial candidates. Nonetheless, 58 percent of Michigan voters favored banning racial preferences. Following voter approval of the referendum, the president of the University of Michigan announced her intention "not ro allow our University" to end its affirmative action efforts.

Public Policy and Hispanic Americans

Hispanic Americans are now the nation's largest minority. The experience of Hispanics—a term that the U.S. Census Bureau uses to refer to Mexican Americans, Puerto Ricans, Cubans, and others of Spanish-speaking ancestry and culture—differs significantly from that of African Americans. It is true, of course, that the Equal Protection Clause of the Fourteenth Amendment protects "any person" and the Civil Rights Act of 1964 specifically identifies "national origin" as a category coming under its protection. Thus, the Constitution and laws of the United States offer Hispanics protection against discrimination.

Elite Exploitation.   Some Mexican Americans are descendants of citizens who lived in the Mexican territory annexed by the United States in 1848, but most have come to the United States in accelerating numbers in recent decades. For many years, agricultural businesses encouraged immigration of Mexican farm labor willing to endure harsh conditions for low pay. Farm workers were not covered by the federal National Labor Relations Act; thus, they were not guaranteed a minimum wage or protected in the right to organize labor unions. It was not until the 1960s that civil rights activity among Hispanic farm workers, under the leadership of Cesar Chávez and the United Farm Workers union, began to make improvements in the wages and living conditions of Mexican farm workers. The movement (often referred to as *La Raza*) encouraged Mexican Americans throughout the Southwest to engage in political activity.

However, inasmuch as many Mexican American immigrants were noncitizens, and many were *indocumentados* (undocumented residents or illegal aliens), they were vulnerable to exploitation by employers. Many continued to work in sub-minimum wage jobs with few or no benefits and under substandard conditions.

Inequalities between Hispanics and whites ("Anglos") can be observed in overall statistics on employment, income, and education (see Table 11–3 earlier in this chapter). Hispanics are included in affirmative action program protections. However, the federal Equal Employment Opportunity Commission receives fewer complaints from Hispanics than from African Americans or women.

Most Hispanics today believe that they confront less prejudice and discrimination than their parents. Nonetheless, in 1994, California voters approved a referendum, Proposition 187, that would have barred welfare and other benefits to persons living in the state illegally. Most Hispanics opposed the measure, believing that it was motivated by prejudice. A federal court later declared major portions of Proposition 187 unconstitutional. Moreover, the U.S. Supreme Court has held that a state may not bar children of illegal immigrants from attending public schools.[32]

Voting Rights.   The Voting Rights Act of 1965, as later amended and as interpreted by the U.S. Supreme Court, extends voting rights protections to "language minorities." Following redistricting after the 1990 census, Hispanic representation in Congress rose substantially. Today about 4 percent of the U.S. House of Representatives are Hispanic, still well below the nation's 15 percent Hispanic population.

The Constitution and Gender Equality

Although the historical context of the Fourteenth Amendment implies its intent to guarantee equality for newly freed slaves, the wording of its Equal Protection Clause applies to "any person." Thus the text of the Fourteenth Amendment *could* be interpreted to bar any gender differences in the law. However, the Supreme Court has never interpreted the Equal Protection Clause to give the same level of protection to gender equality as to racial equality. Indeed, the Supreme Court in the nineteenth century specifically rejected the argument that this clause applied to women; the Court once upheld a state law banning women from practicing law, arguing that "The natural and proper timidity and delicacy which belongs to the female sex evidently unfits it for many of the occupations of civil life."[33]

Early Feminist Politics. The first generation of feminists learned to organize, hold public meetings, and conduct petition campaigns in the pre–Civil War antislavery movement. Following the Civil War, women were successful in changing many state laws that abridged the property rights of married women and otherwise treated them as chattel (property) of their husbands. Activists were also successful in winning some protections for women in the workplace, including state laws improving hours of work, working conditions, and physical demands. At the time, these laws were regarded as progressive. Feminist efforts of the 1800s also centered on the protection of women in families. The perceived threats to women's well-being were their husbands' drinking, gambling, and consorting with prostitutes. Women led the Anti-Saloon League and succeeded in outlawing gambling and prostitution in every state except Nevada and provided the major source of moral support for the Eighteenth Amendment (Prohibition).

The feminist movement in the early twentieth century concentrated on women's suffrage—the drive to guarantee women the right to vote. The early suffragettes employed mass demonstrations, parades, picketing, and occasional disruption and civil disobedience—tactics similar to those of the civil rights movement of the 1960s. The culmination of their efforts was the 1920 passage of the Nineteenth Amendment to the Constitution: "The right of citizens of the United States to vote shall not be denied or abridged by the United States or by any state on account of sex."

Judicial Scrutiny of Gender Classifications. The Supreme Court became responsive to arguments that sex discrimination might violate the Equal Protection Clause of the Fourteenth Amendment in the 1970s. It ruled that sexual classifications in the law "must be reasonable and not arbitrary, and must rest on some ground of difference having fair and substantial relation to . . . important governmental objectives."[34] Thus, for example, the Court has ruled (1) that a state can no longer set different ages for men and women to become legal adults[35] or purchase alcoholic beverages;[36] (2) women cannot be barred from police or firefighting jobs by arbitrary height and weight requirements;[37] (3) insurance and retirement plans for women must pay the same monthly benefits (even though women on the average live longer);[38] and (4) public schools must pay coaches in girls' sports the same as coaches in boys' sports.[39]

Court Recognition of Gender Differences.   Yet the Supreme Court has continued to recognize some gender differences in law. For example, the Court has upheld statutory rape laws that make it a crime for an adult male to have sexual intercourse with a female under the age of 18, regardless of her consent. The Court has upheld Congress's draft registration law for men only, and it has declined to intervene in U.S. Defense Department decisions regarding the assignments of women in the military.

Equal Rights Amendment.   At the center of feminist activity in the 1970s was the Equal Rights Amendment (ERA) to the Constitution. The amendment stated simply, "Equality of rights under the law shall not be denied or abridged by the United States or by any state on account of sex." The ERA passed Congress easily in 1972 and was sent to the states for the necessary ratification by three-fourths (thirty-eight) of them. The amendment won quick ratification in half the states, but a developing "Stop ERA" movement slowed progress and eventually defeated the amendment itself. In 1979, the original seven-year time period for ratification—the period customarily set by Congress for ratification of constitutional amendments—expired. Proponents of the ERA persuaded Congress to extend the ratification period for three more years, to 1982. But despite heavy lobbying efforts in the states and public opinion polls showing national majorities favoring it, the amendment failed to win ratification by the necessary thirty-eight states.*

Public Policy and Gender Equality

Today, women's participation in the labor force is not much lower than men's, and the gap is closing over time. More than 68 percent of married women with school-age children are working; and about 60 percent of married women with children under 6 years of age are working.[40] The movement of women into the American work force shifted feminist political activity toward economic concerns—gender equality in education, employment, pay, promotion, and credit.

Civil Rights Laws.   The Civil Rights Act of 1964, Title VII, prevents sexual (as well as racial) discrimination in hiring, pay, and promotions. The Equal Employment Opportunity Commission (EEOC), the federal agency charged with eliminating discrimination in employment, has established guidelines barring stereotyped classifications of "men's jobs" and "women's jobs." The courts have repeatedly struck down state laws and employer practices that differentiate between men and women in hours, pay, retirement age, and so forth.

The Federal Equal Credit Opportunity Act of 1974 prohibits sex discrimination in credit transactions. Federal law prevents banks, credit unions, savings and loan associations, retail stores, and credit card companies from denying credit because of sex or marital status. However, these businesses may still deny credit for a poor or nonexistent credit rating, and some women who have always maintained accounts in their husbands' name may still face credit problems if they apply in their own name.

---

*By 1982, thirty-four states had ratified the ERA. Three of them-Idaho, Nebraska, and Tennessee-subsequently voted to "rescind" their ratification; but the U.S. Constitution does not mention rescinding votes. The states that had not ratified it by 1982 were Nevada, Utah, Arizona, Oklahoma, Illinois, Indiana, Missouri, Arkansas, Louisiana, Mississippi, Alabama, Georgia, Florida, North Carolina, South Carolina, and Virginia.

The Education Act Amendment of 1972, Title IX, deals with sex discrimination in education. This federal law bars discrimination in admissions, housing, rules, financial aid, faculty and staff recruitment and pay, and—most troublesome of all—athletics. Athletics has proven very difficult because men's football and basketball programs have traditionally brought in the money to finance all other sports, and men's football and basketball have received the largest share of school athletic budgets. But the overall effect of Title IX has been to bring about a dramatic increase in women's participation in sports.

The Earnings Gap.   Overall, women's earnings remain less than men's earnings, although the gap has narrowed over the years (see Figure 11–3). Today, on average, women earn about 78 percent of men's earnings.

The earnings gap is not so much a product of direct discrimination, that is, women in the same job with the same skills, qualifications, experience, and work record being paid less than

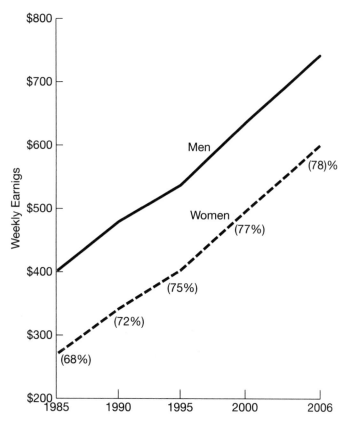

FIGURE 11–3   The Earnings Gap: Median Weekly Earnings of Men and Women Differences in earnings between men and women have narrowed in recent years, yet women continue to lag behind men.
NOTE: Figures in parentheses indicate the ratio of women's to men's median weekly earnings.
SOURCE: *Statistical Abstract of the United States, 2008,* p. 415.

men. This form of direct discrimination has been illegal since the Civil Rights Act of 1964. Rather, the earnings gap is primarily a product of a division in the labor market between traditionally male and female jobs, with lower salaries paid in traditionally female occupations.

The initial efforts of the women's movement were directed toward ensuring that women enjoyed equal access to traditionally male "white-collar" occupations, for example, physician, lawyer, and engineer. Success in these efforts would automatically narrow the wage gap. And indeed, women have been very successful over the last several decades in increasing their representation in prestigious white-collar occupations (see Table 11–4), although most of these occupational fields continue to be dominated by men.

TABLE 11–4   The Dual Labor Market   Gender differences in occupational fields are changing very slowly, with women still concentrated in lower-paying jobs.

"White Collar"

Women are increasingly entering white-collar occupation fields traditionally dominated by men.

	1960	1983	2005
Architects	3	13	24
Computer analysts	11	28	30
College and university teachers	28	36	46
Engineers	1	6	13
Lawyers and judges	4	16	30
Physicians	10	16	32

"Pink Collar"

Women continue to be concentrated in occupational fields traditionally dominated by women.

	1970	1980	2005
Secretaries	98	99	97
Waitresses and waiters	91	88	72
Nurses	97	96	89
Office clerks	75	82	81

"Blue Collar"

Women continue to be excluded from many blue-collar occupational fields traditionally dominated by men, although women bartenders now outnumber men.

	1970	1980	2005
Truck drivers	1	2	5
Carpenters	1	1	2
Auto mechanics	1	1	2
Bartenders	21	44	58

SOURCES: U.S. Department of Labor, *Employment in Perspective: Working Women* (Washington, DC: U.S. Government Printing Office, 1983); National Research Council, National Academy of Sciences, *Women's Work, Men's Work* (Washington, DC: National Academy Press, 1985); *Statistical Abstract of the United States,* 2007, pp. 388–391.

Dual Labor Market. Nonetheless, evidence of a "dual" labor market, with male-dominated "blue-collar" jobs distinguishable from female-dominated "pink-collar" jobs, continues to be a major obstacle to economic equality between men and women. These occupational differences may be attributed to cultural stereotyping, social conditioning, and premarket training and education, which narrow the choices available to women. Progress has been made in recent years in reducing occupational sex segregation (a majority of bartenders are now women). Women are reaching parity as college and university professors; women also constitute about half of law and medical school students today, suggesting parity in the future in these professions (see Table 11–4).

The Glass Ceiling. Few women have climbed the ladder to become president or chief executive officer or director of the nation's largest industrial corporations, banks, utilities, newspapers, or television networks. Large numbers of women are entering the legal profession, but few have made it to senior partner in the nation's largest and most prestigious law firms. Women are more likely to be found in the president's cabinet than in the corporate boardroom.

The barriers to women's advancement to top positions are often very subtle, giving rise to the phrase *the glass ceiling.* There are many explanations for the absence of women at the top, and all of them are controversial: women choose staff assignments rather than fast-track, operating-head assignments. Women are cautious and unaggressive in corporate politics. Women have lower expectations about peak earnings and positions, and these expectations become self-fulfilling. Women bear children, and even during relatively short maternity absences they fall behind their male counterparts. Women are less likely to want to change locations than men, and immobile executives are worth less to a corporation than mobile ones. Women executives in sensitive positions come under even more pressure than men in similar posts. Women executives believe that they get much more scrutiny than men and must work harder to succeed. Finally, it is important to note that affirmative action efforts by governments, notably the EEOC, are directed primarily at entry-level positions rather than senior management posts.

Sexual Harassment. The specific phrase "sexual harassment" does not appear in the Civil Rights Act of 1964. However, Title VII protects employees from sexual discrimination "with respect to compensation, terms, conditions, or privileges of employment." The Supreme Court held in 1986 that "discriminatory intimidation" of employees could be "sufficiently severe" to alter the "conditions" of employment and therefore violate Title VII.

Discriminatory intimidation based on sex (sexual harassment) may take various forms. There seems to be little doubt that it includes (1) conditioning employment or promotion or privileges of employment on the granting of sexual favors by an employee and (2) "tangible" acts of touching, fondling, or forced sexual relations. But sexual harassment has also been defined to include (3) a "hostile working environment." This phrase may include offensive utterances, sexual innuendos, dirty jokes, the display of pornographic material, and unwanted proposals for dates. Several problems arise with this definition. First, it would appear to include speech and hence raise First Amendment questions regarding how far speech may be curtailed by law in the workplace. Second, the definition depends more on the subjective feelings of the individual employee about what is "offensive" and "unwanted" rather than on an objective standard of behavior that is easily understood by all. The Supreme Court wrestled with the definition of a "hostile work environment" in *Harris* v. *Forklift* in 1993. It held that a plaintiff need not show that the utterances caused psychological injury but only that a "reasonable person" would perceive the work environment as hostile or abusive. Presumably a single incident would not constitute harassment; rather, courts should consider "the frequency of the discriminatory conduct," "its severity," and whether it "unreasonably interferes with an employee's work performance."[41]

Abortion and the Right to Life

Abortion is not an issue that can easily be compromised. The arguments touch on fundamental moral and religious principles. Proponents of abortion, who often refer to themselves as "pro choice," argue that a woman should be permitted to control her own body and should not be forced by law to have unwanted children. They cite the heavy toll in lives lost in criminal abortions and the psychological and emotional pain of an unwanted pregnancy. Opponents of abortion, who often refer to themselves as "pro life," generally base their belief on the sanctity of life, including the life of the unborn child, which they believe deserves the protection of law—"the right to life." Many believe that the killing of an unborn child for any reason other than the preservation of the life of the mother is murder.

Early State Laws.   Historically, abortions for any purpose other than saving the life of the mother were criminal offenses under state law. About a dozen states acted in the late 1960s to permit abortions in cases of rape or incest or to protect the physical health of the mother, and in some cases her mental health as well. Relatively few abortions were performed under these laws, however, because of the red tape involved—review of each case by several concurring physicians, approval of a hospital board, and so forth. Then, in 1970, New York, Alaska, Hawaii, and Washington enacted laws that in effect permitted abortion at the request of the woman involved and the concurrence of her physician.

Roe v. *Wade.*   The U.S. Supreme Court's 1973 decision in *Roe* v. *Wade* was one of the most important and far-reaching in the Court's history.[42] The Court ruled that the constitutional guarantee of "liberty" in the Fifth and Fourteenth Amendments included a woman's decision to bear or not to bear a child. The Court also ruled that the word *person* in the Constitution did *not* include the unborn child. Therefore, the Fifth and Fourteenth Amendments to the Constitution, guaranteeing "life, liberty, and property," did not protect the "life" of the fetus. The Court also ruled that a state's power to protect the health and safety of the mother could not justify *any* restriction on abortion in the first three months of pregnancy. Between the third and sixth months of pregnancy, a state could set standards for abortion procedures to protect the health of women, but a state could not prohibit abortions. Only in the final three months could a state prohibit or regulate abortion to protect the unborn.

Government Funding of Abortions.   The Supreme Court's decision did not end the controversy over abortion. Congress defeated efforts to pass a constitutional amendment restricting abortion or declaring that the guarantee of life begins at conception. However, Congress, in what is known as the "Hyde Amendment," banned the use of federal funds under Medicaid (medical care for the poor) for abortions except to protect the life of a woman. The Supreme Court upheld the constitutionality of laws denying tax funds for abortions. Although women retained the right to an abortion, the Court held that there was no constitutional obligation for governments to pay for abortions;[43] the decision about whether to pay for abortion from tax revenues was left to Congress and the states.

Abortions in the United States.   About 1.3 million abortions are currently performed each year in the United States. There are approximately 319 abortions for every 1,000 live births.[44] This abortion rate has *declined* since 1990. About 85 percent of all abortions are performed at abortion clinics; others are performed in physicians' offices or in hospitals, where the cost is significantly higher. Most of these abortions are performed in the first three months; about 10 percent are performed after the third month.

Abortion Battles.   Early efforts by the states to limit abortion ran into Supreme Court opposition. The Court held that states may not interfere with a woman's decision to terminate a pregnancy. However, opponents of abortion won a victory in *Webster* v. *Reproductive Health Services* (1989), when the Supreme Court upheld a Missouri law restricting abortions.[45] The right to abortion under *Roe* v. *Wade* was not overturned, but the Court held that Missouri could deny public funds for abortions that were not necessary for the life of the women and could deny the use of public facilities or employees in performing or assisting in abortions. More important, the Court upheld the requirement for a test of "viability" after twenty weeks and a prohibition on abortions of a viable fetus except to save a woman's life. The Court recognized the state's "interest in the protection of human life when viability is possible." The effect of the *Webster* decision was to rekindle contentious debates over abortion in virtually all state capitols. Various legal restrictions on abortions have been passed in some states, including (1) prohibitions on public financing of abortions; (2) requirements for a test of viability and prohibitions on abortions of a viable fetus; (3) laws granting permission to doctors and hospitals to refuse to perform abortions; (4) laws requiring humane and sanitary disposal of fetal remains; (5) laws requiring physicians to inform patients about the development of the fetus and the availability of assistance in pregnancy; (6) laws requiring that parents of minors seeking abortion be informed; (7) laws requiring that late abortions be performed in hospitals; (8) laws setting standards of cleanliness and care in abortion clinics; (9) laws prohibiting abortion based on the gender of the fetus; (10) laws requiring a waiting period.

Reaffirming *Roe* v. *Wade*.   Abortion has become such a polarizing issue that pro-choice and pro-life groups are generally unwilling to search out a middle ground. Yet the Supreme Court appears to have chosen a policy of affirming a woman's right to abortion while upholding modest restrictions.

When Pennsylvania enacted a series of restrictions on abortion—physicians must inform women of risks and alternatives; a 24-hour waiting period is required; minors must have consent of parents or a judge; spouses must be notified—these restrictions reached the Supreme Court in the case of *Planned Parenthood of Pennsylvania* v. *Casey* in 1992. Justice

Sandra Day O'Connor took the lead in forming a moderate, swing bloc on the Court; her majority opinion strongly reaffirmed the fundamental right of abortion:

> Our law affords constitutional protection to personal decisions relating to marriage, procreation, contraception, family relationships, child rearing and education. . . . These matters, involving the most intimate and personal choices a person may make in a lifetime, choices central to personal dignity and autonomy, are central to the liberty protected by the Fourteenth Amendment. . . . A woman's liberty is not so unlimited, however, that from the outset the State cannot show its concern for the life of the unborn, and at a later point in fetal development the State's interest in life has sufficient force so that the right of the woman to terminate the pregnancy can be restricted. We conclude the line should be drawn at viability, so that before that time the woman has a right to choose to terminate her pregnancy.[46]

Justice O'Connor went on to establish a new standard for constitutionally evaluating restrictions: They must not impose an "undue burden" on women seeking abortion or place "substantial obstacles" in her path. All of Pennsylvania's restrictions were upheld except spousal notification.

Medicaid and Abortion.   Pro-choice and pro-life forces battle in Congress as well as the courts. Pro-choice forces regularly attempt to repeal the Hyde Amendment that prevents states from using federal Medicaid funds to pay for abortions. A Democratic-controlled Congress responded in a limited fashion in 1993 by making abortions in cases of rape and incest eligible for Medicaid payments.

"Partial Birth Abortion."   Following a long and emotional battle, Congress outlawed an abortion procedure known as "partial birth" abortion in 2003. (Congress had passed such a ban in 1996 only to have it vetoed by President Clinton.) This procedure, which is used in less than 1 percent of all abortions, involves partial delivery of a living fetus feet-first, then vacuuming out the brain and crushing the skull to ease complete removal. In 2000 the Supreme Court declared a Nebraska law prohibiting the procedure to be an unconstitutional "undue burden" on a woman's right to an abortion.[47] The Court noted that the Nebraska law failed to make an exception to preserve the life and health of the mother. Congress designed its law to try to meet the Supreme Court's objections, although Congress failed to make an exception for the health of the mother. Abortion rights advocates argue that banning this procedure is a first step in outlawing abortions altogether.

Public Policy and the Disabled

The Americans with Disabilities Act (ADA) of 1990 is a sweeping law that prohibits discrimination against disabled people in private employment, government programs, public accommodations, and telecommunications. The act is vaguely worded in many of its provisions, requiring "reasonable accommodations" for disabled people that do not involve "undue hardship." This means disabled Americans do not have exactly the same standard of protection as minorities or women, who are protected from discrimination *regardless* of hardship or costs. (It also means that attorneys, consultants, and bureaucrats are making handsome incomes interpreting the meaning of these phrases.) Specifically the ADA includes the following protections:

Employment: Disabled people cannot be denied employment or promotion if, with "reasonable accommodation," they can perform the duties of the job. Reasonable accommodation need not be made if doing so would cause "undue hardship" on the employer.

Government programs: Disabled people cannot be denied access to government programs or benefits. New buses, taxis, and trains must be accessible to disabled persons, including those in wheelchairs.

Public accommodations: Disabled people must enjoy "full and equal" access to hotels, restaurants, stores, schools, parks, museums, auditoriums, and the like. To achieve equal access, owners of existing facilities must alter them "to the maximum extent feasible"; builders of new facilities must ensure that they are readily accessible to disabled persons unless doing so is structurally impossible.

Communications: The Federal Communications Commission is directed to issue regulations that will ensure telecommunications devices for hearing- and speech-impaired people are available "to the extent possible and in the most efficient manner."

But the ADA, as interpreted by the Equal Employment Opportunity Commission and federal courts, has begun to generate considerable controversy. Persons who are "learning disabled" have successfully sued colleges and universities, and even state bar associations, not only for admission but also to gain extra time and assistance in passing examinations. Persons claiming various mental disorders have successfully sued employers for being dismissed for chronic tardiness, inability to concentrate on the job, uncooperative and hostile attitudes toward supervisors, and the like.

SUMMARY

Let us try to set forth some propositions that are consistent with elite theory and help describe the development of civil rights policy.

1. Elites and masses in America differ in their attitudes toward minorities. Support for civil rights legislation has come from educated, affluent whites in leadership positions.
2. Mass opinion toward civil rights has generally *followed* public policy and not led it. Mass opinion did not oppose legally segregated schools until after elites had declared national policy in *Brown* v. *Topeka* in 1954.
3. The greatest impetus to the advancement of civil rights policy in the twentieth century was the U.S. Supreme Court's decision in *Brown* v. *Topeka*. Thus, it was the Supreme Court, nonelected and enjoying life terms in office, which assumed the initiative in civil rights policy. Congress did not take significant action until ten years later.
4. The elimination of legal discrimination and the guarantee of equality of opportunity in the Civil Rights Act of 1964 were achieved largely through the dramatic appeals of

middle-class black leaders to the consciences of white elites. Black leaders did not attempt to overthrow the established order but rather to increase opportunities for blacks to achieve success within the American system.

5. Elite support for equality of opportunity does not satisfy the demands of black masses for equality of results. Inequalities between blacks and whites in life chances—income, education, employment, health—persist.

6. Affirmative action programs are pressed on governments, universities, and private employers by federal agencies seeking to reduce inequalities. But white masses generally reject preferences or quotas, which they believe to put working-class and middle-class white males at a disadvantage.

7. The Supreme Court has approved affirmative action programs with racial quotas when there is evidence of current or past discriminatory practices and when the program is narrowly defined to remedy the effects of previous discrimination. The Court has upheld some claims that racial preferences by governments violate the Fourteenth Amendment's guarantee of equal protection of laws when white males are excluded altogether solely on the basis of race, and when there is no "compelling" government objective in classifying people by race.

8. Hispanic Americans are now the nation's largest minority. For many years, elites, especially in agribusiness, encouraged legal and illegal immigration of Mexicans in order to obtain cheap labor. Efforts at immigration reform have been only partially successful.

9. Although representing over half of the nation's population, the women's movement has had to rely on the tactics of minorities—demonstrations, parades, an occasional civil disobedience—to convince governing elites to recognize women's rights. Women did not secure the right to vote in the U.S. Constitution until 1920. Women failed to secure ratification by three-quarters of states for the Equal Rights Amendment. The protection of women's rights relies primarily on the Civil Rights Act of 1964, together with subsequent laws of Congress prohibiting gender discrimination.

10. Abortion was prohibited by most of the states until the Supreme Court decided in *Roe v. Wade* in 1973 that women have a constitutional right to terminate pregnancies. Thus, the Court established as a constitutional right what pro-choice forces had failed to gain through political processes. Despite heated battles over abortion policy, the Supreme Court has steered a moderate policy, affirming a woman's right to abortion while upholding restrictions that do not impose an "undue burden" on women.

Notes

1. *Civil Rights Cases,* 100 U.S. 3 (1883).
2. *Plessy* v. *Ferguson,* 163 U.S. 537 (1896).
3. *Sweatt* v. *Painter,* 339 U.S. 629 (1950).
4. *Brown* v. *Board of Education of Topeka, Kansas,* 347 U.S. 483 (1954).
5. *Alexander* v. *Holmes County Board of Education,* 396 U.S. 19 (1969).
6. Harold W. Stanley and Richard G. Niemi, *Vital Statistics on American Politics,* 2005–2006 (Washington, DC: CQ Press, 2006), p. 380.

7. U.S. Commission on Civil Rights, *Racial Isolation in the Public Schools* (Washington, DC: U.S. Government Printing Office, 1966).

8. *Swann* v. *Charlotte-Mecklenburg County Board of Education,* 402 U.S. 1 (1971).

9. *Milliken* v. *Bradley,* 418 U.S. 717 (1974).

10. *Statistical Abstract of the United States, 2007,* p. 39.

11. *Board of Education* v. *Dowell,* U.S. (1991), 111 S. Ct. 630.

12. *Adarand Construction* v. *Pena,* 515 U.S. 200 (1995).

13. *Parents Involved in Community Schools* v. *Seattle School District,* June 28, 2007.

14. For an inspiring essay on nonviolent direct action and civil disobedience, read Martin Luther King, Jr., "Letter from Birmingham City Jail," April 16, 1963.

15. Ibid.

16. See David H. Rosenbloom, "The Civil Service Commission's Decision to Authorize the Use of Goals and Timetables in Federal Equal Employment Opportunity Programs," *Western Political Quarterly* 26 (June 1973), pp. 236–251.

17. *Regents of the University of California* v. *Bakke,* 438 U.S. 265 (1978).

18. *United Steelworkers* v. *Weber,* 443 U.S. 193 (1979).

19. *United States* v. *Paradise,* 480 U.S. 149 (1987).

20. *Firefighters Local Union* v. *Stotts,* 467 U.S. 561 (1984).

21. *Richmond* v. *Crosen,* 109 S. Ct. 706 (1989).

22. *Plessy* v. *Ferguson,* 163 U.S. 537 (1896), dissenting opinion.

23. See Justice Antonin Scalia's dissenting opinion in *Johnson* v. *Transportation Agency of Santa Clara County,* 480 U.S. 616 (1987).

24. *Wards Cove Packing Co., Inc.* v. *Atonio,* 490 U.S. 642 (1989).

25. *Adarand Construction* v. *Pena,* 515 U.S. 200 (1995).

26. *Grutter* v. *Bollinger,* 539 U.S. 306 (2003).

27. *Gratz* v. *Bollinger,* 539 U.S. 244 (2003).

28. Gallup Poll, 2003, as reported in *The Polling Report, www.pollingreport.com.*

29. *The Federalist,* Number 20.

30. Council of State Governments, *Book of the States,* annual publication.

31. *Coalition for Economic Equity* v. *Wilson,* Ninth Circuit Court of Appeals, April 1997.

32. *Plyer* v. *Doe,* 457 U.S. 202 (1982).

33. *Bradwell* v. *Illinois,* 16 Wall 130 (1873).

34. *Reed* v. *Reed,* 404 U.S. 71 (1971).

35. *Stanton* v. *Stanton,* 421 U.S. 7 (1975).

36. *Craig* v. *Borden,* 429 U.S. 190 (1976).

37. *Dothard* v. *Rawlinson,* 433 U.S. 321 (1977).

38. *Arizona* v. *Norris,* 103 S. Ct. 3492 (1983).

39. *EEOC* v. *Madison Community School District,* 55 U.S.L.W. 2644 (1987).

40. *Statistical Abstract of the United States, 2007,* p. 380.

41. *Harris* v. *Forklift,* 510 U.S. 17 (1993).

42. *Roe* v. *Wade,* 410 U.S. 113 (1973).

43. *Harris* v. *McRae,* 448 U.S. 297 (1980).

44. *Statistical Abstract of the United States,* 2007, p. 74.

45. *Webster* v. *Reproductive Health Services,* 492 U.S. 111 (1989).

46. *Planned Parenthood* v. *Casey,* 112 S. Ct. 2791 (1992).

47. *Stenburg* v. *Carhart,* 530 U.S. 914 (2004).

Bibliography

CONWAY, M. MARGARET. *Women and Public Policy*, 3rd ed. Washington, DC: CQ Press, 2004.

MCGLEN, NANCY E., et al. *Women, Politics, and American Society*, 4th ed. New York: Longman, 2005.

National Urban League. *The State of Black America*. New York: National Urban League, 2000.

ROSE, MELODY. *Safe, Legal, and Unavailable? Abortion Politics in the United States*. Washington, DC: CQ Press, 2006.

THERNSTORM, STEPHEN, and ABIGAIL THERNSTORM. *America in Black and White*. New York: Simon & Schuster, 1997.

WALTON, HANES JR., and ROBERT C. SMITH. *American Politics and the African-American Quest for Universal Freedom*, 7th ed. New York: Longman, 2008.

WHITAKER, LOIS DUKE. *Women in Politics*, 4th ed. Upper Saddle River, NJ: Prentice Hall, 2006.

Web Sites

CENTER FOR AMERICAN WOMEN AND POLITICS. Information on women in national and state elected office. *www.rci.rutgers.edu/-cawp*

NATIONAL ASSOCIATION FOR THE ADVANCEMENT OF COLORED PEOPLE (NAACP). Oldest civil rights organization working on behalf of African Americans. Information on political, social, and economic equality issues. *www.naacp.org*

NATIONAL COUNCIL OF LA RAZA. National organization working on behalf of civil rights and economic opportunities for Hispanics. Information on issues confronting Hispanic Americans. *www.nclr.org*

NATIONAL URBAN LEAGUE. Social service and civil rights organization, with information on issues confronting minorities. *www.nul.org*

CENTER FOR EQUAL OPPORTUNITY. Organization opposed to racial preferences. Policy briefs on issues relating to race, ethnicity, and public policy, including affirmative action. *www.ceousa.org*

AMERICAN CIVIL RIGHTS INITIATIVE. Advocacy organization seeking an end to racial preferences. Provided leadership for California Civil Rights Initiative. *www.acri.org*

JOINT CENTER FOR POLITICAL AND ECONOMIC STUDIES. Information on black elected officials in national and state office. *http://jointcenter.org*

12

American Federalism

Institutional Arrangements and Public Policy

American Federalism

Virtually all nations of the world have some units of local government—states, provinces, regions, cities, counties, towns, villages. Decentralization of policymaking is required almost everywhere. But nations are not truly *federal* unless both national and subnational governments exercise separate and autonomous authority, both elect their own officials, and both tax their own citizens for the provision of public services. Moreover, federalism requires the powers of the national and subnational governments to be guaranteed by a constitution that cannot be changed without the consent of both national and subnational populations.*

The United States, Canada, Australia, India, Germany, and Switzerland are generally regarded as federal systems, but Great Britain, France, Italy, and Sweden are not. Although these latter nations have local governments, they depend on the national government for their powers. They are considered *unitary* rather than federal systems because their local governments can be altered or even abolished by the national government acting alone. In contrast, a system is said to be *confederal* if the power of the national government is dependent on local units of government. While these terms—*federal, unitary,* and *confederal*—can be defined theoretically, in the real world of policymaking it is not so easy to distinguish between governments that are truly federal and

---

*Other definitions of federalism in American political science: "Federalism refers to a political system in which there are local (territorial, regional, provincial, state, or municipal) units of government, as well as a national government, that can make final decisions with respect to at least some governmental authorities and whose existence is especially protected." James Q. Wilson and John J. DiIulio, Jr., *American Government*, 7th ed. (Boston: Houghton Mifflin, 1998), p. 52. "Federalism is the mode of political organization that unites smaller polities within an overarching political system by distributing power among general and constituent units in a manner designed to protect the existence and authority of both national and subnational systems enabling all to share in the overall system's decision making and executing processes." Daniel J. Elazar, *American Federalism: A View from the States* (New York: Thomas Y. Crowell, 1966), p. 2.

those that are not. Indeed, it is not clear whether government in the United States today retains its federal character.

There are more than 89,000 separate governments in the United States, more than 60,000 of which have the power to levy their own taxes. There are states, counties, municipalities (cities, boroughs, villages), school districts, and special districts (see Table 12–1). However, only the national government and the states are recognized in the U.S. Constitution; all local governments are subdivisions of states. States may create, alter, or abolish these governments by amending state laws or constitutions.

Why Federalism?

Why have state and local governments anyway? Why not have a centralized political system with a single government accountable to national majorities in national elections—a government capable of implementing uniform policies throughout the country?

Protection against Tyranny.   The nation's Founders understood that "republican principles"—periodic elections, representative government, political equality—would not be sufficient in themselves to protect individual liberty. These principles may make governing elites more responsive to popular concerns, but they do not protect minorities or individuals, "the weaker party or an obnoxious individual," from government deprivations of liberty or property. Indeed, according to the Founders, "the great object" of constitution writing was both to preserve popular government and at the same time to protect individuals from "unjust and interested" *majorities.* "A dependence on the people is, no doubt, the primary control of government, but experience has taught mankind the necessity of auxiliary precautions."[1]

Among the most important "auxiliary precautions" devised by the Founders to control government was federalism, which was viewed as a source of constraint on big government. They sought to construct a governmental system incorporating the notion of "opposite and rival interests." Governments and government officials could be constrained by competition with other governments and other government officials.[2]

TABLE 12–1   Governments in the United States There are more than 87,000 governments in the United States.

U.S. government	1
State governments	50
Counties	3,033
Municipalities	19,492
Townships	16,579
School districts	13,051
Special districts	37,381
Total	89,587

SOURCE: *Cencus of Governments, 2007.*

Policy Diversity.   Today, federalism continues to permit policy diversity. The entire nation is not straitjacketed with a uniform policy to which every state and community must conform. State and local governments may be better suited to deal with specific state and local problems. Washington bureaucrats do not always know best about what to do in Commerce, Texas.

Conflict Management.   Federalism helps manage policy conflict. Permitting states and communities to pursue their own policies reduces the pressures that would build up in Washington if the national government had to decide everything. Federalism permits citizens to decide many things at the state and local levels of government and avoid battling over single national policies to be applied uniformly throughout the land.

Dispersal of Power.   Federalism disperses power. The widespread distribution of power is generally regarded as an added protection against tyranny. To the extent that pluralism thrives in the United States, state and local governments have contributed to its success. They also provide a political base for the survival of the opposition party when it has lost national elections.

Increased Participation.   Federalism increases political participation. It allows more people to run for and hold political office. Nearly a million people hold some kind of political office in counties, cities, townships, school districts, and special districts. These local leaders are often regarded as closer to the people than Washington officials. Public opinion polls show that Americans believe that their local governments are more manageable and responsive than the national government.

Improved Efficiency.   Federalism improves efficiency. Even though we may think of 89,000 governments as an inefficient system, governing the entire nation from Washington would be even worse. Imagine the bureaucracy, red tape, delays, and confusion if every government activity in every community in the nation—police, schools, roads, firefighting, garbage collection, sewage disposal, street lighting, and so on—were controlled by a central government in Washington.

Ensuring Policy Responsiveness.   Federalism encourages policy responsiveness. Multiple, competing governments are more sensitive to citizens' views than a centralized, monopoly government. The existence of multiple governments offering different packages of benefits and costs allows a better match between citizens' preferences and public policy. People and businesses can vote with their feet by relocating to those states and communities that most closely conform to their own policy preferences. Mobility not only facilitates a better match between citizens' preferences and public policy, it also encourages competition among states and communities to offer improved service at lower costs.

Encouraging Policy Innovation.   Federalism encourages policy experimentation and innovation. Federalism may be perceived today as a conservative idea, but it was once viewed as the instrument of progressivism. A strong argument can be made that the groundwork for the New Deal was built in state policy experimentation during the Progressive Era. Federal programs as diverse as income tax, unemployment compensation, countercyclical public works, Social Security, wage and hour legislation, bank deposit insurance, and food stamps all had antecedents at the state level. Much of the current liberal policy agenda—health insurance, child-care programs, government support of industrial research and development—has been embraced by various states. Indeed, the compelling phrase "laboratories of democracy" is generally attributed to the great progressive jurist Supreme Court Justice Louis D. Brandeis, who used it in defense of state experimentation with new solutions to social and economic problems.

Politics and Institutional Arrangements

Political conflict over federalism—over the division of responsibilities and finance between national and state/local governments—has tended to follow traditional liberal and conservative political cleavages. Generally, liberals seek to enhance the power of the *national* government. Liberals believe that people's lives can be changed by the exercise of government power to end discrimination, abolish poverty, eliminate slums, ensure employment, uplift the downtrodden, educate the masses, and cure the sick. The government in Washington has more power and resources than state and local governments have, and liberals have turned to it to cure America's ills. State and local governments are regarded as too slow, cumbersome, weak, and unresponsive. It is difficult to achieve change when reform-minded citizens must deal with 50 state governments or 89,000 local governments. Moreover, liberals argue that state and local governments contribute to inequality in society by setting different levels of services in education, welfare, health, and other public functions. A strong national government can ensure uniformity of standards throughout the nation. The government in Washington is seen as the principal instrument for liberal social and economic reform.

Generally, conservatives seek to return power to *state and local* governments. They are more skeptical about the good that Washington can do. Adding to the power of the national government is not an effective way of resolving society's problems. On the contrary, conservatives often argue that "government is the problem, not the solution." Excessive government regulation, burdensome taxation, and inflationary government spending combine to restrict individual freedom, penalize work and savings, and destroy incentives for economic growth. Government should be kept small, controllable, and close to the people.

Institutional Arenas and Policy Preferences.   Debates about federalism are seldom constitutional debates; rather, they are debates about policy. People decide which level of government—national, state, or local—is most likely to enact the policy they prefer. Then they argue that that level of government should have the responsibility for enacting the policy. Political scientist David Nice explains "the art of intergovernmental politics" as "trying to reduce, maintain, or increase the scope of conflict in order to produce the policy decisions you want." Abstract debates about federalism or other institutional arrangements, devoid of policy implications, hold little interest for most citizens or politicians. "Most people have little interest in abstract debates that argue which level of government should be responsible for a given task. What people care about is getting the policies they want."[3]

Thus, the case for centralizing policy decisions in Washington is almost always one of substituting the policy preferences of national elites for those of state and local officials. It is not seriously argued on constitutional grounds that national elites better reflect the policy preferences of the American people. Rather, federal intervention is defended on policy grounds—the assertion that the goals and priorities that prevail in Washington should prevail throughout the nation.

Concentrating Benefits to Organized Interests.   The national government is more likely to reflect the policy preferences of the nation's strongest and best-organized interest groups than are 89,000 state and local governments. This is true, first, because the costs of "rent seeking"—lobbying government for special subsidies, privileges, and protections—are less in Washington in relation to the benefits available from national legislation than the combined costs of rent seeking at 89,000 subnational centers. Organized interests, seeking concentrated benefits for themselves and dispersed costs to the rest of society, can concentrate their own resources in Washington. Even if state and local governments individually are more vulnerable to the lobbying efforts of wealthy, well-organized special interests, the prospect of influencing all 50 separate state governments or, worse, 89,000 local governments is discouraging to them. The costs of rent seeking at 50 state capitols, 3,000 county courthouses, and tens of thousands of city halls, while not multiplicative by these numbers, are certainly greater than the costs of rent seeking in a single national capitol.

Moreover, the benefits of national legislation are comprehensive. A single act of Congress, a federal executive regulation, or a federal appellate court ruling can achieve what would require the combined and coordinated action by hundreds, if not thousands, of state and local government agencies. Thus, the benefits of rent seeking in Washington are greater in relation to the costs.

Dispersing Costs to Unorganized Taxpayers.   Perhaps more important, the size of the national constituency permits interest groups to disperse the costs of specialized, concentrated benefits over a very broad constituency. Cost dispersal is the key to interest group success. If costs are widely dispersed, it is irrational for individuals, each of whom bear only a tiny fraction of these costs, to expend time, energy, and money to counter the claims of the special interests. Dispersal of costs over the entire nation better accommodates the strategies of special interest groups than the smaller constituencies of state and local government.

In contrast, state and local government narrows the constituencies over which costs must be spread, thus increasing the burdens to individual taxpayers and increasing the likelihood that they will take notice of them and resist their imposition. Economist Randall G. Holcombe explains: "One way to counteract this [interest group] effect is to provide public goods and services at the smallest level of government possible. This concentrates the cost on the smallest group of taxpayers possible and thus provides more concentrated costs to accompany the concentrated benefits."[4] He goes on to speculate whether the tobacco subsidies granted by Washington to North Carolina farmers would be voted by the residents of that state if they had to pay their full costs.

The rent-seeking efficiencies of lobbying in Washington are well known to the organized interests. As a result, the policies of the national government are more likely to reflect the preferences of the nation's strongest and best-organized interests.

American Federalism: Variations on the Theme

American federalism has undergone many changes in the more than 200 years since the Constitution of 1787. That is, the meaning and practice of federalism have transformed many times.

State-Centered Federalism (1787–1865). From the adoption of the Constitution of 1787 to the end of the Civil War, the states were the most important units in the American federal system. People looked to the states for the resolution of most policy questions and the provision of most public services. Even the issue of slavery was decided by state governments. The supremacy of the national government was frequently questioned, first by the Antifederalists (including Thomas Jefferson) and later by John C. Calhoun and other defenders of slavery and secession.

Dual Federalism (1865–1913). The supremacy of the national government was decided on the battlefields of the Civil War. Yet for nearly a half-century after that conflict, the national government narrowly interpreted its delegated powers and the states continued to decide most domestic policy issues. The resulting pattern has been described as dual federalism, in which the state and the nation divided most government functions. The national government concentrated its attention on the delegated powers—national defense, foreign affairs, tariffs, commerce crossing state lines, money, standard weights and measures, post office and post roads, and admission of new states. State governments decided the important domestic policy issues—education, welfare, health, and criminal justice. The separation of policy responsibilities was once compared to a "layer cake," with local governments at the base, state governments in the middle, and the national government at the top.[5]

Cooperative Federalism (1913–1964). The distinction between national and state responsibilities gradually eroded in the first half of the twentieth century. American federalism was transformed by the Industrial Revolution and the development of a national economy; the federal income tax in 1913, which shifted financial resources to the national government; and the challenges of two world wars and the Great Depression. In response to the Great Depression of the 1930s, state governors welcomed massive federal public works projects under President Franklin D. Roosevelt's New Deal. In addition, the federal government intervened directly in economic affairs, labor relations, business practices, and agriculture. Through its grants-in-aid, the national government cooperated with the states in public assistance, employment services, child welfare, public housing, urban renewal, highway building, and vocational education.

This new pattern of federal–state relations was labeled cooperative federalism. Both the nation and the states exercised responsibilities for welfare, health, highways, education, and criminal justice. This merging of policy responsibilities was compared to a marble cake: "As the colors are mixed in a marble cake, so functions are mixed in the American federal system."[6]

Yet even in this period of shared national–state responsibility, the national government emphasized cooperation in achieving common national and state goals. Congress generally acknowledged that it had no direct constitutional authority to regulate public health, safety, or welfare. It relied primarily on its powers to tax and spend for the general welfare in order to provide financial assistance to state and local governments to achieve shared goals. Congress did not legislate directly on local matters. For example, Congress did not require the teaching of vocational education in public high schools because public education was not an "enumerated power" of the national government in the U.S. Constitution. But Congress could offer money to states and school districts to assist in teaching vocational education and even threaten to withdraw the money if federal standards were not met. In this way the federal government involved itself in fields "reserved" to the states.

Centralized Federalism (1964–1980).   Over the years it became increasingly difficult to maintain the fiction that the national government was merely assisting the states in performing their domestic responsibilities. By the time President Lyndon B. Johnson launched the Great Society in 1964, the federal government had clearly set forth its own "national" goals. Virtually all problems confronting American society—from solid waste disposal and water and air pollution to consumer safety, street crime, preschool education, and even rat control—were declared to be national problems. Congress legislated directly on any matter it chose, without regard to its "enumerated powers." The Supreme Court no longer concerned itself with the "reserved" powers of the states, and the Tenth Amendment lost most of its meaning. The pattern of national–state relations became centralized. As for the cake analogies, one commentator observed, "The frosting had moved to the top, something like a pineapple upside-down cake."[7]

The states' role under centralized federalism is that of responding to federal policy initiatives and conforming to federal regulations established as conditions for federal grant money. The administrative role of the states remained important; they helped implement federal policies in welfare, Medicaid, environmental protection, employment training, public housing, and so on. But the states' role was determined not by the states themselves but by the national government.

Bureaucracies at the federal, state, and local levels became increasingly indistinguishable. Coalitions of professional bureaucrats—whether in education, public assistance, employment training, rehabilitation, natural resources, agriculture, or whatever—worked together on behalf of shared goals, whether they were officially employed by the federal government, the state government, or a local authority. State and local officials in agencies receiving a large proportion of their funds from the federal government feel very little loyalty to their governor or state legislature.

New Federalism (1980–1985).   Efforts to reverse the flow of power to Washington and return responsibilities to state and local government have been labeled the *new federalism.* The phrase originated in the administration of President Richard M. Nixon, who used it to describe general revenue sharing, that is, federal sharing of tax revenues with state and local governments, with few strings attached. Later the phrase "new federalism" was used by President Ronald Reagan to describe a series of proposals designed to reduce federal involvement in domestic programs and encourage states and cities to undertake greater policy responsibilities themselves. These efforts included the consolidation of many categorical grant programs into fewer block grants, an end to general revenue sharing, and less reliance by the states on federal revenue.

Coercive Federalism (1985–?).   It was widely assumed before 1985 that Congress could not directly legislate how state and local governments should perform their traditional functions. Congress was careful not to issue direct orders to the states; instead, it undertook to grant or withhold federal aid money, depending on whether states and cities abided by congressional "strings" attached to these grants. In theory, at least, the states were free to ignore conditions established by Congress for federal grants and forgo the money.

However, in its 1985 *Garcia* decision, the U.S. Supreme Court removed all barriers to direct congressional legislation in matters traditionally "reserved" to the states.[8] The case arose after Congress directly ordered state and local governments to pay minimum wages to their employees. The Court reversed earlier decisions that Congress could not legislate directly state and local government matters. It also dismissed arguments that the nature of American federalism and the Reserved Powers Clause of the Tenth Amendment prevented Congress from directly legislating state affairs. It said that the only protection for state powers was to be found in the states' role in electing U.S. senators, members of Congress, and the president—a concept known as "representational federalism."

Representational Federalism.   The idea behind representational federalism is that there is *no* constitutional division of powers between states and nation—federalism is defined by the role of the states in electing members of Congress and the president. The United States is said to retain a federal system because its national officials are selected from subunits of government—the president through the allocation of electoral college votes to the states, and the Congress through the allocation of two Senate seats per state and the apportionment of representatives based on state population. Whatever protection exists for state power and independence must be found in the national political process—in the influence of state and district voters on their senators and members of Congress.

The Supreme Court rhetorically endorsed a federal system in the *Garcia* decision but left it up to the national Congress, rather than the Constitution or the courts, to decide what powers should be exercised by the states and the national government. In a strongly worded dissenting opinion, Justice Lewis Powell argued that if federalism is to be retained, the Constitution must divide powers, not the Congress. "The states' role in our system of government is a matter of constitutional law, not legislative grace. . . [This decision] today rejects almost 200 years of the understanding of the constitutional status of federalism."

Federal Preemptions.   The supremacy of federal laws over those of the states, spelled out in the National Supremacy Clause of the Constitution, permits Congress to decide whether or not there is *preemption* of state laws in a particular field by federal law. In *total preemption,* the federal government assumes all regulatory powers in a particular field—for example, copyrights, bankruptcy, railroads, and airlines. No state regulations in a totally preempted field are permitted. *Partial preemption* stipulates that a state law on the same subject is valid as long as it does not conflict with the federal law in the same area. For example, the Occupational Safety and Health Act of 1970 specifically permits state regulation of any occupational safety or health issue on which the federal Occupational Safety and Health Administration (OSHA) has *not* developed a standard; but once OSHA enacts a standard, all state standards are nullified. Yet another form of the partial preemption, the *standard partial preemption,* permits states to regulate activities in a field already regulated by the federal government, as long as state regulatory standards are at least as stringent as those of the federal government. Usually states must submit their regulations to the responsible federal agency for approval; the federal agency may revoke a state's regulating power if it fails to enforce the approved standards. For example, the federal Environmental Protection Agency (EPA) permits state environmental regulations that meet or exceed EPA standards.

Federal Mandates.   Federal mandates are direct orders to state and local governments to perform a particular activity or service, or to comply with federal laws in the performance of their functions. Federal mandates occur in a wide variety of areas, from civil rights to minimum wage regulations. Their range is reflected in some examples of federal mandates to state and local governments:

- *Age Discrimination Act of 1986* Outlaws mandatory retirement ages for public as well as private employees, including police, firefighters, and state college and university faculty.
- *Asbestos Hazard Emergency Act of 1986* Orders school districts to inspect for asbestos hazards and remove asbestos from school buildings when necessary.
- *Safe Drinking Water Act of 1986* Establishes national requirements for municipal water supplies; regulates municipal waste treatment plants.
- *Clean Air Act of 1990* Bans municipal incinerators and requires auto emission inspections in certain urban areas.
- *Americans with Disabilities Act of 1990* Requires all state and local government buildings to promote handicapped access.
- *National Voter Registration Act of 1993* Requires states to register voters at driver's license, welfare, and unemployment compensation offices.
- *No Child Left Behind Act of 2001* Requires states and their school districts to test public school pupils.
- *Help America Vote Act of 2002* Requires states to modernize registration and voting procedures.
- *Real ID Act of 2005* Requires that each state produce a "Real ID" driver's license that meets standards set by the Department of Homeland Security.

State and local governments frequently complain that compliance with federal government mandates such as these imposes costs on them that are seldom reimbursed.

"Unfunded" Mandates.   Federal mandates often impose heavy costs on states and communities. When no federal monies are provided to cover these costs, the mandates are said to be *unfunded mandates.* Governors, mayors, and other state and local officials have often urged Congress to halt the imposition of unfunded mandates on states and communities. Private industries have long voiced the same complaint. Regulations and mandates allow Congress to address problems while pushing the costs of doing so onto others.

Money and Power Flow to Washington

Money and power go together. As institutions acquire financial resources they become more powerful. The centralization of power in Washington has come about largely as a product of growth in the national government's financial resources—its ability to tax, spend, and borrow money.

Federal Grants-in-Aid.   The federal grant-in-aid has been the principal instrument for the expansion of national power. As late as 1952, federal intergovernment transfers amounted to about 10 percent of all state and local government revenue. Federal transfers creeped up slowly for a few years; rose significantly after 1957 with the National Defense (Interstate) Highway Program and a series of post-Sputnik educational programs; and then surged in the welfare, health, housing, and community development fields under President Lyndon B. Johnson's Great Society programs (1965–1968). President Nixon not only expanded these Great Society transfers but also added his own general revenue-sharing program. Federal financial interventions continued to grow despite occasional rhetoric in Washington about state and local responsibility. By 1980, more than 27 percent of all state and local revenue came from the federal government. So dependent had state and local governments become on federal largess that the most frequently voiced rationale for continuing federal grant programs was that states and communities had become accustomed to federal money and could not survive without it (see Figure 12–1).

President Ronald Reagan briefly challenged the nation's movement toward centralized government. The Reagan administration succeeded in consolidating many categorical grant programs in larger block grants, allowing for greater local control over revenue allocation. Categorical grants are awarded to specific projects approved by a federal department distributing designated funds. A block grant is a payment to a state or local government for a general function, such as community development or education. State and local officials may use such funds for their stated purposes without seeking the approval of federal agencies for specific projects.

Today, federal grants again account for about one-quarter of all state and local government spending. It is unlikely that centralizing tendencies in the American federal system can ever be permanently checked or reversed. It is not likely that presidents or members of Congress will ever be moved to restrain national power. People expect them to "Do something!" about virtually every problem that confronts individuals, families, communities, states, or the nation. Politicians risk appearing "insensitive" if they respond by saying that a particular problem is not a federal concern.

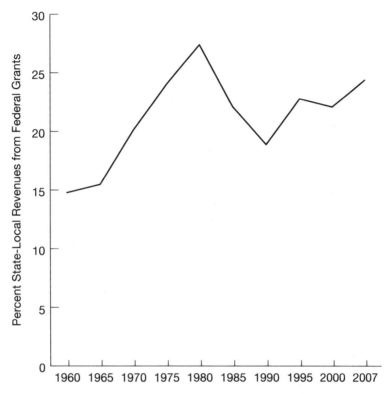

FIGURE 12–1   State and Local Government Dependency on Federal Grants
State and local government dependency on federal money rose sharply prior to
1980; during the Reagan presidency federal grants were curtailed, but have risen
again in recent years.

Federal Grant Purposes.   Federal grants are available in nearly every major category of state
and local government activity. So numerous and diverse are they that there is often a lack of
information about their availability, purpose, and requirements. In fact, federal grants can be
obtained for the preservation of historic buildings, the development of minority-owned
businesses, aid to foreign refugees, the drainage of abandoned mines, riot control, and
school milk. However, health (including Medicaid for the poor) and welfare (including
family cash aid and food stamps), account for more than two-thirds of federal aid money
(see Figure 12–2).

Federalism Revived?

Controversies over federalism are as old as the nation itself. And while over time the flow of
power has been toward Washington, occasionally Congress and even the Supreme Court have
reasserted the constitutional division of power between the federal government and the states.

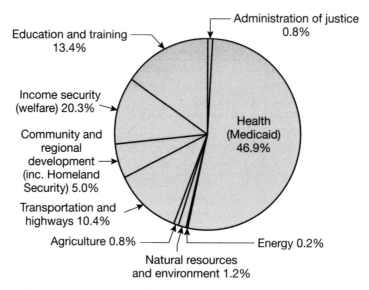

FIGURE 12–2   Purposes of Federal Grant-in-Aid Money Medicaid is the largest category of federal grant money, followed by welfare, education, and transportation.
SOURCE: *Budget of the United States Government*, 2009.

Welfare Reform and "Devolution."   In 1995, with new Republican majorities in both houses of Congress, "Devolution" became a popular catch word. Devolution meant the passing down of responsibilities from the national government to the states, and welfare reform turned out to be the key to devolution. Since Franklin D. Roosevelt's New Deal, with its federal guarantee of cash Aid to Families with Dependent Children (AFDC), low-income mothers and children had enjoyed a federal "entitlement" to welfare benefits. But in 1996 the welfare reform bill passed by Congress and signed by President Clinton (after two earlier vetoes) turned over responsibility for determining eligibility for cash aid to the states, ending the sixty-year federal entitlement. The Temporary Assistance to Needy Families established block grants to the states and gave them broad responsibility for determining eligibility and benefits levels. But Congress did add some "strings" to these grants: states must place a two-year limit on continuing cash benefits and a five-year lifetime limit. This was a major change in federal welfare policy (see Chapter 5).

Supreme Court Revival of Federalism.   Recent decisions of the U.S. Supreme Court suggest at least a partial revival of the original constitutional design of federalism.

In 1995, the Supreme Court issued its first opinion in more than sixty years that recognized a limit on Congress's power over interstate commerce and reaffirmed the Founders' notion of a national government with only the powers enumerated in the Constitution. The Court found that the federal Gun-Free School Zones Act was unconstitutional because it exceeded Congress's powers under the Interstate Commerce Clause. Chief Justice William H. Rehnquist, writing for the majority in a 5-to-4 decision in *United States* v. *Lopez,* even cited James Madison with approval: "The powers delegated by the proposed Constitution are few and defined. Those which are to remain in the state governments are numerous and indefinite."[9]

The Supreme Court also invalidated a provision of a very popular law of Congress, the Brady Handgun Violence Protection Act. The Court decided in 1997 that the law's command to local law enforcement officers to conduct background checks on gun purchasers violated "the very principle of separate state sovereignty." The Court affirmed that the federal government may "neither issue directives requiring the states to address particular problems, nor command the states' officers, or those of their political subdivisions, to administer or enforce the federal regulatory program."[10]

These decisions run counter to most of the Court's twentieth-century holdings that empowered the national government to do just about anything it wished to do under a broad interpretation of the Interstate Commerce Clause. The narrowness of the Court votes in these decisions (5–4) suggested that this revival of federalism might be short-lived. But in 2000, to the surprise of many observers, the Supreme Court held that Congress's Violence Against Women Act was an unconstitutional extension of federal power into the reserved police powers of states. Citing its earlier *Lopez* decision, the Court held that noneconomic crimes are beyond the power of the national government under the Interstate Commerce Clause. "Gender-motivated crimes of violence are not, in any sense, economic activity." The Court rejected Congress's argument that the aggregate impact of crime nationwide has a substantial effect on interstate commerce. "The Constitution requires a distinction between what is truly national and what is truly local, and there is no better example of the police power, which the Founders undeniably left reposed in the States and denied the central government, than the suppression of violent crime and vindication of its victims."[11] But this decision, too, was made by a 5–4 vote of the justices, suggesting that the replacement of justices might reverse this current trend toward federalism by the Supreme Court.

Comparing Public Policies of the States

An overview of state and local government spending suggests the variety of policy areas in which these governments are active. Education is by far the most expensive function of state and local governments: Education accounts for about 35 percent of all state–local spending. Most of this money goes to elementary and secondary schools, but about 9 percent nationwide goes to state universities and community colleges. Welfare, health and hospitals (including Medicaid), and highways place a heavy financial burden on states and communities (see Figure 12–3).

The American states provide an excellent setting for comparative analysis and the testing of hypotheses about the determinants of public policies. Policies in education, welfare, health, highways, natural resources, public safety, and many other areas vary a great deal from state to state, which allows us to inquire about the causes of divergent policies.

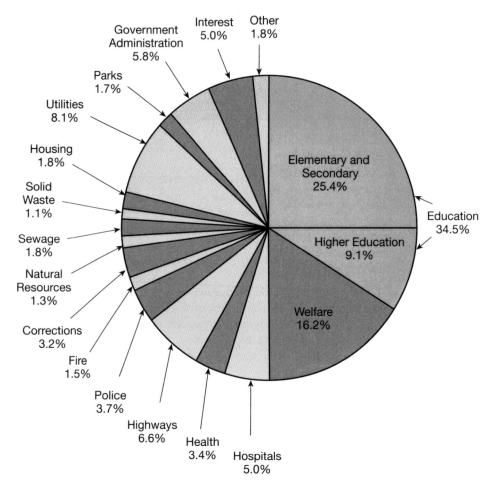

FIGURE 12–3   State–Local Government Expenditures by Function   State and local governments spend more money on education than any other function.
SOURCE: Data from U.S. Bureau of Census, *Governmental Finances 2002,* April 28, 2005.

Variations in State Educational Spending.   Spending for elementary and secondary education varies a great deal among the states (see Table 12–2). Some states (for example New Jersey, New York, Connecticut) spend well over twice as much as other states (for example Utah, Idaho, Arizona, Oklahoma) for the education of the average pupil in public schools. How can we explain such policy variation among the states?

Economic Resources and Public Policy.   Economic research very early suggested that public policies were closely related to the level of economic resources in a society. We can picture this relationship by viewing a "plot" between per capita personal income and per pupil spending in public schools, as shown in Figure 12–4. Per capita income is measured on the horizontal, or *X,* axis, and per pupil spending is measured on the vertical, or *Y,* axis. Each

TABLE 12–2   Policy Variation among the States Federalism allows wide variation among the states in public policies including spending for public schools.

Per Pupil Spending for Public Elementary and Secondary Education

1.	New Jersey	14,954
2.	New York	14,615
3.	Connecticut	13,072
4.	Vermont	12,805
5.	Rhode Island	12,609
6.	Massachusetts	12,564
7.	Delaware	11,621
8.	Alaska	11,476
9.	Wyoming	11,437
10.	Maryland	10,909
11.	Maine	10,841
12.	Pennsylvania	10,723
13.	New Hampshire	10,396
14.	Wisconsin	9,993
15.	Hawaii	9,876
16.	Ohio	9,692
17.	Michigan	9,577
18.	Virginia	9,445
19.	West Virginia	9,440
20.	Nebraska	9,324
21.	Minnesota	9,159
22.	Illinois	9,113
23.	Indiana	8,929
24.	North Dakota	8,728
25.	Oregon	8,645
26.	Kansas	8,644
27.	Montana	8,626
28.	Georgia	8,595
29.	Louisiana	8,486
31.	Iowa	8,355
31.	New Mexico	8,354
32.	California	8,301
33.	Missouri	8,273
34.	Colorado	8,166
35.	South Carolina	8,120
36.	Arkansas	8,030
37.	Washington	7,984
38.	Florida	7,812
39.	South Dakota	7,775
40.	Alabama	7,683
41.	Kentucky	7,668
42.	Texas	7,480
43.	North Carolina	7,396
44.	Nevada	7,177
45.	Mississippi	7,173
46.	Tennessee	7,004
47.	Oklahoma	6,941
48.	Arizona	6,515
49.	Idaho	6,469
50.	Utah	5,464

SOURCE: Data from the National Center for Education Statistics, *http://nces.ed.gov/pups2008.*

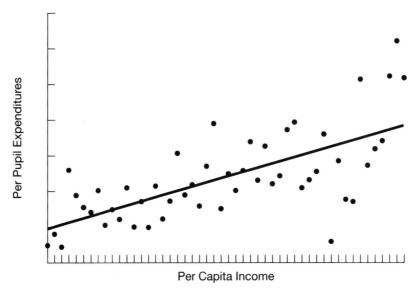

FIGURE 12–4   Fifty States Arranged According to per Capita Personal Income and per Pupil Educational Expenditures   Personal income is the principal determinent of how much states spend on the education of each pupil.

state is plotted in the graph according to its values on these two measures. The resulting pattern—states arranged from the lower left to the upper right—shows that increases in income are associated with increases in educational spending. The diagonal line is a representation of the hypothesis that income largely determines educational spending.

SUMMARY

American federalism creates unique problems and opportunities in public policy. For two hundred years, since the classic debates between Alexander Hamilton and Thomas Jefferson, Americans have argued the merits of policymaking in centralized versus decentralized institutions. The debate continues today.

1. Eighty-seven thousand separate governments—states, counties, cities, towns, boroughs, villages, special districts, school districts, and authorities—make public policy.

2. Proponents of federalism since Thomas Jefferson have argued that it permits policy diversity in a large nation, helps to reduce conflicts, disperses power, increases political participation, encourages policy innovation, and improves governmental efficiency.

3. Opponents of federalism argue that it allows special interests to protect positions of privilege, frustrates national policies, distributes the burdens of government unevenly, hurts poorer states and communities, and obstructs action toward national goals.

4. The nature of American federalism has changed radically over two centuries, with the national government steadily growing in power. "Coercive federalism" refers to Washington's direct mandates to state governments in matters traditionally reserved to the states. "Representational federalism" contends that there is no constitutional division of powers between nation and states and federalism is defined only by the states' role in electing the president and Congress.

5. Over time, power has flowed toward Washington and away from the states, largely as a result of the greater financial resources of national government and its involvement in grant-in-aid programs to state and local governments. These governments are obliged to abide by federal regulations as a condition of receiving federal money. And these governments have become increasingly reliant on federal aid. Today federal aid constitutes about one-quarter of state–local government revenue.

6. Federalism, however, has enjoyed a modest revival in recent years. Congress strengthened federalism in the Welfare Reform Act of 1996 by ending a sixty-year-old federal guarantee of cash assistance and "devolving" the responsibility for cash welfare aid to the states. Nonetheless, Congress attached many "strings" to its welfare grants to the states in the Temporary Assistance to Needy Families program.

7. Federalism has also been strengthened by a series of (narrow 5–4) decisions by the Supreme Court limiting the national government's power under the Commerce Clause and reasserting the authority of the states in the exercise of their police powers.

8. Considerable policy variations exist among the fifty states. For example, tax burdens in some states are more than twice as high as other states, and educational spending per pupil is almost three times greater in some states than others. Economic resources are an important determinant of overall levels of taxing, spending, and services in the states.

Notes

1. James Madison, Alexander Hamilton, John Jay, *The Federalist,* Number 51 (New York: Modern Library, 1958).
2. See Thomas R. Dye, *American Federalism: Competition among Governments* (Lexington, MA: Lexington Books, 1990).
3. David C. Nice, *Federalism: The Politics of Intergovernmental Relations* (New York: St. Martin's Press, 1987), p. 24.
4. Randall G. Holcombe, *An Economic Analysis of Democracy* (Carbondale: Illinois University Press, 1986), p. 174.
5. Morton Grodzins, *The American System* (Chicago: Rand McNally, 1966), pp. 8–9.
6. Ibid., p. 265.
7. Charles Press, *State and Community Governments in the Federal System* (New York: John Wiley, 1979), p. 78.
8. *Garcia* v. *San Antonio Metropolitan Transit Authority,* 469 U.S. 528 (1985).
9. Quoting from *The Federalist,* Number 45, in *United States* v. *Lopez,* 514 U.S. 549 (1995).
10. *Printz* v. *United States,* 521 U.S. 890 (1997).
11. *United States* v. *Morrison,* 529 U.S. 598 (2000).

Bibliography

DYE, THOMAS T. *American Federalism: Competition among Governments.* Lexington, MA: Lexington Books, 1990.

DYE, THOMAS R., and SUSAN A. MACMANUS. *Politics in States and Communities,* 13th ed. Upper Saddle River, NJ: Prentice Hall, 2008.

ELAZAR, DANIEL J. *The American Mosaic.* Boulder, CO: Westview, 1994.

GRAY, VIRGINIA, and RUSSELL L. HARRISON. *Politics in the American States,* 9th ed. Washington, DC: CQ Press, 2007.

KEY, V. O., JR. *American State Politics: An Introduction.* New York: Knopf, 1956.

———. *Southern Politics in State and Nation.* New York: Knopf, 1951.

O'TOOLE, LAURENCE J., JR. *American Intergovernmental Relations,* 4th ed. Washington, DC: CQ Press, 2006.

WALKER, DAVID B. *The Rebirth of Federalism.* New York: Chatham House, 2000.

Web Sites

NATIONAL ASSOCIATION OF STATE INFORMATION RESOURCE EXECUTIVES. Information on state governments by category, for example, "criminal justice," "education," and "finance," as well as access to state home pages. *www.nasire.org*

COUNCIL OF STATE GOVERNMENTS. Organization of state governments providing comparative information on the states, especially in its annual publication *The Book of the States. www.csg.org*

NATIONAL CONFERENCE OF STATE LEGISLATURES. Home page of NCSL providing information on state legislatures, membership, partisan composition, and overview of key issues confronting state legislatures. *www.ncsl.org*

NATIONAL LEAGUE OF CITIES. Official organization of 18,000 cities in the nation, with information on policy positions, including grant-in-aid programs. *www.nlc.org*

NATIONAL CIVIC LEAGUE. Reform organization supporting nonpartisan local government, manager system, etc., with information on local government issues. *www.ncl.org*

INTERNATIONAL CITY/COUNTY MANAGEMENT ASSOCIATION. Official organization of professional city and county managers, with data on city and county government in annual *Municipal Yearbook. www.icma.org*

GOVERNING. Home page of *Governing* magazine, the nation's leading monthly publication directed at state and local government officials, contains information on politics, public affairs, and policy issues. *www.governing.com*

NATIONAL GOVERNORS ASSOCIATION. Official Web site of the nation's governors, with news releases and policy positions. *www.nga.org*

U.S. DEPARTMENT OF HOUSING AND URBAN DEVELOPMENT. Official HUD site, with information on grant programs, federal aid, etc. *www.hud.gov*

13

Defense Policy

Strategies for Serious Games

National Security as a Serious Game

Game theory provides an interesting way of thinking about defense policy. Defense policies of major world powers are interdependent. Each nation must adjust its own defense policies to reflect not only its own national objectives but also its expectations of what other powers may do. Outcomes depend on the combination of choices made in world capitals. Moreover, it is not unreasonable to assume that nations strive for rationality in defense policymaking. Nations choose defense strategies (policies) that are designed to achieve an optimum payoff even after considering all their opponents' possible strategies. Thus, national defense policymaking conforms to basic game theory notions. Our use of game theory is limited, however, to suggesting interesting questions, posing dilemmas, and providing a vocabulary for dealing with policymaking in a competitive, interdependent world.

A rational approach to the formulation of defense policy begins with a careful assessment of the range of threats to the nation and its interests. Once major threats have been identified, the next step is to develop strategies designed to counter them and protect the nation's interests. Once strategies have been devised, defense policymaking must determine the appropriate forces (military units, personnel, weapons, training, readiness, and so forth) required to implement them. Finally, budgets must be calculated to finance the required force levels. Thus, a rational game plan proceeds from

Threat Assessments

to

Strategies

to

Force Levels

to

Budget Requests

Of course, differences and uncertainties arise at each step in this process—differing assessments of the nature and magnitude of the threats facing the nation, the right strategies to confront these threats, the force levels necessary to implement the strategies, and the funds required to provide these forces.

Confronting Nuclear Threats

For more than four decades, following the end of World War II in 1945, the United States and the former Union of Soviet Socialist Republics (USSR) confronted each other in a superpower struggle as intense as any in the history of nations. Indeed, nuclear weaponry made the Cold War more dangerous than any national confrontation in the past. The nuclear arsenals of the United States and the former USSR threatened a human holocaust. Yet paradoxically, the very destructiveness of nuclear weapons caused leaders on both sides to exercise extreme caution in their relations with each other. Scores of wars, large and small, were fought by different nations during the Cold War years, yet American and Soviet troops never engaged in direct combat against each other.

Deterrence.   To maintain nuclear peace, the United States relied primarily on the policy of deterrence. Deterrence is based on the notion that a nation can dissuade a *rational* enemy from attacking by maintaining the capacity to destroy the enemy's society *even after* the nation has suffered a well-executed surprise attack by the enemy. It assumes that the worst may happen— a surprise first strike against our own nuclear forces. It emphasizes *second-strike* capability—the ability of a nation's forces to survive a surprise attack by the enemy and then to inflict an unacceptable level of destruction on the enemy's homeland in retaliation. Deterrence is really a psychological defense against attack; no effective physical defenses against a ballistic missile attack exist even today. The strategy of deterrence maintains peace through fear of retaliation.

Strategic Weapons.   To implement the deterrence strategy, the United States relied on a TRIAD of weapons systems: (1) land-based intercontinental ballistic missiles (ICBMs), (2) submarine-launched ballistic missiles (SLBMs), and (3) manned bombers. Each "leg" of the TRIAD was supposed to be an independent, survivable, second-strike force. Thus, each leg posed separate and unique problems for an enemy who sought to destroy the U.S. second-strike deterrent.

Arms Control Games

The United States and the Soviet Union engaged in negotiations over strategic arms for many years. They began in 1970 under President Richard Nixon and his national security advisor, Henry Kissinger, and were originally labeled the Strategic Arms Limitation Talks (SALT).

SALT I.   SALT I, in 1972, was a milestone in that it marked the first effort by the superpowers to limit strategic nuclear weapons. It consisted of a formal treaty halting further development of antiballistic missile systems (ABMs) and an executive agreement placing numerical limits on offensive missiles. The ABM treaty reflected the theory that the populations of each nation should remain *un*defended from a ballistic missile attack in order to hold them hostage against a first strike by either nation. This MAD theory (mutual assured destruction) was based on the idea that no rational government would order an attack on another nuclear superpower knowing that its own population would be wiped out in a retaliatory attack.

SALT II.   After seven more years of difficult negotiations, the United States and the Soviet Union signed the lengthy and complicated SALT II Treaty in 1979. It set an overall limit on "strategic nuclear launch vehicles"—ICBMs, SLBMs, and bombers with cruise missiles—at 2,250 for each side. It also limited the number of missiles that could have multiple warheads (MIRVs). When the Soviet Union invaded Afghanistan, President Carter withdrew the SALT II Treaty from Senate consideration. However, Carter, and later President Reagan, announced that the United States would abide by the provisions of the unratified SALT II treaty as long as the USSR did so too.

START.   In negotiations with the Soviets, the Reagan administration established three central principles of arms control—*reductions, equality*, and *verification*. The new goal was to be reductions in missiles and warheads, not merely limitations on future numbers and types of weapons, as in previous SALT negotiations. To symbolize this new direction, President Reagan renamed the negotiations the Strategic Arms Reductions Talks, or START.

START.   The long-awaited agreement on long-range strategic nuclear weapons was finally signed in Moscow in 1991 by Presidents George H. W. Bush and Mikhail Gorbachev. The START I Treaty reduced the total number of deployed strategic nuclear delivery systems (ICBMs, SLBMs, and manned bombers) to no more than 1,600, a 30 percent reduction from the SALT II level. The total number of strategic nuclear warheads were reduced to no more than 6,000, a reduction of nearly 50 percent. Verification included on-site and short-notice inspections, as well as "national technical means" (satellite surveillance).

START II.   The end of the Cold War was confirmed by the far-reaching START II agreement between President George H. W. Bush and Russian President Boris Yeltsin. This agreement promised to eliminate the threat of a first-strike nuclear attack by either side. Its most important provision called for the elimination of all multiwarhead (MIRV) land-based missiles. It also called for the reduction of overall strategic warheads to 3,500, slashing the nuclear arsenals of both nations by more than two-thirds from Cold War levels (see Figure 13–1).

The Treaty of Moscow.   Strategic nuclear arms reductions progressed further with the Treaty of Moscow, signed by Russian President Vladimir Putin and U.S. President George W. Bush in 2002. This treaty calls for an overall limit of nuclear warheads at 1,700–2,200 by 2012. Each side may determine for itself the composition and structure of its strategic forces consistent with this limit. The provisions of the START treaties remain unchanged. The effect of the Moscow Treaty, together with earlier reductions in nuclear weapons under the START treaties, will be to reduce the nuclear arsenals of the former adversaries by over 80 percent from Cold War levels (see Figure 13–1).

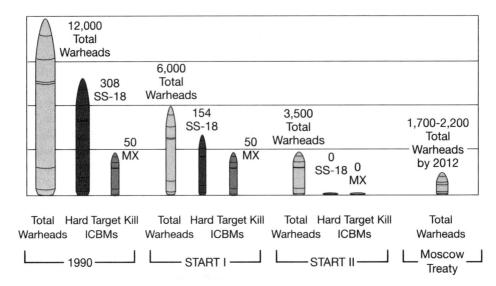

FIGURE 13–1   Strategic Nuclear Arms Reductions   Post–Cold War treaties between United States and Russia have dramatically reduced the number of nuclear warheads held by both nations.

Nuclear Testing and Nonproliferation.   The United States and the former Soviet Union reached an agreement in 1963—the Limited Test Ban Treaty—that prohibited nuclear testing in the atmosphere, under water, or in outer space. The effect was to allow only underground testing, which was believed to reduce radioactivity in the atmosphere. A Threshold Test Ban Treaty was signed in 1974 that prohibited tests of nuclear weapons with explosive power greater than 150 kilotons (equivalent to 150,000 tons of conventional explosives).

In 1992 the Russian government under President Yeltsin announced that it would discontinue *all* nuclear testing if the United States would do the same. President George H. W. Bush declined to make this pledge, but later President Bill Clinton placed a moratorium on U.S. nuclear testing. In 1996, President Clinton signed a Comprehensive Test Ban Treaty, a multilateral agreement that prohibits all nuclear testing. Many nonnuclear-armed nations signed this treaty. But in 1999 the U.S. Senate voted against ratification. Opponents of the treaty noted that testing verified the safety and reliability of weapons, and that several other potentially threatening nuclear nations had refused to sign the treaty, including North Korea, Iran, India, and Pakistan. Russia announced that it was awaiting U.S. ratification before signing the treaty, and China continued testing nuclear weapons.

Yet another multilateral treaty, the nuclear Nonproliferation Treaty, was signed by the United States and the former Soviet Union in 1968. It prohibits nuclear-armed nations from transferring weapons and technologies to nonnuclear nations. Nonnuclear signing nations pledged not to "receive, manufacture, or otherwise acquire nuclear weapons." But the Nonproliferation Treaty has been largely ignored, not only by nations that went on to acquire nuclear weapons (including India, Pakistan, China, and North Korea), but also by nations that have transferred nuclear technology to nonnuclear nations (including France and Russia).

Missile Defenses: The Limits of Deterrence

For over a half-century, since the terrible nuclear blasts of Hiroshima and Nagasaki in Japan in 1945, the world has avoided nuclear war. Peace has been maintained by deterrence—by the threat of devastating nuclear attacks that would be launched in retaliation to an enemy first strike. Nuclear peace has depended on rational leaders who would not endanger their own populations.

Nondeterrable Threats.   But even as the threat of a large-scale nuclear attack recedes, the threats arising from "nondeterrable" sources are increasing. Today, the principal nondeterrable nuclear threats are estimated to be (1) missiles launched by a terrorist nation, or a "rogue" nation whose leaders are prepared to sacrifice their own people to a retaliatory strike, and (2) missile launches by terrorist groups who have acquired nuclear weapons and the means of delivering them. Global nuclear and ballistic missile proliferation steadily increases over time the likelihood of these types of threats. Attacks by rogue nations and terrorist groups are considered nondeterrable because the threat of nuclear retaliation is largely meaningless.

"Star Wars."   In 1993 President Ronald Reagan urged that instead of deterring war through fear of retaliation, the United States should seek a technological defense against nuclear missiles.

> Our nuclear retaliating forces have deterred war for forty years. The fact is, however, that we have no defense against ballistic missile attack. . . . In the event that deterrence failed, a president's only recourse would be to surrender or to retaliate. Nuclear retaliation, whether massive or limited, would result in the loss of millions of lives. . . .[1]

Reagan's Strategic Defense Initiative (SDI) was a research program designed to explore means of destroying enemy nuclear missiles in space before they could reach their targets. Following President Reagan's initial announcement of SDI in March 1983, the press quickly labeled the effort "Star Wars." In theory, a ballistic missile defense (BMD) system could be based in space, orbiting over enemy missile-launching sites. Should an enemy missile get through the space-based defense, a ground-based BMD system would attempt to intercept warheads as they reentered the atmosphere and approached their targets. SDI included research on laser beams, satellite surveillance, computerized battle-management systems, and "smart" and "brilliant" weapons systems. SDI under President Reagan was a very ambitious program with the goal of creating an "impenetrable shield" that would protect not only the population of the United States but the populations of our allies as well.

Protecting against Nuclear Terrorism.   The end of the Cold War refocused missile defense research away from a massive Russian missile attack to much more limited yet more likely threats. Today the principal nuclear threats are missiles launched by terrorist groups or a "rogue state." President George W. Bush notified the Russians in 2002 that the United States was withdrawing from provisions of the SALT I Treaty of 1972 that prohibited the development, testing, or deployment of new ballistic missile defense systems.

Advanced testing has met with both successes and failures. Intercepting an incoming missile has been compared to "hitting a bullet with a bullet." Even this daunting challenge is further complicated by the likelihood of enemy decoys masking the real warhead; a reliable ballistic missile defense must be able to discriminate between decoys and actual warheads. In early 2008 the U.S. Navy successfully intercepted and destroyed a falling reconnaissance satellite with a sea-based anti-ballstic missile.

The actual deployment of a limited number of ground-based and sea-based missile interceptors began in 2004. This initial missile defense capability is designed "to meet the near-term threat to our homeland, our deployed forces, and our friends and allies."[2] It is directed at potential attacks from terrorist states. Currently the U.S. has BMDs based in Alaska, presumably to defend against missiles from North Korea.

President George W. Bush proposed to deploy BMD sites in Poland and the Czech Republic in order to defend Europe against missiles from Iran. But Russia vigorously opposed such a deployment. In 2009 President Barack Obama canceled this deployment, hoping that in exchange Russian President Dimitry Medvedev would help in preventing Iran from acquiring nuclear weapons.

NATO and European Security

The preservation of democracy in Western Europe was the centerpiece of U.S. foreign and military policy for most of the twentieth century. The United States fought in two world wars to preserve democracy in Europe.

Origins of NATO.   In response to aggressive Soviet moves in Europe after World War II, the United States, Canada, Belgium, Britain, Denmark, France, Iceland, Italy, Luxembourg, the Netherlands, Norway, and Portugal joined in the North Atlantic Treaty Organization (NATO). Each nation pledged that "an armed attack against one . . . shall be considered an attack against them all." Greece and Turkey joined in 1952 and West Germany in 1955. To give this pledge credibility, a joint NATO military command was established with a U.S. commanding officer (the first was General of the Army Dwight D. Eisenhower). After the formation of NATO, the Soviets made no further advances in Western Europe. The Soviets themselves, in response to NATO, drew up a comparable treaty among their own Eastern European satellite nations—the Warsaw Pact. It included Poland, Hungary, Czechoslovakia, Romania, Bulgaria, and the German Democratic Republic (the former East Germany).

Collapse of Communism in Eastern Europe.   The dramatic collapse of the communist governments of Eastern Europe in 1989—Poland, Hungary, Romania, Bulgaria, and East Germany—vastly reduced the threat of a military attack on Western Europe. The dismantling of communist governments came about as a direct result of President Mikhail Gorbachev's decision to renounce the use of Soviet military force to keep them in power. For over forty years, the communist governments of Eastern Europe were supported by Soviet tanks; bloody Soviet military operations put down civilian uprisings in Hungary in 1956 and Czechoslovakia in 1968. The threat of Soviet military intervention crushed the Solidarity movement in Poland in 1981, yet that same movement became the government of Poland in

1989. Any effort today by a Russian leader to reimpose control over Eastern European nations would probably result in widespread bloodshed.

Germany United.   The collapse of the Berlin Wall in 1989 and the formal unification of Germany in 1990 rearranged the balance of military power in central Europe. Today Germany is the strongest military power in Western Europe. It remains a member of NATO.

Collapse of the Warsaw Pact and the USSR.   The Warsaw Pact collapsed following the ouster of communist governments in the Eastern European nations and was officially dissolved in 1991. Its former members requested the withdrawal of Russian troops from their territory; the Russian government complied, although withdrawals were slowed by economic conditions in that nation.

At the same time strong independence movements emerged in the republics of the USSR. Lithuania, Estonia, and Latvia—Baltic Sea nations that had been forcibly incorporated into the Soviet Union in 1939—led the way to independence in 1991. Soon all fifteen republics declared their independence, and the Union of Soviet Socialist Republics officially ceased to exist after December 31, 1991. Russian President Boris Yeltsin took over the offices of former Soviet Union President Mikhail Gorbachev. The red flag with its banner and sickle atop the Kremlin was replaced by the flag of the Russian Republic.

NATO and Western Europe.   If Russia, Ukraine, and the other republics of the former Soviet Union make a full transition to democracy and capitalism, the twenty-first century promises much more peace and prosperity for the peoples of the world than the twentieth century. The residual threat to Western Europe posed by Russian forces, even under a hostile regime, is very weak. However, the total withdrawal of U.S. military forces from Western Europe would probably mean an end to the NATO alliance. Proponents of a continued U.S. military presence in Europe argue that it provides reassurance and stability as democracy emerges in Eastern Europe; they note that both our old allies and new friends in Europe have urged the United States to remain involved in European security. Opponents counter that the Western European nations are now quite capable of shouldering the burden of their own security.

NATO Expansion.   Despite Russian objections, NATO extended its membership eastward in 1997 by admitting Poland, Hungary, and the Czech Republic. Proponents of NATO expansion argued successfully that a historic opportunity existed to solidify freedom and democracy in Eastern Europe by admitting those nations to NATO. Russia was reassured that it would be "consulted" on NATO policies, but was given no veto powers over these policies or no guarantee that other Eastern European nations might also be admitted to NATO in the future. Indeed, in 2003 NATO admitted seven former Communist countries of Eastern Europe—Estonia, Latvia, and Lithuania, together with Bulgaria, Romania, Slovakia, and Slovenia. NATO now includes a total of 26 nations (see Figure 13–2).

NATO and Ethnic Conflicts in the Balkans.   Traditionally, NATO forces were never deployed outside of Western Europe. Yet ethnic wars in the former communist nation of Yugoslavia, and the media coverage of the hardships endured by the people there, inspired NATO to intervene and deploy troops to Bosnia in 1995 to halt conflict raging among

FIGURE 13–2 NATO Nations of Europe[*] NATO was originally created to protect the nations of Western Europe from Soviet expansion; the collapse of the Soviet Union in 1991 has led to the expansion of NATO into Eastern European nations formerly dominated by the old Soviet Union.
*NATO members United States and Canada not shown.

Serbs, Croats, and Muslims. The United States provided about one-third of the ground troops deployed in Bosnia as "peacekeepers." Yet some argued that U.S. national security interests were not at stake in southeastern European ethnic conflicts and therefore American troops should not be exposed to the dangers of intervention.

NATO again acted militarily to halt ethnic conflict in Kosovo in 1999. NATO's objective was to force Serbian troop withdrawal from the largely Muslim province. NATO relied exclusively on bombing from the air to force the Serbian withdrawal. Despite some controversy, even among NATO nations, as well as denunciations from Russia and China, NATO aircraft and missiles hit targets in both Kosovo and Serbia itself. (Even the Chinese embassy in the Serbian capital of Belgrade was bombed, apparently by mistake.) Eventually, Serbian troops were withdrawn from Kosovo.

NATO in Afghanistan. The United States turned over command of its military forces in Afghanistan to NATO in 2003. NATO created an International Security Assistance Force, officially under UN auspices, "to assist the Islamic Republic of Afghanistan in creating a stable and secure environment for the people of Afghanistan." Some thirty-seven nations contribute troops to this Force, but the U.S. contributes the largest number. To date NATO forces have failed to capture Osama bin Laden and failed to eliminate Taliban forces from Afghan mountainous regions along the Pakistan border. (See "Using Military Forces: Afghanistan," page 302.)

When to Use Military Force?

All modern presidents have acknowledged that the most agonizing decisions they have made were to send U.S. military forces into combat. These decisions cost lives. The American people are willing to send their sons and daughters into danger—and even to see some of them wounded or killed—but *only* if a president convinces them that the outcome "is worth dying for." A president must be able to explain why they lost their lives and to justify their sacrifice.

To Protect Vital Interests. The U.S. military learned many bitter lessons in its long, bloody experience in Vietnam. Secretary of State Colin Powell was among the younger officers who served in Vietnam. Later General Powell became national security adviser to President Ronald Reagan and then chief of staff during the Gulf War under President George H. W. Bush; still later he would serve as secretary of state under President George W. Bush. The lessons of Vietnam were summarized by the "Powell Doctrine":[4]

- The United States should commit its military forces only in support of vital national interests.

- If military forces are committed, they must have clearly defined military objectives— the destruction of enemy forces and/or the capture of enemy-held territory.

- Any commitment of U.S. forces must be of sufficient strength to ensure overwhelming and decisive victory with the fewest possible casualties.

- Before committing U.S. military forces, there must be some reasonable assurances that the effort has the support of the American people and their representatives in Congress.

- The commitment of U.S. military forces should be a last resort, after political, economic, and diplomatic efforts have proven ineffective.

These guidelines for the use of military force are widely supported within the U.S. military itself. Contrary to Hollywood stereotypes, military leaders are extremely reluctant to go to war when no vital interest of the United States is at stake, where there are no clear-cut military objectives, without the support of Congress or the American people, or without sufficient force to achieve speedy and decisive victory with minimal casualties. They are wary of seeing their troops placed in danger merely to advance diplomatic goals, or to engage in "peacekeeping," to "stabilize governments," or to "build democracy." They are reluctant to undertake humanitarian missions while being shot at. They do not like to risk their soldiers' lives under "rules of engagement" that limit their ability to defend themselves.

In Support of Important Political Objectives. In contrast to military leaders, political leaders and diplomats often reflect the view that "war is a continuation of politics by other means"—a view commonly attributed to nineteenth-century German theorist of war Carl von Clausewitz. Military force may be used to protect interests that are important but not necessarily vital. Otherwise, the United States would be rendered largely impotent in world affairs. A diplomat's ability to achieve a satisfactory result often depends on the expressed or implied threat of military force. The distinguished international political theorist Hans Morganthau wrote: "Since military strength is the obvious measure of a nation's power, its demonstration serves to impress others with that nation's power."[5]
Currently American military forces must be prepared to carry out a variety of missions in addition to the conduct of conventional war:

- Demonstrating U.S. resolve in crisis situations
- Demonstrating U.S. support for democratic governments
- Protecting U.S. citizens living abroad
- Striking at terrorist targets to deter or retaliate
- Peacemaking among warring factions or nations
- Peacekeeping where hostile factions or nations have accepted a peace agreement
- Providing humanitarian aid often under warlike conditions
- Assisting in international efforts to halt drug trafficking

In pursuit of such objectives, recent U.S. presidents have sent troops to Lebanon in 1982 to stabilize the government (Reagan), to Grenada in 1983 to rescue American medical students and restore democratic government (Reagan), to Panama in 1989 to oust drug-trafficking General Manuel Antonio Noriega from power and to protect U.S. citizens (Bush), to Somalia in 1992–1993 to provide emergency humanitarian aid (Bush and Clinton), to Haiti in 1994 to restore constitutional government (Clinton), and to Bosnia in 1995 for peacekeeping among warring ethnic factions and to force Serbian withdrawal from Kosovo in 1999 (Clinton) (see Table 13–1).
Proponents of these more flexible uses of U.S. military forces deny any intent to be the "world's policeman." Rather, they argue that each situation must be judged independently on its own merits—weighing the importance of U.S. goals against expected costs. No military operation is without risk, but some risks may be worth taking to advance important political interests even though these interests may not be deemed "vital" to the United States. The media, particularly television, play an influential role in pressuring the president to use military force. Pictures of torture and killing, starvation and death, and devastation and destruction from around the world provide a powerful emotional stimulus to U.S. military intervention. Generally a president can count on an initial "rally' round the flag" surge in popular support for a military action, despite overall poor public knowledge of international

TABLE 13–1   Major Deployments of U.S. Military Forces since World War II Every president since World War II has found it necessary to deploy U.S. troops abroad.

Year	Area	President
1950–53	Korea	Truman
1958	Lebanon	Eisenhower
1961–64	Vietnam	Kennedy
1962	Cuban waters	Kennedy
1965–73	Vietnam	Johnson, Nixon
1965	Dominican Republic	Johnson
1970	Laos	Nixon
1970	Cambodia	Nixon
1975	Cambodia	Ford
1980	Iran	Carter
1982–83	Lebanon	Reagan
1983	Grenada	Reagan
1989	Panama	Bush
1990–91	Persian Gulf	Bush
1992–93	Somalia	Bush, Clinton
1994–95	Haiti	Clinton
1995–96	Bosnia	Clinton
1999	Kosovo	Clinton
2002–	Afghanistan	Bush, Obama
2003–	Iraq	Bush

politics. But if casualties mount during an operation, if no victory or end appears in sight, then press coverage of body bags coming home, military funeral services, and bereaved families create pressure on a president to end U.S. involvement. Unless the U.S. military can produce speedy and decisive results with few casualties, public support for military intervention wavers and critical voices in Congress arise.

In Support of the War on Terrorism.   The War on Terrorism creates new conditions for the use of military force.[6] Currently U.S. forces are prepared for:

- Direct attacks against terrorist forces to capture or kill them. These operations are usually carried out by highly trained Special Operations Forces.

- Attacks on nations that harbor terrorists, allow terrorists to maintain bases, or supply and equip terrorist organizations. In 1986, the United States struck at Libya in a limited air attack in response to various Libyan-supported acts of terrorism around the world. In 1993, the United States struck Iraq's intelligence center in Baghdad in response to a foiled plot to assassinate former President George H. W. Bush. In 2001, the United States relied principally on Special Forces working in conjunction with tribal forces in Afghanistan to attack Al Qaeda terrorists and to topple the Taliban government that had harbored and supported Al Qaeda (see below).

- Preemptive attacks on regimes that threaten to use weapons of mass destruction—chemical, biological, or nuclear weapons—against the United States or its allies, or to supply terrorist organizations with these weapons. Preemptive military action represents a reversal of traditional U.S. policy. Historically, the United States acted militarily only in response to a direct attack on its own forces or those of its allies. But it is argued that the terrorist attacks of 9/11 initiated the current War on Terrorism and that American military actions in the Middle East, including those in Afghanistan and Iraq, are related to the 9/11 attacks on America. The argument for preemptive military action was summarized by President Bush's National Security Adviser Condoleezza Rice: "We cannot wait until the smoking gun becomes a mushroom cloud."

Threats, Strategies, and Forces

Overall, military force levels in the United States should be threat-driven, that is, determined by the size and nature of the perceived threats to national security. It is true that particular weapons systems or base openings or closings may be driven by political forces such as the influence of defense contractors in Congress or the power of a member of Congress from a district heavily affected by defense spending. And not everyone in the White House and Congress, or even the Defense Department, agrees on the precise nature of the threats confronting the United States now or in the future. Yet defense policy planning and the "sizing" of U.S. military forces should begin with an assessment of the threats confronting the nation.

The End of the Cold War.   The end of the Cold War rationalized deep cuts in military forces and defense budgets in the 1990s. Active duty military personnel declined from 2.1 million to 1.4 million. The Army was reduced to ten active combat divisions and the Air Force to twelve fighter wings (a U.S. Army division includes 15,000 to 18,000 troops; and a Air Force fighter wing includes approximately 70 combat aircraft). The Navy was reduced to twelve and later eleven carrier battle groups (a carrier battle group typically includes one aircraft carrier with sixty-five to seventy-five aircraft, plus defending cruisers, destroyers, frigates, attack submarines, and support ships). The Marine Corps retain all three of its Marine expeditionary forces (each MEF includes one Marine division, one Marine air wing, and supporting services) (see Table 13–2). National Guard and Reserve forces were assigned a larger and more active role. There are an additional 1.2 million persons in the Army, Navy, Air Force, and Marine reserve forces. Military deployments in Iraq and Afghanistan required many of these reserve units to be called to active duty.

The Army continues to maintain the equivalent of ten active duty divisions. However, the Army has been reorganized into thirty-eight Brigade Combat Team (BCTs). Each BCT includes about 3,500 soldiers; BCTs may be armored (tanks), mechanized infantry, airborne (paratroopers), air assault (helicopter borne), or Stryker (combined arms). The Air Force has been reorganized into ten Aerospace Expeditionary Forces (AEFs). Each AEF combines bomber, fighter, attack, refueling, and reconnaissance aircraft.

Confronting Regional Threats.   Following the Gulf War in 1991, U.S. military planning focused on the possibility of *two* regional aggressors attacking at the same time. If U.S. troops were heavily engaged in one regional conflict similar to the Gulf War, defense strategists worried about a second aggressor taking advantage of the U.S. military commitment to

Table 13–2   Military Force Level   Military force levels declined rapidly after the end of the Cold War, igniting criticism that American troops are spread "too thin."

	End of Cold War 1990	2000	2008
Active duty personnel (in millions)	2.1	1.4	1.4
Army divisions	18	10	10 (38 BCTs)
Navy carrier battle groups	15	12	11
Marine expeditionary forces	3	3	3
Air Force fighter wings	24	12	(10 AEFs)

SOURCE: Office of the Secretary of Defense.

Note: BCT = Brigade Combat Team; AEF = Aerospace Expeditionary Forces.

launch its own military action elsewhere against the United States or its allies or interests. The most common scenario for simultaneous regional threats was a heavy U.S. military involvement in the Middle East, and the possibility that an Asian regional power would be tempted to take advantage of that commitment to launch its own aggression (for example North Korea against South Korea, China against Taiwan). While officially recognizing the "Two Major Theaters of War" threat as late as 2002, the U.S. never possessed the forces to prevail in major conflicts in the Middle East and Asia simultaneously. Current force levels make it unlikely that the U.S. could do more than "hold" in one conflict while pursuing victory in another, and then later shifting forces to the second conflict. The United States is most deficient in airlift and sealift forces—the cargo, supply, and weapons and troop-carrying capability required to move combat forces around the world.

Fighting Terrorism.   Confronting terrorism brought a new emphasis in defense policy on nonconventional forces and tactics. Special Operations Forces played a central role in ousting the Taliban regime from Afghanistan. Special Operations Forces on the ground, together with manned and unmanned surveillance aircraft in the skies, provided the targeting intelligence for U.S. air attacks from carriers in the Arabian Sea, attack aircraft based in the Middle East, and even long-range bombers based in the continental United States. These attacks allowed Afghan forces opposed to the regime to capture the capital, Kabul, two months after the initiation of Operation Enduring Freedom.

Asymmetrical Warfare of the Future.   Traditionally the U.S. structured its military tactics and forces to confront conventional threats—national armies with heavy armor, tanks and artillery, mechanized infantry, and combat aircraft. During the Cold War, U.S. forces were designed to confront heavy Soviet armor and artillery in Central Europe, in a manner similar, albeit more violent, to the armies that fought in World War II. The Gulf War in 1991 demonstrated the superiority of American forces in large-scale conventional operations.

The war on terror requires the U.S. to reshape its military planning to confront unconventional (or asymmetrical) wars—lightly armed irregular enemy forces engaging in tactics such as ambushes, hidden explosives, suicide bombings, and hostage takings. America's enemies are fully aware of the overwhelming firepower of conventional U.S. military forces. Consequently they seek to minimize U.S. advantage in firepower in a variety of ways. They choose terrain that inhibits the use of conventional tank artillery and air power—jungles and mountains where these conventional forces cannot operate as effectively as in open country. They also choose built-up urban areas where civilian populations inhibit U.S. forces from employing their full firepower. They avoid direct confrontations with large American units, blending in with the population and seeming to disappear in the presence of U.S. combat forces.

Asymmetrical warfare is the approach of a weaker foe trying to overcome the advantages of a force that is superior in conventional forms of warfare. Traditionally, the U.S. Army preferred that its opponents face it and massed formations on conventional battlefields where overwhelming American power could be brought to bear to destroy the opponent. But an inferior opponent would be foolhardy to cooperate in its own destruction by fighting the war that Americans prefer to fight. Guerrilla warfare, which United States encountered in Vietnam, is one form of asymmetrical warfare. Terrorism is another, which includes consciously targeting civilians.

"In the future the United States is likely to confront a new and radically different form of warfare:

> "in the future there will be no distinctions between civilians and military forces in terms of targeting: society is the battlefield in the new environment. There will be an absence of definable battlefields or fronts, and the places where fighting occurs will be disbursed and undefined: everywhere and nowhere is the front lines. . . . The goal will not be traditional military defeat but instead the internal political collapse of the opponent and its will to continue. The manipulation of the media will be a skill that is highly sought by practitioners [of this kind of warfare], and the targets of much of this activity will be popular support for the government or whatever force against which the campaign is waged."[6]

Counterinsurgency Emphasis. Secretary of Defense Robert Gates expressed his belief that "asymmetric warfare will remain the mainstay of the contemporary battlefield for some time." The experiences in Afghanistan and Iraq are currently shaping U.S. military planning. Among the current developments:

• Expansion of the size of the Army and Marine Corp in recognition of the need for more "boots on the ground."
• Transformation of a division-based Army into one organized in Brigade Combat Teams.
• Heavier reliance on Army Reserve and National Guard units. (Some of these units were called for multiple tours of duty in Afghanistan and Iraq.)
• Introduction of new equipment, including mine resistant and ambush protection vehicles (MAPVs) and unmanned aerial vehicles (UAVs), capable of both reconnaissance and attack missions.
• Overhaul of the counterinsurgency doctrine to shift operations away from "enemy-centric" armed conflict toward a "population-centric" approach emphasizing political goals and the importance of social and cultural factors in military operations.

While many military leaders agree with the new emphasis on asymmetrical threats, others argue that the true lesson of Afghanistan and Iraq is that U.S. forces should avoid protracted commitments to "peacekeeping" and "nationbuilding" and instead undertake only those military operations that promise rapid, decisive results.

Peacekeeping.   U.S. military forces are currently deployed in more than 120 countries around the world. The largest deployments are in Iraq, South Korea, and Afghanistan, but large numbers of U.S. forces are deployed in Qatar, Bahrain, Saudi Arabia, Kuwait, Bosnia, Kosovo, Philippines, Japan, Cuba (Guantanamo), Colombia, Honduras, and the NATO countries, including Great Britain, Germany, Italy, Ireland, and Turkey.

Traditionally U.S. military forces were trained for combat, not "peacekeeping." Currently, however, the U.S. military is tailoring more of its training, doctrine, and equipment to its peacekeeping missions. This means increasing the numbers of military police, civil affairs units, local force trainers, and humanitarian relief supply units.

Stretched Too Thin?   Over the past decade, U.S. military forces have been assigned increasing numbers of war-fighting and peacekeeping missions. Yet force levels have remained minimal.

Experience has taught the U.S. military that casualties can be kept low only when overwhelming military force is employed quickly and decisively. Lives are lost when minimal forces are sent into combat, when they have inadequate air combat support, or when they are extended over too broad a front. Current numbers of Army and Air Force combat units and the limited transport and support services available to the military are inadequate for two major regional conflicts. Potential regional foes—for example, Iran and North Korea—deploy modern heavy armor and artillery forces. Commitments of U.S. troops to peacekeeping and humanitarian missions divert resources, training, and morale away from war-fighting. Morale is also affected when U.S. military forces are deployed abroad for long periods of time; this is especially true for National Guard and Reserve troops.

Using Military Force: The Gulf War

Saddam Hussein's invasion of Kuwait in August, 1990, was apparently designed to restore his military prestige after a long and indecisive war against Iran; to secure additional oil revenues to finance the continued buildup of Iraqi military power; and to intimidate (and perhaps invade) Saudi Arabia and the Gulf states, thereby securing control over a major share of the world's oil reserves. Early in the crisis President George H. W. Bush committed U.S. forces to the Gulf region for the military defense of Saudi Arabia. The president described the early U.S. military deployment as "defensive." But he soon became convinced that neither diplomacy, UN resolutions, nor an economic blockade would dislodge Saddam from Kuwait. He ordered his military commanders to prepare an "offensive" plan that would force the withdrawal of Iraqi forces from Kuwait.

The top military commanders—including the Chairman of the Joint Chiefs of Staff, General Colin Powell, and the commander in the field, General Norman Schwarzkopf—were reluctant to go into battle without the full support of the American people. If ordered to fight, they wanted to employ *overwhelming and decisive military force*; they wanted to avoid gradual escalation, protracted conflict, target limitations, and political interference in the conduct of the war. Accordingly, they presented the president with a plan that called for a very large military buildup. More than 500,000 U.S. military personnel were sent to the Gulf region.

In November 1990, Secretary of State James Baker won the support of the UN Security Council for a resolution authorizing the "use of all necessary means" against Iraq to force its withdrawal from Kuwait. Following a lengthy debate in Congress, in January 1991, President Bush won a similar resolution in the House (250–183) and in the Senate (52–47). President Bush succeeded in putting together a large coalition of nations in support of military action. The British and French sent significant ground combat units, and smaller units from Gulf Arab states also participated.

From Baghdad, CNN reporters were startled on the night of January 16, 1991, when Operation Desert Storm began with an air attack on key installations in the city. After five weeks of air war, intelligence estimated that nearly half of Iraq's tanks and artillery had been destroyed, that demoralized troops were hiding in deep shelters, and that the battlefield had been isolated and prepared for ground operations. On the night of February 24, the ground attack began. Marines breached ditches and minefields and raced directly to the Kuwait airport. Army helicopter assaults lunged deep into Iraq; armored columns raced northward across the desert to outflank Iraqi forces and attack them from the West; and a surge in air attacks kept Iraqi forces holed up in their bunkers. Iraqi troops surrendered in droves, highways from Kuwait City became a massive junkyard of Iraqi vehicles, and Iraqi forces that tried to fight were quickly destroyed. After one hundred hours of ground fighting, President Bush ordered a cease-fire.

The United States had achieved a decisive military victory quickly and with remarkably few casualties. The president resisted calls to expand the original objectives of the war and to go on to capture Baghdad or to kill Saddam, although it was expected that his defeat would lead to his ouster. President Bush chose to declare victory and celebrate the return of American troops. But the results of the war were mixed. In retrospect, the president's decision to end the war after only one hundred hours of ground operations appears to have been premature. With his surviving forces, Saddam maintained his cruel grip on the country and proceeded to attack his regime's opponents brutally, even using chemical weapons against the Kurdish minority in northern Iraq. Tens of thousands of Iraqis were killed in Saddam's retribution following the departure of American troops.

Using Military Force: Iraq

At the end of the Gulf War in 1991, the Iraqi regime of Saddam Hussein agreed to destroy all of its chemical and biological weapons and to end its efforts to acquire nuclear weapons. United Nations inspectors were to verify Iraqi compliance with these conditions. But Saddam's regime refused to cooperate: in 1998 he ordered the inspectors out of the country. Over a twelve-year period Iraq violated at least a dozen UN resolutions. Following a U.S. military buildup in the region in late 2002, Saddam allowed UN inspectors to return but continued to obstruct their work. On March 19, 2003, after giving Saddam a forty-eight-hour warning to leave Iraq, the United States and Great Britain launched air strikes designed to eliminate Saddam and his top command.

Operation Iraqi Freedom. At different times President George W. Bush stated the purposes of Operation Iraqi Freedom as (1) the elimination of Iraq's weapons of mass destruction, (2) a "regime change" for Iraq to end the threat that Saddam posed for his neighbors and to free the Iraqi people from his oppressive rule, and (3) to ensure that Saddam would not harbor or assist terrorist organizations. But President Bush and Secretary of State Colin Powell failed to secure UN Security Council approval for military action. Among the permanent members of the Security Council, only the British, with the strong support of Prime Minister Tony Blair, were prepared to offer significant military support for the war against Saddam. Public opinion in America supported military action, but public opinion in Europe opposed it. France and Germany led the diplomatic opposition; Turkey refused to let U.S. troops use its territory to attack Iraq; and the U.S. was obliged to rely primarily on Kuwait, Qatar, and the other smaller Gulf states for regional support.

The U.S. military wanted to wage war in the fashion of the successful Gulf War—a period of heavy air bombardment to "prepare the battlefield," followed by a massive ground attack using overwhelming military force. But Secretary of Defense Donald Rumsfeld wanted a "leaner" fighting force in Iraq. He deployed fewer than half of the air, ground, and naval forces that had been used in the Gulf War. And he began the air and ground attacks simultaneously.

American and British soldiers and Marines took just twenty-one days to sweep the 350 miles from the Kuwait border to downtown Baghdad. The British 3rd Armored Division with Australian support captured the port city of Basra; the U.S. 3rd Infantry Division moved up the west side of the Euphrates River; and the U.S. 1st Marine Division moved up the east side. Special Operations Forces together with elements of the 101st Airborne Division joined Kurdish forces in northern Iraq. Special Operations Forces also acted quickly to secure Iraq's oil fields and prevent their destruction. At first, progress was hindered by the requirement that soldiers wear heavy chemical protection gear and carry decontamination equipment. But neither chemical nor biological weapons were used against U.S. forces. The advance on Baghdad was speeded up and the city was captured with precious few casualties.

President Bush announced "the end of major combat" on May 1, 2003, but the real war in Iraq had just begun.

What Went Wrong in Iraq?

The war in Iraq was a "preemptive" strike against terrorism, consistent with the declarations of the Bush administration about the necessity of fighting terrorists on their own ground rather than on American soil. American, British, and other intelligence services reported that Iraq had chemical and biological weapons and was in the process of acquiring enriched uranium for the construction of nuclear weapons. Initially public opinion in America supported military action. Yet much of what had been learned at a high cost in Vietnam and summarized by the Powell Doctrine (described above) was ignored.

Limits on the Number of Troops.　Early on, Defense Secretary Donald Rumsfeld decided to place severe limits on the number of troops sent to Iraq. This decision was part of his broader vision of a "lean" military force. And indeed, this force was able to quickly capture Baghdad. Within weeks, however, an insurgent movement developed that soon inflicted far more casualties on U.S. troops than were experienced in the capture of Iraq's capital. U.S. troops were stretched so thin across Iraq that they could not hold cities or neighborhoods after they had been captured. Supply lines could not be defended and the insurgents quickly

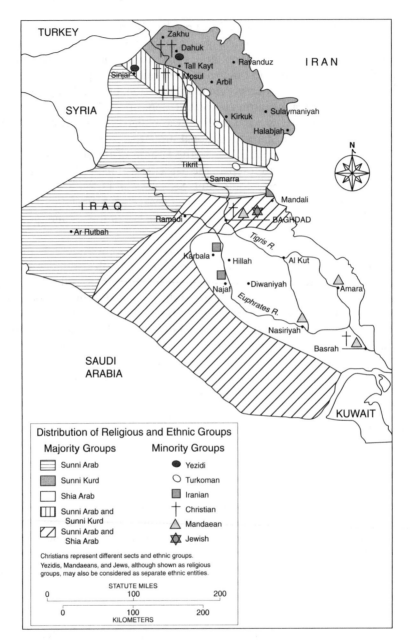

FIGURE 13–3   Religious and Ethnic Groups in Iraq. Iraq encompasses multiple religious and ethnic groups. The principal divisions are between Sunni, Shia, and Kurds.

SOURCE: *Iraq Study Group Report* (2006).

learned to plant IEDs—improvised explosive devices—along routes commonly used by U.S. troops. More casualties were inflicted by these devices than by any other means; the U.S. did not have enough troops to guard supply routes.

American Troops Used for "Nation Building."   The American occupation of Iraq started out poorly and proceeded over time to become worse. Planning for postwar Iraq appeared nonexistent. The U.S. administrator for Iraq, Paul Bremmer, began by dismissing the entire Iraqi Army, sending thousands of well-armed, unemployed young men into the streets. The U.S. promised to restore infrastructure—water, electricity, roads, etc.—yet Bremmer pursued a policy of dismissing virtually all Iraqi managers and technicians on the grounds that they had been Baathists (Saddam's ruling party members). Later, the U.S. would be obliged to begin recruiting and training an Iraqi Army and police force and bringing in U.S. contract workers, managers, and technicians. Bremmer was fired after one year.

Soon, Iraqi street mobs that had earlier torn down Saddam's statue began demonstrations against the American presence. An insurgent movement seemed to surprise Secretary of Defense Donald Rumsfeld. He steadfastly refused to send additional U.S. troops to Iraq to handle the insurgency and insisted that a new Iraqi government could eventually recruit and train enough troops to contain the insurgency.

No weapons of mass destruction were found despite an intensive search. Saddam himself was captured and turned over to the Iraqis. After a bizarre show trial, he was convicted of mass murder and executed by hanging.

Iraq held its first nationwide election in fifty years in 2003, despite violence and threats of violence. Nearly 60 percent of the population participated, many proudly displaying their blue-inked thumbs to signal that they had voted. The result was a new constitution that was approved in a second vote that year. However, a substantial number of Sunnis boycotted the elections, fearing a loss of their power and the ascendancy of the Shiites. The United States officially turned over sovereignty to a new Iraqi government in 2004.

Involvement in Civil Strife.   The population of Iraq is composed of three major factions: the Kurds, who occupy most of northeastern Iraq; the Shiites, who occupy most of southern Iraq; and the Sunnis, who occupy central Iraq. Baghdad itself Is divided between Sunni and Shiite neighborhoods (see Figure 13–3). The Sunnis have long dominated Iraq. Saddam's family was Sunni. Yet the Shiites are the largest faction, with more than half of the total population of Iraq. Over the years, the Kurds have fought for a separate outcome strongly opposed by neighboring Turkey.

By 2006 most of the violence in Iraq was occurring among various factions; thousands of Iraqi were victims of sectarian killings. The Shiites, the majority of Iraq's population, gained power for the first time in more than 1000 years. Above all, the Shiites are interested in preserving that power. The Sunnis fear displacement and the loss of their traditional position of power in Iraq. The Kurds seek at a minimum quasi-independence and control over the oil resources in their region. The Shiites also seek control over oil in southern Iraq. But

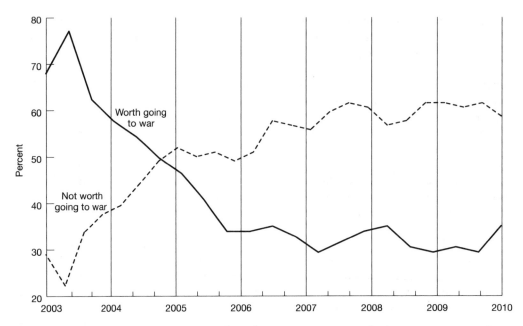

FIGURE 13–4   Changing Public Opinion about the War in Iraq Support for the war in Iraq among the American people declined over time.
SOURCE: *www.pollingreport.com.*

the areas with the largest Sunni population lack oil resources, so the Sunni fight to maintain control of all of Iraq. Corruption is rampant throughout Iraq, the judiciary is weak, oil production is down, and the U.S.-backed government is unable to produce an acceptable plan of national reconciliation.[7]

Costs to the U.S. Military.   American military forces suffered a gruesome toll in lives and limbs. By 2006 over 4,000 American troops had been killed, many from "improvised explosive devices." U.S. Army and Marine forces approached the "breaking point." Nearly every Army and Marine combat unit, and several National Guard and Reserve units, were rotated into Iraq more than once. The strain on U.S. forces worldwide became clearly evident, with both personnel and equipment wearing down.

"Clear Hold and Build."   U.S. policy in Iraq focused primarily on security. The key phrase was "clear, hold, and build." U.S. military forces were to clear neighborhoods, cities, towns, and regions of insurgents, then hold the cleared areas with U.S. trained and equipped Iraqi army and police forces; and then to begin to rebuild infrastructure. U.S. forces were able to "clear" many areas, but there were too few troops to "hold" these areas. Iraqi forces were unable or unwilling to halt insurgents from reoccupying these areas after American troops left. Very little "building" took place. Many members of the Iraqi security forces remained loyal to their sectarian—Shiite or Sunni—goals, rather than the agenda of the national government. Many of these units simply refused to carry out assigned missions.

Nevertheless, President Bush continued to argue that the war in Iraq was central to the worldwide war against terrorism. He argued that an abrupt withdrawal ("cut and run") would encourage radical Islamic terrorists around the world.

> Failure is not an option. Iraq would become a safe haven from which terrorists could plan attacks against American interests abroad, and our allies. Middle East reformers would never again fully trust American assurances of support for democtacy in human rights in the region Iraq is the central front in the global war on terror.[8]

The "Surge." The sweeping Democratic victory in the congressional elections of 2006 was widely attributed to popular disaffection with the war in Iraq. Democrats gained control of both the House and the Senate. Many of their supporters expected them to end the war by cutting off funds for the prosecution of the war. At a minimum, opponents of the war wanted Congress to set a timetable for the reduction of U.S. troops in Iraq. But when staring directly at the prospect of cutting off funds for troops in the field, Congress blinked. Resolutions to end the war failed, as did effects to set a timetable for troop withdrawal.

Instead, President Bush announced a "surge" in troop strength designed to improve security in Iraq and allow the Iraqi government to reach "benchmarks" in resolving civil strife. The "surge" involved increasing U.S. troop levels in Iraq from roughly 138,000 to 160,000. In January 2007 the president appointed a new commander for Iraq, General David Petraeus. Petraeus was unanimously confirmed by the Senate, but Congress stipulated that in September, 2007, the general was to report on progress in Iraq.

Petraeus reported to Congress that the "surge" was working, that progress was being made in stabilizing Iraq and training Iraqi forces, that U.S. troop levels could be reduced to pro-surge levels, but that some U.S. forces may be needed in Iraq for ten years or more. He argued that a timetable for troop reductions would be counterproductive.

Loss of Public Support. Americans demand quick victory in war. With the exception of World War II, American public support for wars, notably Korea (1950–53) and Vietnam (1965–73), declined steadily as casualties rose and no end appeared in sight. The initial "rally round the flag" support for military action begins to wane after the first year of combat Quick victories with few casualties, as in the Gulf War (1991), inspire support for the president and his decision to go to war. Prolonged stalemates with mounting casualties gradually erode public support for war.

Shortly after the war in Iraq began, most Americans thought Iraq was worth going to war over. Indeed, this opinion climbed to 76 percent immediately following the capture of Baghdad. But as American casualties mounted and no end to the fighting appeared in sight, mass opinion in support of the war declined rapidly. By late 2004 the majority of Americans believed that Iraq was "not worth going to war" (see Figure 13–4).

Withdrawal of Combat Forces. In the presidential campaign of 2008, Barack Obama pledged to end the war in Iraq "responsibly." He warned against "an occupation of undetermined length, with undetermined costs and undetermined consequences." Upon taking office in January 2009, Obama ordered the U.S. military to plan for a phased withdrawal of American combat forces from Iraq. The expectation was that the U.S. could "redeploy"

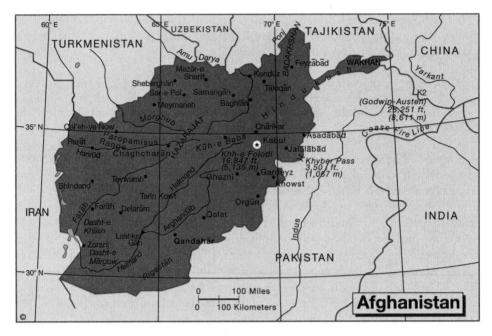

FIGURE 13–5   Afghanistan

combat brigades at a pace of one to two per month over a sixteen-month period, ending in the summer of 2010. A "residual force" was to remain in Iraq—to conduct targeted counterterrorism missions against Al Qaeda and to protect American diplomatic and civilian personnel. This residual force would continue to train and support Iraqi security forces "as long as Iraqi leaders move toward political reconciliation and away from sectarianism."[9]

The thrust of U.S. policy in Iraq was to shift from military to diplomatic efforts. The phased withdrawal itself was expected to encourage Iraqis to provide for their own security and to work toward real political reconciliation among the factions. The political tasks expected of the Iraqis included compromises on oil revenue sharing, equitable provision of services, continued reform of security forces, and the elimination of corruption in government.

Obama pledged to try to achieve comprehensive stability in the region by negotiating with Iran and Syria. The objective would be to secure Iraq's borders, isolate Al Qaeda, support reconciliation among Iraqi factions, and provide support for reconstruction and development.

Using Military Force: Afghanistan

The military phase of the war on terrorism began October 7, 2001, less than one month after September 11. U.S. Air Force and Navy aircraft began attacks on known Al Qaeda bases in Afghanistan and U.S. Special Forces organized and led anti-Taliban fighters, including several tribal groups calling themselves the Northern Alliance, in a campaign against the Taliban regime. A coalition of nations participated in Operation Enduring Freedom; some, including Britain and Canada, contributed troops, while others, including Pakistan, Saudi Arabia, and Uzebekistan, informally allowed U.S. forces to base operations on their territory. Kabul, the capital of Afghanistan, was occupied by anti-Taliban forces on November 13, 2001.

President Bush made it clear that the United States was prepared to act militarily against governments that harbored or gave sanctuary to terrorists. The Taliban regime was ousted from power. By April 2002—six months into Operation Enduring Freedom—Al Qaeda and Taliban forces had been scattered into small groups in the mountainous areas of Afghanistan and neighboring Pakistan (see Figure 13–5). Osama bin Laden himself, however, escaped capture.

A meeting in Bonn, Germany, of various Afghan political and military groups produced general agreement on the installation of a new government in Kabul, headed by Hamid Karzai. The Karzai government has less than full control over Afghanistan various tribal military chiefs, or "warlords," exercise independent power throughout the country.

Al Qaeda Resurgence. While campaigning for the presidency in 2008 Barack Obama drew a sharp distinction between the war in Iraq and the war in Afghanistan. Iraq, he claimed, had diverted America's attention away from the greater dangers posed by Al Qaeda and Taliban forces in Afghanistan. It was Al Qaeda that was responsible for the September 11, 2001, attacks on the New York Trade Center and the Pentagon, and it was the Taliban regime in Afghanistan that provided Al Qaeda with safe haven. And evidence was mounting of a resurgence of Al Qaeda and its Taliban allies in the southern and eastern mountainous areas of Afghanistan and across the border in neighboring Pakistan.

Shortly after entering the White House, President Obama ordered a strategic review of the situation in Afghanistan and Pakistan. The review concluded that the situation was "increasingly perilous," with Al Qaeda and its Taliban allies controlling large sections of both Afghanistan and Pakistan. Additional combat brigades were to be sent to the region as well as thousands of trainees for Afghanistan army and police forces. The U.S. was also to make a heavy financial investment in the economic development of both countries.

Counterinsurgency Operations. The announced goal of U.S. policy is to "disrupt, dismantle, and defeat" Al Qaeda in both Afghanistan and Pakistan. The policy suggests that Al Qaeda will no longer find safe haven across the border in Pakistan. Economic and military aid to Pakistan is to be contingent upon that country's commitment to its own security and its willingness to "confront violent extremists." Afghanistan will offer a test of the U.S. military's concept of asymmetrical (counterinsurgency) warfare.

Limited Objective. U.S. policy recognizes that Afghanistan's 25 million people are divided along ethnic lines. The central government in Kabul exercises little control over a country the size of Texas. U.S. strategy appears to be to win over local tribes and leaders, including Taliban forces that are not allied to Al Qaeda. The objective of U.S. policy is not necessarily to bring Western-style democracy to Afghanistan, but rather to ensure that the country does not become a safe haven for Al Qaeda and its terrorist allies.

SUMMARY

Decisions about defense policy in Washington and in other capitals are interdependent—strategies, force levels, and spending decisions depend on perceived threats posed by other major powers. Game theory provides a way of thinking rationally about decision making in competitive, interdependent situations.

1. During the long Cold War, deterrence strategy prevented nuclear war by making the consequences of a nuclear attack unacceptable to a rational enemy. Deterrence emphasized *second-strike* capability—the ability of a nation's forces to survive an attack and inflict unacceptable levels of destruction on the attacker in retaliation.

2. The end of the Cold War resulted in a decline in overall strategic nuclear forces by two-thirds. The START agreements slashed total nuclear warheads on both sides and required the elimination of all land-based MIRV missiles. The resulting force levels on both sides virtually eliminated the possibility of launching a rational first strike.

3. Current strategic debate focuses on nondeterrable threats—missiles launched by terrorist nations or by terrorist groups. Global nuclear proliferation increases the likelihood of these threats. President Ronald Reagan began a large-scale research program, the Strategic Defense Initiative (SDI), or "Star Wars," to develop a capability to intercept and destroy incoming ballistic missiles. President George W. Bush redirected missile defense from large-scale Russian attacks to smaller attacks by terrorist nations. He withdrew the United States from the SALT I Treaty banning the deployment of missile defenses. The U.S. currently deploys limited land-based (Alaska) and sea-based anti-ballstic missiles.

4. In the NATO alliance the United States and Western European nations pledged that an armed attack against one would be considered an armed attack against all. A joint NATO military command is designated to implement this pledge. The collapse of communist governments in Eastern Europe, the unification of Germany, and the dissolution of the Soviet Union greatly diminished the threat to European security. NATO has expanded to 28 countries including countries formerly in the Soviet orbit.

5. The end of the Cold War rationalized drastic reductions in Army and Air Force combat units. Navy and Marine combat units, traditionally designed for regional wars, endured less drastic cuts. The end of the Cold War also brought dramatic reductions in defense spending.

6. The United States has never adopted clear policy guidelines regarding when to use military force. Most military leaders argue that troops should be used only to protect vital national interests, with clearly defined military objectives, and with the support of Congress and the American people. Furthermore, military force should only be used with sufficient force to achieve speedy and decisive victory with minimum casualties, and only as a last resort.

7. In contrast, many political and diplomatic leaders argue that troops may be used in support of important political objectives and humanitarian goals. These may include demonstrating U.S. resolve in crisis situations, U.S. support for democratic governments,

peacemaking among warring factions or nations, peacekeeping where hostile parties have agreed to a settlement, and the provision of humanitarian aid.

8. The war on terrorism added to the responsibilities of the military, including direct attacks against terrorist forces and attacks against nations that harbor terrorists or that seek to develop weapons of mass destruction. These responsibilities envision preemptive attacks.

9. The attack on Afghanistan in 2001 was successful in dislodging the Taliban government that had aided and assisted Al Qaeda terrorists. But Al Qaeda and Taliban forces regrouped in the mountainous border area with Pakistan.

10. The war in Iraq, beginning in 2002, was expected to eliminate weapons of mass destruction (WMDs), end the regime of Saddam Hussein, and ensure that Iraq would not threaten its neighbors or become a haven for terrorists. Following the rapid capture of Baghdad, however, no WMDs were found and an insurgency grew that eventually caused far more casualties among U.S. and British troops than the capture of Baghdad. Conflict between Shia and Sunni sects threatened civil war.

11. By 2004, a majority of Americans had turned against the War in Iraq, declaring in polls that it was "not worth" the sacrifice in American casualties. A troop "surge" in 2007 appeared to reduce overall violence. Following victories in the 2006 congressional elections, Democrats tried but failed to set dates for the withdrawal of U.S. troops from Iraq.

12. Upon taking office, President Barack Obama ordered the phased withdrawal of American combat forces from Iraq over a sixteen-month period. A residual force was expected to remain to conduct counter-terrorist missions, protect American personnel, and train Iraq security forces.

Notes

1. President Ronald Reagan, *The President's Strategic Defense Initiative,* The White House, January 3, 1985.
2. Office of the President, *National Security Strategy of the United States, 2002* (Washington, DC: U.S. Government Printing Office, 2002).
3. U.S. Department of Defense, *2002 Annual Defense Report* (Washington, DC: Department of Defense, 2002).
4. General Colin Powell, testimony before the Budget Committee of the U.S. Senate, February 1992.
5. Han Morganthau, *Politics among Nations* (New York: Knopf, 1973), p. 27.
6. Donald M. Snow, *National Security for a New Era* (New York: Pearson, 2008), p. 309.
7. *The Iraq Study Group Report* (New York: Vintage Books, 2006).
8. President George W. Bush, *National Strategy in Victory in Iraq,* November 1, 2005, *www.whitehouse.gov.*
9. *www.whitehouse.gov/agenda/Iraq.*

Bibliography

Editors of *Time. 21 Days to Baghdad.* New York: Time Books, 2003.

COMBS, CYNTHIA C. *Terrorism in the 21st Century,* 4th ed. Upper Saddle River, NJ: Prentice Hall, 2006.

Chairman of the Joint Chiefs of Staff, *National Military Strategy to Combat Weapons of Mass Destruction.* Febraury 13, 2006. *www.defenselink.gov*

The Iraq Study Group. New York: Vintage, 2006.

Office of the President. *Quadrennial Defense Review.* Washington, DC: U.S. Government Printing Office, 2003.

SNOW, DONALD M. *National Security for a New Era*, 3rd ed. New York: Longman, 2009.

SUMMERS, HARRY G., JR. *On Strategy II: A Critical Analysis of the Gulf War.* New York: Dell, 1992.

The Military Balance. London: International Institute for Strategic Studies, annually.

Web Sites

U.S. DEPARTMENT OF DEFENSE. Official Web site of the Defense Department, with news column photos, and links to Army, Navy, Air Force, and Marine Web sites, and Web sites of all Unified Commands. *www.defense.link.gov*

CENTRAL INTELLIGENCE AGENCY. Official Web site of the CIA, with history, news, press releases, and links to its *World Factbook* and *Factbook on Intelligence* and other publications. *www.cia.gov*

NORTH ATLANTIC TREATY ORGANIZATION. Official Web site of NATO, with history, membership, facts, and current issues. *www.nato.int*

COUNCIL ON FOREIGN RELATIONS. Home page of the CFR, with information on world trade, globalization, national security and defense, etc. *www.cfr.org*

NATIONAL SECURITY COUNCIL. Official site of the NSC, with membership, functions, press releases, and information on national security issues. *www.whitehouse.gov/nsc*

UNITED NATIONS. Official site of the UN, with news, resolutions, agenda issues, and links to all UN agencies. *www.un.org*

GLOBAL SECURITY. News and information about weapons, forces, and military conflicts around the world. *www.globalsecurity.org*

AMERICAN SECURITY COUNCIL. Organization providing summary information on national security threats. *www.ascusa.org*

14

Homeland Security

Terrorism and Nondeterrable Threats

The Nature of Terrorism

Maintaining peace and security through deterrence assumes *rational* enemies—enemies who are *un*willing to bring death and destruction upon themselves, their own people, or their own nation, in response to their own aggression. For a half-century, before the terrorist attacks on America, September 11, 2001, the defense of the homeland of the United States relied primarily on deterrence—convincing potential enemies that an attack on our nation would result in devastating losses to themselves and their people. But "9/11" awakened America to the threat of terrorism—deliberate attacks on civilian targets by enemies who are willing to sacrifice themselves and their people to their cause.

The attack of "9/11" resulted in 3,000 deaths in New York, Washington, and Pennsylvania. Commercial airliners with civilian passengers were hijacked and flown at high speeds directly into the symbols of America's financial and military power—the World Trade Center in New York and the Pentagon in Washington. Televised images of the collapse of New York City's largest buildings left a lasting impression on Americans.

The Goals of Terrorism.   Terrorism is political violence directed against innocent civilians.* As barbaric as terrorism appears to civilized peoples, it is not without a rationale. Terrorists are not "crazies." Their first goal is to announce in the most dramatic fashion their own grievances, their commitment to violence, and their disregard for human life, often including their own. In its initial phase the success of a terrorist act is directly related to the publicity it receives. Terrorist groups jubilantly claim responsibility for their acts. The more horrendous, the more media coverage, the more damage, the more dead—all add to the success of the terrorists in attracting attention to themselves.

---

*Title 22 of the U.S. Code, Section 2656 (d): "The term 'terrorism' means premeditated, politically motivated violence perpetrated against noncombatant targets by subnational groups or clandestine agents, usually intended to influence an audience."

A prolonged campaign of terrorism is designed to inspire pervasive fear among people, to convince them that their government cannot protect them, and to erode their confidence in their nation's leadership. (The Latin root of the term, *terrere*, means "to frighten.") The horror of terrorist acts and their unpredictability add to public fear—people can neither anticipate nor prepare for tragedies inflicted upon them. Terrorists hope that people will eventually conclude that submission to the terrorists' demands is preferable to living in a continuing climate of anxiety and uncertainty.

Democratic leaders are particularly vulnerable to terrorism. They must respond quickly and effectively to maintain the confidence of their people. But in doing so they are almost always forced to sacrifice some of the very liberties they are dedicated to protect—increased surveillance with cameras, wiretaps, and other detection devices; stopping and searching citizens without cause; searches at airports, terminals, and public gatherings; detention of persons for long periods without trial; crackdowns upon immigrants; and other restrictive measures.

Global Terrorism.   Global terrorism has evolved over the years into highly sophisticated networks operating in many countries. The most notable terrorist attacks extend back over thirty years (see Table 14–1). Prior to the attacks on New York's World Trade Center and the Pentagon on September 11, 2001, most Americans thought of terrorism as foreign. Terrorist acts on American soil had been rare; the most destructive attack—the Oklahoma City

TABLE 14–1 Selected Global Terrorist Acts Major terrorist attacks occur regularly around the world.

Date	Number of People Killed	Description	Prime suspect(s)
September 5, 1972	17	Israeli athletes are killed during the Olympics in Munich, Germany	Black September, a Palestinian guerrilla group
April 18, 1983	63	The American Embassy in Beirut, Lebanon, is bombed	Hezbollah (Party of God)
October 23, 1983	299	Two truck bombs kill U.S. Marines and French paratroopers in Beirut, Lebanon	U.S. blames groups aligned with Iran and Syria
June 23, 1985	329	An Air India jet explodes over the Atlantic Ocean, off the coast of Ireland	The Royal Canadian Mounted Police charge Ajaib Singh Bagri and Ripudaman, two Sikh dissidents, in 2000
November 29, 1987	115	A Korean Air Lines jet explodes over the Burma coast	South Korea suspects North Korean involvement
December 21, 1988	270	Pan Am 103 explodes over Lockerbie, Scotland	One Libyan intelligence officer is convicted in a trial in the Hague in 2001, another is acquitted

TABLE 14–1 **Continued**

Date	Number of People Killed	Description	Prime suspect(s)
February 26, 1993	6	A van filled with explosives explodes in the garage of the World Trade Center, leaving more than 1,000 people wounded	Ramzi Yousef receives a life sentence plus 240 years in 1998; the FBI suspects Osama bin Laden is behind the plot
April 19, 1995	168	Oklahoma City truck bomb destroys Alfred P. Murrah federal building	Timothy McVeigh executed June 11, 2001
August 7, 1998	224	Car bombs destroy U.S. embassies in Nairobi, Kenya, and Dar Es Salaam, Tanzania	Al Qaeda (Osama bin Laden) suspected
October 12, 2000	17	Rubber boat filled with explosives detonates next to USS *Cole* in Yemen	Al Qaeda (Osama bin Laden) suspected
September 11, 2001	2,999	Four U.S. commercial airliners hijacked. Two destroy World Trade Center, one hits the Pentagon, one crashes in Pennsylvania	Al Qaeda (Osama bin Laden) suspected
March 11, 2004	191	Bombing of train in Madrid, Spain	Al Qaeda suspected
September 3, 2004	355 (155 children)	Chechen terrorists attack school in Russia	Chechens
July 7, 2005	58	Four bombs set off London transit system	Unknown
July 11, 2006	209	Mumbai (Bombay) India train bombings	Kashmir muslims
December 27, 2007	22	Benizar Bhutto, Pakistan opposition leader assasinated in bombing	unknown

SOURCE: U.S. National Counterterrorism Center, 2009. *www.nctc.gov.*

bombing of a federal building in 1995—had been carried out by a domestic terrorist. But the 9/11 attacks were on an unprecedented scale and they revealed a sophisticated global plot against America.

A loose-knit network of terrorist cells (Al Qaeda) organized by a wealthy Saudi Arabian, Osama bin Laden, was engaged in global terrorism. Their political grievances included America's support of Israel in Middle East conflicts and an American presence in Islamic holy lands, notably Saudi Arabia. Several nations share these grievances and, more important, provided support and haven to Al Qaeda in similar terrorist organizations. The U.S. State Department lists as terrorist-sponsoring states: Syria, Iran, Iraq, Sudan, Cuba, and North Korea. Countries on the State Department watch list are Afghanistan, Pakistan, Lebanon, and Yemen. But the principal base of support and sanctuary for Al Qaeda was the repressive and violent Taliban regime of Afghanistan.

Post–9/11 Response

On the evening of September 11, 2001, President George W. Bush spoke to the American people from the Oval Office in a nationally televised address:

> The pictures of airplanes flying into buildings, fires burning, huge structures collapsing, have filled us with disbelief, terrible sadness, and a quiet, unyielding anger. These mass murders were intended to frighten our nation into chaos and retreat. But they failed, our country is strong . . . These deliberate and deadly attacks were more than acts of terror. They were acts of war.[1]

The president outlined a broad "response to terrorism" to be fought both at home and abroad through diplomatic, military, financial, investigative, homeland security, and humanitarian means. He warned that the new "war on terrorism" would require a long-term sustained effort.

Aviation Security.   The 9/11 attacks frightened many airline travelers. The first response of Congress was the Aviation and Transportation Security Act of 2001. After some partisan bickering over whether or not airport security people should be federal employees or private contractors, Congress and the president finally agreed to create a new Transportation Security Agency that, among other things, would federalize all airport baggage and passenger screening, require all checked baggage to be screened, authorize federal marshals on domestic and international flights, and tighten airport security throughout the United States. The Transportation Security Agency is now part of the Department of Homeland Security.

The USA Patriot Act.   But an even more sweeping enactment followed: the USA Patriot Act of 2001, officially the Uniting and Strengthening America Act by *P*roviding *A*ppropriate *T*ools *R*equired to *I*ntercept and *O*bstruct *T*errorism. President Bush and Attorney General John Ashcroft successfully lobbied the Congress to increase the federal government's powers of searches, seizures, surveillance, and detention of suspects. The concerns of civil libertarians were largely swept aside. The American public generally supported new restrictions on their liberty. The act was passed nearly unanimously in the Senate (98–1) and overwhelmingly in the House (337–66), with the support of both Democrats and Republicans.

Among the key provisions of the Patriot Act:

- *Roving Wiretaps.* Allows wiretaps of any telephones that suspects might use, instead of requiring separate warrants for each line.

- *Internet Tracking.* Allows law enforcement authorities to track Internet communications, that is, to "surf the Web" without obtaining warrants.

- *Business Records.* Allows investigators to obtain information from credit cards, bank records, consumer purchases, libraries, schools and colleges, and so on.

- *Foreign Intelligence Surveillance Court.* A special Foreign Intelligence Surveillance Court (FISA) may issue search warrants on an investigator's assertion that the information sought is relevant to a terrorist investigation. No showing of "probable cause" is required. The warrant is not made public, in order to avoid "tipping off" the subject.

- *Property Seizure.* Authorizes the seizure of the property of suspected terrorists. Persons whose property is seized bear the burden of proof that the property was not used for terrorist purposes in order to secure the return of their property.

- *Detention.* Allows the detention of suspected terrorists for lengthy periods.

- *Aliens Reporting and Detention.* Authorizes the Immigration and Customs Enforcement (ICE) to require reporting by aliens of selected nations and indefinite detention of illegal aliens suspected of terrorist connections.

- *Prohibits Harboring of Terrorists.* Creates a new federal crime: knowingly harboring persons who have committed, or are about to commit, a terrorist act.

Surveillance Powers. Congress passed a Foreign Intelligence Surveillance Act (FISA) in 1978 that established a special court to oversee requests for surveillance warrants against suspected domestic terrorists and foreign intelligence agents operating inside the United States. The FBI is the principal agency requesting FISA warrants. The FISA court is a "secret court"—hearings are closed and records are not available to the public.

The National Security Agency (NSA) has the responsibility for monitoring foreign electronic intelligence. NSA is an important component of the intelligence community (see Figure 14–3 later in this chapter). NSA is not authorized to undertake surveillance of domestic targets. But controversy arose following the 9/11 attack's regarding NSA surveillance of international calls between one party located within the United States and another party in a foreign country.

President George W. Bush authorized NSA to intercept international telephone calls made to and from the United States. These intercepts were done without warrants from the FISA court. President Bush argued that obtaining warrants from the FISA court was too slow, and that the president, as commander in chief during wartime, could authorize the gathering of intelligence by means of his choosing. But critics charged that the president acted lawlessly in authorizing warrantless telephone intercepts.

At President Bush's urgent request, Congress passed a Protect America Act in 2007. It authorizes warrantless surveillance of electronic communications of targets "reasonably believed" to be outside of the United States. It authorizes warrantless intercepts of calls and e-mails between overseas targets and persons located within the United States. It also allows warrantless monitoring of foreign communications that travel through telecommunications equipment located in the United States. Domestic-to-domestic communications still cannot be intercepted without a FISA warrant. Congress also dismissed lawsuits against communications companies that had cooperated earlier in the president's surveillance program.

Enemy Combatants. The U.S. military detains hundreds of "enemy combatants." These include people captured in the fighting in Afghanistan and Iraq as well as terrorists captured in other nations. Traditionally, prisoners of war are not entitled to rights under the U.S. Constitution; but they are protected by the Geneva Convention. They may be detained for the duration of a war. However, detainees in the war on terrorism are not uniformed soldiers of a sovereign nation, and therefore are not officially prisoners of war. Some have been detained for many years without trial and without prospects for release. Relatively few could be convicted in traditional jury trials. Among the detainees are persons deemed to be extremely dangerous—persons who are likely to resume terrorist activities if released.

The U.S. Supreme Court held in 2004 that detainees in the war on terrorism, even those captured on foreign battlefields and held outside the U.S., are entitled to a judicial hearing under the Constitution's guarantee of the writ of habeas corpus.[2] And in a controversial 2008 decision the Supreme Court held that detainees at Guantánamo "have the constitutional privilege of habeas corpus"—access to federal courts to challenge their detention. Although the Constitution recognizes that habeas corpus can be suspended "in cases of Rebellion or Invasion" this Suspension Clause does not apply to current enemy combatants. "Some of the petitioners have been in custody for six years with no definitive judicial determination as to the legality of their detention. Their access to the writ [of habeas corpus] is a necessity to determine the lawfulness of their status. . . ."[3] In a stinging dissent, Justice Scalia wrote: "Today for the first time in our nation's history, the Court confers a constitutional right to habeas corpus on alien enemies detained abroad by military forces in the course of an ongoing war. . . . It will almost certainly cause more Americans to be killed."[4]

Shortly after taking office, President Barack Obama ordered the prison at the U.S. naval base in Guantánamo, Cuba, to be closed within a year. The U.S. military had held hundreds of enemy combatants in the prison since 2002; approximately 250 detainees remained at the time of the president's order. Some of these detainees were transferred to prisons in the United States, some were returned to their country of origin, and others were released.

Interrogation.   Following national security crises, the CIA and FBI come under intense pressure both to find terrorist perpetrators and to prevent subsequent attacks. After "9/11" the CIA was pressured to break terrorist suspects and obtain information through "enhanced interrogation techniques," including sleep deprivation and simulated drowning ("water boarding"). (Accounts vary regarding how successful these techniques were in identifying terrorists and heading off new attacks.) The Justice Department's Office of Legal Council ruled that various techniques did not violate laws and treaties banning "torture," in effect granting approval for the use of these techniques. But civil libertarians objected, and when the Obama Administration came to Washington, pressure mounted to investigate and prosecute Bush administration officials for allowing torture tactics. Against the advice of former CIA directors, President Obama ordered the release of memos describing enhanced interrogation techniques. (Intelligence professionals warned that even the publication of these techniques aided terrorists by providing them with information to use in training future terrorists to resist interrogation.) President Obama ruled out prosecuting agents who conducted interrogations relying upon legal advice from the Justice Department. But he did not rule out the prosecution of officials who gave their approval.

The Department of Homeland Security

Presidents often create new bureaucratic organizations to symbolize their commitment to a policy direction. On October 8, 2001, less than one month after the 9/11 terrorist attacks, President George W. Bush issued an executive order establishing the Office of Homeland Security. Then later in 2002, in response to growing criticism that he had not done enough to reassure the American public of the federal government's commitment to protect them from terrorism, President Bush proposed a new Department of Homeland Security.

Organization. The creation of the Department of Homeland Security involved a significant reorganization of the federal bureaucracy. The new department incorporated the U.S. Customs Service (formerly part of the Department of Treasury), the Immigration and Naturalization Service and the Border Patrol (formerly parts of the Department of Justice), the Transportation Security Administration (formerly part of the Department of Transportation), the United States Coast Guard (formerly part of the Department of Treasury), the Secret Service (formerly part of the Department of Treasury), and FEMA, the Federal Emergency Management Agency (formerly an independent agency) (see Figure 14–1).

The Security Advisory System. A highly publicized activity of the Department of Homeland Security is its "Security Advisory System," a scale of five conditions indicating increasing risk of terrorist attack (see Figure 14–2). The colored conditions have had little effect on the general public. However, the "Elevated," "High," and "Severe" conditions require federal, state, and local law enforcement agencies, as well as the Armed Forces, to take increasingly restrictive measures (for example, restricting public access to certain facilities or closing them altogether).

Effectiveness. Reorganization alone seldom solves policy problems. The agencies transferred to the Department of Homeland Security remain largely intact, each with its own continuing problems. In all, some twenty-two agencies employing nearly 200,000 workers were moved into the new department; it was the largest federal reorganization in more than a half-century. Indeed, the administrative problems created by reorganization may overshadow the mission of the department—fighting terrorism.

But perhaps the greatest obstacle to effectiveness is that the federal agencies with the greatest involvement in homeland security—the Federal Bureau of Investigation (FBI), the Central Intelligence Agency (CIA), and intelligence and anti-terrorist units of the Department of Defense—remain beyond the authority of the Department of Homeland Security. Rather, the new Secretary of Homeland Security is charged with the responsibility for "coordinating" with these agencies. This requires integrated analysis of all foreign and domestically collected threat information—a daunting task. Indeed, bureaucratic obstacles to the flow of information between federal intelligence agencies may have contributed to the "9/11" disaster.[5] It is by no means certain that the new department can gain access to all the sources of intelligence relating to the threats of terrorism against the U.S. homeland.

Fighting Terrorism with Intelligence

Success in the war on terrorism requires actions to prevent terrorist attacks before they occur. A proactive war on terrorism requires the collection, analysis, and dissemination of relevant foreign and domestic information to federal, state, and local government agencies, and to the American people. This is the responsibility of America's intelligence community.

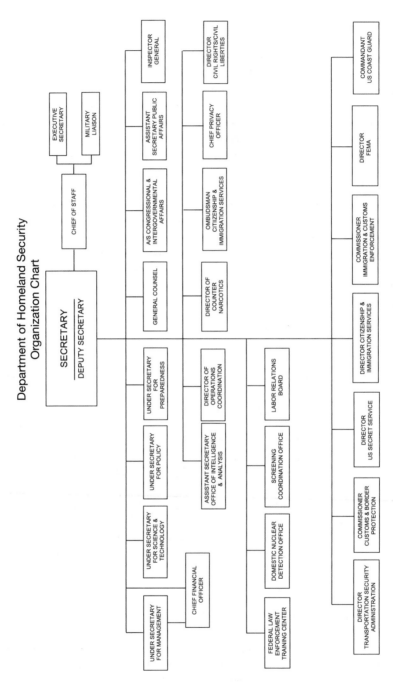

Department of Homeland Security
Organization Chart

FIGURE 14–1 Department of Homeland Security Organization Chart The key operating agencies are at the bottom of the chart.
SOURCE: U.S. Department of Homeland Security.

FIGURE 14–2 Security Advisory System A color-coded "Security Advisory System" is supposed to indicate the risk of terrorist attack.

The Intelligence Community. The intelligence community refers to a broad array of organizations within the federal government that collect, analyze, and disseminate information to intelligence "consumers"—from the president and other top Washington policymakers to battlefield commanders (see Figure 14–3). The principal components of the intelligence community are as follows:

Director of National Intelligence. The Director of National Intelligence (DNI) oversees the entire intelligence community. (The DNI replaced the CIA director's role as the principal intelligence advisor to the president. The CIA director now concentrates on the responsibilities of the CIA itself.) The DNI must unify the budget for national intelligence as well as approve and submit nominations for individuals to head various agencies of the intelligence community. The DNI also manages the nation's counterterrorism effort, with the assistance of a new National Counterterrorism Center, which assembles and analyzes information on terrorists gathered both at home and abroad.

Independent Agency. The Central Intelligence Agency (CIA) is the lead agency in assembling, analyzing, and disseminating intelligence from all other agencies in the intelligence community. It prepares the President's Daily Briefing (PDB), which summarizes all intelligence reports from all agencies for the president each day. The CIA also prepares National Intelligence Estimates (NIEs)—more thorough studies of specific topics, for example, North Korea's nuclear capabilities. In addition, the CIA is charged with responsibility for human intelligence collection (recruiting agents around the world and supervising their work), and it also oversees covert operations, including paramilitary special operations, with a special "presidential finding" authorizing such operations.

AGENCIES WITHIN THE DEPARTMENT OF DEFENSE

Defense Intelligence Agency (DIA)—provides timely and objective military intelligence to warfighters, policymakers, and force planners.

The Intelligence Community

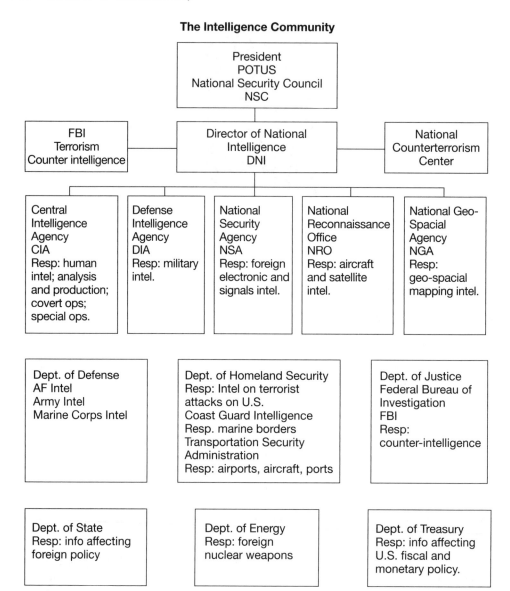

FIGURE 14–3   The Intelligence Community The "intelligence community" includes a variety of agencies, now under the direction of the Director of National Intelligence who reports to the president.

NOTE: The CIA, DIA, NSA, NRO, and NGA are concerned exclusively with intelligence. The Departments of Defense, Homeland Security, Justice, State, Energy, and Treasury are concerned primarily with other missions, but do have intelligence responsibilities.

National Security Agency (NSA)—collects and processes foreign electronic signals intelligence information for our nation's leaders and warfighters, and protects critical U.S. information security systems from compromise.

National Reconnaissance Office (NRO)—collects information from airplane and satellite reconnaissance.

National Imagery and Mapping Agency (NIMA)—provides timely, relevant, and accurate geospatial intelligence in support of national security.

Army, Navy, Air Force, and Marine Corps Intelligence Agencies—each collects and processes intelligence relevant to their particular service needs. Each is closely integrated with its respective military commands.

AGENCIES WITHIN OTHER DEPARTMENTS

State Department—collects and analyzes information affecting U.S. foreign policy.

Energy Department—performs analyses of foreign nuclear weapons, nuclear nonproliferation, and energy-security related intelligence issues in support of U.S. national security policies, programs, and objectives.

Treasury Department—collects and processes information that may affect U.S. fiscal and monetary policy.

Federal Bureau of Investigation—deals with counterespionage, domestic and foreign terrorist organizations, and international criminal cases.

Department of Homeland Security—collects and coordinates information relevant to domestic security including infrastructure protection, Internet communication protection, technology security, and biological and chemical defenses. It assembles intelligence collected from the Secret Service, U.S. Coast Guard, the Transportation Security Administration, National Bio-Weapons Defense Analysis Center, and the Border Patrol.

The Organization of Intelligence. The ultimate responsibility for all intelligence activities rests with the President of the United States. Presidents have undertaken intelligence activities since the founding of the nation. During the Revolutionary War, General George Washington nurtured small groups of patriots living behind British lines who supplied him with information on Redcoat troop movements. Today, the president relies principally on the Director of National Intelligence (DNI) to coordinate the activities of the Intelligence Community. The DNI reports directly to the president and is a member of the National Security Council, the president's inner cabinet.

Covert Actions. The CIA is responsible for the collection of human intelligence—reports obtained from foreign sources by CIA caseworkers around the world. The CIA's responsibilities also include supervision of all covert actions—activities in support of the national interest of the United States that would be ineffective or counterproductive if their sponsorship by the United States were to be made public. Most covert actions consist of routine transfers of economic aid and military training and equipment to pro–U.S. forces that do not wish to acknowledge such aid publicly. (For example, one of the largest covert actions ever taken by the United States was the support for nearly ten years of the Afghan rebels fighting Soviet occupation of their country from 1978 to 1988. These rebels did not wish to acknowledge such aid in order to avoid being labeled as "puppets" of the United States.)

Integrating Foreign and Domestic Intelligence. Perhaps the most troublesome problem in intelligence and counterterrorism in the past had been the lack of coordination between the CIA and the FBI. Fighting global terrorism requires close surveillance of individuals and terrorist organizations both within and outside of the United States. But in the original National Security Act of 1947 that established the CIA, this agency was specifically prohibited from engaging in any activities, including surveillance of individuals and organizations, *inside the borders of the United States*. Only the FBI has the authority to act against terrorists inside the United States. Intelligence reorganization encouraged greater cooperation between these agencies, and the Patriot Act now permits both agencies to undertake surveillance of communications relevant to terrorism both within United States and abroad. However, the FBI and the intelligence community each continues to operate largely separately from the other, and it is not clear whether their communication and coordination problems have been resolved.

The congressional Joint Inquiry into the 9/11 tragedy concluded:

> . . . prior to September 11, the Intelligence Community was neither well organized nor equipped, and did not adequately adapt to meet the challenge posed by global terrorists focused on targets within the domestic United States . . . Within the Intelligence Community, agencies did not share relevant counterterrorism information . . . not only between different Intelligence Community agencies but also within individual agencies, and between the intelligence and the law-enforcement agencies. Serious problems in information sharing also persisted between the Intelligence Community and other federal agencies as well as state and local authorities.[6]

FBI Counterterrorist Activity. The principal responsibility for combating domestic terrorism rests with the FBI. Indeed, the FBI has specifically designated counterterrorism as its top priority. (Previously, its top priorities were federal crimes, drug trafficking, public corruption, civil rights protection, and the support of state and local law enforcement.) The FBI has established Joint Terrorism Task Forces in all of its regional offices; these forces include members of other agencies such as the Immigration and Customs Enforcement (ICE), and the Bureau of Alcohol, Tobacco and Firearms (ATF) as well as state and local law enforcement. The FBI also sponsors a National Joint Terrorism Task Force and promises to integrate its intelligence activities with the CIA and the new Department of Homeland Security.

However, the traditional missions and methods of the FBI may not be well suited to fighting terrorism. It is widely acknowledged that counterterrorism must be preventative. Investigation and apprehension of terrorists *after* a terrorist act has been committed is not enough. Rather, terrorist attacks must be preempted. Preemption frequently requires the identification and surveillance of suspected terrorists, undercover penetration of suspected terrorist organizations, "watch lists" of persons who may be connected to terrorist organizations, and the preventative disruption of terrorist plans. These kinds of activities raise issues of personal liberty and privacy.

The FBI operates under congressional restraints on its methods. Following a congressional investigation in the 1970s of FBI surveillance of anti-Vietnam War and civil rights groups, Congress enacted a series of laws restricting FBI surveillance of individuals and organizations. The Foreign Intelligence Surveillance Act of 1978 requires the FBI to obtain warrants from a special Foreign Intelligence Surveillance Court in order to watch or wiretap aliens living in the United States. Warrants to place U.S. citizens under surveillance must be obtained from federal courts; law enforcement agencies seeking such warrants must set forth "probable cause" to believe that a crime has been committed. The Patriot Act relaxed some of these restrictions, but the FBI continues to confront criticism from civil rights groups for undertaking surveillance of individuals and groups who have not (yet?) committed any crimes.

Security versus Liberty

The war on terrorism promises to be a long one. Americans must become accustomed to greater restrictions on their travel, increased surveillance of their activities, and new intrusions into their privacy. With the tragedy of 9/11 fresh in their minds, most Americans approved of increased restrictive measures. But over time Americans became increasingly concerned with the losses of personal liberty inspired by the war on terrorism.

Historic Trade-Offs. Historically, threats to national security have resulted in challenges to individual liberty. Abraham Lincoln suspended the writ of habeas corpus (the requirement that authorities bring defendants before a judge and show cause for their detention) during the Civil War. (Only after the war did the U.S. Supreme Court hold that he had no authority to suspend the writ.[7]) In the wake of World War I, Congress passed the Espionage Act, which outlawed "any disloyal, profane, scurrilous, or abusive language intended to cause contempt, scorn, contumely, or disrepute" to the government. Socialist presidential candidate Eugene V. Debs was imprisoned for speaking against the war and the draft: his conviction was upheld by the U.S. Supreme Court, as were the convictions of other antiwar protesters of that era.[8] In February 1942, shortly after the Japanese attack on Pearl Harbor, President Franklin D. Roosevelt authorized the removal and internment of Japanese Americans living on the West Coast. The U.S. Supreme Court upheld this flagrant violation of the Constitution.[9] Not until 1988 did the U.S. Congress vote to make reparations and public apologies to the surviving victims. During the Cold War, the U.S. government prosecuted top leaders of the Communist party for violating the Smith Act, which made it unlawful "to knowingly and willfully advocate, abet, advise, or teach the duty, necessity, or propriety of overthrowing any government in the United States by force or violence." Again, the U.S. Supreme Court upheld their convictions.[10] Not until the 1960s did the Court begin to reassert freedom of expression including the advocacy of revolution. Only when the perceived crisis appears to fade do American elites again reassert their commitment to fundamental liberties.

The Costs to Liberty. The war on terrorism has inspired development of a new arsenal of antiterrorist weapons—laws, executive orders, and military actions—many of which raise serious questions about individual liberty. The Patriot Act expands the authority of federal law enforcement agencies in the surveillance of citizens, including tracking their communications, credit card, and Internet use. It also authorizes the seizure of property of persons suspected of terrorist connections; such seizures may occur prior to, and in the absence of, their conviction of any crime. (The same type of seizure provisions can be found in the RICO Act designed to fight the "war on drugs." See Chapter 4.) The legal standard to obtain warrants for searches and seizures of persons suspected of connections with terrorist organizations or activities has been lowered from "probable cause" to merely suspected connection with terrorism. Finally, the act allows lengthy detention of suspected terrorists.

Evolving Public Opinion.   Immediately after the terrorist attacks on New York and Washington on September 11, 2001, public opinion strongly supported restrictions on civil liberties in the interests of security. But over time, as the threat of terrorism appeared to recede in their minds, Americans became less willing to sacrifice personal liberties:

In order to curb terrorism in this country, do you think it will be necessary for the average person to give up some civil liberties, or not?

	Necessary	Not Necessary
2001	55%	35%
2008	40	54

Public opinion today is less concerned about an imminent attack. In 2001 almost three-quarters of Americans believed that another terrorist attack was very or somewhat likely over the next several weeks. With time, the perceived threat has receded:

How likely is it that there will be further acts of terrorism in the United States over the next several weeks?

	Very Likely	Somewhat Likely	Not Too Likely	Not at All Likely
2001	24	50	16	6
2005	4	31	45	18
2008	8	27	45	20

Over time Americans have become less confident that the United States is "adequately prepared to deal with another terrorist attack":

In general, do you think the United States is adequately prepared to deal with another terrorist attack, or not?

	Is	Is Not	Unsure
2003	64	29	7
2005	49	44	7
2008	39	55	5

And Americans are less satisfied with the government's efforts to reduce the threat of terrorism:

Do you approve or disapprove of the job the government is doing to protect the country from terrorism?

	Approve	Disapprove	Unsure
2003	71	19	10
2005	53	38	9
2007	50	39	10

In short, as the threat of terrorism recedes in the minds of Americans, they become more critical of government anti-terrorist efforts and less willing to sacrifice personal liberties.[11]

SUMMARY

1. The United States traditionally relied on deterrence to protect itself, including protection against a direct attack on its homeland. However, the attacks on the U.S. on September 11, 2001, demonstrated that terrorism is a nondeterrable threat. Terrorists deliberately attack civilian targets and sacrifice themselves and their people to their cause.

2. Terrorism is political violence directed against innocent civilians. It is designed to inspire fear in people and erode their confidence in the ability of their government to protect them. Global terrorism has developed over the years into highly sophisticated networks operating in many countries.

3. The American people initially responded to the 9/11 attacks with strong support for the nation's leadership and for security measures designed to reduce the threat of terrorism.

4. The USA Patriot Act was supported in Congress by large majorities of both parties. It gave federal law enforcement authorities sweeping new powers of searches, seizures, surveillance, and detention of suspects in fighting the war on terrorism.

5. A new Department of Homeland Security was created, reorganizing the federal bureaucracy. The new department includes the Customs and Border Protection, Citizenship and Immigration Services, Immigration and Customs Enforcement, Coast Guard, Federal Emergency Management Agency, Secret Service, and the Transportation Security Administration.

6. Success in fighting terrorism depends heavily on intelligence—information that allows government authorities to act to prevent terrorist attacks before they occur. The U.S. intelligence community refers to a broad array of organizations of the federal government, not all of which have effectively communicated with each other in the past.

7. The war on terrorism has placed greater restrictions on the liberties of Americans. As in the past, Americans have tolerated restrictions on their liberties when confronted with perceived serious threats. As the threat recedes, they are less willing to sacrifice individual liberties.

Notes

1. President George W. Bush, Remarks to the Nation, September 11, 2001.
2. *Rasul* v. *United States,* 542 U.S. 466 (2004).
3. *Boumediene* v. *Bush,* June 12, 2008.
4. Ibid.
5. *The 9/11 Commission Report* (New York: Norton, 2005).
6. Senate Select Committee on Intelligence and House Permanent Select Committee on Intelligence Joint Inquiry into the Terrorist Attacks of September 11, 2001, *Final Report* (Washington, DC: U.S. Government Printing Office, 2003).
7. *Ex Parte Milligan (1866).*
8. *Debs* v. *United States,* 249 U.S. 211 (1919); *Schenk* v. *United States,* 249 U.S. 47 (1919).
9. *Korematsu* v. *United States,* 323 U.S. 214 (1944).
10. *Dennis* v. *United States,* 341 U.S. 494 (1951).
11. Various polls as reported in *The Polling Report, www.pollingreport.com.* Accessed July, 2008.

Bibliography

Department of Homeland Security. *Strategic Plan 2008–2013*. Washington, DC: U.S. Government Printing Office, 2008.

GERTZ, BILL. *Breakdown: How America's Intelligence Failures Led to September 11*. New York: Regnery, 2002.

GUNARATNA, ROHAN. *Inside Al Queda*. New York: Columbia University Press, 2002.

KETTL, DONALD F. *System Under Stress: Homeland Security and American Politics*. 2nd ed. Washington, DC: CQ Press, 2006.

LOWENTHAL, MARK M. *Intelligence: From Secrets to Policy*, 4th ed. Washington, DC: CQ Press, 2008.

National Commission on Terrorist Attacks upon the United States. *The 9/11 Commission Report*. New York: Norton, 2005.

SYLES, RICHARD. *Disaster Policy and Politics: Emergency Management and Homeland Security*. Washington DC: CQ Press, 2008.

WHITE, JONATHAN R. *Terrorism and Homeland Security*, 6th ed. Belmount, CA: Wadsworth, 2009.

Web Sites

DEPARTMENT OF HOMELAND SECURITY. Official government site for homeland security, with information on travel, transportation, immigration, threats, and homeland protection. *www.dhs.gov*

U.S. IMMIGRATION AND CUSTOMS ENFORCEMENT. The official government site (of agency replacing INS), with immigration laws, regulations, etc. *www.ice.gov*

FEDERAL EMERGENCY MANAGEMENT AGENCY. Official site of FEMA, with information on current disasters, how to get help, etc. *www.fema.gov*

INSTITUTE FOR HOMELAND SECURITY. Private think tank devoted to research, education, and public awareness of homeland security issues. *www.homelandsecurity.org*

ELECTRONIC PRIVACY INFORMATION CENTER. Advocacy organization for privacy rights, opposed to many homeland security measures. *www.epic.org*

AMERICAN CIVIL LIBERTIES UNION. Advocacy organization for civil liberties, opposed to homeland security measures believed to violate civil rights. *www.aclu.org*

SENATE SELECT COMMITTEE ON INTELLIGENCE AND HOUSE PERMANENT SELECT COMMITTEE ON INTELLIGENCE JOINT INQUIRY. Report of activities of U.S. intelligence community in connection with attacks of September 11, 2001. *www.gpoaccess.gov/serialset/creports/all*

PRESERVING LIFE AND LIBERTY. U.S. Department of Justice defense of the Patriot Act. *www.lifeandliberty.gov*

15

Policy Evaluation

Finding Out What Happens After a Law Is Passed

Americans often assume that once we pass a law, create a bureaucracy, and spend money, the purpose of the law, the bureaucracy, and the expenditure will be achieved. We assume that when Congress adopts a policy and appropriates money for it, and when the executive branch organizes a program, hires people, spends money, and carries out activities designed to implement the policy, the effects of the policy will be felt by society and will be those intended. Unfortunately, these assumptions are not always warranted. The national experiences with many public programs indicate the need for careful appraisal of the real impact of public policy.

Does the government really know what it is doing? Generally speaking, no. Governments usually know how much money they spend; how many persons ("clients") are given various services; how much these services cost; how their programs are organized, managed, and operated; and, perhaps, how influential interest groups regard their programs and services. But even if programs and policies are well organized, efficiently operated, widely utilized, adequately financed, and generally supported by major interest groups, we may still want to ask, So what? Do they work? Do these programs have any beneficial effects on society? Are the effects immediate or long range? Positive or negative? What is the relationship between the costs of the program and the benefits to society? Could we be doing something else with more benefit to society with the money and work force devoted to these programs? Unfortunately, governments have done very little to answer these more basic questions.

Policy Evaluation: Assessing the Impact of Public Policy

Policy evaluation is learning about the consequences of public policy. Other, more complex definitions have been offered: "Policy evaluation is the assessment of the overall effectiveness of a national program in meeting its objectives, or assessment of the relative effectiveness of two or more programs in meeting common objectives."[1] "Policy evaluation research is the objective, systematic, empirical examination of the effects ongoing policies and public programs have on their targets in terms of the goals they are meant to achieve."[2]

Some definitions tie evaluation to the stated "goals" of a program or policy. But since we do not always know what these "goals" really are, and because we know that some programs and policies pursue conflicting "goals," we will not limit our notion of policy evaluation to their achievement. Instead, we will concern ourselves with all of the consequences of public policy, that is, with "policy impact."

The impact of a policy is all its *effects on real-world conditions*, including

1.   Impact on the target situation or group
2.   Impact on situations or groups other than the target (spillover effects)
3.   Impact on future as well as immediate conditions
4.   Direct costs, in terms of resources devoted to the program
5.   Indirect costs, including loss of opportunities to do other things

All the benefits and costs, both immediate and future, must be measured in both symbolic and tangible effects.

Measuring Impact, Not Output.   "Policy impact" is not the same as "policy output." In assessing policy impact, we cannot be content simply to measure government activity. For example, the number of dollars spent per member of a target group (per pupil educational expenditures, per capita welfare expenditures, per capita health expenditures) is not really a measure of the impact of a policy on the group. It is merely a measure of government activity—that is, a measure of *policy output*. Unfortunately many government agencies produce reams of statistics measuring outputs—such as welfare benefits paid, criminal arrests and prosecutions, Medicare payments, and school enrollments. But this "bean counting" tells us little about poverty, crime, health, or educational achievement. We cannot be satisfied with measuring how many times a bird flaps its wings; we must know how far the bird has flown. In describing public policy, or even in explaining its determinants, measures of policy output are important. But in assessing *policy impact*, we must identify changes in society that are associated with measures of government activity.

Target Groups.   The target group is that part of the population for whom the program is intended—such as the poor, the sick, the ill-housed. Target groups must first be identified and then the desired effect of the program on the members of these groups must be determined. Is it to change their physical or economic circumstances—for example, the percentage of minorities or women employed in professional or managerial jobs, the income of the poor, the infant death rate? Or is it to change their knowledge, attitudes, awareness, interests, or behavior? If multiple effects are intended, what are the priorities among different effects? What are the possible unintended effects (side effects) on target groups?

Nontarget Groups.   All programs and policies have differential effects on various segments of the population. Identifying important nontarget groups for a policy is a difficult process. For example, what is the impact of the welfare reform on groups *other* than the poor—government bureaucrats, social workers, local political figures, working-class families who are not on welfare, taxpayers, and others? Nontarget effects may be expressed as benefits as well as costs, such as the benefits to the construction industry of public housing projects.

Short-Term and Long-Term Effects.   When will the benefits or the costs be felt? Is the program designed for short-term emergencies? Or is it a long-term, developmental effort? If it is short term, what will prevent the processes of incrementalism and bureaucratization from turning it into a long-term program, even after the immediate need is met? Many impact studies show that new or innovative programs have short-term positive effects—for example, Operation Head Start and other educational programs. However, the positive effects frequently disappear as the novelty and enthusiasm of new programs wear off. Other programs experience difficulties at first, as in the early days of Social Security, but turn out to have "sleeper" effects, as in the widespread acceptance of Social Security today. Not all programs aim at the same degree of permanent or transient change.

Indirect and Symbolic Costs and Benefits.   Programs are frequently measured by their direct costs. Government agencies have developed various forms of cost-benefit analysis to identify the direct costs (usually, but not always, in dollars) of government programs. But it is very difficult to identify the indirect and symbolic benefits or costs of public programs. Rarely can all these factors be included in a formal decision-making model. Cost-accounting techniques developed in business were designed around units of production—automobiles, airplanes, tons of steel, and so on. But how do we identify and measure units of social well-being? Often political intuition is the best guide available to policymakers in these matters.

Calculating Net Benefits and Costs.   The task of calculating the *net* impact of a public policy is truly awesome. It would be all the symbolic and tangible benefits, both immediate and long range, minus all the symbolic and tangible costs, both immediate and future (see Table 15–1). Even if all these costs and benefits are known (and everyone agrees on what is a "benefit" and

TABLE 15–1   Assessing Policy Impact A rational approach to policy evaluation tries to calculate the difference between all present and future, target and nontarget, costs and benefits.

	BENEFITS			COSTS	
	Present	**Future**		**Present**	**Future**
Target Groups and Situations Nontarget Groups and Situations (Spillover)	Symbolic Tangible Symbolic <u>Tangible</u> Sum Present Benefits	Symbolic Tangible Symbolic <u>Tangible</u> Sum Future Benefits		Symbolic Tangible Symbolic <u>Tangible</u> Sum Present Costs	Symbolic Tangible Symbolic <u>Tangible</u> Sum Future Costs
	<u>Sum</u> all benefits	=	Minus <u>Net</u> policy impact	<u>Sum</u> all costs	

what is a "cost"), it is still very difficult to come up with a net balance. Many of the items on both sides of the balance would defy comparison—for example, how do you subtract a tangible cost in dollars from a symbolic reward in the sense of well-being felt by individuals or groups?

The Symbolic Impact of Policy

The impact of a policy includes both its symbolic and tangible effects. Its symbolic impact deals with the perceptions that individuals have of government action and their attitudes toward it. Even if government policies do not succeed in eliminating poverty, preventing crime, and so on, the failure of government to *try* to do these things would be even worse. Individuals, groups, and whole societies frequently judge public policy in terms of its good intentions rather than tangible accomplishments. Sometimes very popular programs have little positive tangible impact.

The policies of government may tell us more about the aspirations of a society and its leadership than about actual conditions. Policies do more than effect change in societal conditions; they also help hold people together and maintain an orderly state.

Once upon a time politics was described as "who gets what, when, and how." Today it seems that politics centers on "who *feels* what, when, and how." The smoke-filled room where patronage and pork were dispensed has been replaced with the talk-filled room where rhetoric and image are dispensed. What governments say is as important as what governments do. Television has made the image of public policy as important as the policy itself. Systematic policy analysis concentrates on what governments do, why they do it, and what difference it makes. It devotes less attention to what governments say. Perhaps this is a weakness in policy analysis. Our focus has been primarily on activities of governments rather than their rhetoric.

Program Evaluation: What Governments Usually Do

Most government agencies make some effort to review the effectiveness of their own programs. These reviews usually take one of the following forms:

Hearings and Reports.   The most common type of program review involves hearings and reports. Government administrators are asked by chief executives or legislators to give testimony (formally or informally) on the accomplishments of their own programs. Frequently, written annual reports are provided by program administrators. But testimonials and reports of administrators are not very objective means of program evaluation. They frequently magnify the benefits and minimize the costs of the program.

Site Visits.   Occasionally teams of high-ranking administrators, expert consultants, legislators, or some combination of these people will decide to visit agencies or conduct inspections in the field. These teams can pick up impressionistic data about how programs are being run, whether they are following specific guidelines, whether they have competent staffs, and sometimes whether or not the clients (target groups) are pleased with the services.

Program Measures.   The data developed by government agencies themselves generally cover policy output measures: the number of recipients in various welfare programs, the number of persons in work-force training programs, the number of public hospital beds available, the tons of garbage collected, or the number of pupils enrolled. But these program measures rarely indicate what impact these numbers have on society: the conditions of life confronting the poor, the success of work-force trainees in finding and holding skilled jobs, the health of the nation's poor, the cleanliness of cities, and the ability of graduates to read and write and function in society.

Comparison with Professional Standards.   In some areas of government activity, professional associations have developed standards of excellence. These standards are usually expressed as a desirable level of output: for example, the number of pupils per teacher, the number of hospital beds per one thousand people, the number of cases for each welfare worker. Actual government outputs can then be compared with ideal outputs. Although such an exercise can be helpful, it still focuses on government outputs and not on the impact of government activities on the conditions of target or nontarget groups. Moreover, the standards themselves are usually developed by professionals who are really guessing at what ideal levels of benefits and services should be. There is rarely any hard evidence that ideal levels of government output have any significant impact on society.

Evaluation of Citizens' Complaints.   Another common approach to program evaluation is the analysis of citizens' complaints. But not all citizens voluntarily submit complaints or remarks about governmental programs. Critics of government programs are self-selected, and they are rarely representative of the general public or even of the target groups of government programs. There is no way to judge whether the complaints of a vocal few are shared by the many more who have not spoken up. Occasionally, administrators develop questionnaires for participants in their program to learn what their complaints may be and whether they are satisfied or not. But these questionnaires really test public opinion toward the program and not its real impact on the lives of participants.

Surveys of Public Opinion.   Occasionally governments undertake to survey citizens about their satisfaction or dissatisfaction with various programs and services. This is more common at the local level of government. Yet even polls focused on federal government services can be instructive (see Table 15–2).

Program Evaluation: What Governments Can Do

None of the common evaluative methods just mentioned really attempts to weigh *costs* against *benefits*. Indeed, administrators seldom calculate the ratio of costs to services—the dollars required to train one worker, to provide one hospital bed, to collect and dispose of one ton of garbage. It is even more difficult to calculate the costs of making specific changes in society—the dollars required to raise student reading levels by one grade, to lower the infant death rate by one point, to reduce the crime rate by 1 percent. To learn about the real impact of governmental programs on society, more complex and costly methods of program evaluation are required.

TABLE 15–2   **Public Satisfaction/Dissatisfaction with Federal Government Programs**   Polls can reflect general satisfaction or dissatisfaction with federal programs. Often the military ranks at or near the top of public esteem; the public is decidedly less satisfied with energy policy, health care, poverty programs, and the nation's finances.

Next we are going to name some major areas the federal government handles. For each one please say whether you are satisfied or dissatisfied with the work the government is doing.

	Satisfied	Dissatisfied	Unsure
National parks	71	27	2
Military and national defense	59	40	1
Agriculture and farming	56	38	5
Transportation	56	42	2
Homeland security	50	49	1
Environmental issues	48	51	1
Public housing/urban development	47	49	4
Criminal justice	47	52	1
Labor and employment issues	44	54	2
Foreign affairs	41	58	1
Education	41	59	0
Job creation/economic growth	39	60	1
Responding to natural disasters	33	66	1
Energy policy	27	71	2
Health care	24	75	1
Poverty programs	24	75	1
The nation's finances	23	76	1

SOURCE: *The Polling Report*, accessed April 1, 2008. www.pollingreport.com.

Systematic program evaluation involves comparisons—comparisons designed to estimate what changes in society can be attributed to the program rather than nonprogram factors. Ideally, this means comparing what "actually happened" to "what would have happened if the program had never been implemented." It is not difficult to measure what happened; unfortunately too much program evaluation stops there. The real problem is to measure what would have happened without a program and then compare the two conditions of society. The difference must be attributable to the program itself and not to other changes that are occurring in society at the same time.

Before versus After Comparisons.   There are several common research designs in program evaluation. The most common is the before-and-after study, which compares results in a jurisdiction at two times—one before the program was implemented and the other some time after. Usually only target groups are examined. These before-and-after comparisons are designed to show program impacts, but it is very difficult to know whether the changes observed, if any, came about as a result of the program or as a result of other changes that were occurring in society at the same time (see Design 1, Figure 15–1).

Projected Trend Line versus Postprogram Comparisons.   A better estimate of what would have happened without the program can be made by projecting past (preprogram) trends into the postprogram time period. Then these projections can be compared with what actually

Design 1
Before vs. After

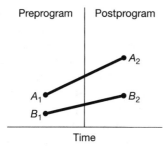

Preprogram | Postprogram

• A_2

A_1•

Time

■ $A_2 - A_1$ = Estimated Program Effect

Design 2
Projected vs. Postprogram

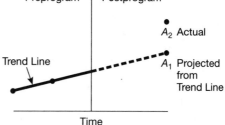

Preprogram | Postprogram

A_2 Actual

Trend Line

A_1 Projected from Trend Line

Time

■ $A_2 - A_1$ = Estimated Program Effect

Design 3
With vs. Without Program

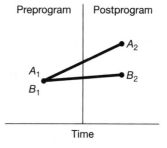

Preprogram | Postprogram

A_2

A_1

B_2

B_1

Time

■ *A* has Program; *B* does not.
■ $(A_2 - A_1) - (B_2 - B_1)$ = Estimated Program Effect.
■ Or difference between *A* and *B* in rate of change equals Estimated Program Effect.

Design 4
The Classic Research Design: Control vs. Experimental Groups

Preprogram | Postprogram

A_2

A_1

B_2

B_1

Time

■ *A* has Program; *B* does not.
■ *A* and *B* identical in preprogram period.
■ $A_2 - B_2$ = Estimated Program Effect

FIGURE 15–1 **Policy Evaluation Research Designs** Policy evaluation can utilize a variety of research designs.

happened in society after the program was implemented. The difference between the projections based on preprogram trends and the actual postprogram data can be attributed to the program itself. Note that data on target groups or conditions must be obtained for several time periods before the program was initiated, so that a trend line can be established (see Design 2, Figure 15–1). This design is better than the before-and-after design, but it requires more effort by program evaluators.

Consider, for example, efforts at evaluating welfare reform (see the section "Evaluation: Is Welfare Reform Working?" in Chapter 5). To date, most evaluations of welfare reform have followed the trend line research design. If the goal of the reform is to reduce welfare rolls, there is ample evidence that the program has contributed to that goal (see Figure 5–6). The "target group" (recipients of cash welfare payments) has been reduced by over half since the ending of the federal cash entitlement program, Aid to Families with Dependent Children, and its substitution with the federally aided state program, Temporary Assistance for Needy Families, in 1996. But it is not clear exactly what proportion of this reduction is due to the policy itself and what proportion is due to other economic factors. All we really know is that the welfare rolls are declining.

Some of the decline may be attributable to the deterrent effect of the new job training and search requirements on prospective welfare enrollees. We do not know exactly how many people were forced off welfare rolls by the two-year time limit or work or training requirements. We do not know whether the people who left the rolls actually found jobs that lifted them out of poverty. We do not know whether the people involuntarily cut from the rolls are actually suffering hardship. And we do not know whether welfare rolls can continue to decline, or whether a certain hard core of recipients must remain on welfare due to physical, mental, or emotional problems that prevent them from finding and keeping jobs.

Comparisons between Jurisdictions with and without Programs.   Another common evaluation design is to compare individuals who have participated in programs with those who have not, or to compare cities, states, or nations which have programs with those that do not. Comparisons are sometimes made in the postprogram period only; for example, comparisons of the job records of those who have participated in work-force training programs with those who have not, or comparisons of homicide rates in states that have the death penalty with the homicide rates in states without the death penalty. But so many other differences exist between individuals or jurisdictions that it is difficult to attribute differences in their conditions to differences in government programs. For example, persons who voluntarily enter a work-force training program may be more motivated to find a job or have different personal characteristics than those who do not. States with the death penalty may tend to be rural states, which have lower homicide rates than urban states, which may or may not have the death penalty.

Some of the problems involved in comparing jurisdictions with and without programs can be resolved if we observe both kinds of jurisdictions before and after the introduction of the program. This enables us to estimate differences between jurisdictions before program efforts are considered. After the program is initiated, we can observe whether the differences between jurisdictions have widened or not (see Design 3, Figure 15–1). This design provides some protection against attributing differences to a particular program when underlying socioeconomic differences between jurisdictions are really responsible for different outcomes.

Comparisons between Control and Experimental Groups before and after Program Implementation.   The classic research design involves the careful selection of control and experimental groups that are identical in every way, the application of the policy to the experimental group only, and the comparison of changes in the experimental group with changes in the control group after the application of the policy. Initially, control and experimental groups must be identical, and the preprogram performance of each group must be measured and found to be the same. The program must be applied only to the experimental group. The postprogram differences between the experimental and control groups must be carefully measured (see Design 4, Figure 15–1). This classic research design is preferred by scientists because it provides the best opportunity of estimating changes that derived from the effects of other forces in society.

Federal Evaluation: The General Accountability Office

The General Accountability Office (GAO) is an arm of Congress. It has broad authority to audit the operations and finances of federal agencies, to evaluate their programs, and to report its findings to Congress. For most of its history, the GAO confined itself to financial auditing and management and administrative studies. In recent years, however, it has increasingly undertaken evaluative research on government programs.

The GAO was established by Congress as an independent agency in 1921, in the same Budget and Accounting Act that created the first executive budget; its authority to undertake evaluation studies was expanded in the Congressional Budget and Impoundment Control Act of 1974, the same act that established the House and Senate Budget Committees and the Congressional Budget Office (see Chapter 7). The GAO is headed by the Comptroller General of the United States. Most GAO reports are requested by Congress, although the office can also undertake studies on its own initiative.

According to the GAO, "Program evaluation—when it is available and of high quality—provides sound information about what programs are actually delivering, how they are being managed, and the extent to which they are cost-effective."[3] The GAO believes that evaluation efforts by federal agencies fall woefully short of what is required for rational decision making. It has been especially critical of the Defense Department for failing to test weapons systems adequately, to monitor defense contractors and their charges, or to adjust its future plans to expected reductions in defense spending (see Chapter 13). The GAO has criticized the Environmental Protection Agency for measuring its own success in terms of input measures—numbers of inspections performed and enforcement actions undertaken—rather than actual improvements in environmental conditions, such as in water quality or air quality (see Chapter 10). The GAO has also reported on the Social Security trust fund and the dangers of spending trust fund money on current governmental operations (see Chapter 5). It has reported on the high and growing cost of medical care in the United States, especially Medicaid and Medicare, and noted the lack of correlation between medical spending and measures of the nation's health (see Chapter 5). It has undertaken to assess the overall impact of drug control policies (see Chapter 4), and it has studied the default rate on student loans and recommended collection of overdue loans by withholding tax refunds (see Chapter 6). In short, the GAO has been involved in virtually every major policy question confronting the nation.[4]

Experimental Policy Research

Many policy analysts argue that policy experimentation offers the best opportunity to determine the impact of public policies. This opportunity rests on the main characteristics of experimental research: the systematic selection of experimental and control groups, the application of the policy under study to the experimental group only, and the careful comparison of differences between the experimental and the control groups after the application of the policy. But government-sponsored experimental policy research raises a series of important questions.

A Bias toward Positive Results.   First, are government-sponsored research projects predisposed to produce results supportive of popular reform proposals? Are social scientists, whose personal political values are generally liberal and reformist, inclined to produce findings in support of liberal reform measures? Moreover, successful experiments—in which the proposed policy achieves positive results—will receive more acclaim and produce greater opportunities for advancement for social scientists and administrators than will unsuccessful experiments—in which the policy is shown to be ineffective. Liberal, reform-oriented social scientists expect liberal reforms to produce positive results. When reforms appear to do so, the research results are immediately accepted and published; but when results are unsupportive or negative, the social scientists may be inclined to go back and recode their data, redesign their research, or reevaluate their results because they believe a "mistake" must have been made. The temptation to "fudge the data," "reinterpret" the results, coach participants on what to say or do, and so forth will be very great. In the physical and biological sciences the temptation to "cheat" in research is reduced by the fact that research can be replicated and the danger of being caught and disgraced is very great. But social experiments can seldom be replicated perfectly, and replication seldom brings the same distinction to a social scientist as does the original research.

The Hawthorne Effect.   People behave differently when they know they are being watched. Students, for example, generally perform at a higher level when something—anything—new and different is introduced into the classroom routine. This "Hawthorne effect" may cause a new program or reform to appear more successful than the old, but it is the newness itself that produces improvement. The term is taken from early experiments at the Hawthorne plant of Western Electric Company in Chicago in 1927. It was found that worker output increased with *any* change in routine, even decreasing the lighting in the plant.[5]

Generalizing Results to the Nation.   Another problem in policy research is that results obtained with small-scale experiments may differ substantially from those that would occur if a large-scale nationwide program were adopted. For example, years ago a brief experiment involving a small number of families purported to show that a government-guaranteed income did not change the work behavior of recipients; they continued to behave as their neighbors did—searching for jobs and accepting employment when it was offered.[6] Subsequent studies of the effects of a guaranteed government income challenged even these experimental group findings but also predicted that a *nationwide* program would produce much more dramatic changes in working behavior. If everyone in the nation were guaranteed a minimum annual income, cultural standards might be changed nationwide; the resulting work disincentives might "seriously understate the expected cost of an economy-wide program."[7]

Ethical and Legal Issues.   Experimental strategies in policy impact research raise still other problems. Do government researchers have the right to withhold public services from individuals simply to provide a control group for experimentation? In the medical area, where giving or withholding treatment can result in death or injury, the problem is obvious and many attempts have been made to formulate a code of ethics. But in the area of social experimentation, what are we to say to control groups who are chosen to be similar to experimental groups but denied benefits in order to serve as a base for comparison? Setting aside the legal and ethical issues, it will be politically difficult to provide services for some people and not others.

Political Interpretations of Results. Finally, we must acknowledge that the political milieu shapes policy research. Politics helps decide what policies and policy alternatives will be studied in the first place. Politics can also affect findings themselves, and certainly the interpretations and uses of policy research are politically motivated.

Despite these problems, the advantages of policy experimentation are substantial. It is exceedingly costly for society to commit itself to large-scale programs and policies in education, welfare, housing, health, and so on without any real idea about what works.

Program Evaluation: Why It Fails So Often

Occasionally government agencies attempt their own policy evaluations. Government analysts and administrators report on the conditions of target groups before and after their participation in a new program, and some effort is made to attribute observed changes to the new program itself. Policy experimentation is less frequent; seldom do governments systematically select experimental and control groups of the population, introduce a new program to the experimental group only, and then carefully compare changes in the conditions of the experimental group with a control group that has not benefited from the program. Let us turn first to some of the problems confronting policy evaluation.

1. The first problem confronting anyone who wants to evaluate a public program is to determine what the goals of the program are. What are the target groups and what are the desired effects? But governments often pursue incompatible goals to satisfy very diverse groups. Overall policy planning and evaluation may reveal inconsistencies in public policy and force reconsideration of fundamental societal goals. Where there is little agreement on the goals of a public program, evaluation studies may engender a great deal of political conflict. Government agencies generally prefer to avoid conflict, and hence to avoid studies that would raise such questions.

2. Many programs and policies have primarily symbolic value. They do not actually change the conditions of target groups but merely make these groups feel that the government "cares." A government agency does not welcome a study that reveals that its efforts have no tangible effects; such a revelation itself might reduce the symbolic value of the program by informing target groups of its uselessness.

3. Government agencies have a strong vested interest in "proving" that their programs have a positive impact. Administrators frequently view attempts to evaluate the impact of their programs as attempts to limit or destroy their programs or to question the competence of the administrators.

4. Government agencies usually have a heavy investment—organizational, financial, physical, psychological—in current programs and policies. They are predisposed against finding that these policies do not work.

5. Any serious study of policy impact undertaken by a government agency would involve some interference with ongoing program activities. The press of day-to-day business generally takes priority over study and evaluation. More important, the conduct of an experiment may necessitate depriving individuals or groups (control groups) of services to which they are entitled under law; this may be difficult, if not impossible, to do.

6. Program evaluation requires funds, facilities, time, and personnel, which government agencies do not like to sacrifice from ongoing programs. Policy impact studies, like any research, cost money. They cannot be done well as extracurricular or part-time activities. Devoting resources to studies may mean a sacrifice in program resources that administrators are unwilling to make.

How Bureaucrats Explain Negative Findings

Government administrators and program supporters are ingenious in devising reasons why negative findings about policy impacts should be rejected. Even in the face of clear evidence that their favorite programs are useless or even counterproductive, they will argue that

1. The effects of the program are long range and cannot be measured at the present time.

2. The effects of the program are diffuse and general in nature; no single criterion or index adequately measures what is being accomplished.

3. The effects of the program are subtle and cannot be identified by crude measures or statistics.

4. Experimental research cannot be carried out effectively because to withhold services from some persons to observe the impact of such withholding would be unfair to them.

5. The fact that no difference was found between persons receiving the services and those not receiving them means that the program is not sufficiently intensive and indicates the need to spend *more* resources on the program.

6. The failure to identify any positive effects of a program is attributable to inadequacy or bias in the research itself, not in the program.

Political scientist James Q. Wilson formulated two general laws to cover all cases of social science research on policy impact:

Wilson's First Law: All policy interventions in social problems produce the intended effect—if the research is carried out by those implementing the policy or by their friends.

Wilson's Second Law: No policy intervention in social problems produces the intended effect—if the research is carried out by independent third parties, especially those skeptical of the policy.

Wilson denies that his laws are cynical. Instead he reasons that

> Studies that conform to the First Law will accept an agency's own data about what it is doing and with what effect; adopt a time frame (long or short) that maximizes the probability of observing the desired effect; and minimize the search for other variables that might account for the effect observed. Studies that conform to the Second Law will gather data independently of the agency; adopt a short time frame that either minimizes the chance for the desired effect to appear or, if it does appear, permits one to argue that the results are "temporary" and probably due to the operation of the "Hawthorne Effect" (i.e., the reaction of the subjects to the fact that they are part of an experiment); and maximize the search for other variables that might explain the effects observed.[8]

Why Government Programs Are Seldom Terminated

Government programs are rarely terminated. Even when evaluative studies produce negative findings; even when policymakers themselves are fully aware of fraud, waste, and inefficiency; even when highly negative benefit-cost ratios are reported, government programs manage to survive. Once policy is institutionalized within a government, it is extraordinarily difficult to terminate.

Why is it so difficult for governments to terminate failed programs and policies? The answer to this question varies from one program to another, but a few generalizations are possible.

Concentrated Benefits, Dispersed Costs.   Perhaps the most common reason for the continuation of inefficient government programs and policies is that their limited benefits are concentrated in a small, well-organized constituency, while their greater costs are dispersed over a large, unorganized, uninformed public. Although few in number, the beneficiaries of a program are strongly committed to it; they are concerned, well informed, and active in their support. If the costs of the program are spread widely among all taxpayers, no one has a strong incentive to become informed, organized, or active in opposition to it. Although the costs of a failed program may be enormous, if they are dispersed widely enough so that no one individual or group bears a significant burden, there will be little incentive to organize an effective opposition. (Consider the case of a government subsidy program for peanut growers. If $300 million per year were distributed to 5,000 growers, each would average $60,000 in subsidy income. If each grower would contribute 10 percent of this subsidy to a political fund to reward friendly legislators, the fund could distribute $30 million in campaign contributions. If the costs of the program could be dispersed evenly among 300 million Americans, each would pay only $1. No one would have a sufficient incentive to become informed, organized, or active in opposition to the subsidy program. So it would continue, regardless of its limited benefits and extensive costs to society.) When program costs are widely dispersed, it is irrational for individuals, each of whom bears only a tiny fraction of these costs, to expend the time, energy, and money to counter the support of the program's beneficiaries.

Legislative and Bureaucratic Interests.   Among the beneficiaries of any government program are those who administer and supervise it. Bureaucratic jobs depend on a program's continuation. Government positions with all of their benefits, pay, prerequisites, and prestige, are at stake. Strong incentives exist for bureaucrats to resist or undermine negative evaluations of their programs, to respond to public criticism by making only marginal changes in their programs or even by claiming that their programs are failing because not enough is being spent on them.

Legislative systems, both in Congress and in state capitals, are structured so that legislators with the most direct control over programs are usually the most friendly to them. The committee system, with its fragmentation of power and invitation to logrolling ("You support my committee's report and I'll support yours") favors retention of existing programs and policies. Legislators on committees with jurisdiction over the programs are usually the largest recipients of campaign contributions from the organized beneficiaries of the programs. These legislators can use their committee positions to protect failed programs, to minimize reform, and to block termination. Even without the incentives of bureaucratic position and legislative power, no public official wants publicly to acknowledge failure.

Incrementalism at Work.   Governments seldom undertake to consider any program as a whole in any given year. Active consideration of programs is made at the margin—that is, attention is focused on proposed changes in existing programs rather than on the value of programs in their entirety. Usually this attention comes in the budgetary process (see Chapter 7), when proposed increases or decreases in funding are under discussion in the bureaucracy and legislature. Negative evaluative studies can play a role in the budgetary process—limiting increases for failed programs or perhaps even identifying programs ripe for budget cutting. But attention is almost always focused on changes or reforms, increases or decreases, rather than on the complete termination of programs. Even mandating "sunset" legislation, used in many states (requiring legislatures periodically to reconsider and reauthorize whole programs), seldom results in program termination.

Politics as a Substitute for Analysis

Policy analysis, including systematic policy evaluation, is a rational process. It requires some agreement on what problems the government should undertake to resolve; some agreement on the nature of societal benefits and costs and the weights to be given to them; and some agreement on the formulation of a research design, the measurement of benefits and costs, and the interpretation of the results. Value conflicts intrude at almost every point in the evaluation process, but policy analysis cannot resolve value conflicts.

Politics is the management of conflict. People have different ideas about what are the principal problems confronting society and about what, if anything, the government should do about them. Value conflicts explain why policymakers rely so little on systematic policy analysis in the formulation, selection, or evaluation of policy. Instead, they must rely on political processes.

A political approach to policy analysis emphasizes

- The search for common concerns that might form the basis for identification of societal problems
- Reasonable trade-offs among conflicting values at each stage of the policymaking process

- The search for mutually beneficial outcomes for diverse groups; attempting to satisfy diverse demands
- Compromise and conciliation and a willingness to accept modest net gains (half a loaf) rather than suffer the loss of more comprehensive proposals
- Bargaining among participants, even in separate policy areas, to win allies ("I'll support your proposals if you support mine.")

At best, policy analysis plays only a secondary role in the policymaking process. But it is an important role, nonetheless. Political scientist Charles E. Lindblom explains "the intelligence of democracy":

> Strategic analysis and mutual adjustment among political participants, then, are the underlying processes by which democratic systems achieve the level of intelligent action that they do. . . .
>
> There is never a point at which the thinking, research, and action is "objective," or "unbiased." It is partisan through and through, as are all human activities, in the sense that the expectations and priorities of those commissioning and doing the analysis shape it, and in the sense that those using information shape its interpretation and application.
>
> Information seeking and shaping must intertwine inextricably with political interaction, judgment, and action. Since time and energy and brainpower are limited, strategic analysis must focus on those aspects of an issue that participating partisans consider to be most important for persuading each other. There is no purely analytical way to do such focusing, it requires political judgments: about what the crucial unknowns are, about what kind of evidence is likely to be persuasive to would-be allies, or about what range of alternatives may be politically feasible.[9]

The Limits of Public Policy

Never have Americans expected so much of their government. Our confidence in what governments can do seems boundless. We have come to believe that they can eliminate poverty, end racism, ensure peace, prevent crime, restore cities, clean the air and water, and so on, if only they will adopt the right policies.

Perhaps confidence in the potential effectiveness of public policy is desirable, particularly if it inspires us to continue to search for ways to resolve societal problems. But any serious study of public policy must also recognize the limitations of policy in affecting these conditions.

1. Some societal problems are incapable of solution because of the way in which they are defined. If problems are defined in *relative* rather than *absolute* terms, they may never be resolved by public policy. For example, if the poverty line is defined as the line that places one-fifth of the population below it, poverty will always be with us regardless of how well off the "poor" may become. Relative disparities in society may never be eliminated. Even if income differences among classes were tiny, tiny differences may come to have great symbolic importance, and the problem of inequality would remain.

2. Expectations may always outrace the capabilities of governments. Progress in any policy area may simply result in an upward movement in expectations about what policy should accomplish. Public education never faced a dropout problem until the 1960s, when for the first time a majority of boys and girls were graduating from high school. At the turn of the century, when high school graduation was rare, there was no mention of a dropout problem.

3. Policies that solve the problems of one group in society may create problems for other groups. In a plural society, one person's solution may be another person's problem. For example, solving the problem of inequality in society may mean redistributive tax and spending policies, which take from persons of above-average wealth to give to persons with below-average wealth. The latter may view this as a solution, but the former may view it as creating serious problems. There are *no* policies that can simultaneously attain mutually exclusive ends.

4. It is quite possible that some societal forces cannot be harnessed by governments, even if it is desirable to do so. It may turn out that the government cannot stop urban location patterns of whites and blacks, even if it tries to do so. Whites and blacks may separate themselves regardless of government policies in support of integration. Some children may not be able to learn much in public schools no matter what is done. In other words, governments may not be *able* to bring about some societal changes.

5. Frequently people adapt themselves to public policies in ways that render the policies useless. For example, we may solve the problem of poverty by government guarantees of a high annual income, but by so doing we may reduce incentives to work and thus swell the number of dependent families beyond the fiscal capacities of government to provide guarantees. The possibility always exists that adaptive behavior may frustrate policy.

6. Societal problems may have multiple causes, and a specific policy may not be able to eradicate the problem. For example, job training may not affect the hardcore unemployed if their employability is also affected by chronic poor health.

7. The solution to some problems may require policies that are more costly than the problem. For example, it may turn out that certain levels of public disorder—including riots, civil disturbances, and occasional violence—cannot be eradicated without the adoption of very repressive policies—the forceable breakup of revolutionary parties, restrictions on the public appearances of demagogues, the suppression of hate literature, the addition of large numbers of security forces, and so on. But these repressive policies would prove too costly in democratic values—freedom of speech and press, rights of assembly, freedom to form opposition parties. Thus, a certain level of disorder may be the price we pay for democracy. Doubtless there are other examples of societal problems that are simply too costly to solve.

8. The political system is not structured for completely rational decision making. The solution of societal problems generally implies a rational model, but government may not be capable of formulating policy in a rational fashion. Instead the political system may reflect group interests, elite preferences, institutional forces, or incremental change, more than rationalism. Presumably, a democratic system is structured to reflect mass influences, whether these are rational or not. Elected officials respond to the demands of their constituents, and this may inhibit completely rational approaches to public policy.

Notes

1. Joseph S. Wholey, et al., *Federal Evaluation Policy* (Washington, DC: Urban Institute, 1970), p. 25.
2. David Nachmias, *Public Policy Evaluation* (New York: St. Martin's Press, 1979), p. 4.
3. *Federal Evaluation Issues* (Washington, DC: General Accounting Office, 1989).
4. *Annual Index of Reports Issued* (Washington, DC: General Accountability Office, annually).
5. See David L. Sills, ed., *International Encyclopedia of the Social Sciences*, vol. 7 (New York: Free Press, 1968), p. 241.
6. David Kershaw and Jerelyn Fair, eds., *Final Report of the New Jersey Graduated Work Incentive Experiment* (Madison: University of Wisconsin, Institute for Research on Poverty, 1974).
7. John F. Cogan, *Negative Income Taxation and Labor Supply: New Evidence from the New Jersey–Pennsylvania Experiment* (Santa Monica, CA: Rand Corporation, 1978). See also SRI International, *Final Report of the Seattle–Denver Income Maintenance Experiment* (Washington, DC: U.S. Government Printing Office, 1983), for experimental results suggesting that government job training has no effect on a person's subsequent earnings or employment and that a guaranteed income significantly lowers earnings and hours of work and contributes to marital dissolutions.
8. James Q. Wilson, "On Pettigrew and Armor," *The Public Interest* 31 (Spring 1973), pp. 132–134.
9. Charles E. Lindblom and Edward J. Woodhouse, *The Policy-Making Process*, 3rd ed. (Englewood Cliffs, NJ: Prentice Hall, 1993), pp. 31–32.

Bibliography

AMMONS, DAVID N. *Tools for Decision-Making: A Practical Guide for Local Government.* Washington, DC: CQ Press, 2002.

BARDACH, EUGENE. *A Practical Guide for Policy Analysis*, 2nd ed. Washington, DC: CQ Press, 2004.

BINGHAM, RICHARD D., and CLAIRE L. FELBINGER. *Evaluation in Practice*, 2nd ed. Washington, DC: CQ Press, 2002.

HEINEMAN, ROBERT A., et. al. *The World of the Policy Analyst.* Washington, DC: CQ Press, 2001.

POSAVAC, EMIL J., and RAYMOND G. CAREY. *Program Evaluation*, 7th ed. Upper Saddle River, NJ: Prentice Hall, 2007.

PRESSMAN, JEFFREY L., and AARON WILDAVSKY. *Implementation.* Berkeley: University of California Press, 1974.

WEIMER, DAVID, L., and AIDAN R. VINING. *Policy Analysis: Concepts and Practices*, 4th ed. Upper Saddle River, NJ: Prentice Hall, 2005.

WILDAVSKY, AARON. *Speaking Truth to Power.* New York: John Wiley, 1979.

Web Sites

GENERAL ACCOUNTABILITY OFFICE. The GAO is the investigative and evaluative arm of the Congress. Its purpose is to hold the executive branch accountable to the Congress. Its reports cover a wide variety of issues. *www.gao.gov*

OFFICE OF MANAGEMENT AND BUDGET. In addition to preparing the Budget of the United States, OMB performs management studies, including reports on financial management and regulatory matters. *www.whitehouse.gov/omb*

ASSOCIATION FOR PUBLIC POLICY ANALYSIS AND MANAGEMENT. Academic organization that publishes the *Journal of Policy Analysis and Management*, with articles on public administration and management. *www.appam.org*

AMERICAN SOCIETY FOR PUBLIC ADMINISTRATION. Organization of academic and professional public administrators, with news, job listings, and publication—*Public Administration Review. www.aspanet.org*

RAND CORPORATION. Originally devoted almost exclusively to research on defense and weapons systems, RAND studies now include space research, Internet technology, information protection, and assessments of government programs across a wide spectrum. *www.rand.org*

CATO INSTITUTE, *Regulation* magazine. Articles assessing the costs and effectiveness of government programs, especially regulatory programs and agencies. *www.cato.org/pubs/regulation*

Index

Operation Iraqi Freedom, 296–302
Orszag, Peter R., 188

PACs, 40–41
parties, 43
Patriot Act, 79, 310
Paulson, Henry, 152
Pechman, Joseph A., 188
Peters, Guy B., 9
Peterson, Paul E., 145
Petraeus, David, 301
Pierce v. Society of Sisters, 145
Planned Parenthood of Pennsylvania v. Casey,
    258, 262
plea bargaining, 78
Plessy v. Ferguson, 235, 246, 260
Plyer v. Doe, 208, 261
police, 64–65
policy
    analysis, 5–8
    civil rights, 232–262
    criminal justice, 54–87
    defense, 281–306
    definition, 1–3
    economic, 147–168
    education, 116–146
    elitism, 20–22, 189–208, 232–262
    energy, 222–231
    environmental, 210–231
    game theory, 24–25, 281–306, 307–322
    group theory, 19–20, 116–145, 169–188
    health, 105–114
    homeland security, 307–322
    implementation, 199–207
    immigration, 199–207
    incrementalism, 17–19, 147–167
    legitimation, 41–45
    models, 11–27
    monetary, 147–149, 156–157
    processes, 14, 28–53
    public choice, 25–27, 210–231
    rationalism, 15–17, 54–86, 88–115
    social security, 96–100
    study of, 3–8
    tax, 169–188
    trade, 189–209
    welfare, 88–105
Pollocks v. Farmers Loan, 187
Posavac, Jeffery L., 339
poverty, 90–95

Powell, Colin, 289, 295
prayer, (in schools), 141–143
preemptions, federal, 270–271
president, 33, 43–44
Press, Charles, 279
Pressman, Jeffrey L., 339
Printz v. United States, 279
prisons, 80–81, 85
process, policy, 14, 28–53
progressivity (in taxes), 175–176
protectionism, 192
public assistance, 100–101
public choice theory, 22–24, 25–27, 210–231

quotas (trade), 191–192

R.A.V. v. City of St. Paul, 85
Rabuska, Alvin, 188
race, 232–249
Rahm, Dianne, 167
Rasul v. United States, 321
rationalism, 15–17, 54–86, 88–115
Reagan, Ronald, 178–179, 285
recession, 151–156
Reconstruction, 235
recycling, 212–213
Reed v. Reed, 261
Regents of the University of California v. Bakke,
    245–246
regulation, 48–49
religion, 139–143
research (policy), 328–333
Rice, Condoleezza, 92
Richmond v. Crosen, 246, 261
RICO, 78–79
Rio Treaty, 221
Rodgers, Harold R., 115
Rodriguez v. San Antonio, 144
Roe v. Wade, 256–258, 261
Roper v. Simmons, 86
Rose, Melody, 262
Rosenbaum, Walter A., 230
Rosenburger v. University of Virginia, 145
Rossi, Peter H., 85, 114
Rossman, David, 85
Rumsfeld, Donald, 297–299
Rushevsky, Mark E., 10, 115

"Star Wars," 285
Saddam, Hussien, 295–296

Introduction to International Relations

Introduction to
International Relations
Theories and approaches

Robert Jackson
Georg Sørensen

OXFORD
UNIVERSITY PRESS

OXFORD

UNIVERSITY PRESS

Great Clarendon Street, Oxford OX2 6DP

Oxford University Press is a department of the University of Oxford.
It furthers the University's objective of excellence in research, scholarship,
and education by publishing worldwide in

Oxford New York

Auckland Cape Town Dar es Salaam Hong Kong Karachi
Kuala Lumpur Madrid Melbourne Mexico City Nairobi
New Delhi Shanghai Taipei Toronto

With offices in

Argentina Austria Brazil Chile Czech Republic France Greece
Guatemala Hungary Italy Japan Poland Portugal Singapore
South Korea Switzerland Thailand Turkey Ukraine Vietnam

Oxford is a registered trade mark of Oxford University Press
in the UK and in certain other countries

Published in the United States
by Oxford University Press Inc., New York

© Robert Jackson and Georg Sørensen, 2007

British Library Cataloguing in Publication Data

Data available

Library of Congress Cataloging in Publication Data

Jackson, Robert H.
Introduction to international relations : theories and approaches /
Robert Jackson, Georg Sørensen.—3rd ed.
   p. cm.
Includes bibliographical references and index.
ISBN-13: 978–0–19–928543–3
ISBN-10: 0–19–928543–8
 1. International relations. 2. International relations—Philosophy.
I. Sørensen, Georg, 1948– II. Title.
JZ1242.J33 2007
327.1—dc22   2006023286

Typeset by Newgen Imaging Systems (P) Ltd., Chennai, India
Printed in Great Britain
on acid-free paper by
Bath Press Ltd, Bath

ISBN 0–19–928543–8   978–0–19–928543–3

1 3 5 7 9 10 8 6 4 2

To our students

▌ ACKNOWLEDGEMENTS

This third revised and expanded edition of the book has benefited from very helpful comments made by the readers of the first two editions. We were encouraged to stay with the basic aim and format of the book: a succinct and readable introduction to the major IR theories and approaches. This third edition retains those features. We also received suggestions for expanded coverage. This third edition has two new chapters: one on 'Social Constructivism' and one on 'Foreign-Policy Analysis'. All chapters are brought up to date in the light of current international events and ongoing debates in the discipline.

This new edition has several additional features to enhance students' access to international relations theories and approaches. The supporting Online Resource Centre (ORC) has been revised and expanded, and there is a closer connection between book and ORC; each chapter of the book now provides specific references to relevant web links. There are web links to theoretical debates as well as to information on world situations in specific geographical locations, thus giving students a perspective on how theory can be used in the real world. There is a map of the world in the new edition, and there are links to further maps on the ORC. A glossary with key terms is included at the end of the book.

We are grateful for support and encouragement from a large number of people. Tim Barton of Oxford University Press warmly supported the project from the very start. Several anonymous readers made constructive suggestions for revisions and clarifications. Many colleagues provided advice or encouragement: Will Bain, Derek Beach, Michael Corgan, Kenneth Glarbo, Hans Henrik Holm, Kal Holsti, Peter Viggo Jakobsen, Brian Job, Knud Erik Jørgensen, Anne Mette Kjær, Tonny Brems Knudsen, Mehdi Mozaffari, Liselotte Odgaard, Jørgen Dige Pedersen, Thomas Pedersen, Nikolaj Petersen, Jennifer Jackson Preece, Mette Skak, Sasson Sofer, Mark Zacher, and Clemens Stubbe Østergaard.

We owe special thanks to those readers who provided us with useful comments on the second edition, including ten anonymous referees. We have tried to deal with their many excellent suggestions for improvement without sacrificing the existing qualities of the book which most of them commented on very favourably. We are confident that both instructors and students will find that this third expanded edition has managed to achieve that goal.

Ruth Anderson was a great help as commissioning editor for this third edition. Jonna Kjær again handled the paperwork with her usual efficiency and punctuality. Eva Dyrberg Pedersen and Bethany Boucher did an excellent job collecting and systematizing the links for the book's web site. Elsebeth Søndergaard compiled an overview of recent IR literature. Dennis Flanders contributed to the preparation of the glossary.

Finally, we owe special thanks to our wives and children for their support in our continuing endeavour to produce an IR textbook that can communicate to readers not only in North America and Europe but everywhere that international relations is taught and studied as an academic discipline.

Aarhus and Boston
March 2006

▌ CONTENTS

▌DETAILED CONTENTS

Today virtually the entire population of the world lives within the borders of those separate territorial communities we call states—about six billion people are citizens or subjects of one state or another. For more than half a billion people living in the developed countries of Western Europe, North America, Australia, New Zealand and Japan, basic security and welfare are often taken more or less for granted, because it is guaranteed and sometimes directly provided by the state. But for several billions of people who live in the developing countries of Asia, Africa and the former Soviet Union, basic security and welfare is not something that can be taken for granted. Protection, policing, law enforcement and other civil conditions of minimal safety for all cannot be guaranteed. For many people it is a daily challenge to provide adequate food, clean water, housing and similar socioeconomic necessities. The academic subject of international relations (IR) seeks to understand how people are provided, or not provided, with the basic values of security, freedom, order, justice and welfare.

What is in the Book?

First and foremost this book is an introduction to the academic *discipline* of IR. What is a 'discipline'? It is a branch of knowledge, aimed at the systematic understanding of a subject. As is often the case in the social sciences, in IR there is no one best way to master the subject. Instead, what we have are several significant theories and theoretical traditions: realism, liberalism, International Society, social constructivism and International Political Economy. They interact and overlap in interesting and important ways that we investigate in the chapters which follow. However, each one explores the subject of IR in its own distinctive way. Realism, for example, is focused on the basic value of security, because according to realists war is always a possibility in a system of sovereign states. Liberals, on the other hand, argue that international relations can be cooperative and not merely conflictive. That belief is based on the idea that the modern, liberal state can bring progress and opportunities to the greatest number of people around the world.

All the most important theories and theoretical traditions of IR are presented in the chapters which follow. There is no need to give a detailed account of each chapter here. But a brief consumer guide may be helpful. What is it that this book has to offer? The main elements can be summarized as follows:

- This third edition provides an introduction to the analytical tools that the discipline has on its shelves: IR theories and approaches. Some theories have proved to be of more enduring importance than others. In the central chapters we focus on those theories, which we call 'established' or 'main theoretical' traditions. They are realism, liberalism, International Society, and important theories of International Political Economy (IPE).

This edition also includes a chapter on a major new approach, social constructivism, as well as a chapter on theories involved in foreign-policy analysis. Finally, we review 'post-positivist' theories that have gained prominence in recent years.

- Theories are presented faithfully, by focusing on both their strengths and their weaknesses. The main points of contention between theories are thoroughly discussed. The book makes clear how major theoretical debates link up with each other and structure the discipline of IR.

- The book places emphasis on the relationship between 'IR theory' (academic knowledge of international relations) and 'IR practice' (real world events and activities of world politics). Theories matter for their own sake, and theories also matter as a guide to practice. The book carefully explains how particular theories organize and sharpen our view of the world. We often assume that the sword is mightier than the pen, but it is the pen, our guiding ideas and assumptions, which usually shapes the ways that swords are put to use.

Every chapter is guided by our aim to enable students to acquire knowledge of IR as an evolving academic discipline. Although we have written the book with introductory level courses foremost in mind, it also contains much information and analysis that will prove valuable in higher level courses, making it possible for students to advance more swiftly in their study of IR.

■ GUIDED TOUR OF TEXTBOOK FEATURES

This text is enriched with a range of pedagogic tools to help you navigate the text material and reinforce your knowledge of International Relations. This guided tour shows you how to get the most out of your textbook package and do better in your studies.

Chapter Summaries

■ Summary

This chapter introduces the historical and social basis of international relations or IR. The aim of the chapter is to emphasize the practical reality of international relations in our everyday lives and to connect that practical reality with the academic study of international relations. The chapter makes that connection by focusing on the core historical subject matter of IR: modern sovereign states and the international relations of the state system. Three main topics are discussed: the significance of international relations in everyday life and the main values that states exist to foster, the historical evolution of the state system and world economy in brief outline, and the changing contemporary world of states.

Brief summaries at the beginning of every chapter set the scene for upcoming themes and issues to be discussed, and indicate the scope of coverage within each chapter topic.

Boxes

BOX 4.2	Classical liberalism	
	FOCUS:	
	freedom, cooperation, peace, progress	
	EARLY THINKERS:	
Locke (1632–1704)	**Bentham** (1748–1832)	**Kant** (1724–1804)
The rule of law	Liberal states respect	'Republics will establish
'Rechtsstaat'	international law	perpetual peace'

A number of topics benefit from further explanation or exploration in a manner that does not disrupt the flow of the main text. Throughout the book, boxes provide you with extra information on particular topics that complement your understanding of the main chapter text.

Glossary Terms

pluralism Along with solidarism, one of two International Society approaches to the potential conflict between state sovereignty and respect for human rights. A pluralist view of the state system emphasizes the primacy of state sovereignty: a policy of non-intervention must be maintained even when another state is experiencing (or complicit in) a humanitarian crisis within its borders. Civil rights (within states) take precedence over human rights (between states).

positivism A methodology in IR that employs most of the attitudes and assumptions of behaviouralism but does so in a more sophisticated way. Positivism is a fundamentally scientific approach. Its advocates and adherents believe that there can be objective knowledge of the social and political dimensions of the world, and that this knowledge is obtainable through the careful development and testing of empirical propositions. The social scientist is no different from any other scientist in this regard.

Key terms are bold-faced in the text and defined in a glossary at the end of the text, to aid you in exam revision.

Key Points

KEY POINTS

- The focus of social constructivism is on human awareness or consciousness and its place in world affairs. The international system is constituted by ideas, not by material forces.

- Social theory is the more general theory about the social world. In social theory, constructivists emphasize the social construction of reality. The social world is not a given. The social world is a world of human consciousness: of thoughts and beliefs, of ideas and concepts, of languages and discourses. Four major types of ideas are: ideologies; normative beliefs; cause–effect beliefs; and policy prescriptions.

- Constructivist Alexander Wendt rejects the neorealist position of anarchy necessarily leading to self-help. That cannot be decided a priori; it depends on the interaction between states. In these processes of interaction the identities and interests of states are created.

- Martha Finnemore argues that identities and interests are defined by international forces, that is, by the norms of behaviour embedded in international society.

Each chapter ends with a set of Key Points that summarize the most important arguments developed within each chapter topic.

Further Reading

GUIDE TO FURTHER READING

Brown, C., Nardin, T., and Rengger, N. (2002). 'Introduction', in C. Brown, T. Nardin, and N. Rengger (eds), *International Relations in Political Thought*. Cambridge: Cambridge University Press.

Bull, H. (1969). 'International Theory: The Case for a Classical Approach', in K. Knorr and J. Rosenau (eds), *Contending Approaches to International Politics*. Princeton: Princeton University Press.

Jackson, R. (2005). *Classical and Modern Thought on International Relations: From Anarchy to Cosmopolis*. New York: Palgrave Macmillan.

To take your learning further, reading lists have been provided as a guide to find out more about the issues raised within each chapter topic and to help you locate the key academic literature in the field.

Online Resource Centre

WEB LINKS

Web links mentioned in the chapter plus additional links can be found an the Online Resource Centre that accompanies this book.

www.oxfordtextbooks.co.uk/orc/jackson_sorensen3e/

Each chapter provides references to relevant annotated web links which can be found on the Online Resource Centre that accompanies this book.

▌GUIDED TOUR OF ONLINE RESOURCE CENTRE

www.oxfordtextbooks.co.uk/orc/jackson_sorensen3e/

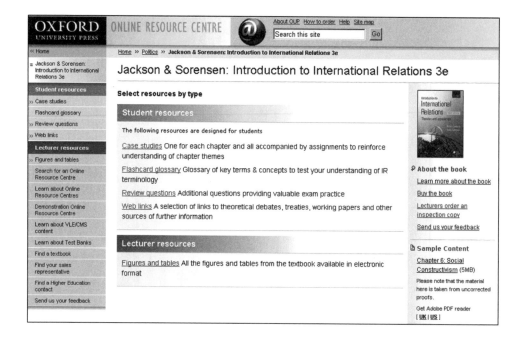

The Online Resource Centre that accompanies this book provides students and instructors with ready-to-use teaching and learning materials. These resources are free of charge and designed to maximize the learning experience.

Case-Studies

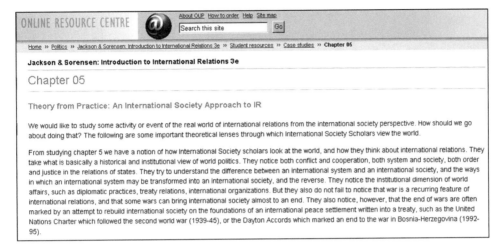

Each chapter is supplemented with a short case-study accompanied by assignments, designed to reinforce students' understanding of chapter themes.

Review Questions

Chapter 07

1) Are mercantilists right when they assert that the economy should be subordinated to the primary goal of increasing state power?
2) Are the Japanese, the Koreans, and the Chinese thinking mercantilist terms as claimed in box 7.2?
3) What should be the role of the state according to economic liberalism?
4) Is Ricardo's theory of comparative advantage confirmed when looking at today's international trade?
5) Are the advanced industrialized countries characterized by class struggle as the Marxist view assumes?
6) Discuss Lenin's view of 'uneven development'-is it a correct view?
7) Does foreign investment in the Third World by the industrialized countries lead to exploitation as Gunder Frank claims?
8) Discuss the pros and cons of Robert Cox's analytical framework as set out in box 7.9.
9) Will the capitalist world-economy always be a hierarchy as Wallerstein says?
10) Marxists maintain that economic power is the basis for political power; discuss.

Additional questions allow students to test themselves and provide valuable exam practice.

Web Links

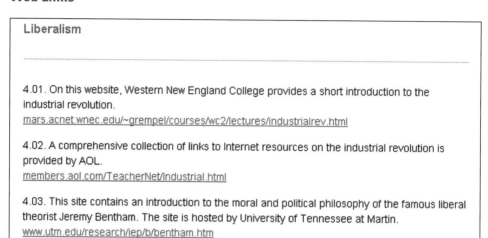

A series of annotated web links organized by chapter have been provided to point you in the direction of different theoretical debates, important treaties, working papers, articles and other relevant sources of information.

There are also web links on maps, countries, essential international organizations and the Iraq War.

Flashcard Glossary

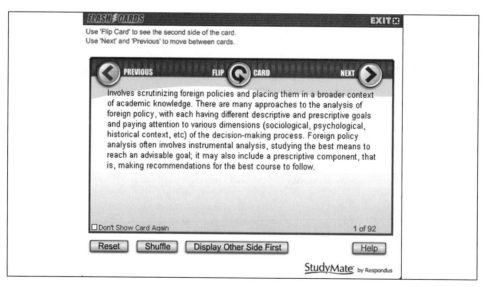

A series of interactive flashcards containing key terms and concepts have been provided to test your understanding of IR terminology.

Figures and Tables from the Text (instructors only)

Click on the thumbnails below to download full-size versions of the figures and tables in part one. Alternatively, you can download a zip file containing all the figures from chapter 03.

For best results when printing these images:
- Click on the thumbnail to open the full-size version, then go to **File > Save As** to save the image to your computer.
- Insert the image into a document (e.g. Word, PowerPoint) by clicking on **Insert > Picture > From file**.

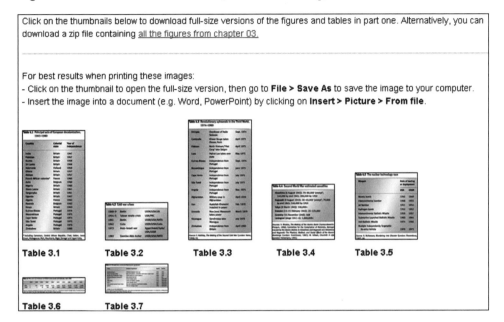

Table 3.1   Table 3.2   Table 3.3   Table 3.4   Table 3.5

Table 3.6   Table 3.7

All figures and tables from the text have been provided in high resolution format for downloading into presentation software or for use in assignments and exam material.

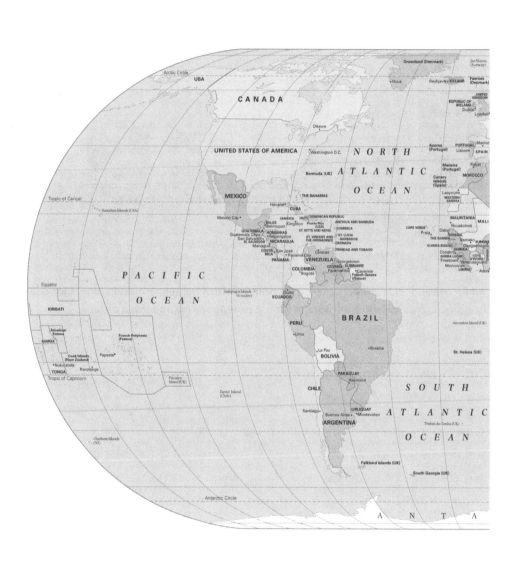

CHAPTER 1

Why Study IR?

▌ Summary

This chapter introduces the historical and social basis of international relations or IR. The aim of the chapter is to emphasize the practical reality of international relations in our everyday lives and to connect that practical reality with the academic study of international relations. The chapter makes that connection by focusing on the core historical subject matter of IR: modern sovereign states and the international relations of the **state system**. Three main topics are discussed: the significance of international relations in everyday life and the main values that states exist to foster, the historical evolution of the state system and world economy in brief outline, and the changing contemporary world of states.

International Relations in Everyday Life

IR is the shorthand name for the academic subject of international relations. The main reason why we should study IR is the fact that the entire population of the world is divided into separate political communities, or independent states, which profoundly affect the way people live. A state may be defined as a clear-cut and bordered territory, with a permanent population, under the jurisdiction of supreme government that is constitutionally independent of all foreign governments: a sovereign state. Together those states form an international state system that is global in extent. At the present time there are almost 200 independent states. With very few exceptions, everybody on earth not only lives in one of those countries but is also a citizen of one of them and very rarely of more than one. So virtually every man, woman and child on earth is connected to a particular state, and via that state to the state system which affects their lives in important ways that they may not be fully aware of.

States are independent of each other, at least legally: they have sovereignty. But that does not mean they are isolated or insulated from each other. On the contrary, they adjoin each other and affect each other and must therefore somehow find ways to coexist and to deal with each other. In other words, they form a state system, which is a core subject of IR. Furthermore, states are usually embedded in international markets which affect the policies of their governments and the wealth and welfare of their citizens. That requires that they enter into relations with each other. Complete isolation is usually not an option. When states are isolated and cut off from the state system, either by their own government or by foreign powers, the people usually suffer as a result. That has been the situation recently with regard to Burma, Libya, North Korea, Iraq and Iran. Like most other social systems, the state system can have certain advantages and disadvantages for the states involved and their people. IR is the study of the nature and consequences of these international relations.

The state system is a distinctive way of organizing political life on earth which has deep historical roots. There have been state systems at different times and places in different parts of the world: for example, in ancient India, in ancient Greece and in Renaissance Italy (Watson 1992). However, the subject of IR conventionally dates back to the early modern era (sixteenth and seventeenth centuries) in Europe, when sovereign states based on adjacent territories were initially established. Ever since the eighteenth century the relations between such independent states have been labelled 'international relations'. In the nineteenth and twentieth centuries the state system was expanded to encompass the entire territory of the earth. The world of states is basically a territorial world: it is a way of politically organizing the world's populated territory, a distinctive kind of territorial political organization, based on numerous different governments that are legally independent of each other. The only large territory that is not a state is Antarctica, and it is administered by a consortium of states. Today IR is the study of the global state system from various scholarly perspectives, the most important of which shall be discussed in this book.

To understand the significance of IR it is necessary to grasp what living in states basically involves. What does it imply? How important is it? How should we think about it? This book is centrally concerned with these questions and especially with the last one. The chapters which follow deal with various answers to that fundamental question. This chapter examines the core historical subject matter of IR: the evolution of the state system and the changing contemporary world of states.

To begin to respond to these questions it may be helpful to examine our everyday life as citizens of particular states to see what we generally expect from a state. There are at least five basic social values that states are usually expected to uphold: security, freedom, order, justice and welfare. These are social values that are so fundamental to human well-being that they must be protected or ensured in some way. That could be by social organizations other than the state: e.g. by family, clan, ethnic or religious organizations. In the modern era, however, the state has usually been involved as the leading institution in that regard: it is expected to ensure these basic values. For example, people generally assume that the state should and would underwrite the value of security, which involves the protection of citizens from internal and external threat. That is a fundamental concern or interest of states. However, the very existence of independent states affects the value of security: we live in a world of many states, almost all of which are armed at least to some degree. Thus states can both defend and threaten people's security, and that paradox of the state system is usually referred to as the 'security dilemma'. In other words, just like any other human organization, states present problems as well as provide solutions.

Most states are likely to be friendly, non-threatening and peace-loving. But a few states may be hostile and aggressive and there is no world government to constrain them. That poses a basic and age-old problem of state systems: national security. To deal with that problem most states possess armed forces. Military power is usually considered a necessity so that states can coexist and deal with each other without being intimidated or subjugated. Unarmed states are extremely rare in the history of the state system. That is a basic fact of the state system that we should never lose sight of. Many states also enter into alliances with other states to increase their national security. To ensure that no great power succeeds in achieving a hegemonic position of overall domination, based on intimidation, coercion or the outright use of force, it is also necessary to construct and maintain a balance of military power. Security is obviously one of the most fundamental values of international relations. That approach to the study of world politics is typical of realist theories of IR (Morgenthau 1960). It operates on the assumption that relations of states can be best characterized as a world in which armed states are competing rivals and periodically go to war with each other.

The second basic value that states are usually expected to uphold is freedom, both personal freedom and national freedom or independence. A fundamental reason for having states and putting up with the burdens that governments place on citizens, such as taxes or obligations of military service, is the condition of national freedom or independence that states exist to foster. We cannot be free unless our country is free too: that was made very clear to millions of Czech, Polish, Danish, Norwegian, Belgian and Dutch citizens, as well as citizens of other countries that were invaded and occupied by Nazi Germany during the Second World War. Even if our country is free we may still not be free personally, but at least then the problem of our freedom is in our own hands. War threatens and sometimes destroys freedom. Peace fosters freedom. Peace also makes progressive international change possible, that is, the creation of a better world. Peace and progressive change are obviously among the most fundamental values of international relations. That approach to the study of world politics is typical of liberal theories of IR (Claude 1971). It operates on the assumption that international relations can be best characterized as a world in which states cooperate with each other to maintain peace and freedom and to pursue progressive change.

The third and fourth basic values that states are usually expected to uphold are order and justice. States have a common interest in establishing and maintaining international order so that they can coexist and interact on a basis of stability, certainty and predictability. To that end, states are expected to uphold international law: to keep their treaty commitments and to observe the rules, conventions and customs of the international legal order. They are also expected to follow accepted practices of diplomacy and to support international organizations. International law, diplomatic relations and international organizations can only exist and operate successfully if these expectations are generally met by most states most of the time. States are also expected to uphold human rights. Today there is an elaborate international legal framework of human rights—civil, political, social and economic—which has been developed since the end of the Second World War. Order and justice obviously are among the most fundamental values of international relations. That approach to the study of world politics is typical of International Society theories of IR (Bull 1995). It operates on the assumption that international relations can be best characterized as a world in which states are socially responsible actors and have a common interest in preserving international order and promoting international justice.

The final basic value that states are usually expected to uphold is the population's socio-economic wealth and welfare. People expect their government to adopt appropriate policies to encourage high employment, low inflation, steady investment, the uninterrupted flow of trade and commerce, and so forth. Because national economies are rarely isolated from each other, most people also expect that the state will respond to the international economic environment in such a way as to enhance or at least defend and maintain the national standard of living.

States nowadays try to frame and implement economic policies which can maintain the stability of the international economy upon which they are all increasingly dependent. That usually involves economic policies that can deal adequately with international markets, with the economic policies of other states, with foreign investment, with foreign exchange rates, with international trade, with international transportation and communications, and with other international economic relations that affect national wealth and welfare. Economic interdependence, meaning a high degree of mutual economic dependence among countries, is a striking feature of the contemporary state system. Some people consider that to be a good thing because it may increase overall freedom and wealth by expanding the global marketplace and thereby increasing participation, specialization, efficiency and productivity. Other people consider it to be a bad thing because it may promote overall inequality by allowing rich and powerful countries, or countries with financial or technological advantages, to dominate poor and weak countries that lack those advantages. But either way, wealth and welfare obviously are among the most fundamental values of inter-national relations. That approach to the study of world politics is typical of IPE (Interna-tional Political Economy) theories of IR (Gilpin 1987). It operates on the assumption that international relations can be best characterized as fundamentally a socioeconomic world and not merely a political and military world.

Most people usually take these basic values (security; freedom; order and justice; welfare) for granted. They only become aware of them when something goes wrong—for example, during a war or a depression, when things begin to get beyond the control of individual states. On those learning occasions people wake up to the larger circumstances of their lives which in normal times are a silent or invisible background. At those moments they are likely to become sharply aware of what they take for granted, and of how important these values really are in their everyday lives. We become aware of national security when a foreign power rattles its sabre or engages in hostile actions against our country or one of our allies. We become aware of national independence and our freedom as citizens when peace is no longer guaranteed. We become aware of international order and justice when some states, especially major powers, abuse, exploit, denounce or disregard international law, or trample on human rights. We become aware of national welfare and our own personal socio-economic well-being when foreign countries or international investors use their economic clout to jeopardize our standard of living.

There were significant moments of heightened awareness of these major values during the twentieth century. The First World War made it dreadfully clear to most people just how devastatingly destructive of lives and living conditions modern mechanized warfare between major powers can be, and just how important it is to reduce the risk of war between great powers (see web link 1.09). Such recognition led to the first major developments of IR thought which tried to find effective legal institutions—e.g. the Covenant of the League of Nations—to prevent great-power war (see web link 1.10). The Great Depression brought home to many people around the world how their economic livelihood could be adversely affected, in some cases destroyed, by market conditions not only at home but also in other countries (see web link 1.11). The Second World War not only underlined the reality of the dangers of great-power war, but also revealed how important it is to prevent any great power from getting out of control and how unwise it is to pursue a policy of appeasement—which was adopted by Britain and France in regard to Nazi Germany just prior to the war with disastrous consequences for everybody, including the German people.

There also were moments of heightened awareness of the fundamental importance of these values after the Second World War. The Cuban missile crisis of 1962 brought home to many people the dangers of nuclear war. The anti-colonial movements in Asia and Africa of the 1950s and 1960s and the secessionist movements in the former Soviet Union and former Yugoslavia at the end of the Cold War made it clear how important self-determination and political independence continue to be. The global inflation of the 1970s and early 1980s, caused by a sudden dramatic increase in oil prices by the OPEC cartel of oil-exporting coun-tries, was a reminder of how the interconnectedness of the global economy can be a threat to national and personal welfare anywhere in the world. For example, the oil shock of the 1970s made it abundantly clear to countless American, European and Japanese motorists—among others—that economic policies of Middle East and other major oil-producing countries could suddenly raise the price of gas or petrol at the pump and lower their standard of living. The Gulf War (1990–1) and the conflicts in the Balkans, particularly Bosnia (1992–5) and Kosovo (1999), were a reminder of the importance of international order and respect for human rights. The attacks on New York and Washington (2001) awakened many people in the United States and elsewhere to the dangers of international terrorism (see web link 1.16).

For a long time there has been a basic assumption that life inside properly organized and well-managed states is better than life outside states or without states at all. For example, the Jews spent more than half a century trying to get a state of their own in which they could be secure: Israel. As long as states and the state system manage to maintain the foregoing core values, that assumption holds. That has generally been the case for developed countries, especially the states of Western Europe, North America, Japan, Australia, New Zealand and some others. That gives rise to more conventional IR theories which regard the state system as a valuable core institution of modern life. The traditional IR theories discussed in this book tend to adopt that positive view. They recognize the significance of these basic values even if they disagree about which ones are most important—e.g. realists emphasize the importance of security and order, liberals emphasize freedom and justice, and IPE scholars emphasize economic equality and welfare.

But if states are not successful in that regard the state system can easily be understood in the opposite light: not as upholding basic social conditions and values, but rather as undermining them. That is the case with regard to many states in the Third World, especially sub-Saharan Africa. It is also the case with regard to some states which emerged as a result of the break-up of the Soviet Union and Yugoslavia at the end of the Cold War. Many of these states more or less fail to provide or protect even to a minimal standard at least some of the five basic values discussed above. More than a few states fail to ensure any of them. The plight of countless men, women and children in those countries puts into question the credibility and perhaps even the legitimacy of the state system. It promotes a corresponding assumption that the international system fosters or

BOX 1.1	IR values and theories	
FOCUS		**THEORIES**
• **Security** power politics, conflict and war		• **Realism**
• **Freedom** cooperation, peace and progress		• **Liberalism**
• **Order and justice** shared interests, rules and institutions		• **International Society**
• **Welfare** wealth, poverty and equality		• **IPE theories**

BOX 1.2	Views of the state

TRADITIONAL VIEW

States are valuable institutions: they provide security, freedom, order, justice and welfare

People benefit from the state system

ALTERNATIVE VIEW

States and the state system create more problems than they solve

The majority of the world's people suffer more than they benefit from the state system

at least tolerates human suffering, and that the system should be changed so that people everywhere can flourish, and not just those in the developed countries of the world. That gives rise to more critical IR theories which regard the state and the state system as a less beneficial and more problematical institution. The alternative IR theories discussed later in this book tend to adopt that critical view.

To sum up thus far: states and the system of states are territory-based social organizations which exist primarily to establish, maintain and defend basic social conditions and values, including, particularly, security, freedom, order, justice and welfare. These are the main reasons for having states. Many states and certainly all developed countries uphold these conditions and values at least to minimal standards and often at a higher level. Indeed, they have been so successful in doing that for the past several centuries that the standards have steadily increased and are now higher than ever. These countries set the international standard for the entire world. But many states and most underdeveloped countries fail to meet even minimal standards, and as a consequence their presence in the contemporary state system raises serious questions not only about those states but also about the state system of which they are an important part. That has provoked a debate in IR between traditional theorists who by and large accept the existing state system and radical theorists who by and large reject it.

Brief Historical Sketch of the State System

States and the state system are such basic features of modern political life that it is easy to assume that they are permanent features: that they have always been and will always be present. That assumption is false. It is important to emphasize that the state system is a historical institution. It is not ordained by God or determined by Nature. It has been fashioned by certain people at a certain time: it is a social organization. Like all social organizations, the state system has advantages and disadvantages which change over time. There is nothing about the state system that is necessary to human existence, even though there may be many things about it that are advantageous to better living conditions.

BOX 1.3   **The Roman Empire**

Rome began as a city state in central Italy . . . Over several centuries the city expanded its authority and adapted its methods of government to bring first Italy, then the western Mediterranean and finally almost the whole of the Hellenistic world into an empire larger than any which had existed in that area before . . . This unique and astonishing achievement, and the cultural transformation which it brought about, laid the foundations of European civilization . . . Rome helped to shape European and contemporary practice and opinion about the state, about international law and especially about empire and the nature of imperial authority.

Watson (1992: 94)

People have not always lived in sovereign states. For most of human history people have organized their political lives in different ways, the most common being that of political empire such as the Roman Empire. In the future the world may not be organized into a state system either. People may eventually give up on sovereign statehood and abandon the institution. People throughout history have abandoned many other ways of organizing their political lives, including city-states, feudalism and colonialism, to mention a few. It is not unreasonable to suppose that a form of global political organization that is better or more advanced than states and the state system will eventually be adopted. Some IR scholars discussed in later chapters believe that such an international transformation, connected with growing interdependence among states (i.e. globalization), is already well under way. But the state system has been a central institution of world politics for a very long time, and still remains so. Even though world politics is in flux, in the past states and the state system have always managed to adapt to significant historical change. But nobody can be sure that that will continue to be the case in the future. This issue of present and future international change is discussed later in the chapter.

There were no clearly recognizable sovereign states before the sixteenth century, when they first began to be instituted in Western Europe. But for the past three or four centuries, states and the system of states have structured the political lives of an ever-increasing number of people around the world. They have become universally popular. Today the system is global in extent. The era of the sovereign state coincides with the modern age of expanding power, prosperity, knowledge, science, technology, literacy, urbanization, citizenship, freedom, equality, rights and so on. This could be a coincidence, but that is not very likely when we remember how important states and the state system have been in shaping the five fundamental human values discussed above. Of course, it is difficult to say whether states were the effect or the cause of modern life, and whether they will have any place in a postmodern age. Those questions must be set aside for later.

However, we do know that the state system and modernity are closely related historically. In fact, they are completely coexistent: the system of adjoining territorial states arose in Europe at the start of the modern era. And the state system has been a central if not a defining feature of modernity ever since. Although the sovereign state emerged in Europe, it extended to North America in the late eighteenth century and to South America in the early nineteenth century. As modernity spread around the world the state system spread with it.

Only slowly did it expand to cover the entire globe. Sub-Saharan Africa, for example, remained isolated from the expanding Western state system until the late nineteenth century, and it only became a regional state system after the middle of the twentieth century. Whether the end of modernity will also bring the end of the state system is an important question that must be left for later in this book.

Of course, there is evidence of political systems that resembled sovereign states long before the modern age. They obviously had relations of some sort with each other. The historical origin of international relations in that more general sense lies deep in history and can only be a matter of speculation. But, speaking conceptually, it was a time when people began to settle down on the land and form themselves into separate territory-based political communities. The first examples of that date back more than 5,000 years.

Each political group faced the inescapable problem of coexisting with neighbouring groups whom they could not ignore or avoid because they were right there next door. Each political grouping also had to deal with groups that were further away but were still capable of affecting them. Their geographical closeness must have come to be regarded as a zone of political proximity, if not a frontier or border of some kind. Where group contact occurred, sometimes it must have involved rivalry, disputes, threats, intimidation, intervention, invasion, conquest, and other hostile and warlike interactions. But sometimes, and perhaps most of the time, it must also have involved mutual respect, cooperation, commerce, conciliation, dialogue, and similar friendly and peaceful relations. A very significant form of dialogue between autonomous political communities—diplomacy—has ancient roots. There are recorded formal agreements among ancient political communities which date as far back as 1390 BC, and records of quasi-diplomatic activity as early as 653 BC (Barber 1979: 8–9). Here in prototype is the classical problem of IR: war and peace; conflict and cooperation. Here, too, are the different aspects of international relations emphasized by realism and liberalism.

These relations between independent political groups make up the core problem of international relations. They are built on a fundamental distinction between our collective selves and other collective selves in a territorial world of many such separate collective selves in contact with each other. Here we arrive at a preliminary definition of a state system: it stands for relations between politically organized human groupings which occupy distinctive territories, are not under any higher authority or power, and enjoy and exercise a measure of independence from each other. International relations are primarily relations between such independent groups.

BOX 1.4	City-states and empires
500 BC–100 BC	Greek city-states
200 BC–AD 500	Roman Empire
500–1500	Catholic Christendom: the Pope in Rome
Medieval Christian world	Orthodox Christendom: Byzantine Empire, Constantinople
Other historical empires	Persia, India, China

The first relatively clear historical manifestation of a state system is that of ancient Greece (500–100 BC), then known as *Hellas* (see web link 1.01). Ancient Greece was not a nation-state the way it is today. Rather, it was a system of many, mostly small city-states (Wight 1977; Watson 1992). Athens was the largest and most famous, but there were also many other city-states, such as Sparta and Corinth. Together they formed the first state system in Western history. There were extensive and elaborate relations between the city-states of Hellas. But the ancient Greek city-states were not modern sovereign states with extensive territories. They were far smaller in population and territory than most modern states. Greek intercity relations also lacked the institution of diplomacy, and there was nothing comparable to international law and international organization. The state system of Hellas was based on a shared language and a common religion more than anything else.

The ancient Greek state system was eventually destroyed by more powerful neighbouring empires, and in due course the Greeks became subjects of the Roman Empire (200 BC–AD 500). The Romans developed a huge empire in the course of conquering, occupying and ruling most of Europe and a large part of the Middle East and North Africa (see web link 1.02). The Romans had to deal with the numerous political communities that occupied these areas, but they did that by subordinating them rather than recognizing them. Instead of international relations or quasi-international relations, under the Roman Empire the only option for political communities was either submission to Rome or revolt. Eventually those communities on the periphery of the empire began to revolt; the Roman army could not contain the revolts and began to retreat, and on several occasions the city of Rome itself was invaded and shattered by the 'barbarian' tribes. In that way the Roman Empire was finally brought to an end after many centuries of political success and survival.

Empire was the prevalent pattern of political organization that gradually emerged in Christian Europe over several centuries after the fall of the Roman Empire. Rome's two main successors in Europe also were empires: in Western Europe the medieval (Catholic) empire based at Rome (Christendom); in Eastern Europe and the near east the Byzantine (Orthodox) empire centred on Constantinople or what is today Istanbul (Byzantium). Byzantium claimed to be the continuation of the Christianized Roman Empire. The European medieval Christian world (500–1500) was thus divided geographically most of the time into two politico-religious empires. There were other political systems and empires further afield. North Africa and the Middle East formed a world of Islamic civilization which originated in the Arabian peninsula in the early years of the seventh century (see web link 1.15). There were empires in what are today Iran and India. The oldest empire was the Chinese which survived, under different dynasties, for about 4,000 years until the early twentieth century. Perhaps it still exists in the form of the Chinese Communist state, which resembles an empire in its hierarchical political and ideological structure. The Middle Ages were thus an era of empire and the relations and conflicts of different empires (see web links 1.03, 1.04 and 1.05). But contact between empires was intermittent at best: communications were slow and transportation was difficult. Consequently, most empires at that time were a world unto themselves.

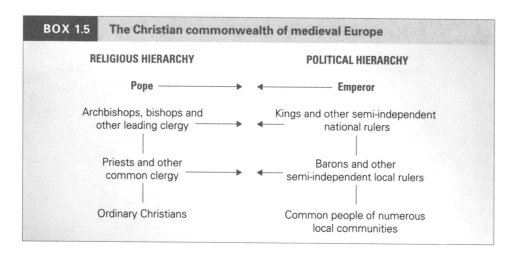

Can we speak of 'international relations' in Western Europe during the medieval era? Only with difficulty because, as already indicated, medieval Christendom was more like an empire than a state system. States existed, but they were not independent or sovereign in the modern meaning of these words. There were no clearly defined territories with borders. The medieval world was not a geographical patchwork of sharply differentiated colours which represented different independent countries. Instead, it was a complicated and confusing intermingling of lines and colours of varying shades and hues. Power and authority were organized on both a religious and a political basis: the Pope and the Emperor were the heads of two parallel and connected hierarchies, one religious and the other political. Kings and other rulers were subjects of those higher authorities and their laws. They were not fully independent. And much of the time local rulers were more or less free from the rule of kings: they were semi-autonomous but they were not fully independent either. The fact is that territorial political independence as we know it today was not present in medieval Europe.

The medieval era was also one of considerable disarray, disorder, conflict and violence which stemmed from this lack of clearly delineated of territorial political organization and control. Sometimes wars were fought between religious civilizations—for example, the Christian Crusades against the Islamic world (1096–1291). Sometimes wars were fought between kings—for example, the Hundred Years War between England and France (1337–1453). But often war was feudal and local, and was fought between rival groups of knights whose leaders had a quarrel. The authority and power to engage in war was not monopolized by the state: kings did not control war as they were later able to do. Instead, war-making rights and capacities belonged to members of a distinctive caste—the armed knights and their leaders and followers—who fought sometimes for the Pope, sometimes for the Emperor, sometimes for their king, sometimes for their master, and sometimes and indeed quite regularly for themselves. There was no clear distinction between civil war and international war. Medieval wars were more likely to be fought over issues of rights and wrongs: wars to defend the faith, wars to resolve conflicts over dynastic inheritance, wars to

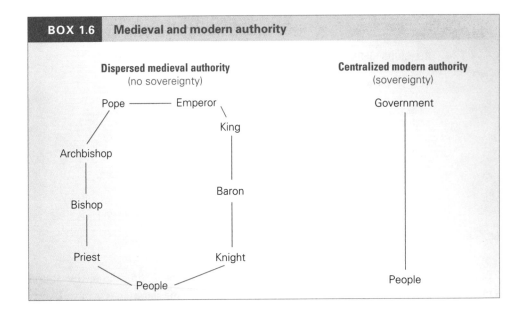

BOX 1.6   Medieval and modern authority

Dispersed medieval authority
(no sovereignty)

Centralized modern authority
(sovereignty)

Pope ——— Emperor

King

Archbishop

Bishop

Baron

Priest

Knight

People

Government

People

punish outlaws, wars to collect debts and so on. (Howard 1976: ch. 1). Wars were less likely to be fought over the exclusive control of territory or over state or national interests. In medieval Europe there was no exclusively controlled territory, and no clear conception of the nation or the national interest.

The values connected with sovereign statehood were arranged differently in medieval times. The key to that difference is the fact that no one political organization, such as the sovereign state, catered for all these values. Instead, they were looked after by different organizations which operated at different levels of social life. Security was provided by local rulers and their knights who operated from fortified castles and towns. Freedom was not freedom for the individual or the nation; rather, it was freedom for feudal rulers and their followers and clients. Order was the responsibility of the Emperor, but his capacity to enforce order was very limited and medieval Europe was punctuated by turbulence and discord at all levels of society. The provision of justice was the responsibility of both political and religious rulers, but it was a highly unequal justice. Those higher up in the political and religious hierarchies had easier access to justice than those at the bottom. There were different courts for different classes of people. There was no police force, and often justice was meted out by people themselves in the form of revenge or reprisal. The Pope was responsible not only for ruling the Church through his hierarchy of bishops and other clergy, but also for overseeing political disputes between kings and other semi-independent national rulers. Members of the clergy were often senior advisers to kings and other secular rulers. Kings were sometimes 'Defenders of the Faith'—such as Henry VIII of England. Knights often thought of themselves as Christian soldiers. Welfare was connected to security and was based on feudal ties between local rulers and common people in which those rulers provided protection in exchange for a share of the labour, crops and other resources and products of a local peasant economy. Peasants were not free to live wherever they wished. Instead, they were tied to feudal landlords who could be members of the nobility or the clergy or both.

What did the political change from medieval to modern basically involve? The short answer is: it eventually consolidated the provision of these values within the single framework of one unified and independent social organization: the sovereign state. In the early modern era European rulers liberated themselves from the overarching religious-political authority of Christendom. They also freed themselves from their dependence on the military power of barons and other local feudal leaders. The kings subordinated the barons and defied the Emperor and the Pope. They became defenders of state sovereignty against internal disorder and external threat. Peasants began their long journey to escape from their dependence on local feudal rulers to become the direct subjects of the King: they eventually became 'the people'.

In short, power and authority were concentrated at one point: the King and his government. The King now ruled a territory with borders which were defended against outside interference. The King became the supreme authority over all the people in the country, and no longer had to operate via intermediate authorities and rulers. That fundamental political transformation marks the advent of the modern era.

One of the major effects of the rise of the modern state was its monopoly of the means of warfare. The King first created order at home and became the sole centre of power within the country. Knights and barons who had formerly controlled their own armies now took orders from the King. Many kings then looked outward with an ambition to expand their territories. As a result international rivalries developed which often resulted in wars and the enlargement of some countries at the expense of others. At various times Spain, France, Austria, England, Denmark, Sweden, Holland, Poland, Russia, Prussia and other states of the new European state system were at war. Some wars were spawned by the Protestant Reformation which profoundly divided the European Christian population in the sixteenth and seventeenth centuries. But other wars, and increasingly most wars, were provoked by the mere existence of independent states whose rulers resorted to war as a means of defending their interests, pursuing their ambitions and, if possible, expanding their territorial holdings. War became a key international institution for resolving conflicts between sovereign states.

BOX 1.7	The Thirty Years War (1618–48)

Starting initially in Bohemia as an uprising of the Protestant aristocracy against Spanish authority, the war escalated rapidly, eventually incorporating all sorts of issues . . . Questions of religious toleration were at the root of the conflict . . . But by the 1630s, the war involved a jumble of conflicting stakes, with all sorts of cross-cutting dynastic, religious, and state interests involved . . . Europe was fighting its first continental war.

Holsti (1991: 26–8)

> ### BOX 1.8   The Peace of Westphalia (1648)
>
> The Westphalian settlement legitimized a commonwealth of sovereign states. It marked the triumph of the *stato* [the state], in control of its internal affairs and independent externally. This was the aspiration of princes [rulers] in general—and especially of the German princes, both Protestant and Catholic, in relation to the [Holy Roman or Habsburg] empire. The Westphalian treaties stated many of the rules and political principles of the new society of states . . . The settlement was held to provide a fundamental and comprehensive charter for all Europe.
>
> Watson (1992: 186)

The political change from medieval to modern thus basically involved the construction of the independent territorial state. The state captured its territory and turned it into state property, and it captured the population of that territory and turned them into subjects and later citizens. In many countries, indeed most, the Christian churches fell under state control. There was no room within modern states for semi-independent territory or people or institutions. In the modern international system territory is consolidated, unified and centralized under a sovereign government. The population of the territory owe allegiance to that government and have a duty to obey its laws. That includes bishops as well as barons; merchants as well as aristocrats. All institutions are now subordinate to state authority and public law. The familiar territorial patchwork map of the world is in place, in which each patch is under the exclusive jurisdiction of a particular state. All of the territory of Europe and eventually the entire planet became partitioned in that way by independent governments. The historical end-point of the medieval era and the starting-point of the modern international system, speaking very generally, is usually identified with the Thirty Years War (1618–48) and the Peace of Westphalia which brought it to an end (see web link 1.06).

From the middle of the seventeenth century states were seen as the only legitimate political systems of Europe, based on their own separate territories, their own independent governments and their own political subjects. The emergent state system had several prominent characteristics which can be summarized. First, it consisted of adjoining states whose legitimacy and independence was mutually recognized. Second, that recognition of states did not extend outside of the European state system. Non-European political systems were not members of the state system. They were usually regarded as politically inferior and most of them were eventually subordinated to European imperial rule. Third, the relations of European states were subject to international law and diplomatic practices. In other words, they were expected to observe the rules of the international game. Fourth, there was a balance of power between member states which was intended to prevent any one state from getting out of control and making a successful bid for hegemony, which would in effect re-establish an empire over the continent.

There were several major attempts by different powers to impose their political hegemony on the continent. The Habsburg Empire (Austria) made the attempt during the Thirty Years

War (1618–48), and was blocked by a coalition led by France and Sweden. France made the attempt under King Louis XIV (1661–1714) and was blocked by an English–Dutch alliance. Napoleon (1795–1815) made the attempt and was blocked by Britain, Russia, Prussia and Austria. A post-Napoleonic balance of power among the great powers (the Concert of Europe) held for most of the period between 1815 and 1914. Germany made the attempt under Hitler (1939–45) and was blocked by the United States, the Soviet Union and Britain. For the past 350 years the European state system has managed to resist the main political tendency of world history, which is the attempt by strong powers to bend weaker powers to their political will and thereby establish an empire. Whether the sole remaining superpower after the Cold War, the United States, was becoming a global hegemon was an issue at the time of writing (see web link 1.08).

The Global State System and the World Economy

Yet, while Europeans resisted empire in Europe, at the very same time they also constructed vast overseas empires and a world economy by which they controlled most non-European political communities in the rest of the world. The Western states that could not dominate each other succeeded in dominating much of the rest of the world both politically and economically. That outward control of the non-European world by Europeans began at the start of the early modern era in the sixteenth century, at the same time that the European state system was coming into existence. It lasted down to the middle of the twentieth century, when the last non-Western peoples finally broke free of Western colonialism and acquired political independence. The fact that Western states were never able to dominate each other but were capable of dominating almost everybody else has been crucially important in shaping the modern international system. The global ascendancy and supremacy of the West is vital for understanding IR even today.

The history of modern Europe is a history of political and economic conflict and war between its sovereign states. States made war, and war made and unmade states (Tilly 1992). European state rivalries were conducted not only in Europe but wherever European ambitions and power could be projected—and that was, eventually, throughout the world. European states entered into competition with each other to penetrate and control militarily useful and economically desirable areas in other parts of the world. European states felt they had every right to do that. The idea that non-Western peoples had rights of independence and self-determination only came much later. Huge non-European territories and populations consequently fell under the control of European states, by military conquest, commercial domination or political annexation.

Western imperial expansion made possible for the first time the formation and operation of a global economy (Parry 1966) and a global polity (Bull and Watson 1984). The expansion of trade between the Western world and the non-Western world began at about the same time that the modern state was emerging in Europe—around the year 1500. That expansion was based on the long-distance and heavily armed sailing-ship used by Europeans both for transporting goods and for projecting military and political power. By such means European states expanded their power far beyond Europe. The American continents were gradually brought into the world trading system via the mining of silver and other precious metals, the trade in furs and the production of agricultural commodities—much of it produced on large plantations by slave labour. About the same time the East Indies and then continental parts of South Asia and South-East Asia came under European colonization and control. While the Spanish, the Portuguese, the Dutch, the English and the French expanded their empires overseas, the Russians expanded theirs overland. By the late eighteenth century the Russian empire based on the fur trade extended across Siberia, into Alaska and down the west coast of North America as far as northern California. The Western powers also forced the opening of trade with China and Japan—although neither country was colonized politically. Large territories of the non-European world were settled by Europeans and later became independent member states of the state system under the control of their settler populations: the United States, the states of Latin America, Canada, Australia, New Zealand and—for a long time—South Africa. The Middle East and tropical Africa were the last continents that Europeans colonized.

During the era of economic and political imperialism by European states a few funda-mental points should be kept in mind which shed light on the state system at that time (see web link 1.07). First, European states made expedient alliances with non-European political systems—such as the alliances arranged by the British and by the French with different Indian 'tribes' (i.e. nations) of North America. Second, almost wherever they could, European states conquered and colonized those non-Western political systems and made them a subordinate part of their empires. Third, those far-flung empires became a basic source of the wealth and power of the European states for several centuries. Thus the devel-opment of Europe was achieved in significant part on the basis of the control of extensive territories outside Europe and by the exploitation of their natural and human resources. Fourth, some of those overseas colonies fell under the control of European settler

---

BOX 1.9   President McKinley on American imperialism in the Philippines (1899)

When I realized that the Philippines [a Spanish colony] had dropped into our laps [as a result of America's military defeat of Spain] . . . I did not know what to do . . . one night late it came to me this way . . . (1) That we could not give them back to Spain—that would be cowardly and dishon-orable; (2) that we could not turn them over to France or Germany—our commercial rivals in the Orient—that would be bad business and discreditable; (3) that we could not leave them to them-selves—they were unfit for self-government—and they would soon have anarchy and misrule over there worse than Spain's was; and (4) that there was nothing left for us to do but take them . . . [and] put the Philippines on the map of the United States . . .

Bridges et al. (1969: 184)

populations, and many of those new 'settler states' eventually became members of the state system. The successful American Revolution against the British Empire first opened that door in the late eighteenth century. That launched the transition from a European state system to a Western state system. Lastly, throughout the era of Western imperialism, from the sixteenth century until the early twentieth century, there was no interest or desire to incorporate non-Western political systems into the state system on a basis of equal sovereignty. That only happened on a large scale after the Second World War (see web link 1.12).

The first stage of the globalization of the state system was via the incorporation of non-Western states that could not be colonized by the West. Not every non-Western country fell under the political control of a Western imperial state; but countries that escaped colonization were still obliged to accept the rules of the Western state system. The Ottoman Empire (Turkey) is one example: it was forced to accept those rules by the Treaty of Paris in 1854. Japan is another example: it acquiesced to them later in the nineteenth century. Japan rapidly acquired the organizational substance and constitutional shape of a modern state, and by the early twentieth century that country had become a great power—as demonstrated by its military defeat of an existing great power, Russia, on the battlefield: the Russo-Japanese war of 1904–5. China was obliged to accept the rules of the Western state system during the nineteenth and early twentieth century. China was not acknowledged and fully recognized as a great power until 1945. The second stage of the globalization of the state system was brought about via anti-colonialism by the colonial subjects of Western empires. In that struggle indigenous political leaders made political claims for decolonization and independence based on European and American ideas of self-determination (see web link 1.13). That 'revolt against the West', as Hedley Bull put it, was the main vehicle by which the state system expanded dramatically after the Second World War (Bull and Watson 1984). In a short period of some twenty years, beginning with the independence of India and Pakistan in 1947, most colonies in Asia and Africa became independent states and members of the United Nations.

BOX 1.10	**President Ho Chi-minh's 1945 declaration of independence of the Republic of Vietnam**

'All men are created equal. They are endowed by their Creator with certain inalienable rights, among these are life, liberty and the pursuit of happiness.'. . . All the peoples on the earth are equal from birth, all the peoples have a right to live, be happy and free . . . We members of the provisional Government, representing the whole population of Vietnam, have declared and renew here our declaration that we break off all relations with the French people and abolish all the special rights the French have unlawfully acquired in our Fatherland . . . We are convinced that the Allied nations which have acknowledged at Teheran and San Francisco the principles of self-determination and equality of status will not refuse to acknowledge the independence of Vietnam . . . For these reasons we . . . declare to the world that Vietnam has the right to be free and independent.

Bridges et al. (1969: 311–12)

BOX 1.11	Global expansion of the state system
	1600s Europe (European system)
	1700s + North America (Western system)
	1800s + South America, Japan (globalizing system)
	1900s + Asia, Africa, Caribbean, Pacific (global system)

European decolonization in the Third World more than tripled the membership of the UN from about 50 states in 1945 to over 160 states by 1970. About 70 per cent of the world's population were citizens or subjects of independent states in 1945 and were thus represented in the state system. By 1995 that figure was virtually 100 per cent. The spread of European political and economic control beyond Europe thus eventually proved to be an expansion of the state system which became completely global in the second half of the twentieth century. The final stage of the globalization of the state system was the dissolution of the Soviet Union together with the simultaneous break-up of Yugoslavia and Czechoslovakia at the end of the Cold War. That expanded UN membership to almost 200 states at the end of the twentieth century.

Today the state system is a global institution that affects the lives of virtually everybody on earth whether they realize it or not. That means that IR is now more than ever a universal academic subject. That also means that world politics at the start of the twenty-first century must accommodate a range and variety of states that are far more diverse—in terms of their cultures, religions, languages, ideologies, forms of government, military capacity, technological sophistication, levels of economic development, etc.—than ever before. That is a fundamental change in the state system and a fundamental challenge for IR scholars to theorize.

IR and the Changing Contemporary World of States

Many important questions in the study of IR are connected with the theory and practice of sovereign statehood which, as indicated, is the central historical institution of world politics. But there are other important issues as well. That has led to ongoing debates about the proper scope of IR. At one extreme the scholarly focus is exclusively on states and interstate relations; but at another extreme IR includes almost everything that has to do with human relations across the world. It is important to study these different perspectives if we hope to have a balanced and rounded knowledge of IR.

Our reason for linking the various IR theories to states and the state system is to acknowledge the historical centrality of that subject. Even theorists who seek to get beyond the state usually take it as a starting-point: the state system is the main point of reference both for traditional and for new approaches. Later chapters will explore how each tradition of IR scholarship has attempted to come to grips with the sovereign state. There are debates about how we should conceptualize the state and different IR theories take somewhat different approaches. In later chapters we shall present contemporary debates on the future of the state. Whether its central importance in world politics may now be changing is a very important question in contemporary IR scholarship. But the fact is that states and the state system remain at the centre of academic analysis and discussion in IR.

We must of course be alert to the fact that the sovereign state is a contested theoretical concept. When we ask the questions 'what is the state?' and 'what is the state system?' there will be different answers depending on the theoretical approach adopted: the realist answer will be different from the liberal answer, and those answers will be different from the International Society answer and from the answer given by IPE theories. None of these answers is strictly speaking either correct or incorrect because the truth is: the state is a multifaceted and somewhat confusing entity. There is disagreement about the scope and purpose of the state. The state system consequently is not an easy subject to understand, and it can be understood in different ways and with different points of emphasis.

But there are ways of simplifying. It is helpful to think of the state as having two different dimensions, each divided into two broad categories. The first dimension is the state as a government versus the state as a country. Viewed from within, the state is the national government: it is the highest governing authority in a country: it possesses internal sovereignty. That is the *internal* aspect of the state. The main questions in regard to the internal aspect concern *state–society* relations: how the government rules the domestic society, the means of its power and the sources of its legitimacy, how it deals with the demands and concerns of individuals and groups which compose that domestic society, how it manages the national economy, what its domestic policies are, and so forth.

Viewed internationally, however, the state is not merely a government: it is a populated territory with a national government and a society. In other words, it is a country. From that angle, both the government and the domestic society make up the state. If a country is a sovereign state it will be generally recognized as such. That is the *external* aspect of the state in which the main questions concern *interstate* relations: how the governments and societies of states relate to each other and deal with each other, what the basis of those interstate relations are, what the foreign policies of particular states are, what the international organizations of the states are, how people from different states interact with each other and engage in transactions with each other, and so forth.

That brings us to the second dimension of the state, which divides the external aspect of sovereign statehood into two broad categories. The first category is the state viewed as a *formal* or legal institution in its relations with other states. That is the state as an entity which is constitutionally independent of all foreign states, is recognized as sovereign or independent by most of those states, enjoys membership in international organizations and possesses various international rights. We shall refer to that first category as 'juridical' statehood. Constitutional independence and recognition are essential elements of juridical statehood. Constitutional independence indicates that no foreign state claims or has any legal authority over a state. Recognition acknowledges that fact of independence. That paves the way for membership of International Society, including membership of the United

BOX 1.12	External dimension of statehood

The state as a country:
- Territory, government, society

Legal, juridical statehood:
- Recognition by other states

Actual, empirical statehood:
- Political institutions, economic basis, national unity

Nations. The absence of constitutional independence and recognition denies it. Not every country is independent and recognized as such: an example is Quebec, which is a province of Canada. To become independent it must be separate from Canada and be recognized as such by existing sovereign states, by far the most important of which for Quebec are first Canada and second the United States.

The countries that are sovereign states are always fewer than the countries, like Quebec, that are not sovereign but conceivably could become sovereign. That is because independence is generally regarded as politically valuable. But the countries that presently are sovereign states usually have no desire to see new countries emerge because it would involve partition: existing states would lose territory, population, resources, power, status and so on. If partition became an accepted practice it would undermine international stability. Partition would set a dangerous precedent that could destabilize the state system if a growing number of currently subordinated but potentially independent countries lined up to demand sovereign statehood. So there may always be somebody knocking on the door of state sovereignty, but there is a great reluctance to open the door and let them in. That would be disruptive of the present state system—especially now that there are no more colonies and the entire inhabited territory of the world is enclosed within one global state system. So juridical statehood is carefully rationed by existing sovereign states.

The second category is the state viewed as a *substantial* political-economic organization. That category has to do with the extent to which states have developed efficient political institutions, a solid economic basis and a substantial degree of national unity, that is, of popular unity and support for the state. We shall refer to that second category as 'empirical' statehood. Some states are very strong in the sense that they have a high level of empirical statehood. Most states in the West are like that. Many of those states are small, for example Sweden, Holland and Luxembourg. A strong state in the sense of a high level of empirical statehood should be held separate from the notion of a strong power in the military sense. Some strong states are not militarily powerful; Denmark is an example. Some powers in the military sense, such as Russia, are not strong states. Canada is the unusual case of a highly developed country with an effective democratic government but with a major weakness in its statehood: the threat of Quebec to secede. On the other hand, the United States is both a strong state and a strong power: indeed, it is the strongest power on earth.

This distinction between empirical statehood and juridical statehood is of fundamental importance because it helps to capture the very significant differences that exist between the almost 200 currently independent and formally equal states of the world. States differ

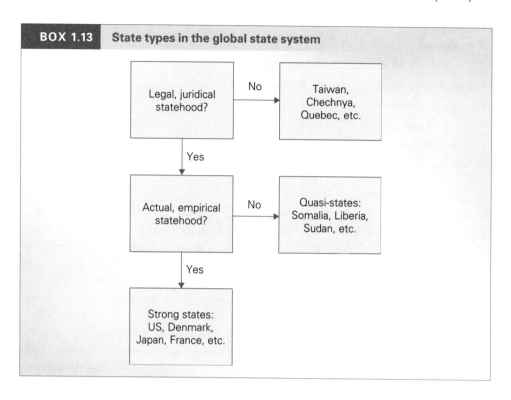

BOX 1.13   State types in the global state system

BOX 1.14   Strong/weak states—strong/weak powers

	STRONG POWER	WEAK POWER
Strong state	USA, France, UK, Japan	Denmark, Switzerland, New Zealand, Singapore
Weak state	Russia, Iraq, Pakistan	Somalia, Liberia, Chad, etc.

enormously in the legitimacy of their political institutions, the effectiveness of their governmental organizations, their economic wealth and productivity, their political influence and status, and their national unity. Not all states possess effective national governments. Some states, including both large and small, are solid and capable organizations: they are strong states. Most states in the West are more or less like that. Some tiny island microstates in the Pacific Ocean are so small that they can hardly afford to have a government at all. Other states may be fairly large in terms of territory or population or both—e.g. Nigeria or the Congo (formerly Zaïre)—but they are so poor, so inefficient and so corrupt that they are barely able to carry on as an effective government. A large number of states,

---

BOX 1.15   **The global state system**

- 5 great powers: US, Russia, China, Britain, France
- Approx. 30 highly substantial states: Europe, N. America, Japan
- Approx. 75 moderately substantial states: Asia and Latin America
- Approx. 90 less substantial quasi-states: Africa, Asia, Caribbean, Pacific
- Numerous unrecognized territorial political systems submerged in existing states

---

especially in the Third World, have a low degree of empirical statehood. Their institutions are weak, their economic basis is frail and underdeveloped, there is little or no national unity. We can refer to these states as quasi-states: they possess juridical statehood but they are severely deficient in empirical statehood (Jackson 1990). If we summarize the various distinctions made here, we get the picture of the global state system shown in Box 1.15.

One of the most important conditions that throws light on the existence of so many quasi-states in the Third World is that of economic underdevelopment. Their poverty and consequent shortages of investment, infrastructure (roads, schools, hospitals, etc.), modern technology, trained and educated people, and other socioeconomic assets or resources are among the most important factors that help us to understand why these states are so weak. The government and its institutions in these countries demonstrate little in the way of a solid foundation. The weakness of these states is a mirror of their poverty and technological backwardness, and as long as those conditions persist their incapacity as states is likely to persist as well. That profoundly affects the nature of the state system and also, therefore, the character of our IR theories.

Different conclusions can be drawn from the fact that empirical statehood varies so widely in the contemporary state system, from economically and technologically advanced and mostly Western states at one extreme to economically and technologically backward and mostly non-Western states at the other. Realist IR scholars focus mainly on the states at the centre of the system: the major powers and especially the great powers. They see Third World states as marginal players in a system of power politics that has always rested on 'the inequality of nations' (Tucker 1977). Such marginal or peripheral states do not affect the system in any very significant way. Other IR scholars, usually liberals and International Society theorists, see the adverse conditions of quasi-states as a fundamental problem for the state system which raises issues not only of international order but also of international freedom and justice.

Some IPE scholars, usually Marxists, make underdevelopment of peripheral countries and the unequal relations between the centre and the periphery of the global economy the crucial explanatory element of their theory of the modern international system (Wallerstein 1974). They investigate international linkages between the poverty of the Third World, or the South, and the enrichment of America, Europe and other parts of the North. They see

BOX 1.16	Insiders and outsiders in the state system
PREVIOUS STATE SYSTEM	**PRESENT STATE SYSTEM**
Small core of insiders, all strong states	Virtually all states are recognized insiders, posessing formal or juridical statehood
Many outsiders: colonies, dependencies, etc.	Big differences between insiders: some strong states, some weak quasi-states

the international economy as one overall 'world system', with the developed capitalist states at the centre advancing at the expense of the weak, underdeveloped states at the periphery. According to these scholars, legal equality and political independence—what we have designated as juridical statehood—are scarcely more than a polite facade that merely obscures the extreme vulnerability of poor Third World states and their domination and exploitation by the rich capitalist states of the West.

The underdeveloped countries certainly disclose in a striking way the profound empirical inequalities of contemporary world politics. But it is their possession of juridical statehood, reflecting their membership of the state system, that places that issue in sharp perspective, for it highlights the fact that the populations of some states—the developed countries—enjoy far better living conditions in virtually every respect than the populations of other states, that is, the underdeveloped countries. The fact that underdeveloped countries belong to the same global state system as developed countries raises different questions from those that would arise if they belonged to entirely separate systems, the situation that existed before the global state system was created. We can see the issues of security, freedom and progress, order and justice, and wealth and poverty far more clearly when they involve members of the same international system. For *inside* a system the same general standards and expectations apply. So, if some states cannot meet common standards or expectations because of their underdevelopment, that becomes an international problem and not only a domestic problem or somebody else's problem. That is a major change from the past when most non-Western political systems either were *outside* the state system and operated according to different standards, or were colonies of Western imperial powers that were responsible for them as a matter of domestic policy rather than foreign policy.

These developments are a reminder that the world of states is a dynamic, changing world and not a static, unchanging one. In international relations, as in other spheres of human relations, nothing stands still for very long. International relations change along with everything else: politics, economics, science, technology, education, culture and the rest. An obvious case in point is technological innovation, which has profoundly shaped international relations from the beginning and continues to shape it in significant ways which are never entirely predictable. Over the centuries new or improved military technology has had a profound impact on the balance of power, arms races, imperialism and colonialism, military alliances, the nature of war, and much else. Economic growth has permitted greater wealth to be devoted to military budgets, and has provided a foundation for the development of larger, better-equipped and more effective military forces. Scientific discoveries have made possible new technologies, such as transportation or information technologies, which have had the effect of knitting the world more closely together and making national borders more permeable. Literacy, mass education and expanded higher education have enabled governments to increase the capacity of their state and expand their activities into more and more specialized spheres of society and economy.

It cuts both ways, of course, because highly educated people do not like being told what to think or what to do. Changing cultural values and ideas have affected not only the foreign policy of particular states but also the shape and direction of international relations. For example, the ideologies of anti-racism and anti-imperialism that were first articulated by intellectuals in Western countries eventually undermined Western overseas empires in Asia and Africa, and helped bring about the decolonization process by making the moral justification of colonialism increasingly difficult and eventually impossible.

The examples of the impact of social change on international relations are almost endless in their number and variety. However, this should suffice to make the point that social change affects states and the state system. The relationship is undoubtedly reversible: the state system also has an impact on politics, economics, science, technology, education, culture and the rest. For example, it has been compellingly argued that it was the development of a state system in Europe that was decisive in propelling that continent ahead of all other continents during the modern era. The competition of the independent European states within their state system—their military competition, their economic competition, their scientific and technological competition—catapulted those states ahead of non-European political systems which were not spurred by the same degree of competition. One scholar has made the point as follows: 'The states of Europe . . . were surrounded by actual or potential competitors. If the government of one were lax, it impaired its own prestige and military security . . . The state system was an insurance against economic and technological stagnation' (Jones 1981: 104–26). We should not conclude, therefore, that the state system merely reacts to change; it is also a cause of change.

The fact of social change raises a more fundamental question. At some point should we expect states to change so much that they are no longer states in the sense discussed here (see web links 1.18, 1.22, 1.23 and 1.24)? For example, if the process of economic globalization continues and makes the world one single marketplace and one single production site, will the state system then be obsolete? We have in mind the following activities which might bypass states: ever-increasing international trade and investment, expanding multinational business activity, enlarged NGO (non-governmental organization) activities, increasing regional and global communications, the growth of the Internet, expanding and ever-extending transportation networks, exploding travel and tourism, massive human migration, cumulative environmental pollution, expanded regional integration, the growth of trading communities, the global expansion of science and technology, continuous downsizing of government, increased privatization and other activities which have the effect of increasing interdependence across borders.

Or will sovereign states and the state system find ways of adapting to those social changes, just as they have adapted time and again to other major changes during the past 350 years? Some of those changes were just as fundamental: the scientific revolution of the seventeenth century, the Enlightenment of the eighteenth century, the encounter of Western and non-Western civilizations over the course of several centuries, the growth of Western imperialism and colonialism, the Industrial Revolution of the eighteenth and nineteenth centuries, the rise and spread of nationalism in the nineteenth and twentieth centuries, the revolution of anti-colonialism and decolonization in the twentieth century, the spread of mass public education, the growth of the welfare state, and much else (see web link 1.27). These are some of the most fundamental questions of contemporary IR scholarship, and we should keep them in mind when we speculate about the future of the state system.

Conclusion

The state system is a historical institution, fashioned by people. The population of the world has not always lived in sovereign states. For most of recorded human history people have lived under different kinds of political organization. In medieval times, political authority was chaotic and dispersed. Most people were dependent on a large number of different authorities—some of them political, some religious—with diverse responsibilities and power, from the local ruler and landlord to the King in a distant capital city, from parish priest to the Pope in far-away Rome. In the modern state, authority is centralized in one legally supreme government, and people live under the standard laws of that government. The development of the modern state went a long way towards organizing political authority and power along rational and national lines.

The state system was European in the first instance. During the era of Western imperialism the rest of the world was dominated by Europeans, both politically and economically. Only with Asian and African decolonization, after the Second World War, did the state system become a global institution. The globalization of the state system vastly increased the variety of its member states and consequently its diversity. The most important difference is between strong states with a high level of empirical statehood and weak quasi-states, which have formal sovereignty but very little substantial statehood. In other words, decolonization contributed to a huge and deep internal division in the state system between the rich North and the poor South: i.e. between developed countries at the centre, which dominate the system politically and economically, and underdeveloped countries at the peripheries, which have limited political and economic influence.

People often expect states to uphold certain key values: security, freedom, order, justice and welfare. IR theory concerns the ways in which states do or do not ensure those values. Historically the system of states consists of many heavily armed states, including a small number of great powers which often have been military rivals and sometimes have gone to war with each other. That reality of the state as a war machine underlines the value of security. That is the starting-point for the realist tradition in IR. Until states cease to be armed rivals, realist theory will have a firm historical basis. Following the end of the Cold War there are some signs that that may be changing: the great powers have cut back their military budgets very significantly and reduced the size of their armed forces. They have modernized their armies and navies and air forces, but they have not even considered abandoning their armed forces. That suggests that realism will be a relevant IR theory for some time to come.

But it is also a fact that most of the time states cooperate with each other more or less routinely, and without much political drama, for mutual advantage. They carry on diplomatic relations, they trade, they support international markets, they exchange scientific and technological knowledge, and they open their doors to investors, businesspeople, tourists and travellers from other countries. They collaborate in order to deal with various common problems, from the environment to the traffic in illegal drugs. They commit themselves to bilateral and multilateral treaties for that purpose. In short, states interact in accordance with norms of reciprocity. The liberal tradition in IR is based on the idea that the modern state in that quiet and routine way makes a strategic contribution to international freedom and progress.

How do states uphold order and justice in the state system? It is mainly through the rules and norms of international law, and through international organizations and diplomatic activity. There has been a huge expansion of those elements of international society since 1945. The International Society tradition in IR emphasizes the importance of such international relations. Finally the system of states is also a socioeconomic system; wealth and welfare are core concerns of most states. That fact is the starting-point for the IPE theories in IR. IPE theorists also discuss the consequences of Western expansion and the eventual incorporation of the Third World into the state system. Is that process bringing modernization and progress to the Third World, or is it bringing inequality, underdevelopment and misery? This question also leads to the larger issue of whether the state system is worth upholding and defending or whether it ought to be replaced by another system. IR theories are not in agreement on this issue; but the discipline of IR is based on the conviction that sovereign states and their development are of crucial importance for understanding how basic values of human life are being, or not being, provided to people around the world.

The following chapters will introduce the theoretical traditions of IR in further detail. We begin this task by introducing IR as an academic discipline. Whereas this chapter has concerned the actual development of states and the state system, the next chapter will focus on how our thinking about states and their relations has developed over time.

KEY POINTS

- The main reason why we should study IR is the fact that the entire population of the world is living in independent states. Together those states form a global state system.

- The core values that states are expected to uphold are security, freedom, order, justice and welfare. IR theory is about the effects that states and the state system have for these core values.

- The system of sovereign states emerged in Europe at the start of the modern era, in the sixteenth century. Medieval political authority was dispersed; modern political authority is centralized, residing in the government and the head of state.

- The state system was European first; now it is global. The global state system contains states of very different type: great powers and small states; strong, substantial states and weak quasi-states.

- There is a link between the expansion of the state system and the establishment of a world market and a global economy. Some Third World countries have benefited from integration into the global economy; others remain poor and underdeveloped.

- Economic globalization and other developments challenge the sovereign state. We cannot know for certain whether the state system is now becoming obsolete, or whether states will find ways of adapting to new challenges.

QUESTIONS

- What is a state? Why do we have them? What is a state system?

- When did independent states and the modern system of states emerge? What is the difference between a medieval and a modern system of political authority?

- We expect states to sustain a number of core values: security, freedom, order, justice and welfare. Do states meet our expectations?

- What are the effects on Third World countries of integration into the global economy?

- Should we strive to preserve the system of sovereign states? Why or why not?

- Explain the main differences between strong, substantial states, weak quasi-states, great powers and small powers. Why is there such diversity in the state system?

GUIDE TO FURTHER READING

Bull, H. and Watson, A. (eds) (1984). *The Expansion of International Society*. Oxford: Clarendon Press.

Osiander, A. (1994). *The States System of Europe, 1640–1990*. Oxford: Clarendon Press.

Tilly, C. (1992). *Coercion, Capital and European States*. Oxford: Blackwell.

Wallerstein, I. (1974). *The Modern World System*, i. New York: Academic Press.

Watson, A. (1992). *The Evolution of International Society*. London: Routledge.

WEB LINKS

Web links mentioned in the chapter plus additional links can be found on the Online Resource Centre that accompanies this book.

www.oxfordtextbooks.co.uk/orc/jackson_ sorensen3e/

CHAPTER 2

IR as an Academic Subject

▌ Summary

This chapter shows how thinking about **international relations** has evolved since IR became an academic subject around the time of the First World War. Theoretical approaches are a product of their time: they address those problems of international relations that are seen as the most important ones in their day. The established traditions deal nonetheless with international problems that are of lasting significance: war and peace, conflict and cooperation, wealth and poverty, development and underdevelopment. In this chapter we shall focus on four established IR traditions. They are **realism**, **liberalism**, **International Society** and **International Political Economy (IPE)**. We shall also introduce some recent, alternative approaches which challenge the established traditions.

Introduction

The traditional core of IR has to do with issues concerning the development and change of sovereign statehood in the context of the larger system or society of states. That focus on states and the relations of states helps explain why war and peace is a central problem of traditional IR theory. However, contemporary IR is concerned not only with political relations between states but also with a host of other subjects: economic interdependence, human rights, transnational corporations, international organizations, the environment, gender inequalities, development, terrorism and so forth. For this reason, some scholars prefer the label 'International Studies' or 'World Politics'. We shall stay with the label 'International Relations' but we shall interpret it to cover the broad range of issues.

There are four major theoretical traditions in IR: realism, liberalism, International Society and IPE. In addition, there is a more diverse group of alternative approaches which have gained prominence in recent years. The most important of these is social constructivism. The main task of this book is to present and discuss all these theories. In this chapter we shall examine IR as an evolving academic subject. IR thinking has developed through distinct phases, characterized by specific debates between groups of scholars. At most times during the twentieth century there has been a dominant way of thinking about IR and a major challenge to that way of thinking. Those debates and dialogues are the main subject of this chapter.

There are a great many different theories in IR. They can be classified in a number of ways; what we call a 'main theoretical tradition' is not an objective entity. If you put four IR theorists in a room you will easily get ten different ways of organizing theory, and there will also be disagreement about which theories are relevant in the first place! At the same time, we have to group theories into main categories. Without drawing together main paths in the development of IR thinking, we are stuck with a large number of individual contributions, pointing in different and sometimes rather confusing directions. But the reader should always be wary of selections and classifications, including the ones offered in this book. They are analytical tools created to achieve overview and clarity; they are not objective truths that can be taken for granted.

Of course, IR thinking is influenced by other academic subjects, such as philosophy, history, law, sociology or economics. IR thinking also responds to historical and contemporary developments in the real world. The two world wars, the Cold War between East and West, the emergence of close economic cooperation between Western states, and the persistent development gap between North and South are examples of real-world events and problems that stimulated IR scholarship in the twentieth century. And we can be certain that future events and episodes will provoke new IR thinking in the years to come: that is already evident with regard to the end of the Cold War, which is stimulating a variety of innovative IR thought at the present time. The terrorist attacks that began on 11 September 2001 are the latest major challenge to IR thinking.

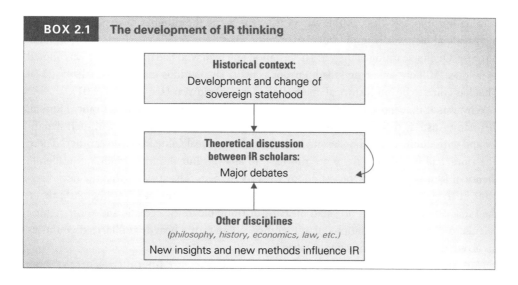

BOX 2.1   The development of IR thinking

Historical context:
Development and change of sovereign statehood

↓

Theoretical discussion between IR scholars:
Major debates

↑

Other disciplines
(philosophy, history, economics, law, etc.)
New insights and new methods influence IR

There have been three major debates since IR became an academic subject at the end of the First World War and we are now in the early stages of a fourth. The first major debate is between utopian liberalism and realism; the second between traditional approaches and behaviouralism; the third between neorealism/neoliberalism and neo-Marxism. The emerging fourth debate is between established traditions and post-positivist alternatives. We shall review these major debates in this chapter because they provide us with a map of the way the academic subject of IR has developed over the past century. We need to become familiar with that map in order to comprehend IR as a dynamic academic subject which continues to evolve, and to see the directions of that continuing evolution of IR thought.

Utopian Liberalism: The Early Study of IR

The decisive push to set up a separate academic subject of IR was occasioned by the First World War (1914–18), which produced millions of casualties; it was driven by a widely felt determination never to allow human suffering on such a scale to happen again. That desire not to repeat the same catastrophic mistake required coming to grips with the problem of total warfare between the mechanized armies of modern industrial states which were capable of inflicting mass destruction. The war was a devastating experience for millions of people, and particularly for young soldiers who were conscripted into the armies and were slaughtered by the million, especially in the trench warfare on the Western Front. Some battles resulted in tens of thousands and sometimes a hundred thousand casualties or even more. The famous Battle of the Somme (France) in July–August 1916 inflicted casualties on that scale. It was referred to as a 'bloody holocaust' (Gilbert 1995: 258). The justification for all that death and destruction became less and less clear as the war years went by, as the number of casualties kept on increasing to historically unprecedented levels, and as the war failed to disclose any rational purpose. On first learning of the war's devastation one man who had been isolated was quoted as follows: 'Millions are being killed. Europe is mad. The world is mad' (Gilbert 1995: 257). That has come to be our historical image of the First World War (see web link 2.01).

Why was it that the war began in the first place? And why did Britain, France, Russia, Germany, Austria, Turkey and other powers persist in waging war in the face of such slaughter and with diminishing chances of gaining anything of real value from the conflict? These questions and others like them are not easy to answer. But the first dominant academic theory of IR was shaped by the search for answers to them. The answers that the new discipline of IR came up with were profoundly influenced by liberal ideas. For liberal thinkers, the First World War was in no small measure attributable to the egoistic and short-sighted calculations and miscalculations of autocratic leaders in the heavily militarized countries involved, especially Germany and Austria.

Unrestrained by democratic institutions and under pressure from their generals, these leaders were inclined to take the fatal decisions that led their countries into war. And the democratic leaders of France and Britain, in turn, allowed themselves to be drawn into the conflict by an interlocking system of military alliances. The alliances were intended to keep the peace, but they propelled *all* the European powers into war once *any* major power or alliance embarked on war. When Austria and Germany confronted Serbia with armed force, Russia was duty-bound to come to the aid of Serbia, and Britain and France were treaty-bound to support Russia. For the liberal thinkers of that time the 'obsolete' theory of the balance of power and the alliance system had to be fundamentally reformed so that such a calamity would never happen again.

Why was early academic IR influenced by liberalism? That is a big question, but there are a few important points that we should keep in mind in seeking an answer. The United States was eventually drawn into the war in 1917. Its military intervention decisively determined the outcome of the war: it guaranteed victory for the democratic allies (US, Britain, France) and defeat for the autocratic central powers (Germany, Austria, Turkey). At that time the United States had a President, Woodrow Wilson, who had been a university professor of

---

BOX 2.2   Leadership misperceptions and war

It is my conviction that during the descent into the abyss, the perceptions of statesmen and generals were absolutely crucial. All the participants suffered from greater or lesser distortions in their images of themselves. They tended to see themselves as honorable, virtuous, and pure, and the adversary as diabolical. All the nations on the brink of the disaster expected the worst from their potential adversaries. They saw their own options as limited by necessity or 'fate', whereas those of the adversary were characterized by many choices. Everywhere, there was a total absence of empathy; no one could see the situation from another point of view. The character of each of the leaders was badly flawed by arrogance, stupidity, carelessness, or weakness.

Stoessinger (1993: 21–3)

BOX 2.3	Making the world safe for democracy

We are glad now that we see the facts with no veil of false pretense about them, to fight thus for the ultimate peace of the world and for the liberation of its peoples, the German peoples included: for the right of nations great and small and the privilege of men everywhere to choose their way of life and of obedience. The world must be made safe for democracy. We have no selfish ends to serve. We desire no conquest, no dominion. We seek no indemnities for ourselves, no material compensation for the sacrifices we shall freely make. We are but one of the champions of the right of mankind. We shall be satisfied when those rights have been made as secure as the faith and the freedom of nations can make them.

Woodrow Wilson, from 'Address to Congress Asking for Declaration of War', 1917. Quoted in Vasquez (1996: 35–40)

political science and who saw it as his main mission to bring liberal democratic values to Europe and to the rest of the world. Only in that way, he believed, could another great war be prevented. In short, the liberal way of thinking had a solid political backing from the most powerful state in the international system at the time. Academic IR developed first and most strongly in the two leading liberal-democratic states: the United States and Great Britain. Liberal thinkers had some clear ideas and strong beliefs about how to avoid major disasters in the future; e.g. by reforming the international system, and also by reforming the domestic structures of autocratic countries.

President Wilson had a vision of making the world 'safe for democracy' that had wide appeal for ordinary people. It was formulated in a fourteen-point programme delivered in an address to Congress in January 1918 (see web link 2.02). He was awarded the Nobel Peace Prize in 1919. His ideas influenced the Paris Peace Conference which followed the end of hostilities and tried to institute a new international order based on liberal ideas. Wilson's peace programme calls for an end to secret diplomacy: agreements must be open to public scrutiny. There must be freedom of navigation on the seas and barriers to free trade should be removed. Armaments should be reduced to 'the lowest point consistent with domestic safety'. Colonial and territorial claims shall be settled with regard to the principle of self-determination of peoples. Finally, 'a general association of nations must be formed under specific covenants for the purpose of affording mutual guarantees of political independence and territorial integrity of great and small nations alike' (Vasquez 1996: 40). This latter point is Wilson's call to establish a League of Nations (see web link 2.05), which was instituted by the Paris Peace Conference in 1919.

Two major points in Wilson's ideas for a more peaceful world deserve special emphasis (Brown 1997: 24). The first concerns his promotion of democracy and self-determination. Behind this point is the liberal conviction that democratic governments do not and will not go to war against each other. It was Wilson's hope that the growth of liberal democracy in Europe would put an end to autocratic and warlike leaders and put peaceful governments in their place. Liberal democracy should therefore be strongly encouraged. The second major point in Wilson's programme concerned the creation of an international organization that would put relations between states on a firmer institutional foundation than the realist notions of the Concert of Europe and the balance of power had provided in the past. Instead, international relations would be regulated by a set of common rules of international law. In essence that was Wilson's concept of the League of Nations. The idea that international institutions can promote peaceful cooperation among states is a basic element of liberal thinking; so is the notion about a relationship between liberal democracy and peace. We shall return to both ideas in Chapter 4.

Wilsonian idealism can be summarized as follows. It is the conviction that, through a rational and intelligently designed international organization, it should be possible to put an end to war and to achieve more or less permanent peace. The claim is not that it will be possible to do away with states and statespeople, foreign ministries, armed forces, and other agents and instruments of international conflict. Rather, the claim is that it is possible to tame states and statespeople by subjecting them to the appropriate international organizations, institutions and laws. The argument liberal idealists make is that traditional power politics—so-called 'Realpolitik'—is a 'jungle', so to speak, where dangerous beasts roam and the strong and cunning rule, whereas under the League of Nations the beasts are put into cages reinforced by the restraints of international organization, i.e. into a kind of 'zoo'. Wilson's liberal faith that an international organization could be created that could guarantee permanent peace is clearly reminiscent of the thought of the most famous classical liberal IR theorist: Immanuel Kant in his pamphlet *Perpetual Peace*.

Norman Angell (see web link 2.06) is another prominent liberal idealist of the same era. In 1909 Angell published a book entitled *The Great Illusion*. The illusion is that many statespeople still believe that war serves profitable purposes; that success in war is beneficial for the winner. Angell argues that exactly the opposite is the case: in modern times territorial conquest is extremely expensive and politically divisive because it severely disrupts international commerce. The general argument set forth by Angell is a forerunner of later liberal thinking about modernization and economic interdependence. Modernization demands that states have a growing need of things 'from "outside"—credit, or inventions, or markets or materials not contained in sufficient quantity in the country itself' (Navari 1989: 345). Rising interdependence, in turn, effects a change in relations between states. War and the use of force become of decreasing importance, and international law develops in response to the need for a framework to regulate high levels of interdependence. In sum, modernization and interdependence involve a process of change and progress which renders war and the use of force increasingly obsolete.

The thinking of Wilson and Angell is based on a liberal view of human beings and human society: human beings are rational, and when they apply reason to international relations they can set up organizations for the benefit of all. Public opinion is a constructive force; removing secret diplomacy in dealings between states and, instead, opening diplomacy to public scrutiny assures that agreements will be sensible and fair. These ideas had some success in the 1920s; the League of Nations was indeed established and the great powers took some further steps to assure each other of their peaceful intentions. The high point of these efforts came with the Kellogg–Briand pact of 1928, which practically all countries signed.

The pact was an international agreement to abolish war; only in extreme cases of self-defence could war be justified. In short, liberal ideas dominated in the first phase of academic IR. In the international relations of the 1920s these ideas could claim some success.

Why is it, then, that we tend to refer to such ideas by the somewhat pejorative term of 'utopian liberalism', indicating that these liberal arguments were little more than the projection of wishful thinking? One plausible answer is to be found in the political and economic developments of the 1920s and 1930s. Liberal democracy suffered hard blows with the growth of fascist and Nazi dictatorship in Italy, Germany and Spain. Authoritarianism also increased in many of the new states of Central and Eastern Europe—for example, Poland, Hungary, Romania and Yugoslavia—that were brought into existence as a result of the First World War and the Paris Peace Conference and were supposed to become democracies. Thus, contrary to Wilson's hopes for the spread of democratic civilization, it failed to happen. In many cases what actually happened was the spread of the very sort of state that he believed provoked war: autocratic, authoritarian and militaristic states.

The League of Nations never became the strong international organization that liberals hoped would restrain powerful and aggressively disposed states. Germany and Russia failed to sign the Versailles Peace Treaty initially, and their relationship to the League was always strained. Germany joined the League in 1926 but left in the early 1930s. Japan also left at about that time, while embarking on war in Manchuria. Russia finally joined in 1934, and was expelled in 1940 because of the war with Finland. But by that time the League was effectively dead. Although Britain and France were members from the start, they never regarded the League as an important institution and refused to shape their foreign policies with League criteria in mind. Most devastating, however, was the refusal of the United States Senate to ratify the covenant of the League. Isolationism had a long tradition in US foreign policy, and many American politicians were isolationists even if President Wilson was not; they did not want to involve their country in the entangling and murky affairs of Europe. So, much to Wilson's chagrin, the strongest state in the international system—his own—did not join the League. With a number of important states outside the League,

---

BOX 2.4   The League of Nations

The League of Nations (1920–46) contained three main organs: the Council (fifteen members including France, the United Kingdom and the Soviet Union as permanent members) which met three times a year; the Assembly (all members) which met annually and a Secretariat. All decisions had to be by unanimous vote. The underlying philosophy of the League was the principle of collective security which meant that the international community had a duty to intervene in international conflicts: it also meant that parties to a dispute should submit their grievances to the League. The centre-piece of the [League] Covenant was Article 16, which empowered the League to institute economic or military sanctions against a recalcitrant state. In essence, though, it was left to each member to decide whether or not a breach of the Covenant had occurred and so whether or not to apply sanctions.

Evans and Newnham (1992: 176)

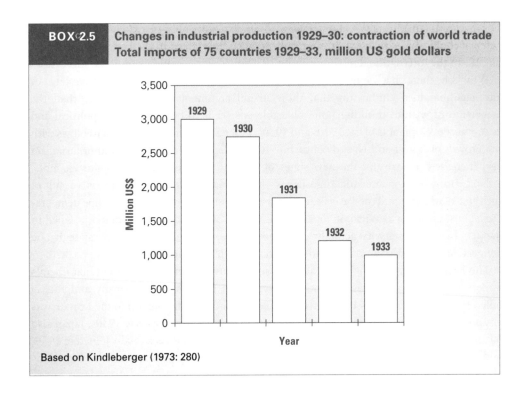

BOX 2.5   **Changes in industrial production 1929–30: contraction of world trade**
Total imports of 75 countries 1929–33, million US gold dollars

Based on Kindleberger (1973: 280)

including the most important, and with the two major powers inside the organization lacking any real commitment to it, the League never achieved the central position marked out for it in Wilson's blueprint.

Norman Angell's high hopes for a smooth process of modernization and interdependence also foundered on the harsh realities of the 1930s. The Wall Street crash of October 1929 marked the beginning of a severe economic crisis in Western countries that would last until the Second World War and would involve severe measures of economic protectionism. World trade shrank dramatically, and industrial production in developed countries declined rapidly to become only one third of what it was a few years before. In ironic contrast to Angell's vision, it was every country for itself, each country trying as best it could to look after its own interests, if necessary to the detriment of others—the 'jungle' rather than the 'zoo'. The historical stage was being set for a less hopeful and more pessimistic understanding of international relations.

Realism and the Twenty Years' Crisis

Liberal idealism was not a good intellectual guide to international relations in the 1930s. Interdependence did not produce peaceful cooperation; the League of Nations was helpless in the face of the expansionist power politics conducted by the authoritarian regimes in Germany,

Italy and Japan. Academic IR began to speak the classical realist language of Thucydides, Machiavelli and Hobbes in which the grammar and the vocabulary of power was central.

The most comprehensive and penetrating critique of liberal idealism was that of E. H. Carr, a British IR scholar. In *The Twenty Years' Crisis* (1964 [1939]) Carr argued that liberal IR thinkers profoundly misread the facts of history and misunderstood the nature of international relations. They erroneously believed that such relations could be based on a harmony of interest between countries and people. According to Carr, the correct starting-point is the opposite one: we should assume that there are profound conflicts of interest both between countries and between people. Some people and some countries are better off than others. They will attempt to preserve and defend their privileged position. The underdogs, the 'have-nots', will struggle to change that situation. International relations is in a basic sense about the struggle between such conflicting interests and desires. That is why IR is far more about conflict than about cooperation. Carr astutely labelled the liberal position 'utopian' as a contrast to his own position, which he labelled 'realist', thus implying that his approach was the more sober and correct analysis of international relations (see web links 2.10 and 2.11).

The other significant realist statement from this period was produced by a German scholar who fled to the United States in the 1930s to escape from the Nazi regime in Germany: Hans J. Morgenthau. More than any other European émigré scholar Morgenthau brought realism to the US, and with great success. His *Politics among Nations: The Struggle for Power and Peace*, first published in 1948, was for several decades the most influential American book on IR (Morgenthau 1960). There were other authors writing along the same realist lines: among the most important were Reinhold Niebuhr, George Kennan and Arnold Wolfers. But Morgenthau gave the clearest summary of realism's core claims and had the widest appeal to IR scholars and their students.

For Morgenthau, human nature was at the base of international relations. And humans were self-interested and power-seeking and that could easily result in aggression. In the late 1930s it was not difficult to find evidence to support such a view. Hitler's Germany, Mussolini's Italy and Imperial Japan pursued blatantly aggressive foreign policies aimed at conflict, not cooperation. Armed struggle for the creation of *Lebensraum*, of a larger and stronger Germany, was at the core of Hitler's political programme. Furthermore, and ironically from a liberal perspective, both Hitler and Mussolini enjoyed widespread popular support despite the fact that they were autocratic and even tyrannical leaders. Even the most horrendous component of Hitler's political project—elimination of the Jews—enjoyed such popular support (Goldhagen 1996).

Why should international relations be egoistic and aggressive? Observing the growth of fascism in the 1930s, Einstein wrote to Freud that there must be 'a human lust for hatred and destruction' (Ebenstein 1951: 802–4). Freud confirmed that such an aggressive impulse did indeed exist, and he remained deeply sceptical about the possibilities for taming it.

Another possible explanation draws on Christian religion. According to the Bible, humans have been endowed with original sin and a temptation for evil ever since Adam and Eve were thrown out of Paradise. The first murder in history is Cain's killing of his brother Abel out of pure envy. Human nature is plain bad; that is the starting-point for realist analysis.

The second major element in the realist view concerns the nature of international relations. 'International politics, like all politics, is a struggle for power. Whatever the ultimate

---

BOX 2.6   Freud's reply to Einstein

Freud's reply [to Einstein] drew on his theoretical work . . . We see this necessity for repression, Freud explained, in the imposition of discipline by parents over children, by institutions over individuals, and by the state over society. From this he deducted, and Einstein agreed, that a world government was needed to impose the necessary discipline on the otherwise dangerously anarchic international system. But whereas Einstein became a supporter of the United World Federalists and other groups working toward the establishment of world government, Freud doubted that humans have the requisite capacity to overcome their irrational attachments to national and religious groups. The father of psychoanalysis, therefore, remained deeply pessimistic about the prospects for fundamentally reducing the role of war in world politics.

Brown (1994: 10–11)

---

aims of international politics, power is always the immediate aim' (Morgenthau 1960: 29). There is no world government. On the contrary, there is a system of sovereign and armed states facing each other. World politics is an international anarchy. The 1930s and 1940s appeared to confirm this proposition. International relations was a struggle for power and for survival. The quest for power certainly characterized the foreign policies of Germany, Italy and Japan. The same struggle, in response, applied to the Allied side during the Second World War. Britain, France and the United States were the 'haves' in Carr's terms, the satisfied powers who wanted to hold on to what they already had, and Germany, Italy and Japan were the 'have-nots'. So it was only natural, according to realist thinking, that the 'have-nots' would try and redress the international balance through the use of force.

Following realist analysis, the sole appropriate response to such attempts is the creation of countervailing power and the intelligent utilization of that power to provide for national defence and to deter potential aggressors. In other words, it was essential to maintain an effective balance of power as the only way to preserve peace and prevent war. This is a view of international politics that denies that it is possible to reorganize the 'jungle' into a 'zoo'. The strongest animals will never allow themselves to be captured and put in cages. Germany following the First World War was seen as proof of that truth. The League of Nations failed to put Germany in a cage. It took a world war, millions of casualties, heroic sacrifice and vast material resources finally to defeat the challenge from Nazi Germany, Fascist Italy and Imperial Japan. All of that might have been avoided if a realistic foreign policy based on the principle of countervailing power had been followed by Britain, France and the United States right from the start of Germany's, Italy's and Japan's sabre-rattling. Negotiations and diplomacy by themselves can never bring security and survival in world politics.

The third major component in the realist view is a cyclical view of history. Contrary to the optimistic liberal view that qualitative change for the better is possible, realism stresses continuity and repetition. Each new generation tends to make the same sort of mistake as previous generations. Any change in this situation is highly unlikely. As long as sovereign states are the dominant form of political organization, power politics will continue and states will have to look after their security and prepare for war. In other words, the Second World War was no extraordinary event; neither was the First World War. Sovereign states can live in peace with each other for long periods when there is a stable balance of power. But every now and then that precarious balance will break down and war is likely to follow. There can of course be many different causes of such breakdown. Some realist scholars think that the Paris Peace Conference of 1919 contained the seeds of the Second World War because of the harsh conditions that the peace treaty imposed on Germany. But domestic developments in Germany, the emergence of Hitler and many other factors are also relevant in accounting for that war.

In sum, the classical realism of Carr and Morgenthau combines a pessimistic view of human nature with a notion of power politics between states which exist in an international anarchy. They see no prospects of change in that situation: for classical realists, independent states in an anarchic international system are a permanent feature of international relations. The classical realist analysis appeared to capture the essentials of European politics in the 1930s and world politics in the 1940s far better than liberal optimism. When international relations took the shape of an East–West confrontation, or Cold War, after 1945 realism again appeared to be the best approach for making sense of what was going on.

The utopian liberalism of the 1920s and the realism of the 1930s–1950s represent the two contending positions in the first major debate in IR (see Box 2.7).

The first major debate was clearly won by Carr, Morgenthau and the other realist thinkers. Realism became the dominant way of thinking about international relations not only among scholars but also among politicians and diplomats. Morgenthau's summary of realism in his 1948 book became the standard introduction to IR in the 1950s and 1960s. Yet it is important to emphasize that liberalism did not disappear. Many liberals conceded that realism was the better guide to international relations in the 1930s and 1940s, but they saw this as an extreme and abnormal historical period. Liberals of course rejected the deeply pessimistic realist idea that humans were 'plain bad' (Wight 1991: 25) and they had some strong counter-arguments to that effect, as we shall see in Chapter 4. Finally, the post-war period was not only about a struggle for power and survival between the United States and the Soviet Union and their political-military alliances. It was also about cooperation and international institutions, such as the United Nations and its many special organizations. Although realism had won the first debate, there were still competing theories in the discipline that refused to accept permanent defeat.

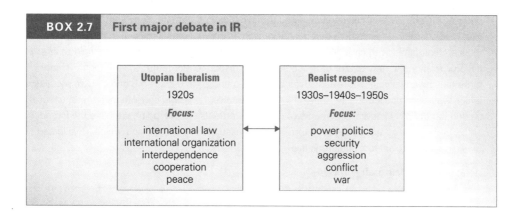

The Voice of Behaviouralism in IR

The second major debate in IR concerns methodology. In order to understand how that debate emerged, it is necessary to be aware of the fact that the first generations of IR scholars were trained as historians or academic lawyers, or were former diplomats or journalists. They often brought a humanistic and historical approach to the study of IR. This approach is rooted in philosophy, history and law, and is characterized 'above all by explicit reliance upon the exercise of judgment' (Bull 1969). Locating judgement at the heart of international theory serves to emphasize the normative character of the subject which at its core involves some profoundly difficult moral questions that neither politicians nor diplomats nor anyone else who is involved can escape, such as the deployment of nuclear weapons and their justified uses, military intervention in independent states and so forth. That is because the deployment and use of power in human relations, military power especially, always has to be justified and can thus never be divorced completely from normative considerations. This way of studying IR is usually referred to as the traditional, or classical, approach.

After the Second World War, the academic discipline of IR expanded rapidly. That was particularly the case in the United States, where government agencies and private foundations were willing to support 'scientific' IR research which they could justify as being in the national interest. That support produced a new generation of IR scholars who adopted a rigorous methodological approach. They were usually trained in political science, economics or other social sciences, sometimes in mathematics and the natural sciences, rather than diplomatic history, international law or political philosophy. These new IR scholars thus had a very different academic background and equally different ideas concerning how IR should be studied. These new ideas came to be summarized under the term 'behaviouralism' (see web link 2.15), which signified not so much a new theory as a novel methodology which endeavoured to be 'scientific' in the natural-science meaning of that term.

BOX 2.8	Behaviouralist science in brief

Once the investigator has mastered the existing knowledge, and has organized it for his purposes, he pleads a 'meaningful ignorance': 'Here is what I know; what do I not know that is worth knowing?' Once an area has been selected for investigation, the questions should be posed as clearly as possible, and it is here that quantification can prove useful, provided that mathematical tools are combined with carefully constructed taxonomic schemes. Surveying the field of international relations, or any sector of it, we see many disparate elements . . . wondering whether there may be any significant relationships between A and B, or between B and C. By a process which we are compelled to call 'intuition' . . . we perceive a possible correlation, hitherto unsuspected or not firmly known, between two or more elements. At this point, we have the ingredients of a hypothesis which can be expressed in measurable referents, and which, if validated, would be both explanatory and predictive.

Dougherty and Pfaltzgraff (1971: 36–7)

Just as scholars of science are able to formulate objective and verifiable 'laws' to explain the physical world, the ambition of behaviouralists in IR is to do the same for the world of international relations. The main task is to collect empirical data about international relations, preferably large amounts of data, which can then be used for measurement, classification, generalization, and, ultimately, the validation of hypotheses, i.e. scientifically explained patterns of behaviour. Behaviouralism is thus not a new IR theory; it is a new method of studying IR. Behaviouralism is more interested in observable facts and measurable data, in precise calculation, and the collection of data in order to find recurring behavioural patterns, the 'laws' of international relations. According to behaviouralists, facts are separate from values. Unlike facts, values cannot be explained scientifically. The behaviouralists were therefore inclined to study facts while ignoring values. The scientific procedure that behaviouralists support is laid out in Box 2.9.

The two methodological approaches to IR briefly described above, the traditional and the behavioural, are clearly very different. The traditional approach is a holistic one that accepts the complexity of the human world, sees international relations as part of the human world and seeks to understand it in a humanistic way by getting *inside* it. That involves imaginatively entering into the role of statespeople, attempting to understand the moral dilemmas in their foreign policies, and appreciating the basic values involved, such as security, order, freedom and justice. To approach IR in that traditional way involves the scholar in understanding the history and practice of diplomacy, the history and role of international law, the political theory of the sovereign state, and so forth. IR is on that view a broadly humanistic subject; it is not and could never be a strictly scientific or narrowly technical subject.

The other approach, behaviouralism, has no place for morality or ethics in the study of IR because that involves values, and values cannot be studied objectively, i.e. scientifically. Behaviouralism thus raises a fundamental question which continues to be discussed today: can we formulate scientific laws about international relations (and about the social world, the world of human relations, in general)? Critics emphasize what they see as a major mistake in that method: the mistake of treating human relations as an external phenomenon in the same general category as nature so that the theorist stands *outside* the subject—like an anatomist dissecting a cadaver. The anti-behaviouralists hold that the theorist of human affairs is a human being who can never divorce himself or herself completely from human

---

| **BOX 2.9** | **The scientific procedure of behaviouralists** |

The hypothesis must be validated through testing. This demands the construction of a verifying experiment or the gathering of empirical data in other ways . . . The results of the data-gathering effort are carefully observed, recorded and analyzed, after which the hypothesis is discarded, modified, reformulated or confirmed. Findings are published and others are invited to duplicate this knowledge-discovering adventure, and to confirm or deny. This, very roughly, is what we usually mean by 'the scientific method'.

Dougherty and Pfaltzgraff (1971: 37)

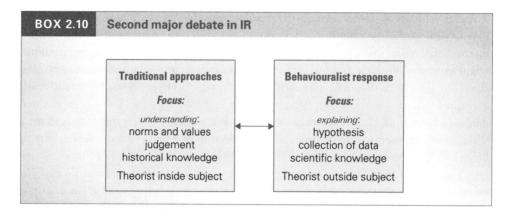

BOX 2.10	Second major debate in IR

Traditional approaches	Behaviouralist response
Focus:	*Focus:*
understanding:	*explaining*:
norms and values	hypothesis
judgement	collection of data
historical knowledge	scientific knowledge
Theorist inside subject	Theorist outside subject

relations: he or she is always *inside* the subject (Hollis and Smith 1990; Jackson 2000). The scholar can strive for detachment and moral neutrality but can never succeed completely. Some scholars attempt to reconcile these approaches: they seek to be historically conscious about IR as a sphere of human relations while also trying to come up with general models that seek to explain and not merely understand world politics. Morgenthau might be an example of that. In studying the moral dilemmas of foreign policy he is in the traditionalist camp; yet he also sets forth general 'laws of politics' which are supposed to apply at all times in all places, and that would appear to put him in the behaviouralist camp.

The behaviouralists did not win the second major debate, but neither did the traditionalists. After a few years of vigorous controversy the second great debate petered out. A compromise resulted which has been portrayed as 'different ends of a continuum of scholarship rather than completely different games . . . Each type of effort can inform and enrich the other and can as well act as a check on the excesses endemic in each approach' (Finnegan 1972: 64). Yet behaviouralism did have a lasting effect in IR. That was largely because of the domination of the discipline after the Second World War by US scholars, the vast majority of whom supported the quantitative, scientific ambitions of behaviouralism. They also led the way in setting a research agenda focused on the role of the two superpowers, especially the United States, in the international system. That paved the way to new formulations of both realism and liberalism that were heavily influenced by behaviouralist methodologies. These new formulations—neorealism and neoliberalism—led to a replay of the first major debate under new historical and methodological conditions.

Neoliberalism: Institutions and Interdependence

Having won the first major debate, realism remained the dominant theoretical approach in IR. The second debate about methodology did not immediately change that situation. After 1945 the centre of gravity in international relations was the Cold War struggle between the United States and the Soviet Union. The East–West rivalry lent itself easily to a realist interpretation of the world.

Yet during the 1950s, 1960s and 1970s a good deal of international relations concerned trade and investment, travel and communication, and similar issues which were especially prevalent in the relations between the liberal democracies of the West. Those relations provided the basis for a new attempt by liberals to formulate an alternative to realist thinking that would avoid the utopian excesses of earlier liberalism. We shall use the label 'neoliberalism' for that renewed liberal approach. Neoliberals share old liberal ideas about the possibility of progress and change, but they repudiate idealism. They also strive to formulate theories and apply new methods which are scientific. In short, the debate between liberalism and realism continued, but it was now coloured by the post-1945 international setting and the behaviouralist methodological persuasion.

In the 1950s a process of regional integration was getting under way in Western Europe which caught the attention and imagination of neoliberals. By 'integration' we refer to a particularly intensive form of international cooperation. Early theorists of integration studied how certain functional activities across borders (trade, investment, etc.) offered mutually advantageous long-term cooperation. Other neoliberal theorists studied how integration fed on itself: cooperation in one transactional area paved the way for cooperation in other areas (Haas 1958; Keohane and Nye 1975). During the 1950s and 1960s Western Europe and Japan developed mass-consumption welfare states, as the United States had done already before the war. That development entailed a higher level of trade, communication, cultural exchange, and other relations and transactions across borders.

This provides the basis for sociological liberalism, a strand of neoliberal thinking which emphasizes the impact of these expanding cross-border activities. In the 1950s Karl Deutsch and his associates argued that such interconnecting activities helped create common values and identities among people from different states and paved the way for peaceful, cooperative relations by making war increasingly costly and thus more unlikely. They also tried to measure the integration phenomenon scientifically (Deutsch et al. 1957).

In the 1970s Robert Keohane and Joseph Nye developed such ideas further. They argued that relationships between Western states (including Japan) are characterized by complex interdependence: there are many forms of connections between societies in addition to the political relations of governments, including transnational links between business

BOX 2.11	OECD countries, total import/export, million current US$				
	1965	1970	1975	1980	2000
Imports, c.i.f.	10,804	18,803	48,945	114,086	4,379,185
Exports, f.o.b.	10,455	18,333	47,315	103,487	4,041,170

Based on OECD and UNCTAD trade statistics

corporations. There is also an 'absence of hierarchy among issues': i.e. military security does not dominate the agenda any more. Military force is no longer used as an instrument of foreign policy (Keohane and Nye 1977: 25). Complex interdependence portrays a situation that is radically different from the realist picture of international relations. In Western democracies there are other actors besides states, and violent conflict clearly is not on their international agenda. We can call this form of neoliberalism *interdependence liberalism*. Robert Keohane and Joseph Nye (1977) are among the main contributors to this line of thinking.

When there is a high degree of interdependence, states will often set up international institutions to deal with common problems. Institutions promote cooperation across international boundaries by providing information and by reducing costs. Institutions can be formal international organizations, such as the WTO or EU or OECD, or they can be less formal sets of agreements (often called regimes) which deal with common activities or issues, such as agreements about shipping, aviation, communication or the environment. We can call this form of neoliberalism *institutional liberalism*. Robert Keohane (1989a) and Oran Young (1986) are among the main contributors to this line of thinking.

The fourth and final strand of neoliberalism—*republican liberalism*—picks up on a theme developed in earlier liberal thinking. It is the idea that liberal democracies enhance peace because they do not go to war against each other. It has been strongly influenced by the rapid spread of democratization in the world after the end of the Cold War, especially in the former Soviet satellite countries in Eastern Europe. An influential version of the theory of democratic peace was set forth by Michael Doyle (1983). Doyle finds that the democratic peace is based on three pillars: the first is peaceful conflict resolution between democratic states; the second is common values among democratic states—a common moral foundation; the final pillar is economic cooperation among democracies. Republican liberals are generally optimistic that there will be a steadily expanding 'Zone of Peace' among liberal democracies even though there may also be occasional setbacks.

These different strands of neoliberalism are mutually supportive in providing an overall consistent argument for more peaceful and cooperative international relations. They consequently stand as a challenge to the realist analysis of IR. In the 1970s there was a general feeling among IR scholars that neoliberalism was on the way to becoming the dominant theoretical approach in the discipline. But a reformulation of realism by Kenneth Waltz (1979) once again tipped the balance towards realism. Neoliberal thinking could make convincing reference to relations between industrialized liberal democracies to argue its case about a more cooperative and interdependent world. But the East–West confrontation

BOX 2.12	Neoliberalism: progress and cooperation
Sociological liberalism	Cross-border flows, common values
Interdependence liberalism	Transactions stimulate cooperation
Institutional liberalism	International institutions, regimes
Republican liberalism	Liberal democracies living in peace with each other

remained a stubborn feature of international relations in the 1970s and 1980s. The new reflections on realism took their cue from that historical fact.

Neorealism: Bipolarity and Confrontation

Kenneth Waltz broke new ground in his book *Theory of International Politics* (1979), which sets forth a substantially different realist theory inspired by the scientific ambitions of behaviouralism. His theory is most often referred to as 'neorealism', and we shall employ that label. Waltz attempts to formulate 'law-like statements' about international relations that achieve scientific validity. He thus departs sharply from classical realism in showing virtually no interest in the ethics of statecraft or the moral dilemmas of foreign policy—concerns that are strongly evident in the realist writings of Morgenthau (see web link 2.31).

Waltz's focus is on the 'structure' of the international system and the consequences of that structure for international relations. The concept of structure is defined as follows. First, Waltz notes that the international system is an anarchy; there is no worldwide government. Second, the international system is composed of like units: every state, small or large, has to perform a similar set of government functions such as national defence, tax collection and economic regulation. However, there is one respect in which states are different and often very different: in their power, what Waltz calls their relative capabilities. Waltz thus draws a very parsimonious and abstract picture of the international system with very few elements. International relations is thus an anarchy composed of states that vary in only one important respect: their relative power. Anarchy is likely to endure, according to Waltz, because states want to preserve their autonomy.

The international system that came into existence after the Second World War was dominated by two superpowers, the United States and the Soviet Union: i.e. it was a bipolar system (see web link 2.32). The demise of the Soviet Union has resulted in a different system with several great powers but with the United States as the predominant power in the system: i.e. it is moving towards a multipolar system. Waltz does not claim that these few pieces of information about the structure of the international system can explain everything about international politics. But he believes that they can explain 'a few big and important things' (Waltz 1986: 322–47). What are they? First, great powers will always tend to balance each other. With the Soviet Union gone, the United States dominates the system. But 'balance-of-power theory leads one to predict that other countries . . . will try to bring American power into balance' (Waltz 1993: 52). Second, smaller and weaker states will have a tendency to align themselves with great powers in order to preserve their maximum autonomy. In making this argument Waltz departs sharply from the classical realist argument based on human nature viewed as 'plain bad' and thus leading to conflict and confrontation. For Waltz states are power-seeking and security-conscious not because of human nature but rather because the structure of the international system compels them to be that way.

This last point is also important because it is the basis for neorealism's counter-attack against the neoliberals. Neorealists do not deny all possibilities for cooperation among states. But they do maintain that cooperating states will always strive to maximize their relative power and preserve their autonomy. In other words, just because there is cooperation, as for example in relations between industrialized liberal democracies (e.g. between the United States and Japan), it does not mean that the neoliberal view has been vindicated. We shall return to the details of this debate in Chapter 4. Here we merely draw attention to the fact that neorealism succeeded in putting neoliberalism on the defensive in the 1980s. Theoretical arguments were significant in this development. But historical events also played an important role. In the 1980s the confrontation between the United States and the Soviet Union reached a new level. US President Ronald Reagan referred to the Soviet Union as an 'evil empire', and in that hostile international climate the arms race between the superpowers was sharply intensified. At about that time the United States was also feeling the increasing competitive pressure from Japan and to some extent from Europe too. Armed conflict between the liberal democracies was certainly not on the agenda; but there were 'trade wars' and other disputes between the Western democracies which appeared to confirm the neorealist hypothesis about competition between self-interested countries that were fundamentally concerned about their power position relative to each other.

During the 1980s some neorealists and neoliberals came close to sharing a common analytical starting-point that is basically neorealist in character: i.e. states are the main actors in what is still an international anarchy and they constantly look after their own best interests (Baldwin 1993). Neoliberals still argued that institutions, interdependence and democracy led to more thoroughgoing cooperation than is predicted by neorealists. But many current versions of neorealism and neoliberalism were no longer diametrically opposed. In methodological terms there was even more common ground between neorealists and neoliberals. Both strongly supported the scientific project launched by the behaviouralists, even though republican liberals were a partial exception in that regard.

As indicated earlier, the debate between neorealism and neoliberalism can be seen as a continuation of the first major debate in IR. But unlike the earlier debate this one resulted in most neoliberals accepting most of the neorealist assumptions as starting-points for analysis. Robert Keohane (1986) attempted to formulate a synthesis of neorealism and neoliberalism coming from the neoliberal side. Barry Buzan et al. (1993) made a similar attempt coming from the neorealist side. However, there is still no complete synthesis between the two traditions. Some neorealists (e.g. Mearsheimer 1993; 1995b) and neoliberals (e.g. Rosenau 1990) are far from reconciled to each other and keep arguing exclusively in favour of their side of the debate. The debate is therefore a continuing one (see web link 2.34).

International Society: The English School

The behaviouralist challenge was most strongly felt among IR scholars in the United States. The neorealist and neoliberal acceptance of that challenge also came predominantly from the American academic community. As indicated earlier, during the 1950s and 1960s American scholarship completely dominated the developing but still youthful IR discipline. Stanley Hoffman made the point that the discipline of IR was 'born and raised in America', and he analysed the profound consequences of that fact for thinking and theorizing in IR (Hoffmann 1977: 41–59). Among the most important of such consequences is the fact that IR continues to be dominated by American scholars even though their pre-eminence may be declining. In the 1970s and 1980s the IR agenda was preoccupied with the neoliberalism/neorealism debate. In the 1990s after the end of the Cold War American predominance in the discipline became less pronounced. IR scholars in Europe and elsewhere became more self-confident and less ready to accept an agenda largely written by US scholars.

In the United Kingdom a school of IR had existed throughout the period of the Cold War which was different in two major ways. It rejected the behaviouralist challenge and emphasized the traditional approach based on human understanding, judgement, norms and history. It also rejected any firm distinction between a strict realist and a strict liberal view of international relations. The IR school to which we refer is sometimes called 'the English School'. But that name is far too narrow: it overlooks the fact that several of its leading figures were not English and many were not even from the United Kingdom; rather, they were from Australia, Canada and South Africa. For that reason we shall use its other name: International Society. Two leading International Society theorists of the twentieth century are Martin Wight and Hedley Bull (see web links 2.35 and 2.36).

International Society theorists recognize the importance of power in international affairs. They also focus on the state and the state system. But they reject the narrow realist view that world politics is a Hobbesian state of nature in which there are no international norms at all. They view the state as the combination of a *Machtstaat* (power state) and a *Rechtsstaat* (constitutional state): power and law are both important features of international relations. It is true that there is an international anarchy in the sense that there is no world government. But international anarchy is a social and not an anti-social condition: i.e. world politics is an 'anarchical society' (Bull 1995). International Society theorists also recognize the importance of the individual, and some of them argue that individuals are prior to states. Unlike many contemporary liberals, however, International Society theorists tend to regard IGOs and NGOs (intergovernmental and non-governmental organizations) as marginal rather than central features of world politics. They emphasize the relations of states and they play down the importance of transnational relations.

International Society theorists find that realists are correct in pointing to the importance of power and national interest. But if we push the realist view to its logical conclusion, states

---

BOX 2.13	International Society

A *society of states* (or international society) exists when a group of states, conscious of certain common interests and common values, form a society in the sense that they conceive themselves to be bound by a common set of rules in their relations with one another, and share in the working of common institutions. My contention is that the element of a society has always been present, and remains present, in the modern international system.

Bull (1995: 13, 39)

would always be preoccupied with playing the tough game of power politics; in a pure anarchy, there can be no mutual trust. That view is clearly misleading; there is warfare, but states are not continually preoccupied with each other's power, nor do they conceive of that power exclusively as a threat. On the other hand, if we take the liberal idealist view to the extreme, it means that all relations between states are governed by common rules in a perfect world of mutual respect and the rule of law. That view too is clearly misleading. Of course there are common rules and norms that most states can be expected to observe most of the time; in that sense relations between states constitute an international society. But these rules and norms cannot by themselves guarantee international harmony and cooperation; power and the balance of power still remain very important in the anarchical society.

The United Nations system demonstrates how both elements—power and law—are simultaneously present in international society (see web links 2.38 and 2.39). The Security Council is set up according to the reality of unequal power among states. The great powers (the United States, China, Russia, Britain, France) are the only permanent members with the authority to veto decisions. That simply recognizes the reality of unequal power in world politics. The great powers have a de facto veto anyway: it would be very difficult to force them to do anything that they were not prepared to do. That is the 'realist power and inequality element' in international society. The General Assembly—by contrast with the Security Council—is set up according to the principle of international equality: every member state is legally equal to every other state; each state has one vote, and the majority rather than the most powerful prevail. That is the rationalist 'common rules and norms' element in international society. Finally, the UN also provides evidence about the importance of individuals in international affairs. The UN has promoted the international law of human rights, beginning with the Universal Declaration of Human Rights (1948). Today there is an elaborate structure of humanitarian law which defines the basic civil, political, social, economic and cultural rights that are intended to promote an acceptable standard of human existence in the contemporary world. That is the cosmopolitan or solidarist element of international society.

For International Society theorists the study of international relations is not about singling out one of these elements and disregarding the others. They do not seek to make and test hypotheses with the aim of constructing scientific laws of IR. They are not trying to explain international relations scientifically; rather, they are trying to understand it and interpret it. International Society theorists thus take a broader historical, legal and philosophical approach to international relations. IR is about discerning and exploring the complex presence of all these elements and the normative problems they present to state leaders. Power and national interests matter; so do common norms and institutions. States are important, but so are human beings. Statesmen and stateswomen have a national responsibility to their own nation and its citizens; they have an international responsibility to observe and follow international law and respect the rights of other states; and they have a humanitarian responsibility to defend human rights around the world. But, as the 1990s crises in Bosnia, Somalia and the Persian Gulf clearly demonstrated, carrying out these responsibilities in a justifiable way is no easy task (Jackson 2000).

In sum, International Society is an approach which tells us something about a world of sovereign states where power and law are both present. The ethics of prudence and the

BOX 2.14	International Society (The English School)

METHODOLOGICAL FOCUS	MAIN ELEMENTS IN THE INTERNATIONAL SYSTEM
• Understanding	1. Power, national interest (realist element)
• Judgement	2. Rules, procedures, international law (liberal element)
• Values	
• Norms and historical knowledge	3. Universal human rights, one world for all (cosmopolitan element)
Theorist inside subject	

national interest claim the responsibilities of statespeople alongside their duty to observe international rules and procedures. World politics is a world of states but it is also a world of human beings, and it will often be difficult to reconcile the demands and claims of both. The main elements of the International Society approach are summarized in Box 2.14.

The challenge posed by the International Society approach does not count as a new major debate. It should rather be seen as an extension of the first debate and a repudiation of the seeming behaviouralist triumph in the second debate. International Society builds on classical realist and liberal ideas, combining and expanding them in ways which provides an alternative to both. International Society adds another perspective to the first great debate between realism and liberalism by rejecting the sharp division between them. Although International Society scholars did not enter that debate directly, their approach clearly suggests that the difference between realism and liberalism is drawn too sharply: the historical world does not choose between power and law in quite the categorical way that the debate implies. As regards the second great debate between the traditionalists and the behaviouralists, International Society theorists did enter that debate by firmly rejecting the latter approach and upholding the former approach (Bull 1969). International Society scholars do not see any possibility of the construction of 'laws' of IR on the model of the natural sciences. For them, that project is flawed: it is based on an intellectual misreading of the character of international relations. For International Society scholars IR is entirely a field of human relations: it is thus a normative subject and it cannot be fully understood in non-normative terms. IR is about understanding, not explaining; it involves the exercise of judgment: putting oneself in the place of statespeople to try better to understand the dilemmas they confront in their conduct of foreign policy. The notion of an international society also provides a perspective for studying issues of human rights and humanitarian intervention which figured prominently on the IR agenda at that time.

To sum up: International Society scholars emphasize the simultaneous presence in international society of both realist and liberal elements. There is conflict and there is cooperation; there are states and there are individuals. These different elements cannot be simplified and abstracted into a single theory that emphasizes only one explanatory variable—e.g.

power. That would be a much too simple view of world politics and would distort reality. International Society theorists argue for a humanist approach that recognizes the simultaneous presence of all these elements, and the need for holistic and historical study of the problems and dilemmas that arise in that complex situation.

International Political Economy (IPE)

The academic IR debates presented so far are mainly concerned with international politics. Economic affairs play a secondary role. There is little concern with the weak states in the Third World. As we noted in Chapter 1, the decades after the Second World War were a period of decolonization. A large number of 'new' countries appeared on the map as the old colonial powers gave up their control and the former colonies were given political independence. Many of the 'new' states are weak in economic terms: they are at the bottom of the global economic hierarchy and constitute a 'Third World'. In the 1970s Third World countries started to press for changes in the international system to improve their economic position in relation to the developed countries. Around this time, neo-Marxism emerged as an attempt to theorize about economic underdevelopment in the Third World.

This became the basis for a third major debate in IR about international wealth and international poverty—i.e. about International Political Economy or IPE for short. IPE is basically about who gets what in the international economic and political system (see web links 2.43 and 2.44). The third debate takes the shape of a neo-Marxist critique of the capitalist world economy together with liberal IPE and realist IPE responses concerning the relationship between economics and politics in international relations.

Neo-Marxism is an attempt to analyse the situation of the Third World by applying the tools of analysis first developed by Karl Marx. Marx, a famous nineteenth-century political economist, focused on capitalism in Europe; he argued that the bourgeoisie or capitalist class used its economic power to exploit and oppress the proletariat, or working class. Neo-Marxists extend that analysis to the Third World by arguing that the global capitalist economy controlled by the wealthy capitalist states is used to impoverish the world's poor countries. 'Dependence' is a core concept for neo-Marxists. They claim that countries in the Third World are not poor because they are inherently backward or undeveloped. Rather, it is because they have been actively underdeveloped by the rich countries of the First World. Third World countries are subject to unequal exchange: in order to participate in the global capitalist economy they must sell their raw materials at cheap prices, and they have to buy finished goods at high prices. In marked contrast, rich countries can buy low and sell high. It is important to emphasize that for neo-Marxists that situation is imposed upon poor countries by the wealthy capitalist states.

Andre Gunder Frank claims that unequal exchange and appropriation of economic surplus by the few at the expense of the many are inherent in capitalism (Frank 1967). As long as the capitalist system exists there will be underdevelopment in the Third World.

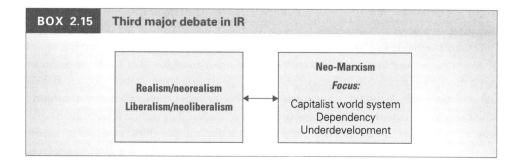

BOX 2.15   Third major debate in IR

Realism/neorealism
Liberalism/neoliberalism

Neo-Marxism

Focus:

Capitalist world system
Dependency
Underdevelopment

A similar view is taken by Immanuel Wallerstein (1974; 1983), who has analysed the over-all development of the capitalist world system since its beginning in the sixteenth century. Wallerstein (see web link 2.47) allows for the possibility that some Third World countries can 'move upwards' in the global capitalist hierarchy. But only a few can do that; there is no room at the top for everybody. Capitalism is a hierarchy based on the exploitation of the poor by the rich, and it will remain that way unless and until it is replaced.

The liberal view of IPE is very different and almost exactly the opposite. Liberal IPE scholars argue that human prosperity can be achieved by the free global expansion of capitalism beyond the boundaries of the sovereign state, and by the decline of the signifi-cance of these boundaries. Liberals draw from the economic analysis of Adam Smith and other classical liberal economists, who argue that free markets together with private prop-erty and individual freedom create the basis for self-sustaining economic progress for everybody involved. People would not conduct exchange on the free market unless it was to their benefit: 'Since the household always has the alternative of producing directly for itself, it need not enter into any exchange unless it benefits from it. Hence, no exchange will take place unless both parties do benefit from it' (Friedman 1962: 13–14). Thus, whereas Marxist IPE views international capitalism as an instrument for the exploitation of the Third World by the developed countries, liberal IPE views it as an instrument of progressive change for all countries regardless of their level of development (see web link 2.48).

Realist IPE is different again. It can be traced back to the thought of Friedrich List, a nineteenth-century German economist. It is based on the idea that economic activity should be put in the service of building a strong state and supporting the national interest. Wealth should thus be controlled and managed by the state; that statist IPE doctrine is often referred to as 'mercantilism' or 'economic nationalism'. For mercantilists, the creation of wealth is the necessary basis for increased power of the state. Wealth is there-fore an instrument in the creation of national security and national welfare. Moreover, the smooth functioning of a free market depends on political power. Without a dominant or hegemonic power, there can be no liberal world economy (Gilpin 1987: 72). The United States has had the role of hegemon since the end of the First World War. But beginning in the early 1970s the US was increasingly challenged economically by Japan and by Western Europe. And according to realist IPE that decline of US leadership has weakened the liberal world economy, because there is no other state that can perform the role of global hegemon.

These different views of IPE show up in analyses of three important and related IPE issues of recent years. The first issue concerns economic globalization: that is, the spread and intensification of all kinds of economic relations between countries. Does economic globalization undermine 'national' economies by erasing national borders and by subjecting national economies to the exigencies of the global economy? The second issue is about who wins and who loses in the process of economic globalization. The third issue concerns how we should view the relative importance of economics and politics. Are global economic relations ultimately controlled by states who set out the framework of rules that economic actors have to observe? Or are politicians increasingly subject to anonymous market forces over which they have lost effective control? Underlying many of these questions is the issue of state sovereignty: are the forces of global economics making the sovereign state obsolete? The three approaches to IPE come up with very different answers to these questions, as we shall see in Chapter 8.

In short, the third major debate further complicates the discipline of IR because it shifts the subject away from political and military issues and towards economic and social issues, and because it introduces the distinct socioeconomic problems of Third World countries. It is not a debate like the previous two IR debates discussed above. Rather, it is a marked expansion of the academic IR research agenda to include socioeconomic questions of welfare as well as political-military questions of security. Yet both the realist and the liberal traditions have specific views on IPE, and those views have been attacked by neo-Marxism. And all three perspectives are in rather sharp disagreement with each other: they take fundamentally different views of the international political economy in terms of both concepts and values. In that sense we do indeed have a third debate. The debate was focused on North–South relations at first, but it has long since expanded to include IPE issues in all areas of international relations. There was no clear winner in the third debate, as we shall see in Chapter 8.

Dissident Voices: Alternative Approaches to IR

The debates introduced so far have concerned the established theoretical traditions in the discipline: realism, liberalism, International Society and the theories of International Political Economy (IPE). Currently a fourth debate is under way in IR. It involves various critiques of the established traditions by alternative approaches, sometimes identified as post-positivism (Smith et al. 1996).

There have always been 'dissident voices' in the discipline of IR: philosophers and scholars who have rejected established views and tried to replace them with alternatives. But in recent years these voices have increased in number.

BOX 2.16	Post-positivist approaches

In the last few years a number of powerful attacks on realism have been mounted by scholars from a diffuse grouping of positions . . . there are four main groupings involved in this challenge. The first comes from critical theory. A second strand of thought has developed . . . under the general heading of historical sociology . . . The third grouping comprises feminist writers . . . Finally there are those writers concerned to develop postmodern readings of international relations.

Smith (1995: 24–5)

Two factors help explain that development. The end of the Cold War changed the international agenda in some fundamental ways. In place of a clear-cut East/West conflict dominated by two contending superpowers a number of diverse issues emerged in world politics, including, for example, state partition and disintegration, civil war, terrorism, democratization, national minorities, humanitarian intervention, ethnic cleansing, mass migration and refugee problems, environmental security, and so forth. An increasing number of IR scholars expressed dissatisfaction with the dominant Cold War approach to IR: the neorealism of Kenneth Waltz. Many IR scholars now take issue with Waltz's claim that the complex world of international relations can be squeezed into a few law-like statements about the structure of the international system and the balance of power. They consequently reinforce the anti-behaviouralist critique first put forward by International Society theorists such as Hedley Bull (1969). Many IR scholars also criticize Waltzian neorealism for its conservative political outlook: there is not much in neorealism which can point to change and the creation of a better world.

In sum, there are new debates in IR that address methodological issues (i.e. *how* to approach the study of IR) (see web link 2.56) and substantial issues (i.e. *which* issues should be considered the most important ones for IR to study). We have chosen to present these developments in three chapters.

Chapter 6 introduces social constructivism. Constructivists claim that neorealism and neoliberalism are 'materialist' theories; they focus on material power, such as military forces and economic capabilities. Constructivists argue that the international system is constituted by ideas, not material power. The chapter presents constructivist theories of IR. Chapter 10 addresses 'non-traditional' (or rediscovered) issues in IR. We shall look into five important issues that have captured the attention of IR scholars since the end of the Cold War: international terrorism; the environment; gender; sovereignty; and changes in statehood. They are rival answers to the question: what is the most important issue or concern in world politics now that the Cold War has come to an end, and IR's realist preoccupation with superpower rivalry and nuclear security along with it? Finally, Chapter 11 takes up the discussion on methodology. We examine different methodological currents in post-positivist IR. These different methodologies are rival answers to the question: if behaviouralist methodology, as employed by neorealism and neoliberalism, is abandoned, what should it be replaced with? The various currents are thus in agreement about criticizing the behaviouralist attempts to

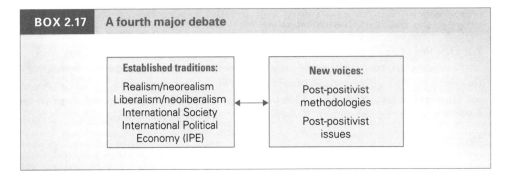

BOX 2.17   A fourth major debate

Established traditions:		New voices:
Realism/neorealism Liberalism/neoliberalism International Society International Political Economy (IPE)	←→	Post-positivist methodologies Post-positivist issues

formulate scientific laws of international relations; but they disagree about what is the best replacement for the methods that are now being rejected.

Social constructivism and the non-traditional issues and methodologies mentioned here have something in common: they claim that established traditions in IR fail to come to grips with the post-Cold War changes of world politics. These recent approaches should thus be seen as 'new voices' that are trying to point the way to an academic IR discipline that is more in tune with international relations at the start of a new millennium. In short, many scholars argue that a fourth IR debate has been thrown open in the 1990s between the established traditions on the one hand and these new voices on the other.

Which Theory?

This chapter has introduced the main theoretical traditions in IR. It is necessary to be familiar with theory, because facts do not speak for themselves. We always look at the world, consciously or not, through a specific set of lenses; we may think of those lenses as theory. Is development taking place in the Third World or is it underdevelopment? Is the world a more secure or a more dangerous place since the end of the Cold War? Are contemporary states more prone to cooperate or to compete with each other? The facts alone cannot answer these questions; we need help from theories. They tell us which facts are important and which are unimportant, that is, they structure our view of the world. They are based on certain values, and often they also contain visions of how we want the world to be. Early liberal thinking about IR, for example, was driven by the determination never to repeat the disaster of the First World War. Liberals hoped the creation of new international organizations would foster a more peaceful and cooperative world.

Because theory is necessary in thinking systematically about the world it is better to get the most important theories out in the open and subject them to scrutiny. We should examine their concepts, their claims about how the world hangs together and what the important facts are; we should probe their values and visions. That is what we set out to do in the following chapters. The presentation of different theories always begs a big question: which theory is best? It may seem an innocent question, but it raises a number of difficult and complex issues. One answer is that the question about the best theory is not really meaningful, because different theories, such as realism and liberalism, are like different games, played by different people (Rosenau 1967; see also Smith 1997). If there was only one game, say tennis, we could easily find one winner by setting up a tournament. But when there is more than one game, say both tennis and badminton, the badminton player will not stop playing just because a tennis player comes along and claims that tennis is a much better game. Maybe the theories that most appeal to us are like the games that we most enjoy watching or playing.

Another answer to the question about the best theory is that even if theories are different in many ways, it does make sense to rank them, just as it makes sense to point out the athlete of the year even if the candidates for that honour compete in very different athletic disciplines. What would be the criteria for identifying the best theory? We may think of several relevant criteria, among them:

- Coherence: the theory should be consistent, i.e. free of internal contradictions.
- Clarity of exposition: the theory should be formulated in a clear and lucid manner.
- Unbiased: the theory should not be based on purely subjective valuations. No theory is value-free, but the theory should strive to be candid about its normative premises and values.
- Scope: the theory should be relevant for a large number of important issues. A theory with limited scope, for example, is a theory about US decision-making in the Gulf War. A theory with wide scope is a theory about foreign policy decision-making in general.
- Depth: the theory should be able to explain and understand as much as possible of the phenomenon which it purports to tackle. For example, a theory of European integration has limited depth if it explains only some part of that process and much more depth if it explains most of it.

Other possible criteria could be set forth (see Chapter 11); but it must be emphasized that there is no objective way of choosing between the evaluative criteria. And it is clear that some criteria can load the dice in favour of some types of theory and against others. There is no simple way around the problem. A further complication is that people's values and political priorities play a role in choosing one theory ahead of another.

As textbook writers, we see it as our duty to present what we consider the most important theories in a way that draws out the strength of each theory but is also critical of its weaknesses and limitations. This book is not aimed at guiding the reader towards one single theory which we see as the best; it is aimed at identifying the pros and cons of several important theories in order to enable the reader to make his or her own well-considered choices from the available possibilities.

Conclusion

The foregoing traditional and alternative theories constitute the main analytical tools and concerns of contemporary IR. We have seen how the subject developed through a series of debates between different theoretical approaches. We noted that these debates were not conducted in splendid isolation from everything else: they were shaped and influenced by historical events, by the major political and economic problems of the day. They were also influenced by methodological developments in other areas of scholarship. These elements are summarized in Box 2.1.

No single theoretical approach has clearly won the day in IR. The main theoretical traditions and alternative approaches that we have outlined are all actively employed in the discipline today. That situation reflects the necessity of different approaches to capture different aspects of a very complicated historical and contemporary reality. World politics is not dominated by one single issue or conflict; on the contrary, it is shaped and influenced by many different issues and conflicts. The pluralist situation of IR scholarship also reflects the personal preferences of different scholars: they often prefer particular theories for reasons that may have as much to do with their personal values and world-views as with what takes place in international relations and what is required to understand those events and episodes.

 KEY POINTS

- IR thinking has evolved in stages that are marked by specific debates between groups of scholars. The first major debate is between *utopian liberalism* and *realism*; the second debate is on method, between *traditional approaches* and *behaviouralism*. The third debate is between *neorealism/neoliberalism* and *neo-Marxism*; and an emerging fourth debate is between *established traditions* and *post-positivist alternatives*.

- The first major debate was won by the realists. During the Cold War realism became the dominant way of thinking about international relations not only among scholars but also among politicians, diplomats and so-called 'ordinary people'. Morgenthau's (1960) summary of realism became the standard introduction to IR in the 1950s and 1960s.

- The second major debate is about method. The contenders are traditionalists and behaviouralists. The former try to understand a complicated social world of human affairs and the values fundamental to it, such as order, freedom and justice. The latter approach, behaviouralism, finds no place for morality or ethics in international theory. Behaviouralism wants to classify, measure and explain through the formulation of general laws like those formulated in the 'hard' sciences of chemistry, physics, etc. The behaviouralists seemed to triumph for a time but in the end neither side won the debate. Today both types of method are used in the discipline. There was a revival of traditional normative approaches to IR after the end of the Cold War.

- In the 1960s and 1970s, neoliberalism challenged realism by arguing that interdependence, integration and democracy are changing IR. Neorealism responded that anarchy and the balance of power are still at the heart of IR.

- International Society theorists maintain that IR contains both 'realist' elements of conflict and 'liberal' elements of cooperation, and that these elements cannot be collapsed into a single theoretical synthesis. They also emphasize human rights and other cosmopolitan features of world politics, and they defend the traditional approach to IR.

- The third debate is characterized by a neo-Marxist attack on the established positions of realism/neorealism and liberalism/neoliberalism. This debate concerns International Political Economy (IPE). It creates a more complex situation in the discipline because it expands the terrain towards economic issues and because it introduces the distinct problems of Third World countries. There is no clear winner of the third debate. Within IPE, the discussion between the main contenders continues.

- Currently a fourth debate is under way in IR; it involves an attack on the established traditions by alternative approaches, sometimes identified as 'post-positivist alternatives'. The debate raises both methodological issues (i.e. *how* to approach the study of an issue) and substantial issues (i.e. *which* issues should be considered the most important ones). Some of these approaches also reject the scientific claims of neorealism and neoliberalism.

QUESTIONS

- Identify the major debates within IR. Why do the debates often linger on without any clear winner emerging?
- Which are the established theoretical traditions in IR? How can they be seen as 'established'?
- Why was early IR strongly influenced by liberalism?
- Seen over the long term, realism is the dominant theoretical tradition in IR. Why?
- Why do scholars have pet theories? What are your own theoretical preferences?

GUIDE TO FURTHER READING

Angell, N. (1909). *The Great Illusion*. London: Weidenfeld & Nicolson.

Burchill, S. et al. (2001). *Theories of International Relations*. Basingstoke: Palgrave Macmillan.

Carr, E. H. (1964). *The Twenty Years' Crisis*. New York: Harper & Row.

Cox, M. (ed.) (2002). 'The World Crisis and the Origins of International Relations', *International Relations*, 16/1, April (issue on the origins of the IR discipline).

Jackson, R. (2005). *Classical and Modern Thought on International Relations: From Anarchy to Cosmopolis.* New York: Palgrave Macmillan

Kahler, M. (1997) 'Inventing International Relations: International Relations Theory after 1945', in M. Doyle and G. J. Ikenberry (eds), *New Thinking in International Relations Theory.* Boulder: Westview, 20–54.

Knutsen, T. L. (1997). *A History of International Relations Theory.* Manchester: Manchester University Press.

Nye, J. S. (2004). *Understanding International Conflicts: An Introduction to Theory and History.* Harlow: Pearson Higher Education/Longman—with foreword by Stanley Hoffmann.

Schmidt, B. C. (1998). *The Political Discourse of Anarchy: A Disciplinary History of International Relations.* Albany: SUNY Press.

Smith, S. (1995). 'The Self-Images of a Discipline: A Genealogy of International Relations Theory', in K. Booth and S. Smith (eds), *International Relations Theory Today.* University Park: Pennsylvania State University Press; Cambridge: Polity, 1–38.

Vasquez, J. A. (1996). *Classics of International Relations*, 3rd edn. Upper Saddle River, NJ: Prentice-Hall.

WEB LINKS

Web links mentioned in the chapter plus additional links can be found on the Online Resource Centre that accompanies this book.

www.oxfordtextbooks.co.uk/orc/jackson_sorensen3e/

Realism

▌ Summary

This chapter sketches the realist tradition in IR. The chapter takes note of an important dichotomy in realist thought between classical and contemporary approaches to realism. Classical and neoclassical realists emphasize the normative aspects of realism as well as the empirical aspects. Most contemporary realists pursue a social scientific analysis of the structures and processes of world politics, but they tend to ignore norms and values. The chapter discusses both classical and contemporary strands of realist thought. It examines a debate among realists concerning the wisdom of NATO expansion into Eastern Europe. It also reviews two critiques of realist doctrine: an International Society critique and an emancipatory critique. The concluding section assesses the prospects for the realist tradition as a research programme in IR.

Introduction: Elements of Realism

Basic realist ideas and assumptions are: (1) a pessimistic view of human nature; (2) a conviction that international relations are necessarily conflictual and that international conflicts are ultimately resolved by war; (3) a high regard for the values of national security and state survival; and (4) a basic scepticism that there can be progress in international politics that is comparable to that in domestic political life (see web link 3.01). These ideas and assumptions steer the thought of most leading realist IR theorists, both past and present.

In realist thought humans are characterized as being preoccupied with their own well-being in their competitive relations with each other. They desire to be in the driver's seat. They do not wish to be taken advantage of. They consequently strive to have the 'edge' in relations with other people—including international relations with other countries. In that regard at least, human beings are considered to be basically the same everywhere. Thus the desire to enjoy an advantage over others and to avoid domination by others is universal. This pessimistic view of human nature is strongly evident in the IR theory of Hans Morgenthau (1965; 1985), who was probably the leading realist thinker of the twentieth century. He sees men and women as having a 'will to power'. That is particularly evident in politics and especially international politics: 'Politics is a struggle for power over men, and whatever its ultimate aim may be, power is its immediate goal and the modes of acquiring, maintaining, and demonstrating it determine the technique of political action' (Morgenthau 1965: 195).

Thucydides, Machiavelli, Hobbes, and indeed all classical realists, share that view to a greater or lesser extent. They believe that the goal of power, the means of power and the uses of power are a central preoccupation of political activity. International politics is thus portrayed as—above all else—'power politics': an arena of rivalry, conflict and war between states in which the same basic problems of defending the national interest and ensuring the continued survival of the state repeat themselves over and over again.

Realists thus operate with a core assumption that world politics unfolds in an international anarchy: i.e. a system with no overarching authority, no world government. The state is the pre-eminent actor in world politics. International relations are primarily relations of states. All other actors in world politics—individuals, international organizations, NGOs, etc.—are either less important or unimportant. The main point of foreign policy is to project and defend the interests of the state in world politics. But states are not equal: on the contrary, there is an international hierarchy of power among states. The most important states in world politics are the great powers. International relations are understood by realists as primarily a struggle between the great powers for domination and security.

The normative core of realism is national security and state survival: these are the values that drive realist doctrine and realist foreign policy. The state is considered to be essential for the good life of its citizens: without a state to guarantee the means and conditions of security and to promote welfare, human life is bound to be, in the famous phrase of Thomas

Hobbes (1946: 82), 'solitary, poor, nasty, brutish and short'. The state is thus seen as a protector of its territory, of the population, and of their distinctive and valued way of life. The national interest is the final arbiter in judging foreign policy. Human society and morality is confined to the state and does not extend into international relations, which is a political arena of considerable turmoil, discord and conflict between states in which the great powers dominate everybody else.

The fact that all states must pursue their own national interest means that other countries and governments can never be relied upon completely. All international agreements are provisional and conditional on the willingness of states to observe them. All states must be prepared to sacrifice their international obligations on the altar of their own self-interest if the two come into conflict. That makes treaties and all other agreements, conventions, customs, rules, laws and so on between states merely expedient arrangements which can and will be set aside if they conflict with the vital interests of states. There are no international obligations in the moral sense of the word—i.e. bonds of mutual duty—between independent states. As indicated above, the only fundamental responsibility of statespeople is to advance and to defend the national interest. That is nowhere stated more brutally than by Machiavelli in his famous book *The Prince* (see Box 3.3).

That means that there can be no progressive change in world politics comparable to the developments that characterize domestic political life. That also means that realist IR theory is considered to be valid not only at particular times but at all times, because the foregoing basic facts of world politics never change. That, at any rate, is what most realists argue and evidently believe.

There is an important distinction in realist IR theory between classical realism and contemporary realism. Classical realism is one of the 'traditional' approaches to IR that was prominent prior to the behaviouralist revolution of the 1950s and 1960s as outlined in Chapter 2. It is basically normative in approach, and focuses on the core political values of national security and state survival. Classical realists have lived in many different historical periods, from ancient Greece right down to the present time. Contemporary realism, on the other hand and as the name implies, is a recent IR doctrine: it is basically scientific in approach and focuses on the international system or structure. It is largely (although not exclusively) American in origin. Indeed, it has been and perhaps still is the most prominent IR theory in the United States, which is home to by far the largest number of IR scholars in the world. That fact alone makes contemporary realism a particularly important IR theory.

Classical Realism

What is classical realism? Who are the leading classical realists? What are their key ideas and arguments? In this section we shall examine, briefly, the international thought of three outstanding classical realists of the past: (1) the ancient Greek historian Thucydides; (2) the Renaissance Italian political theorist Niccolò Machiavelli; and (3) the seventeenth-century

English political and legal philosopher Thomas Hobbes. In the next section we shall single out for special treatment the neoclassical realist thought of the twentieth-century German-American IR theorist Hans J. Morgenthau.

Thucydides

What we call inter*national* relations Thucydides saw as the inevitable competitions and conflicts between ancient Greek city-states (which together composed the cultural-linguistic civilization known as Hellas) and between Hellas and neighbouring non-Greek empires, such as Macedonia or Persia (see web links 3.03 and 3.04). Neither the states of Hellas nor their non-Greek neighbours were in any sense equal. On the contrary, they were substantially unequal: there were a few 'great powers'—such as Athens, Sparta and the Persian Empire, and many smaller and lesser powers—such as the tiny island statelets of the Aegean Sea. That inequality was considered to be inevitable and natural. A distinctive feature of Thucydides' brand of realism is thus its naturalist character. Aristotle said that 'man is a political animal'. Thucydides said in effect that political animals are highly unequal in their powers and capabilities to dominate others and to defend themselves. All states, large and small, must adapt to that given reality of unequal power and conduct themselves accordingly. If states do that, they will survive and perhaps even prosper. If states fail to do that, they will place themselves in jeopardy and may even be destroyed. Ancient history is full of many examples of states and empires, small and large, that were destroyed.

So Thucydides emphasizes the limited choices and the restricted sphere of manoeuvre available to statespeople in the conduct of foreign policy. He also emphasizes that decisions have consequences: before any final decision is made a decision-maker should have carefully thought through the likely consequences, bad as well as good. In pointing that out, Thucydides is also emphasizing the ethics of caution and prudence in the conduct of foreign policy in an international world of great inequality, of restricted foreign-policy choices, and of ever-present danger as well as opportunity. Foresight, prudence, caution and judgement are the characteristic political ethics of classical realism which Thucydides and most other classical realists are at pains to distinguish from private morality and the principle of justice.

BOX 3.1	International relations in Ancient Greece

The Greeks established the Hellenic League . . . and placed it under the leadership of Sparta and Athens. Despite the semblance of Greek unity during the Persian Wars (492–477 BC) there were serious conflicts between members of the League, mostly occasioned by the smaller city-states' fear of Athenian imperialism and expansion. Thus, after the Greek victories over the Persians, Athens' competitors, led by Sparta, formed a rival organization, the Peloponnesian League, an intricate alliance and collective security system designed to deter further Athenian expansion . . . A bitter competition over trade and naval supremacy between Corinth and Athens led ultimately to the Peloponnesian Wars involving the two military alliances.

Holsti (1988: 38–9)

If a country and its government wish to survive and prosper, they had better pay attention to these fundamental political maxims of international relations.

In his famous study of the Peloponnesian War (431–404 BC) Thucydides (1972: 407) put his realist philosophy into the mouths of the leaders of Athens—a great power—in their dialogue with the leaders of Melos—a minor power—during a moment of conflict between the two city-states in 416 BC. The Melians made an appeal to the principle of justice, which to them meant that their honour and dignity as an independent state should be respected by the powerful Athenians. But, according to Thucydides, justice is of a special kind in international relations. It is not about equal treatment for all; it is about knowing your proper place, about adapting to the natural reality of unequal power. Thucydides therefore let the Athenians reply to the Melian appeal as set out in Box 3.2.

That is probably the most famous example of the classical realist understanding of international relations as basically an anarchy of separate states that have no real choice except to operate according to the principles and practices of power politics in which security and survival are the primary values and war is the final arbiter.

Machiavelli

Power (the Lion) and deception (the Fox) are the two essential means for the conduct of foreign policy, according to the political teachings of Machiavelli (1984: 66). The supreme political value is national freedom, i.e. independence. The main responsibility of rulers is always to seek the advantages and to defend the interests of their state and thus ensure its survival. That requires strength: if a state is not strong it will be a standing invitation for others to prey upon it; the ruler must be a lion. That also requires cunning and—if necessary—ruthlessness in the pursuit of self-interest: the ruler must also be a fox. If rulers are not astute, crafty and adroit they might miss an opportunity that could bring great advantages or benefits to them and their state. Even more importantly, they might fail to notice a menace or threat which if not guarded against might harm or even destroy them, their regime and possibly even the state as well. That statesmen and stateswomen must be both lions and foxes is at the heart of Machiavelli's (1984: 66) realist theory. Classical realist IR theory is primarily a theory of survival (Wight 1966).

BOX 3.3   Machiavelli on the Prince's obligations

A prince . . . cannot observe all those things for which men are considered good, for in order to maintain the state he is often obliged to act against his promise, against charity, against humanity, and against religion. And therefore, it is necessary that he have a mind ready to turn itself according to the way the winds of fortune and the changeability of [political] affairs require . . . as long as it is possible, he should not stray from the good, but he should know how to enter into evil when necessity commands.

Machiavelli (1984: 59–60)

The overriding Machiavellian assumption is that the world is a dangerous place (see web link 3.05). But it is also, by the same token, an opportune place too. If anybody hopes to survive in such a world, he or she must always be aware of dangers, must anticipate them and must take the necessary precautions against them. And if they hope to prosper, to enrich themselves and to bask in the reflected glory of their accumulated power and wealth, it is necessary for them to recognize and to exploit the opportunities that present themselves and to do that more quickly, more skilfully and—if necessary—more ruthlessly than any of their rivals or enemies. The conduct of foreign policy is thus an instrumental or 'Machiavellian' activity based on the intelligent calculation of one's power and interests as against the power and interests of rivals and competitors.

That shrewd outlook is reflected in some typical Machiavellian maxims of realist statecraft, including the following. Be aware of what is happening. Do not wait for things to happen. Anticipate the motives and actions of others. Do not wait for others to act. Act before they do. The prudent state leader acts to ward off any threat posed by his or her neighbours. He or she should be prepared to engage in pre-emptive war and similar initiatives. The realist state leader is alert to opportunities in any political situation, and is prepared and equipped to exploit them.

Above all, according to Machiavelli, the responsible state leader must not operate in accordance with the principles of Christian ethics: love thy neighbour, be peaceful, and avoid war except in self-defence or in pursuit of a just cause; be charitable, share your wealth with others, always act in good faith, etc. Machiavelli sees these moral maxims as the height of political irresponsibility: if political leaders act in accordance with Christian virtues, they are bound to come to grief and they will lose everything. Not only that: they will sacrifice the property and perhaps the freedom and even the lives of their citizens, who depend upon their statecraft. The implication is clear: if a ruler does not know or respect the maxims of power politics, his or her statecraft will fail, and with it the security and welfare of the citizens who depend absolutely upon it. In other words, political responsibility flows in a very different vein from ordinary, private morality. The fundamental, overriding values are the security and the survival of the state: that is what must guide foreign policy.

Machiavelli's realist writings are sometimes portrayed (Forde 1992: 64) as 'manuals on how to thrive in a completely chaotic and immoral world'. But that view is misleading. It overlooks the responsibilities of rulers not merely to themselves or to their personal regimes but also to their country and its citizens: what Machiavelli, thinking of Florence, refers to as 'the republic'. This is the civic-virtue aspect of Machiavellian realism: rulers have to be both lions and foxes because their people depend upon them for their survival and prosperity. That dependence of the people upon their ruler, and specifically upon the wisdom of his or her foreign policy, is owing to the fact that their fate is entangled in the same state: that is the normative heart not only of Machiavellian realism but of classical realism generally.

Hobbes and the Security Dilemma

Thomas Hobbes thinks we can gain a fundamental insight into political life if we imagine men and women living in a 'natural' condition prior to the invention and institution of the sovereign state. He refers to that pre-civil condition as the 'state of nature'. For Hobbes (1946: 82) the 'state of nature' is an extremely adverse human circumstance in which there is a permanent 'state of war' 'of every man against every man': in their natural condition every man, woman and child is endangered by everybody else, life is constantly at risk, and nobody can be confident about his or her security and survival for any reasonable length of time. People are living in constant fear of each other. Hobbes characterizes that pre-civil condition as shown in Box 3.4. It is obviously not only desirable but also extremely urgent to escape from those intolerable circumstances at the earliest moment if that is possible (see web link 3.06).

Hobbes believes that there is an escape route from the state of nature into a civilized human condition, and that is via the creation and maintenance of a sovereign state. The means of escape is by men and women turning their fear of each other into a joint collaboration with each other to form a security pact that can guarantee each other's safety. Men and women paradoxically cooperate politically because of their fear of being hurt or killed by their neighbours: they are 'civilized by fear of death' (Oakeshott 1975: 36). Their mutual fear and insecurity drives them away from their natural condition: the war of all against all. In other words, they are basically driven to institute a sovereign state not by their reason (intelligence) but, rather, by their passion (emotion). With the value of peace and order firmly in mind, they willingly and jointly collaborate to create a state with a sovereign government that possesses absolute authority and credible power to protect them from both internal disorders and foreign enemies and threats. In the civil condition—i.e. of peace and order—under the protection of the state men and women have an opportunity to flourish in relative safety: they no longer live under the constant threat of injury and death. Being

BOX 3.4	Hobbes on the state of nature

In such condition, there is no place for industry; because the fruit thereof is uncertain: and consequently no culture of the earth, no navigation, nor use of the commodities that may be imported by sea; no commodious building . . . no arts; no letters; no society, and which is worst of all, continual fear, and danger of violent death; and the life of man, solitary, poor, nasty, brutish, and short.

Hobbes (1946: 82)

secure and at peace, they are now free to prosper. As Hobbes puts it, they can pursue and enjoy 'felicity', i.e. happiness, well-being.

However, that statist solution to the problem of the natural condition of humankind automatically poses a serious political problem. The very act of instituting a sovereign state to escape from the fearful state of nature simultaneously creates another state of nature between states. That poses what is usually referred to as 'the security dilemma' in world politics: the achievement of personal security and domestic security through the creation of a state is necessarily accompanied by the condition of national and international insecurity that is rooted in the anarchy of the state system.

There is no escape from the international security dilemma in the way that there is an escape from the personal security dilemma, because there is no possibility of forming a global state or world government. Unlike individual men and women in the primary state of nature, sovereign states are not willing to give up their independence for the sake of any global security guarantee. That is because the international state of nature between states is not as threatening and dangerous as the original state of nature: it is easier for states to provide security than it is for individual men and women to do it on their own; states can mobilize the collective power of large numbers of people; states can arm themselves and defend themselves against foreign-security threats in a credible and continuous way. Individual men and women are vulnerable because they sometimes have to let their guard down: e.g. they have to sleep. But states never sleep: while some citizens sleep, other citizens are awake and on guard. If states do their job of protecting their own people, then the international state of nature can even be seen as a good thing because it gives particular groups of people freedom from other groups of people. In other words, international anarchy based on sovereign states is a system of freedom for groups. But the main point about the international state of nature is that it is a condition of actual or potential war; there can be no permanent or guaranteed peace between sovereign states. War is necessary, as a last resort, for resolving disputes between states that cannot agree and will not acquiesce.

According to Hobbes, states can also contract treaties with each other to provide a legal basis for their relations: international law can moderate the international state of nature by providing a framework of agreements and rules that are of advantage to all states. The classical realism of Hobbes thus emphasizes both military power and international law. But international law is created by states, and it will only be observed if it is in the security and survival interests of states to do that; otherwise it will be ignored. For Hobbes, as for

BOX 3.5	**Basic values of three classical realists**	
THUCYDIDES	**MACHIAVELLI**	**HOBBES**
• Political fate	• Political agility	• Political will
• Necessity and security	• Opportunity and security	• Security dilemma
• Political survival	• Political survival	• Political survival
• Safety	• Civic virtue	• Peace and felicity

Machiavelli and Thucydides, security and survival are values of fundamental importance. But the core value of Hobbesian realism is domestic peace—peace within the framework of the sovereign state—and the opportunity that only civil peace can provide for men and women to enjoy felicity. The state is organized and equipped for war in order to provide domestic peace for its subjects and citizens.

We can summarize the discussion thus far by briefly stating what these classical realists basically have in common. First, they agree that the human condition is a condition of insecurity and conflict which must be addressed and dealt with. Second, they agree that there is a body of political knowledge, or wisdom, to deal with the problem of security, and each of them tries to identify the keys to it. Finally, they agree that there is no final escape from this human condition, which is a permanent feature of human life. In other words, although there is a body of political wisdom—which can be identified and stated in the form of political maxims—there are no permanent or final solutions to the problems of politics—including international politics. This sober and somewhat pessimistic view is at the heart of the IR theory of the leading neoclassical realist of the twentieth century, Hans J. Morgenthau.

Morgenthau's Neoclassical Realism

According to Morgenthau (1965), men and women are by nature political animals: they are born to pursue power and to enjoy the fruits of power. Morgenthau speaks of the *animus dominandi*, the human 'lust' for power (Morgenthau 1965: 192). The craving for power dictates a search not only for relative advantage but also for a secure political space within which to maintain oneself and to enjoy oneself free from the political dictates of others. That is the security aspect of the *animus dominandi*. The ultimate political space within which security can be arranged and enjoyed is, of course, the independent state. Security beyond the state is impossible (see web links 3.07 and 3.08).

The human *animus dominandi* inevitably brings men and women into conflict with each other. That creates the condition of power politics which is at the heart not only of Morgenthau's realism but of all classical and neoclassical realist conceptions of international relations. 'Politics is a struggle for power over men, and whatever its ultimate aim may be, power is its immediate goal and the modes of acquiring, maintaining, and demonstrating it determine the technique of political action' (Morgenthau 1965: 195). Here Morgenthau is clearly echoing Machiavelli and Hobbes. If people desire to enjoy a political space free from the intervention or control of foreigners, they will have to mobilize their power and deploy their power for that purpose. That is, they will have to organize themselves into a capable and effective state by means of which they can defend their interests. The system of states leads to international anarchy and conflict.

The struggle between states in turn leads to the problem of justifying power in human relations. Here we arrive at the central normative doctrine of classical and neoclassical realism. Morgenthau follows in the tradition of Thucydides and Machiavelli: there is one morality for the private sphere and another and very different morality for the public sphere. Political ethics allows some actions that would not be tolerated by private morality. Morgenthau is critical of those theorists and practitioners, such as American President Woodrow Wilson, who believed that it was necessary for political ethics to be brought into line with private ethics. For example, in a famous address to the US Congress in 1917, President Wilson said he could discern 'the beginning of an age in which it will be insisted that the same standards of conduct and of responsibility for wrong shall be observed among nations and their governments that are observed among the individual citizens of civilized states' (Morgenthau 1965: 180).

Morgenthau considers that outlook to be not only ill advised but also irresponsible: it is not only mistaken intellectually but also fundamentally wrong morally. It is a gross intellectual mistake because it fails to appreciate the important difference between the public sphere of politics, on the one hand, and the private sphere or domestic life, on the other hand. According to classical realists, the difference is fundamental. As indicated, Machiavelli made that point by noting that if a ruler operated in accordance with Christian private ethics he or she would come to grief very quickly because political rivals could not be counted on to operate in the same Christian way. It would thus be an ill-advised and irresponsible foreign policy; and all the people who depended on the policy would suffer from the disaster it created.

Such a policy would be reckless in the extreme, and would thus constitute a moral failure because political leaders bear a very heavy responsibility for the security and welfare of their country and its people. They are not supposed to expose their people to unnecessary perils or hardships. Sometimes—for example, during crises or emergencies—it may be necessary to carry out foreign policies and engage in international activities that would clearly be wrong according to private morality: spying, lying, cheating, stealing, conspiring and so on are only a few of the many activities that would be considered at best dubious and at worst evil by the standards of private morality. Sometimes it may be necessary to trample on human rights for the sake of the national interest: during war, for example. Sometimes it may be necessary to sacrifice a lesser good for a greater good and to choose between evils: for realists that tragic situation is virtually a defining feature of international politics, especially during times of war. Here Morgenthau is reiterating an insight into the ethically compromised nature of statecraft

> ## BOX 3.7 President Nixon on the balance of power (1970)
>
> We must remember the only time in the history of the world that we have had any extended periods of peace is when there has been balance of power. It is when one nation becomes infinitely more powerful in relation to its potential competitor that the danger of war arises. So I believe in a world in which the United States is powerful. I think it will be a safer world and a better world if we have a strong, healthy United States, Europe, Soviet Union, China, Japan, each balancing the other, not playing one against the other, an even balance.
>
> Quoted in Kissinger (1994: 705)

> ## BOX 3.8 President Nixon on the American national interest (1970)
>
> Our objective . . . is to support our interests over the long run with a sound foreign policy. The more that policy is based on a realistic assessment of our and others' interests, the more effective our role in the world can be. We are not involved in the world because we have commitments; we have commitments because we are involved. Our interests must shape our commitments, rather than the other way around.
>
> Quoted in Kissinger (1994: 711–12)

that was noted by the ancient Greek philosopher Plato (1974: 82, 121), who spoke of the 'noble lie': 'Our rulers will probably have to make considerable use of lies and deceit for the good of their subjects.'

For Morgenthau the heart of statecraft is thus the clear-headed knowledge that political ethics and private ethics are not the same, that the former cannot be and should not be reduced to the latter, and that the key to effective and responsible statecraft is to recognize this fact of power politics and to learn to make the best of it. That involves statecraft of the kind that Machiavelli advocated, as well as action in defence of the state and the national interest such as Hobbes recommended.

It also involves the distinctive political ethics associated with responsible statecraft. Responsible statesmen and stateswomen are not merely free, as sovereign rulers, to act in an expedient way. They must act in full knowledge that the mobilization and exercise of political power in foreign affairs inevitably involves moral dilemmas, morally tainted acts and sometimes evil actions. The awareness that political ends (e.g. defending the national interest during times of war) must sometimes justify morally questionable or morally tainted means (e.g. the targeting and bombing of cities) leads to situational ethics and the dictates of 'political wisdom': prudence, moderation, judgement, resolve, courage and so on. Those are the cardinal virtues of political ethics. They do not preclude evil actions. Instead, they underline the tragic dimension of international ethics: they recognize the inevitability of moral dilemmas in international politics: that evil actions must sometimes be taken to prevent a greater evil.

Morgenthau (1985: 4–17) encapsulates his IR theory in 'six principles of political realism'. As a conclusion to this section of the chapter we shall briefly reiterate them.

- Politics is rooted in a permanent and unchanging human nature which is basically self-centred, self-regarding and self-interested.

- Politics is 'an autonomous sphere of action' and cannot therefore be reduced to economics (as Marxist scholars are prone to do) or reduced to morals (as Kantian or liberal theorists are prone to do). State leaders should act in accordance with the dictates of political wisdom.

- Self-interest is a basic fact of the human condition: all people have an interest at a minimum in their own security and survival. Politics is the arena for the expression of those interests which are bound to come into conflict sooner or later. International politics is an arena of conflicting state interests. But interests are not fixed: the world is in flux and interests change over time and over space. Realism is a doctrine that responds to the fact of a changing political reality.

- The ethics of international relations is a political or situational ethics which is very different from private morality. A political leader does not have the same freedom to do the right thing that a private citizen has. That is because a political leader has far heavier responsibilities than a private citizen: the leader is *responsible to* the people (typically of his or her country) who depend on him or her; the leader is *responsible for* their security and welfare. The responsible state leader should strive not to do the best but, rather, to do the best that circumstances on that particular day permit. That circumscribed situation of political choice is the normative heart of realist ethics.

- Realists are therefore opposed to the idea that particular nations—even great democratic nations such as the United States—can impose their ideologies on other nations and can employ their power in crusades to do that. Realists oppose that because they see it as a dangerous activity that threatens international peace and security. Ultimately, it could backfire and threaten the crusading country.

- Statecraft is a sober and uninspiring activity that involves a profound awareness of human limitations and human imperfections. That pessimistic knowledge of human beings as they are and not as we might wish them to be is a difficult truth that lies at the heart of international politics.

BOX 3.9	Morgenthau's concept of neoclassical realist statecraft	
HUMAN NATURE (basic condition)	**POLITICAL SITUATION** (means and context)	**POLITICAL CONDUCT** (goals and values)
• *Animus dominandi*	• *Power politics*	• *Political ethics (prudence, etc.)*
• *Self-interest*	• *Political power*	• *Human necessities (security, etc.)*
	• *Political circumstances*	• *National interest*
	• *Political skills*	• *Balance of power*

Schelling and Strategic Realism

Classical and neoclassical realists—including Thucydides, Machiavelli, Hobbes and Morgenthau—provide a normative analysis as well as an empirical analysis of IR. Power is understood to be not only a fact of political life but also a matter of political responsibility. Indeed, power and responsibility are inseparable concepts. For example, the balance of power is not merely an empirical statement about the way that world politics are alleged to operate. The balance of power is also a basic value: it is a legitimate goal and a guide to responsible statecraft on the part of the leaders of the great powers. In other words, for classical realists the balance of power is a desirable institution and a good thing to strive for because it prevents hegemonic world domination by any one great power. It upholds the basic values of international peace and security.

Since the 1950s and 1960s new realist approaches have emerged which are a product of the behaviouralist revolution and the quest for a positivist social science of IR. Many contemporary realists seek to provide an empirical analysis of world politics. But they hold back from providing a normative analysis of world politics because that is deemed to be subjective and thus unscientific. That attitude to the study of values in world politics marks a fundamental divide between classical and neoclassical realists on the one hand and contemporary strategic realists and neorealists on the other. In this section we shall examine strategic realism which is exemplified by the thought of Thomas Schelling (1980; 1996). Schelling does not pay much attention to the normative aspects of realism, although he does notice their presence in the background. In the next section we shall turn to neorealism which is associated most closely with Kenneth Waltz (1979). Waltz tends to ignore the normative aspects of realism.

Strategic realism focuses centrally on foreign policy decision-making. When state leaders confront basic diplomatic and military issues they are obliged to think strategically—i.e. instrumentally—if they hope to be successful. Schelling (1980; 1996) seeks to provide analytical tools for strategic thought. He views diplomacy and foreign policy, especially that of the great powers and particularly the United States, as a rational-instrumental activity that can be more deeply understood by the application of a form of logical analysis called 'game theory' (see web links 3.09 and 3.10). He summarizes his thought as shown in Box 3.10.

A central concept that Schelling employs is that of a 'threat': his analysis concerns how statespeople can deal rationally with the threat and dangers of nuclear war. For example, writing about nuclear deterrence Schelling (1980: 6–7) makes the important observation that

the efficacy of . . . [a nuclear] threat may depend on what alternatives are available to the potential enemy, who, if he is not to react like a trapped lion, must be left some tolerable recourse. We have come to realize that a threat of all-out retaliation . . . eliminates lesser courses of action and forces him to choose between extremes . . . [and] may induce him to strike first.

BOX 3.10	Schelling on diplomacy

Diplomacy is bargaining: it seeks outcomes that, though not ideal for either party, are better for both than some of the alternatives . . . The bargaining can be polite or rude, entail threats as well as offers, assume a status quo or ignore all rights and privileges, and assume mistrust rather than trust. But . . . there must be some common interest, if only in the avoidance of mutual damage, and an awareness of the need to make the other party prefer an outcome acceptable to oneself. With enough military force a country may not need to bargain.

Schelling (1980: 168)

This is a good example of strategic realism which basically concerns how to employ power intelligently in order to get our military adversary to do what we desire and, more importantly, to avoid doing what we fear. The statement from President Kennedy in 1963 (Box 3.11) gives an example of the need for bargaining between strongly armed nuclear powers.

For Schelling the activity of foreign policy is technically instrumental and thus free from moral choice. It is not primarily concerned about what is good or what is right. It is primarily concerned with the question: what is required for our policy to be successful? These questions are clearly similar to those posed above by Machiavelli. Schelling (1980) identifies and dissects with sharp insight various mechanisms, stratagems and moves which, if followed by the principal actors, could generate collaboration and avoid disaster in a conflict-ridden world of nuclear-armed states. But Schelling does not base his instrumental analysis on an underlying political or civic ethics the way that Machiavelli does. The normative values at stake in foreign policy are largely taken for granted. That marks an important divide between classical and neoclassical realism, on the one hand, and contemporary strategic realism and neorealism, on the other.

One of the crucial instruments of foreign policy for a great power, like the United States, is that of armed force. And one of the characteristic concerns of strategic realism is the use of armed force in foreign policy. Schelling devotes considerable thought to this issue. He observes (1996: 169–70) that there is an important distinction between brute force and coercion: 'between taking what you want and making someone give it to you'. He goes on to notice that 'brute force succeeds when it is used, whereas the power to hurt is most successful when held in reserve. It is the threat of damage . . . that can make someone yield or comply.' He adds that to make the use of our coercive apparatus effective 'we need to know what an adversary treasures and what scares him[sic]', and we also need to communicate clearly to him 'what will cause the violence to be inflicted [on him] and what will cause it to be withheld'.

Schelling goes on to make a fundamentally realist point: for coercion to be effective as a foreign policy 'requires that our interests and our opponent's [interests] are not absolutely opposed . . . coercion requires finding a bargain'. Coercion is a method of bringing an adversary into a bargaining relationship and getting the adversary to do what we want him or her to

BOX 3.11	**President Kennedy on US/Soviet relations (1963)**

Among the many traits the people of [the United States and the Soviet Union] have in common, none is stronger than our mutual abhorrence of war. Almost unique among the major world powers, we have never been at war with each other . . .

Today, should total war ever break out again—no matter how—our two countries would become the primary targets. It is an ironical but accurate fact that the two strongest powers are the two in most danger of devastation . . . We are both caught up in a vicious and dangerous cycle in which suspicion on one side breeds suspicion on the other and new weapons beget counter weapons.

In short, both the United States and its allies, and the Soviet Union and its allies, have a mutually deep interest in a just and genuine peace and in halting the arms race . . .

So let us not be blind to our differences, but let us also direct attention to our common interests and to the means by which those differences can be resolved. And If we cannot end now our differences, at least we can help make the world safe for diversity.

Quoted in Kegley and Wittkopf (1991: 56)

BOX 3.12	**Schelling on diplomacy and violence**

The power to hurt is nothing new in warfare, but . . . modern technology . . . enhances the importance of war and threats of war as techniques of influence, not of destruction; of coercion and deterrence, not of conquest and defense; of bargaining and intimidation . . . War no longer looks like just a contest of strength. War and the brink of war are more a contest of nerve and risk-taking, of pain and endurance . . . The threat of war has always been somewhere underneath international diplomacy . . . Military strategy can no longer be thought of . . . as the science of military victory. It is now equally, if not more, the art of coercion, of intimidation and deterrence . . . Military strategy . . . has become the diplomacy of violence.

Schelling (1996: 168, 182)

do without having to compel it—i.e. the use of brute force, which is usually far more difficult, far less efficient and far more dangerous (see web links 3.11 and 3.12). Schelling (1996: 181) summarizes his analysis of the modern diplomacy of violence in Box 3.12.

There obviously are striking similarities between the realism of Machiavelli and that of Schelling. However, unlike Machiavelli the strategic realism of Schelling (1980) usually does not probe the ethics of foreign policy; it merely presupposes basic foreign goals without comment. The normative aspects of foreign policy and the justifications of intelligent strategy in a dangerous world of nuclear-armed superpowers are intimated by his argument but largely hidden beneath the surface of his text. Schelling speaks quite readily of the 'dirty' and 'extortionate' heart of strategic realism. But he does not inquire why that kind of diplomacy could be called 'dirty' or 'extortionate', and he does not say whether that can be justified. Schelling's realism is fundamentally different from Machiavelli's realism in that important respect.

BOX 3.13	Realist statecraft: instrumental realism and strategic realism	
	MACHIAVELLI'S RENAISSANCE STATECRAFT	**SCHELLING'S NUCLEAR STATECRAFT**
Mode	Instrumental realism	Strategic realism
Means	Strength and cunning	Intelligence, nerve and risk-taking
	Opportunism and luck	Logic and art of coercion
Goals	Security and survival	Security and survival
Values	Civic virtue	Value-neutral; non-prescriptive

Strategic realism thus presupposes values and carries normative implications. Unlike classical realism, however, it does not examine them or explore them. For example, Schelling (1980: 4) is well aware that rational behaviour is motivated not only by a conscious calculation of advantages but also by 'an explicit and internally consistent value system'. But the role of value systems is not explicitly investigated by Schelling beyond making it clear that behaviour is related to values, such as vital national interests. The character and *modus operandi* of the specific values involved in nuclear strategy—threats, mutual distrust, promises, reprisals and so forth—are not investigated. Values are taken as given and treated instrumentally. In other words, the fundamental point of behaving the way that Schelling suggests foreign policymakers *ought* to behave is not explored, clarified or even addressed. He provides a strategic analysis but not a normative theory of IR. That is a characteristic of much contemporary realism in IR.

Here we come to a fundamental difference between classical or neoclassical realism and contemporary realism. Here is where Schelling differs fundamentally from Machiavelli. For Machiavelli, the point was the survival and flourishing of the nation. It was the responsibility of state leaders to achieve that desirable political condition which required civic (i.e. political) virtue on their part. Classical realists are conscious of the basic values at stake in world politics and they are explicitly concerned about them: they provide a political and ethical theory of IR. Contemporary realists are mostly silent about them and seem to take them more or less for granted without commenting on them or building them into their realist IR theories. They limit their analyses to political structures and processes and they largely ignore political ends. That is evident from a brief analysis of contemporary neorealism.

Waltz and Neorealism

The leading contemporary neorealist thinker is undoubtedly Kenneth Waltz (1979). He takes some elements of classical and neoclassical realism as a starting-point—e.g. independent states existing and operating in a system of international anarchy. But he departs from that

BOX 3.14	Waltz's neorealist theory: structure and outcomes

INTERNATIONAL STRUCTURE	**INTERNATIONAL OUTCOMES**
(state units and relations)	*(effects of state competition)*
International anarchy	Balance of power
States as 'like units'	International recurrence and repetition
Unequal state capability	International conflict, war
Great power relations	International change

BOX 3.15	Waltz on the importance of structure

The ruler's, and later the state's, interest provides the spring of action; the necessities of policy arise from the un-regulated competition of states; calculation based on these necessities can discover the policies that will best serve the state's interests; success is the ultimate test of policy, and success is defined as preserving and strengthening the state ... structural constraints explain why the methods are repeatedly used despite differences in the persons and states who use them.

Waltz (1979: 117)

tradition by ignoring its normative concerns and by trying to provide a scientific IR theory (see web link 3.14). Unlike Morgenthau (1985), he gives no account of human nature and he ignores the ethics of statecraft. Waltz's *Theory of International Politics* (1979) seeks to provide a scientific explanation of the international political system. His explanatory approach is heavily influenced by positivist models of economics. A scientific theory of IR leads us to expect states to behave in certain predictable ways. In Waltz's view the best IR theory is a neorealist systems theory that focuses centrally on the structure of the system, on its interacting units, and on the continuities and changes of the system. In classical realism, state leaders and their subjective valuations of international relations are at the centre of attention. In neorealism, by contrast, the structure of the system, in particular the relative distribution of power, is the central analytical focus. Actors are less important because structures compel them to act in certain ways. Structures more or less determine actions.

According to Waltz's neorealist theory, a basic feature of international relations is the decentralized structure of anarchy between states. States are alike in all basic functional respects—i.e. in spite of their different cultures or ideologies or constitutions or personnel, they all perform the same basic tasks. All states have to collect taxes, conduct foreign policy and so on. States differ significantly only in regard to their greatly varying capabilities. In Waltz's own words, the state units of an international system are 'distinguished primarily by their greater or lesser capabilities for performing similar tasks . . . the structure of a system

BOX 3.16   John Gaddis' portrait of the long bipolar peace during the Cold War

1. The postwar bipolar system realistically reflected the facts of where military power resided at the end of World War II . . .

2. The post-1945 bipolar structure was a simple one that did not require sophisticated leadership to maintain it . . .

3. Because of its relatively simple structure, alliances in this bipolar system have tended to be more stable than they had been in the 19th century and in the 1919–1939 period. It is striking that the North Atlantic Treaty Organization has equalled in longevity the most durable of the pre-World War I alliances, that between Germany and Austria-Hungary; it has lasted almost twice as long as the Franco-Russian alliance, and certainly much longer than any of the tenuous alignments of the interwar period . . .

In short, without anyone's having designed it . . . the nations of the post-war era lucked into a system of international relations that because it has been based upon realities of power, has served the cause of order—if not justice—better than one might have expected.

Gaddis (1987: 221–2)

changes with changes in the distribution of capabilities across the system's units' (Waltz 1979: 97). In other words, international change occurs when great powers rise and fall and the balance of power shifts accordingly. A typical means of such change is great-power war.

As indicated, the states that are crucially important for determining changes in the structure of the international system are the great powers. A balance of power between states can be achieved, but war is always a possibility in an anarchical system. Waltz distinguishes between bipolar systems—such as existed during the Cold War between the United States and the Soviet Union—and multipolar systems—such as existed both before and after the Cold War. Waltz believes that bipolar systems are more stable and thus provide a better guarantee of peace and security than multipolar systems. 'With only two great powers, both can be expected to act to maintain the system' (Waltz 1979: 204). That is because in maintaining the system they are maintaining themselves. According to that view, the Cold War was a period of international stability and peace.

That hypothesis may be historically problematical insofar as the United States and the Soviet Union took joint (i.e. cooperative) actions in the early 1990s to terminate their international military rivalry and thus to bring the bipolar system and the Cold War to an end. In the course of that historical change the Soviet Union failed to survive and a number of smaller successor states emerged in its place, the most important of which is Russia. In the light of the ending of the Cold War, presumably, Waltzian neorealism will have to be revised to incorporate the historical possibility that two great powers may in certain circumstances terminate a bipolar system rather than perpetuate it without engaging in a war in which one of them is defeated. It is a matter of debate among IR scholars whether the United States defeated the Soviet Union in the Cold War or the Soviet government, particularly President Gorbachev, terminated it by withdrawing from the contest. Neorealists are inclined to take the first view.

As indicated, Waltz takes classical and neoclassical realism as a starting-point and develops some of its core ideas and assumptions. For example, he employs the concept of international anarchy and focuses exclusively on states. He also focuses on the central feature of anarchical state systems: power politics. He assumes that the fundamental concern of states is security and survival. He also assumes that the major problem of great-power conflict is war, and that the major task of international relations among the great powers is that of peace and security.

But Waltz departs from classical and neoclassical realism in some fundamental ways which make his approach different from that, say, of Morgenthau. There is no discussion of human nature, such as Morgenthau provides and even Schelling clearly assumes. The focus is on the structure of the system and not on the human beings who create the system or operate the system. State leaders are prisoners of the structure of the state system and its determinist logic which dictates what they must do in their conduct of foreign policy. There is no room in Waltz's theory for foreign policymaking that is independent of the structure of the system. Thus, in the above example, neorealists would view Gorbachev's policy of disengaging from the Cold War as dictated by the Soviet Union's 'defeat' at the hands of the United States. On that view, Gorbachev could not have initiated the policy for domestic reasons or for ideological reasons. Waltz's image of the role of state leaders in conducting foreign policy comes close to being a mechanical image in which their choices are shaped by the international structural constraints that they face, as emphasized in Box 3.15.

Unlike Schelling's strategic realism, Waltz's neorealist approach does not provide explicit policy guidance to state leaders as they confront the practical problems of world politics. That is presumably because they have little or no choice, owing to the confining international structure in which they must operate. Waltz (1979: 194–210) does address the question of 'the management of international affairs'. However, that discussion is far more about the structural constraints of foreign policy than it is about what Schelling clearly understands as the logic and art of foreign policy. Schelling operates with a notion of situated choice: the rational choice for the situation or circumstances in which leaders find themselves. The choice may be sharply confined by the circumstances but it is a choice nevertheless and it may be made intelligently or stupidly, skilfully or maladroitly, etc. The main point of Schelling's analysis is to reveal the logic and art of making rational foreign policy choices. Waltz's neorealism makes far less provision for statecraft and diplomacy than Schelling's strategic realism. Waltz's argument is at base a determinist theory in which structure dictates policy. This takes the classical realist idea of the importance of international structure in foreign policy to a point beyond classical or neoclassical realism, which always makes provision for the politics and ethics of statecraft (Morgenthau 1985).

However, just beneath the surface of Waltz's neorealist text, and occasionally on the surface, there is a recognition of the ethical dimension of international politics which is virtually identical to classical realist IR. The core concepts that Waltz employs have a normative aspect. For example, he operates with a concept of state sovereignty: 'To say that a state is sovereign means that it decides for itself how it will cope with its internal and external problems' (Waltz 1979: 96). Thus state sovereignty means being in a position to decide, a condition which is usually signified by the term 'independence': sovereign states are postulated as independent of other sovereign states. But what is independence? Waltz (1979: 88) says that each state is formally 'the equal of all the others. None is entitled to command; none is required to obey.' But to say that independence is an 'entitlement' is to take notice of a *norm* which is acknowledged: in this case the norm of 'equal' state sovereignty. Because to say that states are the formal or legal equals of each other is to make not only an empirical statement but also a normative statement. For Waltz, all states are equal only in a formal-legal sense; they are unequal, often profoundly so, in a substantive or material sense. But that means that a norm of state equality exists which all states without exception are expected to observe in their relations with each other regardless of their substantive inequalities of power. Waltz also assumes that states are worth fighting for. That, too, indicates that neorealism is imbued with normative values: those of state security and survival.

Waltz (1979: 113) operates, as well, with a concept of the national interest: 'each state plots the course it thinks will best serve its interests'. For classical realists the national interest is the basic guide of responsible foreign policy: it is a moral idea that must be defended and promoted by state leaders. For Waltz, however, the national interest seems to operate like an automatic signal commanding state leaders when and where to move. The difference here is: Morgenthau believes that state leaders are duty bound to conduct their foreign policies by reference to the guidelines laid down by the national interest, and they may be condemned for failing to do that. Waltz's neorealist theory hypothesizes that they will always do that more or less automatically. Morgenthau thus sees states as organizations guided by leaders whose foreign policies are successful or unsuccessful, depending on the astuteness and wisdom of their decisions. Waltz sees states as structures that respond to the impersonal constraints and dictates of the international system.

Similarly, Waltz (1979: 195) argues that the great powers manage the international system. Classical and neoclassical realists argue that they ought to manage that system and that they can be criticized when they fail to manage it properly—i.e. when they fail to maintain international order. The notion that the Great Powers must be Great Responsibles is not only a traditional realist idea; it is also a core idea of the International Society tradition (see Chapter 5). Great powers are understood by Waltz to have 'a big stake in their system' and for them management of the system is not only something that is possible but also something that is 'worthwhile'. It is perfectly clear that Waltz values international order. It is clear, too, that he is convinced that international order is more likely to be achieved in bipolar systems than in multipolar systems. That discloses his normative values. The difference between neorealism and classical and neoclassical realism in this regard is that Waltz takes it as a given that that will happen, whereas Morgenthau and classical realists take it as an important norm for judging the foreign policy of the great powers.

A distinctive characteristic of neorealism emerges at this point. Waltz wants to present a scientific *explanation* of international politics; but he cannot avoid employing what are inherently normative concepts, and he cannot avoid making what are implicitly normative assumptions and indeed resting his entire case on normative foundations of a traditional realist kind. Thus, although he makes no explicit reference to values or ethics and avoids normative theory, the basic assumptions and concepts he uses and the basic international issues he is concerned with are normative ones. In that respect his neorealism is not as far removed from classical or neoclassical realism as his claims about scientific theory imply. This demonstrates how attempts at scientific explanation can frequently rest on unidentified norms and values (see Chapter 9).

Neorealist Stability Theory

Both strategic realism (Schelling 1980; 1996) and neorealism (Waltz 1979) were intimately connected with the Cold War. They were distinctive IR theory responses to that special, if not unique, historical situation. Being strongly influenced by the behaviouralist revolution in IR (see Chapters 2 and 8) they both sought to apply scientific methods to the theoretical and practical problems posed by the conflict between the United States and the Soviet Union. Schelling tried to show how a notion of strategy based on game theory could shed light on the nuclear rivalry between the two superpowers. Waltz tried to show how a structural analysis could shed light on 'the long peace' (Gaddis 1987) that was produced by the rivalry between the United States and the Soviet Union during the Cold War (see web link 3.15). The end of the Cold War thus raises an important question about the future of realist theories that were developed during what could be regarded as an exceptional period of modern international history. In this section we shall address that question in connection with neorealism.

In a widely discussed essay John Mearsheimer (1993) takes up the neorealist argument of Waltz (1979) and applies it to both the past and the future. He says that neorealism has continued relevance for explaining international relations: neorealism is a general theory that applies to other historical situations besides that of the Cold War. He also argues that neorealism can be employed to predict the course of international history beyond the Cold War.

Mearsheimer builds on Waltz's (1979: 161–93) argument (outlined in the previous section) concerning the stability of bipolar systems as compared with multipolar systems (see web link 3.18). These two configurations are considered to be the main structural arrangements of power that are possible among independent states. As indicated, Waltz claims that bipolar systems are superior to multipolar systems because they provide greater international stability and thus greater peace and security. There are three basic reasons why bipolar systems are more stable and peaceful. First, the number of great-power conflicts is fewer, and that reduces the possibilities of great-power war. Second, it is easier to operate an effective system of deterrence because fewer great powers are involved. Finally, because only two powers dominate the system the chances of miscalculation and misadventure are lower. There are fewer fingers on the trigger. In short, the two rival superpowers can keep their eye steadily fixed on each other without the distraction and confusion that would occur if there were a larger number of great powers, as was the case prior to 1945 and arguably has been the case since 1990 (Mearsheimer 1993: 149–50).

The question Mearsheimer (1993: 141) poses is: what would happen if the bipolar system were replaced by a multipolar system? How would that basic system change affect the chances for peace and the dangers of war in post-Cold War Europe? The answer Mearsheimer (p. 142) gives is as follows:

the prospects for major crises and war in Europe are likely to increase markedly if . . . this scenario unfolds. The next decades in a Europe without the superpowers would probably not be as violent as the first 45 years of this century, but would probably be substantially more prone to violence than the past 45 years.

What is the basis for that pessimistic conclusion? Mearsheimer (pp. 142–3) argues that the distribution and nature of military power are the main sources of war and peace and says, specifically, that 'the long peace' between 1945 and 1990 was a result of three fundamentally important conditions: the bipolar system of military power in Europe; the approximate military equality between the United States and the Soviet Union; and the reality that both of the rival superpowers were equipped with an imposing arsenal of nuclear weapons. The withdrawal of the superpowers from the European heartland would give rise to a multipolar system consisting of five major powers (Germany, France, Britain, Russia and perhaps Italy) as well as a number of minor powers. That system would be 'prone to instability'. 'The departure of the superpowers would also remove the large nuclear arsenals they now maintain in Central Europe. This would remove the pacifying effect that these weapons have had on European politics' (Mearsheimer 1993: 143).

Thus, according to Mearsheimer (p. 187), the Cold War between the United States and the Soviet Union 'was principally responsible for transforming a historically violent region into a very peaceful place'. Mearsheimer even argues that the demise of the bipolar Cold War order and the emergence of a multipolar Europe will produce a highly undesirable return to the bad old ways of European anarchy and instability and even a renewed danger of international conflict, crises and possibly war. He makes the following highly controversial point:

The West has an interest in maintaining peace in Europe. It therefore has an interest in maintaining the Cold War order, and hence has an interest in the continuation of the Cold War confrontation; developments that threaten to end it are dangerous.

By way of conclusion, we should notice some contemporary historical places where Mearsheimer's thesis seems to be confirmed by events, and other places where it seems to be refuted by them. His hypothesis seems to be confirmed by the outbreak of conflict and war in the former Yugoslavia (Croatia, Bosnia-Herzegovina and Kosovo in Serbia) and in the former Soviet Union (Azerbaijan, Armenia, Georgia, Moldova and Russia itself—in Chechnya).

It is worth pointing out, however, that these places are outside the Central European heartland where the neorealist thesis about the instability of the post-Cold War era is meant to apply most. In that part of Europe since the late 1950s something entirely different has been happening that may raise questions about Mearsheimer's neorealist hypothesis: the integration of the European nation-states into the European Union, the core of which consists of Germany and France, who have created a close partnership over the past several decades. The end of the Cold War has not put an end to that relationship; if anything, it made it more important. In other words, the European Union and particularly its

BOX 3.17	Mearsheimer's neorealist stability theory

CONDITIONS OF STABLE BIPOLARITY	CONDITIONS OF UNSTABLE MULTIPOLARITY
• Europe during the Cold War	• Europe before 1945 and after 1990
• Two superpowers	• Several great powers
• Rough superpower equality	• Unequal and shifting balances of power
• Nuclear deterrence	• Conventional military rivalry
• Conquest is difficult	• Conquest is less difficult and more tempting
• Superpower discipline	• Great power indiscipline and risk-taking

Franco-German core discloses a new international relationship between the major and minor powers of Europe that neorealism's thesis about bipolarism versus multipolarism faces some difficulties in comprehending.

Mearsheimer's arguments raise the important question of how realists should understand the post-Cold War era. There have been two major debates that offer insights into how realism looks upon international relations and particularly the relations of the great powers after the Cold War. The first debate was over the expansion of NATO to include East European countries, most of which were former members of the Soviet-dominated Warsaw Pact that ceased to exist after the end of the Cold War. The second debate concerned the paramount place of the United States in the international system and whether that would provoke a new balance of power by other states against American domination. These issues are discussed in the next two sections.

Realism after the Cold War: The Issue of NATO Expansion

In 1995, the North Atlantic Treaty Organization conducted a study on the pros and cons of NATO enlargement via expansion into Eastern Europe (http://www.nato.int/issues/enlargement/index.html). It concluded that the end of the Cold War provided a unique opportunity to improve security and stability for the entire Euro-Atlantic area and not merely Western Europe and North America. The study further concluded that enlargement would reinforce democratic reforms in Eastern Europe, not least by establishing 'civilian and democratic control over military forces', by fostering 'patterns and habits of cooperation, consultation and consensus-building relations' among newer and older members of the alliance, and by 'promoting good-neighbourly relations'. It would also increase 'transparency in defence planning and military budgets', thereby reinforcing confidence among states, and 'would reinforce the overall tendency toward closer integration and cooperation in Europe'. The study concluded that enlargement would strengthen the alliance's ability to contribute to European and international security and strengthen and broaden the transatlantic partnership.

From the time the alliance was created in 1949, NATO's membership has expanded from twelve founding members to twenty-six members in 2005. The twelve founders are Belgium, Canada, Denmark, France, Iceland, Italy, Luxembourg, the Netherlands, Norway, Portugal, the United Kingdom and the United States. The first round of enlargement took place in 1952 with the admission of Greece and Turkey, thereby extending NATO to South-eastern Europe. Three years later, in 1955, the Federal Republic of Germany became NATO's fifteenth member. Spain became the sixteenth member when it joined in 1982. None of that expansion was controversial, because it was seen to strengthen NATO in its effort to confront and contain the Soviet Union and the Soviet-organized Warsaw Pact (see web link 3.19).

The end of the Cold War saw new rounds of expansion into Eastern Europe. The Czech Republic, Hungary and Poland were invited to begin accession talks at the Alliance's Madrid Summit in 1997 and on 12 March 1999 they became the first former members of the Warsaw Pact to join NATO. Enlargement remains an on-going process, based upon Article 10 of the NATO Treaty, which declares that membership is open to any 'European State in a position to further the principles of this Treaty and to contribute to the security of the North Atlantic area'. In March 2004, seven more countries joined the alliance: Bulgaria, Estonia, Latvia, Lithuania, Romania, Slovakia and Slovenia. That was the largest round of enlargement in the alliance's history. According to NATO as of 2005 it 'may not be the last'. At that time, three more countries—Albania, Croatia and Macedonia—were being considered for membership, and were being assisted 'to meet NATO standards and prepare for possible future membership'. Unlike the earlier expansions noted above, the expansion of NATO into the former Soviet Union's sphere of influence and control in Eastern Europe has been controversial.

NATO expansion is a complicated and in some respects a highly technical subject—especially concerning the equipment and deployment of military forces (see web links 3.21 and 3.22). But the heart of the process involves questions of military strategy and ultimately questions of international politics at the highest level. Reduced to essentials, there have been two opposing arguments regarding NATO expansion into Eastern Europe. Both arguments disclose realist ideas and concerns. The controversy demonstrates there can be debates within realism—and by implication within every IR theory discussed in this book. Each argument can be summarized as follows (see web links 3.23 and 3.24).

Those who argue in favour of NATO expansion into Eastern Europe (Ball 1998: 52–67) claim that 'the prime objective' is greater regional security. They base their argument on the claim that it could deter Russia from entertaining or engaging in territorial revisionism to recover lost territories or to intimidate its neighbours. It could also promote stability and security in the region by providing reassurance not only to its new East European member states but also to other countries in the region that are not NATO members, for example Ukraine. If NATO expanded eastward, Russia would be obliged to take into account the strategic fact that any threat or use of force against its neighbours would provoke a response from the alliance. With NATO in the area Russia would have to stop and consider the consequences of any such threats or actions. It could not intimidate smaller and weaker neighbours such as the Baltic republics (Lithuania, Latvia, Estonia).

NATO expansion can provide greater security to all European states, provided that the proper balance among deterrence, reassurance, and diplomatic linkage is maintained. The single best argument for NATO expansion is that the next war is likely to arise out of the uncoordinated pursuit of security by the Central European states, not unprovoked hostile actions by Russia. The fears that Central European countries have about their future security are not unreasonable. Opponents of NATO expansion downplay or ignore the consequences of those fears. The key to the success of NATO expansion is conducting diplomacy that tempers all Central European states' foreign policy while reassuring them of their security.

Ball (1998: 67)

Proponents of NATO expansion claim that it will confer benefits on Russia too. For example, it would restrain Russia's East European neighbours—such as Poland—from taking advantage of any weakness of Russia, thereby provoking regional instability. In other words, it would place a positive West European control on East European states with a history of suspicion, fear and even enmity vis-à-vis Russia. It would also forestall East European states from searching for security outside the alliance. Such states would not have to fear for their security if they became members of NATO. They would not be tempted by nationalism or chauvinism which could provoke regional instability, nor would they be tempted to develop and equip their armed forces with nuclear weapons. They would not be tempted to form alliances among themselves that would complicate the task of building a regional security community, and they would not tempt a united Germany to play a more independent security role in the region. The risk of any East European state going it alone and becoming a problem for everybody else would be averted if NATO were in charge in the region. The risk of a regional arms race would be lowered if not eliminated, because NATO could ensure that weaponry was consistent with the overall defensive goals of the alliance.

The eastward expansion of NATO, proponents argue, would largely pre-empt any plans and actions by Russia to regard its security in Cold War terms: i.e. the mistake—as a senior US State Department official put it—of 'defining [Russia's] security at the expense of everyone else's' (Strobe Talbott, quoted by Ball 1998: 60). Instead, with NATO present there would be greater opportunities for cooperative as opposed to competitive security arrangements between Russia and the states to the west. Russian security unilateralism would decrease; consultation would increase. The possibilities of agreements between Russia and NATO to reduce the level of military forces in Eastern Europe would be very much greater in a climate of consultation and agreement than in one of rivalry and suspicion. In short, security in Eastern Europe and international order and stability beyond that region is likely to be worse—i.e. more uncertain, more provocative, more unpredictable, more combative, and ultimately more dangerous—if NATO does not expand.

Those who argue against NATO expansion raise several concerns which they believe are very serious. In June 1997 in an open letter to US President Clinton a group of fifty leading former US Senators, cabinet members in previous administrations, ambassadors, arms control experts and foreign-policy specialists registered their opposition to expansion in the following stark terms: 'the current US-led effort to expand NATO . . . is a policy error of historical importance' (McGwire 1998: 23, 42). They based their negative assessment on four fundamental arguments.

First, it would place in doubt 'the entire post-Cold War settlement' (McGwire 1998: 23). That is because it would threaten Russia. It would drastically undermine those Russian politicians and officials who were in favour of closer and more cooperative relations with the United States and who wanted to bring about democratic reforms in Russia that would align that nation's political system more closely with those of the West. Russia expressed grave concerns about the prospect of NATO eastward expansion. If its concerns were ignored, that would be a sign in Russian eyes that the West did not take Russia seriously and was contemptuous of its fundamental security interests. Further, expansion would undermine NATO's claim to be a purely defensive and peace-loving alliance. It would provoke the antagonism of many Russian politicians and embolden those who were opposed to negotiations with the United States to reduce nuclear and other strategic weapons. It would strengthen those Russian parties and politicians, including Communists, who were opposed to democratic reform. In short, NATO expansion into the former Soviet sphere of Eastern Europe might unite all those nationalist and xenophobic political forces in Russia who opposed closer collaboration between their country and the West, particularly the United States. There was a real and deeply worrying possibility that it would reopen the Cold War division between East and West.

Second, it would draw a new and deep line of division between those former Soviet satellite countries which had moved inside NATO (Poland, the Czech Republic, Slovakia, Hungary) and those which remained outside. It would reduce the security of those nations that were not included: they would be left to fend for themselves and perhaps to seek other security alliances. That would provoke greater instability rather than less.

Third, within NATO itself, expansion would reduce the alliance's credibility at the politically most fundamental point: its promise to defend without exception any member in the event of an attack. As the alliance expanded eastward, according to this argument, its capacity to defend its member states' security and independence would diminish, and maybe its political will to do that would diminish too—if that undertaking risked all-out war with Russia. A significant factor in this argument is that some of those would-be NATO member states are much nearer to Russia, some of them harbour strong historical resentments and animosities towards Russia, some of them have domestic Russian minority problems, and some of them have unstable and undeveloped systems of government. In other words, these states are in awkward locations, have unfortunate historical memories, and lack the political foundations to be solid and reliable members of the alliance. 'NATO could be entrapped by Central European [member] states' (Ball 1998: 49).

Finally, NATO expansion into areas of Europe that are inherently more unstable and more difficult to defend might put in jeopardy the United States' commitment to the alliance. That is because of the always latent and sometimes active strain of isolationism in American political culture. This could be a fatal weakening of the alliance, because the United States has always been and would have to continue to be the political and military key to NATO's

| **BOX 3.19** | **Against NATO expansion** |

Russian ultranationalist Vladimir Zhirinovsky said Saturday that Eastern Europe would become a battlefield in another world war if any of its countries try to join NATO: 'Our neighbors must know that if they let NATO soldiers approach Russia's borders, Russia would destroy both NATO and the territories that are putting the world on the brink of war,' Zhirinovsky said.

Many Russian leaders, including President Boris Yeltsin, have spoken out strongly against NATO's proposed eastward expansion, although none has gone so far as firebrand Zhirinovsky.

Associated Press, 11 February 1996

success as a defensive military organization. NATO expansion might very well encourage American isolationism, which would be a fatal blow to international peace and security.

What are the implications of this important historical debate for realism after the Cold War? It clearly reveals a fundamental point that is often obscured by IR scholars: that realists can have honest and open differences of opinion among themselves on important issues of foreign policy. Both arguments are basically realist in their values: they are both concerned with national security, regional stability, international peace and so on. They both employ instrumental language such as 'danger', 'risk', 'uncertainty', 'threat', 'capability', 'credibility', 'deterrence', 'fear', 'reassurance', 'confidence'. They both clearly understand international relations in strategic realist terms, in which the primary aim is to use foreign policy and military power to defend national interests and promote international order.

In that connection, realists who favour expansion and realists who oppose it both understand statecraft as an activity that involves the responsible use of power. They both operate within the same general realist ethics of statecraft. Their differences only emerge at this point. They are concerned with the same values and they both employ the same language, but they differ in their *judgements* of the proposed policy and their assessments of the circumstances in which it must be carried out. One side views expansion as promoting basic realist values and the other side views it as undermining the same values. Where those in favour see an opportunity in NATO expansion that must be seized, those against see a risk that must be avoided. So each side assesses opportunity and risk differently but both sides are fully alerted to risk and both are concerned about the fundamental values of security and stability.

In that regard, the debate on NATO expansion into Eastern Europe discloses the classical and neoclassical realist emphasis on responsible statecraft and political virtues such as prudence and judgement. Responsible statecraft and political virtue are moral concerns. To understand such concerns involves normative inquiry. That cannot be grasped by neorealism, which aims at scientific explanation that repudiates normative analysis, i.e. the study of values and norms. That brings to the surface one important advantage that classical and neoclassical realism has over neorealism in IR: its ability to engage in inquiry into foreign policy issues that involve basic questions of values: for example, given the fundamental importance of the value of security and stability in world politics, *should* NATO expand eastward or should it stay where it is? Because that is a normative question that involves political judgement, there can be honest differences on the part of both practitioners and observers and there can be no scientific or objective answer. The failure to address such value questions is a clear limitation of neorealism as an IR approach.

Hegemony and the Balance of Power

The end of the Cold War raised questions about the applicability of realism as an IR theory: was it now less relevant or more relevant than previously? Did the changed circumstances render other IR theories, such as liberalism, more applicable to the situation? Did they call for any revision to realist theory? Different responses to such questions are possible. That will depend in part on how theorists read the new situation. Is the international system becoming a more integrated world based on globalization and non-state actors, in which nation-states are less significant than in the past? That is a thesis characteristic of liberal IR theories. Is international relations becoming a more hegemonic world, owing to the disintegration of the Soviet Union and the emergence of the United States as the only remaining superpower (see web link 3.17)? That is a thesis characteristic of realist IR theories. Realist IR theories also raise the question of how US primacy in the post-Cold War international system relates to the balance of power. Does the United States operate to defend and maintain the balance of power, or does America operate to overcome the balance of power and establish its own supremacy in world politics?

There have been debates within realism on these questions, one of the main focuses of which has been the realist arguments of John J. Mearsheimer (2001). Like other realists, Mearsheimer argues that the state is the principal actor in international politics, and that states are of necessity preoccupied with the balance of power. Furthermore, the power in question is military force: realists give much attention to the use of force and to questions that involve the various political and military uses of armed force: deterrence, nuclear weapons, war, armed intervention and so forth. As indicated earlier in this chapter, that is the case with the realist theories of Hans J. Morgenthau, Thomas Schelling and Kenneth Waltz, among many others.

Mearsheimer differs from these realist thinkers in several ways. Unlike Morgenthau but like Waltz, he regards the behaviour of states as shaped if not indeed determined by the anarchical *structure* of international relations. Morgenthau sees that behaviour as dictated by human nature and the prudential ethics of statespeople seeking security and survival in an anarchical world. He differs from Waltz whom he characterizes as a 'defensive realist': i.e. someone who recognizes that states must and do seek power in order to be secure and to survive, but who believe that excessive power is counterproductive, because it provokes hostile alliances by other states. For Waltz, it does not make sense, therefore, to strive for excessive power beyond that which is necessary for security and survival. Mearsheimer speaks of Waltz's theory as 'defensive realism'.

Mearsheimer agrees with Waltz that anarchy compels states to compete for power. However, he argues that states seek hegemony, that they are ultimately more aggressive than Waltz portrays them as being. The goal for a country, such as the United States, is to dominate the entire system, because only in that way could it rest assured that no other state or combination of states would even think about going to war against the United States. In the Western hemisphere, for example, the United States has long been by far the most powerful state. No other state—Canada, Mexico, Brazil—would even think about threatening or employing armed force against the United States. All major powers strive for that ideal situation. But the planet is too big for global hegemony. The oceans are huge barriers. No state would have the necessary power. Mearsheimer therefore argues states can only become the hegemon in their own region of the world.

Regional hegemons can see to it, however, that there are no other regional hegemons in any other part of the world. They can prevent the emergence and existence of a peer competitor. According to Mearsheimer, that is what the United States is trying to ensure. That is because a peer competitor might try to interfere in a regional hegemon's sphere of influence and control. For almost two centuries, since the Monroe Doctrine of 1823, the United States endeavoured to ensure that no great power intervened militarily in the Western hemisphere. As a great power for the past half century and longer, America has made great efforts to ensure that there is no regional hegemon in either Europe or East Asia, the two areas where there are other major or great powers and a potential peer competitor could emerge: Germany in Europe and China in East Asia. The United States confronted Imperial Germany in the First World War, Nazi Germany in the Second World War, and the Soviet Union in the Cold War, because if any of those states had gained hegemony in Europe it would be free to intervene in the Western hemisphere, and possibly threaten the security of the United States.

According to Mearsheimer, all states want to become regional hegemons. He argues that Germany will become the dominant European state and that China will likely emerge as a potential hegemon in Asia. For example, his theory leads one to believe that China eventually will want to dominate East Asia. By the same theory, if that were to happen one would also expect the United States to react to try to prevent or undercut Chinese power in East Asia. Indeed, if China became a peer competitor America could be expected to go to great lengths to contain China's influence and prevent China from intervening in other regions of the world where American national interests are at stake. That is why he refers to his theory as 'offensive realism' which rests on the assumption that great powers 'are always searching for opportunities to gain power over their rivals, with hegemony as their final goal' (p. 29). Mearsheimer, like other realists, believes that his argument has general application to all places at all times. There will always be a struggle between nation-states for power and domination in the international system. There has always been conflict, there is conflict, and there always will be conflict over power. And there is nothing that anyone can do to prevent it. This is why the title of one of his books is *The Tragedy of Great Power Politics*.

Mearsheimer's theory of offensive realism has come in for criticism from many quarters. Some of those criticisms are levelled by liberal IR theorists. He debunks the liberal theory that democracies are less likely to wage war with each other. His theory of offensive realism has been criticized for failing to explain peaceful change and cooperation between great powers, such as that between Britain and the United States for the past century and longer. Critics also argue, for example, that it fails to explain the emergence of the European Union, which involves the pooling of sovereignty by states in an international community. However, we shall be concerned only with selected criticisms from within realism itself. At least one potential regional hegemon has been involved in the process of European unification: Germany. Mearsheimer would explain that by the military presence of the United States in Europe, which checks Germany's military expansion. But from within his own theory one could ask: why do American armed forces remain in Europe more than a decade after the disintegration of the Soviet Union and in the absence of any other great power trying to dominate the region?

A realist like Morgenthau would probably criticize Mearsheimer's argument for ignoring the responsibilities of statecraft, and for leaving the impression that states are conflicting power machines that behave without any human involvement as to their management or mismangement. There are no misadventures, misunderstandings or mistakes in the behaviour of great powers; there is only power, conflict, war, hegemony, subjugation and so on. That same criticism of a mechanistic model could be directed against Waltz's defensive theory. A related criticism is the theory's deficiency in empirical perceptiveness and subtlety. Mearsheimer sees no significant difference in the current and future power relationships between states in Western Europe as compared with those in East Asia. Here, it has been pointed out, 'he is at odds with that more famous realist, Henry Kissinger, who in his book, *Does America Need a Foreign Policy?*, convincingly argues that for the foreseeable future there is little or no likelihood of the nations of Western Europe going to war with each other or with the United States, but that war is much more possible among the nations of Asia or between America and Asian powers' (Francis Sempa http://www.unc.edu/depts/diplomat/). That leads to a more general criticism: the limitations and distortions that result when the usually complicated process of historical contingency and change is explained exclusively by means of a single factor theory: in this case 'offensive realism'. Mearsheimer's offensive realist theory has also been criticized for failing to look at historical experiences which are contrary to his thesis, or in other words for not being sufficiently open-minded and eclectic in seeking to explain relations between great powers and the balance of power. Eclecticism, however, means opening one's approach to the possibility of factors and forces not predicted by one's theory. Ultimately, eclecticism would also transform theory into history. That is not what neorealist theories are content with. Mearsheimer, like Waltz, wants to come up with explanations that satisfy the concept of a 'scientific' theory in accordance with philosophy of science criteria. How successful they have been in that regard is still being debated.

Two Critiques of Realism

The dominance of realism in IR during the second half of the twentieth century, especially in the United States, spawned a substantial literature that criticizes many of its core assumptions and arguments (see web link 3.25). As indicated in Chapter 2, realism itself rose to a position of academic pre-eminence in the 1940s and 1950s by effectively criticiz-ing the liberal idealism of the interwar period. Contemporary neorealism has been involved in a renewed debate with contemporary liberalism. We shall investigate that debate in Chapter 4. Here we shall confine our discussion to two important critiques of realism: an International Society critique and an emancipatory critique.

The International Society tradition (see Chapter 5) is critical of realism on two counts. First, it regards realism as a one-dimensional IR theory that is too narrowly focused. Second, it claims that realism fails to capture the extent to which international politics is a dialogue of different IR voices and perspectives. The International Society tradition is not critical of every aspect of realist thought in IR. On the contrary, International Society scholars acknowl-edge that classical and neoclassical realism provide an important angle of vision on world politics. They agree that there is a strain in human nature that is self-interested and combat-ive. They share a focus of analysis in which states loom large. They operate with a concep-tion of international relations as anarchical. They agree that power is important and that international relations consist significantly of power politics. They also agree that interna-tional theory is in some fundamental respects a theory of security and survival. They recog-nize that the national interest is an important value in world politics. In short, International Society scholars incorporate several elements of realism into their own approach.

However, they do not believe that realism captures all of IR or even its most important aspects. They argue that realism overlooks, ignores or plays down many important facets of international life. It overlooks the cooperative strain in human nature. It ignores the extent to which international relations form an anarchical *society* and not merely an anarchical sys-tem. States are not only in conflict, they also share common interests and observe common rules which confer mutual rights and duties. It ignores other important actors besides states, such as human beings and NGOs. Realism plays down the extent to which the relations of states are governed by international law. It also plays down the extent to which international politics are progressive, i.e. cooperation instead of conflict can prevail. International Society theorists recognize the importance of the national interest as a value, but they refuse to accept that it is the only value that is important in world politics.

Martin Wight (1991), a leading representative of the International Society approach, places a great deal of emphasis on the character of international politics as a historical dia-logue between three important philosophies/ideologies: realism (Machiavelli), rationalism (Grotius) and revolutionism (Kant). In order to acquire a holistic understanding of IR it is necessary, according to Martin Wight, to comprehend the dialectical relations of these three basic normative perspectives (see Chapter 5).

At least one leading neoclassical realist appears to agree with Martin Wight. In a monumental study of diplomacy, the American scholar and statesman Henry Kissinger (1994: 29–55) explores the long-standing and continuing dialogue in diplomatic theory and practice between the foreign-policy outlook of pessimistic realism and that of optimistic lib-eralism. For example, Kissinger discerns that dialogue in the contrasting foreign policies of US Republican President Theodore Roosevelt and Democratic President Woodrow Wilson in the early twentieth century. Roosevelt was 'a sophisticated analyst of the balance of power' while Wilson was 'the originator of the vision of a universal world organization, the League of Nations'. Both perspectives have shaped American foreign policy historically. That dialogue between realism and liberalism is not confined to past and present American foreign policy; it is also evident in British foreign policy historically. Kissinger contrasts the politically cautious and pragmatic nineteenth-century British foreign policy of Conservative Prime Minister Benjamin Disraeli and the morally aroused and interventionist foreign policy of his Liberal counterpart, William Gladstone. Kissinger implies that both these perspectives have a legitimate place in American foreign policy and in British foreign policy, and that neither of them should be ignored. Here, then, is an implied criticism of realism: that it is inclined to ignore or at least to downplay the liberal and democratic voice in world affairs.

We thus have reason to ask whether Kissinger should be classified as a realist at all? Is he a secret member of the International Society school? We believe the correct answer to the first question is 'yes' and to the latter question 'no'. Kissinger should be regarded as a neoclassical realist. Although he portrays the Wilsonian voice in American foreign policy and the Gladstonian voice in British foreign policy as legitimate and important, it is abundantly clear from his lengthy analysis that his preferred basis for any successful foreign policy for America and Britain is the realist outlook disclosed by Roosevelt and Disraeli, with whom Kissinger strongly identifies.

Neoclassical realists could thus reply to the critique as follows. International Society scholars can be criticized for failing to recognize that while the liberal voice is important in world politics the realist voice is always first in importance. That is because it is the best perspective on the core problem of IR: war. According to realists, difficult times, such as war, demand hard choices that realists are better able to clarify than any other IR scholars or practitioners. Liberals—according to classical/neoclassical realists—tend to operate on the assumption that foreign-policy choices are easier and less dangerous than they really may be: they are the foremost theorists of peaceful, prosperous and easy times. For realists the problem with that is: what shall we do when times are difficult? If we follow the liberals we may fail to respond adequately to the challenge with appropriate hard choices and we may thus place ourselves—and those who depend on our policies and actions—at risk. In other words, realism will always be resorted to during times of crisis when hard choices have to be made, and some criteria for making those choices are required.

An alternative and very different critique of realism is that of emancipatory theory. Because realism has been such a dominant IR theory, emancipatory theorists direct their energies at providing what they consider to be a root-and-branch critique of realist assumptions and arguments. That is intended to pave the way for a complete reconceptualization of IR. Their critique of realism is central to their project of global human emancipation. Emancipatory theorists argue that IR should seek to grasp correctly how men and women are prisoners of existing international structures. IR theorists should indicate how they can be liberated from the state and from other structures of contemporary world politics which have the effect of oppressing them and thus preventing them from flourishing as they otherwise would. A central aim of emancipatory theory, then, is the transformation of the realist state-centric and power-focused structure of international politics. The goal is human liberation and fulfilment. The role of the emancipatory IR theorist is to determine the correct theory for guiding the practice of human liberation.

An emancipatory critique of realism has been developed by Ken Booth (1991). Booth (pp. 313–26) builds his critique on a familiar realist view of the 'Westphalian system': i.e. it is 'a game' that is 'played by diplomats and soldiers on behalf of statesmen'. The 'security game' that states learned to play was 'power politics, with threats producing counterthreats, alliances, counteralliances and so on'. In IR that produced an 'intellectual hegemony of realism': a conservative or 'status quo' theory based on the security and survival of existing states, and focused on strategic thinking in which the concept of military (sometimes nuclear) threats was the core of realist thought. In other words, Booth is specifically criticizing strategic realism associated with thinkers such as Thomas Schelling (1980) discussed above.

Booth claims that the realist game of power politics and military (including nuclear) strategy is now obsolete because security is now a local problem within disorganized and sometimes failed states. It is no longer primarily a problem of national security and national defence. Security is now more than ever both cosmopolitan and local at the same time: a problem of individual humans (e.g. citizens in failed states) and of the global community of humankind (facing, for example, ecological threats or nuclear extinction). Security is different in scope; it is also different in character: emancipation is the freeing of people (as individuals and groups) from those physical and human constraints which stop them carrying out what they would freely choose to do. War and the threat of war is one of those constraints, together with poverty, poor education, political oppression and so on. Security and emancipation are two sides of the same coin. Emancipation, not power or order, produces true security (Booth 1991: 319).

Implicit in this argument is the Kantian 'categorical imperative': the moral idea 'that we should treat people as ends and not means. States, however, should be treated as means and not ends' (Booth 1991: 319). In other words, people always come first; states are merely tools that can be discarded if they are no longer useful.

In a similar vein Andrew Linklater (1989) disputes the realist view of IR and offers an alternative emancipatory perspective to take its place (Box 3.20). Both Booth and Linklater claim that world politics can be constructed along these universal solidarist lines, with IR

BOX 3.20   Linklater's emancipatory vision of global politics

A new framework for world politics, based on

1. the construction of a 'global legal and political system' which goes beyond the state and 'affords protection to all human subjects';

2. the decline of self-interest and competitiveness which, according to realist thinking, sustains the state and fosters international conflict and ultimately war;

3. the rise and spread of human generosity that transcends state boundaries and extends to people everywhere;

4. the consequent development of a community of humankind to which all people owe their primary loyalty.

Linklater (1989: 199)

theorists leading the way. Not only that: they also claim that this social movement away from the anarchical society based on states and power politics and towards a cosmopolitan idea of global human security is well under way. The consequence of that for IR is clear: realism is becoming obsolete as a theoretical apparatus for studying IR, and irrelevant as a practical attitude to world politics.

The realist response to such emancipatory critiques could be expected to include some of the following observations. Linklater's and Booth's declaration of the death of the independent state and thus of the anarchical state system, like the famous mistaken announcement of the death of Mark Twain, is premature. People across the world in their almost countless millions continue to cling to the state as their preferred form of political organization. We need only recall the powerful attraction of self-determination and political independence based on the state for the peoples of Asia, Africa and the Middle East during the demise of European colonialism and for the peoples of Eastern Europe during the demise of the Soviet empire. When states fragment—as in the case of Yugoslavia at the end of the Cold War—the fragments turn out to be new (or old) states—e.g. Slovenia, Croatia, Bosnia. In historical terms all these major movements towards the sovereign state occurred recently—i.e. in the latter half of the twentieth century. Security continues to be based primarily on the state and the state system. It is not based on a global political-legal organization: such an entity does not exist (at least not yet). Where security is based on other social organizations, such as the family or the clan, as sometimes happens in Africa and some other parts of the world, that is because the local state has failed as a security organization. The people are trying to make the best of a bad situation. Their own state has failed them, but that does not mean they have given up on the state. What they want is what the people of many other countries already have: a developed and democratic state of their own. What they do not want is a 'global legal and political system' such as Linklater describes: that would be scarcely distinguishable from Western colonialism which they have just escaped from.

It is also necessary to mark the continuing significance of the major states. Realists underline the centrality of great powers in world politics. Great-power relations shape the international relations and influence the foreign policies of most other states. That is why realists concentrate their attention on the great powers. There is little reason to doubt that the United States, China, Japan, Russia, Germany, France, Britain, India and a few other core states will continue to assert their leading roles in world politics. There also is little reason to doubt that the people of the world depend on those states, before all others, for maintaining international peace and security. There is nobody else to provide that fundamental service.

Research Prospects and Programme

Realism is a theory, first about the security problems of sovereign states in an international anarchy, and second about the problem of international order. The normative core of realism is state survival and national security. If world politics continues to be organized on the basis of independent states with a small group of powerful states largely responsible for shaping the most important international events, then it seems clear that realism will continue to be an important IR theory. The only historical development that could render it obsolete is a world historical transformation that involved abandoning the sovereign state and the anarchical state system. That does not appear very likely in the foreseeable future.

This chapter has discussed the various main strands of realism; a major distinction was made between classical (and neoclassical) realism on the one hand and contemporary strategic realism and neorealism on the other. Which strand of realism contains the most promising research programme? John Mearsheimer (1993) says that neorealism is a general theory that applies to other historical situations besides that of the Cold War. He argues that neorealism can be employed to predict the course of international history after the Cold War. We have noted that neorealism formulates a number of important questions about the distribution of power in the international system and the power-balancing of the leading powers. Yet we have also emphasized some limitations of neorealist theory, especially as regards the analysis of cooperation and integration in Western Europe after the end of the Cold War. Some neorealists think that these patterns of cooperation can be addressed without major difficulty through the further development of neorealist analysis (see e.g. Grieco 1997). On a more sceptical view, neorealism (and also strategic realism) appears closely tied to the special historical circumstances of the East/West conflict: (1) a bipolar system based on two rival superpowers (the United States and the Soviet Union) each implacably opposed to the other and prepared to risk nuclear war for the sake of its ideology; and (2) the development of nuclear weapons and the means to deliver them to any point on earth.

Since the end of the Cold War the Soviet Union has disappeared and the bipolar system has given way to one in which there are several major powers, but the United States arguably is now the only genuine superpower. Nuclear weapons remain in existence, of course. There is now a greater danger than before of the spread of nuclear weapons. In 1998 both India and Pakistan tested nuclear-weapon devices and in so doing turned the sub-continent of South Asia into an openly nuclear-weapons region. In 2002 they came to the brink of war which raised widespread anxiety about nuclear conflict and provoked the United States and some members of the European Union into concerted diplomatic efforts to defuse the situation. But none of the major powers that possess nuclear weapons—including Russia and China—gives any indication of wishing to restore the Cold War system of nuclear coercion.

We believe that leaves neoclassical realism with the most promising future research programme. We have tried to show how the debate on NATO expansion in Eastern Europe emphasized the need for discussing important questions of values when conducting inquiry into foreign policy issues. Neorealists are right in pointing to the risk of a new Cold War, but it is classical realism which is focused on analysing how the difficult choices made by state leaders may or may not bring about a new Cold War. In the debate on NATO expansion it is clearly evident that both realists in favour of expansion and realists against expansion were very concerned about this, and that they both wanted to avoid a second Cold War—even though they came to opposite conclusions about whether or not expansion would diminish or increase the risks of that happening. Their debate was a good example of the honest differences between neoclassical realists.

On this view, a future research programme for realism would build on the work of Hans Morgenthau rather than that of Schelling or Waltz or Mearsheimer, and would address important issues of the post-Cold War state system that the narrower focus of strategic realism and neorealism cannot so readily come to grips with. Among those issues are five key ones. (1) The emergence of the United States as an unrivalled great power following the demise of the Soviet Union, and the reduced significance of Russia in world politics. The role of the United States as a paramount power is somewhat comparable to Great Britain in the nineteenth century. At that time Britain refrained from engaging in wars of conquest in Europe and remained content with employing its political skill and military assets to maintain the balance of power. The United States at the dawn of the twenty-first century is even more benign than Britain was at that time: the US appears prepared to devote itself not only to defending its own national interest but also, albeit to a lesser extent, to being a responsible defender of international peace and security. (2) The return to a contemporary version of the Concert system of great powers in which the permanent members of the UN Security Council assume the main responsibility for safeguarding international peace and security under the leadership of the United States. (3) The threat posed by peripheral 'rogue states' such as Iraq which are prepared to threaten regional peace and security but are not in a position to threaten the global balance of power. (4) The problems posed by 'failed states' and the issue of great power responsibility for the protection of human rights in a world of states. (5) The security crisis presented by audacious acts of international terrorism, particularly the 11 September 2001 attacks on New York and Washington DC, which threaten the personal security of citizens more than either the national security of states or international peace and security.

A plausible research strategy for post-Cold War realism, therefore, would involve the attempt to understand the role of an unrivalled but also a benign paramount power in an international system which must face several fundamental problems: the protection of global peace and security, the coming to grips with 'rogue states' and 'failed states' on the periphery of the state system, and the protection of citizens, particularly those of Western countries, from international terrorism.

 KEY POINTS

- Realists usually have a pessimistic view of human nature. Realists are sceptical that there can be progress in international politics that is comparable to that in domestic political life. They operate with a core assumption that world politics consists of an international anarchy of sovereign states. Realists see international relations as basically conflictual, and they see international conflicts as ultimately resolved by war.

- Realists believe that the goal of power, the means of power and the uses of power are a central preoccupation of political activity. International politics is thus portrayed as 'power politics'. The conduct of foreign policy is an instrumental activity based on the intelligent calculation of one's power and one's interests as against the power and interests of rivals and competitors.

- Realists have a high regard for the values of national security, state survival, and international order and stability. They usually believe that there are no international obligations in the moral sense of the word—i.e. bonds of mutual duty—between independent states. For classical and neoclassical realists there is one morality for the private sphere and another and very different morality for the public sphere. Political ethics allows some actions that would not be tolerated by private morality.

- Realists place a great deal of importance on the balance of power, which is both an empirical concept concerning the way that world politics are seen to operate and a normative concept: it is a legitimate goal and a guide to responsible statecraft on the part of the leaders of the great powers. It upholds the basic values of peace and security.

- Many contemporary realists seek to provide an empirical analysis of world politics. But they hold back from providing a normative analysis of world politics because that is deemed to be subjective and thus unscientific. That attitude marks a fundamental divide between classical and neoclassical realists on the one hand and contemporary strategic realists and neorealists on the other.

- Schelling seeks to provide analytical tools for strategic thought. He views diplomacy and foreign policy, especially that of the great powers and particularly the United States, as a rational-instrumental activity that can be more deeply understood by the application of a form of mathematical analysis called 'game theory'. Coercion is a method of bringing an adversary into a bargaining relationship and getting the adversary to do what we want him or her to do without having to compel it—i.e. employ brute force which, in addition to being dangerous, is usually far more difficult and far less efficient.

- Neorealism is an attempt to explain international relations in scientific terms by reference to the unequal capabilities of states and the anarchical structure of the state system, and by focusing on the great powers whose relations determine the most important 'outcomes' of international politics. A scientific theory of IR leads us to expect states to behave in certain predictable ways. Waltz and Mearsheimer believe that bipolar systems are more stable and thus provide a better guarantee of peace and security than multipolar systems. According to that view, the Cold War was a period of international stability and peace.

- The International Society tradition is critical of realism on two counts. First, it regards realism as a one-dimensional IR theory that is too narrowly focused. Second, it claims that realism fails to capture the extent to which international politics is a dialogue of different IR voices and perspectives. Emancipatory theory claims that power politics is obsolete because security is now a local problem within disorganized and sometimes failed states, and at the same time is a cosmopolitan problem of people everywhere regardless of their citizenship. It is no longer exclusively or even primarily a problem of national security and national defence.

QUESTIONS

- Realists are pessimistic about human progress and cooperation beyond the boundaries of the nation-state. What are the reasons given for that pessimism? Are they good reasons?

- Why do realists place so much emphasis on security? Does that make sense? How important is security in world politics?
- Identify the major differences between the neoclassical realism of Hans Morgenthau and the neorealism of Kenneth Waltz. Which approach is best suited for analysing international relations after the Cold War?
- Outline the main arguments for and against NATO expansion. State your own position including supporting arguments.
- What is the emancipatory critique of realism? Does it make sense?

GUIDE TO FURTHER READING

Kennan, G. (1954). *Realities of American Foreign Policy*. Princeton: Princeton University Press.

Machiavelli, N. (1984). *The Prince*, trans. P. Bondanella and M. Musa. New York: Oxford University Press.

Mearsheimer, J. (2001) *The Tragedy of Great Power Politics*. New York: W.W. Norton.

Morgenthau, H. (1985). *Politics among Nations: The Struggle for Power and Peace*, 6th edn. New York: Knopf.

Schelling, T. (1980). *The Strategy of Conflict*. Cambridge, Mass.: Harvard University Press.

Waltz, K. (1979). *Theory of International Politics*. New York: McGraw-Hill.

WEB LINKS

Web links mentioned in the chapter plus additional links can be found on the Online Resource that accompanies this book.

www.oxfordtextbooks.co.uk/orc/jackson_sorensen3e/

CHAPTER 4

Liberalism

▌ Summary

This chapter sets forth the liberal tradition in IR. Basic liberal assumptions are: (1) a positive view of human nature; (2) a conviction that international relations can be cooperative rather than conflictual; and (3) a belief in progress. In their conceptions of international cooperation liberal theorists emphasize different features of world politics. Sociological liberals highlight transnational non-governmental ties between societies, such as communication between individuals and between groups. Interdependence liberals pay particular attention to economic ties of mutual exchange and mutual dependence between peoples and governments. Institutional liberals underscore the importance of organized cooperation between states; finally, republican liberals argue that liberal democratic constitutions and forms of government are of vital importance for inducing peaceful and cooperative relations between states. The chapter discusses these four strands of liberal thought and a debate with neorealism to which it has given rise. The concluding section evaluates the prospects for the liberal tradition as a research programme in IR.

Introduction: Basic Liberal Assumptions

Why read a chapter on the liberal tradition in IR? The short answer is that you need to know the liberal tradition to form your own opinion about one of the most keenly debated issues in IR: the pessimistic view of realism versus the optimistic view of liberalism. The previous chapter introduced the realist tradition, with its focus on power and conflict. This chapter is about the sharply contrasting liberal view. How can liberals be optimistic? Why do they see a more peaceful world down the road? What are their arguments and beliefs?

The liberal tradition in IR is closely connected with the emergence of the modern liberal state. Liberal philosophers, beginning with John Locke in the seventeenth century, saw great potential for human progress in modern civil society and capitalist economy, both of which could flourish in states which guaranteed individual liberty. Modernity projects a new and better life, free of authoritarian government and with a much higher level of material welfare.

The process of modernization unleashed by the scientific revolution led to improved technologies and thus more efficient ways of producing goods and mastering nature. That was reinforced by the liberal intellectual revolution which had great faith in human reason and rationality. Here is the basis for the liberal belief in progress: the modern liberal state invokes a political and economic system that will bring, in Jeremy Bentham's famous phrase, 'the greatest happiness of the greatest number' (see web link 4.03).

Liberals generally take a positive view of human nature. They have great faith in human reason and they are convinced that rational principles can be applied to international affairs. Liberals recognize that individuals are self-interested and competitive up to a point. But they also believe that individuals share many interests and can thus engage in collaborative and cooperative social action, domestically as well as internationally, which results in greater benefits for everybody at home and abroad. In other words, conflict and war are not inevitable; when people employ their reason they can achieve mutually beneficial cooperation not only

BOX 4.1	Modernization

Between 1780 and 1850, in less than three generations, a far- reaching revolution, without precedent in the history of Mankind, changed the face of England. From then on, the world was no longer the same. The Industrial Revolution transformed Man from a farmer-shepherd into a manipulator of machines worked by inanimate energy . . . [It] opened up a completely different world of new and untapped sources of energy such as coal, oil, electricity and the atom. From a narrow technological point of view, the Industrial Revolution can be defined as the process by which a society gained control of vast sources of inanimate energy; but such a definition does not do justice to this phenomenon . . . as regards its economic, cultural, social and political implications.

Cipolla (1977: 7–8)

within states but also across international boundaries. Liberal theorists thus believe that human reason can triumph over human fear and the lust for power. But they disagree about the magnitude of the obstacles on the way to human progress (Smith 1992: 204). For some liberals it is a long-term process with many setbacks; for others, success is just around the corner. However, all liberals agree that in the long run cooperation based on mutual interests will prevail. That is because modernization constantly increases the scope and the need for cooperation (Zacher and Matthew 1995: 119).

The belief in progress is a core liberal assumption. But it is also a point of debate among liberals (see Pollard 1971: 9–13). How much progress? Scientific and technological for sure, but also social and political? What are the limits of progress? Are there any limits? Progress for whom? A small number of liberal countries or the entire world? The scope and degree of liberal optimism as regards progress has fluctuated over time. Many early liberals were inclined to be thoroughly optimistic; we have also noted the surge of utopian liberalism around the First World War. After the Second World War, however, liberal optimism became more muted. Robert Keohane, for example, cautiously notes that liberals at a minimum believe 'in at least the possibility of cumulative progress' (Keohane 1989a: 174). Yet there was another surge of liberal optimism after the end of the Cold War, propelled by the notion of 'the end of history' based on the defeat of communism and the expected universal victory of liberal democracy (Fukuyama 1989; 1992). However, the terrorist attacks in New York and Washington of 11 September 2001, followed by the attacks in Madrid, London and elsewhere, are a setback for liberal optimism.

Progress for liberals is always progress for individuals. The core concern of liberalism is the happiness and contentment of individual human beings. John Locke (see web link 4.05) argued that states existed to underwrite the liberty of their citizens and thus enable them to live their lives and pursue their happiness without undue interference from other people. In contrast to realists, who see the state first and foremost as a concentration and instrument of power, a *Machtstaat*, liberals see the state as a constitutional entity, a *Rechtsstaat*, which establishes and enforces the rule of law that respects the rights of citizens to life, liberty and property. Such constitutional states would also respect each other and would deal with each other in accordance with norms of mutual toleration. That argument was enlarged by Jeremy Bentham—an eighteenth-century English philosopher—who coined the term 'international law'. He believed that it was in the rational interests of constitutional states to adhere to international law in their foreign policies (Rosenblum 1978: 101). The argument was further expanded by Immanuel Kant, an eighteenth-century German philosopher. He thought that a world of such constitutional and mutually respectful states—he called them 'republics'—could eventually establish 'perpetual peace' in the world (Gallie 1978: 8–36). Box 4.2 summarizes the focus of leading classical liberal thinkers.

In summary, liberal thinking is closely connected with the emergence of the modern constitutional state. Liberals argue that modernization is a process involving progress in most areas of life. The process of modernization enlarges the scope for cooperation across international boundaries. Progress means a better life for at least the majority of individuals. Humans possess reason, and when they apply it to international affairs greater cooperation will be the end result.

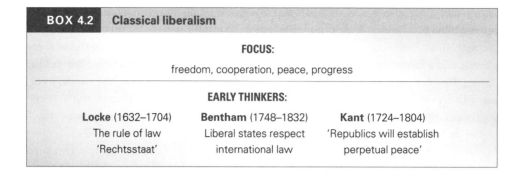

BOX 4.2   **Classical liberalism**

FOCUS:

freedom, cooperation, peace, progress

EARLY THINKERS:

Locke (1632–1704)	**Bentham** (1748–1832)	**Kant** (1724–1804)
The rule of law	Liberal states respect	'Republics will establish
'Rechtsstaat'	international law	perpetual peace'

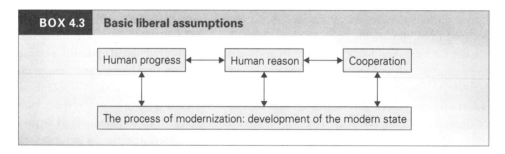

BOX 4.3   **Basic liberal assumptions**

Human progress ←→ Human reason ←→ Cooperation

The process of modernization: development of the modern state

In Chapter 2, we presented the utopian or idealist liberalism of the 1920s. This chapter focuses on liberal theory after the Second World War. It is useful to divide post-war liberalism into four main strands of thinking: sociological liberalism; interdependence liberalism; institutional liberalism; and republican liberalism (Nye 1988: 246; Keohane 1989a: 11; Zacher and Matthew 1995: 121). The following sections of this chapter will focus on each one in turn. It will not be possible to address all the relevant scholarly works or to demonstrate in detail how contemporary liberal thought builds on classical liberal thinking. Our focus will be on important contributions that represent each of these strands. We have chosen this division into four major strands because we find that they bring out the most important aspects of current liberal ideas about international relations.

Sociological Liberalism

For realists, IR is the study of relations between the governments of sovereign states. Sociological liberalism rejects this view as too narrowly focused and one-sided. IR is not only about state–state relations; it is also about transnational relations, i.e. relations between people, groups and organizations belonging to different countries. We should note that this emphasis on society as well as the state, on many different types of actor and not just national governments, has led some to identify liberal thought by the term 'pluralism'.

Transnational relations are considered by sociological liberals to be an increasingly important aspect of international relations (see web links 4.09 and 4.10). James Rosenau defines transnationalism as follows: 'the processes whereby international relations conducted by governments have been supplemented by relations among private individuals, groups, and societies that can and do have important consequences for the course of events' (Rosenau 1980: 1). In focusing on transnational relations, sociological liberals return to an old theme in liberal thinking: the notion that relations between people are more cooperative and more supportive of peace than are relations between national governments. Richard Cobden, a leading nineteenth-century liberal thinker, put the idea as follows: 'As little intercourse betwixt the Governments, as much connection as possible between the nations of the world' (Cobden 1903: 216; Taylor 1957: 49). By 'nations' Cobden was referring to societies and their membership.

Karl Deutsch was a leading figure in the study of transnational relations during the 1950s. He and his associates attempted to measure the extent of communication and transactions between societies. Deutsch argues that a high degree of transnational ties between societies leads to peaceful relations that amount to more than the mere absence of war (Deutsch et al. 1957). It leads to a security community: 'a group of people which has become "integrated"'. Integration means that a 'sense of community' has been achieved; people have come to agree that their conflicts and problems can be resolved 'without resort to large-scale physical force' (1957: 5). Such a security community has emerged, argues Deutsch, among the Western countries in the North Atlantic area. He lists a number of conditions that are conducive to the emergence of security communities: increased social communication; greater mobility of persons; stronger economic ties; and a wider range of mutual human transactions (see web link 4.12).

Many sociological liberals hold the idea that transnational relations between people from different countries help create new forms of human society which exist alongside or even in competition with the nation-state. In a book called *World Society* John Burton (1972) proposes a 'cobweb model' of transnational relationships. The purpose is to demonstrate how any nation-state consists of many different groups of people which have different types of external tie and different types of interest: religious groups, business groups, labour groups and soon. In marked contrast, the realist model of the world often depicts the system of states as a set of billiard balls: i.e. as a number of independent, self-contained units. According to sociological liberals like Burton, if we map the patterns of communication and transactions between various groups we will get a more accurate picture of the world because it would represent actual patterns of human behaviour rather than artificial boundaries of states (see web link 4.15).

Burton implies that the cobweb model points to a world driven more by mutually beneficial cooperation than by antagonistic conflict. In this way the cobweb model builds on an earlier liberal idea about the beneficial effects of cross-cutting or overlapping group memberships. Because individuals are members of many different groups, conflict will be muted if not eliminated; overlapping memberships minimize the risk of serious conflict between any two groups (Nicholls 1974: 22; Little 1996: 72).

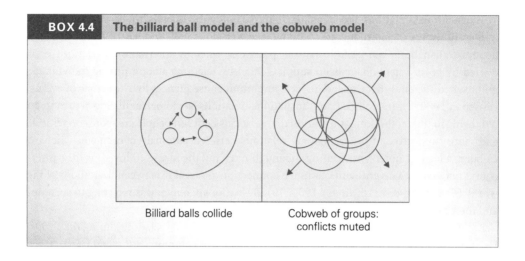

BOX 4.4	The billiard ball model and the cobweb model

Billiard balls collide   Cobweb of groups: conflicts muted

James Rosenau has further developed the sociological liberal approach to transnational relations (Rosenau 1990; 1992). He focuses on transnational relations at the macro-level of human populations in addition to those conducted at the micro-level by individuals. Rosenau argues that individual transactions have important implications and consequences for global affairs. First, individuals have greatly extended their activities owing to better education and access to electronic means of communication as well as foreign travel. Second, states' capacity for control and regulation is decreasing in an ever more complex world. The consequence is a world of better-informed and more mobile individuals who are far less tied than before to 'their' states. Rosenau thus sees a profound transformation of the international system that is underway: the state-centric, anarchic system has not disappeared but a new 'multi-centric world has emerged that is composed of diverse "sovereignty-free" collectivities which exist apart from and in competition with the state-centric world of "sovereignty-bound" actors' (Rosenau 1992: 282). Rosenau thus supports the liberal idea that an increasingly pluralist world, characterized by transnational networks of individuals and groups, will be more peaceful. In some respects it will be a more unstable world, because the old order built on state power has broken down; but only rarely will conflicts lead to the use of force, because the numerous new cosmopolitan individuals that are members of many overlapping groups will not easily become enemies divided into antagonistic camps.

We can summarize sociological liberalism as follows. IR is not only a study of relations between national governments; IR scholars also study relations between private individuals, groups and societies. Overlapping interdependent relations between people are bound to be more cooperative than relations between states because states are exclusive and, according to sociological liberalism, their interests do not overlap and cross-cut. A world with a large number of transnational networks will thus be more peaceful.

| BOX 4.5 | The importance of individuals in global politics |

Citizens have become important variables . . . in global politics . . . [for] at least five reasons:

1. The erosion and dispersion of state and governmental power.

2. The advent of global television, the widening use of computers in the workplace, the growth of foreign travel and the mushrooming migrations of peoples, the spread of educational institutions . . . has enhanced the analytic skills of individuals.

3. The crowding onto the global agenda of new, interdependence issues (such as environmental pollution, currency crises, the drug trade, AIDS, and terrorism) has made more salient the processes whereby global dynamics affect the welfare and pocketbooks of individuals.

4. The revolution of information technologies has made it possible for citizens and politicians literally to 'see' the aggregation of micro actions into macro outcomes. People can now observe support gather momentum as street rallies, the pronouncements of officials, the responses of adversaries, the comments of protesters . . . and a variety of other events get portrayed and interpreted on television screens throughout the world.

5. This new-found capacity of citizens to 'see' their role in the dynamics of aggregation has profoundly altered . . . possibly even reduced, the extent to which organization and leadership are factors in the mobilization of publics . . . Leaders are increasingly becoming followers because individuals are becoming increasingly aware that their actions can have consequences.

Rosenau (1992: 274–6)

Interdependence Liberalism

Interdependence means mutual dependence: peoples and governments are affected by what happens elsewhere, by the actions of their counterparts in other countries. Thus, a higher level of transnational relations between countries means a higher level of interdependence. That also reflects the process of modernization, which usually increases the level of interdependence between states. The twentieth century, especially the period since 1950, has seen the rise of a large number of highly industrialized countries. Richard Rosecrance (1986; 1995; 1999) has analysed the effects of these developments on the policies of states. Throughout history states have sought power by means of military force and territorial expansion. But for highly industrialized countries economic development and foreign trade are more adequate and less costly means of achieving prominence and prosperity. That is because the costs of using force have increased and the benefits have declined. Why is force less beneficial for states and trade increasingly so? The principal reason, according to Rosecrance, is the changing character and basis of economic production, which is linked to modernization. In an earlier age the possession of territory and ample natural resources were the key to greatness. In today's world that is no longer the case; now a highly qualified labour force, access to information and financial capital are the keys to success.

The most economically successful countries of the post-war period are the 'trading states' such as Japan and Germany. They have refrained from the traditional military-political option of high military expenditure and economic self-sufficiency; instead, they have chosen the trading option of an intensified international division of labour and increased interdependence. Many small countries are also 'trading states'. For a long time the very large countries, most notably the former Soviet Union and the United States, pursued the traditional military-political option, thereby burdening themselves with high levels of military expenditure. That has changed in recent decades. According to Rosecrance, the end of the Cold War has made that traditional option less urgent and thus less attractive. Consequently, the trading-state option is increasingly preferred even by very large states (see web links 4.16 and 4.17).

Basically these liberals argue that a high division of labour in the international economy increases interdependence between states, and that discourages and reduces violent conflict between states. There still remains a risk that modern states will slide back to the military option and once again enter into arms races and violent confrontations. But that is not a likely prospect. It is in the less developed countries that war now occurs, according to Rosecrance, because at lower levels of economic development land continues to be the dominant factor of production, and modernization and interdependence are far weaker.

During the Second World War, David Mitrany (1966) set forth a functionalist theory of integration, arguing that greater interdependence in the form of transnational ties between countries could lead to peace. Mitrany believed, perhaps somewhat naïvely, that cooperation should be arranged by technical experts, not by politicians. The experts would devise solutions to common problems in various functional areas: transport, communication, finance and so on. Technical and economic collaboration would expand when the participants discovered the mutual benefits that could be obtained from it. When citizens saw the welfare improvements that resulted from efficient collaboration in international organizations, they would transfer their loyalty from the state to international organizations. In that way, economic interdependence would lead to political integration and to peace (see web link 4.21).

Ernst Haas developed a so-called neofunctionalist theory of international integration that was inspired by the intensifying cooperation between the countries of Western Europe that began in the 1950s. Haas builds on Mitrany. But he rejects the notion that 'technical' matters can be separated from politics. Integration has to do with getting self-interested political élites to intensify their cooperation. Integration is a process whereby 'political actors are persuaded to shift their loyalties . . . toward a new center whose institutions possess or demand jurisdiction over the preexisting national states' (Haas 1958: 16). This 'functional' process of integration depends on the notion of 'spillover', when increased cooperation in one area leads to increased cooperation in other areas. Spillover would ensure that political elites marched inexorably towards the promotion of integration. Haas saw that happening in the initial years of West European cooperation in the 1950s and early 1960s.

From the mid-1960s, however, West European cooperation entered a long phase of stagnation and even backsliding. That was due primarily to President de Gaulle of France, who opposed the limitations on French sovereignty that resulted from interdependence. Functional and neofunctional theory did not allow for the possibility of setbacks in cooperation; integration theorists had to rethink their theories accordingly. Haas concluded that regional integration ought to be studied in a larger context: 'theory of regional integration ought to be subordinated to a general theory of interdependence' (Haas 1976: 179).

It was indeed such a general theory of interdependence that was attempted in the next phase in liberal thinking. But we should also note that theories of integration have seen a revival in the 1980s and 1990s due to a new momentum in West European cooperation (Moravcsik 1991; Tranholm-Mikkelsen 1991; Keohane and Hoffmann 1991). A core issue in these recent studies concerns whether integration is best explained by a liberal, neofunctionalist approach, or by a realist approach emphasizing national interest? We return to that debate between liberals and realists below.

An ambitious attempt to set forth a general theory of what they called 'complex interdependence' was made in the late 1970s in a book by Robert Keohane and Joseph Nye,

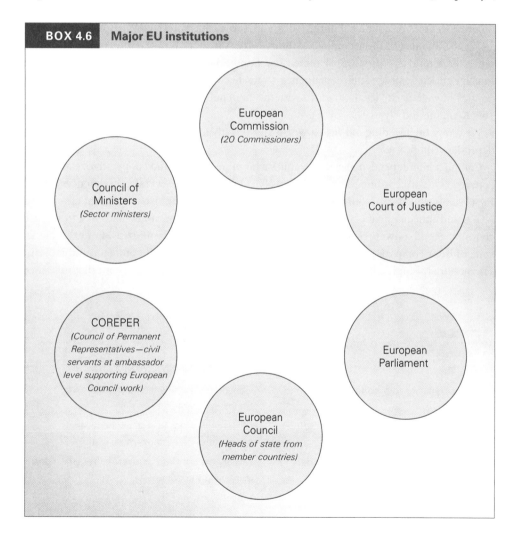

BOX 4.6   Major EU institutions

European Commission
(20 Commissioners)

European Court of Justice

Council of Ministers
(Sector ministers)

COREPER
(Council of Permanent Representatives—civil servants at ambassador level supporting European Council work)

European Parliament

European Council
(Heads of state from member countries)

Power and Interdependence (1977; 2001). They argue that post-war 'complex interdependence' is qualitatively different from earlier and simpler kinds of interdependence. Previously, international relations were directed by state leaders dealing with other state leaders. The use of military force was always an option in the case of conflict between those national leaders. The 'high politics' of security and survival had priority over the 'low politics' of economics and social affairs (Keohane and Nye 1977: 23). Under conditions of complex interdependence, however, that is no longer the case, and for two reasons. First, relations between states nowadays are not only or even primarily relations between state leaders; there are relations on many different levels via many different actors and branches of government. Second, there is a host of transnational relations between individuals and groups outside of the state. Furthermore, military force is a less useful instrument of policy under conditions of complex interdependence.

Consequently, international relations are becoming more like domestic politics: 'Different issues generate different coalitions, both within governments and across them, and involve different degrees of conflict. Politics does not stop at the water's edge' (Keohane and Nye 1977: 25). In most of these conflicts military force is irrelevant. Therefore, power resources other than military ones are of increasing importance, for example, negotiating skills. Finally, under complex interdependence states become more preoccupied with the 'low politics' of welfare and less concerned with the 'high politics' of national security (Nye 1993: 169; Keohane and Nye 1977: 24–6).

We typify the receding old realist world and the advancing new world of complex interdependence in Box 4.7.

Complex interdependence clearly implies a far more friendly and cooperative relationship between states. According to Keohane and Nye (1977: 29–38) several consequences follow. First, states will pursue different goals simultaneously and transnational actors, such as NGOs and transnational corporations, will pursue their own separate goals free from state control. Second, power resources will most often be specific to issue areas. For example, in spite of their comparatively small size, Denmark and Norway will command influence in international shipping because of their large merchant and tanker fleets, but that influence

BOX 4.7	**Types of international relations**
REALISM	**COMPLEX INTERDEPENDENCE**
States dominant actors and coherent units	Transnational actors increasingly important States coherent units
Force usable and effective	Military force less useful. Economic and institutional instruments more useful
Military security dominates the agenda	Military security less important. Welfare issues increasingly important
Based on Keohane and Nye (1977)	

does not easily translate to other issue areas. Third, the importance of international organizations will increase. They are arenas for political actions by weak states, they animate coalition formation and they oversee the setting of international agendas.

Where do we locate complex interdependence in time and space? On the time dimension, it appears to be connected with social modernization or what Keohane and Nye (1977: 227) call 'the long-term development of the welfare state' which picked up speed after 1950. In space, complex interdependence is most evident in Western Europe, North America, Japan, Australia and New Zealand: in short, the industrialized, pluralist countries (1977: 27). The relevance of complex interdependence grows as modernization unfolds, and it is thus especially applicable to the relations between advanced Western countries.

Keohane and Nye are nevertheless at pains to emphasize that realism is not irrelevant or obsolete:

> It is not impossible to imagine dramatic conflict or revolutionary change in which the use of threat of military force over an economic issue or among advanced industrial countries might become plausible. Then realist assumptions would again be a reliable guide to events.
>
> (Keohane and Nye 1977: 28)

In other words, even among industrialized countries of the West an issue could still become 'a matter of life and death' (p. 29), because even that world is still in some basic respects a world of states. In that eventuality, realism would be the more relevant approach to events.

Realists claim that any issue can become a matter of life and death in an anarchic world. Interdependence liberals will reply that that is too simplistic and that a large number of issues on the international agenda are important bread-and-butter items in line with the complex interdependence assumptions. Therefore, interdependence liberals suggest a compromise:

> The appropriate response to the changes occurring in world politics today is not to discredit the traditional wisdom of realism and its concern for the military balance of power, but to realize its limitations and to supplement it with insights from the liberal approach.
>
> (Nye 1990: 177)

Interdependence liberals are thus more balanced in their approach than some other liberals for whom everything has changed for the better and the old world of violent conflict, unbridled state power and the dictatorship of the national interest is gone forever. However, in adopting this middle-of-the-road position interdependence liberals face the problem of deciding exactly how much has changed, how much remains the same and what the precise implications are for IR. We return to this debate later in the chapter.

Meanwhile, interdependence liberalism can be summarized as follows. Modernization increases the level and scope of interdependence between states. Under complex interdependence, transnational actors are increasingly important, military force is a less useful instrument, and welfare—not security—is becoming the primary goal and concern of states. That means a world of more cooperative international relations.

Institutional Liberalism

This strand of liberalism picks up on earlier liberal thought about the beneficial effects of international institutions. In Chapter 2, we noted Woodrow Wilson's vision about transforming international relations from a 'jungle' of chaotic power politics to a 'zoo' of regulated and peaceful intercourse. This transformation was to be achieved through the building of international organizations, most importantly the League of Nations. Present-day institutional liberals are less optimistic than their more idealist predecessors. They do agree that international institutions can make cooperation easier and far more likely, but they do not claim that such institutions can by themselves guarantee a qualitative transformation of international relations, from a 'jungle' to a 'zoo'. Powerful states will not easily be completely constrained. However, institutional liberals do not agree with the realist view that international institutions are mere 'scraps of paper', that they are at the complete mercy of powerful states. International institutions are more than mere handmaidens of strong states. They are of independent importance, and they can promote cooperation between states (Keohane 1989a; Young 1989; Rittberger 1993; Levy et al. 1995).

What is an international institution? According to institutional liberals, it is an international organization, such as NATO or the European Union; or it is a set of rules which govern state action in particular areas, such as aviation or shipping. These sets of rules are also called 'regimes'. Often the two go together: the trade regime, for example, is shaped primarily by the World Trade Organization (WTO). There may also be regimes without formal organizations: for example, the Law of the Sea conferences held under the auspices of the United Nations do not have a formal international organization. Finally, we should note that there is an additional type of international institution which is of a more fundamental kind, such as state sovereignty or the balance of power. These fundamental institutions are not what institutional liberals focus on; but they are main objects of study for International Society theorists, as we shall see in Chapter 5.

Institutional liberals claim that international institutions help promote cooperation between states. In order to evaluate that claim, institutional liberals adopt a behaviouralistic, scientific approach. An empirical measure of the extent of institutionalization among states is devised. The extent to which these international institutions have helped advance cooperation is then assessed. The extent of institutionalization can be measured on two dimensions: scope and depth. 'Scope' concerns the number of issue areas in which there are institutions. Are they only in a few crucial economic areas, such as trade and investment, or are they in many other economic areas as well, and also in military and sociopolitical areas? For assessing the 'depth' of institutionalization, three measures have been suggested:

- **Commonality**: the degree to which expectations about appropriate behaviour and understanding about how to interpret action are shared by participants in the system.
- **Specificity**: the degree to which these expectations are clearly specified in the form of rules.

- **Autonomy**: the extent to which the institution can alter its own rules rather than depending on outside agents (i.e. states) to do so.

(From Keohane 1989a: 4)

Current research on international institutions has two main aims. First, there is an effort to collect more data on the existence of regimes in various issue areas of international relations. Second, a number of theoretical questions require further study, as indicated in a recent survey (Levy et al. 1995: 268):

- Under what conditions and through what mechanisms do international regimes come into existence?
- Do regimes persist even when the circumstances in which they came into existence change?
- What consequences of regimes for state behavior and problem-solving can we observe?
- What long-term effects do regimes have on national political systems and the structure of world politics?

It is clear that a thorough analysis of the scope and depth of institutionalization among a group of states is a substantial research task. A complete absence of institutionalization is highly unlikely; there will always be some rules of coordination. The difficulty is to determine the exact level of institutionalization. A number of studies have addressed the question about the extent to which institutions have helped advance cooperation (Krasner 1983; Keohane 1984; 1989a; Rittberger 1993; Underdal 1992; Young 1989; Oye 1986; Haftendorn et al.

BOX 4.8	A typology of international and transnational organizations		
		GOAL OF ORGANIZATION	
		Specific	*General*
Regional	*Intergovernmental*	NATO NAFTA	AU (African Union)
	Supranational	ECSC (European Coal and Steel Community) EURATOM	European Union
	Transnational	European Anti-Poverty Network	European Movement
Universal	*Intergovernmental*	WHO (World Health Organization) IAEA (International Atomic Energy Agency)	UN
	Supranational	–	–
	Transnational	Amnesty International	World Federalist Association

*(Left vertical label: **TERMS OF MEMBERSHIP**)*

Adapted from Heurlin (1996)

1999; Lake 2001; Botcheva and Martin 2001). One way of doing that is to look at a group of states where we immediately believe that the scope and depth of institutionalization are high and then evaluate the ways in which institutions matter.

One such group of states is Europe, especially the European Union countries (see web link 4.31). EU countries cooperate so intensively that they share some functions of government, for example in agricultural and industrial policies; they have established the regulatory framework for a single market in the economic sector, and they are in the process of intensifying their cooperation in other areas. EU Europe, in other words, is a good test case for examining the importance of institutions. Institutional liberals do claim that institutions have made a significant difference in Western Europe after the end of the Cold War (Keohane et al. 1993). Institutions acted as 'buffers' which helped absorb the 'shocks' sent through Western Europe by the end of the Cold War and the reunification of Germany.

One way to assess the institutional liberal view is to set it against that of neorealist analysis. Neorealists argue that the end of the Cold War is most likely to bring the return of instability to Western Europe which could lead to a major war. It threatens to be a repetition of the first half of the twentieth century. Peace in Europe during the Cold War rested on two pillars that made up the balance of power between the United States and the Soviet Union. They were, first, bipolarity with its stable distribution of military power and, second, the large arsenals of nuclear weapons almost entirely monopolized by those superpowers. With the revival of multipolarity, however, instability and insecurity is sharply increased. At the root of all this is the anarchic structure of the international system. According to neorealist John Mearsheimer, '[a]narchy has two principal consequences. First, there is little room for trust among states. . . . Second, each state must guarantee its own survival since no other actor will provide its security' (Mearsheimer 1993: 148).

The argument made by institutional liberals (Keohane 1989a: 2; Nye 1993: 38; Keohane et al. 1993) is that a high level of institutionalization significantly reduces the destabilizing effects of multipolar anarchy identified by Mearsheimer. Institutions make up for lack of trust between states. They do that by providing a flow of information between their member states, which consequently are much less in the dark about what other states are doing and why. Institutions thus help reduce member states' fear of each other. In addition, they provide a forum for negotiation between states. For example, the European Union has a number of fora with extensive experience in negotiation and compromise, including the Council of Ministers, the European Commission and the European Parliament. Institutions provide continuity and a sense of stability. They foster cooperation between states for their mutual advantage. For example, European states can use the EU machinery to try to ensure that the other parties will respect commitments already made. Institutions help 'create a climate in which expectations of stable peace develop' (Nye 1993: 39). The constructive role of institutions as argued by institutional liberals is summarized in Box 4.9.

Institutional liberalism can be summarized as follows. International institutions help promote cooperation between states and thereby help alleviate the lack of trust between states and states' fear of each other which are considered to be the traditional problems associated with international anarchy. The positive role of international institutions for advancing cooperation between states continues to be questioned by realists. We return to that debate below.

> **BOX 4.9**   **Institutional liberalism: the role of institutions**
>
> - Provide a flow of information and opportunities to negotiate;
> - Enhance the ability of governments to monitor others' compliance and to implement their own commitments – hence their ability to make credible commitments in the first place;
> - Strengthen prevailing expectations about the solidity of international agreements.
>
> **Based on Keohane (1989a: 2)**

Republican Liberalism

Republican liberalism is built on the claim that liberal democracies are more peaceful and law-abiding than are other political systems. The argument is not that democracies never go to war; democracies have gone to war as often as have non-democracies. But the argument is that democracies do not fight each other. This observation was first articulated by Immanuel Kant (1992) in the late eighteenth century in reference to republican states rather than democracies. It was resurrected by Dean Babst in 1964 and it has been advanced in numerous studies since then. One liberal scholar even claims that the assertion that democracies do not fight each other is 'one of the strongest nontrivial or nonautological statements that can be made about international relations' (Russett 1989: 245). This finding, then, is the basis of the present optimism among many liberal scholars and policymakers concerning the prospects of long-term world peace (see web link 4.36). Their reasoning goes as follows. Because the number of democracies in the world has increased rapidly in recent years we can look forward to a more peaceful world with international relations characterized by cooperation instead of conflict (parts of this section draw on Sørensen 1993a).

Why are democracies at peace with one another? The answer to that question has been most systematically addressed by Michael Doyle (1983; 1986) (see web links 4.37 and 4.38). Doyle based his argument on the classical liberal treatment of the subject by Immanuel Kant. There are three elements behind the claim that democracy leads to peace with other democracies (see Box 4.11). The first is the existence of domestic political cultures based on peaceful conflict resolution. Democracy encourages peaceful international relations because democratic governments are controlled by their citizens, who will not advocate or support wars with other democracies.

The second element is that democracies hold common moral values which lead to the formation of what Kant called a 'pacific union'. The union is not a formal peace treaty; rather, it is a zone of peace based on the common moral foundations of all democracies. Peaceful ways of solving domestic conflict are seen as morally superior to violent behavior, and this attitude is transferred to international relations between democracies. Freedom of expression and free communication promote mutual understanding internationally, and help to assure that political representatives act in accordance with citizens' views.

BOX 4.10	Democracy's progress

The Freedom House Index Classification of Free Countries (with greater than one million inhabitants), 2005 (data from 2004)

(1 = highest rating)

Average rating: 1

Andorra	France	Norway
Australia	Germany	Palau
Austria	Hungary	Poland
Bahamas	Iceland	Portugal
Barbados	Ireland	San Marino
Belgium	Italy	Slovakia
Canada	Kiribati	Slovenia
Cape Verde	Liechtenstein	Spain
Chile	Luxembourg	Sweden
Costa Rica	Malta	Switzerland
Cyprus	Marshall Islands	Tuvalu
Czech Republic	Mauritius	United Kingdom
Denmark	Micronesia	United States
Dominica	Nauru	Uruguay
Estonia	Netherlands	
Finland	New Zealand	

Average rating: 1.5

Belize	Latvia	St Vincent and Grenadines
Bulgaria	Monaco	South Africa
Greece	Panama	South Korea
Grenada	St Kitts and Nevis	Suriname
Japan	St Lucia	Taiwan

Average rating: 2

Antigua and Barbuda	Ghana	Mongolia
Argentina	Guyana	Samoa
Benin	Israel	Sao Tome and Principe
Botswana	Lithuania	Vanuatu
Croatia	Mali	
Dominican Republic	Mexico	

Average rating: 2.5

Brazil	Lesotho	Romania
El Salvador	Namibia	Senegal
India	Peru	Serbia and Montenegro
Jamaica	Philippines	Thailand

Based on data from *www.freedomhouse.org*. The index employs one dimension for political rights and one dimension for civil liberties. For each dimension a seven-point scale is used, so that the highest ranking countries (that is, those with the highest degree of democracy) are one-ones (1–1s) and the lowest ranking are seven-sevens (7–7s). Countries with an average rating between 1 and 2.5 are considered free.

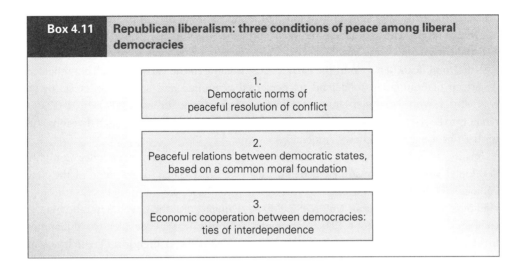

Box 4.11   Republican liberalism: three conditions of peace among liberal democracies

1.
Democratic norms of
peaceful resolution of conflict

2.
Peaceful relations between democratic states,
based on a common moral foundation

3.
Economic cooperation between democracies:
ties of interdependence

Finally, peace between democracies is strengthened through economic cooperation and interdependence. In the pacific union it is possible to encourage what Kant called 'the spirit of commerce': mutual and reciprocal gain for those involved in international economic cooperation and exchange.

Of the different strands of liberalism considered in this chapter, republican liberalism is the one with the strongest normative element. For most republican liberals there is not only confidence but also hope that world politics is already developing and will develop far beyond rivalry, conflict and war between independent states. Republican liberals are optimistic that peace and cooperation will eventually prevail in international relations, based on progress towards a more democratic world. Not only that (and here the normative element shows itself clearly): they see it as their responsibility to promote democracy worldwide, for in doing so they are promoting peace, which is one of the most fundamental of all political values.

The end of the Cold War helped launch a new wave of democratization; that led to growing liberal optimism as regards the future of democracy. Yet most liberals are well aware of the fragility of democratic progress. When republican liberals examine the conditions for a democratic peace in the light of recent democratic transformations in Eastern Europe, Latin America and Africa, the evidence is not supportive of any profound optimism. With regard to the first condition (see Box 4.11), it is evident that a democratic culture with norms of peaceful conflict resolution has not yet taken root in the new democracies. Democratic norms must be ingrained before the domestic basis of the democratic peace will be secure, and such development of the political culture usually takes a long time. There will be setbacks; some countries will revert to non-democratic forms of rule. For example, Russia took a step backwards in 2004 and is now classified by Freedom House as a 'Not Free' country.

As regards the second condition, peaceful relations have indeed developed between the consolidated democracies of the West. There is reason to hope that the new democracies of Eastern Europe will come to be included in this zone—provided that there are no severe setbacks in their further democratization. The democracies of the South are more problematic in that regard. The foundations between North and South are not strong. During the Cold War the United States was hostile and even aggressive towards some southern democracies, e.g. the Dominican Republic in the early 1960s or Chile in the early 1970s. That reflected American determination to defend its perceived economic and security interests in its competition with the Soviet Union (for further analysis, see Sørensen 1993a: 101–12). It remains to be seen whether the end of the Cold War will also put an end to such divisions and mistrust between old and new democracies.

Turning to the final condition, economic cooperation and interdependence is highly developed among the consolidated democracies of the West. At least some of the new democracies of Eastern Europe are integrated into these economic networks through membership of the European Union, e.g. Poland, Hungary and the Czech Republic. Yet the complex negotiations about EU enlargement demonstrate the considerable difficulties involved in close economic cooperation between countries at highly different levels of development. For the democracies of the South, continued one-sided economic dependence on the North rather than interdependence is the order of the day, even after the end of the Cold War. That relation of basic inequality augurs less well for the development of peaceful relations even if both parties have democratic governments.

In short, the emergence of a global pacific union embracing all the new and old democracies is not guaranteed. Indeed, most of the new democracies fail to meet at least two of the three conditions for a democratic peace identified above. And instead of exhibiting further progress, they may backslide towards authoritarian rule. Most republican liberals are therefore less optimistic than was Francis Fukuyama when he predicted 'the end of history as such: that is, the end point of mankind's ideological evolution and the universalization of Western liberal democracy as the final form of human government' (1989: 4). Most liberals argue that there is a democratic 'zone of peace' among the consolidated liberal democracies, including Western Europe, North America and Japan. But the expansion of that zone is far from assured (Russett 1993: 138).

Most republican liberals thus emphasize that democratic peace is a dynamic process rather than a fixed condition. A pacific union does not spring into existence between countries as soon as they meet a minimum definition of democracy. Peace is built on all three foundation stones (Box 4.11) only over a long period of time. There can be setbacks. There can even be reversions to non-democratic rule. There is a weakness even in this qualified republican liberal argument, however. Republican liberals need to specify the exact ways in which democracy leads to peace, and they need to sort out in more precise terms when there is a democratic peace between a group of democracies and why. In that context a more thorough evaluation of the current processes of democratization is necessary. There are already a number of contributions that address these issues (Thompson 1996; Sørensen 1992; Adler and Barnett 1996; Schweller 1992; Lake 1992; Russett 1993; Lipson 2003; for a new critique, see Rosato 2003).

Republican liberalism can be summarized as follows. Democracies do not go to war against each other owing to their domestic culture of peaceful conflict resolution, their common moral values, and their mutually beneficial ties of economic cooperation and interdependence. These are the foundation stones upon which their peaceful relations are based. For these reasons an entire world of consolidated liberal democracies could be expected to be a peaceful world.

We have already introduced a number of specific points where realists are sceptical of liberalism. Realists are sceptical about this version of liberalism too. Behind their disbelief is a larger debate which sets liberalism against realism in IR. The core question in that debate is: can a liberal world escape the perils of anarchy? Will a more liberal world, with more democracies, with a higher level of interdependence and with more international institutions, mean that anarchy is eclipsed? Will it mean that war is permanently ended? The next two sections take up the most important debates between liberals and neorealists.

Neorealist Critiques of Liberalism

Liberalism's main contender is neorealism. We saw in Chapter 2 that the first major debate in IR was between idealist liberalism and pessimist realism. The debate between liberalism and realism continues to this day. We shall see that this debate has created divisions in the liberal camp. There is now a group of 'weak liberals' who have moved closer to the realist camp; and there is a group of 'strong liberals' who continue to support a more distinctively liberal view of world politics.

A main point of contention in previous debates between liberals and realists, around the Second World War, concerned 'human nature'. We have seen that liberals generally take a positive view of human nature whereas realists tend to hold a negative view: they see human beings as capable of evil. That issue was at the core of Hans Morgenthau's realist critique of liberals. The substance of that critique can be expressed as follows: 'You have misunderstood politics because you have misestimated human nature' (Waltz 1959: 40).

These diverging views of human nature continue to separate realists from liberals. But 'human nature' is no longer a major point of debate for two reasons. First, it was increasingly realized among neorealists as well as liberals that 'human nature' is highly complex. It is behind 'good' things as well as 'bad' things: peace and war, philanthropy and robbery, Sunday schools and brothels. Our attention must therefore shift to the social and political context to help us explain when humans (having the potential for being good as well as bad) will behave in either one way or another way (Waltz 1959: 16–41). Second, there was the influence from the behavioural movement in political science. That influence led scholars away from the study of human actions and their 'internal' moral qualities and capabilities towards the analysis of observable facts and measurable data in the 'external' world, i.e. overt evidence of patterns of human behaviour. How should scholars conceive of the external world? How should we view history?

We noted earlier that classical realists have a non-progressive view of history. States remain states in spite of historical change. They continue to reside in an unchanging anarchical system. Anarchy leads to self-help: states have to look after themselves; nobody will do it for them. To be secure they arm themselves against potential enemies; one state's security is another state's insecurity. The result can be an arms race and, eventually, war. That was the case 2,000 years ago. According to neorealists it is still the case today, because the basic structure of the state system remains the same. History is 'the same damn things over and over again' (Layne 1994: 10).

For liberals, however, history is at least potentially progressive. We identified the main conditions of liberal progress earlier and summarized them in the four major strands of liberal thought. Neorealists are not impressed. They note that such 'liberal' conditions have existed for a long time without being able to prevent violent conflict between states. For example, economic interdependence is nothing new. As a percentage of world GNP, world exports in 1970 were below the 1880–1910 level. Put differently, the rapid increase in world trade between 1950 and 1975 which liberals view as the great era of interdependence was nothing more than a recovery from abnormally low levels of interdependence caused by two world wars and the Great Depression in the first half of the twentieth century.

Financial flows reveal a similar story. Measured as a percentage of GNP, total foreign investment from Western developed countries was much higher over the entire period from 1814 to 1938 than during the 1960s and 1970s. International banking has been important for more than two centuries (Thompson and Krasner 1989). In sum, economic interdependence is nothing new, and in the past it has done little to prevent wars between states, such as the Second World War.

Neorealists are also critical of the role that liberals attach to international institutions. While states cooperate through institutions, they still do it solely on the basis of their own decision and self-interest. The strong prevail in international relations. Institutions are no

BOX 4.12	Trade as percentages of world GNP, various years

YEAR	WORLD EXPORTS/ WORLD GNP
1830	4.6
1840	5.7
1850	6.8
1860	9.3
1870	9.8
1880	11.4
1890	11.1
1900	10.4
1910	10.4
1913	11.4
1950	8.1
1960	9.2
1970	10.0
1980	16.9

Based on tables in Thompson and Krasner (1989: 199, 201)

more than theatre stages where the power play unfolds. But the play has been written by the playwright: the states. Institutions are not important in their own right (Mearsheimer 1995b: 340). Finally, as we indicated, neorealists are critical of republican liberalism (Gowa 1999). They emphasize that there is always the possibility that a liberal or democratic state will revert to authoritarianism or another form of non-democracy. Furthermore, today's friend might very well turn out to be tomorrow's enemy, whether they are a democracy or not.

There is thus a common thread running through the realist critique of the various strands of liberalism: the persistence and permanence of anarchy and the insecurity that that involves. According to neorealists, anarchy cannot be eclipsed. Anarchy means that even liberal states must contemplate the possibility that their liberal friends will some day perhaps turn against them. 'Lamentably, it is not possible for even liberal democracies to transcend anarchy' (Mearsheimer 1993: 123). No amount of sociological, interdependence, institutional or republican liberalism can do the trick. And, as long as anarchy prevails, there is no escape from self-help and the security dilemma. Liberal optimism is not warranted.

The Retreat to Weak Liberalism

Liberals have reacted to these neorealist objections in basically two different ways. One group is somewhat defensive, accepting several realist claims including the essential point about the persistence of anarchy. We shall call this group 'weak liberals'. Another group, whom we shall call the 'strong liberals', will not budge; they claim that the world is changing in some fundamental ways which are in line with liberal expectations. Note that the labels 'weak' and 'strong' say nothing about the solidity of the arguments made. They are purely descriptive labels, indicating different degrees of disagreement with realism.

The work of Robert Keohane, one of the leading scholars in the debate between liberals and neorealists, illustrates how a liberal adjusted to realist critiques. As indicated, his early work with Joseph Nye (Keohane and Nye 1971) is characteristic of sociological liberalism. In that work they draw an important distinction between a 'state-centric' paradigm and a 'world politics paradigm'; the former focus is on 'interstate interactions' whereas the latter focus is on 'transnational interactions' in which non-governmental actors play a significant role (1971: xii, 380). The implication is that world politics is changing dramatically from a state system to a transnational political system. That argument is an example of strong liberalism.

This sociological liberal view was popular in the early 1960s; realists were on the defensive. But sociological liberalism appeared to be a prisoner of history and the circumstances of the time. It turned out that the flutter of transnational relations upon which sociological liberals built their argument could only develop smoothly within a framework created by dominant American power (Little 1996: 78). That was true for a period following the Second World War. Then came a period when American power appeared to wane; the country was tied up in a difficult and unpopular war in Vietnam. On the economic front there was also trouble; President Nixon terminated the dollar's convertibility into gold in 1971. The United States' political and economic distress sent shock waves through the entire international system. That put realism back on the offensive: if sociological liberalism only worked within a realist framework of power, progress had hardly gone very far.

Keohane turned his attention away from transnational relations and back towards states. The result was the theory of complex interdependence described earlier. That analysis was a movement in the direction of realism: the primary importance of states was acknowledged. But it was unclear to what extent realism should be supplemented with liberal insights. Keohane increasingly focused his analysis on international institutions. That brought him one step closer to neorealism. The analytical starting-point is now clearly realist. States are the major actors, the international system is anarchical, and the power of states is highly significant. The strong can prevail over the weak. Still, as we saw above, a liberal core remained, namely the idea that international institutions can facilitate cooperation.

Even though this brand of liberalism is fairly close to a neorealist position, most such realists remained dissatisfied with the revised and very much weakened liberal thesis. They claim that Keohane as well as several other liberal institutionalists overlook one crucial item, that of relative gains. 'Gains' are benefits that accrue to participants that cooperate. Institutional liberals claim that institutions facilitate cooperation and thus make it less likely that states will cheat on each other. That is because international institutions are transparent. They provide information to all member states and they thus foster an environment in which it is easier for states to make reliable commitments. Neorealists reply that cheating is not the main problem in negotiation between states. The main problem is relative gains. States must worry that other states gain more from cooperation than they do. Neorealists claim that institutional liberals take no account of that problem; they 'ignore the matter of relative gains . . . in doing so, they fail to identify a major source of state inhibitions about international cooperation' (Grieco 1993: 118) (see web link 4.50).

This neorealist critique led Keohane to emphasize a qualification which further moderated his liberal position. That qualification concerned the conditions for cooperation between states. The single most important condition is the existence of common interests between states (Keohane 1989a: 3; 1993: 277). If states have interests in common they will not worry about relative gains. In that situation institutions can help advance cooperation. In the absence of common interests states will be competitive, apprehensive and even fearful. In those circumstances institutions will not be of much help.

This way of responding to the neorealist critique does make the liberal position less vulnerable to realist attacks, and it does help us to understand why there can be cooperation under anarchy. But it leads liberalism closer and closer to neorealism: less and less remains of a distinctive and genuine liberal theory. In other words, liberal institutionalism is open to the criticism that it is merely neorealism 'by another name' (Mearsheimer 1995a: 85). If we define weak liberals as those who accept basic neorealist assumptions as a starting-point for analysis, other members of that group include Axelrod (1984), Lipson (1984) and Stein (1990). However, the end of the Cold War gave a strong boost to a more pronounced liberal posture.

The Counter-attack of Strong Liberalism

The neorealist attack on liberal theory looks strong. Their spare and parsimonious theory builds on two basic assumptions: history is 'the same damn things over and over again';

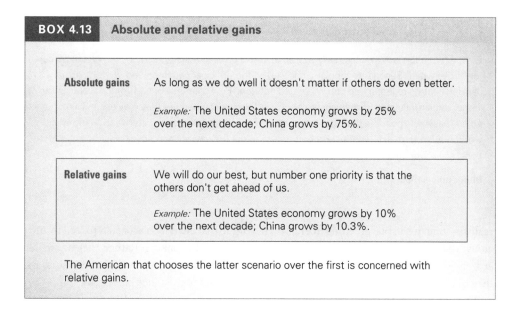

BOX 4.13	Absolute and relative gains

Absolute gains	As long as we do well it doesn't matter if others do even better. *Example:* The United States economy grows by 25% over the next decade; China grows by 75%.

Relative gains	We will do our best, but number one priority is that the others don't get ahead of us. *Example:* The United States economy grows by 10% over the next decade; China grows by 10.3%.

The American that chooses the latter scenario over the first is concerned with relative gains.

there is anarchy leading to insecurity and the risk of war. A terse and bold starting-point makes for strong statements. But parsimony can also be a weakness, because so many things are not taken into consideration. Can we really seriously believe that nothing has changed in international relations over the past several hundred years? Neorealism, as one experienced observer noticed, 'manages to leave most of the substance of the field [of IR] outside the straitjacket' (Hoffmann 1990). In order to argue for such a bald thesis, you have to close your eyes to a lot of things.

That is where 'strong liberals' begin their counter-attack on neorealism. They maintain that qualitative change has taken place. Today's economic interdependence ties countries much closer together; economies are globalized; production and consumption take place in a worldwide marketplace. It would be extremely costly in welfare terms for countries to opt out of that system (Holm and Sørensen 1995; Cerny 1993). Today there is also a group of consolidated liberal democracies for whom reversion to authoritarianism is next to unthinkable, because all major groups in society support democracy. These countries conduct their mutual international relations in new and more cooperative ways. For them there is no going back; historical change is irreversible. 'Strong liberals' include Rosenau (1990), Doyle (1983), Deutsch (1957), Burton (1972), Rosecrance (1986), Zürn (1995), Russett (1993) and Deudney and Ikenberry (1999).

Neorealists do not insist that there has been no change at all; but they do maintain that such change has not led to the disappearance of anarchy. The self-help system of states remains in place. In that fundamental respect the realist analysis continues to apply. From this fact, neorealists draw the conclusion that there is a huge difference between domestic and international politics. In domestic affairs there is 'authority, administration and law', while international politics 'is the realm of power, struggle, and of accommodation' (Waltz 1979: 113). Strong liberals, however, dispute that crucial premise: the assertion that anarchy—as understood by

| | | |

BOX 4.14   Globalization in practice

First, information is now universally available, in real time, simultaneously, in every financial center of the world. Second, technology has tied all the principal countries and world financial and banking centers together into one integrated network. Few countries or parts of the world can any longer remain insulated from financial shocks and changes, wherever they may occur. Third, technology has made possible the establishment of a new, comprehensive system and highly efficient world market to match lenders and borrowers, to pool resources and share risks on an international scale without regard to boundaries.

Blumenthal (1988)

realists—remains in place. Strong liberals do not argue that anarchy has been replaced by hierarchy: that a world government has been created or is in the making. Rather, they argue that anarchy is a far more complex international relationship than is recognized by neorealists, and they question the conclusions that neorealists draw from the existence of anarchy.

What does it mean that there is anarchy in the international system? It means that there is no single, overarching government. It does not mean that there is no government at all. It follows that the distinction between domestic and international politics is not as clear as neorealists claim. The fact is that some states lack an effective and legitimate system of government, e.g. Chad, Somalia, Liberia, Afghanistan, Bosnia. The fact also is that some groups of states are acquiring a governmental system, e.g. the EU. Politics is not 'stopping at the water's edge'. Anarchy does not necessarily mean complete absence of legitimate and effective authority in international politics.

Strong liberals take their cue from that reality. International politics need not be a 'raw anarchy' with fear and insecurity all around. There can be significant elements of legitimate and effective international authority. And strong liberals see examples in the international relations of firmly consolidated, liberal democracies, because here we have combined the key elements of sociological liberalism, interdependence liberalism, institutional liberalism and republican liberalism. One way of characterizing these relations is by Karl Deutsch's term, 'security communities'. The consolidated liberal democracies of Western Europe, North America and Japan constitute a security community (Singer and Wildawsky 1993). It is extremely unlikely—indeed, it is unthinkable—that there will be violent conflict between any of these countries in the future.

Strong liberals thus underline the need for a more nuanced view of peace and war. Peace is not merely the absence of war, as most realists believe. There are different kinds or degrees of peace. The 'warm peace' between the countries of the security community of liberal democracies is far more secure than the 'cold peace' between, say, the United States and the Soviet Union during the height of the Cold War (Boulding 1979; Adler and Barnett 1996). A more nuanced view of war is also required. War has changed dramatically in the course of history. War has grown more and more destructive, spurred by technological and industrial development, culminating in the two world wars of the twentieth century. In addition, there is now the risk of unlimited destruction through nuclear war. Strong liberals argue that

BOX 4.15	The obsolescence of major war

Dueling and slavery no longer exist as effective institutions and have faded from human experience except as something one reads about in books . . . There are signs that, at least in the developed world . . . [war] . . . has begun to succumb to obsolescence. Like dueling and slavery, war does not appear to be one of life's necessities—it is not an unpleasant fact of existence that is somehow required by human nature or by the grand scheme of things. One can live without it, quite well in fact. War may be a social affliction, but in important respects it is also a social affliction that can be shrugged off.

John Mueller (1990: 13)

these developments increase the incentives for states to cooperate (Mueller 1990; 1995); neorealists do not deny that nuclear weapons help decrease the risk of war (Waltz 1993). But strong liberals go one step further. They argue that large-scale war has moved 'toward terminal disrepute because of its perceived repulsiveness and futility' (Mueller 1990: 5).

Strong liberals, then, argue that in important parts of the world anarchy does not produce the insecurity that realists claim. Peace is fairly secure in many important places. There are two main types of peace in the world today. The first type is among the heavily armed powers, especially the nuclear powers, where total war threatens self-destruction. It rests primarily (but not solely) on the balance created by military power. It is the least secure peace. The second main type of peace is among the consolidated democracies of the OECD. This is a far more secure, 'liberal' peace, predicated upon liberal democratic values, a high level of economic interdependence, and a dense network of institutions facilitating cooperation (Cooper 1996; Russett 1993; Maoz and Russett 1993; Sørensen 1992; 1997; Lipson 2003).

For these reasons strong liberals remain optimistic about the future. They argue that genuine progress is possible, and that it is taking place in important parts of the world. There is no world government, of course, but in several areas the world has moved far beyond the neorealist condition of raw anarchy, with all its negative consequences for international relations. Liberals thus appear better equipped than most realists when it comes to the study of change as progress. Whereas many realists always see more of the same in international relations, namely anarchy and power politics, most liberals have a notion of modernization and progress built into their theoretical foundation which makes them more receptive to the study of social, economic, institutional and political change. The end of the Cold War has boosted the liberal position; the world seems to be moving in a more liberal direction. At the same time, liberals are less well prepared for lack of progress or retrogress. For example, we saw how liberal theories of integration did not allow for setbacks in the process of cooperation in Europe. In the Third World a number of very poor countries have experienced lack of development and even state collapse in some instances. Liberal theory has difficulty handling such cases because it is fundamentally based on a conception of irreversible modernization (Zacher and Matthew 1995: 138). It is the beneficial consequences of that process that are the core theme of liberal thinking. Consequently, when that process does not take place for some reason or when it backfires, liberal analysis falters.

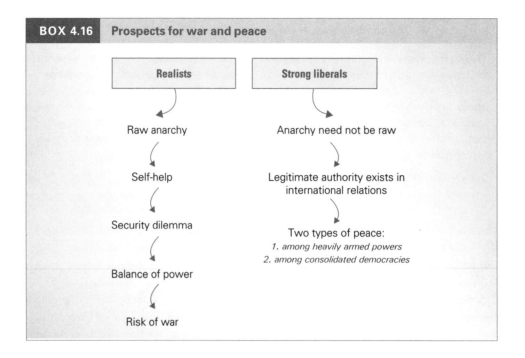

BOX 4.16   Prospects for war and peace

Realists	Strong liberals
Raw anarchy	Anarchy need not be raw
Self-help	Legitimate authority exists in international relations
Security dilemma	Two types of peace: *1. among heavily armed powers* *2. among consolidated democracies*
Balance of power	
Risk of war	

Liberals also are not as precise in their claims as realists are. How much has actually changed? How secure is a democratic peace? What is the exact link between the various liberal elements in international relations—such as democracy or transnational relations—and more peaceful and cooperative relations between governments? Liberals have problems with these questions. That is because liberals try to theorize historical change, which is by its very nature complex, fluid, open-ended, and thus uncertain in the course it will take.

Recent liberal thinking has gone to work on these problems. Andrew Moravcsik has set forth a reformulation of liberal theory that attempts to be 'non-ideological and non-utopian' (Moravcsik 1997: 513). The fundamental actors in international politics are rational individuals and private groups. The policies of states represent what individuals and groups in society (and inside the state apparatus) want. In other words, government policy reflects the preferences of different combinations of groups and individuals in domestic society. In the international system, each state seeks to realize its preferences—to get what it wants—under the constraints imposed by the preferences of other states.

This reformulation of liberal theory avoids prior assumptions about the prevalence of cooperation over conflict or the inavoidability of progress. At the same time, it contains both a 'domestic' component (state preferences) and an international, 'systemic' component (state preferences constrained by other states). The core element in the theory is the set of preferences pursued by states. The preferences may be influenced by liberal factors. To the extent that they are, peace and cooperation may follow. To the extent that they are not, conflict may prevail. According to Moravcsik, there are three major variants of liberal theory: ideational, commercial and republican. Republican liberalism, for example, 'stresses the impact on state behavior of varying forms of domestic representation and the resulting incentives for social groups to engage in rent seeking' (Moravcsik 1997).

Moravcsik's effort demonstrates the attempt to provide a 'a general restatement of positive liberal IR theory' (p. 515) which is based on strong liberal assumptions. The assertion is that such a liberal theory is better than both realism and neoliberal institutionalism at explaining foreign policy, historical change in the international system and the peaceful relations between consolidated liberal democracies.

Liberalism and World Order

Another recent attempt by strong liberals to update liberal thinking is the theory of 'structural liberalism' by Daniel Deudney and G. John Ikenberry (1999). They seek to characterize the major features of the Western order, that is, the relations between Western liberal democracies. Five elements of that order are singled out:

- security co-binding
- penetrated reciprocal hegemony
- semi-sovereign and partial great powers
- economic openness
- civic identity.

Security co-binding refers to the liberal practice of states locking one another into mutually constraining institutions, such as NATO. That organization has joint force planning, coordinated military command structures, and a network for making political and military decisions. Penetrated reciprocal hegemony is the special way in which the United States leads the Western order. The US is an open and diverse political system that is also receptive to pressures from its partners. Transnational and transgovernmental political networks play an increasing role in this.

Semi-sovereign and partial great powers refers to the special status of Germany and Japan. They have imposed constraints on themselves as great powers; an important part of that is that they have foregone the acquisition of nuclear weapons. The features of these 'trading states' are an anomaly seen from neorealism, but from a liberal view they are an integrated part of the Western political order. Economic openness is another major aspect of the Western liberal order. In a world of advanced industrial capitalism, the benefits from absolute gain derived from economic openness are so great that liberal states try to cooperate so as to avoid the incentive to pursue relative gains. Finally, civic identity expresses a common Western support for the values of political and civil liberties, market economics and ethnic toleration.

Deudney and Ikenberry argue that these features of the Western liberal order are so strong and entrenched that they will survive the collapse of the common external threat, the Soviet Union. In short, the liberal order rests on a liberal foundation, not on a particular balance of power or a certain external threat.

It is clear that recent events question the liberal optimism in Deudney and Ikenberry's analysis. The coming to power of George W. Bush in the United States and the US security strategy focused on a 'war on terrorism' has strained relations across the Atlantic (Ikenberry 2002). According to one (realist) commentator (Kagan 2003), Europeans and Americans live in different worlds in the sense that they have very different views of world order: 'Americans are from Mars and Europeans are from Venus,' says Kagan, meaning that Europeans live in a 'Kantian world' of 'peace and relative prosperity', whereas the 'United States remains mired in history, exercising power in an anarchic Hobbesian world where international laws and rules are unreliable, and where true security and the defense and promotion of a liberal order still depend on the possession and use of military might' (Kagan 2003: 3).

But the question is whether Kagan overstates the differences between Europe and the United States. There is no prospect whatsoever that the transatlantic disagreements will lead to violent conflict: the security community based on liberal values, interdependence and common institutions remains in place. So instead of a confrontation between the US and Europe, the disagreement is sooner about the best ways of confronting the terrorist threat. In the US, the neoconservative strategy of aggressively confronting states thought to have 'weapons of mass destruction' (WMD) has dominated so far; in Europe, there is stronger support for the view that 'the best response to transnational terrorist networks is networks of cooperating government agencies' (Nye 2003: 65).

Nevertheless, these events illustrate that there are tensions in the liberal view of world order. What values should a liberal foreign policy seek to realize? The answer from the Liberal International is clear: 'Freedom, responsibility, tolerance, social justice, and equality of opportunity' (Liberal International Manifesto 1997). Of course liberals will seek freedom. But freedom is no uniform entity; Isaiah Berlin (1969) pursued a now classical distinction between negative and positive liberty. Negative liberty is an individual sphere of autonomy, of non-interference of state authorities of any kind. The core element in this kind of freedom is property rights: liberty is a right that flows from property in one's own person; property of person and possessions is a crucial condition for liberty and happiness. The critical task of political authority is to ensure these rights (see web link 4.55).

Positive liberty, by contrast, is the liberty of 'being one's own master', according to Berlin. Positive freedom is only possible when certain conditions are met: one must have health, economic resources, education and so on. To be really free, individuals must have more than negative liberty affords and the state should take care to provide such conditions for all.

Individuals are not states and domestic conditions are not like the conditions in the international system. Even so, we can trace the presence of negative and positive liberty in liberal internationalism. Negative liberty emphasizes a Liberalism of Restraint, of holding back, of providing room for states to conduct their own affairs unobstructed by others. Non-intervention as a core element in the classical institution of sovereignty emphasizes negative liberty: let states choose on their own, but also let them take the responsibility if they fail. International institution-building and international law is also part of a Liberalism of Restraint: it entails the fencing-in of raw power and the principle of negotiation to resolve discord.

Positive liberty, by contrast, points to a different kind of liberal internationalism. It forms the basis for a Liberalism of Imposition, of going out and radically changing the world in order to provide the universal basis for the 'good (i.e. liberal) life'. Woodrow Wilson's dictum of 'making the world safe for democracy' is Liberalism of Imposition; so is John Kennedy's willingness to 'pay any price, bear any burden . . . to assure the success of liberty' (inauguration speech). Most recently, President Bush has declared that the US and the UK 'seek the advance of freedom and the peace that freedom brings'. Charles Krauthammer has identified this Liberalism of Imposition as the motive behind the wars in Afghanistan and Iraq (Krauthammer 2004: 11). In Europe, Tony Blair's adviser, Robert Cooper, has argued in favour of 'a new kind of imperialism, one acceptable to a world of human rights and cosmopolitan values' (Cooper 2002).

In sum, Liberalism of Restraint wants to live and let live, to quietly sort out differences via negotiation and collaboration, to persuade via the argument rather than via the sword. Liberalism of Imposition sees this as much too defensive and ineffective; it wants to go out and forcefully change the world in a liberal direction, using force when necessary. Both liberalisms have a home in liberal thinking. It is quite clear that in face of the world's problems, a Liberalism of Restraint can be too little (i.e. not solving the problems), and a Liberalism of Imposition can be too much (i.e. undermining the liberal values it seeks to promote, cf. Rhodes 2003).

We do not have space in the present context to further pursue this liberal dilemma. Our point here is a simple one: with liberal values preponderant in the present world order, the contradictions of liberalism cannot fail to be further exposed and sharpened. When this happens, the foreign policies of liberal states will increasingly be confronted with the question of how to master this core tension in liberalism. Those who favour Restraint must point to ways of avoiding that this leads to quiet acceptance of massive human suffering. Those who favour Imposition must point to ways of ensuring the result will not be illiberal outcomes and illegitimate policies. In sum, this essential dilemma in liberalism is a central key to appreciating the challenges faced by a liberal foreign policy.

Liberalism: The Current Research Agenda

With the end of the Cold War some traditional issues on the liberal research agenda have been endowed with a new urgency. More than previously, it is now important to know precisely how democracy leads to peace, and to understand the exact extent to which new democracies need to be consolidated in order to secure a democratic peace. The concept of the 'security community' proposed by Karl Deutsch requires further development. This notion is helpful in emphasizing that peace is more than merely the absence of war. However, it is less precise than it ought to be as an effective research tool (for current research building on Deutsch, see e.g. Adler and Barnett 1996; Kacowicz 1995; Schneider 1995; Deudney 1996; Parish and Peceny 2002; Lindberg 2005).

A similar urgency of need for more solid knowledge pertains to international institutions. Newer institutions, such as the OSCE (Organization for Security and Cooperation in Europe) and the WTO (World Trade Organization), have appeared on the world stage. Older institutions, such as NATO, are changing significantly. (Core questions regarding the emergence, change and effects of institutions were set forth in the section on institutional liberalism.)

Sociological and interdependence liberals have emphasized the importance of the development of transnational relations. It appears that this process is continuing with increasing intensity, at least among some countries (Keohane and Milner 1996; Risse-Kappen 1995; Scholte 2005). In Western Europe it has helped foster a policy of integration with qualitatively new elements: states are pooling their sovereignty in order to improve their collective capacity for regulation (Keohane 1995; Zürn 1995). (For an overview of the prospects and problems involved, see Keohane and Hoffmann 1991; Lodge 1993; Baun 1996; Pollack 2005.)

The tensions in the liberal view of world order were discussed above. As already indicated, the atrocities of 11 September 2001 present a challenge to liberal IR theory. Mass murder terrorism, such as the attacks on New York and Washington DC, obviously is a very ominous threat to the physical security of citizens of Western liberal democracies, especially the United States. It clearly is the case that easy movement of people across international boundaries around the world has a dark side. Some individuals may exploit that freedom to plot and carry out acts of mass murder against citizens of the country in which they are residing. That new security threat demands greater police and intelligence surveillance within countries. That could extend to infringing on some of the civil liberties associated with liberal democracy—as in the case of the US PATRIOT Act passed in the aftermath of the attacks (Waldron 2003). It also demands greater security at international borders and other entry points of countries. That could extend to closer inspection of the international transport of goods. It could interfere with the open borders advocated by liberals. At the same time, however, the event could also strengthen international cooperation between countries that perceive a terrorist threat to the security of their citizens. This has happened in connection with the terrorist attacks on New York and Washington DC. The main point is: such events may oblige theorists to rethink their theories, and that includes liberals and liberalism.

In sum, all students of IR need to take note of the processes of change which are taking place, and to evaluate the possible consequences for international relations. That is an important lesson that liberal IR theory teaches us.

 KEY POINTS

- The theoretical point of departure for liberalism is the individual. Individuals plus various collectivities of individuals are the focus of analysis: first and foremost states, but also corporations, organizations and associations of all kinds. Liberals maintain that not only conflict but also cooperation can shape international affairs.
- Liberals are basically optimistic: when humans employ their reason they can arrive at mutually beneficial cooperation. They can put an end to war. Liberal optimism is closely connected with the rise of the modern state. Modernization means progress in most areas of human life, including international relations.

- Liberal arguments for more cooperative international relations are divided into four different strands: sociological liberalism, interdependence liberalism, institutional liberalism and republican liberalism.

- Sociological liberalism: IR not only studies relations between governments; it also studies relations between private individuals, groups and societies. Relations between people are more cooperative than relations between governments. A world with a large number of transnational networks will be more peaceful.

- Interdependence liberalism: modernization increases the level of interdependence between states. Transnational actors are increasingly important, military force is a less useful instrument, and welfare, not security, is the dominant goal of states. That 'complex interdependence' signifies a world of more cooperative international relations.

- Institutional liberalism: international institutions promote cooperation between states. Institutions alleviate problems concerning lack of trust between states and they reduce states' fear of each other.

- Republican liberalism: democracies do not go to war against each other. That is due to their domestic culture of peaceful conflict resolution, to their common moral values, and to their mutually beneficial ties of economic cooperation and interdependence.

- Neorealists are critical of the liberal view. They argue that anarchy cannot be eclipsed and therefore that liberal optimism is not warranted. As long as anarchy prevails, there is no escape from self-help and the security dilemma.

- Liberals react differently to these neorealist objections. One group of 'weak liberals' accepts several neorealist claims. Another group, 'strong liberals', maintains that the world is changing in fundamental ways that are in line with liberal expectations. Anarchy does not have the exclusively negative consequences that neorealists claim: there can be positive anarchy that involves secure peace between consolidated liberal democracies.

 QUESTIONS

- Liberals are optimistic about human progress, cooperation and peace. What are the reasons given for that optimism? Are they good reasons?

- Has international history been as progressive as liberals claim? Use examples.

- Identify the arguments given by the four strands of liberalism discussed in this chapter. Is any strand of liberalism more fundamentally important, or are all strands equally important?

- What arguments can you make, for and against, the assertion that democracy has made striking progress in the world during the past decade?

- Realists argue that anarchy cannot be transcended. Strong liberals say it can. Who is right and for which reasons?

- Was 11 September 2001 a setback for liberal ideas?

- Think of one or two research projects based on liberal theory.

- Identify the tensions in the liberal view of world order. How can these tensions be mastered?

GUIDE TO FURTHER READING

Deudney, D. and Ikenberry, G. J. (1999). 'The Nature and Sources of Liberal International Order', *Review of International Studies*, 25/2: 179–96.

Deutsch, K. W. et al. (1957). *Political Community and the North Atlantic Area*. Princeton: Princeton University Press.

Doyle, M. W. (1986). 'Liberalism and World Politics', *American Political Science Review*, 80/4: 1151–69.

Ikenberry, G. J. (2001a). *After Victory: Institutions, Strategic Restraint and the Rebuilding of Order after Major Wars*. Princeton: Princeton University Press.

Keohane, R. O. (1989a). *International Institutions and State Power: Essays in International Relations Theory*. Boulder: Westview Press.

—— and Nye, J. S. (1977). *Power and Interdependence: World Politics in Transition*. Boston: Little, Brown.

Moravcsik, A. (1997). 'Taking Preferences Seriously: A Liberal Theory of International Politics', *International Organization*, 51/4: 513–53.

Mueller, J. (1990). *Retreat from Doomsday: The Obsolescence of Major War*. New York: Basic Books.

Nye, J. S., Jr. (1988). 'Neorealism and Neoliberalism', *World Politics*, 40/2: 235–51.

Rosecrance, R. (1995). 'The Obsolescence of Territory', *New Perspectives Quarterly*, 12/1: 44–50.

—— (1999). *The Rise of the Virtual State*. New York: Basic Books.

Rosenau, J. N. (2003). *Distant Proximities: Dynamics Beyond Globalization*: Princeton: Princeton University Press.

Zacher, M. and Matthew, R. A. (1995). 'Liberal International Theory: Common Threads, Divergent Strands', in C. W. Kegley, Jr., *Controversies in International Relations: Realism and the Neoliberal Challenge*. New York: St Martin's Press, 107–50.

 WEB LINKS

 Web links mentioned in the chapter plus additional links can be found on the Online Resource Centre that accompanies this book.

www.oxfordtextbooks.co.uk/orc/jackson_sorensen3e/

CHAPTER 5

International Society

▌ Summary

The International Society tradition—sometimes labelled the 'English School' of IR—is a historical and institutional approach to world politics that focuses on human beings and their political values (see web link 5.01). Central to this approach is the study of ideas and ideologies that shape world politics. The basic assumptions are: (1) a claim that international relations are a branch of human relations at the heart of which are basic values such as independence, security, order and justice; (2) a human-focused approach: the IR scholar is called upon to interpret the thoughts and actions of the people involved in international relations; and (3) acceptance of the premise of international anarchy. But International Society scholars argue that world politics is an 'anarchical society' with distinctive rules, norms and institutions that statespeople employ in conducting foreign policy. The chapter discusses contributions of the International Society tradition as well as critiques of the tradition. The concluding section evaluates the current research agenda of the tradition and its prospects.

Basic International Society Approach

According to a leading exponent of this approach (Wight 1991: 1) international politics 'is a realm of human experience' with its own distinctive characteristics, problems and language. To study IR means 'entering this tradition' and 'joining in the conversation' with the aim of understanding it. The main point of this approach is that international relations ought to be understood as a 'society' of sovereign states.

Understanding the society of states is not a question of applying social science models. Rather, it is a question of becoming familiar with the history of international relations as it is experienced by the people involved, the most important of whom are statespeople: presidents, prime ministers, foreign ministers, defence ministers, diplomats, military commanders and other people who act on behalf of states in foreign affairs. IR scholars should try to understand what inclines the practitioners of international relations to act the way they do by seeking to gain insight into the ideas and thought behind their foreign policies. In short, IR scholarship involves getting as close as possible to the social world of international relations by trying to grasp the experience of practitioners past as well as present.

Hedley Bull (1969: 20) summarized this 'traditional' International Society approach as follows: it derives from 'philosophy, history and law' and it 'is characterized above all by explicit reliance upon the exercise of judgement' (see web link 5.02). By 'the exercise of judgement' Bull meant that IR scholars should fully understand that foreign policy sometimes presents difficult moral choices to the statespeople involved—i.e. choices about conflicting political values and goals. IR scholars should be able to evaluate those choices in terms of the situations in which they are made and the values at stake. A difficult foreign-policy choice in this regard would be the decision to go to war or the decision to engage in humanitarian intervention. Two recent examples of such decisions are discussed later in this chapter: the 1990 UN Security Council decision to use armed force to expel the Iraqi army from occupied Kuwait and the 1995 UN and NATO decisions to intervene in former Yugoslavia.

One of the important IR debates identified in Chapter 2 was that between traditionalists and behaviouralists (Bull 1969). International Society scholars are squarely on the traditionalist side of that debate. They do not see IR theory as a value-neutral science in which models and hypotheses are applied and tested. They reject 'positivist' social science methodologies. They disagree fundamentally with Kenneth Waltz's claim that there is a 'structure' of international politics which operates with 'law-like regularity', and which thus makes possible a 'scientific' theory of international politics from which 'predictions' can be derived (Waltz 1979). States are not things: they do not exist or interact on their own. States do not have an existence separate from the human beings—the citizens and governments—who compose them and who act on their behalf. International Society theorists view international relations as a special branch of human

BOX 5.1	Traditionalism and behaviouralism
TRADITIONAL CLASSICAL APPROACH	**BEHAVIOURALIST APPROACH**
Human-focused	Structure-focused
Interpretive	Explanatory
Normative	Positive
Historical-concrete	Analytical-abstract

relations that occur in historical time and involve rules, norms and values. IR is a study of that historical human world.

The International Society tradition is one of the classical IR approaches. But it seeks to avoid the stark choice between (1) state egotism and conflict and (2) human goodwill and cooperation presented by the debate between realism and liberalism. On the one hand, International Society scholars reject classical realists' singularly pessimistic view of states as self-sufficient and self-regarding political organizations which relate to each other and deal with each other only on an instrumental basis of narrow self-interest: international relations conceived as a state 'system' that is prone to recurrent discord, conflict and—sooner or later—war. On the other hand, they reject classical liberalism's singularly optimistic view of international relations as a developing world community that is conducive to unlimited human progress and perpetual peace.

The International Society tradition is a middle way in classical IR scholarship: it carves out a place between classical realism and classical liberalism and builds that place into a separate and distinctive IR approach. It regards international relations as a 'society' of states in which the principal actors are statespeople who are specialized in the practice of statecraft. It views statecraft as a very important human activity that encompasses foreign policy, military policy, trade policy, political recognition, diplomatic communication, intelligence-gathering and spying, forming and joining military alliances, threatening or engaging in the use of armed force, negotiating and signing peace treaties, entering into commercial agreements, joining and participating in international organizations, and engaging in countless international contacts, interactions, transactions and exchanges. That means that the foreign-policy inclinations of states and statespeople must be a central focus of analysis: their interests, concerns, intentions, ambitions, calculations and miscalculations, desires, beliefs, hopes, fears, doubts, uncertainties and so forth.

The discussion so far can be summarized: international relations consist of the foreign-oriented policies, decisions and activities of statespeople who act on behalf of territory-based political systems that are independent of each other and are subject to no higher authorities than themselves, i.e. sovereign states. 'International organizations', 'non-governmental organizations', 'multinational corporations' and so forth are important human organizations that are also involved in international relations. But they are subordinate to sovereign states. They cannot act completely independently of those states. That is why International Society theorists consider sovereign states to be the foundation of world politics. That is the basic image of the 'society of states' that International Society scholars operate with.

For International Society theorists IR typically is a study of war and peace; of declaring war, making peace and rejecting or accepting peace offers; of giving assurances, forming alliances and entering into secret pacts; of sabre-rattling and appeasing; of negotiating and breaking off negotiations; of establishing and severing diplomatic communications; of attacking and defending; of intervening, liberating, isolating, terrorizing, 'ethnic cleansing', hostage-taking and spying; of broadcasting propaganda and jamming foreign broadcasts; of trading and investing, claiming and offering humanitarian assistance, receiving and repatriating refugees; and of many other distinctive international activities in which humans engage. All these international activities have important normative aspects which are of central concern to International Society scholars.

At the heart of the International Society approach are states conceived as human organizations. As indicated, the key concept is that of a 'society of states' (Wight 1977). International politics is understood to be that special branch of politics that is lacking in hierarchical authority—i.e. there is no world 'government' that is above sovereign states. To that extent they agree with classical realists. However, there are still common interests, rules, institutions and organizations which are created and shared by states and which help to shape the relations of states. That international social condition is summed up by Hedley Bull's (1995) phrase 'the anarchical society': there is a worldwide social order of independent states. Bull made an important distinction between an 'international system' and an 'international society' (see Box 5.2).

The 'system of states' is a realist concept; the 'society of states' is a liberal concept. The more international relations constitute a society and the less international relations merely compose a system is an indication of the extent to which world politics forms a distinctive human civilization with its own norms and values. For example, during the Cold War international society between the United States and the Soviet Union was reduced to being not much more than a system in which the foreign policy of each side was based on its calculation about the intentions and capabilities of the other side (see web link 5.11). After the

BOX 5.2	International system, international society

A system of states (or international system) is formed when two or more states have sufficient contact between them, and have sufficient impact on one another's decisions . . . to make the behaviour of each a necessary element in the calculations of the other. A society of states (or international society) exists when a group of states, conscious of certain common interests and common values, form a society in the sense that they conceive themselves to be bound by a common set of rules in their relations with one another and share in the working of common institutions.

Bull (1995: 9–13)

Cold War, however, Russia became associated and involved with the Western-centred world of international organizations such as the G-8 (Group of Eight—the United States, Canada, Britain, Germany, France, Italy, Russia and Japan), OECD (Organization for Economic Cooperation and Development), IMF (International Monetary Fund), EBRD (European Bank for Reconstruction and Development), OSCE and NATO. In order to do that Russia had to take on board the common interests and observe the common values and obligations of those international organizations—in short, Russia had to become a reliable citizen of Western-centred international society.

Another important set of distinctions are the concepts of realism, rationalism and revolutionism (Wight 1991). These are three different ways of looking at the relations of states. The first concept views states as power agencies that pursue their own interests. It thus conceives of international relations solely as instrumental relations. That is the realist view of Machiavelli (see web link 5.04). The second concept views states as legal organizations that operate in accordance with international law and diplomatic practice (see web links 5.15 and 5.16). It thus conceives of international relations as rule-governed activities based on the mutually recognized authority of sovereign states. That is the rationalist view of Grotius (see web link 5.05). The third concept downplays the importance of states and places the emphasis on human beings. Humans are seen to compose a primordial 'world community' or 'community of humankind' that is more fundamental than the society of states. That is the revolutionist view of Kant (see web links 5.06 and 5.07).

According to Martin Wight (1991), however, IR cannot be adequately understood through any one of these conceptualizations alone. IR can only be adequately understood through all of them together. If properly carried out, the International Society approach should be an exploration of the conversation or dialogue between these three different theoretical perspectives. Realists, rationalists and revolutionists each represent a distinctive normative position, or 'voice', in a continuing dialogue about the conduct of foreign policy and other international human activities. That will be set out in the next section.

All three voices broadcast the fact that international relations is basically a human activity concerned with fundamental values. Two of the most fundamental values are given special attention by Hedley Bull (1995): international order and international justice. By 'international order' Bull means 'a pattern or disposition of international activity that sustains' the basic goals of the society of states. By 'international justice' he means the moral rules which 'confer rights and duties upon states and nations' such as the right of self-determination, the right of non-intervention and the right of all sovereign states to be treated on a basis of equality (Bull 1995: 78). These two basic values of the international society tradition will be discussed in a later section.

Two international values that are closely related to order and justice are given special emphasis by John Vincent (1986): state sovereignty and human rights. On the one hand, states are supposed to respect each other's independence; that is the value of state sovereignty and non-intervention. On the other hand, international relations involve not only states but also human beings, who possess human rights regardless of the state of which they happen to be a citizen (see web links 5.25, 5.26 and 5.28). There can be and sometimes there is a conflict between the right of non-intervention and human rights. When that happens, which of these values should have priority? If human rights are being massively violated from within a state, does the government retain its right of non-intervention? In such circumstances, is there a right of humanitarian intervention to rescue people (see web links 5.29 and 5.32)? How should the two rights be balanced? That is one of the basic value conflicts of international relations at the present time.

The International Society approach presents two main answers to these questions. The first answer is *pluralist*, stressing the importance of state sovereignty. According to this view, rights and duties in the international society are conferred upon sovereign states; individuals have only the rights given to them by their own states. Therefore, the principles of respect for sovereignty and non-intervention always come first. States have no right to intervene in other states for humanitarian reasons. The second answer given by the International Society approach to the above questions is *solidarist*, stressing the importance of individuals as the ultimate members of international society. On this view, there is both a right and a duty for states to conduct intervention in order to mitigate extreme cases of human suffering.

We return to this discussion later. Here we may stress that, according to the International Society approach, problems of intervention and human rights can be studied normatively, i.e. philosophically, historically and legally. But they cannot be studied scientifically because they are essentially human issues and are thus value-laden. There can be no value-neutral scientific answer to them. There can be no abstract or general answer either. Every answer will be affected by the situation and will thus be essentially historical in character.

The International Society approach views world politics as a totally human world. That means that it is attuned to the normative aspects and value dilemmas of international relations. That also means that the approach is basically situational or historical. World

BOX 5.3.	**Basic International Society apporach**	
Methodology	Humanism	
	Interpretation	
	Historical, jurisprudential, philosophical	
Core concepts	Human relations	
	States	
	Anarchical society	
	State system	
	Society of states	
Basic values	Order	
	Justice	
	State sovereignty	
	Human rights	

politics is open to all the potential that human beings have for improving their lives, including the progress and peace that classical liberals emphasize. But world politics is also exposed to all the shortcomings and limitations that human beings exhibit, with all the possibilities of risk, uncertainty, danger, conflict and so on that that implies; including the insecurity and disorder emphasized by classical realists. The International Society approach refuses to choose between liberal optimism and realist pessimism; that may be its main strength.

The Three Traditions: Theory

Martin Wight (1991) taught that the leading ideas of the most outstanding classical theorists of IR—theorists such as Machiavelli, Grotius and Kant—fall into three basic categories: realist, rationalist and revolutionist. Realists are those who emphasize and concentrate on the aspect of 'international anarchy'; rationalists are those who emphasize and concentrate on the aspect of 'international dialogue and intercourse'; and revolutionists are those who emphasize and concentrate on the aspect of 'moral unity' of international society (Wight 1991: 7–8). Wight considered these to be the foundational ideas of international relations. As indicated, the three Rs are not isolated from each other but are in dialogue, and all three voices must be heard by IR scholarship. Wight sees IR as a never-ending dialogue between realist, revolutionist and rationalist ideas. All three Rs are necessary for gaining a rounded and balanced understanding of IR. However, there is a tendency for International Society theorists to listen most carefully to the moderate voice of Grotian rationalism.

The key to the International Society approach is the role of these leading ideas in world politics. While history is emphasized, it is the history of ideas that is at the heart of the tradition. None of these ideas is 'true' and none is 'false'. They simply represent different basic normative outlooks on world politics that compete with each other. Each is incomplete in that it only captures one aspect or dimension of international relations. Each by itself is an inadequate theory of IR. But together they play an indispensable role in IR theory. Realism is the 'controlling' or disciplining factor, revolutionism is the 'vitalizing' or energizing factor, and rationalism is the 'civilizing' or moderating factor in world politics.

Realism is the doctrine that rivalry and conflict between states is 'inherent' in their relations. Realists emphasize 'the element of anarchy, of power politics, and of warfare' (Wight 1991: 15–24). Realism concentrates on the actual—what is—rather than the ideal—what ought to be. It thus involves the avoidance of wishful thinking and 'the frank acceptance of the disagreeable side of life'. Realists therefore tend to be pessimistic about human nature: humankind is divided into 'crooks and fools', and realists survive and succeed by outsmarting the crooks and taking advantage of those who are stupid or naïve. That implies that world politics cannot progress but always remains basically the same from one time or place to another. Realism taken to the extreme is a denial that an international society exists; what exists is a Hobbesian state of nature. The only political society and, indeed, moral community is the state. There are no international obligations beyond or between states.

Rationalists are those theorists who believe that humans are reasonable, can recognize the right thing to do, and can learn from their mistakes and from others (Wight 1991: 14–24). Rationalists believe that people can reasonably manage to live together even when they share no common government, as in the anarchical condition of international relations. Rationalism taken to the extreme—if it is possible to push to the limit that which is the soul of moderation—is a perfect world of mutual respect, concord and the rule of law between states. In this way rationalism defines a 'middle road' of international politics, separating the pessimistic realists on one side from the optimistic revolutionists on the other side.

Revolutionists are those theorists who identify themselves with humanity and believe in 'the moral unity' of human society beyond the state (Wight 1991: 8–12). They are 'cosmopolitan' rather than state-centric thinkers, solidarists rather than pluralists, and their international theory has a progressive and even a missionary character in that it aims at changing the world for the better. Revolutionary social change is the goal. That involves bringing into existence an ideal world of some kind, whether that ideal world is based on a revolutionary religion, such as Christianity, or a revolutionary ideology, such as republican liberalism or Marxism-Leninism. For revolutionists history is not merely a sequence of events and happenings. Rather, history has a purpose; human beings have a destiny. Revolutionists are optimistic about human nature: they believe in human perfectibility. The ultimate purpose of international history is to enable humans to achieve fulfilment and freedom. For Kant, revolution involved instituting a system of constitutional states—'Republics'—that could jointly build perpetual peace. For Marx, revolution involved destroying the capitalist state, overthrowing the class system upon which it was based and instituting a classless society. When that was achieved, humanity would be not only liberated but also reunited, and there would be no place either for states or for international relations. Revolutionism taken to the extreme is a claim that the only real society on earth is a world society consisting of every human being, that is, humankind.

BOX 5.4	Wight's three IR traditions	
REALISM	**RATIONALISM**	**REVOLUTIONISM**
Anarchy	Society	Humanity
Power politics	Evolutionary change	Revolutionary change
Conflict and warfare	Peaceful coexistence	Anti-state
Pessimism	Hope without illusions	Utopianism

The Three Traditions: Practice

When Wight (1991) elaborated on realism or rationalism or revolutionism, he illustrated and illuminated his argument with historical and contemporary examples that probed the thought of statespeople or leading commentators. During the depths of the Cold War in 1956, for example, the leader of the Soviet Union, Nikita Khrushchev, was quoted as saying: 'a little country doesn't count any more in the modern world. In fact, the only two countries that matter are Russia and the United States. And Russia is superior. The other countries have no real say' (Wight 1991: 33). This comment is an expression of the idea of realism in world politics.

Wight (1991: 47) distinguishes moderate realism from both realism proper and extreme realism. Extreme realists deny the existence of an international society: they see international relations as a morally neutral and thus instrumental condition between sovereign states; society is possible within states but not between states. No sovereign state has the authority to command any other sovereign state. No sovereign state has the obligation to obey any other sovereign state. Moderate realists are closer to rationalists in recognizing international law. But they see international law as based on the interests and responsibilities of the great powers.

Wight draws no important distinctions within rationalism. He does, however, draw a distinction between rationalism and moderate realism. Wight quotes George Kennan, an influential American commentator on US foreign policy during the Cold War: 'I do not wish ever to see the conduct of this nation in . . . its foreign relations animated by anything else than decency, generosity, moderation and consideration for others' (Wight 1991: 120–1). Kennan recognized the guiding importance of the national interest in the conduct of foreign policy. But he also recognized the legitimacy of the national interest of other countries and not merely of his own country, including rivals and even enemies. Kennan is

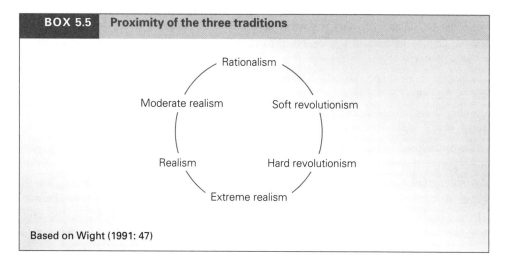

BOX 5.5	Proximity of the three traditions

Based on Wight (1991: 47)

> **BOX 5.6** **The Covenant of the League of Nations (1920)**
>
> The High Contracting Parties, in order to promote international co-operation and to achieve international peace and security, by the acceptance of obligations not to resort to war, by the prescription of open, just and honorable relations between nations, by the firm establishment of the understandings of international law as the actual rule of conduct among Governments and by the maintenance of justice and a scrupulous respect for all treaty obligations in the dealings of organized peoples with one another, agree to this Covenant of the League of Nations.

> **BOX 5.7** **The authority of the Security Council under the UN Charter (1945)**
>
> The Security Council shall determine the existence of any threat to the peace, breach of the peace, or act of aggression and shall make recommendations, or decide what measures shall be taken [Article 39] . . . it may take action by air, sea or land forces as may be necessary to maintain or restore international peace and security.
>
> [Article 42]

usually seen as a moderate realist, but these remarks come very close to expressing ideas characteristic of rationalism. Wight (p. 267) claims: 'Kennan is really a rationalist because he maintains that the national interest should be guided by justice.'

Realist and rationalist ideas are also embedded in international organization. Wight regards the UN Charter as an instance of moderate realism by giving commanding authority on questions of peace and security to five great powers. He points to the UN Security Council: the Council is given the exclusive constitutional responsibility for maintaining international peace and security, and in that way it acts as 'the Hobbesian sovereign of the United Nations' (see web links 5.08 and 5.09). States can join the United Nations or remain outside, but either way they have no right to refuse the commands of the Security Council, which is controlled by five great powers that possess a permanent veto: the United States, Russia, China, Britain and France. On the other hand, Wight regards the Covenant of the League of Nations as an instance of rationalism by binding 'the organs of the League to observe the rules of law and existing treaties' much more definitely and explicitly than does the UN. In short, according to Wight, the League Covenant was based on the *consent* of member states, whereas the UN Charter is based on the *interests* of the great powers (Wight 1991: 34).

Revolutionism, as its name implies, is a doctrine of overthrowing and eradicating existing regimes, if necessary by violence. There is no particular ideology associated with the doctrine: revolutionists could be left-wing or right-wing. Wight quotes a leading Russian Communist during the Russian civil war in 1920 and an interview with the leader (Franco) of the Spanish Fascists during the Spanish civil war in 1936: both disclose the same basic attitude to revolutionary violence (see Box 5.8). Wight (1991: 228) notes that each of

BOX 5.8	Revolutionist ideology: left and right

Comrades! Brothers! The time has come when you can start on the organization of a true and holy people's war against the robbers and oppressors . . . The Communist International turns today to the peoples of the East and says to them: 'Brothers we summon you to a holy war, in the first place against English imperialism.'

Soviet Communist Grigory Zinoviev, 1920

How long . . . is the massacre to go on? There can be no compromise, no truce. I shall go on preparing my advance to Madrid. I shall advance. I shall take the capital. I shall save Spain from Marxism, at whatever cost. That means you will have to shoot half Spain. I repeat, at whatever cost.

Spanish Fascist Francisco Franco, 1936
Quoted in Wight (1991: 223, 226)

these revolutionary leaders 'expresses very simply the revolutionist principle of holy war: divide mankind into good and bad on a criterion provided by your doctrine, and then kill all the bad'. That is the 'hard' version of militant and violent revolutionism. Hard revolutionists seek the violent destruction of the system or society of sovereign states and its replacement by a world government or global order of some kind which is based on an exclusive ideology. Among hard revolutionists he names Lenin. They are close to the tough-minded position of extreme realists—except that hard revolutionists want to destroy the state system, whereas extreme realists want to preserve it.

There is also a 'soft' version of revolutionism that proclaims 'a world society of individuals which overrides nations or states . . . rejects the idea of a society of states and says that the only true international society is one of individuals' (Wight 1991: 45). Christian pacifists and secular humanitarians are examples of soft revolutionists. Soft revolutionists also want to abolish states and the state system but they are committed to achieve that peacefully by a revolution of ideas rather than by violence. Among the soft revolutionists he names the German philosopher Immanuel Kant, American President Woodrow Wilson and India's first Prime Minister, Jawaharlal Nehru. One could add the names of the Indian pacifist Mohandas K. Gandhi and his disciple, the American civil rights leader Martin Luther King. Soft revolutionists are close to the tender-minded position of the rationalist.

This cosmopolitan world society idea is not as far-fetched as it may seem. For example, there is a historical tendency in American foreign policy to be suspicious of secret diplomacy and to be in favour of open relations between the citizens of different countries (see web links 5.12 and 5.14). President Woodrow Wilson made a famous speech in 1918 containing Fourteen Points for ending the First World War and establishing a world safe for democracy. That outlook, discussed in Chapters 2 and 4, is usually referred to as the 'idealist' or 'liberal' tendency in American foreign policy and is undoubtedly rooted in the democratic traditions of the United States.

BOX 5.9 **President Wilson's 1917 war message**

There is one choice we cannot make . . . we will not choose the path of submission and suffer the most sacred rights of our nation and our people to be ignored or violated . . . We have no quarrel with the German people. We have no feeling towards them but one of sympathy and friendship. It was not upon their impulse that their government acted in entering this war. It was not with their previous knowledge or approval. It was a war determined upon as wars used to be . . . in the old, unhappy days when peoples were nowhere consulted by their rulers and wars were provoked and waged in the interest of dynasties or of little groups of ambitious men who were accustomed to use their fellow men as pawns and tools . . .

Address to Congress Asking for Declaration of War, 2 April 1917
Quoted in Vasquez (1996: 35–40)

Henry Kissinger explored in great historical detail the diplomatic dialectic of American foreign policy between an outward impulse towards idealism and the creation of a new world order based on human freedom, and a countervailing inward pull of national self-indulgence and isolationism. According to Kissinger, American statespeople and citizens have to balance 'hope and possibility': 'the fulfillment of America's ideals will have to be sought in the patient accumulation of partial successes' (Kissinger 1994: 836). The world cannot be made permanently safe for democracy: that is a naïve hope that cannot be fulfilled. But in recognizing that impossibility it is not necessary or desirable to retreat into Fortress America, because that would leave the management of international order to others by default, and that would not be in the national interest of the United States. According to Kissinger, American foreign policy has to be guided by a realistic assessment of the limited choices available, even for a superpower like the United States, in a far-flung and diverse world of numerous independent states expressing different foreign policies, political ideologies, systems of government, cultures, civilizations and so on. Here Kissinger discloses his own moderately realist and almost rationalist foreign-policy philosophy: his doctrine of 'hope and possibility' is virtually identical to the rationalist position of 'hope without illusions'.

There are four key emphases in International Society theory. The first is the emphasis on leading operative ideas that are seen to shape the thought, policies and activities of the people involved in international relations: statespeople especially. The second is the emphasis on the dialogue between the leading ideas, values and beliefs which come into play in the conduct of foreign policy. A proper academic understanding cannot be obtained by adopting only a realist or only a revolutionist or only a rationalist approach. To adopt only one of these approaches is to give a one-dimensional and thus partial and incomplete analysis which distorts our understanding of international relations. The third is the emphasis on the historical dimension of international relations. To ignore history is to fail to appreciate the great length of time these traditions have been in existence and the significance of that. The fourth is the emphasis on the most fundamental and the least ephemeral aspect of

BOX 5.10	Walter Lippmann (a famous American journalist) on Cold War containment of the Soviet Union (1947)

For more than a hundred years all Russian governments have sought to expand over Eastern Europe. But only since the Red Army reached the Elbe River [in Germany, 1945] have the rulers of Russia been able to realize the ambitions of the Russian Empire and the ideological purposes of communism . . . American power must be available, not to 'contain' the Russians at scattered points, but to hold the whole Russian military machine in check, and to exert a mounting pressure in support of a diplomatic policy which has as its concrete objective a settlement that means withdrawal [from Germany and other occupied countries of Eastern Europe].

Quoted in Kissinger (1994: 465)

BOX 5.11	President Gorbachev on Soviet–US collaboration (1985)

You asked me what is the primary thing that defines Soviet–American relations. I think it is the immutable fact that whether we like one another or not, we can either survive or perish only together. The principal question that must be answered is whether we are at last ready to recognize that there is no other way to live at peace with each other and whether we are prepared to switch our mentality and our mode of acting from a warlike to a peaceful track.

Quoted in Kissinger (1994: 790)

international relations: the normative aspect as seen in a historical light. To ignore the normative dimension is to fail to understand the essentially human character of international relations and the extremely difficult moral problems involved.

Order and Justice

As indicated, the International Society approach emphasizes philosophy and history as well as law. Martin Wight was essentially a diplomatic historian who reflected on the dynamic interplay of foundational ideas in international relations. Hedley Bull, on the other hand, was primarily a philosopher of world politics who tried to work out a systematic theory of international society (Jackson 1995: 110–28). Both Wight and Bull saw IR theory as a branch of political theory. They believed that it was only possible to theorize IR within the context of concrete historical events and episodes. They were deeply sceptical of abstract social science theorizing based on game theory or other scientific models that are divorced from history and human experience.

The main point of the anarchical society, according to Bull (1995: 16–19), is promotion and preservation of international order, which is defined as 'a pattern or disposition of international activity that sustains those goals of the society of states that are elementary, primary or universal'. He identifies four such goals: preservation of international society; upholding the independence of member states, maintaining peace and helping to secure the normative foundations of all social life, which includes 'the limitation of violence' (expressed in the laws of war); 'the keeping of promises' (expressed in the principle of reciprocity); and 'the stability of possession' (expressed in the principle of mutual recognition of state sovereignty). According to Bull, these are the most fundamental goals of the anarchical society. All these goals are moral in character: they are not merely instrumental or wholly self-interested; they are for others as well as ourselves. Bull, like most other International Society theorists, presents a normative analysis of world politics.

Bull distinguishes three kinds of order in world politics (Bull 1995: 3–21). The first kind is 'order in social life', which is an essential element of human relations regardless of the form taken; the second is 'international order', which is order between states in a system or society of states; and the last is 'world order', which is order among humankind as a whole. He goes on to say that 'world order is more fundamental and primordial than international order because the ultimate units of the great society of all mankind are not states . . . but individual human beings'. States and the society of states are merely temporary—i.e. historical—arrangements of human relations, but 'individual human beings . . . are permanent and indestructible in a sense in which groupings of them . . . are not'. That is a cosmopolitan or solidarist inclination of Bull's IR theory. But most of Bull's analysis is concerned with states and the society of states: it is pluralist rather than solidarist.

The responsibility for sustaining international order—order between states—belongs to the great powers, and is achieved by 'managing their relations with one another'. Bull adds the important qualifier that this is not an empirical statement about what great powers actually do. Rather, it is a normative statement of their special role and responsibility in world politics which derives from the reality of the profound inequality of power between states. He notes that 'great powers, like small powers, frequently behave in such a way as to promote disorder rather than order' (Bull 1995: 199–201). That of course happened on two

---

BOX 5.12   Bull's rationalist conception of war as an institution

War is organized violence carried on by political units against each other . . . We should distinguish between war in the loose sense of organized violence which may be carried out by any political unit (a tribe, an ancient empire, a feudal principality, a modern civil faction) and war in the strict sense of international or interstate war, organized violence waged by sovereign states. Within the modern states system only war in the strict sense, international war, has been legitimate; sovereign states have sought to preserve for themselves a monopoly of the legitimate use of violence . . . In any actual hostilities to which we can give the name 'war', norms or rules, whether legal or otherwise, invariably play a part.

Bull (1995: 178)

major occasions in the twentieth century which shook the foundations of world politics: the First World War (1914–18) and the Second World War (1939–45). The latter in particular was a profound failure of responsibility on the part of the great powers whose fundamental duty is to maintain the balance of power and prevent any great power from getting out of hand and creating a disaster—as Germany and Japan did in the 1930s and 1940s. Bull argued that during the 1960s and early 1970s the United States and the Soviet Union made some attempt to act 'as responsible managers of the affairs of international society as a whole'. The Cold War at times produced international order. But he also said that at certain other times during the Cold War, specifically in the late 1970s and early 1980s, the two superpowers behaved more like 'the great irresponsibles' (Bull and Watson 1984: 437). That clearly is a more ambivalent view of the Cold War than that held by contemporary neorealists (see Chapter 3).

Bull's argument on the balance of power comes very close to that of a moderate realist in Wight's terms. He employed history to draw some important distinctions, for example between a 'simple balance of power' and a 'complex balance of power'. The former corresponds roughly to the realist concept of bipolarity; the latter corresponds roughly to the realist concept of multipolarity. In the same vein, he went on to use historical illustrations to distinguish between a general balance of power and a local balance of power, and between an objective balance of power and a subjective balance of power. The general balance of power between the United States and the Soviet Union during the Cold War could be distinguished from the local balance of power between Israel and the Arab states in the Middle East, or between India and Pakistan in South Asia.

BOX 5.13 | **President de Gaulle on national responsibility (1961)**

It is intolerable for a great State [France] to leave its destiny up to the decisions and action of another State [the United States], however friendly it may be . . . the integrated country loses interest in its national defense, since it is not responsible for it.

Quoted in Kissinger (1994: 605)

BOX 5.14 | **President Franklin Roosevelt on international responsibility (1945)**

Nothing is more essential to the future peace of the world than continued cooperation of the nations which had to muster the force necessary to defeat the conspiracy of the Axis powers to dominate the world. While the great states have a special responsibility to enforce the peace, their responsibility is based upon the obligations resting upon all states, large and small, not to use force in international relations except in defense of law.

Quoted in Kissinger (1994: 427)

The objective balance of power is a factual reality, but the subjective balance is a matter of belief and even faith: the doctrine of promoting and maintaining a balance of power to achieve and maintain the value of international order. That is the fundamental moral point of the balance of power which scientific theories often fail to grasp. Writing in the 1970s Bull (1995: 109) noted that at that time there was no general agreement between the great powers that the maintenance of the balance of power was a common objective, much less a valuable goal for them to pursue. That is misleading, because the Soviet Union and the United States did in fact work out rules between themselves for regulating nuclear weapons and other military aspects of their relationship: they collaborated in the pursuit of nuclear peace, and in doing so they disclosed a recognition of shared interests and at least a minimal sociability in their Cold War relationship (Hoffmann 1991).

Hedley Bull also uses historical and contemporary illustrations to make his argument about the nature of war in an anarchical society. In writing on war his argument is characteristic of a rationalist in Wight's terms. That is clear from his definition of war as an institution. Bull employs historical and contemporary examples to illustrate this rationalist notion of war. He notes (1995: 179) that war between states is often contrasted unfavourably with peace between states, but that can be misleading. He points out that 'the historical alternative to war between states was more ubiquitous violence', such as the social anarchy that existed during the medieval era before modern states monopolized the activity and means of warfare (see Chapter 1). Historically the state system has sought to suppress such violence by restricting warfare to armed combat between states. So the monopoly of war by states has promoted the value of order.

Since 1945 international society has succeeded in limiting interstate war but not intrastate war. Wars between great powers have been almost non-existent—except for 'wars fought "by proxy" between the superpowers', such as the Korean War or the Vietnam War (Bull 1995: 187). The wars that have occurred since 1945 have predominantly been revolutionary wars, wars of national liberation, civil wars, secessionist wars, the 'war' against international terrorism and so forth. These are the non-state 'wars of a third kind' (Holsti 1996) that characterize the contemporary era. Bull notes that 'international war, as a determinant of the shape of the international system, has declined in relation to civil war', which he attributed largely to the Cold War stand-off between the superpowers, but which could also be attributed to the norms of the UN Charter, which outlaw aggressive war, and to international public opinion which stands behind them.

During the Cold War social science positivists—such as strategic realists and neorealists— saw the rivalry between the United States and the Soviet Union in instrumental or structural terms (see Chapter 3). They did not see the Cold War in normative terms as involving basic human values. However, as an exponent of the International Society tradition, Hedley Bull saw nuclear deterrence and other aspects of the American/Russian rivalry as a conflict involving fundamental human values. For Bull (1995: 112–21, emphasis added) nuclear deterrence was an '*institution* or quasi-institution' involving human values which could be captured in the following statement: 'To say that Country A deters Country B from something is to imply . . . that Country A conveys to Country B a threat to inflict *punishment* or deprivation of values if it embarks on a certain course of action.' Bull points out that mutual

BOX 5.15	Order and justice	
	ORDER	**JUSTICE**
	Order in social life	Human justice
	International order	Interstate justice
	World order	World justice

nuclear deterrence is a special case of general deterrence which has always been a defence policy of states. It is special in the sense that it becomes 'a prime object of policy' because of the reluctance of nuclear armed powers 'to use nuclear weapons in actual war'. Clearly what is at stake in deterrence, and what is at greater stake in the case of nuclear deterrence, is human *values*: security, survival, the continuation of a national way of life, international order and so on. Those normative goals are the fundamental purpose of the game of nuclear deterrence.

According to Bull, international society involves concern not only about order but also about *justice*. He identifies various conceptions of justice, but he draws particular attention to the distinction between commutative justice and distributive justice in international relations. Commutative justice is about procedures and reciprocity. It involves 'a process of claim and counter-claim' among states. States are like firms in the marketplace; each firm does its best to succeed within the framework of economic competition. That presupposes a level playing field: all firms play by the same rules of the market; all states play by the same rules of international society. Justice is fairness of the rules of the game: the same rules are applied in the same way to everybody. The rules of the game are expressed by international law and diplomatic practices. That is commutative justice, the principal form of international justice.

Distributive justice is about goods. It involves the issue of how goods should be distributed between states, as 'exemplified by the idea that justice requires a transfer of economic resources from rich countries to poor'. Distributive justice is the idea that the poor and weak deserve special treatment, such as development aid. That means that not all states play by the same rules: some get special treatment. That form of justice takes a back seat to commutative justice because sovereign states are usually understood as the most appropriate framework *within* which normative issues of distributive justice ought to be resolved: in other words, distributive justice is usually understood as an issue of domestic politics rather than international politics. However, in the twentieth century issues of distributive justice have increasingly encroached on international relations as the globe has shrunk.

Bull distinguishes three levels of justice in world politics: 'international or interstate justice', which basically involves the notion of equal state sovereignty; 'individual or human justice', which basically involves ideas of human rights; and 'cosmopolitan or world justice', which basically involves 'what is right or good for the world as a whole', as evident, for example, in global environmental standards. Historically the interstate level has usually prevailed in world politics. In the twentieth century the latter two levels of justice became more prominent, but they did not overtake the interstate level which is the level at which most issues of justice in world politics are still addressed.

Bull ends his discussion of order and justice by considering the relative weight of these two values in world politics. In that comparison, order is seen to be more fundamental: 'it is a condition for the realization of other values' (Bull 1995: 93). Order is prior to justice. However, Bull makes a point of saying that that is a general statement, but in any particular case justice may come first. An example is the international justice of self-determination and state sovereignty for colonized peoples in Asia and Africa that was widely regarded as morally prior to the international order of Western colonialism in those parts of the world. Bull's main point is that world politics involves questions of both order and justice, and that world politics cannot be adequately understood by focusing on either value to the exclusion of the other.

Statecraft and Responsibility

The International Society approach leads to the study of moral choices in foreign policy that responsible statespeople are confronted with (Jackson 2000). We can discern at least three distinctive dimensions or levels of responsibility which correspond to Wight's three traditions noted above: (1) devotion to one's own nation and the well-being of its citizens; (2) respect for the legitimate interests and rights of other states and for international law; and (3) respect for human rights.

National Responsibility

According to this conception, statespeople are responsible for the well-being of their citizens. The only fundamental standard of conduct that they should adhere to in their foreign policies is that of national self-interest. National security is the foundational value that they are duty-bound to protect. This realist standard for evaluating foreign policies gives rise to Machiavellian precepts such as the following: always put your nation and its citizens first; avoid taking unnecessary risks with their security and welfare; collaborate with other

Box 5.16	Four dimensions of responsibility	
	RESPONSIBLE TO WHOM?	RESPONSIBLE FOR WHAT?
National	Our citizens	National security
International	Other states	International peace

countries when it is advantageous or necessary but avoid needless foreign entanglements; do not subject your population to war unless it is absolutely necessary. These normative considerations are characteristic of a system of autonomous states, i.e. realism.

What is the normative basis for claiming that statespeople are only responsible for defending the national interest of their own country? The answer can be derived from a familiar theory of political obligation which regards the state—whether it is formed by a social contract, by historical evolution, by conquest or by any other method—as a self-contained political community that is morally prior to any international associations it may subsequently join. That normative view is typical of many American policymakers who regard the United States Constitution as above international law. States have no international obligations that come before their national interests: international law and international organizations are merely instrumental considerations in determining the national interest of states. Human beings have rights only by virtue of being citizens of states: each statesperson is responsible for defending his or her own citizens, but not the citizens of other states.

International Responsibility

According to this conception, statespeople have foreign obligations deriving from their state's membership of international society, which involves rights and duties as defined by international law. This interstate standard for evaluating foreign policies gives rise to Grotian precepts such as the following: be a good citizen of international society; recognize that other states have international rights and legitimate interests which deserve respect; act in good faith; observe international law; and comply with the laws of war. These normative considerations are characteristic of a pluralist society of states based on international law, i.e. rationalism.

What is the normative basis for believing that statespeople have a separate responsibility to international society and its members? The usual answer comes from a conception of international obligation: states are not isolated or autonomous political entities, responsible only to themselves. On the contrary, states are related to each other, and constitute the external sovereignty of each other by the practices of recognition, diplomacy, commerce and so on. States consequently have foreign obligations to other states and to international society as a whole from which they derive important rights and benefits. Those foreign obligations are independent of and additional to the domestic obligations of statespeople.

Humanitarian Responsibility

According to this conception, statespeople first and foremost are human beings and as such they have a fundamental obligation to respect human rights not only in their own country but in all countries around the world. This cosmopolitan standard for evaluating foreign policies gives rise to Kantian precepts such as the following: always remember that people in other countries are human beings just like yourself; respect human rights; give sanctuary

BOX 5.17	**Russian Foreign Minister Andrei Kozyrev on humanitarian responsibility**

Wherever threats to democracy and human rights occur, let alone violations thereof, the international community can and must contribute to their removal . . . Such measures are regarded today not as interference in internal affairs but as assistance and cooperation ensuring everywhere a 'most favored regime' for the life of the peoples—one consistent with each state's human rights commitments under the UN Charter, international covenants and other relevant instruments.

Quoted in Weller (1993)

to those who are fleeing from persecution; assist those who are in need of material aid which you can supply at no sacrifice to yourself; in waging war spare non-combatants. These normative considerations are characteristic of a solidarist world society based on the community of humankind, i.e. revolutionism.

This cosmopolitan criterion of responsible statecraft obviously goes well beyond international responsibility. What is the normative basis for believing that statespeople are responsible for human rights around the world? The usual answer derives from a theory of human obligation: before one can be a citizen of a state and a member of its government, one must be a human being. This naturally entails fundamental obligations that every human being must observe. The traditional way of expressing one's obligations as a human being is by claiming that there is a natural law, a universal law of reason and of conscience, and natural rights—what we now call 'human rights'—which statespeople no less than anyone else are duty-bound to respect.

If these criteria and precepts are operative standards of conduct, it becomes clear that we should expect normative dilemmas and conflicts to be a feature of contemporary statecraft. It is equally clear that all three of these dimensions of responsibility must be a focus of analysis. To reduce responsible statecraft to only one or two of these dimensions is to carry out at best a partial analysis and at worse a biased account which would underestimate the normative complexity of international relations and consequently the actual difficulty of making normatively defensible choices in foreign policy. No criterion can predictably trump all other considerations in all circumstances. There is an underlying normative pluralism which statespeople cannot escape from, which IR scholars should not ignore, and which perhaps is what Wight (1991) is referring to when he says he encountered all three perspectives when he canvassed his own mind on such questions. That is evident from two important post-Cold War conflicts: the Gulf War and the crisis in Bosnia (Mayall 1996).

When the armed forces of Saddam Hussein's Iraq invaded Kuwait in August 1990, other countries and international society as a whole were presented with a military action that was in clear violation of the UN Charter and threatened the legitimate national interests of many states. Some response had to be made. But no response would be easy. Even the decision to do nothing would be difficult, owing to the extreme seriousness of Iraq's offence against international law and the threat it posed to the Persian Gulf and its huge oil supplies, upon which many states were heavily dependent. As it happened, a series of major decisions were taken by the UN Security Council and its member states which eventually led to a war against Iraq. It is convenient and instructive to assess those decisions from an International Society perspective (Jackson 1992). The decision to commit member states of the UN to a war with Iraq was taken with reluctance, and only after extensive debate and many previous decisions failed to persuade Saddam Hussein to withdraw his armed forces from occupied Kuwait.

The difficulty of the decision is clearly indicated by a debate in the US Congress in January 1991 regarding whether the United States should participate in the UN action against Iraq by committing its armed forces. Senators and Congressmen had to make that decision jointly with the President. They were attentive to the seriousness of their decision, i.e. the anticipated consequences of passing the resolution versus the expected consequences of defeating the resolution. On the one hand, they were acutely aware that an affirmative decision would inevitably result in the wounding and killing of American and Allied soldiers; it would also bring death, destruction and suffering to the people of Kuwait and Iraq where the war would be waged. On the other hand, they were equally aware that a negative decision would probably allow Iraq to get away with a serious act of aggression that heaped contempt upon the UN Charter and particularly the principle of non-intervention and on the value of international peace and security, and that threatened to disrupt the flow of Middle East oil supplies. As it turned out, the US Senate passed the resolution by a narrow vote of 52 to 47. That is a telling indication of the normative weight and difficulty of the decision.

In short, all three normative criteria of responsible statecraft were evident in the Gulf War. Realists would notice that the West's vital interest in an uninterrupted supply of Middle East oil—i.e. the norm of national responsibility—was uppermost in the minds of US President George Bush and other Western leaders when they embarked upon a course of war to evict Saddam Hussein's armed forces from Kuwait in January 1991. Rationalists

---

BOX 5.18   **United States declared foreign policy in the Persian Gulf**

1. The immediate, unconditional and complete withdrawal of all Iraqi forces from Kuwait;

2. the restoration of Kuwait's legitimate government;

3. the security and stability of the Persian Gulf region;

4. the protection of American citizens abroad, and the release of all those held hostage by Iraq; and

5. the fostering of a new world order, free from the threat of terror, stronger in the pursuit of justice, and more secure in the quest for peace.

Weller (1993: 276)

BOX 5.19   President Bush's justification of war against Iraq (January 1991)

Just 2 hours ago, allied air forces began an attack on military targets in Iraq and Kuwait . . . This military action, taken in accord with United Nations resolutions and with the consent of the United States Congress, follows months of constant and virtually endless diplomatic activity on the part of the United Nations, the United States, and many, many other countries . . . the 28 countries with forces in the Gulf area have exhausted all reasonable efforts to reach a peaceful resolution— have no choice but to drive Saddam Hussein from Kuwait by force . . . . Our objectives are clear. Saddam Hussein's forces will leave Kuwait. The legitimate government of Kuwait will be restored to its rightful place, and Kuwait will once again be free . . . it is our hope that [in the future] Iraq will live as a peaceful and cooperative member of the family of nations, thus enhancing the security and stability of the Gulf.

Quoted in Weller (1993: 279)

BOX 5.20   UN Security Council Resolution 688 on safe havens in Iraq

The Security Council, mindful of its duties and its responsibilities under the Charter of the United Nations for the maintenance of international peace and security . . .

1. *Condemns* the repression of the Iraqi civilian population in many parts of Iraq, including most recently in Kurdish populated areas, the consequences of which threaten international peace and security in the region;
2. *Demands* that Iraq . . . immediately end this repression . . .
3. *Insists* that Iraq allow immediate access by international humanitarian organizations to all those in need of assistance in all parts of Iraq . . .

UN Security Council, 5 April 1991
Quoted in Weller (1993: 13)

---

would notice the nearly universal condemnation of Iraq's invasion and occupation of Kuwait. Iraq's conduct in this episode was widely construed as an act of aggression and thus a violation of the UN Charter—i.e. the norm of international responsibility was also evident. Soft revolutionists would notice that many UN Security Council resolutions addressed the problem of human rights violations by Iraq: against citizens of occupied Kuwait, against Western citizens living in Kuwait and Iraq, and against Iraqi citizens who belong to minority groups, such as the Kurds. It is clear that the norm of humanitarian responsibility was evident in the Gulf War too.

The most perplexing post-Cold War conflict was the war in the former Yugoslav republic of Bosnia-Herzegovina (1992–5). Statespeople were confronted with three basic courses of action: absolute non-intervention, in which responsibility for events would reside in the hands of the parties to the conflict (the Bosnian army and the Serbian and Croatian militias);

full-scale military intervention, in which international society would assume a heavy responsibility for events; or a path somewhere between these extremes. The course that was embarked upon and followed during most of the conflict was a normatively ambiguous middle way of muddling through, by means of a limited UN humanitarian intervention which attempted to protect non-combatants, deliver humanitarian aid and arrange a negotiated settlement. That path was finally abandoned in 1995, when NATO became involved in a major armed peace enforcement operation in Bosnia.

For three years (1992–5) the UN Security Council in cooperation with the European Union were reluctant to commit to that second course of action. The leading argument against intervention was the moderate realist claim that it was a civil war, that it presented no threat to international peace and security, and that it did not affect the vital national interests of the great powers. But there was already a major international intervention in Bosnia-Herzegovina. In 1992 the country became a sovereign state as a direct result of recognition by member states of the European Union and the United States. They bore a crucial international responsibility for Bosnia's independence from Yugoslavia. Furthermore, international society subsequently intervened massively by imposing an arms embargo on former Yugoslavia, which put the Bosnian government at a big military disadvantage. The Serbian and Croatian militias were supplied with arms by their kindred states, Serbia and Croatia. That made it possible for them to carry out an undeclared war of state partition against Bosnia-Herzegovina.

By 1994–5 the leaders of the great powers began to be confronted by a difficult decision that grew out of the failure of their initial middle course. Should they continue with a restricted UN intervention that was proving to have morally intolerable consequences, such as its failure to persuade the parties to settle their conflict at the peace table and its failure to prevent 'ethnic cleansing' and other human rights violations? Or should they engage in a stepped-up major military intervention, with all the risks and dangers that that would involve? Withdrawal was clearly out of the question, and in the meantime the human

---

BOX 5.21   UN Security Council Resolution 713 on Yugoslavia

The Security Council . . .

1. *Appeals urgently to and encourages* all parties to settle their disputes peacefully and through negotiation . . .

2. *Decides*, under Chapter VII of the Charter of the United Nations, that all States shall, for the purposes of establishing peace and stability in Yugoslavia, immediately implement a general and complete embargo on all deliveries of weapons and military equipment to Yugoslavia . . .

3. *Calls on* all States to refrain from any action which might contribute to increasing tension and to impeding or delaying a peaceful and negotiated outcome to the conflict in Yugoslavia, which would permit all Yugoslavs to decide upon and to construct their future in peace . . .

UN Security Council, 21 September 1995
Quoted in Mayall (1996: 174–5)

BOX 5.22 **The General Framework Agreement for Peace in Bosnia and Herzegovina (Dayton Agreement)**

The parties shall conduct their relations in accordance with the principles set forth in the United Nations Charter, as well as the Helsinki Final Act . . . In particular, the parties shall fully respect the sovereign equality of one another . . . and shall refrain from any action, by threat or use of force or otherwise, against the territorial integrity or political independence of Bosnia and Herzegovina or any other state. [Article I]

The Federal Republic of Yugoslavia and the Republic of Bosnia and Herzegovina recognize each other as sovereign independent States within their international borders. [Article X]

Dayton Peace Accord, 21 November 1995

---

tragedy of Bosnia was continuing and even deepening. The United States began to assert its leadership role. NATO air power was employed in 1994, and eventually the military option was used as a threat to bring the parties to a peace conference. In late 1995 a peace treaty was signed and a substantial NATO force was deployed to Bosnia to implement the terms of the Dayton Agreement and to help bring about a permanent settlement of the conflict (see web link 5.34).

The International Society approach to responsible statecraft says that we must imagine ourselves in the shoes of the statespeople at the time they are confronted by a moral dilemma. If we do that in the case of Bosnia, it is not so difficult to understand why a middle course of muddling through was originally chosen: it is the response that one would expect from any statesman or stateswoman who had a genuine desire to safeguard humanitarian values but no compelling national interest to become directly involved in a conflict and persuasive prudential reasons to stay out. Non-intervention would involve disregarding the compelling humanitarian claims of the Bosnian people; but full military intervention would involve taking incalculable risks with the lives of everybody involved, civilians as well as soldiers. As it turned out, the middle course of limited UN humanitarian intervention probably prolonged the conflict and proved to have tragic consequences. But that was not clear in advance. In world politics only hindsight gives the full picture.

The length, intensity and circuitous course of the debate over Bosnia did not indicate an exclusively realist preoccupation with national interests or any lack of humanitarian concern. If national responsibility was all that mattered, the Bosnia–Herzegovina conflict would have been left to the people who live in those countries to sort out themselves. In fact, the humanitarian crisis in Bosnia created a great deal of frustration and anguish for the leaders of major Western powers. What that debate did indicate was an absence of confidence that military intervention in Bosnia-Herzegovina would be successful; many statespeople feared that it would actually make the problem worse. The Bosnia-Herzegovina case illustrates the deeply troubling moral choices that sometimes confront statespeople in a pluralist world in which they have a responsibility to safeguard their own country and its citizens but also a responsibility to defend international law and protect human rights around the world. In other words, the case is a reminder of how statesmen and stateswomen must try to come to grips with and find a way to reconcile their diverging foreign policy responsibilities.

In order to construe these episodes in the correct light, according to the International Society approach, it is necessary to take account of all dimensions of responsible statecraft. National responsibility (realism) is a necessary, but it is not a sufficient guide to the ethics of statecraft in contemporary world politics. To account for the normative complexity and ambiguity of international relations today, IR scholarship must also take into account international responsibility (rationalism) and humanitarian responsibility (revolutionism).

Critiques of International Society

Several major criticisms can be made of the International Society approach to IR. First, there is the realist critique that the evidence of international norms as determinants of state policy and behavior is weak or non-existent. Second, there is the liberal critique that the International Society tradition downplays domestic politics—e.g. democracy—and cannot account for progressive change in international politics. Third, there is the IPE critique that it fails to give an account of international economic relationships. Finally, there are several solidarist critiques that emerge from within the International Society tradition itself that focus on its limitations as a theory of political modernity that cannot come to grips with an emerging postmodern world.

The realist critique of the International Society approach rests on a deep scepticism that there is an 'international society' as Hedley Bull (1995: 13) characterizes it: a group of states that 'conceive themselves to be bound by a common set of rules in their relations with one another, and share in the working of common institutions'. Realists believe that states are bound only by their own national interests. Where is the evidence, realists ask, that states are also 'bound by certain rules . . . that they should respect one another's claims to independence, that they should honour agreements into which they enter, and that they should be subject to certain limitations in exercising force against one another' (Bull 1995: 13)? Realists are sceptical that states really do behave that way. States may respect such rules, but only because it is in their interest to do so. If it is not deemed to be in their interest they are

BOX 5.23	Three traditional critiques of International Society	
REALISM	**LIBERALISM**	**IPE**
Weak evidence of norms	Ignores domestic society	Ignores economics
Interests dominate	Ignores democracy	Ignores Third World
	Ignores progress	

not likely to respect them. Realists thus see states as being 'bound by a common set of rules in their relations with one another' only as long as there is an advantage in doing that. When there is a conflict between international obligations and national interests the latter will always win, because the fundamental concern of states is always their own advantage and ultimately their security and survival. That is the concern that guides foreign policy.

The International Society approach is not as soft a target as the realist critique claims. As pointed out, realism is built into the approach as one of its three basic elements. Wight (1966) characterizes IR as a 'theory of survival' which is an acknowledgement of the primacy of states, their right to exist and the legitimacy of their interests. But the International Society approach does not stop there. It emphasizes that states bind themselves to other states via treaties, and that the justification for that can be more than merely self-interest (realism) or even enlightened self-interest (moderate realism). It emphasizes that states have legitimate interests that other states recognize and respect; it also emphasizes that states recognize the general advantages of observing a principle of reciprocity in international affairs (rationalism). Likewise, it notices that states do not observe treaties only when it is in their best interests to do so. Rather, they enter into treaty commitments with caution because they know that they are binding themselves to the terms of such treaties. If states really acted the way realists claim there would be no binding treaties, because no state could be expected to keep their promise when it was no longer in their interest to do so. Yet binding treaties are commonplace in world politics.

A more damaging criticism of the International Society approach is the theoretical incoherence that could result from trying to combine realism, rationalism and revolutionism within a single framework of interpretation, and from emphasizing not only international order but also international justice.

Liberals have directed most of their critical attention at realism, and the debate between liberals (or idealists) and realists was the most conspicuous IR debate in the twentieth century. However, one implied liberal critique is the lack of interest of International Society theorists in the role of domestic politics in international relations. Like realists, International Society theorists draw a firm line between international relations and the internal politics of states. They are not inclined to investigate the domestic aspects of foreign policy. A second implied liberal critique derives from the claim that liberal democracies are more peace-loving than non-democratic political systems. Here, republican liberals are criticizing not only realists but also—by implication—International Society theorists who tend to ignore the subject. A third implied liberal critique is the inability of the International Society approach to account for progressive change in international relations. Wight (1966: 33) claims that domestic politics is a sphere of progressive change, but that international politics is a sphere of recurrence and repetition and IR is a 'theory of survival'. That view is identical to that of realism.

The implied liberal critique does not really hit the mark. Wight's concept of rationalism and Bull's concept of International Society are very close to ideas of institutional liberalism which focus on institution-building and reject the realist claim that institutions are 'scraps of paper'. There is also room in Wight's notion of revolutionism and Bull's notion of international justice for progressive change. Both notions take the Kantian cosmopolitan

Box 5.24	Three soldarist critiques of International Society

TRANSNATIONAL SOCIETY	GLOBAL SOCIETY	GLOBAL INJUSTICE
State and non-state	Anti-statist	Anti-statist
Transnational activities	Complex global relations	Global protection racket
International civil society	World society	Human wrongs
Public–private coexistence		World injustice

tradition into account, and that is the philosophical basis for the republican liberal claim that democracies do not fight each other.

The main criticism that IPE scholars could direct at the International Society approach is its neglect of economics and the social-class aspect of international relations. International Society scholars have only a limited defence against such a criticism, because the fact is that Martin Wight and Hedley Bull give their overwhelming attention to international politics and largely ignore international economics. There is little discussion of economic issues in their writings, and it is possible to conclude from reading them that economics has little role in IR. However, economics are not entirely ignored. Wight (1991: 1) includes in his definition of rationalism the idea of 'commerce' as one of the basic relations between sovereign states. Bull (1995: 261–9) explores the role of 'economic factors in international relations' and specifically that of 'multinational corporations', 'regional economic associations' and 'transnational society'. Robert Jackson (1990: 109–38) investigates the role of 'international development assistance', 'Third World debt' and the obstacles that existing international society based on state sovereignty presents to Third World development.

The 'transnational society' critique basically argues that international society conceived in terms of a 'society of states' is deficient because it fails to take into account 'the transnational activities of individuals, firms, interest associations and social groups' (Peterson 1992: 371). The state 'does not monopolize the public sphere' and, accordingly, the relations of states do not exhaust international relations. These transnational actors and activities should be neither underestimated nor overestimated: they 'coexist' with sovereign states and interstate relations. International relations are both public and private. There is an international 'civil society' that consists of various transnational actors, but the operation of that society 'relies on the state' to provide 'the conditions under which it can flourish' (Peterson 1992: 376). Those conditions include peace, security, reciprocity—in other words, Bull's basic goals of international order.

That pinpoints the debate between the traditional International Society theorists of IR, discussed above, and their transnational critics. The question is: how important are these conditions, and how important is the state in providing them (see web link 5.17)? It is hard to see any practical and viable alternative to the state at present. If the state is the only institution that can provide these conditions, then the transnational critique loses much of its force, and becomes merely an added, secondary feature of international society which is still, basically, a society of states. If transnational society flourishes in the conditions of the society of states, the transnational critique is less a critique of the traditional International Society approach than a modest reform which expands on that approach.

The 'global society' critique basically argues that International Society is deficient because it operates with 'a fundamentally state-centric approach' that regards states as actors 'akin to individuals', and neglects 'the complex social relations which bind individuals and states' (Shaw 1992: 423–8). International Society theory is really a thinly disguised ideology which basically serves the purpose of justifying the system of sovereign states. It also is blind to 'world society', which it is ill equipped to come to grips with conceptually. 'World society exists through the social relations involved in global commodity production and exchange, through global culture and mass media, and through the increasing development of world politics' (Shaw 1992: 429). That global society has priority, including moral priority, over the society of states (see web link 5.31). It involves 'global responsibility' for human needs, human rights and the environment regardless of state jurisdiction and international boundaries. To the extent that national leaders fail to exercise global responsibility they disclose the moral bankruptcy of traditional International Society based on independent states and, at the same time, the conceptual inadequacy and ideological blinkers of International Society theory.

The core of this critique is the Marxist claim that there is a primary world society in existence in relation to which the society of states is secondary and subordinate. World society is the basic structure. The corresponding claim is that International Society theorists ignore that underlying 'reality' and dispense an 'ideology' of state primacy, the national interest, the law of nations and so on. The reader has to decide whether the state and, by extension, the society of states is more or less substantial and important than other international relations in world politics. A response that International Society theorists might make to Shaw's critique is to point to the way that statespeople actually conceive of and exercise responsibility in world politics, which is by giving priority first to their own citizens (national responsibility), second to other states (international responsibility) and only third to human beings, regardless of their citizenship or to the world as a whole. In other words, the ethic of pluralism is more significant than that of solidarism in shaping and taking responsibility in world politics.

The 'global injustice' critique acknowledges that state interests and concerns still have primacy in world politics, but goes on to make a cosmopolitan critique of the morality, or rather the immorality, of the sovereign state. Ken Booth (1995) argues that international society conceived in terms of a 'society of states' sacrifices human beings on the altar of the sovereign state (see web links 5.31 and 5.32). Statism is the problem rather than the solution as far as human well-being is concerned. Far from ensuring the protection of citizens in particular states primarily through the mechanisms of respect for state sovereignty and defence of the national interest, international society actually 'bears an uncomfortable resemblance to a global protection racket'. Ordinary people in many underdeveloped countries are 'slaves' who are abused and exploited by their rulers, the 'slave-masters'. Instead of protecting human rights, the state system actually produces 'human wrongs' on a global scale.

Booth thus extends Shaw's critique by arguing that statespeople, far from acting responsibly, have created an exclusive club—the society of states—whose rules of equal sovereignty and non-intervention exist to serve their own selfish interests at the expense of a suffering humanity. International Society theorists, by trying to understand and appreciate the difficult choices that statespeople face, actually end up by apologizing for their actions and being 'fetishizers of Foreign Offices' (Booth, quoted by Wheeler 1996: 129). However, this critique ignores or plays down the goal of international order and coexistence without which, arguably, there can be no global justice. It also ignores the fact that Hedley Bull was a critical theorist and anything but an apologist when it came to the behaviour of the great powers, and specifically the United States and the Soviet Union, which he said were 'not well suited to fulfil the normative requirements of great powerhood' (1984: 437–47).

The Current Research Agenda

Since the end of the Cold War the research agenda of International Society has expanded and changed to a degree. The central normative concern has moved at least some distance away from order and towards justice in world politics. Not only has there been a shift of scholarly concern in the direction of justice in world politics, but there has also been a movement away from a concern about international justice and towards a concern about human justice. There has also been an enlargement of the subject to include issues of world justice—such as environmental protection or the law of the sea—and the question of what shape International Society might take in the future if state sovereignty ceases to be the foundation institution of world politics as it has been for the past three and a half centuries.

This raises the age-old question of state sovereignty. We still live in a world of state sovereignty and non-intervention and there is a strong feeling, in our age of democracy, that countries should govern themselves and should not be governed by foreigners, whether they are colonial powers or international trusteeships. However, the same democratic age has produced numerous declarations of human rights which reduce, at least in theory, the sphere of state sovereignty and non-intervention. John Vincent observes that 'boundaries' between domestic societies and international society became 'fuzzier' in the last half of the twentieth century with the accumulation of many international declarations and conventions on human rights (Vincent 1990: 254–5). In other words, there is an ambiguous and confusing relation in international law today between the responsibilities of citizenship, on the one hand, and universal human rights, on the other. A leading item on the research agenda of International Society has been the analysis of that ambiguity in contemporary world politics.

John Vincent and Peter Wilson (1993: 128–9) have argued in more reformist International Society terms that a new idea of 'international legitimacy' is emerging because the international law of human rights 'opens up the state to scrutiny from outsiders and propels us beyond non-intervention'. There is a 'new order of things' which is the interdependent and transnational world propelled by the technological revolution in communications that is 'nudging international society in the direction of a world society'. They argue that the pluralist society of states based on the principle of non-intervention 'has now been replaced by a much more complex world'. There must be a 'new order of thoughts' that explores the conceivable directions that such a change could and should take in the future. They call for a cosmopolitan or solidarist theory of International Society 'which recognizes that the principle of non-intervention no longer sums up the morality of states'. That theory could be pursued by developing a new idea of international legitimacy in which presumably the sovereign state no longer has pride of place, but is instead merely one component, along with human beings and the world itself, of an expanded and far more complex international society: a world society in Hedley Bull's terms.

Another area where we can see an expanding research agenda is 'the greening' of International Society theory (Hurrell and Kingsbury 1992). It is often believed that the environment presents normative problems to which international society cannot respond in the usual terms of state sovereignty and international law. For example, Robert Goodin (1990: 93) considers 'that the traditional structure of international law—guided as it is by notions of autonomous national actors with strong rights that all other national actors similarly share—is wildly inappropriate to many of the new environmental challenges'. That argument suggests that traditional international society based on state sovereignty is beyond its useful life, and now serves more as an obstacle than an asset as far as addressing world environmental problems is concerned. International Society theorists argue that the society of states is more flexible and adaptable than that critique implies. The clear implication is that international society can be green (Jackson 1996a). Indeed, only if sovereign states get involved will environmental problems gain the recognition and environmental norms the respect that they deserve. On that view, international law has not obstructed or even discouraged environmental concerns; on the contrary, it has been employed and adjusted to accommodate and indeed to promote such concerns (Birnie 1992: 51–84) by fitting them into the practices of state sovereignty.

As the above discussion indicates, there has been an enlargement of the scope of International Society theory well beyond its traditional focus on state sovereignty and the society of states. That raises a final question: what shape should international society be expected to take in the future if these trends continue? Are they an indication that state sovereignty will eventually cease to be the foundation institution of world politics, as it has been for the past three and a half centuries? Or are they an indication that state sovereignty is an adapting, evolving international institution which has presented a somewhat different face to the world in the past, and which can be expected to change its shape and substance again in the future?

Hedley Bull (1995: 254–66) speculated on whether the classical society of states based on state sovereignty 'may be giving place to a secular reincarnation of the system of overlapping or segmented authority that characterized medieval Christendom' (see Chapter 1). He saw preliminary evidence of such a trend in 'five features of contemporary world politics': (1) the regional integration of states, such as the European Union; (2) the disintegration of states, such as the break-up of the Soviet Union and former Yugoslavia; (3) the expansion of private international violence, such as the rise of international terrorism; (4) the growth of transnational organizations, including the rise of multinational corporations; and (5) the increasing 'unification' of the world by means of advancing technology, such as the spread of electronic communications. Richard Falk (1985: 651) answered that question in the affirmative: 'the reorganization of international life has two principal features—increased central guidance and increased roles for non-territorial actors'. Bull disagreed with Falk's revolutionist assessment: 'there is no clear evidence that in the next few decades the states system is likely to give place to any of the alternatives to it that have been nominated'. However, Bull did emphasize 'that there is now a wider world political system of which the states system is only a part'. That larger system is a 'world-wide network of interaction' that embraces not only states but also other political actors, both 'above' the state and 'below' it.

In short, the difference between Falk and Bull on the question of the future of International Society is a matter of scholarly judgement. Falk judges world politics to be in a process of fundamental, revolutionary change. Bull judges world politics to be in a process of evolutionary adaptation. The reader will have to make up his or her own mind as to which of these theorists is closer to getting it right.

KEY POINTS

- The International Society approach is a middle way in classical IR scholarship: it carves out a place between classical realism and classical liberalism and builds that place into a separate and distinctive IR approach. It regards international relations as a 'society' of states in which the principal actors are statespeople who are specialized in the art of statecraft.

- A system of states is formed when two or more states have sufficient contact between them to make the behaviour of each a necessary element in the calculations of the other. A society of states exists when a group of states form a society in the sense that they conceive themselves to be bound by a common set of rules in their relations with one another.

- IR is a never-ending dialogue between realism, rationalism and revolutionism. Realism emphasizes anarchy and power politics. Rationalism emphasizes society and international law. Revolutionism emphasizes humanitarianism, human rights and human justice.

- The main point of international society is the promotion and preservation of international order. The responsibility for sustaining order between states belongs to the great powers.

- International society also involves concerns about justice. Commutative justice is the principal form of international justice. But issues of distributive justice are of increasing importance on the international agenda.

- Statespeople face difficult dilemmas because of the different kinds of responsibility that they have to consider. There are three distinctive dimensions of responsibility: national, international and humanitarian.

QUESTIONS

- What are the core elements of the International Society approach?

- What is the difference between order and justice in world politics? Is Hedley Bull correct in claiming that order comes before justice?

- Compare the realist, rationalist and revolutionist views of the (1990) Gulf War. Which view is the most persuasive?

- What are the most important responsibilities that state leaders in international society must take into consideration when deciding their course of action in cases such as Bosnia?

- Some International Society theorists argue that human rights are of increased importance in world politics since the end of the Cold War. Are they correct? What is the evidence in favour of such a view?

- International Society theorists are sometimes accused of being realists in disguise. Is that accusation warranted?

GUIDE TO FURTHER READING

Bain, W. (2003). *Between Anarchy and Society*. Oxford: Oxford University Press.

Bellamy, A. J. (ed.) (2005). *International Society and its Critics*. Oxford: Oxford University Press.

Bull, H. (1995). *The Anarchical Society: A Study of Order in World Politics*, 2nd edn. London: Macmillan.

Bull, H. and Watson, A. (eds) (1984). *The Expansion of International Society*. Oxford: Clarendon Press.

Buzan, B. (2004). *From International to World Society?* Cambridge: Cambridge University Press.

Foot, R., Gaddis, J. L. and Hurrell, A. (eds) (2003). *Order and Justice in International Relations*. Oxford: Oxford University Press.

Jackson, R. (2000). *The Global Covenant: Human Conduct in a World of States*. Oxford: Oxford University Press.

Keene, E. (2002). *Beyond the Anarchical Society*. Cambridge: Cambridge University Press.

Vincent, R. J. (1990). 'Grotius, Human Rights, and Intervention', in H. Bull, B. Kingsbury and A. Roberts (eds), *Hugo Grotius and International Relations*. Oxford: Clarendon Press.

Wight, M. (1991). *International Theory: The Three Traditions*. Leicester: Leicester University Press.

Williams, J. and Little, R. (2006). *Anarchical Society in a Globalized World* (New York: Palgrave Macmillan.

WEB LINKS

Web links mentioned in the chapter plus additional links can be found on the Online Resource Centre that accompanies this book.

www.oxfordtextbooks.co.uk/orc/jackson_sorensen3e/

CHAPTER 6

Social Constructivism

▌ Summary

This chapter introduces social constructivist theory of IR. We first clarify where constructivism comes from and why it has established itself as an important approach in IR. Constructivism is examined both as a meta-theory about the nature of the social world and as a substantial theory of IR. Several examples of constructivist IR theory are presented, followed by reflections on the strengths and weaknesses of the approach.

Introduction

The focus of social constructivism (in shorthand: constructivism) is on human awareness or consciousness and its place in world affairs. Much IR theory, and especially neorealism, is *materialist*; it focuses on how the distribution of material power, such as military forces and economic capabilities, defines balances of power between states and explains the behaviour of states. Constructivists reject such a one-sided material focus. They argue that the most important aspect of international relations is social, not material. Furthermore, they argue that this social reality is not objective, or external, to the observer of international affairs. The social and political world, including the world of international relations, is not a physical entity or material object that is outside human consciousness. Consequently, the study of international relations must focus on the ideas and beliefs that inform the actors on the international scene as well as the shared understandings between them (see web link 6.01).

The international system is not something 'out there' like the solar system. It does not exist on its own. It exists only as an intersubjective awareness among people; in that sense the system is constituted by *ideas*, not by material forces. It is a human invention or creation not of a physical or material kind but of a purely intellectual and ideational kind. It is a set of ideas, a body of thought, a system of norms, which has been arranged by certain people at a particular time and place.

If the thoughts and ideas that enter into the existence of international relations change, then the system itself will change as well, because the system consists in thoughts and ideas. That is the insight behind the oft-repeated phrase by constructivist Alexander Wendt: 'anarchy is what states make of it' (1992). The claim sounds innocent but the potential consequences are far-reaching: suddenly the world of IR becomes less fixated in an age-old structure of anarchy; change becomes possible in a big way because people and states can start thinking about each other in new ways and thus create new norms that may be radically different from old ones.

This chapter introduces constructivist theory of IR. We first clarify where constructivism comes from and why it has established itself as an important approach in IR over a short period of time. The nature of constructivist theory is examined: is it a meta-theory about the nature of the social world or is it a substantial theory of IR, or is it both? That leads to a brief presentation of the constructivist contributions to IR theory and some reflections on the strengths and weaknesses of the approach.

The Rise of Constructivism in IR

Beginning in the 1980s, constructivism has become an increasingly significant approach, especially in North American IR. During the Cold War there was a clear pattern of power balancing between two blocs, led by the United States and the Soviet Union respectively.

After the end of the Cold War and following the dissolution of the Soviet Union, the situation turned much more fluid and open. It soon became clear that the parsimonious neorealist theory was not at all clear about the future developments of the balance of power. Neorealist logic dictates that other states will balance against the US because offsetting US power is a means of guaranteeing one's own security; such balancing will lead to the emergence of new great powers in a multipolar system. But since the end of the Cold War, this has not happened; Waltz argues that it will eventually happen 'tomorrow' (2002). Another neorealist, Christopher Layne, speculates that it could take some fifty years before Japan and Germany start balancing against the US (1993). The constructivist claim is that neorealist uncertainty is closely connected to the fact that the theory is overly spare and materialist; and constructivists argue that a focus on thoughts and ideas leads to a better theory about anarchy and power balancing.

Some liberals (see Chapter 4) have basically accepted neorealist assumptions as a starting point for analysis; they are of course vulnerable to much of the critique directed against neorealism by constructivists. Other liberals did begin to focus more on the role of ideas after the Cold War ended. When Francis Fukuyama proclaimed 'the end of history' (1989), he was endorsing the role of ideas and especially the progress of liberal ideas in the world. But he and other liberals are mostly interested in the concrete advance of liberal, democratic government in the world. Even if constructivists are sympathetic to several elements of liberal thinking, their focus is less on the advance of liberal ideas; it is on the role of thinking and ideas in general.

So the historical context (i.e. the end of the Cold War) and the theoretical discussion between IR scholars (especially among neorealists and liberals) helped set the stage for a constructivist approach. And constructivism became especially popular among North American scholars, because that environment was dominated by the neorealist/neoliberal approaches. In Europe, the International Society approach (see Chapter 5) had already to a significant extent included the role of ideas and the importance of social interaction between states in their analysis. In that sense, there was less intellectual space in Europe for constructivists to fill out.

At the same time, constructivists were inspired by theoretical developments in other social science disciplines, including philosophy and sociology. In sociology, Anthony Giddens (1984) proposed the concept of structuration as a way of analysing the relationship between structures and actors (see web link 6.02). According to Giddens, structures (i.e. the rules and conditions that guide social action) do not determine what actors do in any mechanical way, an impression one might get from the neorealist view of how the structure of anarchy constrains state actors. The relationship between structures and actors involves intersubjective understanding and meaning. Structures do constrain actors, but actors can also transform structures by thinking about them and acting on them in new ways. The notion of structuration therefore leads to a less rigid and more dynamic view of the relationship between structure and actors. IR constructivists use this as a starting-point for suggesting a less rigid view of anarchy.

We have noted some recent historical and theoretical developments that help explain the rise of social constructivism in IR. But constructivism has deeper roots; it is not an entirely new approach. It also grows out of an old methodology that can be traced back at least to the eighteenth-century writings of the Italian philosopher Giambattista Vico (Pompa 1982). According to Vico, the natural world is made by God, but the historical world is made by Man (Pompa 1982: 26). History is not some kind of unfolding or evolving process that is external to human affairs. Men and women make their own history. They also make states which are historical constructs. States are artificial creations and the state system is artificial too; it is made by men and women and if they want to, they can change it and develop it in new ways (see web link 6.03).

Immanuel Kant is another forerunner of social constructivism (Hacking 1999: 41). Kant argued that we can obtain knowledge about the world, but it will always be subjective knowledge in the sense that it is filtered through human consciousness. Max Weber emphasized that the social world (i.e. the world of human interaction) is fundamentally different from the natural world of physical phenomena. Human beings rely on 'understanding' of each other's actions and assigning 'meaning' to them. In order to comprehend human interaction, we cannot merely describe it in the way we describe physical phenomena, such as a boulder falling off a cliff; we need a different kind of interpretive understanding, or 'verstehen' (Morrison 1995: 273–82). Is the pat of another person's face a punishment or a caress? We cannot know until we assign meaning to the act. Weber concluded that 'subjective understanding is the specific characteristic of sociological knowledge' (Weber 1977: 15). Constructivists rely on such insights to emphasize the importance of 'meaning' and 'understanding' (Fierke and Jørgensen (eds) 2001).

Constructivism as Social Theory

We can distinguish between theories at different levels of abstraction. Social theory is the more general theory about the social world, about social action, and about the relationship between structures and actors. Substantive IR theory is theory about some aspect of international relations. Constructivism is both a social theory and a number of different substantive theories of IR; this section is about constructivism as a social theory; the next section is about constructivist theories of IR.

In social theory, constructivists emphasize the social construction of reality. Human relations, including international relations, consist of thought and ideas and not essentially of material conditions or forces. This is the philosophically idealist element of constructivism which contrasts with the materialist philosophy of much social science positivism (see Chapter 11). According to constructivist philosophy, the social world is not a given: it is not something 'out there' that exists independent of the thoughts and ideas of the people involved in it. It is not an external reality whose laws can be discovered by scientific research and explained by scientific theory as positivists and behaviouralists argue. The social and political world is not part of nature. There are no natural laws of society or economics or politics. History is not an evolving external process that is independent of human thought

BOX 6.1	Wendt's constructivist conception of social structures

Social structures have three elements: shared knowledge, material resources, and practices. First, social structures are defined, in part, by shared understandings, expectations, or knowledge. These constitute the actors in a situation and the nature of their relationships, whether cooperative or conflictual. A security dilemma, for example, is a social structure composed of intersubjective understandings in which states are so distrustful that they make worst-case assumptions about each other's intentions, and as a result define their interests in self-help terms. A security community is a different social structure, one composed of shared knowledge in which states trust one another to resolve disputes without war. This dependence of social structure on ideas is the sense in which constructivism has an idealist (or 'idea-ist') view of structure.

Wendt (1992: 73)

and ideas. That means that sociology or economics or political science or the study of history cannot be objective 'sciences' in the strict positivist sense of the word.

Everything involved in the social world of men and women is made by them. The fact that it is made by them makes it intelligible to them. The social world is a world of human consciousness: of thoughts and beliefs, of ideas and concepts, of languages and discourses, of signs, signals and understandings among human beings, especially groups of human beings, such as states and nations. The social world is an intersubjective domain: it is meaningful to people who made it and live in it, and who understand is precisely because they made it and they are at home in it.

The social world is in part constructed of physical entities. But it is the ideas and beliefs concerning those entities which are most important: what those entities signify in the minds of people. The international system of security and defence, for example, consists of territories, populations, weapons and other physical assets. But it is the ideas and understandings according to which those assets are conceived, organized and used—e.g. in alliances, armed forces, etc.—that is most important. The physical element is there, but it is secondary to the intellectual element which infuses it with meaning, plans it, organizes it and guides it. The thought that is involved in international security is more important, far more important, than the physical assets that are involved because those assets have no meaning without the intellectual component: they are mere things in themselves.

It is helpful to emphasize the contrast between a materialist view held by neorealists (and neoliberals) and the ideational view held by constructivists. According to the materialist view, power and national interest are the driving forces in international politics. Power is ultimately military capability, supported by economic and other resources. National interest is the self-regarding desire by states for power, security or wealth (Wendt 1999: 92). Power and interest are seen as 'material' factors; they are objective entities in the sense that because of anarchy states are compelled to be preoccupied with power and interest. In this view, ideas matter little; they can be used to rationalize actions dictated by material interest. In the ideational view held by social constructivists ideas always matter. 'The starting premise is that the material world is indeterminate and is interpreted within a larger context of meaning.

> **BOX 6.2**   **The social constructivist view of ideas**
>
> The claim is *not* that ideas are more important than power and interest, or that they are autonomous from power and interest. The claim is rather that power and interest have the effects they do in virtue of the ideas that make them up. Power and interest explanations *presuppose* ideas, and to that extent are not rivals to ideational explanations at all . . . Let me [propose] a rule of thumb for idealists: when confronted by ostensibly 'material' explanations, always inquire into the discursive conditions which make them work. When Neorealists offer multipolarity as an explanation for war, inquire into the discursive conditions that constitute the poles as enemies rather than friends. When Liberals offer economic interdependence as an explanation for peace, inquire into the discursive conditions that constitute states with identities that care about free trade and economic growth. When Marxists offer capitalism as an explanation for state forms, inquire into the discursive conditions that constitute capitalist relations of production. And so on.
>
> Wendt (1999: 135–6)

Ideas thus define the meaning of material power' (Tannenwald 2005: 19). This constructivist view of ideas is emphasized by Wendt in Box 6.2.

The core ideational element upon which constructivists focus is intersubjective beliefs (and ideas, conceptions and assumptions) that are widely shared among people. Ideas must be widely shared to matter; nonetheless they can be held by different groups, such as organizations, policymakers, social groups or society. 'Ideas are mental constructs held by individuals, sets of distinctive beliefs, principles and attitudes that provide broad orientations for behaviour and policy' (Tannenwald 2005: 15). There are many different kinds of ideas. Nina Tannenwald identifies four major types: 'ideologies or shared belief systems, normative beliefs, cause–effect beliefs, and policy prescriptions' (Tannenwald 2005: 15); they are described in Box 6.3.

Constructivism is an empirical approach to the study of international relations—empirical in that it focuses on the intersubjective ideas that define international relations. The theory displays some distinctive research interests and approaches. If the social and political world consists, at base, of shared beliefs, how does that affect the way we should account for important international events and episodes? Constructivists, as a rule, cannot subscribe to mechanical positivist conceptions of causality. That is because the positivists do not probe the intersubjective content of events and episodes. For example, the well-known billiard ball image of international relations is rejected by constructivists because it fails to reveal the thoughts, ideas, beliefs and so on of the actors involved in international conflicts. Constructivists want to probe the inside of the billiard balls to arrive at a deeper understanding of such conflicts (see web links 6.05 and 6.07).

Constructivists generally agree with Max Weber that they need to employ interpretive understanding (*verstehen*) in order to analyse social action (Ruggie 1998). But they are not in agreement about the extent to which it is possible to emulate the scientific ideas of the natural sciences and produce scientific explanations based on hypotheses, data collection

> **BOX 6.3   Four types of ideas**
>
> Ideologies or shared belief systems are a systematic set of doctrines or beliefs that reflect the social needs and aspirations of a group, class, culture, or state. Examples include the Protestant ethic or political ideologies such as liberalism, Marxism, and fascism . . .
>
> Normative (or principled) beliefs are beliefs about right and wrong. They consist of values and attitudes that specify criteria for distinguishing right from wrong or just from unjust and they imply associated standards of behaviour, [for example] the role of human rights norms at the end of the Cold War . . .
>
> Causal beliefs are beliefs about cause–effect, or means–end relationships. They . . . provide guidelines or strategies for individuals on how to achieve their objectives . . . [for example], Soviet leaders' changing beliefs about the efficacy (or more precisely non-efficacy) of the use of force influenced their decision in 1989 not to use force to keep Eastern Europe under Soviet control.
>
> Finally, policy prescriptions are the specific programmatic ideas that facilitate policymaking by specifying how to solve particular policy problems. They are at the center of policy debates and are associated with specific strategies and policy programs.
>
> Tannenwald (2005: 15–16)

and generalization (see Chapter 11). On the one hand, constructivists reject the notion of objective truth; social scientists cannot discover a 'final truth' about the world which is true across time and place. On the other hand, constructivists do make 'truth claims about the subjects they have investigated . . . while admitting that their claims are always contingent and partial interpretations of a complex world' (Price and Reus-Smit 1998: 272).

At the same time, it is fair to say that constructivists do not agree entirely on this issue (Fierke 2001). The view expressed here is closer to what has been called 'conventional' constructivism (Hopf 1998) represented by such scholars as Alexander Wendt (1999), Peter Katzenstein (1996b), Christian Reus-Smit (1997), John Ruggie (1998), Emanuel Adler and Michael Barnett (1998), Ted Hopf (2002) and Martha Finnemore (2003). 'Critical' constructivists are much more sceptical about this position; they argue that 'truth claims' are not possible because there is no neutral ground where we can decide about what is true. What we call truth is always connected to different, more or less dominant, ways of thinking about the world. Truth and power cannot be separated; indeed, the main task of critical constructivism is to unmask that core relationship between truth and power, to criticize those dominant versions of thinking that claim to be true for all. Critical constructivists include David Campbell (1998), Jim George (1994), James Der Derian (1987), R. B. J. Walker (1993), Andrew Linklater (1998) and Ann Tickner (1992). Our presentation of constructivist scholarship focuses on 'conventional' constructivism. Salient aspects of 'critical' constructivism, which we label postmodernism, are discussed in Chapter 11.

Constructivist Theories of International Relations

Constructivism was introduced to IR by Nicholas Onuf (1989) who coined the term. It gathered a larger following among scholars with a series of influential articles and a book by Alexander Wendt (1987; 1992; 1994; 1995; 1999). We begin this brief and selective overview of constructivist IR theory with Wendt's contribution.

The core of Wendt's argument is the rejection of the neorealist position, according to which anarchy must necessarily lead to self-help. Whether it does or not cannot be decided a priori; it depends on the interaction between states. In these processes of interaction the identities and interests of states are created. For neorealists, identities and interests are given; states know who they are and what they want before they begin interaction with other states. For Wendt, it is the very interactions with others that 'create and instantiate one structure of identities and interests rather than another; structure has no existence or causal powers apart from process' (Wendt 1992: 394). States want to survive and be secure; neorealists and constructivists agree about that. But what kind of security policy follows from this? Do states seek to become as powerful as possible or are they content with what they have? Wendt argues that we can only find out by studying identities and interests as they are shaped in the interaction between states.

In concrete terms, 'if the United States and the Soviet Union decide that they are no longer enemies, "the cold war is over". It is collective meanings that constitute the structures which organize our actions. Actors acquire identities—relatively stable, role-specific understanding and expectations about self—by participating in such collective meaning' (Wendt 1992: 397). West European states need not start power balancing against each other because the Cold War is over, four decades of cooperation may have led to a new 'European identity' of cooperation and friendship between them (Wendt 1992: 418) (see web links 6.16 and 6.17).

Wendt's 1999 book further develops the argument introduced in the earlier articles. His point of departure is the same as Waltz's: interaction between states in a system characterized by anarchy. But anarchy need not lead to self-help; that calls for further study of the discursive interaction between states in order to discover what specific 'culture of anarchy' has developed between them. Wendt suggests three major ideal types of anarchy: Hobbesian, Lockean and Kantian (1999: 257). In the Hobbesian culture, states view each other as enemies; the logic of Hobbesian anarchy is 'war of all against all'. States are adversaries and war is endemic because violent conflict is a way of survival. Hobbesian anarchy, according to Wendt, dominated the state system until the seventeenth century.

In the Lockean culture, states consider each other rivals, but there is also restraint; states do not seek to eliminate each other, they recognize the other states' right to exist. Lockean anarchy became a characteristic of the modern state system after the Peace of Westphalia in 1648. Finally, in a Kantian culture, states view each other as friends, settle disputes peacefully and support each other in the case of threat by a third party (Wendt 1999: 299). A Kantian culture has emerged among consolidated liberal democracies since the Second World War (see web link 6.14).

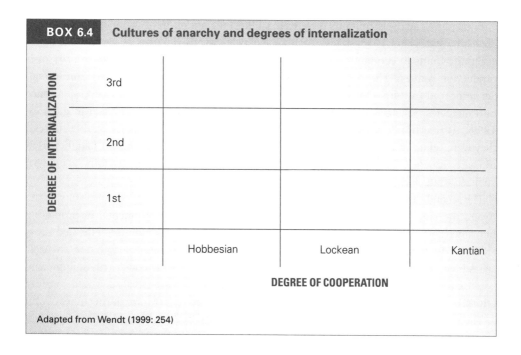

BOX 6.4	**Cultures of anarchy and degrees of internalization**

Adapted from Wendt (1999: 254)

The three different cultures of anarchy can be internalized in different degrees; that is to say, the way states view each other may be more or less deeply shared. Wendt makes a distinction between three degrees of 'cultural internalization' (Wendt 1999: 254): the first degree is a relatively weak commitment to shared ideas; the third degree a strong commitment. We get a three-by-three table of 'degrees of cooperation' and 'degrees of internalization' respectively (see Box 6.4).

Wendt drives home the point that constructivism is not merely about 'adding the role of ideas' to existing theories of IR. Material power and state interest are fundamentally formed by ideas and social interaction. Therefore, states in an anarchic system may each possess military and other capabilities which can be seen as potentially threatening by other states; but enmity and arms races are not inevitable outcomes. Social interaction between states can also lead to more benign and friendly cultures of anarchy.

Wendt's analysis is systemic; it focuses on interaction between states in the international system and disregards the role of domestic factors. Martha Finnemore has proposed another variant of constructivist, systemic analysis in her 1996 book, *National Interests in International Society*. Her starting-point is the definition of states' identities and interests. But instead of looking at the social interaction between states, focus is on the norms of international society and the way in which they affect state identities and interests. State behaviour is defined by identity and interest. Identity and interests are defined by international forces, that is, by the norms of behaviour embedded in international society. The norms of international society are transmitted to states through international organizations. They shape national policies by 'teaching' states what their interests should be (see web link 6.18).

Finnemore's analysis contains three case-studies: the adoption of science policy bureaucracies by states after 1955; states' acceptance of rule-governed norms of warfare; and states accepting limits to economic sovereignty by allowing redistribution to take priority over production values. The first case-study argues that the United Nations Educational, Scientific and Cultural Organization (UNESCO) has taught states how to develop science bureaucracies. Science policy bureaucracies did not exist in many states prior to the mid-1950s. At that time UNESCO began a drive to establish them, with considerable success: they were set up in merely fourteen countries in 1955; by 1975, the number had increased to nearly ninety. UNESCO successfully propagated the idea that in order to be a 'modern civilized' state, having a science policy bureaucracy was a necessary ingredient.

The second case-study is about how states came to accept rule-governed norms of warfare. Again, the argument is that an international organization was instrumental in promoting humanitarian norms in warfare; in this case it is the International Committee of the Red Cross (ICRC). The ICRC succeeded in prescribing what was 'appropriate behaviour' for 'civilized' states involved in war. This would appear to be a 'hard case' for the constructivist approach, because the ICRC could push through new norms in an area that neorealists would consider critical for national interests, namely the right to unconstrained use of force during times of war.

The third and final case-study concerns the acceptance by Third World states of poverty alleviation as a central norm of economic policy. Until the late 1960s the overriding objective of economic policy was to increase production by focusing on economic growth. By the early 1970s welfare improvement through economic redistribution became a principal goal of economic policy. Finnemore argues that this normative shift was pushed by the World Bank. The bank's president—Robert McNamara—played an essential role; he was convinced that the bank should actively promote poverty alleviation in developing countries.

Martha Finnemore thus argues that international norms promoted by international organizations can decisively influence national guidelines by pushing states to adopt these norms in their national policies. Against neorealism, she argues that the changes brought forward by the case-studies cannot be explained by pure national interests in power-maximation. They need to be explained by a constructivist analysis emphasizing the central role of norms in international society.

Systemic constructivists such as Finnemore and Wendt stress the importance of the international environment in shaping state identities. Other constructivists put more

---

BOX 6.5   Martha Finnemore on norms in international society

The fact that we live in an international society means that what we want and, in some ways, who we are are shaped by the social norms, rules, understandings, and relationships we have with others. These social realities are as influential as material realities in determining behaviour. Indeed, they are what endow material realities with meaning and purpose.

In political terms, it is these social realities that provide us with ends to which power and wealth can be used.

Finnemore (1996: 128)

emphasis on the domestic environment. One way of moving in this direction is to study how international norms have dissimilar effects in different states and then speculate about the domestic factors responsible for such variation. A volume edited by Thomas Risse (1999) takes on this task in the area of international human rights norms. The authors demonstrate how regime type, the experience of civil war and the presence of domestic human rights organizations impinge on on the degree to which states are ready to comply with international human rights norms (see web link 6.19).

The book edited by Peter Katzenstein, *The Culture of National Security: Norms and Identity in World Politics* (1996a) aims to drive home the general constructivist claim that culture, norms and identity matter, also in the core area of national security. In this context, many essays put special emphasis on domestic norms. Alastair Johnston, for example, takes up the case of Maoist China in order to see 'how far ideational arguments can go in accounting for realpolitik behaviour' (Johnston 1996: 217). He identifies a specific 'hard realpolitik' strategic culture in the Chinese tradition that informs and shapes Chinese security policies. The argument is that Chinese decision-makers have 'internalized this strategic culture' and that it 'has persisted across vastly different interstate systems, regime types, levels of technology, and types of threat' (Johnston 1996: 217). In other words, neorealist accounts of Chinese behaviour are incomplete because they fail to include such a notion of an idea-based strategic culture; and precisely because its presence can be shown across different systems it is clear that 'anarchy' is not sufficient to account for the Chinese position.

Peter Katzenstein has written a book on Japan which further develops a constructivist argument about the role of domestic norms in the area of national security (Katzenstein 1996b). Systemic theorizing is inadequate, says Katzenstein, because it does not sufficiently appreciate how the internal make-up of states affects their behaviour in the international system. The emphasis in his analysis is on the domestic normative structure and how it influences state identity, interests and policy. A major puzzle addressed is the shift from a militaristic foreign policy before 1945 to a pacifist foreign policy after the world war. The analysis explains why there was a broad consensus favouring a militaristic foreign policy before the war and how the norms on which that consensus was based became profoundly contested as a result of the war. The military's position within the government was severely weakened; furthermore, the new

---

BOX 6.6   **Peter Katzenstein on the importance of culture and identity**

Today's problem is no longer that of E. H. Carr, one of avoiding the sterility of realism and the naïveté of liberalism. Our choice is more complex. We can remain intellectually riveted on a realist world of states balancing power in a multipolar system. We can focus analytically with liberal institutionalists on the efficiency effects that institutions may have on the prospects for policy coordination between states. Or, acknowledging the partial validity of these views, we can broaden our analytical perspective, as this book suggests, to include as well culture and identity as important causal factors that help define the interests and constitute the actors that shape national security policies and global insecurities.

Katzenstein (1996a: 537)

constitution committed Japan to a pacifist standing and put a low ceiling on defence expenditures (1 per cent of the national income). Again, the argument is constructivist, but a systemic analysis is rejected in favour of an analysis of the domestic environment.

Ted Hopf has made a study of Soviet and Russian foreign policy that also focuses on the domestic formation of identity in order to understand how national interests are defined and what foreign policies they lead to (Hopf 2002). He seeks to provide 'an account of how a state's own domestic identities constitute a social cognitive structure that makes threats and opportunities, enemies and allies, intelligible, thinkable, and possible' (Hopf 2002: 16).

State identity is expressed through key decision-makers. The identity of key decision-makers is uncovered through textual sources, including archives, journals, newspapers, memoirs and textbooks. Two case-studies are undertaken, Moscow 1955 and Moscow 1999. The claim is that the reconstructed domestic identities go a long way in explaining Soviet/Russian foreign policy in 1955 and 1999.

Even if constructivists have a debate about the relative importance of domestic versus international environments, the disagreement between them should not be exaggerated. Constructivists are united by much more than divides them; especially, they all emphasize the importance of culture and identity, as expressed in social norms, rules and understandings. The social and political world is made up of shared beliefs rather than physical entities. For constructivists, that must always be the starting-point for analysis.

Critiques of Constructivism

Since neorealism is the main theoretical opponent for most constructivists, let us begin with a neorealist critique of the constructivist approach. First of all, neorealists are sceptical about the importance that constructivists attach to norms, in particular international norms. Such norms surely exist, but they are routinely disregarded if that is in the interest of powerful states. Ever since the Peace of Westphalia in 1648, writes Stephen Krasner:

Powerful states have violated the autonomy and the integrity of weak ones. The Peace of Westphalia included elaborate provisions concerning religious practices within Germany . . . and specified electoral procedures for the selection of the Holy Roman Emperor. Hardly a testimony to respect for sovereign autonomy. Every other major postwar settlement since 1648 has attempted to restructure domestic political institutions in defeated states . . . If there is an international society out there it has not had much more impact on the behaviour of states than conventional norms about sex, family, and marriage now have on the behaviour of individuals in North America and Europe.

(Krasner 1994: 16–17)

At the same time, neorealists are not ready to accept that states can easily become friends due to their social interaction. Such a goal may be 'desirable in principle, but not realizable in practice, because the structure of the international system forces states to behave as egoists. Anarchy, offensive capabilities, and uncertain intentions combine to leave states with little choice but to compete aggressively with each other. For realists, trying to infuse states with communitarian norms is a hopeless cause' (Mearsheimer 1995b: 367).

The major problem that states face in anarchy, according to neorealists, is a problem that is not sufficiently analysed by constructivists; it is the problem of uncertainty (Copeland 2000). Uncertainty is about the present intentions of other states and it is about future intentions of other states. At any given moment, there may be peace and quiet in the international system. But in anarchy, states are always seeking security; moves in that direction can be misread by other states; that is what the security dilemma is all about. 'Realism only needs states to be uncertain about the present and future interests of the other, and in anarchies of great powers, such uncertainty may often be profound' (Copeland 2000: 200). According to Dale Copeland, Wendt's constructivist analysis overly downplays the fact that states have difficulties in obtaining trustworthy information about the motives and intentions of other states (see web links 6.33 and 6.35).

The problem of uncertainty is significantly increased by the fact of deception. Constructivists tend to assume that social interaction between states is always sincere and that states genuinely attempt to express and understand each others' motives and intentions. But there is a pervasive element of deception in the relations between many states. Deceptive actors 'will stage-manage the situation to create impressions that serve their narrow ends, and other actors, especially in world politics, will understand this' (Copeland 2000: 202). In other words, are states really peaceful or do they merely pretend to be peaceful? In the case of the Hitler–Stalin pact it was probably clear to most that it was not based on good and sincere intentions about cooperation between the two states; but it is easy to find other examples where states say one thing and mean another. The analysis by Ted Hopf introduced above, for example, 'takes at face value comments made by Khrushchev to party gatherings praising China and advocating closer ties. In reality, that is only part of the story. That same year, 1955, Khrushchev warned West German Chancellor Konrad Adenauer in private conversations that China represented a real threat to the USSR and to the West . . . Which is the real

Khrushchevian view of China? One cannot explain Soviet policy in 1955 without engaging in that discussion' (Stent 2005: 185).

Against this critique, constructivists will maintain that anarchy is a more complex entity than posited by neorealists. It need not always lead to self-help, mutual aggression and the risk of violent conflict. The claim by Mearsheimer, that 'realism was the dominant discourse from about the start of the late medieval period in 1300 to 1989, and that states and other political entities behaved according to realist dictates during these seven centuries' (Mearsheimer 1995b: 371), is not accurate; without incorporating a focus on ideas and social interaction, on the formation of interests and identities, it will not be possible, say constructivists, to produce a precise analysis about the nature of anarchy in particular historical periods. Furthermore, it may be true that shared ideas about friendship do not reflect a deep commitment between some states; but that point can be addressed by carefully analysing the 'degree of internalization' (see Box 6.4 above) of shared ideas. Neorealists, in turn, can retort that Wendt's 'first degree of internalization' reflects a thin commitment to shared ideas among states; at the same time this 'first degree' level is commonplace in the real world. Wendt's 'first degree' is thus in effect another way of admitting the core relevance of the neorealist analysis of anarchy.

Another critique by neorealists concerns the constructivist view of change. Constructivists 'provide few insights on why discourses rise and fall . . . [therefore, they] say little about why realism has been the dominant discourse, and why its foundations are so shaky. They certainly do not offer a well-defined argument that deals with this important issue . . . Nevertheless, [constructivists] occasionally point to particular factors that might lead to changes in international relations discourse. In such cases, however, they usually end up arguing that changes in the material world drive changes in discourse' (Mearsheimer 1995b: 369). Robert Jervis contends that constructivists fail to explain 'how norms are formed, how identities are shaped, and how interests are defined as they do . . . [Constructivism] does not, by itself, tell us something about the processes at work in political life, it does not, by itself, tell us anything about the expected content of foreign policies or international relations' (Jervis 1998: 976).

Constructivists claim that they do study change. It is rather neorealism that downplays change by claiming international relations to be 'the same damned things over and over again', that is, a constant logic of anarchy (Wendt 1999: 17). Constructivists study change through the analysis of social interaction. 'Regarding the mechanisms of change, some constructivists emphasize collective learning, cognitive evolution, epistemic change and the "life cycles of norms", all of which involve the institutionalization of people's knowledge, practices and discourses' (Adler 2001: 102).

The analysis of change points to areas where constructivists can cooperate with liberals and international society theorists. Liberals (Chapter 4) focus on processes of democratization, interdependence and international institutions. These processes can act as inspiration for a constructivist interpretation of why actors choose to cooperate, even to become friends. Liberal progress can help create norms and ideas of cooperation. As for International Society theorists (Chapter 5) they emphasize the existence of common interests and common values between states. That is precisely what makes relations between states into an international society instead of a mere 'system of states'. Constructivists can thus cooperate with liberals and International Society theorists. At the same time, International Society theorists may claim that constructivists add little new to the analysis of anarchy already produced by IS-scholars. Wendt readily admits that his identification of three cultures of anarchy is an argument that 'builds directly on Bull's' (Wendt 1999: 253). Yet it would be unfair to say that constructivists bring nothing new. Their emphasis on the importance of social theory and the detailed analyses of social interaction in international relations breaks new ground. And as we have seen above, several constructivists emphasize the role of domestic norms, an area little studied by International Society theorists.

Some Marxists are critical of constructivism. Wallerstein's world system theory focuses on the material structure of global capitalism and its development since the sixteenth century (see Chapter 8). That analysis leaves little room for the social interaction analysed by constructivists. Robert Cox's neo-Marxist view of 'historical structures' (see Chapter 8) makes more room for 'ideas' and will thus be more sympathetic to a constructivist approach.

In sum, neorealism remains the main contender and intellectual opponent for constructivist theory. When it comes to liberal and International Society theory, and even to some versions of neo-Marxist theory, constructivists can find more room for intellectual cooperation.

The Constructivist Research Programme

One ongoing debate among constructivists concerns basic social theory. The outline made above recorded the controversy between 'conventional' and 'critical' constructivists. From the 'conventional' camp, Emanuel Adler argues that in order to make an impact in the discipline of IR, constructivists need to develop 'a coherent constructivist methodological base that suggests a practical alternative to imitating the physical sciences' (Adler 2001: 109). From the 'critical' side, Maja Zehfuss wants to move in a very different direction: 'the assertion of an independently existing reality, which in itself cannot be proved and seems to demand no proof, works to support particular political positions and to exclude others from consideration' (Zehfuss 2002: 245). In other words, clarification of basic social theory is important for the constructivist research programme.

The debate about basic theory is of course relevant for the constructivist ambition of demonstrating that 'ideas matter'. How exactly is it that ideas matter? Do changes in ideas always come before changes in material conditions? Do ideas guide policy or are they justifications for policy? Should ideas be seen as causes of behaviour in IR or should they rather be seen as constitutive elements that define what IR is all about? (See Tannenwald 2005 for an excellent discussion of these questions.) Further clarification in these areas is of vital importance for the constructivist research programme.

An additional vital element in the constructivist research programme concerns the direction scholars will take in building constructivist IR theory. Is emphasis going to be put on systemic or domestic aspects? If emphasis is on systemic aspects, should theorizing focus on interaction between states or should it focus on normative and ideational aspects of international society? If emphasis is on domestic aspects, which domestic norms should be given attention; what are the major domestic sources of state identity? Such questions need not be very problematic. The other major theoretical approaches to IR also have a continuing discussion about the most relevant specific research focus. A comprehensive research programme will always be active in a variety of concrete areas.

Finally, it will be important for constructivists to clarify further the relationship to the approaches that have dominated IR so far: realism, liberalism, International Society and International Political Economy. To what extent are they compatible with constructivism and how far are they capable of fruitful cooperation? For example, early constructivist contributions indicated a deep gulf between materialist neorealism and a norms–idea focused constructivism. The debate has demonstrated that the gulf is much smaller: neorealists do recognize the importance of ideas (Dessler 2000); constructivists do recognize the importance of material factors. That raises the question as to whether constructivists will then be able to further define their own, distinctive approach to IR.

Constructivists have demonstrated that 'ideas matter' in international relations. They have shown that culture and identity help define the interests and constitute the actors in IR. All students of IR should be familiar with the important debates raised by constructivists, about basic social theory and about the different ways in which ideas can matter in international relations.

 KEY POINTS

- The focus of social constructivism is on human awareness or consciousness and its place in world affairs. The international system is constituted by ideas, not by material forces.

- Social theory is the more general theory about the social world. In social theory, constructivists emphasize the social construction of reality. The social world is not a given. The social world is a world of human consciousness: of thoughts and beliefs, of ideas and concepts, of languages and discourses. Four major types of ideas are: ideologies; normative beliefs; cause–effect beliefs; and policy prescriptions.

- Constructivist Alexander Wendt rejects the neorealist position of anarchy necessarily leading to self-help. That cannot be decided a priori; it depends on the interaction between states. In these processes of interaction the identities and interests of states are created.

- Martha Finnemore argues that identities and interests are defined by international forces, that is, by the norms of behaviour embedded in international society.

- Peter Katzenstein argues that the internal make-up of states affects their international behaviour. The approach is employed to explain the shift in Japanese foreign policy from militaristic to pacifist.

- Ted Hopf focuses on the domestic foundation of identity in a study of Soviet and Russian foreign policy. The claim is that the identities of key decision-makers go a long way in explaining foreign policy.

QUESTIONS

- Social constructivists argue in favour of an ideational view and against a materialist view of the world. They claim that the international system is constituted by ideas, not by material forces. Explain the distinction and discuss whether it is valid.
- Is social constructivism primarily a meta-theory about the nature of the social world or is it primarily a substantial set of theories about IR?
- Identify the four types of ideas discussed by Nina Tannenwald and think of ways in which each type can influence international relations.
- Alexander Wendt says that 'if the United States and the Soviet Union decide they are no longer enemies, "the cold war is over" '. Do you agree? Why or why not?

GUIDE TO FURTHER READING

Adler, E. (2001). 'Constructivism and International Relations', in W. Carlsnaes, T. Risse and B. A. Simmons (eds), *Handbook of International Relations*. London: Sage, 95–118.

Fierke, K. M. and Jørgensen, K. E. (eds) (2001). *Constructing International Relations*, Armonk: M. E. Sharpe.

Finnemore, M. (1996). *National Interests in International Society*. Ithaca and London: Cornell University Press.

Katzenstein, P. (1996b). *Cultural Norms and National Security*. Ithaca and London: Cornell University Press.

Ruggie, J. G. (1998). *Constructing the World Polity: Essays on International Institutionalization*. London: Routledge.

Wendt, A. (1999). *Social Theory of International Politics*. Cambridge: Cambridge University Press.

Zehfuss, M. (2002). *Constructivism in International Relations: The Politics of Reality*. Cambridge: Cambridge University Press.

WEB LINKS

Web links mentioned in the chapter plus additional links can be found on the Online Resource Centre that accompanies this book.
www.oxfordtextbooks.co.uk/orc/jackson_sorensen3e/

CHAPTER 7

International Political Economy: Classical Theories

▊ Summary

This chapter is about the relationship between politics and economics, between states and markets in world affairs. Ultimately, IPE is about wealth and poverty, about who gets what in the international economic and political system. The most important classical theories in this area are mercantilism, economic liberalism and neo-Marxism. They are 'theories' in the very broad sense of a set of assumptions and values from which the field of IPE can be approached. We present each of these theories in some detail; the next chapter moves on to the most important debates between them.

Introduction: What is IPE?

In some fundamental ways, our lives are about political economy. To survive, we need food, clothes and many other goods. Most of us obtain these provisions in the marketplace, paying for them with money we have earned. We cannot buy anything without money; to demand goods we need some measure of wealth as opposed to poverty. A modern market is based on political rules (if not, it would be a 'Mafia market' based on threats, bribes and force). Political rules and regulations constitute a framework within which the market functions. At the same time, economic strength is an important basis for political power. If economics is about the pursuit of wealth and politics about the pursuit of power, the two interact in complicated and puzzling ways (Polanyi 1957; Gilpin 1987; 2001). It is this complex interplay in the international context between politics and economics, between states and markets, which is the core of IPE (see web links 7.02 and 7.03).

The theoretical traditions introduced in earlier chapters have issues of war and peace, of conflict and cooperation between states, as their main subject of study. IPE shifts our attention to issues of wealth and poverty, and to who gets what in the international system. The present chapter is also different from the previous ones in that it does not focus on a single theoretical tradition. Instead, it introduces the three most important classical theories within the field of IPE; the next chapter adds the major current theories and debates. This approach reflects the development of the discipline of IR in which International Political Economy has emerged as a field of study in its own right. Some scholars even argue that IPE is the more comprehensive discipline and that IR should consequently be seen as a subfield of IPE. Alternatively, both IR and IPE could be subfields within a broader discipline of International Studies (Strange 1995). Many economists believe that methods and theories from the discipline of economics can be applied in other areas of human affairs, including politics and IR. Many political scientists will argue against this tendency to reduce politics to a branch of economics. This debate is fundamentally about which theories and which research questions are the most important ones.

As we saw in Chapter 2, a core normative argument for the establishment of the academic discipline of IR at the beginning of the twentieth century was that it should help promote a more peaceful world. The focus on war and peace continued during the 1950s and 1960s in the context of the Cold War. For those academics as well as politicians whose international outlook was shaped by the experiences of two world wars this was a natural choice of focus. French President (and General) Charles de Gaulle, for example, considered economic affairs 'quartermaster's stuff' and 'low politics' which could be looked after by lesser minds while statesmen such as himself took care of the 'high politics' which concerned the larger issues of war and peace.

There is another reason for this attitude. It concerns the nature of economic activity in modern society: the separation between a political sphere of the state and an economic sphere of the market is a feature of modern, capitalist society. As we shall see below, economic

---

BOX 7.1 **The Bretton Woods system**

The rules of Bretton Woods . . . provided for a system of fixed exchange rates. Public officials, fresh from what they perceived as a disastrous experience with floating rates in the 1930s, concluded that a fixed exchange rate was the most stable and the most conducive to trade . . . The rules further encouraged an open system, by committing members to the convertibility of their respective currencies into other currencies and to free trade . . .

On August 15, 1971, President Nixon—without consulting the other members of the international monetary system and, indeed, without consulting his own State Department—announced his new economic policy: henceforth, the dollar would no longer be convertible into gold, and the United States would impose a 10 percent surcharge on dutiable imports. August 15, 1971, marked the end of the Bretton Woods period . . .

Spero (1985: 37, 54)

---

liberalism holds that the economic system works most efficiently when left to itself, free from political interference. But this liberal idea should not be taken to mean that economics and politics have nothing to do with each other. The term 'free market' does not imply freedom from politics. Many kinds of political regulation concerning contracts, consumer and producer protection, taxation, working conditions and so on make up the framework within which the 'free market' functions. Politics and economics are entangled in complex ways, even in the most liberal 'free market' economies.

In the 1950s and 1960s one could easily get the impression that many IR scholars committed the misunderstanding of separating economics and politics. For a long time, economics and politics in international relations were seen as almost totally isolated from each other, as qualitatively different activities being studied with qualitatively different approaches. As one scholar pointed out in 1970, international economics and international politics were 'a case of mutual neglect' (Strange 1970). But this sharp distinction between politics and economics was increasingly questioned from the beginning of the 1970s.

Why the change of attitude? First, the system that politicians had set up to foster economic growth and international exchange after the Second World War—the so-called Bretton Woods system—showed signs of crisis (see web link 7.06). In particular, the United States was in economic difficulties which grew out of its deep involvement in the Vietnam War (1961–73). To halt the drain on US gold reserves the gold-convertibility of the American dollar had to be abandoned. That measure was taken by American President Richard Nixon. In other words, political measures were taken that changed the rules of the game for the economic marketplace. The oil crisis from 1973 onwards contributed to a sense of lost invulnerability. In times of economic crisis it usually becomes clearer that politics and economics hang together. Second, decolonization had created a new group of politically weak and economically poor states in the international system. Most newly independent countries were far from satisfied with their subordinate position in the international economic system. At the UN during the 1970s they called for a 'New International Economic Order', i.e. political proposals designed to improve the economic position of Third World countries in the international system (see web links 7.07 and 7.08). Although far less important than the Bretton Woods foreign-exchange crisis, these proposals did reveal how the economic position of countries in the international order is closely connected to political measures. Finally, the end of the Cold War also underlined the connection between politics and economics. After 1989 Eastern Europe and the former Soviet Union began to be reintegrated in the international system created by the West. They wanted both political integration, such as membership of Western organizations, and economic integration, meaning more intensive links of economic interdependence with the advanced economies of Western Europe, North America and Japan.

In summary, there is a complex relationship between politics and economics, between states and markets, that IR has to be able to grasp. That relationship is the subject of IPE. We need different theoretical ways of approaching the connection between politics and economics. From the possible theories to choose from (Caporaso 1993) we have selected three theories which most scholars see as the main theories of IPE: mercantilism, economic liberalism and Marxism. These are 'theories' in the very broad sense of a set of assumptions and values from which the field of IPE can be approached. As will be apparent, the outlook of mercantilism has much in common with realism, while economic liberalism is an addition to liberal theory. These two theories thus represent views on IPE that are basically realist and liberal. Marxism has its own original theoretical position and we will spend a little more time on that because the Marxist approach has not been presented earlier.

Mercantilism

We begin with mercantilism because this theory is intimately connected to the establishment of the modern, sovereign state during the sixteenth and seventeenth centuries. Mercantilism was the world-view of political elites that were at the forefront of building the modern state (see web link 7.11). They took the approach that economic activity is and should be subordinated to the primary goal of building a strong state. In other words, economics is a tool of politics, a basis for political power. That is a defining feature of mercantilist thinking. Mercantilists see the international economy as an arena of conflict between opposing national interests, rather than an area of cooperation and mutual gain. In brief, economic competition between states is a 'zero-sum game' where one state's gain is another state's loss. States have to be worried about relative economic gain, because the material wealth accumulated by one state can serve as a basis for military-political power which can be used against other states. We should notice the close affinity between this mercantilist way of thinking and neorealist thought about competition between states in an anarchic realm.

Economic rivalry between states can take two different forms (Gilpin 1987: 32). The first is called defensive or 'benign' mercantilism: states look after their national economic interests because that is an important ingredient in their national security; such policies need not

---

BOX 7.2 **A mercantilist view**

Anglo-American *theory* instructs Westerners that economics is by nature a 'positive sum game' from which all can emerge as winners. Asian *history* instructs many Koreans, Chinese, Japanese, and others that economic competition is a form of war in which some win and others lose. To be strong is much better than to be weak; to give orders is better than to take them. By this logic, the way to be strong, to give orders, to have independence and control, is to keep in mind the difference between 'us' and 'them'. This perspective comes naturally to Koreans (when thinking about Japan), or Canadians (when thinking about the United States), or Britons (when thinking, even today, about Germany), or to Chinese or Japanese (when thinking about what the Europeans did to their nations).

Fallows (1994: 231)

---

have overly negative effects on other states. The other form, however, is aggressive or 'malevolent' mercantilism. Here states attempt to exploit the international economy through expansionary policies: for example, the imperialism of the European colonial powers in Asia and Africa. Mercantilists thus see economic strength and military-political power as complementary, not competing goals, in a positive feedback loop. The pursuit of economic strength supports the development of the state's military and political power; and military-political power enhances and strengthens the state's economic power.

This contrasts sharply with the liberal view introduced in Chapter 4. Liberals posit a radically different choice: the pursuit of economic prosperity through free trade and open economic exchange versus the pursuit of power by the means of military force and territorial expansion. In other words, states can choose the road of economic development and trade and thus become 'trading states', as did West Germany and Japan after the Second World War. Or they can choose the road of military force and territorial expansion and thus base their prominence on military power, as did Russia under Communist rule. Mercantilists reject that liberal view. More national wealth and more military-political power are complementary stratagems that serve the same fundamental end: a stronger, more powerful state. A choice between the two appears only in specific situations; one example is the limits that Western powers put on economic exchange with the Eastern Bloc during the Cold War. Here, the West makes an economic sacrifice for reasons of military security. Mercantilists see that as an extraordinary situation. Normally, wealth and power can be pursued simultaneously, in support of each other.

Mercantilists maintain that the economy should be subordinated to the primary goal of increasing state power: politics must have primacy over economics. But the content of the concrete policies recommended to serve that goal has changed over time. Sixteenth-century mercantilists noted how Spain benefited from the supply of gold and silver bullion from the Americas; that led them to call for the acquisition of bullion as the main road to national wealth. However, when the Netherlands emerged as the leading country in Europe without directly acquiring bullion, and mainly because of its vast overseas trading empire, mercantilists started to emphasize trade and the creation of the largest possible trade surplus as the road to national prosperity. Ever since Britain obtained a leading role in world politics through industrialization, mercantilists have underlined the need for countries to industrialize as the best way to obtain national power. Mercantilism has been particularly popular in countries which lagged behind Britain in industrial development; they felt an urgent need to catch up industrially in order to compete with Britain. That catching-up could not be left to market forces; it called for political measures to protect and develop local industry.

Mercantilism has been advocated by some eminent politicians and economists. Alexander Hamilton, one of the founding fathers of the United States, was a strong proponent of mercantilism in the form of protectionist policies aimed at promoting domestic industry in the United States. Another eloquent spokesman for mercantilism was Friedrich List, a German economist (see web link 7.12). In the 1840s he developed a theory of 'productive power' which stressed that the ability to produce is more important than the result of producing. In other words, the prosperity of a state depends not primarily on its store of wealth, but on the extent to which it has developed its 'powers of production': 'A nation capable of developing a manufacturing power, if it makes use of the system of protection, thus acts quite in the same spirit as the landed proprietor did who by the sacrifice of some material wealth allowed some of his children to learn a production trade' (List 1966: 145). Recent mercantilist thinking focuses on the successful 'developmental' states in East Asia: Japan, South Korea and Taiwan. They emphasize that economic success has always been accompanied by a strong, commanding role for the state in promoting economic development. In Japan, for example, the Japanese state has played a very comprehensive role in the economic development of the country. The state has singled out strategic industries, protected them from outside competition and supported their development even by regulating the competition between firms. We shall have more to say about these theorists in the next chapter.

In summary, mercantilism posits the economy as subordinate to the polity and, particularly, the government. Economic activity is seen in the larger context of increasing state power. The organization that is responsible for defending and advancing the national interest, namely the state, rules over private economic interests. Wealth and power are complementary, not competing goals. Economic dependence on other states should be avoided as far as possible. When economic and security interests clash, security interests have priority.

BOX 7.3	Mercantilism summarized
Relationship between economics and politics:	Politics decisive
Main actors/units of analysis:	States
The nature of economic relations:	Conflictual, a zero-sum game
Economic goals:	State power

Economic Liberalism

Economic liberalism emerged as a critique of the comprehensive political control and regulation of economic affairs which dominated European state-building in the sixteenth and seventeenth centuries: i.e., mercantilism. Economic liberals reject theories and policies which subordinate economics to politics. Adam Smith (1723–90), the father of economic liberalism, believed that markets tend to expand spontaneously for the satisfaction of human needs—provided that governments do not interfere (see web link 7.16). He builds on the body of liberal ideas that are summarized in Chapter 4. These core ideas include the rational individual actor, a belief in progress and an assumption of mutual gain from free exchange. But Smith also adds some elements of his own to liberal thinking, including the key notion that the economic marketplace is the main source of progress, cooperation and prosperity. Political interference and state regulation, by contrast, are uneconomical, retrogressive and can lead to conflict.

Liberal economics has been called 'a doctrine and a set of principles for organizing and managing economic growth, and individual welfare' (Gilpin 1987: 27). It is based on the notion that if left to itself the market economy will operate spontaneously according to its own mechanisms or 'laws'. These laws are considered to be inherent in the process of economic production and exchange. One example is the 'law of comparative advantage' developed by David Ricardo (1772–1823). He argued that free trade—i.e. commercial activities that are carried on independently of national borders—will bring benefits to all participants because free trade makes specialization possible and specialization increases efficiency and thus productivity (see web link 7.18). Paul Samuelson summarized the argument as follows: 'Whether or not one of two regions is absolutely more efficient in the production of every good than is the other, if each specializes in the product in which it has a comparative advantage (greatest relative efficiency), trade will be mutually profitable to both regions' (Samuelson 1967: 651). In a world economy based on free trade all countries will benefit through specialization and global wealth will increase.

BOX 7.4   **A liberal view**

Under a system of perfectly free commerce, each country naturally devotes its capital and labour to such employments as are most beneficial to each. The pursuit of individual advantage is admirably connected with the universal good of the whole. By stimulating industry, by rewarding ingenuity, and by using most efficaciously the peculiar powers bestowed by nature, it distributes labour most effectively and most economically: while, by increasing the general mass of productions, it diffuses general benefit and binds together, by one common tie of interest and intercourse, the universal society of nations throughout the civilized world.

Ricardo (1973: 81)

Economic liberals thus reject the mercantilist view that the state is the central actor and focus when it comes to economic affairs. The central actor is the individual as a consumer and a producer. The marketplace is the open arena where individuals come together to exchange goods and services. Individuals are rational in pursuing their own economic interests, and when they apply that rationality in the marketplace, all participants gain. Economic exchange via the market is thus a positive-sum game: everybody gains more than they put in because of increased efficiency. Individuals and companies would not be active in the marketplace unless it was to their benefit. Liberal economists find that this view of individuals as rational and self-seeking (wanting to make themselves better off) can be used as a starting-point for understanding not only market economics but also politics. That particular perspective goes under the name of rational choice theory (see Chapter 8). Liberals thus reject the mercantilist zero-sum view where one state's economic gain necessarily is another state's economic loss. The road to human prosperity, then, goes through the unfettered expansion of the free market economy, capitalism, not only in each country but also across international boundaries.

There is a recurring debate among economic liberals, however, about the extent to which political interference by governments may be necessary. Early economic liberals called for laissez-faire: i.e. for the freedom of the market from all kinds of political restriction and regulation. Yet even the early economic liberals were aware of the need for a politically constructed legal framework as a basis for the market. Laissez-faire does not mean the absence of any political regulation whatsoever; it means that the state shall only set up those minimal underpinnings that are necessary for the market to function properly. This is the classical version of economic liberalism. At the present time this view is also put forward under labels such as 'conservatism' or 'neoliberalism'; the content is basically the same, however. The 'conservative/neoliberal' economic policies of Margaret Thatcher in Britain and of Ronald Reagan in the United States were both based on classical laissez-faire doctrines.

Economic liberals have from early on been aware that in some cases the market may not work according to expectations of efficiency and mutual gain; such cases are usually called instances of 'market failure'. Political regulation may be necessary to correct or avoid market failures. Some economic liberals thus argue for a larger degree of state interference in the market. John Stuart Mill was in many ways a laissez-faire economic liberal, but he was also critical of the extreme inequalities of income, wealth and power which he observed in nineteenth-century Britain. That made him call for limited state action in some areas, including education and relief for the poor. In the 1930s John Maynard Keynes, the leading economist of the early twentieth century, went one step further (see web link 7.22). According to Keynes the market economy is a great benefit to people, but it also entails potential evils of 'risk, uncertainty and ignorance'. That situation could be remedied through improved political management of the market. Keynes thus argued in favour of a market which was 'wisely managed' by the state (Keynes 1963: 321).

This positive view of the state amounted to a major shift in liberal economic doctrine. Keynesian ideas paved the way for a significantly reformed liberal theory: one which was still based on a market economy, but with a considerable degree of state interference and direction. That Keynesian view was popular in Europe in the decades following the Second

BOX 7.5	Liberalism summarized
Relationship between economics and politics:	Economics autonomous
Main actors/units of analysis:	Individuals and private firms
The nature of economic relations:	Cooperative, a positive-sum game
Economic goals:	Maximum individual and social well-being

World War. In the 1980s, however, the pendulum swung back to classical laissez-faire liberalism. One major reason for this renewed liberal faith in the unfettered market is the belief that economic globalization will bring prosperity to all. We shall return to that issue in the next chapter.

In summary, economic liberals argue that the market economy is an autonomous sphere of society which operates according to its own economic laws. Economic exchange is a positive-sum game and the market will tend to maximize benefits for the rational, self-seeking individuals, the households and the companies that participate in market exchange. The economy is a sphere of cooperation for mutual benefit among states as well as among individuals. The international economy should thus be based on free trade. Classical liberal economists view the role of the state as that of leaving the market alone, including international markets as well as national markets: laissez-faire. But some twentieth and twenty-first-century economic liberals favour increased state involvement in the marketplace.

Marxism

The political economy of the nineteenth-century German philosopher and economist Karl Marx in many ways represents a fundamental critique of economic liberalism. We saw above that economic liberals view the economy as a positive-sum game with benefits for all. Marx rejected that view. Instead, he saw the economy as a site of human exploitation and class inequality. Marx thus takes the zero-sum argument of mercantilism and applies it to relations of classes instead of relations of states. Marxists agree with mercantilists that politics and economics are closely intertwined; both reject the liberal view of an economic sphere operating under its own laws. But where mercantilists see economics as a tool of politics, Marxists put economics first and politics second. For Marxists, the capitalist economy is based on two antagonistic social classes: one class, the bourgeoisie, owns the means of production; the other class, the proletariat, owns only its labour power which it must sell to the bourgeoisie. But labour puts in more work than it gets back in pay; there is a surplus value appropriated by the bourgeoisie. That is capitalist profit and it is derived from labour exploitation.

Even if a capitalist economy controlled by the bourgeoisie is exploitative of labour, Marx did not see the growth of capitalism as a negative or retrogressive event. On the contrary, capitalism means progress for Marx, in two ways: first, capitalism destroys previous relations of production, such as feudalism, which were even more exploitative, with peasants subsisting under slave-like conditions. Capitalism is a step forward in the sense that labour is free to sell its labour power and seek out the best possible pay. Second, and most important for Marx, capitalism paves the way for a socialist revolution where the means of production will be placed under social control for the benefit of the proletariat who are the vast majority. That is the revolutionary goal that Marxist economic thought is aiming at.

The Marxist view is materialist: it is based on the claim that the core activity in any society concerns the way in which human beings produce their means of existence. Economic production is the basis for all other human activities, including politics. The economic basis consists, on the one hand, of the forces of production: i.e. the technical level of economic activity (e.g. industrial machinery versus artisan handicraft). On the other hand, it consists of the relations of production: i.e. the system of social ownership which determines the actual control over the productive forces (e.g. private ownership versus collective ownership). Taken together, forces of production and relations of production form a specific mode of production, for example capitalism, which is based on industrial machinery and private ownership. The bourgeoisie, which dominates the capitalist economy through control of the means of production, will also tend to dominate in the political sphere because economics is the basis of politics according to Marxists (see web link 7.33).

This brings us to the Marxist framework for the study of IPE. First, states are not autonomous; they are driven by ruling-class interests and capitalist states are primarily driven by the interests of their respective bourgeoisies. That means that struggles between states, including wars, should be seen in the economic context of competition between capitalist classes of different states. For Marxists, class conflict is more fundamental than conflict between states. Second, as an economic system, capitalism is expansive: there is a never-ending search for new markets and more profit. Because classes cut across state borders class conflict is not confined to states; instead, it expands around the world in the wake of capitalism. Such expansion first took the form of imperialism and colonization, but it continues after the colonies have been granted independence. It now takes the form of economic globalization led by giant transnational corporations. The history of IPE can thus be seen by Marxists as the history of capitalist expansion across the globe.

BOX 7.6	A Marxist view

Modern industry has converted the little workshop of patriarchal master into the great factory of the industrial capitalist. Masses of laborers, crowded into the factory, are organized like soldiers. As privates of the industrial army they are placed under the command of a perfect hierarchy of officers and sergeants. Not only are they slaves of the bourgeois class, and of the bourgeois state; they are daily and hourly enslaved by the machine, by the overlooker, and above all, by the individual bourgeois manufacturer himself. The more openly this despotism proclaims gain to be its end and aim, the more petty, the more hateful and the more embittering it is.

Marx and Engels (1955: 17)

Lenin, the Communist leader of the Russian Revolution of 1917, analysed this process. He argued that the process of capitalist expansion must always be unequal or uneven, between countries, industries and firms. For example, Britain was ahead of Germany for most of the eighteenth and nineteenth centuries. Consequently, Britain had secured for itself a vast colonial empire whereas Germany had very little. At the beginning of the twentieth century, however, Germany was catching up economically and Britain was declining. Therefore, Lenin noted, Germany wanted a redivision of the international spheres of influence, according to the new relative strength of the countries. That demand led to war between Germany and Britain. Such disparities and conflicts will always develop under capitalist conditions, argued Lenin. That is the 'law of uneven development'.

The notion of uneven development points to the need for a historical analysis of capitalist expansion. A Marxist analysis must therefore also be clear about history. Events must always be analysed in their specific historical context. For example, there was a high economic interdependence between countries around the time of the First World War; there is also a high economic interdependence between many countries today. But we need to look at the precise nature of that interdependence in its historical context in order to be able to understand the processes taking place and their significance for international relations: interdependence around the First World War was often arms-length import/export relations between independent companies. Today it is frequently integrated circuits of production between subsidiaries of the same transnational company; a Ford car, for example, contains parts produced in many

---

BOX 7.7   Lenin and the Law of Uneven Development

There can be no other conceivable basis under capitalism for the division of spheres of influence . . . than a calculation of the strength of the participants in the division, their general economic, financial, military strength, etc. And the strength of these participants in the division does not change to an equal degree, for under capitalism the development of different undertakings, trusts, branches of industry, or countries cannot be even.

Lenin 1917, quoted from Gilpin (1987: 39)

BOX 7.8   A neo-Marxist view

It is widely believed that the United States and other developed capitalist countries contribute more capital to the underdeveloped countries than they receive from them. Nonetheless, all available statistics . . . show precisely the opposite . . . For the seven largest Latin American countries . . . the United States Department of Commerce's conservatively calculated figures for the years 1950 to 1961 indicate $2,962 million of investment flows on private account out of the United States and remittances of profits and interest of $6,875 million; adding American public loans and their Latin American servicing between the same years still leaves a conservatively calculated net capital outflow of $2,081 million *to* the United States.

Frank (1971: 237–8)

different countries. Such global networks of production make for a different and closer type of economic integration than traditional imports and exports between separate companies.

The difference between Marxist and realist analysis should be brought to attention. Both views agree on the perennial competition and conflict between states. But realists explain this by pointing to the existence of independent states in a condition of anarchy. Therefore, the struggle between states has taken place for several millennia, ever since the emergence of states (i.e. independent political units) on the world stage. Marxists reject that view as abstract and unhistorical. It is abstract because there is no concrete specification of the social forces that actually sustain the conflict between states. These social forces, so the Marxists claim, are exactly the ruling classes of capitalists (and their allies); they ultimately control and determine what 'their' states do. When states are rivals and sometimes come into conflict it is because they pursue the economic and political interests for international dominance and control sought after by the ruling classes.

The realist view is also unhistorical according to Marxists. That is because history is seen as always repeating itself; it's 'the same damned things over and over again': states competing in anarchy. But Marxists argue that conflict between states varies substantially across history. Conflict between capitalist states—and ultimately between capitalist ruling classes—is of course connected to the capitalist historical era. Consequently, competition and conflict of earlier historical phases require a different explanation, tying it in with the contest between the social forces of those periods of feudalism and antiquity.

Realists argue that the Marxist view of the state is reductionist, that is, it reduces the state to a simple tool in the hands of the ruling classes, with no will of its own. States are strong actors in their own right. They embody powerful institutions, they control the means of violence (army, police) and they have substantial economic resources. It is simply wrong to view the state as a mere instrument for others. More recent Marxist analysis has conceded this point. The state has some autonomy from the ruling classes, but it is a *relative* autonomy: the basic function of the capitalist state remains the safeguarding of the capitalist system. Yet, within this general framework, the state should not be reduced to a simple tool of others (Carnoy 1984: ch. 4).

Current Marxist thinking has developed this view further. Robert Cox is a prominent neo-Marxist analyst of world politics and political economy (Cox 1996). Cox begins with the concept of historical structures, defined as 'a particular configuration of forces' (Cox 1996: 97). These historical structures are made up of three categories of forces that interact: material capabilities, ideas and institutions. Note how Cox moves away from the traditional Marxist emphasis on materialism through the inclusion of ideas and institutions. In the next step, historical structures are identified at three different levels; they are labelled 'social forces', 'forms of state' and 'world orders', as outlined in Box 7.9.

'Social forces' are a shorthand for the process of capitalist production. An analysis of this aspect will inform us about the present state of development of the capitalist economy on a global scale. 'Forms of state' point to the ways in which states change in the interplay with the social forces of capitalist development. 'World orders' refer to the current organization of international relations including relations between major states and groups of states, the status of international law, and international institutions.

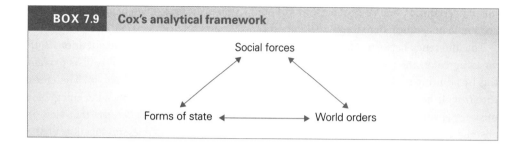

BOX 7.9   Cox's analytical framework

In sum, Cox theorizes a complex interplay between politics and economics, specified as the interaction between social forces, forms of state and world orders. The task for the analyst is to find out how these relationships play out in the current phase of human history. It is not possible to present Cox's analysis of these matters fully here, but the gist of his argument is as follows (Cox 1992). As regards the social forces of capitalism, they are currently involved in an intense process of economic globalization, meaning an internationalizing of production as well as migration movements from South to North. Globalization has been driven by market forces, but Cox foresees that new social movements critical of globalization will grow increasingly strong and this will open a new phase of struggle between social forces concerning the control and regulation of economic globalization.

As regards forms of state, there is variation between states because they link into the global political economy in different ways. States compete for advantage, but they do it on the premise that integration in the global economy is unavoidable. The dominant forces in capitalist states 'concur in giving priority to competitiveness in the global economy and in precluding interventions by whatever authority that are not consistent with this aim' (Cox 2002: 34). Non-territorial power is becoming more important for states; they compete for markets and economic opportunities across the globe. Transnational corporations and civil society organizations operating across borders (i.e. NGOs) are of increasing importance.

Finally, as regards world order, the long-term tendency will be for replacement of the current global US dominance. Several scenarios are possible; one is an international order of 'conflicting power centres' (Cox 1996: 114) structured around leading states or groups of states, such as the EU in Europe and China and Japan in East Asia. Another possibility is a 'post-hegemonic order' (Cox 1992: 142) where states agree on rules and norms of peaceful cooperation for mutual benefit and a common framework for the resolution of possible conflicts. Robert Cox's framework is one example of a recent development of neo-Marxist analysis; we shall return to some of the issues he takes up in the next chapter.

Another major neo-Marxist analysis comes from Immanuel Wallerstein (1974; 1979; 1983). His starting-point is the concept of world system analysis. World systems need not physically include the whole world; they are unified areas characterized by particular economic and political structures. The concept thus ties economics and politics together: a world system is characterized by a certain economic and a certain political structure with the one depending on the other. In human history, there have been two basic varieties of world systems: 'world-empires' and 'world-economies'. In world-empires, such as the Roman Empire, political and economic control is concentrated in a unified centre. World economies, in contrast, are tied together economically in a single division of labour, but politically, authority is decentralized, residing in multiple polities, in a system of states. Wallerstein's key focus is the analysis of the modern world-economy, characterized by capitalism (see web link 7.37).

The capitalist world-economy was established in 'the long 16th century' (1450–1640). It was based on an international division of labour that covered Europe first, but soon expanded to the Western hemisphere and later to other parts of the world as well. Within this division of labour, a process of specialization took place; this happened in a somewhat accidental way at first; for a number of reasons north-west Europe was in a better position to diversify its agriculture and to connect it with industrial advance in textiles and shipping. So the capitalist world-economy is built on a hierarchy of core areas, peripheral areas and semi-peripheral areas. The core areas contain the advanced and complex economic activities (mass-market industries and sophisticated agriculture). Furthermore, these activities are controlled by an indigenous bourgeoisie. Peripheral areas are at the bottom of the hierarchy; they produce staple goods such as grain, wood, sugar and so on. They often employ slavery or coerced labour; what little industrial activity exists is mostly under the external control of capitalists from core countries. Semi-peripheral areas are economically mixed; they are a middle layer between the upper stratum of core countries and the lower stratum of peripheral countries.

A basic mechanism of the capitalist world-economy is unequal exchange. Economic surplus is transferred from the periphery to the core. Surplus is appropriated from low-wage, low-profit producers in the periphery to high-wage, high-profit producers in the core. This transfer is further accentuated by the emergence of strong state machineries in the core and weak state machineries in the periphery. Strong states can enforce unequal exchange on weak ones. Thus capitalism 'involves not only appropriation of surplus value by an owner from a laborer, but an appropriation of surplus of the whole world-economy by core areas. And this was as true in the stage of agricultural capitalism as it is in the stage of industrial capitalism' (Wallerstein 1979: 18).

In the process of unequal exchange, tensions are created in the system. The semi-periphery has an important function in this regard. It provides an element of political stability, because the core countries are not facing a unified opposition; the semi-periphery acts as a buffer or shock absorber. At the same time, the world-economy is not entirely static; any single area of the system may change place from periphery to semi-periphery, from semi-periphery to core, and vice versa. Furthermore, the types of commodities involved in core and peripheral economic activities respectively are subject to dynamic change. Technological advance means that the concrete content of what is 'advanced economic activity' always changes. At one point it was textiles; in a later phase it was industrial machinery; today, it is information- and bio-technology together with financial and other services. But Wallerstein emphasizes that the capitalist system as such does not change: it remains a hierarchy of core, semi-periphery and periphery, characterized by unequal exchange.

Wallerstein sees the end of the Cold War and the destruction of the Soviet bloc as a consequence of the development of the capitalist world-economy. However, the long-term

BOX 7.10	Marxism summarized
Relationship between economics and politics:	Economics decisive
Main actors/units of analysis:	Classes
The nature of economic relations:	Conflictual, zero-sum
Economic goals:	Class interests

prospect is the demise of the capitalist system, because the contradictions of that system are now unleashed on a world scale. Success, not failure, is the real threat to global capitalism; when the possibilities for expansion are all used up, the never-ending quest for more profit will lead to new crises in the world capitalist economy which sooner or later will spell its transformation.

There are some similarities between Wallerstein's world systems analysis of capitalism and Waltz's neorealist analysis of the international system. Both focus on the system rather than on the single units or countries; what happens to countries very much depends on their position in the system. Both see the system as a hierarchy with strong states in the top and weak states in the bottom. But from here the differences take over: Waltz's focus is on relative political-military power in a condition of anarchy; Wallerstein's focus is first and foremost economic power and capability which is then connected with political power. Wallerstein analyses the historical development of capitalism since the sixteenth century, putting economics first and politics second. Waltz analyses the international balance of power in the twentieth century, putting power politics first and economics second. The reader is encouraged to speculate about the advantages and drawbacks of each theory.

It is clear that the contributions by Wallerstein and Cox add a number of nuances to Marxist analysis. In the present context, however, we need to focus on the main thrust of the Marxist approach as compared with liberalism and mercantilism. This basic Marxist view can be summarized as follows: the economy is a site of exploitation and inequality between social classes, especially the bourgeoisie and the proletariat. Politics is to a large extent determined by the socioeconomic context. The dominant economic class is also dominant politically. That means that in capitalist economies the bourgeoisie will be the ruling class. Global capitalist development is uneven and bound to produce crises and contradictions, both between states and between social classes. Marxist IPE thus concerns the history of global capitalist expansion, the struggles between classes and states to which it has given rise around the world, and how a revolutionary transformation of that world might come about.

Conclusion

In an overall summary of this chapter, it is helpful to summarize the three classical theories by combining the information in Boxes 7.3, 7.5 and 7.10. That information is contained in Box 7.11.

BOX 7.11	Three theories of IPE		
	MERCANTILISM	**ECONOMIC LIBERALISM**	**MARXISM**
Relationship between economics and politics:	Politics decisive	Economics autonomous	Economics decisive
Main actors/units of analysis:	States	Individuals	Classes
The nature of economic relations:	Conflictual, zero-sum game	Cooperative, positive-sum game	Conflictual, zero-sum game
Economic goals:	State power	Maximum individual and social well-being	Class interests

In the next chapter we shall introduce the main debates to which the principal IPE theories have given rise in order to convey an impression of the kind of questions and issues which are currently being discussed in IPE.

 KEY POINTS

- The relationship between politics and economics, between states and markets, is the subject matter of International Political Economy (IPE). There are three main theories of IPE: mercantilism, economic liberalism and Marxism.

- Mercantilism posits the economy as subordinate to politics. Economic activity is seen in the larger context of increasing state power: the national interest rules over the market-place. Wealth and power are complementary, not competing goals, but excessive economic dependence on other states should be avoided. When economic and security interests clash, security interests have priority.

- Economic liberals argue that the market economy is an autonomous sphere of society, operating according to its own economic laws. Economic exchange is a positive-sum game and the market will tend to maximize benefits for individuals, households and companies. The economy is a sphere of cooperation for mutual benefit, among states as well as among individuals.

- In the Marxist approach the economy is a site of exploitation and inequality between social classes, especially the bourgeoisie and the proletariat. Politics is to a large extent determined by the socioeconomic context. The dominant economic class is also dominant politically. IPE concerns the history of global capitalist expansion and the struggles between classes and states to which it has given rise. Capitalist development is uneven and bound to produce new crises and contradictions, both between states and between social classes.

QUESTIONS

- What is IPE and why is it important?

- Give the core arguments made by the three main theories of IPE: mercantilism, economic liberalism and Marxism. Which theory, if any, is the best one? Why?

- Politics is in control of economics, say mercantilists. Economics is the basis for everything else, including politics, say Marxists. How should we settle this dispute?

- Economic liberals argue that economic exchange is a positive-sum game. In the Marxist approach the economy is a site of exploitation and inequality. Who is right?

- Do security interests always have priority over economic matters, as mercantilists claim?

- Compare Waltz and Wallerstein. Who has the better theory?

GUIDE TO FURTHER READING

Cox, R. W. (1987). *Production, Power and World Order: Social Forces in the Making of History*. New York: Columbia University Press.

Cox, R. W., with Schechter, M. G. (2002). *The Political Economy of a Plural World: Critical Reflections on Power, Morals, and Civilization*. London: Routledge.

Gilpin, R. (2001). *Global Political Economy: Understanding the International Economic Order*. Princeton: Princeton University Press.

Polanyi, K. (1957). *The Great Transformation: The Political and Economic Origins of Our Time*. New York: Farrar Rinehart.

Schwartz, H. (2000). *States versus Markets: The Emergence of a Global Economy*, 2nd edn. London: Macmillan.

Strange, S. (1988). *States and Markets: An Introduction to International Political Economy*. London: Pinter.

Wallerstein, I. (2004). *World-Systems Analysis: An Introduction*. Durham: Duke University Press.

WEB LINKS

Web links mentioned in the chapter plus additional links can be found on the Online Resource Centre that accompanies this book.

www.oxfordtextbooks.co.uk/orc/jackson_sorensen3e/

CHAPTER 8

International Political Economy: Contemporary Debates

Summary

This chapter presents three important IPE debates. They concern: (1) the exact relationship between politics and economics; (2) development and underdevelopment in the Third World; and (3) the nature and extent of economic globalization. The last part of the chapter presents recent developments in theorizing on IPE. We emphasize that there is a growing concern about issues of wealth and poverty in many countries. For this reason, the IPE research agenda is of increasing importance.

The Relationship between Politics and Economics: The Debate on US Hegemonic Stability

The most important debate stemming from mercantilism concerns the need for a strong state to create a smoothly functioning liberal international economy. A hegemon, a dominant military and economic power, is necessary for the creation and full development of a liberal world market economy, because in the absence of such a power, liberal rules cannot be enforced around the world. That, in its simplest form, is the theory of hegemonic stability which is indebted to mercantilist thinking about politics being in charge of economics (see web links 8.01 and 8.02). But hegemonic stability theory is not exclusively mercantilist. There is also a liberal element: the dominant power does not merely manipulate international economic relations for its own sake; it creates an open world economy based on free trade which is to the benefit of all participating states and not only the hegemon. The version of the theory we present here was first set forth by Charles Kindleberger (1973) and then further developed by Robert Gilpin (1987).

Why is the theory of hegemonic stability important? Because if it is true, we must expect international markets to be dependent on the existence of a liberal dominant power. In the absence of such a hegemon, an open world economy will be much more difficult to sustain. There is a risk that economic relations will deteriorate into nationalistic, self-interested, protectionist competition, as they did during the world economic crisis of the 1930s, when countries pursued national policies the effect of which was 'beggar your neighbour'. The United States was already the largest economic power, but America was not willing to take on the hegemonic responsibility of creating and maintaining a liberal world economic order. That willingness emerged only after the Second World War which put an end to American isolationism.

The war elevated the United States to a position of nearly unrivalled world leadership. A majority of American politicians recognized that the United States had to take on a responsibility for creating a liberal world market economy after the war. With Europe and Japan in ruins and Britain exhausted, there was no other post-war power to perform that global capitalist role. In short, for a liberal economic world order to come into being, the mere capability of a dominant power is not enough; there must also be a willingness to take on the task. And, finally, there must be a commitment to sustain a liberal order once it has been created: to support it not only in good times when the world economy is expanding but also in bad times when it is in recession and participating states may be tempted to beggar their neighbours.

What kinds of power resources are necessary for a hegemon to perform its role? The question is not an easy one to answer, because it involves the complex issue of the fungibility of power. A power resource is fungible if it can be used across several issue areas. For example, military force is not only useful on the battlefield; it can also be used as a lever in other areas of foreign policy. The United States has employed its military power to provide security to

Western Europe against the Soviet threat. That situation has given the United States influence in Europe in other areas, such as trade policies. The provision of military security thus paves the way for leverage in economic areas. In the IR debate about these issues the claim has been made that the fungibility of military power is decreasing (Nye 1990). We cannot pursue that debate here. It is sufficient to say that a dominant state needs a number of different power resources to perform the role of hegemon. In addition to military power, according to Keohane (1984: 32), it requires control over four sets of world economic resources: raw materials, capital, markets, and the hegemon's competitive advantage in the production of goods that can command a very high value.

Why is a hegemon required in order to create and maintain a liberal world economy? Might we not expect that smaller, less powerful states will also be interested in a liberal world economy because that is to the benefit of all? Why would they not cooperate to sustain such an economy? What is the use, then, for a dominant liberal power? According to the theory of hegemonic stability, the need for a hegemon has to do with the nature of the goods which it provides. A liberal world economy is a so-called public or collective good, that is, a good or a service which, once supplied, creates benefits for everybody. Public goods are characterized by non-excludability; others cannot be denied access to them. The air that we breathe is an example of such a good. A lighthouse is another example of a public good; so is a road or a pavement.[1] The elements of a liberal world economy, such as a currency system for international payments, or the possibility to trade in a free market, are examples of public goods. Once created, they are there for the benefit of all.

The problem with public goods is underprovision and what the economists call 'free riding': i.e. making use of the goods without paying for them. Why should anyone sustain the cost to provide such a good in the first place if it is there to be used at no cost, once it is supplied? Existing public goods invite free riding. That is where the hegemon comes in: such a dominant power is needed to provide those goods and to deal with problems created by free riders, for example by penalizing them. Why would the hegemon do that? Because it has a huge stake in the system.

There are two major historical examples of liberal hegemons: Great Britain during the late nineteenth and early twentieth century; and the United States after the Second World War (see web link 8.05). Britain was a global trading power and imperial power and, as such, had a profound interest in maintaining an open world economy based on free trade. Britain lost its position of hegemony in the early twentieth century when other powers began to rival and surpass it, particularly Germany and the United States. After the Second World War, the United States took the lead in setting up new institutions of a reformed liberal world economy: the IMF, the World Bank, the General Agreement on Tariffs and Trade (the GATT, now replaced by the World Trade Organization, the WTO) and the Organization for Economic Cooperation and Development (the OECD). The system was called the Bretton Woods system, named after the small town in the US where the agreement was made in 1944.

---

[1] Yet we know that some roads are closed off, unless you pay a toll; still, many roads are public goods. For further discussion on the difficulties with the distinction see, for example, Hardin (1982).

It was clearly in the United States' own interest to restore the liberal world economy based on new institutions which it could largely control. As the world's dominant industrial power, an open world economy was of great benefit to the US because it gave America better access to foreign markets. Helping in the rebuilding of Western Europe and Japan was also important for American security reasons in its Cold War struggle with the Soviet Union. The United States was not interested in an unstable world, susceptible to Soviet influence, because that would be a threat to United States' political and economic interests. However, it can be argued that there was also an altruistic element in the American effort. The Marshall Plan helped post-war reconstruction get under way. The US accepted unequal treatment by its partners; Japan was allowed to maintain a limited access to its domestic market; Western Europe was allowed to continue its policies of subsidy and protectionism in agriculture.

By the late 1950s or early 1960s the economies of Western Europe and Japan had been rebuilt. The huge US economic lead was disappearing; Japan and Western Europe were catching up economically. There was a growing deficit in the American balance of payments. By the 1970s the US started running trade deficits for the first time in the post-war era. US policies became more oriented towards national interests. Instead of sustaining the post-1945 liberal world economy, the US adopted protectionist measures to support its own economy. America began to act as a 'predatory hegemon' (Jonn Conybeare, quoted from Gilpin 1987). In other words, the US became more concerned about its own national interests, began to lose sight of its role as the defender of an open world economy and perhaps even started to exploit its power position. It was a new era characterized by 'increasing protectionism, monetary instability, and economic crisis' (Gilpin 1987: 351). With the relative decline of the United States, however, there was no longer a clearly dominant power to sustain the liberal world economy. Box 8.1 summarizes the theory of hegemonic stability using the United States as an example.

The line of reasoning summarized in the box has been subject to much debate within IPE. There are several observers that accept the general notion of the need for a hegemon to establish a liberal world economy. But they dispute the idea that US economic power has declined substantially (Strange 1987; Russett 1985; Nye 1990). They make two arguments. First, the United States remains very strong in traditional fungible power resources (military, economy, technology, territory). There has been a relative decline in the economic and technological areas, but that was inevitable since the US lead was unnaturally strong in 1950, when Western Europe and Japan still had to rebuild. The US continues to lead the world in areas of high technology innovation and competition. Second, the ways in which the US position is calculated makes a difference. Susan Strange argues that it is misleading to focus on the territorial economy within United States borders. 'What matters is the share of world output—of primary products, minerals and food and manufactured goods and services—that is under the direction of the executives of US companies' (Strange 1987: 5). That share still puts the US in the lead because of the massive amounts of US foreign investment abroad. Furthermore, as indicated, the US is especially strong in the most advanced, information-rich industries which now count more in terms of economic power than industrial capacity. And, finally, the US also remains strong in non-material power resources, such as 'popular culture'

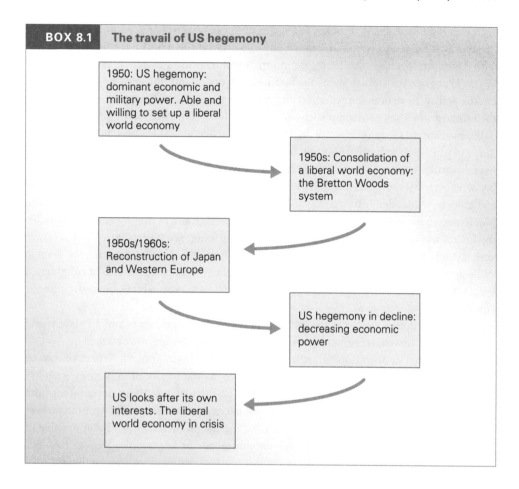

BOX 8.1	The travail of US hegemony

1950: US hegemony: dominant economic and military power. Able and willing to set up a liberal world economy

1950s: Consolidation of a liberal world economy: the Bretton Woods system

1950s/1960s: Reconstruction of Japan and Western Europe

US hegemony in decline: decreasing economic power

US looks after its own interests. The liberal world economy in crisis

BOX 8.2	Power resources of major countries/regions

SOURCE OF POWER	USA	RUSSIA	EUROPE	JAPAN	CHINA
Tangible:					
Basic resources	strong	strong	strong	*medium*	strong
Military	strong	*medium*	*medium*	*weak*	*medium*
Economic	strong	*medium*	strong	strong	*medium*
Science/technology	strong	*weak*	strong	strong	*weak*
Intangible:					
National cohesion	strong	*medium*	*weak*	strong	strong
Universalistic culture	strong	*medium*	strong	*medium*	*medium*
International institutions	strong	*medium*	strong	*medium*	*medium*

Modified from Nye (1990: 174)

with universal appeal: e.g., movies, television, Internet websites and so on. The American lifestyle is attractive to people in many countries around the world. Liberal values in line with American ideology also permeate international institutions such as the IMF and the WTO. That gives the United States a substantial amount of soft power or 'co-optive power': i.e. the ability 'to structure a situation so that other nations develop preferences or define their interests in ways consistent with one's own nation' (Nye 1990: 191).

If we accept these arguments, we are led to the conclusion that US hegemony is still very much in place (see web links 8.09 and 8.10). Why then the tendencies towards crisis in the liberal world economy? Susan Strange has claimed that the United States has made a number of 'managerial decisions of dubious wisdom that accounts quite adequately for financial and monetary disorder' (Strange 1988: 12). In other words, power is not the problem; the problem is about the United States getting its act together and assuming responsibility for the liberal world economy (for a similar line of reasoning, see Nye 1990). More recently, such criticism has also been voiced against the Republican administration of George W. Bush: the US remains the world's supreme power but does not fill the role of enlightened leadership. Instead, US policy is more narrowly focused on satisfying domestic interest groups.

Another IPE debate concerns the issue of the need for a hegemon to run a liberal world economy in the first place. Robert Keohane has argued that hegemonic power helped establish international cooperation in such areas as finance, trade and oil. When US power declined, however, cooperation did not break down, as the theory of hegemonic stability would expect. Keohane concludes that hegemonic power may have been important for the initial establishment of cooperation. But once the necessary international institutions are set up, they have a staying power of their own, they operate on their own, and they are able to promote further cooperation even in the circumstances of hegemonic decline. In other words, we should 'recognize the continuing impact of international regimes on the ability of countries with shared interests to cooperate' (Keohane 1984: 216).

Yet another objection against the theory of hegemonic stability concerns its one-sided emphasis on the leading power, the hegemon. The theory downplays the positive role of smaller powers in the establishment of a liberal world economy. Even the strongest hegemon can accomplish only so much on its own. It calls for the cooperative efforts of other states. Hegemonic stability theory tends to view smaller powers as egoistic free riders. In fact they have contributed greatly to the setting up of a liberal world economy by assisting in the establishment of liberal international regimes. Furthermore, US hegemony was always less altruistic than the theory leads us to believe. During the Cold War the United States had a vital security interest in tying Western Europe and Japan to the liberal camp. The liberal economic order set up by the US was not so much the provision of a public good as it was in the best interest of the US itself (for these arguments see, for example, Gadzey 1994). Of course, that is not to deny that Western Europe was a major beneficiary of the American security guarantee during the Cold War.

Finally, the Marxist position recognizes the importance of hegemony, but connects it to long cycles of economic growth. For Marxists, US hegemony was a specific phase of capitalist expansion in the post-war era. This phase came to an end around 1970 because the preconditions that sustained the long upswing—especially the availability of cheap and skilled labour in Western Europe and Japan—were no longer present. Japan and Western Europe caught up economically (Wallerstein 1984; Amin 1975). US producers were thus squeezed by increasing and intensifying international competition. Robert Cox agrees that the economic decline of the US presents problems for a stable world order. But he follows the Italian Marxist Antonio Gramsci by emphasizing the ideological dimension of hegemony. A stable hegemonic order is based on a shared set of values and understandings derived 'from the ways of doing and thinking of the dominant social strata of the dominant state' (Cox 1996: 517). In other words, US hegemony was based not only on material power but also on values: i.e. a model of society that other countries found attractive and wanted to emulate.

Marxists also point to the elements of inequality and hierarchy inherent in US hegemony. The liberal world economy under US leadership was never truly global. The Third World had a marginal position and the Soviet bloc did not participate. Many Marxists see US hegemony as a vehicle for control over weaker states by the bourgeoisies of the US and other leading Western countries in ways that were to the economic and political benefit of the West (e.g. Frank 1980). On this view, the liberal world economy is a misnomer for economic and political control of the world by a Western capitalist elite for its own benefit. Today, most scholars would agree that the United States is the world's leading power. While some think we are living in an age of US-led empire, others believe that American power is rather fragile and unstable (Hardt and Negri 2000; Mann 2003; Boggs 2005; Münkler 2005).

What can we learn from these discussions about the larger debate concerning the relationship between politics and economics? First, while mercantilism is correct in pointing to the need for a political framework as a foundation for economic activity, that does not mean that there is a one-way relationship in which politics is in control of economics. The economic sphere has a dynamic of its own and unequal economic development between states reshuffles the basis for political power. There is a logic of politics and a logic of economics which influence each other, but economics is not entirely controlled by politics and vice versa. This relationship is summarized in Box 8.3.

Second, the relative decline of the US has not meant a breakdown of the liberal world economy. The end of the twentieth century can hardly be described as a phase of severe international economic crisis, at least seen from the perspective of the industrialized West which has witnessed far greater crises in the past. In other words, political regulation of the

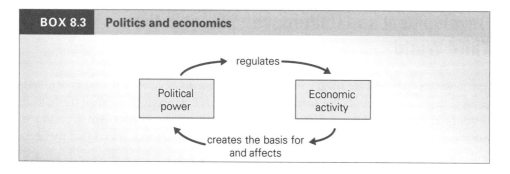

BOX 8.3   Politics and economics

BOX 8.4	Politics and economics in theories of IPE	
	TRUE CLAIM	**FALSE CLAIM**
Mercantilism	Political regulation creates a framework for economic activity	Politics is in full control of economics
Marxism	Economics affects and influences politics	Economics determines politics
Liberalism	The market has an economic dynamic of its own	The market is an autonomous sphere of society

world economy is possible without a highly dominant hegemon; the current regulation appears to rest on the cooperative efforts of the United States, Western Europe and Japan. Should that cooperation break down severely, we might expect the rise of a more regionalized world. But the chances of that are not very great. Finally, the policies of a leading power may be altruistic in the sense that it accepts responsibility for international tasks which others cannot look after, but there will almost always be an important element of self-interest involved. There is a benign as well as a malign aspect of hegemony. The issue of which aspect shall dominate cannot be decided beforehand; it must depend on an analysis of each concrete case (see web link 8.12).

In conclusion, one cannot say that politics is in full control of economics, as mercantilists will have us believe; but it is true that political regulation creates the framework for economic activity. Nor can it be said that economics determines politics, as many Marxists claim; but it is true that economic dynamics affect and influence political power. The liberal claim that the market economy is an autonomous sphere of society is misleading; but it is true that once political regulation has created a market economy, that economy has a dynamic of its own. There is a complex relationship between politics and economics as shown in Box 8.4.

Liberalism, Marxism and mercantilism have each revealed an important aspect of the political-economic relationship. They also disclose distinct shortcomings: they cannot stand alone. We need elements of each theory in order to investigate the complex relationship between politics and economics.

Development and Underdevelopment in the Third World

The most important debate triggered by Marxism concerns development and underdevelopment in the Third World. The Marxist approach to IPE has concentrated on the issue of development and underdevelopment in developing countries (in Asia, Africa and Latin America). The Marxists were reacting to economic liberal ideas so it is best that we begin with the liberal view of development problems.

However, a few preliminary remarks about the development issue itself may be useful. Questions about development problems in the Third World were hardly ever asked before the 1950s. When they were asked it was in terms of colonial development, because most Third World countries were colonies controlled by European states. The development of colonies was an imperial issue but not strictly an international issue. Decolonization, beginning in the 1950s, marked the introduction of development research on a larger, international scale. 'New' states in Africa and Asia became members of the UN and raised their voices about the need to focus on development. The Cold War confrontation between East and West meant that each side was interested in cultivating closer links with the developing world to the disadvantage of the other side.

It was economic liberals who spearheaded development research in the West. Their various contributions were given the label 'modernization theory.' The basic idea was that Third World countries should be expected to follow the same developmental path taken earlier by the developed countries in the West: a progressive journey from a traditional, pre-industrial, agrarian society towards a modern, industrial, mass-consumption society. Development meant overcoming barriers of pre-industrial production, backward institutions and parochial value systems which impeded the process of growth and modernization. Many economic liberals take note of a dualism in Third World countries, i.e. a traditional sector still rooted in the countryside and an emerging modern sector concentrated in the cities. The two sectors exist in relative isolation from each other. The only significant linkage is that the traditional sector functions as a reservoir of labour for the modern sector. This spread of development dynamics from the modern sector to the traditional sector is a core problem in getting economic development underway (Lewis 1970).

The theoretical endeavours among economic liberals, or modernization theorists as they are often called in the development debate, concern identification of the full range of impediments to modernization as well as all factors that promote modernization. Economic liberals underscore the need for an open economy, free of political interference, to help generate the large amounts of investment that is required to foster sustained economic growth and development (Lal 1983). A famous modernization theory by W. W. Rostow (1960; 1978) specifically stressed that the 'take-off', the crucial push in moving from traditional towards modern, is characterized by a marked increase in modern sector investment, to a minimum of 10 per cent of the gross national product (see web link 8.13). Another critical element concerns the relationship of Third World countries to the world market. Close market relations with the developed countries is seen to have a positive developmental effect on Third World economies. Foreign trade is viewed as a road to market expansion and further growth of the modern sector. Foreign direct investment in the Third World by transnational corporations (TNCs) brings in much needed modern technology and production skills. The economic liberal theory can be summarized as shown in Box 8.5.

The liberal understanding of development was subjected to increasing criticism during the 1960s and 1970s. That was partly in reaction to the lack of progress in many Third World countries at that time. While growth rates in the developed world reached unprecedented highs in the post-war decades, many Third World countries had difficulties in getting

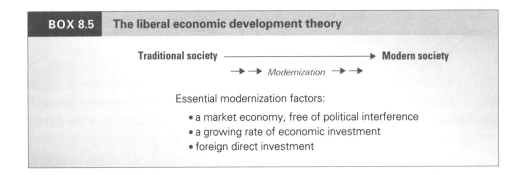

economic development underway. Their economies refused to 'take off'. That naturally led to increasing dissatisfaction with modernization theory.

The most radical critique of economic liberals came from neo-Marxist underdevelopment theory which is also known under the name of dependency theory. It draws on classical Marxist analysis. But it is different from classical Marxism in a basic respect. Unlike Marx, dependency theorists do not expect capitalist development to take root and unfold in the Third World in the same way that capitalism first took place in Western Europe and North America. And, unlike Soviet Marxism, dependency theorists do not support a Soviet model with its centralized and highly authoritarian system. Instead, they argue in favour of a socialist model which is more decentralized and democratic. Their main aim, however, is not so much the formulation of alternative development models to those of capitalism or economic liberalism. Rather, it is to critique the dependency form that capitalist development is seen to take in the Third World (for general overviews, see Kay 1989; Hettne 1995). In short, dependency theory is an attack on late capitalism. It is an effort to provide the theoretical tools by which Third World countries can defend themselves against globalizing capitalism.

We saw earlier that for economic liberals 'traditional society' was the place where all countries started their process of development and modernization. Dependency theory rejects that view. The starting-point for dependency theory is not tradition; it is underdevelopment. Underdevelopment is not a condition which once characterized all countries. It is a process within the framework of the global capitalist system to which Third World countries have been subjected: they have been underdeveloped as an intentional by-product of the development of the West. Underdevelopment is the process by which capitalist forces expand to subdue and impoverish the Third World. Earlier forms of society in the Third World may have been undeveloped; but underdevelopment begins only with the arrival of global capitalism. That is, global capitalism in one single process generates development and wealth (in the industrialized world) and underdevelopment and poverty (in the Third World).

Under such adverse global conditions, how can development be brought to the Third World? Radical dependency theorists, such as Andre Gunder Frank (1969; 1977) and Samir Amin (1976; 1990), do not hesitate to argue that Third World countries have to cut off, or at least severely limit, their ties to the capitalist world market. Through reliance on their own strength, as well as mutual cooperation, real economic development becomes possible,

> **BOX 8.6**   **Dependency theory of underdevelopment**
>
> 1. Underdevelopment is caused by factors external to the poor countries. Third World countries are dominated by foreign interests originating in the developed West.
>
> 2. Underdevelopment is not a phase of 'traditional society' experienced by all countries. Both development and underdevelopment are results of a single process of global capitalist development.
>
> 3. Underdevelopment is due to external, primarily economic, forces; these forces result in crippled and distorted societal structures inside Third World countries.
>
> 4. To overcome underdevelopment a delinking from external dominance is required.

outside the reach of capitalist world market exploitation. Moderate dependency theorists, such as Fernando Henrique Cardoso (Cardoso and Faletto 1979), are less severe in their critique of the capitalist world market. They argue that some development in the Third World is possible even given the ties of external dependence on the capitalist West. We can summarize the radical dependency view as shown in Box 8.6 (see also Evers and Wogau 1973).

Radical dependency theory came under fire during the 1970s and went into decline (see web link 8.21). A number of countries in South-East Asia, most notably the 'Four Tigers' (South Korea, Taiwan, Singapore and Hong Kong), experienced rapid economic growth combined with world market integration. That was a blow to dependency theory's prediction of stagnation and misery and seemed to support liberal modernization theory. Furthermore, dependency theory severely downplayed domestic factors in their analyses, such as the role of the state and domestic social forces. To some extent, the world systems analysis by Wallerstein set forth in Chapter 7 has an answer to such critiques. Wallerstein builds on ideas from dependency theory about unequal exchange and underdevelopment in the periphery. But in his view some countries, such as the 'Four Tigers', may well move ahead; other countries will simply move in the opposite direction and, overall, hierarchy and unequal exchange continues to characterize the capitalist world-economy. Furthermore, Wallerstein would protest against labelling his analysis as economistic; economics and politics affect each other in a dialectical interaction.

In any case, the 1980s saw a strong revival of economic liberal ideas in development thinking. Ronald Reagan's presidency in the US and Margaret Thatcher's administration in the UK both promoted liberal policies which emphasized the role of free market forces and the downsizing of state bureaucracies and state regulations. Third World countries were encouraged to pursue similar policies (Toye 1987).

Yet the late 1980s and early 1990s also saw the return of ideas based on mercantilist thinking. Mercantilism has not set forth a brief and clear statement about Third World development comparable to the ones formulated by economic liberals and dependency theorists. But there is a broad and diverse mercantilist tradition in development which has gained new strength in recent years. The mercantilist view of development strikes a balance between economic liberal and dependency views. Whereas economic liberals argue in favour of world market integration in order to promote development, and dependency

| BOX 8.7 | Development or underdevelopment in sub-Saharan Africa? |

PROGRESS | **DEPRIVATION**

HEALTH

- Between 1960 and 2003 life expectancy at birth increased from 40 to 47 years.
- In the past decade the proportion of the population with access to safe water nearly doubled—from 25% to 43%.

- There is only one doctor for every 18,000 people, compared with 6,000 in the developing world as a whole and 390 in the industrial countries.
- More than ten million people are infected with HIV, two-thirds of all those infected in the world.

EDUCATION

- During the past two decades adult literacy more than doubled—from 27% to 55%.
- Between 1960 and 1991 the net enrolment ratio at the primary level increased from 25% to 50%, and at the secondary level from 13% to 38%.

- Only about half the entrants to grade 1 finish grade 5.
- At the primary and secondary levels more than 80 million boys and girls are still out of school.

INCOME AND POVERTY

- Over the period 1975–2003 four countries—Botswana, Cape Verde, Lesotho and Mauritius—had an annual GDP growth rate of more than 3%.

- About 170 million people (nearly a third of the region's population) do not get enough to eat.
- During the past three decades the ratio of military to social spending increased, from 27% in 1960 to 43% in 1991.

CHILDREN

- Over the past three decades the infant mortality rate dropped from 167 per thousand live births to 97.

- About 23 million children in the region are malnourished, and 16% of babies are underweight.

Sources: The World Bank (1997; 2000); UNDP (1996; 2005)

* Total population in sub-Saharan Africa (1999): 642 million
* GNP per capita (1999): US$ 500

theorists argue for delinking, mercantilists suggest a middle road. Raul Prebisch (1950) and Gunnar Myrdal (1957) had already argued in the 1950s against free trade based on comparative advantage. The economic benefits which liberals said would accrue to the South according to the theory of comparative advantage were not forthcoming. Basically, that was owing to a secular decline in the terms of trade for the South's traditional exports.[2] In other

[2] 'Terms of trade' is the ratio of export and import prices. When Third World countries receive less for their raw material exports and have to pay more for import of industrialized goods, their terms of trade deteriorate.

words, those export commodities lost much of their previous value on world markets whereas industrial and increasingly high technology imports still cost the same or even more. Therefore, it was necessary actively to promote industrialization in the South, even if such industry may be comparatively high-cost in the initial phase. If liberal comparative advantage can be criticized, so can dependency ideas about delinking. Hettne (1995) goes through four cases of 'experiments with delinking' from the 1970s, namely Tanzania, Ghana, Jamaica and Nicaragua, and finds a lack of success in every case, due to a combination of external destabilization and internal resistance, to which should be added wholly unrealistic state economic plans and policies.

Modern mercantilists thus suggest a compromise between the extremes of economic autonomy and full integration into the global capitalist economy. It can be argued that the economic development success of East Asian countries and also Japan is precisely due to their pursuit of a successful mercantilist strategy (Amsden 1989; Toye 1987). A second core area of development where the mercantilists strike a balance concerns the market and the state. Economic liberals argue that free market forces and a minimal role for the state is best for the promotion of economic development. Mercantilists reply that there may be serious flaws in the alleged efficiency of the market (Weiss 1988: 177). Furthermore, there is no firm support in economic theory for maintaining that state intervention is by definition counter-productive. The fact that some interventions are flawed does not constitute a case against intervention per se (Toye 1987: ch. 4). South Korea and Taiwan's development achievements have been based on states actively working towards building desired structures of production (Amsden and Chu 2003; Wade 1985; Ludde-Neurath 1985).

Yet mercantilists recognize that excessive state intervention can involve 'bureaucratic failures' (White 1984: 101) and they do not support the dependency view where there is no significant role at all for market forces. If too much is left to market forces, there is the danger of market failure: for example, monopolies may be created in some areas so that there is no competition among producers any more; or there may be negative side-effects due to unregulated production, such as pollution. Yet if too much is left to state regulation, the result may be bureaucratic failures, that is 'red tape' problems of high cost and inefficiency. The actual balance between state and market will vary across societies and within the same society over time (White 1984). The recent years of prolonged economic crisis in Japan are an indication that after many years of successful growth the political and bureaucratic establishment is unable or unwilling—because there are vested political and economic interests in the current system—to devise new strategies for viable economic development.

Another example of the mercantilist middle road in development thinking concerns the role of transnational corporations (TNCs). Economic liberals often see TNCs as 'engines of growth', bringing progress and prosperity to the South; dependency theory, in contrast, frequently sees TNCs as 'the devil incorporated' (Streeten 1979). Mercantilists note that TNCs have the potential for benefiting Third World development, but only under certain conditions. In weak states with undeveloped local economies, TNCs will totally dominate the host country and that is not helpful for the strengthening of local industry; the TNCs will be local monopolists. In stronger states with some local industry, TNC investment can assist in upgrading local undertakings technologically and otherwise, and thus significantly

| BOX 8.8 | Modern mercantilism |

1. Strike a balance between national autonomy and international integration, i.e. between incorporation into the world market and self-reliance.
2. Strike a balance between state and market, i.e. between free market forces and state regulation.
3. Foreign direct investment by TNCs can be a strong modernization factor, but only provided that TNCs are counterbalanced by local industry and host government supervision.

assist in developing the host economy (Sørensen 1983; Nixson 1988). In other words, TNCs will not bring economic development to the South on their own; there has to be a counter-weight in the form of local industry and a host government strong enough to oversee TNC activity (see web links 8.30 and 8.31). We can summarize the modern mercantilist view of development as shown in Box 8.8.

Modern mercantilism in many ways appears to offer a sensible strategy for economic development. Yet it is not without weaknesses. To follow the path advocated by modern mercantilists, the states of the South need a fairly high political-administrative capacity; otherwise they will not be able to undertake sophisticated state interventions and regulations of the economy. Even if there are a number of states with such developmental strength in East Asia and elsewhere, it is clear that the majority of states in the South are not very strong (Sørensen 1993b; Evans 1989). For example, in sub-Saharan Africa corrupt and self-interested state elites are part of the development problem rather than part of the solution. Under such circumstances, there is little hope of success for the modern mercantilist strategy. Indeed, mercantilist policies might even lead to greater problems by creating conditions in which corruption can flourish.

It ought to be clear from this brief introduction that the problems concerning development and underdevelopment in the Third World continue to provoke debate among scholars who hold different theoretical positions. The popularity of the main positions has waxed and waned yet the development problem remains in place; some 800 million people do not get enough food, and about 500 million are chronically malnourished (UNDP 1996: 20). Economic liberals are right in claiming that a free market economy can be a powerful force promoting growth and modernization; but it is not true that an unregulated market will more or less automatically lead to optimum development for individuals and states in the long run. Dependency theorists have a point when they emphasize how relations of dependence shape and impact development in the Third World. But they are wrong in claiming that integration in the world market must lead to underdevelopment and that developed, Western countries are no more than imperialist exploiters. Modern mercantilism appears to strike a sensible middle road between state and market, between autonomy and integration. But mercantilists tend to rely too much on prudent manoeuvring by Third World states, many of which are quite weak and are led by self-serving and often highly corrupt elites.

In sum, and not surprisingly, each of the main theoretical positions has insights concerning the development problem, and each has blind spots, as shown in Box 8.9.

BOX 8.9	The development problem in theories of IPE	
	TRUE CLAIM	**FALSE CLAIM**
Liberalism	A free market economy promotes growth and development	An unregulated market will lead to the best result for individuals and states
Dependency theory	Dependence shapes Third World development	Integration in the world market must lead to underdevelopment
Modern mercantilism	Development benefits from a sensible mix of state and market, autonomy and integration	Governments are always able to regulate the economy in an optimum fashion

In recent years the debate on development has grown more complex (Payne 2005). It almost had to happen, for two reasons. First, the major theories discussed above claim relevance for development problems everywhere, that is, they are general theories. But there are specific problems in many regions and countries, due to particular historical experiences and variation in local conditions. Africa south of the Sahara, South Asia, East Asia, Latin America and Eastern Europe are examples of regions with very dissimilar historical trajectories of development and very different local conditions. And even within these regions there is great variation. Current development thinking (for overviews see Martinussen 1997 and Nederveen Pieterse 2000) is much more aware of such differences. Consequently, development thinking is becoming increasingly complex: issues and recommendations cannot always travel from one region, or even from a sub-region, to other places.

Second, the whole debate about development has been opened up in the sense that many different voices participate: grass-root organizations, NGOs, peasant movements, political parties, governments, international institutions, the development research community and so on. These participants make up different stakeholders in the process of development. Therefore, they often have different views about what the important issues are and what should be done about them.

One result of this increased complexity is a renewed debate about the concept of development itself. We saw earlier how liberal thinking conceived of development in terms of acquiring the characteristics of modern, capitalist countries: when less developed countries get economic growth and modernization, they develop. That view was promoted in the UN system in the 1950s and 1960s, because there was a need to identify those countries that were eligible for development aid. That group was simply defined in terms of not having achieved much in terms of economic growth per capita.

Dependency theory and mercantilist theory never disputed this liberal concept of development. Where they differ is in the strategies for achieving these results. So there is a mainstream concept of development that focuses on growth and modernization. In recent years this mainstream concept has become somewhat more nuanced. Development is not merely growth—it is distribution and welfare; and development is not merely satisfaction of material needs—it is also democracy, participation, freedom and self-realization. But the core of the concept remains in place: modernization and growth.

There was always a critique of this mainstream concept of development. In recent years it has grown stronger. The critics are not a unified group. Some are directly anti-development; they reject the whole idea of development as progress. In this view, living conditions should be decided by local, autonomous communities steering their own course (cf. Sachs 1992). Many other critics favour some form of alternative development (Hettne 1995). Their visions vary, but there are also some common traits: a sceptical view of modernity and industrialization; a favourable attitude towards traditional values and practices in pre-industrial society; anti-materialism; and an embrace of ultra-democratic values involving a high degree of popular participation and control.

Liberal modernization theory is ready to accept that modernity is somewhat more complex than 'emulating the West'; therefore modernization is a much less uniform transformation than originally believed. It can move in different directions. There may also be aspects of 'tradition' worth preserving in a process of development. In the 1980s the World Bank and the IMF were convinced that 'more market and less state' was the appropriate road to development; today these institutions are less neoliberal. They accept a significant role for the state and they also emphasize the need for democratic accountability and the involvement of civil society in development.

Other international institutions, such as the UNDP, emphasize the need for a broad process of human development, making ordinary people better off, in contrast to a mere quest for economic growth. The construction of a Human Development Index (based on measures of life expectancy at birth, adult literacy rate, years of schooling and real GDP per capita) has drawn attention to other aspects of the development process. The UNDP annual Human Development Report examines female–male gaps, child nutrition, health profiles, rural–urban gaps and North–South gaps (UNDP 2005). International institutions, such as the IMF and the UNDP, heavily influence the debate in development. In 2000, the UN General Assembly adopted the Millennium Declaration and the Millennium Development Goals (MDGs). MDGs are a set of ambitious targets for reducing poverty, inequality and child mortality, and for promoting education, health and a better environment in the Third World.

Critics continue to question the mainstream view of development. A new critique has been provided by discourse analysis (Escobar 1995). The mainstream view is seen as a dominant discourse which defines 'the truth' about development in a certain way and thereby also becomes an instrument of power because it defines what is common sense about development and thereby excludes alternative interpretations. Discourse analysis wants to unmask the dominant 'common sense' in order to make way for alternative ways of thinking about development.

These remarks are meant to indicate that we have only touched the tip of the iceberg of the large and complex development issue; development has to do with much more than IPE. It also involves all the different disciplines that deal with human and social affairs. The three main theoretical positions discussed above will nevertheless continue to influence our thinking about development problems.

Economic Globalization and a Changing Role for States

Economic liberals have sparked a number of debates on various issues. We have chosen to concentrate on the issue of change in the context of economic globalization. The phenomenon of globalization has received a great deal of attention from IPE. Globalization is the spread and intensification of economic, social and cultural relations across international borders (see web links 8.35 and 8.37). This means that globalization covers almost everything; it concerns economics, politics, technology, communication and more. Such a concept of globalization is very difficult to theorize; in social science one cannot have a theory about 'everything', because different aspects of reality have to be analysed in different ways. So, in order to move on, it is helpful to 'unpack' the concept, that is, to look at different major aspects of globalization. Because this is a chapter on IPE, we shall concentrate on the economic aspect of globalization, but it should be remembered that this is only one, albeit very important, aspect of globalization. It is related to interdependence, which was discussed in Chapter 4.

A growing level of economic interconnection between two national economies, for example in the form of more external trade or foreign investment, is one aspect of economic globalization. We might call it 'intensified interdependence'. But there is an additional aspect which signifies a shift towards a truly global economic system. Intensified economic interdependence involves more of the same in the sense that economic intercourse between national economies increases. True economic globalization, however, involves a qualitative shift towards a world economy that is no longer based on autonomous national economies; rather, it is based on a consolidated global marketplace for production, distribution and consumption. In this latter case, the single global economy 'dominates' the numerous national economies contained within it (Hirst and Thompson 1992: 199). Some scholars call this process 'deep integration' in contrast to intensified interdependence which can be seen as 'shallow integration'. Deep integration is first and foremost organized by TNCs. They increasingly organize the production of goods and services on a global scale. The various segments of production, from development and design, to manufacture and assembly, are each placed in locations that offer the best conditions for that particular segment in terms of labour cost, input availability, proximity of markets and so on. At the same time, TNCs set up networks with local firms that act as suppliers and subcontractors.

Globalization is pushed by several factors: the most important is technological change which is driven by relentless economic competition between firms. The measures taken by states (e.g. trade and finance liberalization) are also important catalysts. The three main theoretical approaches to IPE are in agreement that economic globalization is taking place. But they disagree about the actual content of the process (shallow or deep integration); they also disagree about the consequences of economic globalization for states. Many economic liberals have an optimistic view of economic globalization. One example is the famous American economist Milton Friedman who celebrates the fact that it is now 'possible to

BOX 8.10	Two aspects of economic globalization		

		Indicator: Global exports (as % of GDP)	
	'More of the same'	1990:	2002:
ECONOMIC GLOBALIZATION		19%	24%
		Indicator: Intrafirm trade (as % of total US trade, 2001)	
	'Qualitative shift'	Exports:	Imports:
		32%	47%

Source: UNDP (2005)

produce a product anywhere, using resources from anywhere, by a company located anywhere, to be sold anywhere' (Friedman 1993). That is because states no longer interfere with production and consumption the way they used to. According to John Naisbitt (1994), such a world offers tremendous economic opportunities: the possibilities for economic advance are 'far greater than at any time in human history', not only for companies and institutions but also for individuals and families (1994: 59). A number of economic liberals share this optimistic view (e.g. Reich 1992; Ohmae 1993).

Globalization also means that the component parts of the world become smaller and far more numerous. Small is beautiful not only in the economic sphere but also in the political sphere. This process has profound consequences for the state. In a unified global economy, small, flexible economic players can grow increasingly powerful as national economies become obsolete. As globalization progresses, says Naisbitt, people become more and more conscious of their 'tribal' identities (e.g. language and culture), and that is driving the formation of an increasing number of smaller countries. Naisbitt foresees a thousand—maybe even two thousand—countries by sometime in the twenty-first century. That would entail the decline and fall of the nation-state as we have known it for the past several centuries.

The idea that the Westphalian nation-state is becoming too small for some things and too big for other things in an era of globalization resonates with many economic liberals (e.g. Zacher 1992). They argue that the nation-state is pressured 'from above' in the sense that globalization creates cross-border activities which states are no longer able to control on their own—such as global economic transactions and environmental problems. And the nation-state is also pressured 'from below': there is a trend towards ever stronger identification with the local community where people live their daily lives. The economic liberal view of economic globalization and its consequences can be summarized as shown in Box 8.11.

Mercantilists have not formulated a view of globalization that can rival the economic liberal analysis in scope and ambition. But there is what could be termed a mercantilist position in the globalization debate. That position is highly critical of the economic liberal analysis, both as regards the content of economic globalization and as regards the supposed consequences for the nation-state. Mercantilists remain unconvinced that a qualitative shift

---

BOX 8.11   **Economic liberals' view of globalization**

1. Economic globalization means a qualitative shift towards a global economic system.
2. Economic globalization will bring increased prosperity to individuals, families and companies.
3. The nation-state loses power and influence as it is pressed from above and from below.

BOX 8.12   **Selected top 100 TNCs, ranked by transnationality index,[1] 1995**

CORPORATION	ECONOMY	INDUSTRY	TRANSNATIONALITY INDEX
Nestlé SA	Switzerland	Food	94.0
Electrolux AB	Sweden	Electronics	88.3
Shell, Royal Dutch	United Kingdom/ Netherlands	Oil, gas, coal and related services	73.0
Bayer AG	Germany	Chemicals	69.3
Sony Corporation	Japan	Electronics	59.1
IBM	United States	Computers	54.9
Honda Motor Co	Japan	Automotive	52.6
Transnationalization index, top 100 world TNCs			51.0
Daewoo Corporation	South Korea	Diversified	47.7
GTE Corporation	United States	Telecommunication	14.9

[1] The 'transnationality index' is calculated from the average ratios of foreign assets to total assets, foreign sales to total sales, and foreign employment to total employment.

Based on United Nations (1997b)

---

towards a global economic system has taken place. In other words they do not believe there is a phenomenon called 'globalization'. Instead, they see economic globalization as 'more of the same', that is, a process of intensified interdependence between national economies. Furthermore, they argue that trade and investment flows between countries were at a very high level before the First World War. In other words, there is little news in the fact of economic interdependence (Thompson and Krasner 1989). Mercantilists also reject the claim made by many economic liberals (see Reich 1992: 301–17) that corporations have lost their national identity in pursuit of their ambition to become truly global economic players. Instead, mercantilists argue, states and their national corporations remain 'closely linked' in spite of the noteworthy increase in world trade and investment flows since the end of the Second World War (Kapstein 1993: 502).

Mercantilists thus reject the idea that nation-states are being pressured and are somehow losing out in the process of economic globalization. They say liberals fail to take into account the increased capacity of nation-states to respond to the challenges of economic globalization.

BOX 8.13   **The realist-mercantilist view of globalization**

1. Economic globalization is 'more of the same', i.e. intensified economic interdependence; nothing much new in that.

2. Corporations do not lose their national identities because they are global payers; they remain tied to their home countries.

3. The nation-state is not threatened by globalization; the state's capacity for regulation and surveillance has increased rather than decreased.

The technological developments that foster globalization have also helped increase the state's capacity for regulation and surveillance. States are stronger than ever in their capacity to extract economic surplus, such as taxes, from their citizens. Their ability to control and regulate all kinds of activities in society has also increased dramatically. The long-term trend is towards more, not less state autonomy. 'Economic development has made it generally easier for states to finance their activities . . . from internal sources rather than international borrowing' (Krasner 1993: 314). And, lastly, the sovereign state remains the preferred form of political organization around the world. No serious competitor has emerged. We can summarize the realist-mercantilist view of economic globalization as shown in Box 8.13.

The neo-Marxist view of economic globalization differs from that of both economic liberalism and mercantilism. We shall concentrate on the neo-Marxist contribution of Robert Cox which contains both aspects introduced above: economic globalization involves both intensified interdependence and a qualitative shift towards a global economy. According to Cox, there is a new global economy that exists alongside that classical capitalist world economy, but the tendency is that the former 'incrementally supersedes' the latter (Cox 1994: 48). Cox finds that in the process of economic globalization nation-states have lost substantial power over the economy. However, the continued process of economic globalization requires the political framework provided by nation states; in particular, it requires 'the military-territorial power of an enforcer' (Cox 1994: 54). The United States has assumed that role. But America is beset by a contradiction between decreasing economic strength and increasing projection of military power on a world scale. Being the world's 'policeman' requires a strong economic base but that is diminishing under the pressures of economic globalization. The macro-regions (headed by the USA in North and South America, by Japan in East Asia and by the European Union in Europe) are the new political-economic frameworks of capital accumulation. Yet the macro-regions continue to be part of the larger, global economic system, as the global effects of the 1998 economic crisis in Asia amply demonstrated.

Robert Cox and other neo-Marxists thus stress the uneven, hierarchical nature of economic globalization. The global economy is characterized by dependence rather than interdependence. Economic power is increasingly concentrated in the leading industrialized countries, including the United States, Japan and the states of Western Europe. That means that economic globalization will not benefit the impoverished masses of the Third World. Nor will it improve the living standards of the poor in the highly industrialized countries. For that situation to change, social forces from below, such as workers and students, will have to be successful in their struggle to reclaim political control over the economic forces of globalization (Cox 1994). In short, globalization is a form of capitalism, and as such it perpetuates capitalist class domination and the exploitation of poor people around the world. We can summarize the neo-Marxist view of economic globalization as set forth by Robert Cox as shown in Box 8.14.

The debate on economic globalization is not easily settled because each of the three theoretical positions outlined above can point to some empirical evidence which supports their views (see web links 8.43 and 8.45). It is true, as economic liberals claim, that globalization has the potential of bringing increased prosperity to individuals and companies; but it is also true, as emphasized by neo-Marxists, that current processes of globalization are uneven and may have little to offer large groups of underprivileged people. Economic liberals are perhaps right in claiming that globalization is a challenge to the nation-state; but it is equally true, as stressed by mercantilists, that states remain strong players and that they have proved themselves able to adapt to many new challenges. Neo-Marxists correctly emphasize that 'intensified interdependence' and the creation of a global economy are simultaneously present. On that issue, however, economic liberals and mercantilists are too one-sided—they emphasize either one or the other aspect of globalization. In sum, we can, again, find useful insights in each of the theoretical positions, but also weak components in each (see Box 8.15).

BOX 8.14	The neo-Marxist view of globalization

1. Economic globalization is both 'intensified interdependence' and the creation of a global economy.
2. Nation-states remain important regulators of globalization, but they are losing power over the economy. In response, they form macro-regions.
3. Economic globalization is an uneven, hierarchical process, where economic power is increasingly concentrated in leading industrialized countries.

BOX 8.15	Economic globalization and theories of IPE	
	TRUE CLAIM	**FALSE CLAIM**
Economic liberalism	Economic globalization has the potential of bringing increased prosperity to all. Economic globalization challenges the state.	Economic globalization benefits everybody. Economic globalization spells the demise of the state.
Realist mercantilists	States adapt to challenges of economic globalization. States remain strong players.	States are in full control of economic globalization. Economic globalization is merely more interdependence.
Neo-Marxism	Economic globalization is an uneven, hierarchical process.	Economic globalization benefits only a tiny minority.

There is no doubt about the existence of sharp inequalities in today's world. At the turn of the twenty-first century, the richest 20 per cent of the world's population had:

- 86% of world GDP—the bottom fifth had 1%.
- 82% of world export markets—the bottom fifth had 1%.
- 68% of foreign direct investment—the bottom fifth had 1%.
- 74% of world telephone lines—the bottom fifth had 1.5%.
- 93.3% of all Internet users—the bottom fifth had 0.2%. (UNDP 1999:3)

It is important to understand that the poorest countries—and people—are in difficulty not because of economic surplus being taken from them by the rich. Rather it is because they are marginalized participants in the process of economic globalization. Their markets are not attractive to foreign investors because people's purchasing power is low; political institutions are inefficient and corrupt so there is a lack of stability and political order. Less than 2 per cent of total FDI goes to sub-Saharan Africa.

There is a clear relationship between measures of inequality and progress in terms of industrialization. When industrialization began in earnest in Western Europe in the nineteenth century, the gap between the richest and the poorest fifth in the world was not very large; it stood at 3 to 1 in 1820. Today, the gap is much more dramatic:

1820   3 to 1

1870   7 to 1

1913   11 to 1

1960   30 to 1

1990   60 to 1

1997   74 to 1. (UNDP 1999:3)

Ironically, the poorest countries are not excluded from the global economic system. They are integrated in the sense that much of what they produce is agricultural goods or raw materials for export. As much as 30 per cent of sub-Saharan Africa's GDP goes to export. But demand for what they have to offer has been stagnant; so have prices. And upgrading to more advanced products has proved difficult because of domestic political and economic conditions. At the same time, restricted access to global markets for Africa's agricultural products has added to the problem.

Inequality exists not merely between rich and poor at the global level. It tends to be growing between groups within the OECD countries themselves. Groups in these countries with less or no education above basic schooling and groups in agriculture and traditional industrial sectors tend to lose out in the process of economic globalization. The better educated in the advanced sectors of the economy stand to win. The OECD countries have seen big increases in inequality since the 1980s. This is especially true for the United States, the United Kingdom and Sweden.

Against this background, the process of economic globalization has led to the formation of new social movements in many parts of the world. Manuel Castells has analysed what he calls 'resistance identity', 'generated by those actors that are in positions/conditions devalued and/or stigmatized by the logic of domination' (Castells 1998: 8). It includes a large number of different movements, based on religious fundamentalism, nationalism, ethnic identity and territorial identity (urban movements and local communities). His case-studies include the Zapatistas in Mexico, the American militia and the Japanese cult Aum Shinrikyo.

Economic globalization has also led to the formation of transnational resistance movements. The best known is probably the ATTAC (Association for the Taxation of Financial Transactions for the Aid of Citizens). The movement has set forth four core demands aimed at countering the inequalities of globalization: (1) taxation of cross-border currency speculation; (2) writing off the international debt of poor countries; (3) outlawing tax havens; and (4) more democratic control of large pension funds.

The growth of such movements demonstrates that economic globalization is much more than anonymous transactions across borders: it involves political struggle about the extent to which economic transfers should be put under political control and how the benefits from globalization should be distributed among countries and groups of people. This struggle also involves taking a stance in the debate between the three classical approaches to IPE discussed above. Note, for example, how there are elements of all three in the ATTAC movement: (1) a liberal element: there are potential benefits from globalization that all countries can get to share; (2) a mercantilist element: countries have the right to protect themselves against the negative consequences of globalization; (3) a Marxist element: there is hierarchy and exploitation involved in globalization and measures need to be taken to distribute the benefits in a more just and even manner. An important part of the globalization struggle concerns the extent to which the process of globalization should take place in a primarily liberal, a primarily mercantilist or a primarily Marxist framework.

The debate on economic globalization obviously will be highly influenced by the course of future events and developments. Will the world become more regionalized? How will the benefits of globalization be distributed among countries and other groups or classes of people? What level of regulatory control will nation-states have over the process? We have to wait for more history to occur before we can answer such questions. But it is important to pose them. And that is what IPE theorists who study globalization are contributing to our understanding of world politics.

Recent Theoretical Developments in IPE

The previous chapter presented the three classical theories of IPE: mercantilism, economic liberalism and Marxism. They are theories in the very broad sense of sets of assumptions and values from which the field of IPE can be interrogated. They are also macro-theories, with specific views of the relationship between politics and economics and the major institutions connected with politics and economics, namely states and markets.

Economic liberalism appears to be the approach with most success in practice. So-called 'free market' economies have been highly successful; state-led economies have not. This has certainly helped increase the confidence of economic liberals in the validity of their views. Over the past few decades, the theoretical views (often called 'neoclassical economics') of professional economists have dominated, not merely in the study of economic matters, but also in the general field of IPE and indeed also in other areas of political and social science.

The reason for this is not so much the content of ecomic macro-theory of liberalism which we have discussed above. It has to do with the micro-theory supported by economists. Neoclassical economics present a simple model of individuals and their basic behaviour. That model—called rational choice theory—is relevant, so the economists claim, not merely for economics, but for every other sphere of human behaviour (see web link 8.54). Many scholars believe that it is a valid claim. It is appropriate, therefore, to discuss rational choice theory briefly here.

As indicated, rational choice begins with individuals. Whatever happens in the social world, including in international relations, can be explained by individual choices. What a state or any other organization does can be explained by choices made by individuals as well. This view is called methodological individualism. Furthermore, individual actors are rational and self-interested. They want to make themselves better off. This is true for everybody: not merely for sellers and buyers in economic markets, but also for bureaucrats and politicians. Finally, when individuals act in a rational and self-interested way, the overall result or outcome for states or systems will be the best possible. Just as 'the invisible hand' in liberal economics leads from individual greed to the best possible economic result for all, so the individual actions by bureaucrats and politicians lead to the best possible outcome. So if we want to understand what governments do, our first priority must be to understand the preferences, that is the goals, of public officials. They will be looking for private benefits: re-election, promotion, prestige and so on. Once we understand how these preferences condition their behaviour, we are in a position to understand how state policies are affected. That is a basic claim of rational choice theory (Nunn 1996).

Neoclassical economists have gone one step further in their claim for the relevance of their analytical tools. Not merely their view of individual behaviour—the rational choice theory sketched above—but also a number of other key concepts from economic theory, such as marginal utility, optimization and equilibrium, are relevant for a more general study of human affairs including international relations. Amongst other things, this leads in the direction of using game theory and theories of strategic interaction as analytical frameworks (Carlson 2002).

Methodological individualism has been used in other ways as well. New institutional theory—which also goes under the name of 'New Economics of Organization'—starts with the rational and self-interested individual actor. But in contrast to neoclassical economic analysis, institutions are not neglected. They play an independent role for outcomes and so they should, according to new institutional theory, be made a centrepiece of analysis (Spruyt 2002). New institutionalism is the analysis of how institutions affect individual behaviour and policy outcomes. An electoral system is an example of an institution; different electoral systems lead to different behaviour of parties and candidates (Lijphart 1994). In IPE, a major research area for this type of analysis is how international institutions affect cooperation and conflict between states (see Chapter 4). Another research area concerns the processes which lead to the creation and preservation of international institutions; that points towards the debate about hegemony and hegemonic stability introduced earlier in this chapter.

Neo-Marxist and other critical theories have reacted against the entry of methods and theories from neoclassical economics into IPE. They especially argue against the basic idea that individuals are always rational and self-seeking and that they always know what they want, namely to be better off. Rational cost–benefit analysis has limitations in explaining much individual behaviour. Given the cost of going to the polls, why would anyone vote when there are no visible benefits (one single vote cannot really affect the outcome of the election)? Why would anyone engage in the altruistic behaviour of helping others in need when there are no tangible benefits for oneself? Furthermore, individuals don't always know beforehand what they really want. Their preferences—what they want—are created in a process of interaction with others. Consequently, what happens in human affairs including IPE is decided in a much more open-ended and not so precisely predictable process of human interaction (Palan 2002). This view creates its own challenge for the critics, namely how to combine such analysis with other critical insights about the larger development prospects of capitalism and the role of class conflict.

In sum, much recent theorizing in IPE has been inspired by neoclassical economics and its methodological individualism. It is quite clear that neoclassical economics has an important role to play in IPE. Furthermore, the focus on individuals and their behaviour has helped other theories think about how they themselves look at individuals; in other words, methodological individualism helps sharpen the micro-theoretical foundations for theorizing in IPE.

At the same time, the neoclassical view does not really consider the larger sociopolitical setting within which individual behaviour plays out. It is exactly this larger setting which is the subject of the classical macro-theories of IPE discussed earlier, mercantilism, liberalism and Marxism. While neoclassical micro-theory might yield important insights, it cannot replace the classical macro-theories (for a similar view, see Gilpin 2001). We need the classical theories in order to understand the complex interplay between economics and politics.

Conclusion: The Future of IPE

The issues of wealth and poverty raised by IPE are of increasing importance in world politics. The traditional focus of IR is on war and peace. But the danger of war between states, particularly great-power war, appears to be in decline for reasons discussed elsewhere in this book. Violent conflict nowadays takes place mainly inside states, especially inside weak states. And that violence is bound up with problems of development and under-development, one of the core issues in IPE. In other words, even when we look at the traditional core issue of IR, that of armed conflict, IPE is of increasing importance. IPE also addresses the issue of sovereign statehood: the national economy is a crucially important resource base for the nation-state. When national economies are being integrated into a global economy in the course of economic globalization, the basis of modern state-hood might be expected to change in significant ways. As indicated above, that raises new problems concerning the relationship of states and markets and the ability of states to control and regulate the process of economic globalization. IPE opens up several new research agendas, some of which move away from IR as traditionally understood. Such themes as 'international business', 'micro- and macro-economics', 'economic geography', 'international finance and banking' and 'economic history' are all part of IPE. Such research paths are a good reminder that IR involves a host of other issues studied by additional subdisciplines of the vast area of social science.

We have only been able to introduce the main theoretical approaches in IPE and to sketch the research agenda of a very large research territory. What we call 'economic liberalism' is a discipline in its own right, comprising the study of micro- and macro-economics. Marxism is a vast theoretical edifice, rather like a medieval castle, with many different ramparts, quarters and schools. We have only been able to introduce a few of them. The literature on hegemonic stability, development and underdevelopment in the Third World, and economic globalization has grown to immense proportions with a large number of different contributions. However, we do believe that we have singled out the most important theories and the most important debates. We have also argued in favour of drawing on elements of all three classical theories of IPE. No single theory can stand alone; it needs to be combined with insights from the others. Only in that way can we expect to develop a comprehensive and well-founded IPE.

 KEY POINTS

- The most important debate inspired by mercantilism concerns the need for a strong state to create a smoothly functioning liberal international economy; that is the debate on hegemonic stability. The most important debate triggered by Marxism concerns development and underdevelopment in the Third World. Finally, economic liberals have sparked a number of debates on various issues; one significant controversy is the issue of economic globalization.

- The issues of wealth and poverty raised by IPE are of increasing importance in world politics. The traditional focus of IR is on war and peace; but the danger of war between states appears to be in decline. Violent conflict nowadays takes place mainly inside states, especially inside weak states. And that violence is intimately bound up with problems of development and underdevelopment, one of the core issues in IPE. In other words, even when we look the traditional core issue or IR, that of armed conflict, problems addressed by IPE are of increasing importance.

- IPE also raises the problems of development and change of sovereign statehood in a very direct manner. The national economy is a crucially important resource basis for the nation state. When national economies are in a process of being integrated into a global economy in the context of economic globalization, the whole basis for modern statehood changes in a critical way.

- The theoretical views of professional economists have recently dominated IPE. Neoclassical economics presents a simple model of individuals and their basic behaviour.

That model—called rational choice theory—is relevant, so the economists claim, for all spheres of human behaviour. Neo-Marxist and other critical theories argue against the idea that individuals are always rational and self-seeking. And rational choice theory fails to consider sufficiently the larger context within which individual behaviour plays out. The critics thus claim that the classical theories of IPE are still very much needed.

QUESTIONS

- Should we support the claim that a hegemon is needed in order to create a liberal world economy?
- Is the United States currently an altruistic or a 'predatory' hegemon?
- What is 'soft power' and which countries have it?
- Define the development problem in the Third World and discuss how it should be analysed; which theory is most helpful?
- Can the development problem be solved?
- What is economic globalization? What are the benefits and drawbacks of economic globalization? What are the implications for sovereign statehood?
- Think of one or two research projects based on IPE theory.

GUIDE TO FURTHER READING

Dicken, P. (2003). *Global Shift: Reshaping the Global Economic Map in the 21st Century.* London: Sage.

Martinussen, J. (1997). *State, Society and Market: A Guide to Competing Theories of Development.* New York: St Martin's Press.

Nye, J. S., Jr. (2002). *The Paradox of American Power.* New York: Oxford University Press.

Palan, R. (ed.) (2002). *Global Political Economy. Contemporary Theories.* London: Routledge.

Ravenhill, J. (ed.) (2005). *Global Political Economy.* Oxford: Oxford University Press.

Rodrik, D. (1997). *Has Globalization Gone Too Far?* Washington DC: Institute for International Economics.

Scholte, J. A. (2005). *Globalization: A Critical Introduction*, 2nd edn. London: Macmillan.

Stubbs, R. and Underhill, G. R. D. (2000). *Political Economy and the Changing Global Order.* Oxford: Oxford University Press.

Weiss, L. (1998). *The Myth of the Powerless State.* New York: Cornell University Press.

WEB LINKS

 Web links mentioned in this chapter and additional links can be found on the Online Resource Centre that accompanies this book.

www.oxfordtextbooks.co.uk/orc/jackson_sorensen3e/

CHAPTER 9

Foreign Policy

▌ Summary

This chapter addresses theories and approaches involved in **foreign-policy analysis.** Foreign-policy analysis is a study of the management of external relations and activities of nation-states, as distinguished from their domestic policies. The chapter unfolds as follows: first, the concept of **foreign policy** is outlined. Next, various approaches to foreign-policy analysis are discussed. The arguments of major theories are introduced by using a **'level-of-analysis' approach** that addresses the systemic level, the nation-state level and the level of the individual decision-maker. A case-study on the Gulf War demonstrates how insights from various approaches can be brought together. Some critiques of foreign-policy analysis are reviewed. Finally, a note on foreign-policy experts and **'think tanks'** is included.

The Concept of Foreign Policy

Foreign-policy analysis is a study of the management of external relations and activities of nation-states, as distinguished from their domestic policies. Foreign policy involves goals, strategies, measures, methods, guidelines, directives, understandings, agreements and so on, by which national governments conduct international relations with each other and with international organizations and non-governmental actors (see web link 9.01). It is their attempts and efforts to influence the goals and activities of such actors, whom they cannot completely control because they exist and operate beyond their sovereignty (Carlsnaes 2002: 335). All national governments, by the very fact of their separate international existence, are obliged to engage in foreign policy directed at foreign governments and other international actors.

Policies lay out courses of action for government agencies and their personnel. Foreign policies consist of aims and measures that are intended to guide government decisions with regard to external affairs, particularly relations with foreign countries. Government officials in leading positions—presidents, prime ministers, foreign ministers, defence ministers, finance ministers and so on, along with their closest advisers—are usually the key policymakers. Managing foreign relations calls for carefully considered plans of action that are adapted to the foreign interests and concerns—i.e. goals—of the government (see web links 9.02 and 9.03).

Policymaking involves a means–end way of thinking about goals and actions of government. It is an instrumental concept: what is the problem or goal and what solutions or approaches are available to address them? Instrumental analysis involves thinking of the best available choice or course—e.g. giving correct advice—to make things happen according to one's requirements or wishes. It can be an integral element of studying foreign policy, where the analyst seeks to provide knowledge that is of some relevance to the policymaker. It involves calculating the measures and methods that will most likely enable one to reach a goal, and the costs and benefits of different available options. It may extend to recommending the best course to follow. At that point policy analysis becomes not only instrumental but also prescriptive: it recommends what will best enable a government to solve its foreign-policy problems or achieve its foreign-policy goals.

Foreign-Policy Analysis

Foreign-policy analysis involves scrutinizing foreign policies and placing them in a broader context of academic knowledge. That academic context is usually defined by theories and approaches—such as the ones discussed in previous chapters (see web links 9.08 and 9.09). The relationship between theory and policy is complex, because any one theory does not necessarily lead to any one clear policy option; in most cases there will be several different options. Even so, the choice of theory affects the choice of policy.

That is partly because different theories emphasize different social values. Realists underline the value of national security: national military power and power balancing is the major way of achieving national security. International Society scholars emphasize the values of order and justice: a rule-based and well-ordered international society is a major goal. Freedom and democracy are the core values for liberals: they are convinced that liberal democracies will support peaceful international cooperation based on international institutions.

Foreign-policy theorists concerned with defence or security issues are likely to take a realist approach, emphasizing the inevitable clash of interests between state actors, the outcomes of which are seen to be determined by relative state power (see web link 9.16). On the other hand, those concerned with multilateral questions are just as likely to take a liberal approach, emphasizing international institutions—such as the United Nations or the World Trade Organization—as means of reducing international conflict and promoting mutual understanding and common interests (see web link 9.09). Finally, scholars who emphasize the importance of socioeconomic wealth and welfare as a central goal of foreign policy are likely to take an IPE approach. For them, the promotion of a stable international economic system that can support economic growth and welfare progress is a major goal.

In addition to the general IR theories discussed in previous chapters, there are various approaches that are specific to foreign-policy analysis. Some approaches are derived from IR theories. Some are adapted from other disciplines, such as economics and social psychology. Policy analysis approaches are evident not only in academic scholarship but also in advocacy think tanks and the analyses of experts associated with them (see below). Box 9.1 present major approaches to foreign-policy analysis; they are further explained in what follows.

1. A traditional approach to foreign-policy analysis involves being informed about a government's external policies: knowing their history or at least their background, comprehending the interests and concerns that drive the policies, and thinking through the various ways of addressing and defending those interests and concerns. That includes knowing the consequences of past foreign-policy decisions and actions. It also involves an ability to recognize the circumstances under which a government must operate in carrying out its foreign policy. The traditional approach involves, as well, the exercise of judgement and common sense in assessing the best practical means and courses of action available for carrying out foreign policies.

BOX 9.1	Approaches to foreign-policy analysis

1. Traditional approach: focus on the decision-maker
2. Comparative foreign policy: behaviouralism and 'pre-theory'
3. Bureaucratic structures and processes; decision-making during crisis
4. Cognitive processes and psychology
5. 'Multilevel, multidimensional'; the general theories
6. The constructivist turn: identities before interests

That 'feel' for what is possible under the circumstances is usually derived from experience. It could be said, in that regard, that a satisfactory grasp of a country's foreign policy is best achieved by direct knowledge of its government's foreign affairs: e.g. by serving in a foreign ministry or similar government agency. The next best thing would involve trying to put oneself into the mindset of such an official: attempting to grasp the circumstances of such a person, endeavouring to understand the reasons such an official arrived at a decision, and trying to ascertain its consequences, both good and bad. In short, traditional foreign-policy study is a matter of gaining insight into the activity of foreign policymakers, either from experience or by careful scrutiny of past and present foreign policies.

Foreign-policy analysis was traditionally the domain of diplomatic historians and public commentators. The subject still exists, although it now has many rivals (see web link 9.02). It was rooted in the state system and statecraft of modern Europe as that emerged and acquired its classical characteristics, between the late seventeenth and the early twentieth century. There were several distinctive features of traditional foreign-policy analysis (Carlsnaes 2002). It was seen as a virtually separate sphere from domestic policies and activities of sovereign states. It was the realm of 'high politics' defined and guided by reason of state, now more commonly labelled 'national interests'. It was directed and managed by the leading state officials (emperors, kings, presidents, prime ministers, chancellors, secretaries of state, foreign ministers, defence secretaries, etc., and their closest advisers). It was not subject to popular scrutiny or democratic control. It was an exclusive and often secretive sphere of statecraft.

Traditional foreign-policy analysis, accordingly, was a body of wisdom and insights which could only be acquired by lengthy study and reflection. The main writers on the subject were historians, jurists and philosophers. Some were practitioners as well, such as Machiavelli and Grotius at an early period (see web links 9.10 and 9.11), and George Kennan and Henry Kissinger at a later period (see web links 9.12, 9.13, 9.14 and 9.15). Their commentaries on foreign policy attempted to distil that wisdom and those insights. The approach continues to appeal to historically minded International Society scholars and classical realists, because it gets into the detailed substance of foreign policy.

2. The comparative approach to foreign policy was inspired by the behaviouralist turn (see Chapter 11) in political science. The ambition was to build systematic theories and explanations of the foreign-policy process in general. This was done through the amalgamation of large bodies of data, describing the content and context of the foreign policy of a large number of countries. It was theoretically informed by James Rosenau's (1966) 'pre-theory' of foreign policy. Rosenau identified a large number of possibly relevant sources of foreign-policy decisions and grouped them into five categories which he called: idiosyncratic, role, governmental, societal and systemic variables. He then proposed a ranking of the relative importance of these variables, depending on the issue at hand and on the attributes of the state (e.g. size, political accountability/level of democracy, level of development). A large number of empirical studies of foreign policy employed Rosenau's scheme, but the 'pre-theory' never emerged as a clear explanation of foreign policy; it remained a classification scheme.

3. The bureaucratic structures and processes approach focuses on the organizational context of decision-making, which is seen to be conditioned by the dictates and demands of

the bureaucratic settings in which decisions are made. Analysing processes and channels whereby organizations arrive at their policies is seen to be a superior way to acquire empirical knowledge of foreign policy. The strength of the bureaucratic politics approach is its empiricism: its detailed attention to the concrete way policies are carried out in the bureaucratic milieus within which policymakers work. The approach seeks to find out not only what happened but why it happened the way it did.

The best-known study of this kind is Graham Allison's book on the Cuban missile crisis, *Essence of Decision* (1971; Allison and Zelikow 1999). The analysis suggests three different and complementary ways of understanding American decision-making during the crisis. (1) A 'rational actor approach' that provides models for answering the question: with that information what would be the best decision to move towards one's goal? The assumption is that governments are unified and rational, wanting to achieve well-defined foreign-policy goals. (2) An 'organizational processes' model, according to which a concrete foreign policy emerges from clusters of governmental organizations that look after their own best interests and follow 'standard operating procedures'. And (3) a 'bureaucratic politics model' where individual decision-makers at different levels (each with their own particular goals in mind) bargain and compete for influence. Despite criticism (Bendor and Hammond 1992), Allison's three models have informed much research on foreign policy.

4. The cognitive processes and psychology approach also focuses on the individual decision-maker, this time with particular attention to the psychological aspects of decision-making, such as perceptions of actors. Robert Jervis (1968; 1976) has studied misperception: why do actors misperceive the intentions and actions of others? Jervis gives several reasons: actors see what they want to see instead of what is really going on; they are guided by ingrained, pre-existing beliefs (e.g. the tendency to perceive other states as more hostile than they really are); and they engage in 'perceptual satisficing' and 'wishful thinking'. Another example in this category is the work of Margaret Herman (1984). She studied the personality characteristics of fifty-four heads of government, making the claim that such factors as the leaders' experience in foreign affairs, their political styles, their political socialization and their broader views of the world all should be drawn into the analysis in order to understand the ways in which leaders conduct foreign policy.

5. The 'multilevel, multidimensional' approach has developed because over the past two or three decades, it has become increasingly clear that there will never be one, big, all-encompassing theory of foreign policy, just as there will never be one big theory of IR. Many scholars now use the various major theories presented earlier in this book as approaches to study particular aspects of foreign policymaking. In the realist tradition, studies of balance of power behaviour and of deterrence and security dilemmas are examples of this. Thomas Schelling's strategic realism, which was derived from game theory (see Chapter 3), focuses directly on foreign-policy decision-making. It was applied most successfully in strategic studies during the Cold War, when the United States and the Soviet Union were locked in a struggle involving weapons of mass destruction, including nuclear armed, long-range missiles (Schelling 1960). Schelling won the 2005 Nobel Prize in economics for his innovative application of game theory to foreign policy.

As indicated in Chapter 4, liberals have studied complex interdependence, the role of international institutions, processes of integration and paths of democratization. In the liberal view, all of these elements contribute in their separate ways to foreign policies that are more orientated towards peaceful cooperation for mutual benefit. International Society scholars (Chapter 5) have traced the three traditions (realism, rationalism and revolutionism) in the thought and behaviour of statespeople and have pondered their consequences for foreign policy. In IPE (see Chapter 8) neo-Marxists have focused on the relationship between core and periphery, and have identified the vulnerable position of weak states as the basic explanation of the limitations and constraints on their room for manoeuvre in foreign policy.

6. A focus on the role of ideas and discourse, and identity, as recorded in Chapter 6, is indicative of a social constructivist approach to foreign-policy analysis. Constructivists see foreign policymaking as an intersubjective world, whose ideas and discourse can be scrutinized in order to arrive at a better theoretical understanding of the process. In the analysis of foreign policy, they trace the influence of ideas, as one factor among others, on the processes and outcomes in foreign policy (Goldstein and Keohane 1993). That way of thinking has policy implications, in the sense that the discourse of actors influences not only what they say but also what they do—since many actions are conveyed by speech and writing. A more ambitious version of constructivism is not satisfied with the notion of ideas as one among several factors influencing foreign policy. These constructivists claim that identity, rooted in ideas and discourse, is the basis for a definition of interests and thus lies behind any foreign policy. In that approach, ideas and discourse always constitute foreign policy (see web links 9.24 and 9.25). Some constructivists focus on domestic sources of ideas and identities (Hopf 2002); others focus on the discursive interaction of states (Wendt 1999).

How to Study Foreign Policy: A Level-of-Analysis Approach

We begin from the premise that any country's foreign policy is a complex subject that can only be fully understood through careful examination of the political, economic, psychological and other factors that are at work among both actors and groups of actors at the domestic level and in the patterns of international relations that define the context of foreign policy. In other words, we must assume that the different theories and approaches briefly identified in the previous section can all be of some assistance in the analysis of foreign policy. That of course leaves us with a very comprehensive and complicated research agenda (see web links 9.08 and 9.09). It will not be possible to present all the different theories and approaches in detail here; some considerable simplification is necessary. We propose to demonstrate the arguments of major theories by using a level-of-analysis approach. The level-of-analysis approach was introduced by Kenneth Waltz in his study of the causes of war (Waltz 1959; see also Singer 1961). Waltz searched for the causes of war at three different levels of analysis: the level of the individual (are human beings aggressive by nature?); the level of the state (are some states more aggressive and conflict-seeking than others?); and the level of the system (are there conditions in the international system that lead states towards war?). Following this distinction we can search for explanations of foreign policy at three levels of analysis:

- The systemic level (e.g. the distribution of power among states; their economic and political interdependence).
- The nation-state level (e.g. type of government, democratic or authoritarian; relations between the state apparatus and groups in society; the bureaucratic make-up of the state apparatus).
- The level of the individual decision-maker (his/her way of thinking, basic beliefs, personal priorities).

Theories at the systemic level explain foreign policy by pointing to conditions in the international system that compel or pressure states towards acting in certain ways, that is, to follow a certain foreign policy. Therefore, systemic theories first need to say something about the conditions that prevail in the international system; they then need to create a plausible connection between those conditions and the actual foreign-policy behaviour of states. As we have seen in previous chapters, the various theories of the international system are not in full agreement about the conditions that primarily characterize the system. Realists focus on anarchy and the competition between states for power and security; liberals find more room for cooperation because of international institutions and a common desire by states for progress and prosperity. For many social constructivists, the goals of states are not decided beforehand; they are shaped by the ideas and values that come forward in the process of discourse and interaction between states. For present purposes, these different views of the international system can be summarized as shown in Box 9.2. So different images of the international system lead to different ideas about how states will behave. But, even if we agree on one of these theories, it remains complicated to get from the general description of the system to specific foreign policies by states. Let us focus on realism; it proclaims a resurgence of great-power competition in an anarchic world where states compete for power and security. This would appear to be accurate in the broad sense, for example, that US foreign policy, 'is generally consistent with realist principles, insofar as its actions are still designed to preserve US predominance and to shape a postwar order that advances American interests' (Walt 1998: 37).

But how exactly does anarchy and self-help in the system lead to a certain US foreign policy? For neorealists such as Kenneth Waltz or Stephen Krasner the basic factor explaining state behaviour is the distribution of power among states. With a bipolar distribution of power, the two leading states are compelled to balance against each other, to become rivals. In other words, neorealism:

can offer its most precise explanations when states have few options because they are narrowly constrained by the international distribution of power. Britain was bound to balance

BOX 9.2	Three conceptions of the international system		
	REALISM	**LIBERALISM**	**CONSTRUCTIVISM**
Main theoretical proposition	Anarchy. States compete for power and security	States want progress and prosperity. Commitment to liberal values	Collective norms and social identities shape behavior
Main instruments policy	Military and economic power	Institutions, liberal values, networks of interdependence	Ideas and discourse
Post-Cold War prediction	Resurgence of great-power competition	Increased cooperation as liberal values spread	Agnostic: depends on content of ideas

Strongly modified version of Walt (1998: 174)

against Germany in the First and Second World Wars because Germany was the one state that had the potential to dominate the continent and thereby pose a threat to the British Isles... Realism is less analytically precise when the international system is not tightly constraining. A hegemonic state, for instance, does not have to be concerned with its territorial and political integrity, because there is no other state . . . that can threaten it. (Krasner 1992: 39–40)

In the post-Cold War world, the United States is the predominant power by far. Therefore, the US is not particularly constrained by other states or groups of states in the system. In the absence of constraints the balance of power will be less helpful in understanding the leading state's foreign policy; 'it may be necessary to introduce other arguments, such as domestic social purpose or bureaucratic interests. A realist explanation always starts with the international distribution of power but it may not be able to end there' (Krasner 1992: 41).

As indicated above, there is an additional difficulty in moving from the systemic level to the particular foreign policies of states. Even in cases where the balance of power is tightly constraining, assumptions need to be made about what it is that states want when they compete with other states. An important distinction here is between defensive and offensive realists (Rose 1998; Walt 1998). The former take a benign view of anarchy; states seek security rather than more power. Offensive realists, by contrast, believe that states 'look for opportunities to gain power at the expense of rivals, and to take advantage of those situations when the benefits outweigh the costs. A state's ultimate goal is to be the hegemon in the system' (Mearsheimer 2001: 21). For defensive realists, states are generally pleased with the prevailing balance of power when it safeguards their security; for offensive realists, states are always apprehensively looking to increase their relative power position in the system. It is clear that different foreign policies can follow from adopting either the defensive or the offensive assumption. Finally, it must also be stressed that foreign-policy choices are made by 'actual political leaders and elites, and so it is their perceptions of relative power that matter, not simply relative quantities of physical resources or forces in being. This means that over the short to medium term countries' foreign policies may not necessarily track objective material power trends closely or continuously' (Rose 1998: 147).

In sum, the systemic level is important in the analysis of foreign policy because it defines the basic context within which states have to conduct their foreign policies. At the same time, we have indicated that the systemic level of analysis cannot stand alone; it can say something about the general forces that affect states' foreign-policy behaviour, but it is too blunt an instrument to make us fully understand any given state's foreign policy (see web links 9.15 and 9.16). A productive comprehension of foreign policy will have to include the domestic level of the nation-state as well as the level of the individual decision-maker. Yet for realists, there is no doubt that the systemic distribution of power among states is the central starting-point for understanding foreign policy. In Waltz's formulation: 'the third image [the systemic level] describes the framework of world politics, but without the first and second images there can be no knowledge of the forces that determine policy; the first and second images [the level of the individual and the level of the nation-state] describe the forces in world politics, but without the third image it is impossible to assess their importance or predict their results' (Waltz 1959: 238).

The Level of the Nation-State

Let us now look at the level of the nation-state. One way of approaching an analysis of this level is to examine the relationship between a country's state apparatus and the surrounding society. For many realists, this relationship is important because it says something about the ability of a government to mobilize and manage the country's power resources. 'Foreign policy is made not by the nation as a whole but by its government. Consequently, what matters is state power, not national power. State power is that portion of national power the government can extract for its purposes and reflects the ease with which central decision-makers can achieve their ends' (Zakaria 1998: 9). The United States may be a very powerful country in terms of general power resources, but such resources may not be at the ready disposal of the government. For long periods, the US was a 'weak state' facing a 'strong society': the state was unable to muster the power resources that were present in society. Consequently, the 'weak state' was unable to conduct an expansive foreign policy that matched the actual power resources of the country (see Box 9.3).

This analysis indicates that it is not sufficient to examine the overall power resources of countries, that is, the systemic distribution of power. It is also important to examine the connection between a country's government and its society in order to clarify the government's ability to mobilize resources in society and to extract resources from society for foreign-policy purposes (e.g. military expenditures, involvement in international institutions, foreign aid). 'Weak states' are less capable in this regard and that has consequences for the kind of foreign-policy agenda that they can pursue (see also Christensen 1996; Schweller 1998).

BOX 9.3	Fareed Zakaria on the US as a 'weak state'

The decades after the Civil War saw the beginning of a long period of growth in America's material resources. But this national power lay dormant beneath a weak state, one that was decentralized, diffuse, and divided. The presidents and their secretaries of state tried repeatedly to convert the nation's rising power into influence abroad, but they presided over a federal state structure and a tiny central bureaucracy that could not get men or money from the state governments or from society at large . . . The 1880s and 1890s mark the beginnings of the modern American state, which emerged primarily to cope with the domestic pressures generated by industrialization . . . This transformation of state structure complemented the continuing growth of national power, and by the mid-1890s the executive branch was able to bypass Congress or coerce it into expanding American interests abroad. America's resounding victory in the Spanish-American War crystallized the perception of increasing American power . . . America expanded dramatically in the years that followed.

Zakaria (1998: 10–11)

Liberals take a different approach to the analysis of foreign policy. As emphasized in Chapter 4, liberals believe that individuals, groups and organizations in society play an important role in foreign policy. They not only influence the government; they also conduct international relations (or 'foreign policies') in their own right, creating transnational relations that are an important element in the international interactions between countries. Sociological liberals argue that international relations conducted by governments have been 'supplemented by relations among private individuals, groups, and societies that can and do have important consequences for the course of events' (Rosenau 1980: 1). Interdependence liberals note that international relations are becoming more like domestic politics, where 'different issues generate different coalitions, both within governments and across them, and involve different degrees of conflict. Politics does not stop at the water's edge' (Keohane and Nye 1977: 25; see also Chapter 4). According to these liberals, then, it is too narrow to consider foreign policy as exchanges between state elites from different countries; the complex networks of relations between societies must enter the picture as well.

Another important liberal theory of foreign policy stems from republican liberalism. As explained in Chapter 4, the claim is that foreign policies conducted between liberal democracies are more peaceful and law-abiding than are foreign policies involving countries which are not liberal democracies. This can be seen as a liberal theory of foreign policy: liberal democracies are based on political cultures based on peaceful conflict resolution. That leads to pacific relations with other democracies because democratic governments are controlled by citizens who will not advocate or support wars with other democracies. With processes of democratization taking place in many countries after the end of the Cold War, there is a renewed intense debate about the liberal theory of democratic peace. Some critics claim that on the one hand early processes of democratization may lead to more, rather than less, conflict in the country (Elman 1997); other critics argue that there are serious flaws in the theoretical logic, according to which liberal democracy leads to a more peaceful behaviour in foreign policy (Rosato 2003).

We should take note of a more general difference in the approach of realists and liberals when it comes to foreign-policy analysis focusing on the nation-state level. Realists most often see the state (i.e. the government) as a robust, autonomous unit, capable—at least most of the time—of extracting resources from society and imposing its will on society. Therefore, the analysis of foreign policy should first and foremost focus on the state (government). Liberals, by contrast, most often see the state as a relatively weak entity which follows the bidding of strong groups in society. As noted by liberal scholar Andrew Moravcsik, foreign policy—as indeed government policy in general—reflects the preferences of different combinations of groups and individuals in domestic society (see Chapter 4). Therefore, the analysis of foreign policy should focus on how different groups in society influence and dominate the formulation of state preferences. In both cases the relationship between state and society plays a role in the analysis of foreign policy, but the realist approach is state-centred whereas the liberal approach is society-centred (see web links 9.20 and 9.22).

The foregoing approaches at the nation-state level of analysis focus on different types of relationships between the state (government) and society. The approaches to which we now turn focus on the decision-making process within the state apparatus. They call into question whether the decisions made by states are really based on 'rational choice'. According to rational choice, states are able correctly to identify foreign-policy challenges and to make the best possible decision in terms of benefits and cost, considering the goals and values that the state supports; this is the Rational Actor Model of decision-making in foreign policy (Allison and Zelikow 1999). Is this really the way states make decisions or is it more complicated than that? Two approaches answer in the affirmative. The 'bureaucratic politics' approach questions the standard ways of looking at bureaucracies as streamlined and efficient organizations that always serve their political masters in the best way. The 'groupthink' approach argues that the dynamics taking place in small groups negatively influence the quality of the group's decision-making.

The 'bureaucratic politics' approach rejects the idea of bureaucratic decision-making as a rational process based on clear formal and legal procedures. Bureaucratic politics is much more a bargaining process in which individuals compete for personal position and power. According to Graham Allison, 'the name of the game is politics: bargaining along regularized circuits among players positioned hierarchically within the government. Government behaviour can thus be understood . . . not as organizational outputs, but as results of these bargaining games' (Allison 1971: 144). A study by David Kozak and James Keagle (1988) has identified the core characteristics of the bureaucratic politics model (see Box 9.4). So the foreign policy emerging from a process of bureaucratic politics may not be rational in the sense mentioned above. It is more likely to reflect the narrow self-interests of the bureaucracies involved. Some scholars argue that decision-making during crisis is less prone to bureaucratic politics because such decisions would be made at the top level by a few key decision-makers with access to the best available information. But Allison's study of the

BOX 9.4	The bureaucratic politics model

- Bureaucrats and bureaucracy are driven by agency interests in order to ensure their survival.

- Agencies and bureaucracies are involved in a constant competition for various stakes and prizes. The net effect is a policy process whereby struggles for organizational survival, expansion and growth, and imperialism are inevitable.

- Competition produces an intra-agency bureaucratic culture and behaviour pattern. The axiom 'where you stand depends on where you sit' accurately describes this condition.

- Bureaucracies have a number of advantages over elected officials in the realm of policy-making. They include expertise, continuity, responsibility for implementation and longevity. These characteristics create an asymmetrical power and dependence relationship between the professional bureaucrats and the elected officials.

- Policy made in the arena of bureaucratic politics is characterized by bargaining, accommodation and compromise.

- In the bureaucratic politics system proposals for change are driven by the political considerations. Bureaucracies have a deep-seated interest in self-preservation.

- By its nature, bureaucratic politics raises questions concerning control, accountability, responsiveness and responsibility in a democratic society.

Modified from a longer list in Kozak and Keagle (1988: 3–15)

Cuban missile crisis did recognize a number of bureaucratic failures during that crisis (Allison and Zelikow 1999) (see web link 9.56).

Critics of the bureaucratic politics model claim that it tends to go much too far in its negative view of bureaucracies. Bureaucratic bargaining may lead to better decisions because the values and interest at stake become clearer in the process (George 1972). Furthermore, the bureaucratic approach tends to downplay the role of the President in the American system. He is 'not just another player in a complex bureaucratic game. Not only must he ultimately decide but he also selects who the other players will be, a process that may be critical in shaping the ultimate decisions' (Holsti 2004: 24).

Let us turn to the 'groupthink' approach. The term 'groupthink' was coined by psychologist Irving Janis in 1972. He wanted to describe a process by which a group arrives at bad or irrational decisions. When groupthink occurs, the group fails to consider alternatives and it aims at unanimity rather than at the best possible decision. Janis defined groupthink as follows: 'a mode of thinking that people engage in when they are deeply involved in a cohesive in-group, when the members' strivings for unanimity override their motivation to realistically appraise alternative courses of action' (Janis 1982: 9). When decisions are affected by groupthink, they share a number of characteristics: the objectives are not precisely defined; alternatives roads of action are not fully explored; risks involved in the preferred choice are not scrutinized; the search for information is poor; the information is processed in a biased way; and there is a failure to work out contingency plans (Janis 1982). Janis identified eight primary characteristics of groupthink; they are listed in Box 9.5.

> **BOX 9.5   Characteristics of groupthink**
>
> - Illusion of invulnerability: the group believes that its decision-making is beyond question which creates excessive optimism and extreme risk taking.
> - Belief in the inherent morality of the group: members ignore the moral or ethical consequences of their decisions.
> - Collective rationalization: the group discounts warnings that might have otherwise led them to reconsider their assumptions before they recommit to past policy decisions.
> - Out-group stereotypes: others are framed as too evil or stupid to warrant consideration of their strategies or attempts to negotiate with them.
> - Self-censorship: members feel inclined to avoid deviation from consensus, and minimize the significance of their doubts and counter-arguments.
> - Illusion of unanimity: partly from the silence or self-censorship, members share the belief that they are unanimous in their judgements; silence means consensus.
> - Direct pressure on dissenters: challenges or sanctioning comments are made to those who express strong arguments against the group's stereotypes, illusions or commitments; loyal members do not bring up questions.
> - Self-appointed 'mindguards': these members protect the group from adverse information that might threaten the shared illusions regarding the effectiveness or morality of the group's decisions.
>
> **Based on Janis (1982: 244)**

There are several important cases of groupthink, according to Janis: Pearl Harbor (the US naval commanding group believed that the Japanese would never risk attacking the US; the admiral in charge joked about the idea just before it happened); the Bay of Pigs invasion (the President Kennedy group convinced itself that Castro's army was weak and its popular support shallow; objections were suppressed or overruled); the Vietnam War (the President Johnson group focused more on justifying the war than on rethinking past decisions; dissenters were ridiculed).

At the same time, any kind of groupthink need not always be counterproductive; there are 'successful' cases too, such as the Marshall Plan and the Cuban missile crisis. According to Janis, it is possible to devise a number of remedies that will avoid the negative consequences of groupthink and enhance the capabilities of groups for making better decisions (Janis 1982; see also Hart et al. 1997).

The Level of the Individual Decision-Maker

Just as bureaucracies or small groups may not always make decisions based on the Rational Actor Model of decision-making, this applies to the individual decision-maker as well. A large number of influences and constraints come into play even when making foreign-policy choices; the approaches introduced here emphasize different aspects of these constraints and propose different ways of analysing them.

Human beings have limited capacities for conducting rational and objective decision-making. According to Ole Holsti, the 'cognitive constraints on rationality include limits on the individual's capacity to receive, process, and assimilate information about the situation; an inability to identify the entire set of policy alternatives; fragmentary knowledge about the consequences of each option; and an inability to order preferences on a single utility scale' (Holsti 2004: 27; see also Jervis 1976; Rosati 2000).

These limitations are connected to the way in which individuals perceive and process information. In Alexander George's summation, 'every individual acquires during the course of development a set of beliefs and personal constructs about the physical and social environment. These beliefs provide him with a relatively coherent way of organizing and making sense of what would otherwise be a confusing and overwhelming array of signals and cues picked up from the environment . . . These beliefs and constructs necessarily simplify and structure the external world' (George 1980: 57).

A recent analysis by Jerel Rosati suggests several ways in which human cognition (i.e. the process of acquiring knowledge by the use of reasoning, intuition or perception) and policymaker beliefs matter; they are summarized in Box 9.6.

These effects can be expanded as follows (based on Rosati 2000):

1. The content of policymaker beliefs: an early study by Nathan Leite (1951) identified the belief system of the Soviet Communist elite, summarizing it in an 'operational code' consisting of 'philosophical beliefs' steering the diagnosis of the situation and 'instrumental' beliefs framing the search for courses of action. Stephen Twing (1998) has shown how American cultural myths and traditions helped structure the world-views and decision-making styles of John Foster Dulles, Averell Harriman, and Robert McNamara during the Cold War. Robert Axelrod and others have studied the 'cognitive complexity' in international decision-making, tracing the influence of foreign-policy beliefs in relation to specific issues (Eagly and Chaiken 1993).

2. Organization and structure of policymaker beliefs: the belief systems and images of policymakers can vary in other ways; some belief systems are coherent and comprehensive while others are fragmented and sketchy. The latter type is prone to 'uncommitted

BOX 9.6	The effects of human cognition and policymaker beliefs on foreign policy

1. Through the content of policymaker beliefs
2. Through the organization and structure of policymaker beliefs
3. Through common patterns of perception (and misperception)
4. Through cognitive rigidity (and flexibility) for change and learning

Quoted from Rosati (2000: 53)

thinking' where decision-makers who are 'beset with uncertainty and sitting at the intersection of a number of information channels, will tend at different times to adopt *different* belief patterns for the same decision problem' (Steinbrunner 1974: 136). Jimmy Carter, for example, has been characterized as prone to 'uncommitted thinking' while experienced foreign-policy experts such as Zbigniew Brzezinski and Cyrus Vance displayed more coherent belief systems (Rosati 2000: 58).

3. Common patterns of perception (and misperception): there are several ways in which perception patterns can lead to biased views; one is the creation of a stereotype image of the opponent. Ole Holsti (1967) showed how John Foster Dulles held a hostile image of the Soviet Union during the Cold War, 'regardless of changes in Soviet behaviour. Dulles rejected new information inconsistent with his "inherent bad faith image" of Moscow' (Rosati 2000: 60). Engaging in wishful thinking is another source of bias. American policymakers during the Vietnam War were convinced that the US could not lose the war; that led them down the path of increased involvement in South-East Asia.

4. Cognitive rigidity (and flexibility) for change and learning: deeply held images and beliefs tend to resist change. In a review of Kissinger's foreign-policy beliefs, Harvey Starr demonstrated a very considerable stability in the content of his official, pre-office and post-office beliefs. When core convictions do change, they are most likely to do so following big shocks and setbacks. Mikhail Gorbachev's 'new thinking' emerged in a period of severe Soviet political and economic crisis; American leaders' image of Japan changed dramatically after the attack on Pearl Harbor; the tragedy of the Vietnam War similarly changed elite views on the United States' role in the world (Holsti and Rosenau 1984).

We have briefly looked at various ways in which individual cognitive processes and belief systems can influence foreign-policy decision-making. This whole debate is important for a simple reason: it challenges us to speculate about the assumptions we can make concerning human rationality. When we study the general effects of systemic structures or domestic pressures on decision-makers, the usual assumption is one of rationality, as emphasized by Robert Keohane: 'The link between system structure and actor behaviour is forged by the rationality assumption, which enables theorists to predict that leaders will respond to the incentives and constraints imposed by their environments' (Keohane 1986: 167). The literature on human cognition and belief systems questions this notion of rationality; it requests us to adopt a different notion of cognition: 'International relations theorists should not rely on the overly simplistic and naïve assumptions of rational choice. Instead, they should turn to bounded rationality and a cognitive approach and ground their theories in a more realistic psychology' (Rosati 2000: 74). James Goldgeier underlines the point:

Because the existence of threats depends on the perceptions of individuals and societies, we need to incorporate the psychological dimension of threat perception and identity formation into our more structural analyses . . . The growing attention given by neorealists to perceptual variables, the examination by neoliberals of the role of ideas, and the social constructivist focus on identity, all suggest that models operating at other levels of analysis could be strengthened by incorporating work operating at the psychological level. (Goldgeier 1997: 164–5)

At the same time, taking the road of 'cognition' instead of that of 'rationality' also has a potential downside. Even a somewhat comprehensive study of human cognition in world politics raises an extremely large and complex research agenda that will be very time-consuming both in terms of collecting information and in terms of analysis. Furthermore, 'there is a danger that adding levels of analysis may result in an undisciplined proliferation of categories and variables. It may then become increasingly difficult to determine which are more or less important, and ad hoc explanations for individual cases erode the possibilities for broader generalization across cases' (Holsti 2004: 31–2). However, many scholars are confident about the possibility of combining different theories and modes of analysis in an attempt to bring together insights from competing approaches. The following section introduces a study which attempts to do just that.

Going to War in the Persian Gulf: A Case-Study

On 2 August 1990 Iraq invaded Kuwait; four days later, the country was annexed as Iraq's nineteenth province. Having erased Kuwait from the map, it was feared that Iraq would next invade oil-rich Saudi Arabia. UN resolutions condemned the invasion and demanded Iraq's unconditional withdrawal from Kuwait. Five months of negotiations led nowhere The US-led war to expel Iraq from Kuwait began on 16 January 1991; Iraq was forced to sign a cease-fire some five weeks later, on 27 February. Why did the United States choose to go to war in the Persian Gulf? (See web links 9.35 and 9.37.) The question was recently raised in a book by Steve A. Yetiv (2004). In the attempt to answer it, he applies five different theoretical perspectives. The analysis demonstrates how a combination of different perspectives helps us understand the course of events. The following brief summary of this analysis focuses on what are arguably the three most important approaches. The three theories are: the Rational Actor Model (RAM); the cognitive model; and the groupthink model. They are drawn from the three different levels of analysis introduced above: the systemic level (RAM); the nation-state level (groupthink); and the individual level (the cognitive model).

The baseline model in Yetiv's analysis is the RAM. It treats the United States as a unitary actor driven by a motivation to advance national interests; it also assumes that the decisions made by the US are based on rational choice. The explanation of how and why the United States went to war from a RAM perspective is summarized in Box 9.7.

The RAM perspective would appear to take us a long way in understanding why the United States went to war in the Persian Gulf. It highlights the strategic interaction between the US and Iraq and plausibly explains why going to war was ultimately unavoidable. But there are also elements that leave us in the dark, and assumptions that are not questioned. RAM is clearly premised on a realist model of the international system; it is characterized by anarchy and self-help; therefore, war is always a possibility. This would appear entirely plausible in the present case; but, as noted above (Box 9.2), there are different conceptions of the international system that can lead to different ideas about the systemic pressures on states. We cannot fully know whether the decision-makers were driven by a realist

| BOX 9.7 | Applying the RAM perspective |

The argument is that the United States perceived itself as having vital national interests in the Persian Gulf. In order to protect them, it tried to consider and exhaust diplomatic and economic alternatives to war. It faced an intransigent Iraqi regime, and over time believed that the costs of waiting for sanctions to work increasingly exceeded the benefits. Therefore, taking into consideration Iraq's behaviour in the crisis, and its continuing threat even if it had withdrawn from Kuwait, Washington increasingly saw war as sensible. While Iraq may or may not have reached a similar conclusion, it was also the case that the two sides could not locate or agree upon a negotiated settlement, because their bargaining positions did not overlap much, if at all. This further inclined the United States towards war. Furthermore, the structural condition of anarchy in international relations enforced this logic. In their strategic interaction, the United States could not trust Iraq to withdraw from Kuwait and not to invade it at a later time, and Iraq could not trust the United States not to attack or harass it, if it agreed to withdraw.

Quoted from Yetiv (2004: 32–3)

understanding of the international system until we open up the black box of 'The United States' and further scrutinize their reflections. Nor can we know whether the process of decision-making was fully rational, as the RAM model assumes. Were all possible alternative options to the war decision carefully identified and meticulously examined before the decision was taken? In order to know about this, other theoretical perspectives that further investigate the process of decision-making are necessary.

The cognitive approach focuses on the individual key decision-maker, in this case President Bush Sr. Why did he frequently employ hot-headed and emotional rhetoric against Saddam Hussein? What made him emphatically reject any suggestion of compromise with Saddam? Why did he tend to prefer the war option ahead of his advisers? Yetiv's application of the cognitive approach focuses on the importance of historical analogies: 'it focuses on how decision makers create their own images of reality and simplify decision-making through the use of analogies' (Yetiv 2004: 99). In the Gulf War case, the most important historical analogy for President Bush was that of Munich, as explained in Box 9.8.

The cognitive approach highlights aspects of the US war decision that are not accounted for in the RAM perspective. The notion of historical analogy helps explain why President Bush strongly preferred the war option and rejected compromise with Saddam. Did the strong reliance on historical analogy lead Bush towards acting in a non-rational way? That need not be the case; analogical thinking can help identify the nature of the problem at hand and inform the search for possible courses of action. At the same time, such thinking can also 'undermine rational processes if it introduces significant biases, excludes or restricts the search for novel information, or pushes actors to ignore the facts and options that clash with the message encoded in the analogy' (Yetiv 2004: 61). Did that happen in the Gulf War case? Yetiv's analysis leaves the question open; on the one hand, the analogy supported the efforts of rational thinking; on the other hand, Bush also used the analogy 'to construct the crisis, so that we could say that the analogy was both heartfelt by a president who experienced World War II and used to advance the war option' (Yetiv 2004: 158).

BOX 9.8	Applying the cognitive perspective

For Bush, compromising with Saddam, as many wanted at home and abroad, would have made him a modern-day Neville Chamberlain. As Britain's Prime Minister, he yielded Germany the Sudetenland of Czechoslovakia at the 1938 Munich conference, a borderland area of German speakers that Hitler wanted to reintegrate into Germany. Chamberlain, duped by Hitler, believed that his action at Munich, which followed repeated efforts by Britain to appease Nazi Germany, would bring what he called 'peace in our time'. In fact, Hitler proceeded to seize Czechoslovakia and to invade Poland, forcing a change in British policy and creating the Munich analogy, which referred to the failure of appeasement in the face of brutal aggression. Through the Munich lens, Bush tended to see Saddam as a Hitler-like dictator who could not be accommodated or even offered a minor, veiled carrot . . . The analogy made Bush more likely to personalize the conflict with Saddam, to undermine others' efforts at compromise with Saddam, and to prefer war to the continued use of economic sanctions.

Quoted from Yetiv (2004: 61)

BOX 9.9	Applying the groupthink approach

The exclusive nature of the group of eight and the rejection of methodical decision-making procedures both contributed to groupthink and made it easier for Bush and Scowcroft to advance the war option without carefully considering the costs and benefits of other alternatives. The group of eight had slowly coalesced, behind its strong and partial group leader, around the notion that economic sanctions would fail . . . Bush insisted on that decision ahead of most of his advisers, and it was adopted without consulting the most senior US generals and admirals, including Powell, who was disturbed by it, and Schwarzkopf, who was furious about it. [Chas W.] Freeman [US ambassador to Saudi Arabia], who played a fundamental role with Schwarzkopf in the field and was in communication with Washington, asserted his view that 'the record will show that a lot of issues were not fully discussed'.

Quoted from Yetiv (2004: 118)

The groupthink approach emphasizes critical elements of small-group behaviour that can lead to defective decision-making. Two overlapping groups are of interest in the Gulf War case: the group of four consisted of President Bush, Vice President Dan Quayle, National Security Adviser Brent Scowcroft and Chief-of-Staff John Sununu. The group of eight comprised the group of four plus Secretary of State James Baker, Secretary of Defence Richard Cheney, Chairman of the Joint Chiefs-of-Staff Colin Powell and Deputy National Security Adviser Robert Gates. Yetiv's analysis demonstrates that the conditions promoting groupthink were present and they did lead to defective decision-making in the sense that alternative courses to the war option were not given greater consideration. The elements of groupthink are set forth in Box 9.9.

This section has briefly demonstrated how different analytical perspectives can be brought together and yield insights into a case-study of why the United States chose to go to war in the Persian Gulf in 1991. The RAM is the most general and comprehensive approach. It takes in the challenges to US national interests raised by the Iraqi invasion of Kuwait; it posits how the strategic interaction between Iraq and the US inclined the United States towards going to war. The other approaches are less comprehensive; even so, each of them contributes significantly towards understanding why the war option was preferred over other options. Additional perspectives that will yield other insights can be applied; they will generate further information about the case. Scholars will not agree on any 'best combination' of approaches; some will find that the RAM really tells us enough about the case because it examines the challenge to the US presented by Saddam and accounts for why the war option was the response to that challenge. Others will argue that we must draw in the nation-state level and the level of the individual decision-maker to achieve a full analysis. This discussion may be tainted by hindsight: there can be a tendency to see the war option as rational and effective because the war turned out to be a success. In cases of failure, attention will sooner be directed at elements of defective decision-making as demonstrated by analyses of the Vietnam War, the Bay of Pigs invasion or even the current US-led war in Iraq.

A caution in conclusion: scholars who attempt sophisticated foreign-policy analysis can come across as incredibly bright analysts who are capable of identifying all relevant aspects of the case, and of pointing to various examples of more or less flawed decision-making. Maybe it is relevant to emphasize an observation from the traditional approach to foreign-policy analysis: foreign policymakers do not have the benefit of hindsight; they deal with a diverse and multifaceted world. The international system is composed of separate countries, each with its own interests and concerns, its own national government, which is in a position to make its own policies. Primarily for that reason, foreign policy is more prone to uncertainty and conflict, and less amenable to rational manageable decisions than domestic policy, which does operate under a higher authority, namely the national government. Dealing with foreign governments or issues will often tax to the limit the expertise and experience of the policymakers involved. Not only that: many of the issues and problems that foreign policymakers have to come to grips with are in motion, in flux, and that too will introduce uncertainties and difficulties. Rarely, if ever, can there be 'correct' and 'incorrect' foreign policies. Often that knowledge only becomes evident in retrospect, and that cannot be much consolation to the policymakers involved in the episode. Nor can there usually be 'solutions' to foreign-policy 'problems'. For policymakers, there can only be 'better' or 'worse' foreign policies under the circumstances existing at the time.

Critiques of Foreign-Policy Analysis

We hope to have demonstrated the complexity of foreign-policy analysis: it must reach from the overall macro-level of the international system and its salient dynamics to the micro-level of the individual decision-maker and his or her personal convictions and preconceptions. It must attempt to cover everything in between these levels, such as regional dynamics, domestic politics, societal influences, the role of bureaucratic machineries, the influence of small group practices and much more. Small wonder, then, that there is no unified approach or amalgamated theory of foreign policy. Some scholars find that the field is simply too big and complicated to lend itself to coherent theorizing; others deplore that because of this complexity the field is easily dominated by theoretical fashions and fads that are here today and gone tomorrow.

As noted above, there is a fundamental debate about the extent to which foreign policy can be subjected to rational choice. The Rational Actor Model assumes that foreign policy can be precisely 'managed', that knowledge can be applied in foreign policy, with confidence that outcomes will be those anticipated. But new situations that surprise policymakers are not uncommon in foreign relations. Major acts of foreign policy can be leaps in the dark or leaps of faith. Why, for example, did British and French policymakers fail to foresee the blunder they were about to make by launching a joint military operation to take over the Suez canal zone in 1956, without prior support from the US government, which subsequently condemned the action thereby making it unviable? Which American policymakers foresaw and planned against the terrorist attacks on New York and Washington?

The complexities and uncertainties involved in foreign-policy decision-making can be seen as a warning against streamlined analytical models that propose to take in every possible aspect of the decision-making process. Foreign policy, like international politics more generally, is rarely an exclusively instrumental activity of defining problems and finding solutions, or identifying goals and determining courses of action. Still less is it a technical activity. Foreign policy always involves values as well as interests, hopes as well as fears, confidence as well as overconfidence, clarity as well as uncertainly and doubt, passions and other subjective factors as well as objective calculations. In short, it involves the familiar considerations and concerns that human beings bring to their political activity, from narrow self-interests to expansive ideological goals.

A Note on Experts and 'Think Tanks'

Foreign policy has prompted a great deal of interest and research, much of it directed at influencing and possibly improving the foreign-policy process and goals of countries. Over the past century many so-called think tanks have been established with that aim in mind (see web link 9.27). These are organizations that disseminate useful information and provide expert advice on international issues and problems. It is important to know about them because they have entered into the foreign-policy process in many countries, especially the United States, where their influence is widely registered. They supplement conventional policymaking organizations, such as foreign ministries, departments of defence, ministries of foreign trade and commerce, and so forth. Some think tanks have the status and standing of annexes to government ministries and departments. The Rand Corporation, a well-known American think tank, is a highly trusted policy unit of the United States Department of Defense.

Some of the most important think tanks are private organizations engaged in developing and marketing foreign-policy ideas and strategies with a view to shaping public opinion and influencing government policy. Many of the leading experts on foreign policy are members of these organizations rather than regular university departments of international relations. In the United States such experts have a prominent role as public intellectuals. Included among them at the present time would be Ivo Daalder, Robert Kaplan, Thomas Friedman, Michael Hirsh, Samantha Power, Jonathan Schell, Benjamin Barber and Fareed Zakaria. It is possible to build a successful career in foreign-policy analysis entirely in the private sector outside of both government bureaus and university departments.

The first foreign-policy think tanks emerged in the early part of the twentieth century in the United States. They reflected the desire of leading American philanthropists and public intellectuals, of that time, to create institutions where scholars and leaders could meet to discuss and debate international issues with a view to solving them or at least addressing them more effectively than in the past. Three institutions from that period are particularly significant: the Carnegie Endowment for International Peace (1910) which was established by steel tycoon Andrew Carnegie; the Hoover Institution on War, Revolution and Peace (1919) founded by Herbert Hoover, later US President; and the Council on Foreign Relations (1921) which evolved into one of the most respected foreign-policy institutes in the world. There are approximately 2,000 think tanks in the United States alone. Most are affiliated with universities, but perhaps as many as 500 are private organizations. Major American think tanks such as the American Enterprise Institute, the Brookings Institute, the Rand Corporation and the Council on Foreign Relations, among others, have substantial staffs, which sometimes number into the hundreds, and budgets running into many millions of dollars.

The United States is home to some of the most distinguished foreign-policy institutes (see web link 9.28). But over the past century think tanks have been established in many other countries as well. Of these, the best known is British: the Royal Institute of International Affairs (Chatham House) which was founded around the same time as its US counterpart (1920). Foreign-policy organizations of similar vintage are the Canadian Institute of International Affairs (1928) and the Australian Institute of International Affairs (1933). The historical context of their formation was the misery and destruction caused by the First World War. These organizations were supposed to generate and disseminate practical knowledge of how to bring an end to the problems of war and how to institute peace on a more permanent foundation.

More foreign-policy think tanks were established after the Second World War in Europe and beyond. A few of the more noteworthy include the German Institute for International and Security Affairs (1962), the Stockholm International Peace Research Institute (1966), the Japanese Institute for International Policy Studies (1988), the Netherlands Cicero Foundation on European Integration (1992), the Danish Institute of International Affairs (1995) and the Indian Institute of Peace and Conflict Studies (1996). Such organizations deal with a remarkable diversity of foreign-policy issues, including defence and strategy, terrorism, human rights, global poverty, European integration, peace research, regional conflicts, international trade, energy, science and technology, social policy and much else besides.

| BOX 9.10 | Foreign-policy think tanks |

THE CARNEGIE ENDOWMENT—UNITED STATES

The Carnegie Endowment for International Peace was established in 1910 in Washington, DC, with a gift from Andrew Carnegie. As a tax-exempt operating (not grant-making) foundation, the Endowment conducts programmes of research, discussion, publication and education in international affairs and US foreign policy. The Endowment also publishes the quarterly magazine *Foreign Policy*.

COUNCIL ON FOREIGN RELATIONS—UNITED STATES

The Council on Foreign Relations, established in 1921, is a non-profit, non-partisan membership organization that takes no position on issues but is dedicated to improving the understanding of international affairs and American foreign policy through the free exchange of ideas.

FOREIGN POLICY INSTITUTE—TURKEY

FPI was founded in 1974 as an independent research organization to study issues related to Turkish foreign policy. Since its establishment, it has enlarged its activities to cover strategic and regional studies and international affairs.

FRENCH INSTITUTE OF INTERNATIONAL RELATIONS

Founded in 1979 by Thierry de Montbrial, the French Institute of International Relations—Institut français des relations internationales or Ifri—is France's leading independent international relations centre dedicated to policy-oriented research and analysis of global political affairs.

GEORGE C. MARSHALL EUROPEAN CENTER FOR SECURITY STUDIES—UNITED STATES

Founded on 5 June 1993, the George C. Marshall European Center for Security Studies is dedicated to stabilizing and thereby strengthening post-Cold War Europe. Specifically, it aids defence and foreign ministries in Europe's aspiring democracies to develop national security organizations and systems that reflect democratic principles.

GERMAN COUNCIL ON FOREIGN RELATIONS

The German Council on Foreign Relations (DGAP) is Germany's national foreign policy network. As an independent, private, non-partisan and non-profit organization, the Council actively takes part in political decision-making and promotes the understanding of German foreign policy and international relations.

INTERNATIONAL INSTITUTE FOR STRATEGIC STUDIES—UNITED KINGDOM

The International Institute for Strategic Studies (IISS), founded in 1958, is an independent centre for research, information and debate on the problems of conflict, however caused, that have, or potentially have, an important military content. Its work is grounded in an appreciation of the various political, economic and social problems that can lead to instability, as well as the factors that can lead to international cooperation.

NETHERLANDS INSTITUTE FOR INTERNATIONAL RELATIONS ('CLINGENDAEL')

The leading Dutch international affairs research organization. 'Special attention is devoted to European integration, transatlantic relations, international security, conflict studies, policymaking on national and international energy markets, negotiations and diplomacy, and to the United Nations and other international organizations.'

STOCKHOLM INTERNATIONAL PEACE RESEARCH INSTITUTE

The task of the Institute is to conduct research on questions of conflict and cooperation of importance for international peace and security, with the aim of contributing to an understanding of the conditions for peaceful solutions of international conflicts and for a stable peace.

What differentiates leading American think tanks from their counterparts in other parts of the world is the readiness of government policymakers to turn to them for policy advice and often to follow that advice. Foreign-policy expertise has high visibility and prestige. It is that opportunity and ability to participate in policymaking that leads some scholars to conclude that US think tanks have greater impact on public policy than those of most other countries. Immediately following the terrorist attacks on New York and Washington policy experts from some of America's leading foreign-policy institutes appeared prominently in the mass media to offer their thoughts and advice. Since foreign-policy think tanks market ideas to policymakers and the public, 11 September 2001 came as a great opportunity which they seized with confidence. That is only one example of the expertise that exists in the United States for dealing with foreign-policy issues and problems (see web link 9.05).

Many Americans are receptive to the idea that international problems can be solved if the correct expertise is brought to bear on them. The problem is finding the right methods for coming up with the correct solution. That calls for expertise. Experts can be trained and employed to find those solutions. That rationalist mentality is deeply rooted in American culture and history. Many Americans demonstrate a strong desire to develop foreign policies to make the world a better place. Scepticism is generally low.

After the Second World War and faced with responsibilities of being the pre-eminent world power, decision-makers in Washington sought the advice of experts who could help them to create a new security strategy that could come to terms with the emerging threat of the Soviet Union. They turned to think tanks for expertise, and they particularly found what they were looking for in the new Rand Corporation. It was formed in 1948, by means of government funds, to develop US security policies at the dawn of the nuclear age. It took a technical-scientific approach, was staffed by scientists and economists, and became famous for providing cost–benefit and rational choice analyses of foreign-policy problems. Unlike earlier think tanks, which sought to influence and advise governments from outside, Rand was involved in the development of foreign policy on the inside of government. Rand ushered in a new generation of policy research institutions funded by government departments and agencies whose research was intended to address specific concerns of policymakers.

More recently a new kind of advocacy think tank began to appear in the United States as well as other countries. Unlike policy organizations of an earlier period, such as the Council on Foreign Relations—which was concerned to keep some distance from government—and unlike policy organizations such as Rand—which were directly involved with government in the making of policy—these later organization were not concerned only to give policy advice or provide expertise. They were concerned with advocating policy doctrines and prescribing policy values which they were established to promote. Many human rights organizations are advocacy think tanks: Amnesty International being the most famous of them. Many environmental organizations are advocacy think tanks: Greenpeace being among the most famous.

Some of the most noteworthy American advocacy think tanks on foreign policy are the Center for Strategic and International Studies (1962), the Heritage Foundation (1973) and the CATO Institute (1977). These organizations, and others like them, have given foreign-policy studies a doctrinal and combative tone, especially evident in the mass media, which frequently invites opposing positions in op-ed newspaper articles or in live television interviews on current questions of US foreign policy. Policy analysis turns into doctrinal prescriptions which are difficult to distinguish from ideological or theological positions.

KEY POINTS

- Foreign-policy analysis is a study of the management of external relations and activities of nation-states, as distinguished from their domestic policies. Foreign policy involves goals, strategies, measures, methods, guidelines, directives, understandings, agreements and so on, by which national governments conduct international relations with each other and with international organizations and non-governmental actors.

- The relationship between theory and policy is complex, because any one theory does not necessarily lead to one clear policy option; in most cases there will be several different options. Even so, the choice of theory affects the choice of policy. That is partly because different theories emphasize different social values, as explained in Chapter 1.

- A traditional approach to foreign-policy analysis involves being informed about a government's external policies: knowing their history or at least their background, comprehending the interests and concerns that drive the policies, and thinking through the various ways of addressing and defending those interests and concerns.

- The comparative approach to foreign policy was inspired by the behaviouralist turn (see Chapter 11) in political science. The ambition was to build systematic theories and explanations of the foreign-policy process in general. This was done through the amalgamation of large bodies of data, describing the content and context of the foreign policy of a large number of countries. It was theoretically informed by James Rosenau's (1966) 'pre-theory' of foreign policy.

- Bureaucratic structures and processes. This approach focuses on the organizational context of decision-making, which is seen to be conditioned by the dictates and demands of the bureaucratic settings in which decisions are made. Analysing processes and channels whereby organizations arrive at their policies is seen to be a superior way to acquire empirical knowledge of foreign policy.

- Cognitive processes and psychology. This approach again focuses on the individual decision-maker, this time with a particular attention to the psychological aspects of decision-making. Robert Jervis has studied misperception: why do actors misperceive the intentions and actions of others? Another example in this category is the work of Margaret Herman. She studied the personality characteristics of fifty-four heads of government, making the claim that such factors as the leaders' experience in foreign affairs, their political styles, their political socialization and their broader views of the world, all should be drawn into the analysis in order to understand the ways in which leaders conduct foreign policy.

- 'Multilevel, multidimensional'. Over the past two or three decades, it has become increasingly clear that there will never be one, big, all-encompassing theory of foreign policy, just as there will never be one big theory of IR. Many scholars now use the various major theories presented earlier in this book as approaches to study particular aspects of foreign policymaking. The major theories often contain clear implications for foreign policy or even elements that are directly relevant for foreign policy.

- Social constructivists focus on the role of ideas and discourse, as recorded in Chapter 6. For constructivists, foreign policymaking is an intersubjective world, whose ideas and discourse can be scrutinized in order to arrive at a better theoretical understanding of the process.

- The usual situation facing foreign policymakers is one of having to choose between different possible courses of action. That raises two fundamental questions: what policy choices, if any, are available? Of those, what is the best course to follow? Responding to such questions takes us to the heart of foreign policymaking.

- The RAM approach indicates the comprehensive challenges to US national interests raised by the Iraqi invasion of Kuwait; it posits how the strategic interaction between Iraq and the US inclined the United States towards going to war against Iraq as leader of a military coalition.

- Despite the many approaches to foreign policy and levels of analysis outlined in this chapter, it remains an imperfect and controversial body of knowledge, where even the most knowledgeable experts are likely to disagree on vital issues.

- Foreign-policy think tanks are organizations that disseminate useful information and provide expert advice on international issues and problems. There are many in the United States, where their influence is widely registered. Some of the most important think tanks are private organizations engaged in developing and marketing foreign-policy ideas and strategies with a view to shaping public opinion and influencing government policy.

QUESTIONS

- What is foreign-policy analysis fundamentally concerned with?
- Which is the best approach to foreign-policy analysis, and why?
- Which level of foreign-policy analysis makes most sense, and why?
- Should foreign policy be confined to foreign ministries or state departments (as realists and International Society scholars argue) or should it extend to groups in society as well (as liberals argue)?
- How useful is the RAM approach for explaining why the United States chose to go to war in the Persian Gulf in 1991?
- Can theories of foreign policymaking be applied in making foreign-policy decisions or can they only be used to explain those decisions after they have been made?

GUIDE TO FURTHER READING

Allison, G. and Zelikow, P. (1999). *Essence of a Decision: Explaining the Cuban Missile Crisis*, 2nd edn. New York: Longman.

Carlsnaes, W. (2002). 'Foreign Policy', in W. Carlsnaes, T. Risse and B. Simmons (eds), *Handbook of International Relations*. London: Sage, 331–49.

George, A. (1993). *Bridging the Gap: Theory and Practice in Foreign Policy.* Washington, DC: United States Institute of Peace.

Goldstein, J. and Keohane, R. (1993). *Ideas and Foreign Policy.* Ithaca: Cornell University Press.

Hart, P., Stern, E. K. and Sundelius, B. (eds) (1997). *Beyond Groupthink: Political Dynamics and Foreign Policy-making.* Ann Arbor: University of Michigan Press.

Ikenberry, G. J. (ed.) (2001b). *American Foreign Policy: Theoretical Essays*, 4th edn. Boston: Scott Foresman.

Jervis, R. (1976). *Perception and Misperception in International Politics.* Princeton: Princeton University Press.

Larsen, H. (1997). *Foreign Policy and Discourse Analysis: France, Britain, and Europe.* London: Routledge.

 WEB LINKS

 Web links mentioned in the chapter plus additional links can be found on the Online Resource Centre that accompanies this book.
www.oxfordtextbooks.co.uk/orc/jackson_sorensen3e/

CHAPTER 10

Five Issues in IR

▌ Summary

The theoretical traditions we examined earlier focus on the classical issues of IR: war and peace, cooperation and conflict, wealth and poverty. But other issues have also demanded attention on the IR agenda. This chapter discusses five of the most important of these issues: international terrorism; the environment; gender; sovereignty; and changes in statehood. These issues were evident earlier; but for several reasons they stand higher on the agenda today. The chapter discusses whether the issues are merely additional items on an already crowded agenda, or whether they signal a more profound transformation of IR theory.

Introduction

There have always been dissident voices in IR; scholars unhappy with the traditional focus of the discipline have taken up alternative positions and approaches. Indeed, some scholars claim that they are out to transform the discipline altogether. Whether that is likely to happen will be discussed below. This chapter discusses five of the most important issues raised by current events or by various critics of established approaches: international terrorism; the environment; gender; sovereignty; and changes in statehood involving new security challenges. We could have chosen other issues, but these are sufficient to illustrate how different issues can enter the discipline and change its theoretical focus.

An issue in IR is a topic which is considered to be important in terms of both values and theory. Values come into the picture because the decision on what is important and what is not is always based on certain values. Theory comes in because arguing in favour of an issue must derive from some theoretical idea that this issue is important for the study of IR. For these reasons, raising non-traditional issues often involves new approaches to IR.

The discussion of issues will proceed in the following way. First, we shall examine what the issue is about in empirical terms. What are the problems raised and why are they claimed to be important? Second, we shall consider how the issue in question affects the traditional concerns of international relations: war and peace, wealth and poverty. Finally, we shall discuss the nature of the theoretical challenge that the issues present to IR. Can they be handled by traditional approaches or do they require the cultivation of new approaches and concepts?

We shall start with international terrorism, then proceed to the environment, gender, sovereignty and changes in statehood. The order of presentation is not an indication that one issue is more important than another. The introduction to concrete issues will necessarily have to be brief; the reader is urged to consult the guide to further reading at the end of the chapter for references to in-depth treatment of a particular issue.

BOX 10.1	New issues in IR: terrorism, environment, gender, sovereignty, statehood

1. Concrete content of issue: what is it we should study and why?

2. Consequences of issue for core problems in IR: war and peace, conflict and cooperation, wealth and poverty?

3. Nature of theoretical challenge: does the issue demand new approaches and concepts or can it be covered by traditional approaches?

International Terrorism

Terrorism is the unlawful use or threatened use of violence against civilians, often to achieve political, religious or similar objectives. International terrorism involves the territory or the citizens of more than one country. Terrorism is nothing new; it has probably existed ever since human societies began to regulate the use of violence. It is the unusual scale and intensity of the 11 September 2001 attacks in New York and Washington, and later attacks in Ankara, Madrid, London and elsewhere that has put the issue of international terrorism high on the agenda. It is an issue that concerns IR for obvious reasons; IR is not least about national and international security. When the only superpower in the international system, the United States, defines international terrorism as the first-rank threat to US security (NSS 2002) and goes on to launch a 'war on terror', the issue must rank high on the political and scholarly agenda.

The precise definition of terrorism raises several problems; for that reason the United Nations has not succeeded in coming to agreement on a common definition (see web link 10.01). One controversy concerns the relationship between terrorism and other forms of political violence. Some think that there are legitimate forms of political violence which are then not terrorism. For example, one of the leaders of the Palestinian Fatah movement declared in 1973 that he was 'firmly opposed . . . to terrorism'; but he went on to add that 'I do not confuse revolutionary violence with terrorism, or operations that constitute political acts with others that do not' (Iyad 1983: 146).

Another controversy concerns the inclusion or not of state-sponsored terrorism in the definition. It is clear that states have sponsored terrorism in a number of cases (Stohl and Lopez 1984). At the same time, the mass-murder terrorist attacks of recent years appear not to be directly supported by states, but that is of course not a strong argument for excluding states from the definition altogether. A final controversy concerns the term 'civilians'. Some find the term misleading because attacks on military personnel who are not on active duty should also be considered terrorism. For that reason, some prefer to use the term 'non-combatants' instead of 'civilians'.

Most terrorism is national; it is related to political struggles, most often in weak states where democratic politics is weak or absent and incumbent leaders are considered illegitimate, such as Colombia, Nepal, Sri Lanka or Indonesia. In the weakest states, most of which are in sub-Saharan Africa, terrorism takes place in a context of more-or-less permanent civil war. But more consolidated states have also had severe problems with terrorism, including Britain, India, Spain and Argentina. Such terrorism is national because the enemy is national and often groups can fight as guerrillas, getting support from local sympathizers.

An upsurge in international terrorism, in the form of aircraft hijackings, took place from the late 1960s. Air travel had expanded significantly since the 1950s; there were no effective security systems in the airports; and the international media—in particular television—provided extensive coverage that appealed to groups eager to send their messages to the

| **BOX 10.2** | **UK Terrorism Act 2000, Part I, section 1** |

PART I INTRODUCTORY

1. Terrorism: interpretation

(1) In this Act 'terrorism' means the use or threat of action where—

    (a) the action falls within subsection (2),

    (b) the use or threat is designed to influence the government or to intimidate the public or a section of the public, and

    (c) the use or threat is made for the purpose of advancing a political, religious or ideological cause.

(2) Action falls within this subsection if it—

    (a) involves serious violence against a person,

    (b) involves serious damage to property,

    (c) endangers a person's life, other than that of the person committing the action,

    (d) creates a serious risk to the health or safety of the public or a section of the public, or

    (e) is designed seriously to interfere with or seriously to disrupt an electronic system.

(3) The use or threat of action falling within subsection (2) which involves the use of firearms or explosives is terrorism whether or not subsection (1)(b) is satisfied.

(4) In this section—

    (a) 'action' includes action outside the United Kingdom,

    (b) a reference to any person or to property is a reference to any person, or to property, wherever situated,

    (c) a reference to the public includes a reference to the public of a country other than the United Kingdom, and

    (d) 'the government' means the government of the United Kingdom, of a part of the United Kingdom or of a country other than the United Kingdom.

(5) In this Act a reference to action taken for the purposes of terrorism includes a reference to action taken for the benefit of a proscribed organisation.

Source: www.opsi.gov.uk/acts/acts2000/20000011.htm

world. The hijacking of airliners increased from five incidents in 1966 to ninety-four in 1969 (Kiras 2005: 483). Improved security measures helped in reducing hijacking, but international terrorism did not disappear. During the 1980s there was an increased incidence of radical Muslim groups attacking American targets in Lebanon, Iran, Somalia and elsewhere.

Such attacks continued after the end of the Cold War. International terrorism has become a phenomenon primarily connected with radical Muslim groups (see web links 10.03 and

BOX 10.3	Terrorist groups, according to Council on Foreign Relations

- Al-Qaeda (Afghanistan, Islamists)
- Osama bin Laden (Al-Qaeda leader)
- Hamas, Islamic Jihad (Palestinian Islamists)
- Al-Aqsa Martyrs Brigades (Palestinian nationalists)
- PFLP, DFLP, PFLP-GC (Palestinian leftists)
- Hezbollah (Lebanon, Islamists)
- Jamaat al-Islamiyya, Egyptian Islamic Jihad (Egypt, Islamists)
- Armed Islamic Group (Algeria, Islamists)
- Kashmir Militant Extremists (Kashmir, Islamists)
- Mujahedeen-e-Khalq (Iranian rebel)
- Abu Nidal Organization (Iraq, extremists)
- Kach, Kahane Chai (Israel, extremists)
- Chechnya-based Terrorists (Russia, separatists)
- East Turkestan Islamic Movement (China, separatists)
- Kurdistan Workers' Party (Turkey, separatists)

- Jemaah Islamiyah (South-East Asia, Islamists)
- Abu Sayyaf Group (Philippines, Islamist separatists)
- Liberation Tigers of Tamil Eelam (Sri Lanka, separatists)
- Irish Republican Army (UK, separatists)
- IRA Splinter Groups (UK, separatists)
- Northern Ireland Loyalist Paramilitaries (UK, extremists)
- Basque Fatherland and Liberty (Spain, separatists)
- November 17, Revolutionary People's Struggle (Greece, leftists)
- FARC, ELN, AUC (Colombia, rebels)
- Shining Path, Tupac Amaru (Peru, leftists)
- Aum Shinrikyo (Japan, cultists)
- American Militant Extremists (United States, radicals)
- Ansar al Islam (Iraq, Islamists/Kurdish separatists)

Source: Council on Foreign Relations

10.04). Almost all of the international terrorist groups on the US Department of State list belong to that category (see Box 10.3). The best known of these groups or networks is al-Qaeda (the Base).

International terrorism has revived the spectre of a physical security threat to states and civil societies in the OECD world. With the end of the Cold War, there was hope that this event would signal the end of war and large-scale violence altogether in these countries. Colin Powell made the point in 1991: 'I'm running out of demons. I'm running out of enemies. I'm down to Castro and Kim Il Sung.' The al-Qaeda attacks brought national security in the sense of ordinary people's safety back on the agenda.

In order to address the second question in Box 10.1, we need to evaluate the extent and gravity of the terrorist threat posed by radical Muslim groups. The question is controversial; some think that the threat is of no great concern; others argue that it is highly significant. Those who argue the former view claim that, in general terms, the scale of terrorist operations make them more like crime than like organized warfare. And just like crime has existed in most or all types of societies, terrorism 'has been around forever and will presumably continue to exist' (Mueller 2004: 199) without presenting existential threats to society.

At the same time, just as there can be organized crime, there can be organized terrorism. The al-Qaeda network is a case in point and the 11 September 2001 attacks were of unusual magnitude; during the entire twentieth century, 'fewer than twenty terrorist attacks managed to kill as many as 100 people, and none caused more than 400 deaths. Until [11 September], far fewer Americans were killed in any grouping of years by all forms of international terrorism than were killed by lightning' (Mueller 2004: 110).

On this view, it appears highly unlikely that terrorism as represented by al-Qaeda will grow into a large-scale threat to Western societies. While there are a great number of terrorist groups scattered around the world, especially in weak states, their ambitions remain national, not international; only very few move to become international terrorists. Second, the argument is that this kind of international terrorism is specifically connected to a radical, fundamentalist version of Islam which is not representative of Islam as such. Other cultural-religious belief systems (e.g. Confucianism, Hinduism, Buddhism, Christianity) do not exhibit a similar kind of embittered anti-Westernism.

Finally, those who think that the terrorist threat is not so serious emphasize how the al-Qaeda network is specifically connected to marginalized Muslim groups of *Mujahedin* (fighters for Allah's cause) who joined together to fight against the Soviet occupation of Afghanistan and were able to use that country as a safe haven. These groups are not very large and they no longer have easy access to countries where they can set up bases.

But it can also be argued that the threat of international terrorism is very serious. First of all, open, complex societies are necessarily vulnerable: there are limited possibilities for surveillance and control; suicide terrorists carrying forceful, low-tech bombs cannot easily be stopped. The recent London bomb attacks (2005) demonstrated that Muslims with a relatively 'normal' background as citizens of the UK had been recruited for the assaults. This could be taken to mean that the potential recruiting base for terrorist actions is very large indeed; it is not merely confined to ex-Afghani *Mujahedins*; it also comprises self-selected members of local Muslim societies in the UK and other Western countries. Furthermore, some commentators argue that the US-led war in Iraq leads to 'blowback terrorism', meaning that the war tends to increase, rather than decrease, the recruitment potential to international terrorism (Mann 2003: 159–93) (see web links 10.11 and 10.12).

Finally, there is the danger of international terrorists gaining access to and using weapons of mass destruction (WMD), that is, chemical, biological and nuclear weapons. It is clear that terrorist groups have incentives to use WMD; they would be able to create massive destruction and fear, and that would possibly elevate the groups to a new power position vis-à-vis their adversaries (Schmid 2005). A recent study by Graham Allison argues that a nuclear attack by terrorists on America is more likely than not in the decade ahead (Allison 2004). If policymakers take immediate countermeasures, such an attack is 'preventable'. If they do not, says Allison, the attack is 'inevitable'. Meanwhile, other commentators consider it less likely that terrorists can gain access to and will use WMD (Pearlstein 2004);

Box 10.4	Graham Allison on nuclear terrorism

First, thefts of weapons-usable material and attempts to steal nuclear weapons are not a hypothetical possibility, but a proven and recurring fact . . .

Second, . . . the only high hurdle to creating a nuclear bomb is access to fissionable material . . . as John Foster, a leading American bomb maker, . . . wrote a quarter century ago, 'if the essential nuclear materials are at hand, it is possible to make an atomic bomb using information that is available in the open literature . . .

Third, terrorists would not find it difficult to smuggle such a nuclear device into the United States. The nuclear material in question is smaller than a football.

Allison (2004: 9–11)

the barriers to entry in terms of getting hold of materials and competence required to use them remain significant (see web link 10.20).

What can we conclude about the terrorist threat posed by radical Muslim groups? The question is not easy; no doubt people in Western metropolitan areas such as London, New York or Madrid will be more worried about the threat than many others, and understandably so. On the one hand, the threat is not an overriding, existential menace to the states and civil societies of the world; on the other hand, the threat is real and must be taken seriously. The International Institute of Strategic Studies (IISS) recently said that 'groups and others inspired by bin Laden still pose a clear threat to public security and a challenge to law-enforcement and intelligence agencies. Al-Qaeda may be increasingly dependent on local groups and subject to dispersing impulses, but it remains a viable transnational terrorist organisation' (IISS 2004: 1).

Let us turn to the third question in Box 10.1: the theoretical challenge posed by the issue of international terrorism. On first impression, existing theories of IR would appear to be well suited to deal with international terrorism. It is a security threat, and security problems are at the heart of the realist approach. Liberals can identify terrorist groups as a set of non-state actors that substantially influence the international agenda. IPE theorists can study the political economy of international terror. In short, existing approaches would appear to be able to handle the issue very well. However, a closer look reveals another picture. Realism is focused on security threats *between states*. Non-state actors, such as international terrorist groups, often tend to be ignored by realists, because compared with states they are considered insignificant. One outspoken realist, Colin Gray, simply says that transnational terrorism is 'pretty small beer' (see Box 10.5.) Assessment of terrorist threats clearly depends upon one's perspective.

According to one commentator, this realist view explains why the Bush administration was slow to react in spite of warnings before 11 September 2001. Condoleezza Rice and other top members of the administration are realists. Rice's understanding of international relations 'is state-centric. Her policy ends are filtered through national self-interests. Her privileged means are military. And her self-understanding of world events is demarcated by a

> | **Box 10.5** | International terrorism: a realist view |
> | --- | --- |
>
> . . . it seems improbable that transnational actors such as al-Qaeda will shape the (in)security environment for decades to come. Compared with the unpleasantness in Indo-Pakistani relations, the ambition of China to be sovereign throughout maritime east Asia, and the determination of Russia to regain positions of authority by the imperial marches lost in 1991, transnational terrorism is pretty small beer. Geopolitics, not transnationalisms (including 'civilizations'), shapes the mainstream of historical events.
>
> Gray (2002: 231)

clear division between international and domestic realms' (Klarevas 2004: 21). Furthermore, when realists react to the terrorist threat, they have a tendency to *territorialize* it. That is, given their focus on interstate relations, realists are compelled to believe that international terrorist groups 'can flourish only with some significant measure of official state acquiescence, if not necessarily state sponsorship' (Gray 2002: 231).

In other words, realists tend to translate the terrorist threat into a threat from another state; and some of them tend to think that the response to such threat must be by way of military force. However, there is no necessary link between a realist view of the world and a commitment to the 'war on terror'. John Mearsheimer is a well-known realist. He argues that:

what the United States wants to do is not rely too heavily on military force—in part, because the target doesn't lend itself to military attack, but more importantly, because using military force in the Arab and Islamic world is just going to generate more resentment against us and cause the rise of more terrorists and give people cause to support these terrorists. So I'd privilege diplomacy much more than military force in this war, and I think the Bush administration would be wise if it moved more towards diplomacy and less towards force.

(Mearsheimer interview: 2002, http://globetrotter.berkeley.edu/people2/Mearsheimer)

Liberals, by contrast, appreciate non-state actors. Therefore, they are more ready to accept that international terrorist groups claim priority on the international agenda. At the same time, liberals are more ready to emphasize the need for international cooperation in facing the terrorist threat. Joseph Nye says that 'the best response to transnational terrorist networks is networks of cooperating government agencies' (Nye 2003: 65). He may certainly be right; yet the remark also discloses a liberal leaning towards problem-solving via cooperation.

In sum, both realist and liberal approaches can provide important insights in the analysis of international terrorism. Each perspective also tends to 'shape' the issue so that it fits into the particular theoretical point of view. As IR analysts, we need to evaluate the relative merits of each approach. As indicated, this evaluation is only possible if we also assess the larger question of the character and magnitude of the terrorist threat.

The Environment

Environmental topics have appeared more and more frequently on the international agenda over the past three decades. An increasing number of people, at least in Western countries, believe that human economic and social activity is taking place in a way that threatens the environment. In the past fifty years, more people have been added to the world's population than in all previous millennia of human existence. A vastly increasing global population pursuing higher standards of living is a potential threat to the environment.

Food production is an example of that. World food supply has grown faster than the global population over the past forty years. But the supply is unevenly distributed; there is a huge food surplus in the developed countries in the West and substantial shortages in many poor countries. Where food is scarce, people will often over-exploit the land in order to squeeze out of it what they can; that can lead to deforestation and desertification. Where food is abundant there may still be environmental problems due to the use of pesticides, the depletion of scarce water resources and the energy input required for high productivity agriculture.

Industrial mass production threatens the depletion of scarce resources of raw materials and energy. Local problems of environmental degradation have international ramifications. Air pollution does not stop at borders; acid rain from France, for example, threatens people, groundwater, fish in lakes, and forests, not only in France but also in neighbouring European countries. The production of CFC (chlorofluorocarbon) gases, used for refrigeration, air conditioning, solvents and other industrial products, is a major threat to the ozone layer, the gaseous mantle which protects the earth from the ultraviolet rays of the sun. CFC interacts chemically with the ozone layer so as to deplete it. Carbon dioxide and other chemical compounds lock in heat close to the surface of the earth and thereby produce global warming, the so-called greenhouse effect. Global warming means severe air pollution and rising sea levels, a potential threat to perhaps half of the world's population which lives in coastal areas.

If international security and global economics are the two major traditional issue areas in world politics, some scholars now claim that the environment has emerged as the third major issue area (Porter and Brown 1996: 1). The United Nations created a Conference on the Human Environment which convened for the first time in Stockholm in 1972. The grand meeting in Rio in 1992, the occasion of the UN Conference on Environment and Development, was the first global environmental summit in world history (see web link 10.29).

How serious is the problem of environmental degradation? We do not know precisely, because any assessment will have to rest on uncertain estimates and a number of disputable assumptions about future developments. One side in this debate is taken up by 'modernists' who believe that continued improvement in scientific knowledge and in our technological competence will enhance our capability to protect the environment. In other words,

> **Box 10.6**   **The environment issue**
>
> More than twice as many people inhabit the earth today as when the post-war era began. Indeed, more people have been added to the world's population in the past five decades than in all the previous millennia of human existence . . . Developing countries already have 78 per cent of the people in the world; as much as 94 per cent of the current increase is also taking place in these countries . . .
>
> Evidence has accumulated of widespread ecological degradation resulting from human activity: soils losing fertility or being eroded, overgrazed grasslands, desertification, dwindling fisheries, disappearing species, shrinking forests, polluted air and water. These have been joined by the newer problems of climate change and ozone depletion.
>
> Commission on Global Governance (1995: 25–9)

we shall continue to improve our skills and techniques of producing and consuming in environment-friendly ways. For example, emissions of CFC-gases are being cut down; industrial production requires less input of scarce raw materials than before; more food is grown in ecologically sustainable ways (see for example Simon and Kahn 1984; Lomborg 2001).

The other side in the debate is taken up by 'ecoradicals' who think that the ecosystem has a limited carrying capacity. Such a limit 'defines how large a species population can become before it overuses the resources available in the ecosystem' (Hughes 1991: 410). 'Ecoradicals' believe that human societies on earth are moving dangerously closer to the limits of the planet's carrying capacity; they also think that there are no simple technological fixes that can take care of the problem. Therefore, many 'ecoradicals' call for strict population control and dramatic change in modern lifestyles towards a more environment-friendly, less consumption-oriented and waste-producing way of life (Hughes 1991: 409; see also World Commission on Environment and Development, 1987 (The Brundtland Report)) (see web links 10.30 and 10.35).

Let us turn to the second question mentioned in Box 10.1: the consequences of the environment issue for the core problems in IR. In which ways can environment problems increase international conflict? A current example is the dispute over water resources in the Middle East. Water conflicts in the Middle East are not a new issue at all; they have been present in the area for a long time. The region is extremely arid and conflicts over water date back to the seventh century BC. Today this issue is part of the Arab–Israeli conflict. The relatively small Jordan river basin is shared by Syria, Lebanon, Israel and Jordan; there are not many other sources of water. The Arab League attempted to divert the Jordan away from Israel in the early 1960s; that was one of the major factors in the war between Israel and the Arabs in 1967 which Israel won. More than a third of Israel's current water supplies come from territories occupied since the 1967 war. If a permanent peace in the area is going to be built it will have to be based, at least in part, on a resolution of the conflict over water (Gleick 1993; Lowi 1993). Water in the Middle East is a clear example of how environmental scarcity can exacerbate interstate conflict.

Box 10.7	The environment issue: main positions in the debate

'MODERNISTS'

Environment not a serious problem. Progress in knowledge and technology will enable us to protect the environment.

A modernist statement:

'More people and increased income produce problems in the short run. These problems present opportunity, and prompt the search for solutions. In a free society, solutions are eventually found, though many people fail along the way at cost to themselves. In the long run the new developments leave us better off than if the problems had not arisen.'

Myers and Simon (1994: 65)

'ECORADICALS'

Environment a very serious problem. Drastic change of lifestyles plus population control to promote sustainable development is necessary.

An ecoradical statement:

'[O]nly a thoroughgoing ecocentric Green political theory is capable of providing the kind of comprehensive framework we need to usher in a lasting resolution to the ecological crisis . . . an ecocentric polity would be one in which there is a democratic state legislature (which is part of a multilevelled decision-making structure that makes it less powerful than the existing nation state and more responsive to the political determinations of local, regional, and international democratic decision-making bodies); a greater dispersal of political and economic power both within and between communities; a far more extensive range of macro-controls on market activity; and the flowering of an ecocentric emancipatory culture.'

Eckersley (1992: 179, 185)

As some of the previous chapters indicate, the classical focus of IR is on international conflict, and particularly war between states. Some scholars argue, however, that the typical violent conflict stemming from environment problems is not interstate, but intrastate—i.e. within countries. A research project led by Thomas Homer-Dixon argues that environmental scarcity involves persistent, low-intensity conflict that may not lead to dramatic confrontations, but can wear down governments (Homer-Dixon 1995: 178). For example, it can cause urban migration and unrest, decreased economic productivity, ethnic conflicts and so on. Homer-Dixon argues, in a more speculative vein, that 'countries experiencing chronic internal conflict because of environmental stress will probably either fragment or become more authoritarian . . . Authoritarian regimes may be inclined to launch attacks against other countries to divert popular attention from internal stresses' (1995: 179). Environmental scarcity demonstrates the connection between international conflict and domestic conflict and that is where environmentalist IR scholars focus their analysis.

But environmental problems can also put pressures on states to engage in greater international cooperation. The reason is that environmental degradation can be said to make up a special kind of 'threat' which is a threat not to states but to humanity itself. It is a threat to the 'global commons'—i.e. the oceans, the seas, the ozone layer and the climate system, which are a life support system for humankind as a whole. Consequently, some IR scholars see a need for global cooperation in order to face that threat.

Environmental problems have in fact encouraged international cooperation in recent years. International regimes (see Chapter 4) have been set up in a number of specific areas to address various environment issues, including acid rain; ozone depletion; whaling; toxic waste trade; Antarctic environment; global warming; and biodiversity loss (see Porter et al. 2000). The ozone regime is one of the more prominent examples of international cooperation on the environment. It contains an international agreement to cut back and eventually phase out the production of CFCs and thus aims to reverse the damage to the ozone layer which has occurred in recent decades. Several other regimes, by contrast, have been less promising because of the lack of sufficient commitment and tangible cooperation from participating countries (see Haas et al. 1993). In sum, the environment issue can involve international conflict over scarce resources, such as water, as well as international cooperation to preserve the global commons, such as the ozone regime. It is not possible to predict whether collaboration or discord will prevail because that depends on a number of different, unforeseen circumstances.

It remains to address the third item in Box 10.1: the nature of the theoretical challenge posed by the environment issue. Does the issue demand new approaches and concepts or can it be explained by traditional approaches? Many of the questions raised by the environment issue can be comfortably tackled by traditional approaches. For realists, the environment issue is merely one more explainable source of conflict between states which can be added to an already long list. For liberals, the environment adds one more issue, albeit a very important one, to the agenda of international cooperation and regime formation. For IPE scholars, the environment can be accounted for as an aspect of the global economy. In short, the traditional approaches take us a long way in dealing with the environment issue.

However, some aspects of that issue sit uncomfortably with the traditional approaches. Domestic social and political conflict is one such aspect; the environment cuts across the dividing line between domestic politics and international politics in ways not taken sufficiently into account by the traditional approaches' focus on international relations (Hurrell 1995). IR environmentalist scholars argue that it is necessary to get beyond the traditional focus on states, because so many other actors are important when it comes to the environment: e.g., transnational corporations, NGOs, consumers and so on. Yet it is possible to argue, in reply, that liberals and IPE theorists are used to dealing with domestic conflict and with many different types of actors.

Box 10.8	Environment, cooperation and conflict

Environment as a source of *interstate* conflict: e.g. water in the Middle East

Environment as a source of *intrastate* conflict: e.g. soil erosion; population growth; migration

Environmental pollution and degradation as a *special hazard* requiring international cooperation: e.g. regimes to preserve the global commons

We made a distinction earlier between 'modernists' and 'ecoradicals'. It is the 'ecoradical' position which challenges traditional IR approaches. 'Ecoradicals' call for dramatic changes in lifestyles, including very significant changes in economic and political organization. They criticize arguments, such as the Brundtland Report, which call for environment protection within a framework of sustainable growth. 'Ecoradicals' find that this is 'not a call for abandoning the race, but for changing the running technique' (Sachs 1993: 10). For them, real sustainability means abandoning industrial mass production and reverting to some form of de-industrialized society (Lee 1993). Behind such extreme ideas lies a world-view profoundly different from the 'modernist', anthropocentric view that is dominant in Western secular thinking—i.e. that man is above nature. This point is also dominant in Judaeo-Christian thinking; i.e. in Genesis (see Box 10.9) man is commanded to master the natural environment. The corollary of this view is that man is allowed to exploit nature in pursuit of human destiny and development. The 'ecoradical' world-view is very different; it puts equal value on humans and nature as part of one single biosystem. On this view human beings have no right to exploit nature. They have a duty to live in harmony with nature and to respect and sustain the overall ecological balance (Eckersly 1992; Goodin 1992).

'Ecoradicals' call for profound changes not only in economic but also in political organization. They argue that the state is more of a problem than a solution for environmental problems. The state is part of modern society and modern society is the cause of the environmental crisis (Carter 1993). But there is no agreement among 'ecoradicals' about the role of the state or what to put in place of the state. On the one hand, there is a recognition of the need for centralized, global political control in order to facilitate overall management of the global ecosystem. On the other hand, there is a recognition that small, self-reliant, local communities are best suited to promote non-consumerist lifestyles in ecological balance with specific local conditions (Hurrell 1995; Paterson 1996). It is clear that 'ecoradicals' repudiate the conventional view of international relations based on the state system. If we adopt the 'ecoradical' view, much traditional IR theory will have to be abandoned. International relations would take on a whole new meaning from the viewpoint of a global ecosystem mortally endangered by the arrogance of the human quest for modern living based on high levels of material well-being. If we adopt the 'modernist' view, most traditional IR theory can be retained because it is well suited to deal with collaboration and discord including conflicts arising from the environment issue.

In short, the nature of the challenge to IR posed by the environment issue depends to a large degree on one's position in the environment debate. Depending on that position, the environment issue is either one additional item on an agenda which can comfortably

---

Box 10.9   A Judaeo-Christian view

Then God said, 'Let us make man in our image, after our likeness; and let them have dominion over the fish of the sea, and over the birds of the air, and over the cattle, and over all the earth, and over every creeping thing that creeps upon the earth'.

Genesis, Book 1, Verse 26; extract from *The Oxford Annotated Bible* (1962)

be managed by traditional approaches, or it is a very special issue which requires us to reconstruct our entire way of thinking about international relations.

Gender

Gender issues have received increasing attention in many areas of the social sciences in recent decades. The starting-point for introducing gender to IR is often the debate about basic inequalities between men and women and the consequences of such inequalities for world politics. For example, a recent book on global gender issues (Peterson and Runyan 1993; 1999) argues that compared with men, women are a disadvantaged group in the world. Women own about 1 per cent of the world's property and make up less than 5 per cent of the heads of state and cabinet ministers. Women put in about 60 per cent of all working hours, but they only take home 10 per cent of all income. Women also account for 60 per cent of all illiterates and about (together with their children) 80 per cent of all refugees.

Peterson and Runyan emphasize that these dramatic differences have nothing to do with objective differences between men and women. Very few educated Westerners would argue that men are naturally brighter, wiser and better suited for high-paid jobs than women. They claim that the differences have to do with gender inequality. Gender 'refers to socially learned behaviour and expectations that distinguish between masculinity and femininity' (Peterson and Runyan 1993: 5). The argument is that we presently live in a gendered world in which values associated with 'masculinity' (e.g. rationality, activity, strength) are assigned higher value and status than values associated with 'femininity' (e.g. emotionality, passivity, weakness).

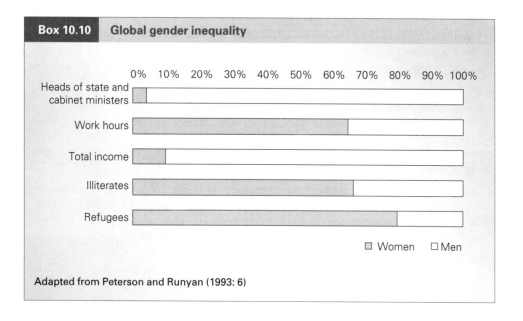

Box 10.10   Global gender inequality

Adapted from Peterson and Runyan (1993: 6)

This amounts to a gender hierarchy: a system of power in which men are privileged over women (see web link 10.38).

Peterson and Runyan go on to argue that most statistical and other indicators of development conceal the unequal position of women. Growth rates, the gross national product per capita, unemployment rates and so on reveal little about the position of women. A gender-sensitive focus on world politics seeks to bring such gender inequalities into the open, to demonstrate empirically the subordinate positions of women and to explain how the working of the international political and economic system 'reproduces' an underprivileged position for women. For example, Peterson and Runyan point out that much work done by men is visible and paid, while much work done by women is invisible and unpaid. Other studies suggest that economic development policies of 'structural adjustment' adopted by the IMF and the World Bank and changes in the international division of labour contribute to an increased 'feminization of poverty' (True 1996: 219). Low-paid, strenuous work in export processing zones in the developing world, sex-tourism and migrant domestic labour are examples of how developments in the international economy involve the exploitation of women. Different forms of gender inequality and discrimination can be found in advanced industrial societies even after many decades of high rates of participation of women in the workforce.

Box 10.11   Women and unpaid work

Much work in society goes unrecognized and unvalued—work in the household and in the community. And most of it is done by women. *Human Development Report 1995* estimated that, in addition to the $23 trillion in recorded world output in 1993, household and community work accounts for another $16 trillion. And women contribute $11 trillion of this invisible output.

In most countries women do more work than men. In Japan women's work burden is about 7% higher than men's, in Austria 11% and in Italy 28% higher. Women in developing countries tend to carry an even larger share of the workload than those in industrial countries—on average about 13% higher than men's share, in rural areas 20% higher. In rural Kenya women do 35% more work than men. In some countries women's work burden is extreme. Indian women work 69 hours a week, while men work 59. Nepalese women work about 77 hours, men 56.

United Nations Development Programme (UNDP) (1996: 15–16)

Box 10.12   Gender dichotomies

Conquering nature, digging out her treasure and secrets . . . these are familiar and currently deadly refrains. The identification of nature as female is not an accident but a historical development that is visible in justifications by elites for territorial and intellectual expansion . . . The gendered dichotomies of culture–nature, subject–object, exploiter–exploited, agency–passivity, and leader–follower are reproduced in the process and justification of exploiting human mothers and 'mother nature'.

Peterson and Runyan (1993: 40)

Feminist IR scholars also argue that the way many conventional IR scholars approach the study of world politics discloses gendered thinking. According to radical feminists, the realist idea of security based on the military defence of states in an international anarchy is a masculinist way of thinking which conceals the continued existence of a gender hierarchy in world politics: i.e. protection from an outside threat is also protection of a domestic jurisdiction which insures a persisting subordination of women (Sylvester 1994).

In sum, a gender-sensitive perspective on IR investigates the inferior position of women in the international political and economic system and analyses how our current ways of thinking about IR tend to disguise as well as to reproduce a gender hierarchy.

Let us turn to the second question in Box 10.1: what are the consequences of the gender issue for core problems in IR? Feminist IR scholars argue that war and peace, conflict and cooperation, are gendered activities, and they believe that a research focus which reveals that fact will provide fresh insights. On the one hand, the military and indeed most activities connected with war and conflict and the conduct of foreign policy are conducted by men and take place in a universe dominated by male values. Nancy McGlen and Meredith Sarkess (1993) have studied the small group of women working close to the top in the US Departments of State and Defense. They point out that women are rarely 'insiders' in those institutions. Foreign policy and military policy is largely a male preserve.

On the other hand, women do play crucial roles in many activities related to war and conflict, and feminist IR scholars show that those roles can be revealed if we care to look for them (see web link 10.41). Women are there as diplomatic wives, as workers for defence contractors, as prostitutes serving military bases, as civilian victims of wars and particularly as refugees (Enloe 1990). In other words, war is not an activity reserved for men or confined to men. Rather, war is a gendered activity with specific, frequently subordinate, positions for women. Yet the dominant ideology sees men as 'Just Warriors' and women as the 'Beautiful Souls' who are being protected (Ehlstain 1987). Feminist scholars argue that this ideology 'keeps women and men from questioning the essential purpose and the negative effects of war, militarization, and violence on their own and other's lives' (Peterson and Runyan 1993: 91).

According to some scholars, gender inequality is in itself a source of conflict. Population analysts argue that a high level of inequality between men and women, particularly inequality of masculine and feminine roles, leads to a faster rate of population growth. This is because there is 'a strong inverse correlation between the adult female literacy rate and the total fertility rate' (Kennedy 1993: 341). In other words, women in poverty without any education marry early, have little knowledge of contraceptives and give birth to a large number of children. Paul Kennedy argues that the population explosion will perhaps be the biggest challenge in the coming century. Successfully confronting that challenge will require a change in gender roles, because 'a change in the status of women would significantly reduce population growth in the developing world' (Kennedy 1993: 342) (see web links 10.44 and 10.45).

We saw in Chapter 2 that the academic discipline of IR was founded around the time of the First World War for the purpose of promoting international peace and cooperation. Yet the discipline has not paid much attention to women's movements for peace and cooperation.

Feminist scholars have tried to change that. For example, Amy Swerdlow argues that the activities of the Women Strike for Peace (WSP) movement in the US in the early 1960s persuaded President Kennedy of the urgent need for a nuclear arms control treaty with the Soviet Union (Swerdlow 1990). Cynthia Enloe argues that the withdrawal of Russian mothers' support for the Soviet army as a result of the war in Afghanistan contributed to the delegitimation of the Communist regime and so helped end the Cold War (Enloe 1994).

We turn now to the third question in Box 10.1, concerning the nature of the theoretical challenge posed by the gender issue. When we look at the gender debate, we can identify a number (see for example Steans 1998) of feminist theories that challenge mainstream IR in different ways. The three major theoretical approaches to gender are: liberal feminism; Marxist/socialist feminism; and radical feminism.

Liberal feminism has equal rights for men and women as its major concern. In Chapter 4 we emphasized that the core concern of liberalism is the freedom and happiness of individual human beings. Liberal feminists point out that basic liberal rights of life, liberty and property have not been extended in equal measure to women. Mary Wollstonecraft wrote *Vindication of the Rights of Woman* in 1792 (see web link 10.39), arguing that women should have the same access as men to economic opportunities and to education (see Steans 1998: 16–18). Contemporary liberal feminists want women to be more active in world politics, to eliminate unequal access to power and influence of men and women, and thus to achieve equal rights for men and women (Tong 1989; Eisenstein 1983; Gatens 1989). Robert Keohane has argued in favour of an alliance between neoliberal republicanism and liberal feminism. He finds that such theory can help examine international relations 'from below'; i.e. from the standpoint of those that have been excluded from power. Furthermore, according to Keohane, such a theory of IR 'could help articulate an institutional vision of international relations—a network view, emphasizing how institutions could promote lateral co-operation among organized entities, states or otherwise' (Keohane 1989b: 248). Yet some feminist scholars are worried by the prospect of such an alliance; they fear that it would involve the subordination of a gender approach to an established mainstream theory which seeks to mould the gender view according to its own priorities (Zalewski 1993: 13–32).

Marxist feminism ascribes the inferior position of women to the economic, social and political structures of the capitalist system. One of the earliest detailed analyses that posits that connection is *The Origins of the Family, Private Property and the State* by Friedrich Engels, close friend of Karl Marx, written in 1884. Engels noted how capitalism established a division between productive work in the factory and 'invisible' work in the private sphere, at home. Men took care of the productive, paid work in the factory while women were at home, taking care of the unpaid, 'invisible' work. This reduced women to second-class citizens. Marxist feminists note how women in the contemporary labour market are mostly in low-paid, low-status jobs. They argue that the only road to equal treatment of women is an overthrow of the capitalist system (Barrett 1980; Tong 1989; Landry and Maclean 1993). Socialist feminism attempts to combine the insights of Marxist feminism with an analysis of patriarchy—i.e. a male-centred and male-dominated household. The oppression of women is seen to follow inevitably from the dual systems of capitalism and patriarchy (Mitchell 1977). Capitalism is the oppressive mode of production; patriarchy is the oppressive mode of reproduction (Steans 1998: 21). Marxist/socialist feminism thus focuses on the ways in which capitalism and patriarchy place women in an underprivileged position. This focus can be connected with IPE theory inspired by Marxism. From the analysis of economic exploitation based on class it is relatively easy to include gender (and race) in the inquiry.

In sum, we can find some common ground between liberal feminism and the liberal tradition in IR, and between Marxist/socialist feminism and the Marxist tradition in IPE. The remaining feminist approach, radical feminism, rejects any such cooperation. Radical feminists want to develop a more genuine and independent feminist analysis that can entirely avoid subordinating gender to traditional IR agendas (Peterson and Runyan 1999; Daly 1979). Only then will it be possible to undertake the theoretical and practical steps necessary to fully develop a gender-sensitive analysis of international relations. We cannot lay out and investigate such an analysis in the present context; we can only sketch the direction it is supposed to take (Peterson and Runyan 1999).

Core concepts of IR, such as violent conflict, security, power and sovereignty, would have to be redefined. For example, violent conflict is not only international; it must include both domestic violence against women and structural violence against women, i.e. the oppression and hardship that women suffer from political and economic structures that subject them to unequal positions. Such aspects of violence demand a concept of security that is radically different from the traditional concept. New theories will be needed that locate gender hierarchies and the question of women's rights and status at the constitutive core. Most probably that will involve a significant downgrading of an autonomous discipline of IR. The gender focus will thus open IR up to a broader tradition of social theory concerned with studies of social power and human emancipation. Finally, gender studies in IR would encourage or even necessitate a methodological move away from the positivism that has been closely connected with neorealism and neoliberalism, towards some of the post-positivist positions introduced in the previous chapter.

Sovereignty

Sovereignty is an international institution, meaning a set of rules that states play by. The rules constitute and regulate the external independence and the domestic authority of states. It is perhaps somewhat surprising to see 'sovereignty' listed among the non-traditional issues in IR. After all, from the beginning the discipline has had the analysis of relations between *sovereign* states as one of its central preoccupations. So what could possibly make sovereignty a 'new issue'? One answer is that the institution of sovereignty is developing and changing in ways not sufficiently foreseen by the traditional approaches. There has been a tendency for many IR scholars, especially realists, to consider sovereignty as a given which, once established, does not change. This assumption has probably never been strictly true. But today there is more reason to question it.

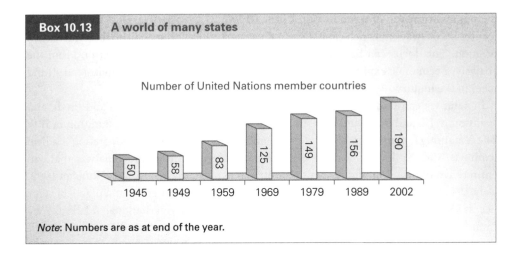

Box 10.13   A world of many states

Number of United Nations member countries

1945	1949	1959	1969	1979	1989	2002
50	58	83	125	149	156	190

Note: Numbers are as at end of the year.

What are the changes that are sparking a new debate about sovereignty? Recall that sovereignty means that a state enjoys political independence from other states. The government has supreme authority to give and enforce the law within its territory. States are juridically equal under international law. In particular, 'No state or group of states has the right to intervene, directly or indirectly, for any reason whatever, in the internal or external affairs of any other state' (UN Declaration of Principles of International Law, 1970). In other words, sovereign governments have a right to control their own territory and to be independent of all other states. Many scholars still think of sovereignty in that way as a basic institution of international society (James 1986).

But a growing number of scholars consider this view to be outdated. These latter authors argue that sovereignty is increasingly challenged from several sides. First, global market forces more easily penetrate borders and affect national economies in unprecedented ways (see web link 10.57): environmental concerns; global communication systems; nuclear weapons; terrorism; the drug trade; all of these and much else are examples of activities and forces that reach across borders and call into question older notions of autonomous sovereign states in full control of their territories (Camilleri and Falk 1992; Lapidoth 1992; Elkins 1995) (see web links 10.50 and 10.51).

Second, the development of norms concerning international protection of human rights and humanitarian law are seen to infringe sovereignty because they challenge the principle of non-intervention—i.e. the right of states to govern their citizens free from outside interference. Several UN General Secretaries have argued in favour of a move away from the norm of non-intervention. In 1991, Javier Perez de Cuellar stated that all nations had a responsibility to live up to the UN Charter requirements concerning human rights and democracy. Failure to do so, he indicated, could provoke UN intervention. In 1992, Boutros Boutros-Ghali claimed that 'the time of absolute and exclusive sovereignty . . . has passed. Its theory was never matched by reality' (quoted from Helman and Ratner 1992–3: 10).

Finally, there is the core area of warfare and control of the means of violence. On the one hand, states are no longer in exclusive control of the means of violence in their domestic jurisdiction. In the United States, for example, expenditures for private security forces are now more than double the amount spent on public police forces (*The Economist*, 19–25 April 1997: 21–3). That is of course legal. But if it was illegal it probably could not be entirely prevented. On the other hand, in weak states the order provided by the government may only extend to some parts but not to all parts of the country; in other areas, dissident groups often control significant territory (see web link 10.58).

In sum, if sovereignty means that governments must actually be in control within their own territory then there is reason to doubt the efficacy and extent of their sovereignty. Some authors think that these developments may even spell an 'end of sovereignty'—at least in the sense that state sovereignty tells us less and less about how states actually function and what type of constraints they really face (Camilleri and Falk 1992). Yet this observation fails to appreciate that sovereignty is an *institution* based on *norms* and there has rarely been a time when those norms have not been challenged or disobeyed by somebody. It must also be stressed that we continue to live in a world of sovereign states. There are no rival forms of political organization which seriously challenge state sovereignty. The sovereign state has out-competed a large number of rival forms of political organization since its first establishment in Europe three or four centuries ago (Tilly 1992). Sovereign statehood also remains very popular around the world. The number of sovereign states has increased more than threefold since 1945. Many ethno-political groups would like to form their own state; Kurds and Palestinians are only two well-known examples from a much larger number of cases (Gurr and Harff 1994).

Finally, new challenges to the state, such as an increasingly internationalized economy, must be seen in context of the state's increased capacities for response. States can exploit modern science and technology as much as anyone. They have been doing just that for centuries. Technological developments have enhanced the state's capacity for surplus extraction, regulation and surveillance. Some scholars argue that the capacity of states to regulate and control their societies has increased over time rather than declined (Krasner 1993). In other words, even if there are challenges to sovereignty as noted above, in the past sovereignty has usually responded and remained a strong and prominent institution (see Box 10.14). We therefore find the 'end of sovereignty' thesis to be somewhat misleading. Sovereignty still remains a supremely important institution of world politics.

Let us recall the second question in Box 10.1: what are the consequences of the foregoing challenges to sovereignty for core problems in IR? It is not possible to address all aspects of this question here. We shall investigate changes in the institution of sovereignty and the consequences of such changes for conflict and cooperation. Talking about change avoids two pitfalls: one is the static view of some traditional approaches (especially neorealism) where sovereignty remains a fixed given: another is the 'endism' view in which all change is taken to mean the demise of sovereignty.

We shall argue that state sovereignty has become a more diversified institution over time as it has encompassed the entire world (Sørensen 1999). Some changes in sovereignty have led to new forms of cooperation among the developed democracies in the North. Other changes have led to new forms of conflict in weak states in the South (Jackson 1990; Sørensen 1997). New forms of cooperation among sovereign states in the North have been

---

Box 10.14   Sovereignty under pressure?

CHALLENGES TO SOVEREIGNTY:

1. Global market forces; environmental concerns; global communication; nuclear weapons; terrorism; drug trade

2. Human rights and humanitarian law

3. Domestic monopoly of violence challenged: terrorism, etc.

ARE STATES THEN WEAKER?

Yes: They face new constraints on sovereignty.

No: They have increased capacities and no rivals exist.

---

pushed by economic globalization which makes it more difficult and costly for countries to control economic developments within their own borders. To resort to isolation—i.e. to shut off the country from outside influence (autarky)—is hardly a way out. In an increasingly interdependent world, isolation is not good for national welfare as demonstrated by North Korea and a few other countries. Globalization obliges advanced states to cooperate with others for mutual benefit; the industrialized democracies reap considerable welfare benefits from globalization. Closer cooperation means that states allow other states to participate in regulating certain mutually beneficial activities within their borders. Each cooperating state does that in return for a similar influence on other states. One scholar has argued that this means sovereignty is becoming 'less a territorially defined barrier than a bargaining resource for a politics characterized by complex transnational networks' (Keohane 1995: 252).

Such forms of cooperation commonly take place among the developed OECD countries but it is the members of the European Union that have gone farthest in that direction. The EU has autonomous authority in certain agreed areas, which has consequences for the sovereignty of participating states. In some areas the EU is able to make binding rules for its members, e.g. matters concerning the Single Market. States involved in that form of concentrated cooperation can be called postmodern states. They are different from modern, Westphalian states in that sovereignty is no longer exclusively vested in the state.[1]

This intense form of cooperation is not anticipated by neorealist and neoliberal approaches. Relations between EU members are not characterized by anarchy and self-help as claimed by neorealists. There is an element of 'authority, administration, and law' in EU relations, words that neorealists exclusively reserve for the analysis of domestic politics (Waltz 1979). EU cooperation has also gone further than the linkages foreseen by republican and interdependence liberalism. EU states are not merely liberal democracies

---

[1] Formally, states retain the freedom of choice: they can opt out of cooperation. But apart from a few special cases, using that possibility would have disastrously negative consequences for the standard of living. See also Keohane (1995: 253).

Box 10.15	New forms of sovereignty and cooperation

Sovereignty changes due to more intense cooperation: countries bargain about influence on each other's internal affairs.

EU members have taken this cooperation farthest: the EU can make binding rules for its members in some areas.

The EU is a special kind of tightly knit security and welfare community: violent conflict among members is out of the question.

that share common moral values; there is an integrated polity that exists beyond the sovereignty of member states. There is not merely economic interdependence; there is an integrated economic space which is no longer based on purely national economies. In such a context, the use of military force to solve conflicts is out of the question. The EU is a special kind of security and welfare community which is not a new state but is substantially more than standard forms of interstate cooperation. The argument is summarized in Box 10.15.

We turn to the Third World to take a closer look at the sovereignty of its weak states and the distinctive patterns of conflict which that involves. These weak states originally were European colonies that achieved sovereignty as a result of decolonization. That process created a new type of 'quasi-state' in the international system which is unable to play by the full set of rules set up by the developed countries (Jackson 1990). Such states have fragile or ineffective political institutions that can claim little or no legitimacy from the population. There is also usually a lack of national unity and most often the economy is poor and underdeveloped. As a consequence, such weak states are not able to stand on their own feet in the international system.

The traditional assumptions of sovereignty do not apply to such weak states. They need special, preferential treatment from the developed world, for example in the form of economic aid. For such states the international system is not one of anarchy and self-help—as argued by neorealists. It is rather a political order which supports the survival of weak states. These states are at best marginal players in the international system. They are often obliged to take what they can get from the richer and stronger countries.

In addition to being vulnerable and dependent externally, weak states have often been incapable of creating domestic order. In extreme cases this has led to a more or less complete breakdown of domestic order, i.e. 'failed states', such as Somalia, Rwanda, Liberia and Sudan. That is the domestic background for humanitarian intervention: i.e. attempts by the UN to intervene in order to safeguard the population (Zartman 1995; Weiss and Collins 1996). In short, the external dependency and internal disorder of weak states has provoked some basic changes in the sovereignty game.

This brief discussion has by no means exhausted the issue. What we do hope to have demonstrated is that it is more accurate to speak of 'changes in sovereignty' than to speak of the 'end of sovereignty'. The changes taking place do not necessarily mean the demise of sovereignty but that does not make them any less important. What they do seem to indicate is important alterations in the nature of independent statehood—both by postmodern states

Box 10.16	Weak states and new forms of conflict

Sovereignty changes with decolonization: Weak states become independent but they are unable to take care of themselves.

The international system supports the survival of weak states. In regard to such states international order is often combined with domestic anarchy.

State failure may lead to humanitarian intervention. That challenges the sovereignty principle of non-intervention.

in the North and by weak states in the South. We further explore some of the most important of these changes in the next section.

Let us recall the third question in Box 10.1. We believe that the analysis of sovereignty does not require wholly new approaches to IR. What it does call for is further development of existing approaches and abandonment of a view of sovereignty as a fixed and unchanging institution. The fact is: sovereignty is a historical and thus an evolving institution. Changes in the institution of sovereignty should be a high priority on the research agenda of IR. There are indications that this is happening. Neorealists have started investigating state sovereignty in a longer historical perspective as well as the concept itself (Krasner 1988; 1993; 1999). Neoliberals are examining how complex interdependence changes sovereignty (Keohane 1995). Scholars working from an International Society perspective are exploring the historical diversity of the institution of state sovereignty (Jackson 1999; Sørensen 1999). Several of the alternative approaches discussed in Chapter 9 also take an active interest in sovereignty (see for example Biersteker and Weber 1996).

Changes in Statehood and New Security Challenges

We emphasized in Chapter 1 that states are historical institutions and we briefly traced the development from city-states and empires to the Christian commonwealth of medieval Europe and finally to the modern state. The modern state, it was also argued in Chapter 1, is usually theorized as a valuable place. It provides, or seeks to provide, security, freedom, order, justice and welfare for the population. Most conventional IR theories, including realism, liberalism and International Society, adopt this view of the state. That is to say, they asume states are valuable institutions. They are not overly concerned with what happens inside states, their *domestic* developments. Their attention is focused on the outside, on the *international* realm, the relations between states.

Many scholars think that this one-sided focus on international relations of states is inadequate today (Sørensen 2001; 2004; Rosecrance 1999; Holsti 1996). That is because the 'modern state' concept fails to indicate how statehood has developed since the mid-twentieth century. Just as the institution of sovereignty has changed so has the substance of the state. And the changes have important implications for the international relations of states, including the way in which these states face problems of security, freedom and welfare for the population. On this view, change in statehood is a new issue of great importance; it challenges the conventional ways of theorizing about the international relations of states.

In order to trace how states have changed it is necessary to identify the basic features of the concept of the modern state as it existed in the mid-twentieth century. That creates a 'baseline model' against which recent developments can be characterized. What is the substance of the modern state—i.e. what is the content of actual, empirical statehood? We can think of it in terms of three different dimensions: the government; the nation; and the economy. The core characteristics of the modern state are set forth in Box 10.17.

The concept of the modern state corresponds to the picture of the state in conventional theories of IR. The modern state is understood to be a valuable place that provides for the good life of its citizens, including their security, their freedom and their welfare. The defence of the realm from external threat and the upholding of domestic order via police and courts provides for security. Freedom is achieved through democratic institutions and a political order based on civil and political rights and liberties. Welfare can be provided by the resources produced in the national economy.

To the extent that this is an accurate picture of current statehood, the conventional theories have no problems. They can proceed to focus on the international relations of states on the assumption that all is well on the domestic front: the modern state actually provides for the good life for its citizens. But states are historical institutions: they are open to change. The modern state emerged from a very long process of development that took place between the seventeenth and twentieth centuries. It came to full maturity in the developed world around the mid-twentieth century. Since then it has not stood still, of course. Changes in

Box 10.17	The modern state
Government	A centralized system of democratic rule, based on administrative, policing and military organizations, sanctioned by a legal order, claiming a monopoly of the legitimate use of force, within a defined territory.
Nation	A people within a territory making up a community of citizens (with political, social and economic rights) and a community of sentiment (based on linguistic, cultural and historical bonds). Nationhood involves a high level of cohesion that binds nation and state together.
Economy	A segregated and self-sustained national economy that comprises the necessary sectors for its reproduction and growth. The major part of economic activity takes place within independent countries.

statehood continue to take place. Nobody can know where they will eventually lead. But it is possible to theorize about those changes. In this section we shall review the main elements of the theory that statehood is undergoing important change.

Some of those changes were discussed earlier. In Chapter 8, we reviewed arguments about how economic globalization was changing the economic basis of states. There are two economic globalization arguments: one is 'more of the same', meaning a higher level of economic intercourse across borders; the other is a 'qualitative shift' towards an integrated world economy. Both processes are taking place, but the latter is most important here. If it is valid, it means that transnational corporations increasingly organize production chains across borders, on a regional and global basis. Most of US manufacturing is now taking place outside of the United States, at foreign production sites that are linked to or integrated with US companies. Production by transnationals outside their home countries exceeds world trade. There is also a globalization trend in the financial sector; instead of purely national financial systems a globally integrated financial market is emerging. So, according to the 'qualitative shift' argument, we must conclude that the economies of the advanced states are no longer aptly described as 'segregated national economies'; the 'national' economy is part of a larger world economy which it is much more difficult for the single state—even if it is a large state—to control.

According to the theory of changing statehood, significant changes are also under way at the political level. In the section on sovereignty in this chapter, we noted the intense cooperation between the members of the EU; in some areas the EU can now make binding rules for its members. Such forms of supranational cooperation are beginning to emerge in other contexts as well, for example in the WTO. Increasingly, governance is changing away from its confinement to the context of national governments towards multilevel governance in several interlocked arenas overlapping each other. The participants are not merely governments and traditional international organizations, but also non-governmental organizations and other non-state actors. Some of that multilevel governance reflects a more intense conventional cooperation between independent states; and some of it reflects a more profound transformation towards supranational governance. To the degree that the latter is happening, modern statehood will be significantly changed.

What about nationhood, the national community? According to the theory of changing statehood, important changes are taking place here also. *Citizen rights* used to be exclusively granted by the state, but other organizations are now active in this area. In the UN system, a set of universal *human* rights have been legally instituted. In some world regions, notably Europe, close cooperation has led to *common* rights for citizens of different countries. Citizens of the European Union enjoy some common rights in all member states, including right of employment and residence and political rights of voting in local and European elections. In Scotland, Northern Italy, Quebec, Spain and elsewhere movements for greater autonomy have emerged; some even seek secession from their respective states.

According to the theory of changing statehood, the community of sentiment appears to be undergoing transformation as well. There appear to be two major developments in different directions. One trend is towards a common civic identity for the Western political order, the core of which is political democracy, individual rights and an economy based on the market and private property (Deudney and Ikenberry 1999). The other trend is towards fragmentation along ethnic, national and religious fault lines which disclose a narrower and more exclusive conception of community (Castells 1998) (see web links 10.54 and 10.64). These changes together would appear to indicate a significant transformation of the modern state. However, the changes are still under way and nobody can be sure where the present process of change is taking us. That is the reason for suggesting the label of 'the postmodern state'. As an ideal type, the postmodern state contains the features shown in Box 10.18.

This change in statehood is a challenge to conventional IR theory because the core problems of the discipline—war and peace, conflict and cooperation—play out in new and unexpected ways. A good example is the 'security dilemma'. Among modern states security must be obtained under conditions of anarchy: states coexist in an international 'state of nature', 'having their weapons pointing, and their eyes fixed on one another' (Hobbes 1946: 101). A world of postmodern states would eliminate this traditional security dilemma. Postmodern states cooperate in far more intense ways. International anarchy is increasingly replaced by authority. Violent conflict is out of the question. These countries are liberal democracies; their level of cooperation through international institutions is very high; they are highly interdependent, both in economic and other areas. And they are developing a common civic identity.

But the changed situation also creates new challenges to postmodern states. The first challenge concerns the definition of 'security'. In the modern state, national security meant defence of the realm: of the national polity, of the national economy, of the nation. Postmodern states, however, are much more integrated with each other; the substance of state is not neatly confined within territorial borders. The economies are deeply integrated across borders; the national polititical systems are parts of a complex multilevel governance; collective identities are projected away from the nation and are no longer linked to the sociopolitical cohesion and thus to the strength of the state. Therefore, the standard way of protecting the state—by strengthening the 'hard shell' (Herz 1950) behind which the good life can be pursued—is no longer a feasible security strategy. And because postmodern statehood does not simply involve the amalgamation of states to larger units, the

Box 10.18	The postmodern state
Government	Multilevel governance in several interlocked arenas overlapping each other. Governance in context of supranational, international, transgovernmental and transnational relations.
Nation	Supranational elements in nationhood, both with respect to the 'community of citizens' and the 'community of sentiment'. Collective loyalties increasingly projected away from the state.
Economy	'Deep integration': major part of economic activity is embedded in cross-border networks. The 'national' economy is much less self-sustained than it used to be.

hard shell cannot be established at any higher level either. The objects of security therefore remain suspended in a space that is not easily territorially demarcated and confined. That is a challenge to all conventional security strategies, because they are predicated upon such demarcated and confined spaces as their objects of security.

A very significant and shocking instance of postmodern insecurity was the terrorist attacks on New York and Washington on 11 September 2001. They clearly revealed the extreme vulnerability of open societies. There is a peculiar security dilemma here: how to create sufficient protection of open societies without shutting down or even reducing their openness. Openness requires freedom of movement, speech, organization and behaviour in general, within constitutional limits. Sufficient protection, however, requires surveillance, undercover intelligence, control of the behaviour and movements of civilians, the citizens. This dilemma is not entirely new of course; it was present during the Cold War also. But it has become much more pertinent after 11 September.

There is another important type of state in the present international system which challenges IR theory because it is neither modern nor postmodern: the weak states of the Third World. These states are unable to provide the political goods that we normally expect from states. There is a decided lack of security, freedom, welfare, justice and order in these states. Most importantly, the state is frequently a significant source of threat to the population, instead of a source of protection and security. Therefore, the basic security problem in weak states is domestic violent conflict and in many cases the state itself is actively taking part in the conflict against large groups of the population. In Rwanda, for example, the mass murder of an entire ethnic group of several hundred thousand people was organized by the state which was under the control of a rival ethnic group.

We cannot offer a detailed treatment of weak statehood (see Sørensen 2001; Jackson 1990). The important point here is: both weak and postmodern states disclose security dilemmas that are markedly different from the classical security dilemma of modern statehood. So in order to understand the most important security challenges facing states, analysis of their external relations is not enough. It is also necessary to look inside states, at their domestic developments. 'Domestic' and 'international' are tied closely together and each significantly affects the other. In order to understand the most important security challenges in the present international system, the transformation of statehood will have to be incorporated in the analysis.

Let us recall the third question in Box 10.1: in what way do these insights challenge conventional IR theories (for a comprehensive discussion, see Sørensen 2001)? The theory of changing statehood challenges the neorealist way of looking at security through the strengthening of the 'hard shell' of the state from external threat. The idea that 'domestic' and 'international' can be sharply separated is also put into question by the dynamic interplay between 'domestic' and 'international' which lies behind the theory of changing statehood.

To sum up: the study of international relations has tended to insulate itself from the study of domestic politics. Traditional IR theory operates on the assumption that sovereign states promote the 'good life' for their citizens. Both postmodern states and weak states present a significant challenge to that view. They suggest that the conventional divorce between the 'international' and the 'domestic' in IR theory should be brought to an end.

Conclusion

We have looked at five issues in IR and discussed their implications for IR theory. The nature of the challenge to IR posed by these issues depends on one's valuation of what is actually at stake. Radical views demand radical solutions. A radical feminist analysis of IR will demand substantial changes of both core concepts and theories in IR. A radical view of the environment issue demands that we reconsider our whole way of thinking about IR.

These radical interpretations point away from traditional IR approaches, but the conceptual and theoretical directions taken are not at all the same. That brings us back to a point made in Chapter 2 about the three main factors which influence IR thinking. The first is changes in the real world which keep throwing up new issues, such as those taken up in this chapter. The second is debates between IR scholars both within and between different traditions. Such debates help us come to a decision about the challenge posed by different issues and what the consequences will be for the discipline. The third element is the influence of other areas of scholarship, especially debates about methodology in a broad sense. We shall see in Chapter 11 how reflections on methodologies help point IR in new directions.

The joint shaping of IR thinking by these three main factors is an ongoing process. There is no end station where scholars can sit back and proclaim that IR thinking is finally developed to perfection. History does not stand still. Intellectual inquiry does not stop. There are always new issues to confront, new methods to apply, and new insights to discover. There are always new generations of scholars inquiring into them. Scholars are not architects working on buildings that will one day be finished. There is no one blueprint. There are several: some plans are abandoned; others are adopted. Scholars are more like travellers with different maps and open-ended tickets. A textbook such as this one is a sort of unfinished travelogue of IR. We know where the journey began and we know about the main stations visited so far. But we are less certain about where IR will go from here because old and new travellers will continue the debate about the best direction to take and the proper places to visit on the way. Some readers of this book might eventually take IR to destinations that we have never heard of.

 KEY POINTS

- An 'issue' in IR is a topic which is considered to be important. The proponents often argue that the issue has received too little attention so far. Non-traditional issues involve both values and theory.
- International terrorism has revived the spectre of physical security threats to states and societies in the OECD world. It is not an overriding, existential menace, but it is a clear threat to public security that must be taken seriously.

- The environment problem is one of several important issues. How serious is the problem of environmental degradation? 'Modernists' believe that continued improvement in human knowledge will enhance our ability to protect and safeguard the environment for future generations. 'Ecoradicals' think that there are no simple technological fixes that can take care of the problem. They want revolutionary changes towards environment-friendly lifestyles.

- Gender is another important issue. A gender focus on world politics seeks to bring inequalities between men and women into the open, to demonstrate the subordinate positions of women, and to explain how the international political and economic system helps reproduce the underprivileged position of women. Radical feminists want to develop an autonomous feminist discipline that addresses the gender issue in a way which avoids subordinating it under traditional analytical agendas.

- Sovereignty is an international institution, meaning a set of rules that states play by. There is a renewed debate about sovereignty in IR. That is because of the challenges to sovereignty by a number of recent developments. It is probably more fruitful to analyse changes in sovereignty than to speak of the 'end of sovereignty'. Changes in sovereignty are connected with new forms of cooperation among the developed democracies in the North and new forms of conflict in weak states in the South. This calls for further development of existing approaches to IR rather than wholly new theories.

- The theory of changing statehood identifies two types of state different from the modern state: the postmodern state and the weak state of the Third World. Each of these types challenges the neorealist way of looking at security through the strengthening of the 'hard shell' of the state from external threat. The idea that 'domestic' and 'international' can be sharply separated is also put into question by the dynamic interplay between 'domestic' and 'international' which lies behind the theory of changing statehood. Traditional IR theory operates on the assumption that sovereign states promote the 'good life' for their citizens. Both postmodern states and weak states present a significant challenge to that view. They suggest that the conventional divorce between the 'international' and the 'domestic' in IR theory should be brought to an end.

- The nature of the challenge to IR posed by these issues depends on one's valuation of what is at stake. A radical view of the environment issue demands that we reconsider our whole way of thinking about IR. A radical feminist analysis of IR will demand wholesale changes of both core concepts and theories in IR. Many scholars who study the non-traditional issues are less radical and more prone to operate within existing traditions in IR.

 QUESTIONS

- Should international terrorism be the top issue on the international agenda? Why or why not?

- How serious is the problem of environmental degradation? What are the consequences for IR?

- Is gender inequality a relevant new issue in IR? Why or why not?

- What does it mean that sovereignty is an institution? Outline the important changes in the institution of sovereignty and discuss the consequences for patterns of conflict and cooperation.

- Outline the characteristics of the postmodern state. How does it challenge traditional thinking about IR?

- Should the 'international' and the 'domestic' always be studied together or should we prefer to uphold conventional IR theory's focus on the 'international'?

- Does the arrival of 'new issues' in IR mean that the discipline will have to be fundamentally changed and some or all of the established ways of thinking will have to be discarded? Why or why not?

GUIDE TO FURTHER READING

Cerny, P. G. (1990). *The Changing Architecture of Politics: Structure, Agency and the Future of the State.* London: Sage.

Diehl, P. F. and Gleditsch, N. P. (eds) (2000). *Environmental Conflict. An Anthology.* Boulder: Westview Press.

Eckersly, R. (2004). *The Green State: Rethinking Democracy and Sovereignty.* Cambridge, Mass.: MIT Press.

Ehlstain, J. B. (1987). *Women and War.* New York: Basic Books.

Enloe, C. (2004). *The Curious Feminist: Searching for Women in a New Age of Empire.* Berkeley: University of California Press.

Goodin, R. E. (1992). *Green Political Theory.* Cambridge: Polity.

Jackson, R. (1990). *Quasi-States: Sovereignty, International Relations and the Third World.* Cambridge: Cambridge University Press.

——(ed.) (1999). 'Sovereignty at the Millennium', *Political Studies*, Special Issue, 47/3: 423–30.

Krasner, S. D. (1999). *Sovereignty: Organized Hypocrisy.* Princeton: Princeton University Press.

Lomborg, B. (2001). *The Sceptical Environmentalist.* Cambridge: Cambridge University Press.

Pearlstein, R. M. (2004). *Fatal Future? Transnational Terrorism and the New Global Disorder.* Austin: University of Texas Press.

Peterson, V. S. and Runyan, A. S. (1999). *Global Gender Issues*, 2nd edn. Boulder: Westview Press.

Porter, G., Brown, J., and Chasek, P. (2000). *Global Environmental Politics.* Boulder: Westview Press.

Schmid, A. P. (2005). 'Terrorism and Human Rights: A Perspective from the United Nations', *Terrorism and Political Violence*, 17: 25–35.

Sørensen, G. (2004). *The Transformation of the State: Beyond the Myth of Retreat.* London and New York: Palgrave Macmillan.

Steans, J. (1998). *Gender and International Relations.* Cambridge: Polity.

WEB LINKS

 Web links mentioned in the chapter plus additional links can be found on
the Online Resource Centre that accompanies this book.

www.oxfordtextbooks.co.uk/orc/jackson_sorensen3e/

CHAPTER 11

Methodological Debates

▌ Summary

Some of the most important IR questions are methodological in nature. Self-consciousness about concepts and terminology was first emphasized in the 1950s and 1960s by the behavioural movement in political science. IR scholars, particularly American scholars, began to apply social scientific or 'positivist' methods to international relations. That prompted a reaction on the part of defenders of traditional or 'classical' approaches which emphasized history, philosophy and law. Several other social science-inspired methodologies were later adopted, such as structural analysis. Positivist methodologies, in turn, provoked some post-positivist approaches, including critical theory, postmodernism and normative theory. All these methodological approaches are elaborate and complicated and each one displays internal disagreements among its advocates. We can only touch on the basics of each. The chapter concludes with a discussion of a fundamental division between IR scholars who think that objective methods can be used to give scientific explanations of international relations and IR scholars who think that is impossible and that the most that IR scholarship can achieve is knowledgeable interpretations of international relations.

Methodological Debates

In most academic disciplines, including IR, there are two fundamental kinds of controversies. One kind involves debates over substantive issues: i.e. questions of fact. Examples of substantive questions include the following. What were the leading causes of the First World War? Does democracy foster peace? Does globalization hinder or help Third World development? The other kind of academic controversy involves debates over methodological issues: i.e. conceptual and philosophical questions that are involved in the way that we carry out our research. Examples of methodological issues include the following. Can IR be studied using objective scientific methods? How plausible are the main assumptions concerning the nature of political reality upon which neorealism is based? Should we accept the realist view of human nature as basically competitive or the liberal view of human nature as basically cooperative? It is also important to notice that substantive questions—including those noted above—also embody conceptual issues. What is 'war'? What are 'causes'? What constitutes 'democracy' or 'peace'? What do we mean by 'globalization' or 'development'? So methodological issues are lurking in almost everything that IR scholars study.

Methodological controversies are an indication that IR has become more of an academic discipline. Such issues became prominent in IR in the second half of the twentieth century, during which time IR became well-established in most universities. In the first half of the century IR was still a subject more than a discipline to which non-academic commentators contributed as much or more than academics. The idealist liberalism of the 1920s involved many leading writers who were not academics or were not based in university departments (see Chapter 2). Many of these commentators were politically active—i.e. they were engaged in making and publishing their arguments about problems of war and peace, freedom and progress, and the like, in the (somewhat naïve) hope that they would be acted upon by political leaders and other foreign policymakers. They were writing and publishing on those problems in an effort to help bring about a better world. They were not writing about them in order to better understand the world. They thought they already understood it perfectly well. The realist reaction to liberal idealism was not basically concerned about methodology either. The realists were preoccupied with correcting what they believed were the fundamental errors and dangers of the idealists and their ideas. The first great debate in IR between the liberal idealists and the realists was about substantive questions of war and peace.

Methodological issues became prominent in connection with the 'behavioural revolution' in American political science which occurred in the 1950s and 1960s. As indicated in Chapter 2, the second great debate between the behaviouralists and the traditionalists concerned methodological issues. The behaviouralists wanted to place IR on a foundation of 'scientific' analysis. Their arguments were particularly influential in the United States where by far the largest number of IR scholars live. The traditionalists became a minority. During most of the Cold War the methodology associated with neorealism prevailed in IR. The new attitude to methodology later came to be known as positivism—i.e. the belief that IR scholarship is an objective inquiry that is concerned with uncovering verifiable facts or regularities of world politics and is based on valid scientific research techniques (see web link 11.03). Positivist methodology was not controversial for most IR scholars at that time.

Since the end of the Cold War, however, methodological issues have returned to centre-stage in a debate between positivist and post-positivist methodologies. The IR theory most strongly attacked by post-positivists is the neorealism of Kenneth Waltz, in part because of its perceived dominance in the discipline, and in part because of its attributed weaknesses. Post-positivists find that those weaknesses are closely related to the positivist methods on which Waltz's theory is based. Post-positivists have thus opened up new and complex questions about IR methodology.

The Behavioural Revolution

In discussing any methodological approach to IR it is important to consider it on its own terms as well as those of its critics. That applies no less to the methodology of behaviouralism than to any other methodology (see web link 11.08). As indicated, beginning in the 1950s and 1960s many political scientists became persuaded by the methodology of behaviouralism. What is the behavioural persuasion in political science? Fundamentally it is a scholarly conviction that there can be a cumulative science of IR of increasing sophistication, precision, parsimony, and predictive and explanatory power. Behaviouralists believe in the unity of science: that social science is not fundamentally different from natural science; that the same analytical methods—including quantitative methods—can be applied in both areas. The behaviouralists also believe in interdisciplinary studies among the social sciences.

Political behaviouralists thus seek to apply scientific attitudes and methods to the inter-disciplinary study of politics. That leads them to hold conceptions of political life which are amenable to scientific research. They ask: how should we look at politics in order to study it scientifically? The answer: focus on human behaviour as it involves politics and government. According to Heinz Eulau (1963: 21), one of the leading advocates of the approach, 'behavioralism investigates acts, attitudes, preferences, and expectations of people in political contexts'. The key elements of the approach are: the individual person is the basic unit of analysis; politics is seen as only one aspect of the behaviour of people; and political behaviour is to be examined at different levels of analysis, including the social level, the cultural level and the personal level. A core focus of the study of political behaviour is the roles of people in social structures. The central social structure is the political system.

The behavioural approach does not reject the analysis of groups or organizations or states. It only rejects any conception of these entities as more than structures of roles occupied by individual people. To speak of 'the state' is to employ a metaphor rather than to speak accurately and empirically. 'Groups, organizations, or nations have no independent status apart from the conduct of the individuals who are related by behaving towards each other in certain ways . . . institutions do not and cannot exist physically apart from the persons who inhabit

> **BOX 11.1**   Easton's political behaviour tenets and credo
>
> 1. Regularities: There are discoverable uniformities in political behavior . . . [which] can be expressed in generalizations or theories with explanatory and predictive value.
> 2. Verification: The validity of such generalizations must be tested empirically.
> 3. Techniques: Rigorous means are necessary to analyze political behavior.
> 4. Quantification: Measurement and quantification are necessary for precision.
> 5. Values: Ethical evaluation and empirical explanation should be kept analytically separate.
> 6. Systematization: Theory and research are intertwined elements of a coherent body of knowledge.
> 7. Pure Science: Explanation of political behavior logically precedes its application in public policy.
> 8. Integration: Political science theory and research is closely tied to other social sciences.
>
> Easton (1965: 7)

them' (Eulau 1963: 14–15). However, some political behaviouralists do employ nation-states as units of analysis. David Easton (1971: 136–41) adopted that perspective in order to conceptualize the domestic political process. Morton Kaplan (1964) adopted a similar perspective in developing a 'systems theory' of IR. States were conceptualized as political systems (Easton 1961: 137): centres of political decision-making in which governments carried out decisions or policies (outputs) in response to demands and supports (inputs). Another way of putting that was to say that politics was about 'who gets what, when, how' (Lasswell 1958). The 'who' could be groups including states as well as individuals.

As indicated, the behavioural approach seeks to transform political science into a true social science by emulating the scientific ideals of the natural sciences. The aim is to collect data which can lead to scientific explanation. That requires scientific methodology and a scientific attitude on the part of the researcher. Then it becomes possible to provide empirical explanations of political behaviour: to determine 'why people behave politically as they do, and why, as a result, political processes and systems function as they do' (Eulau 1963: 25). The scientific study of political behaviour requires rigorous research designs, precise methods of analysis, reliable instruments of analysis, suitable criteria of validation and so forth, all of which are necessary to produce a body of verifiable empirical propositions—i.e. empirical theory—about politics. 'Theory' is not a static body of knowledge; rather, it is a 'tool on the road to knowledge' in the same way that 'facts are not knowledge but only the raw materials' that have to be transformed via 'theorizing activity' into propositions that can be 'tested in the process of empirical research'.

Advocates of the behavioural approach emphasize the correct scientific attitude of mind. The tenets of the behavioural approach were summarized by David Easton, one of its leading advocates (see Box 11.1). Easton (1971: 129–41) attempted to supply a model or analytical framework of a political system which could be employed to frame hypotheses and carry out empirical research into political behaviour. The state was the locus of political decision-making for society. Politics was a ceaseless interactive process of inputs > decisions > outputs > feedback > inputs, etc. That process could be studied empirically and objectively.

Easton was not concerned with the problem of applying his version of the behavioural approach to international relations. But systems theory was further developed by scholars who were interested in doing this. One prominent early example was the approach of Morton Kaplan. Kaplan (1964: 21–53) employed his 'systems analysis' to distinguish different kinds of international state systems: the 'balance of power' system; the loose bipolar system; the tight bipolar system; the universal international system; the hierarchical international system; and the Unit Veto International System. The various international state systems are characterized by different patterns of behaviour, according to Kaplan. Box 11.2 summarizes how Kaplan thinks that states act in a 'balance of power' system. These actions of states lead to certain patterns of alignment in the system which the theory can predict.

If state behaviour does not arise as expected that would have to be investigated and explained further, and if it were more than merely an isolated exception the theory might have to be revised accordingly. In that way empirical research would promote the refinement and improvement of empirical theory. Kaplan (1964: 25) raises the question: was there any time in the history of the 'balance of power' system 'during which the fluctuations in alignments did not shift as the theory predicts'? If there are instances of that happening then 'some other factors must be located to account for the pattern'.

In other words, other variables may have intervened to bring that about. Then it becomes an important research question to investigate and hopefully discover what these intervening variables are and to revise the systems theory accordingly. What we have in this example, and what we find in the behavioural approach to IR and political science more generally, is a specification of independent variables, dependent variables and intervening variables, all of which are involved in explaining domestic and international politics.

BOX 11.2   Kaplan's balance of power system

1. Act to increase capabilities but negotiate rather than fight.

2. Fight rather than pass up an opportunity to increase capabilities.

3. Stop fighting rather than eliminate an essential national actor.

4. Act to oppose any coalition or single actor which tends to assume a position of predominance with respect to the rest of the system.

5. Act to constrain actors who subscribe to supranational organizing principles.

6. Permit defeated or constrained essential national actors to re-enter the system as acceptable role partners . . . Treat all essential actors as acceptable role partners.

Kaplan (1964: 21–53)

Kaplan's systems analysis of IR proved to be flawed in a number of ways. It did not satisfy very well and in some respects not at all Kenneth Waltz's test for empirical theories outlined in Box 11.6 (p. 290). Perhaps the most obvious difficulty is: the rules are both descriptive (empirical) and prescriptive (normative). They indicate not only how state actors in the 'balance of power system' are predicted to behave but also how they ought to behave. But if they do behave in that way there is no need to tell them that that is how they ought to behave. Prescriptions are intended to get people to act in ways that otherwise they might not and perhaps would not act. David Hume, a leading eighteenth-century empiricist philosopher, famously said 'one cannot derive an ought from an is'. In other words, a fact is not a norm and to confuse facts and norms is a fatal error. The propositions of Box 11.2 display that confusion. Kaplan's 'balance of power' system probably received its most severe criticism from Waltz (1979: 50–9) who found it does not provide a satisfactory empirical theory of IR.

As a summary of the discussion so far it is useful to introduce a few preliminary criticisms of the political behaviouralists. Heinz Eulau (1963: 111) claimed that the behavioural persuasion in politics 'aspires to the status of science' and he remarked: 'I take it for granted that a science of politics is both possible and desirable.' Taking that for granted is a controversial issue because it cannot be taken for granted; the validity of that claim must be demonstrated. Most political scientists who sympathize with political behavioralism now recognize that. As a result the philosophy of science which seeks to clarify the grounds for justifying such claims has become far more important in IR. Eulau also claimed that behavioural science develops slowly piece by piece: 'An empirical science is built by the slow, modest, and piecemeal cumulation of theory, methods and data . . . [it is] a gradual "expansion of knowledge"' (Eulau 1963: 116). That can be questioned on the behaviouralists' own empirical grounds. The most one can say is: it remains to be seen whether such an expansion of knowledge will be achieved in political science, including IR.

David Easton (1961: 137) provides a parsimonious 'formula' for a systems analysis of political life: inputs > political process > outputs. The problem with that concept is: human beings rarely conform very well to simple models of their behaviour. They usually disagree, often profoundly, about what is expected or required of them. The model makes reference to 'values' but they are often highly contested. Some of the most fundamental political disagreements and conflicts concern values. Easton's model largely overlooks political disagreement, discord or conflict. And it provides no insight or guidance for resolving disputes or managing conflict.

Finally, Morton Kaplan (1964: 3) acknowledges the reality of historical change in international relations which behavioural research must come to grips with. But he is convinced that history is a 'laboratory' and that the variables that cause change can be brought within a scientific framework of analysis. Unfortunately, historical change is extremely difficult to pin down, explain and predict. How many political scientists correctly predicted the end of the Cold War and its outcome? Are such sceptical observations merely limitations on the scientific enterprise at the present time, an indication that there is still some distance to travel, or are they a fatal blow to the enterprise? That question has not been answered to everybody's satisfaction.

The logic, language and ethos of empirical analysis that the behaviouralists introduced into political science in the 1950s and 1960s have become widespread since that time. Behaviouralism rests upon an assumption that there is an external or 'real' world of international relations that operates in accordance with its own objective regularities or patterns that can be detected and explained in terms of empirical models and theories. For academics who are seeking objective knowledge, that is a very appealing assumption to work with. It probably enhanced the self-esteem and perhaps also the status of political science and IR—especially in the United States where scientific culture is deeper than anywhere else. Since the 1950s this academic orientation has come to be known as positivism. Today, as a result of the behavioural revolution, a large number of IR scholars, particularly in the United States, are positivists. But like any other methodology, positivism is open to criticism and it never was universally followed by IR scholars, even in the United States.

The Classical Approach Strikes Back

The first important reaction to the behavioural revolution in IR was that of the traditional or 'classical' approach that the behaviouralists initially targeted as the main obstacle to creating a truly scientific discipline of political inquiry (see web links 11.10 and 11.11). The most articulate and sophisticated defender of the classical approach is Hedley Bull (1969; 1972; 1975). This section examines his most important arguments in defence of that approach.

Unlike behaviouralism and its positivist successors, and some of their post-positivist critics, the classical approach to IR does not have an explicit methodology in the scientific meaning of the term. It does not frame hypotheses and test them. It does not employ a formal apparatus of research: i.e. models, statistical techniques, analytical tools, etc. It does

---

BOX 11.3	**The traditional and the behavioural approach**

The Traditional Approach: The approach to theorizing which derives from philosophy, history and law, and that is characterized above all by explicit reliance upon the exercise of judgment and by the assumption that if we confine ourselves to strict standards of verification there is very little that can be said of international relations, that general propositions about this subject must therefore derive from a scientifically imperfect process of perception and intuition, and that these general propositions cannot be accorded more than the tentative and inconclusive status appropriate to their doubtful origin.

The Behavioralist Approach: A concern with explanatory rather than normative theory; a concern with recurring patterns rather than the single case; a concern with operational concepts that have measurable empirical reference rather than reified concepts; a concern with the conceptual frameworks; a concern for the techniques of precise data gathering, measurement and presentation.

Quoted from Finnegan (1972: 42, 52)

not gather and organize data. Instead, it has an attitude to scholarship and to some extent an ethic of scholarship. It rejects the view that there can be one correct or valid scientific analysis of international politics. It is restrained about the empirical knowledge that IR scholars can reasonably expect to develop from their research programmes. It is sceptical that there can be a cumulative science of IR of increasing sophistication, precision, parsimony, and predictive and explanatory power. Instead, it sees theories as limited by history (time) and by culture (space).

The classical approach takes the view that sound scholarship is a matter of experience in the practice or vocation of scholarship: i.e. observing, reading, inquiring, reflecting and writing about international relations. Good IR scholarship is not a matter of technical training in correct methods or models or statistical techniques. It is a matter of immersing oneself in the subject by becoming a careful, thoughtful and critical observer of world politics, both contemporary and historical. The classical approach places a premium on an inquiring mind: i.e. curiosity, discernment, judgement and so on. For Hedley Bull, the activity of research basically involves thinking an important topic under investigation through to some conclusions, however preliminary. 'Thinking is also research' was one of his favourite sayings (Holbraad 1990: 193). He dealt with big topics: international security; international order; international justice. One could deal just as well with small topics. But whether a topic is big or small the most important thing in carrying out research is not scientific methodology; it is knowledge of substance and particularly historical knowledge.

The principal elements of traditional scholarly activity are: identifying and ordering the central questions; clarifying the relevant concepts; drawing appropriate distinctions; investigating the historical evidence; and formulating a coherent argument that can comprehend it satisfactorily. The goal is to grasp or understand the substantive topic under study on its own terms. Foreign policies, for example, are intrinsically intelligible activities. They possess inherent meaning. They are not merely data that are waiting for explanation by a scientific observer. Historical or legal or moral problems of world politics cannot be translated into the terms of science without misunderstanding them. The traditional approach operates with what has subsequently come to be known as an interpretive or reflectivist attitude to scholarship. That can be distinguished from the explanatory approach of behaviouralists and other positivists. This distinction is examined at the end of the chapter.

IR is a complex humanistic field of study. According to Bull (1969), it is not a single discipline; rather, it is interdisciplinary and draws heavily on three well-established disciplines: history,

BOX 11.4   Bull on the traditional approach

The tradition of detached and disinterested study of politics is, I believe, a very delicate plant. It exists at all in relatively few countries, and even in these it has a precarious existence. Its survival depends on a form of commitment that is not political, but intellectual and academic: a commitment to inquiry as a distinct human activity, with its own morality and its own hierarchy of priorities . . .

Bull (1975: 284)

political theory or philosophy and international law. History is important because it is the only academic way to grasp the particular characteristics of states and their relations over time: all states are distinctive; they have a history and a geography all their own. Because states have distinctive histories and are located in particular places there are definite limits to our ability to generalize about state systems. History is not only the starting-point for the study of international relations, but also the necessary companion and corrective to IR theory because it is a reminder of the limits of empirical generalization in world politics.

The traditional approach is philosophical and is especially concerned with moral questions which it believes cannot be separated from political questions or legal questions: it calls for a disinterested and detached examination of the moral foundations of international politics and international law. An instance of the classical approach in this regard is evident in a typical International Society question: what is the basic ethic of the NATO Treaty? The answer is evident from the key Article 5 of the Treaty: the obligation of mutual military assistance of all members of the alliance. International law is important because it is a comprehensive body of historical and contemporary knowledge of the rules and norms of Westphalian international society. To overlook international law is to leave out a basic dimension of international relations. Box 11.3 sums up the basic differences between the behavioural and the traditional, or classical, approach.

The central characteristic of the traditional approach, according to Bull (1969), is the exercise of scholarly discernment and judgement in considering historical, legal or philosophical questions of IR. The exercise of scholarly judgement can be informed by reading history and sharpened by thinking about philosophical problems of international relations. But it is rooted in 'everyday assumptions', observation and common sense (Richardson 1990: 162). General propositions about international relations 'must derive from a scientifically imperfect process of perception or intuition' and can have only a 'tentative and inconclusive status' (Bull 1969: 20).

Classical scholars are sceptics about knowledge. They call attention to the limitations of IR scholarship. They see it is an imperfect field of study which can sometimes come up with partial answers to a question but cannot give definitive answers. There cannot be definitive answers to complex historical, legal or philosophical questions of international relations. The traditionalists are critical of overstatement and overconfidence in IR scholarship. This classical view is captured in a famous book by Herbert Butterfield (1973: 51), who was both a leading historian and a member of the 'English School' of IR: 'The historian like every other specialist is quick to over-step the bounds of his subject and elicit from history more than history can really give; and he is forever tempted to bring his stories to a conclusiveness and his judgments to a finality that are not warranted by either the materials or the processes of his research.' This scepticism about the truth claims of IR anticipates a similar post-positivist attitude discussed later in the chapter.

The classical approach emphasizes scholarly disinterestedness and detachment. It is the attitude of scholars who are committed to academic learning rather than technical or scientific expertise. In a humanistic subject, like IR, there can be no experts strictly speaking. For Bull (1972) the 'detached' or 'disinterested' attitude is not the same as a 'value-free' approach. 'There is, of course, no such thing as a "value-free" inquiry into international relations or any other social subject' (Bull 1972: 256). By political detachment Bull means being aware of one's moral and political premises, being frank about them and holding them firmly in check. Box 11.4 contains Bull's own words on IR scholarship and its limits.

It is important to emphasize that the classical approach is not the same as the approach of the interwar liberal idealists (see Chapter 2). Hedley Bull rejected liberal idealism because it was a political and ideological approach that displayed a lot of dogmatism and much naïveté. It was attempting to change the world in favour of its own political values. It was not attempting to understand the world, to make sense of the world, to make world politics more intelligible and to place IR on a more academic foundation. It was not prepared to scrutinize its own values. Although Bull did not live to see the rise of critical theory and other forms of post-positivism in IR (discussed below), the clear implication is that he would also strenuously disagree with critical theorists who believe that IR theory is intrinsically political, whether or not the theorist realizes it or acknowledges it, and that scholarship is a legitimate political engagement. Hedley Bull would probably see critical theorists as born-again idealists wanting to create a better world without making a sufficiently clearheaded and non-subjective analysis of the existing conditions of international relations.

The classical approach has come in for considerable criticism. The reason why Bull originally jumped to its defence was owing to strenuous criticism from the political behavioralists. They criticized the 'traditionalists' on several grounds: for engaging in historicism rather than empiricism (Easton 1971: 234–65); for providing idiographic (descriptive and particularistic) studies rather than nomothetic (explanatory and generalizing) studies; for being satisfied with ivory tower theory that is never tested against reality; for 'the comfortable assumption that theory is the same thing as knowledge' rather than merely being a tool. But there are some similarities too. Both approaches shared a dislike of ideology masquerading as scholarship. Although the behaviouralists were ambitious in their scientific aims and goals, they also emphasized careful and scrupulous analysis—empiricism—based on clear concepts which avoid ideological bias (see web link 11.04).

Contrary to a widely held impression, the behaviouralists were not totally critical of the classical approach. According to Eulau (1963: 9–10) it is a 'mistake' to see the behavioural persuasion as 'a revolt against the classical tradition'. Rather, it is 'a continuation of the classical tradition' because it 'represents an attempt, by modern modes of analysis, to fulfill the quest for political knowledge begun by the classical political theorists'. Eulau (1963: 32) finally adds: 'the behavioral persuasion is a continuation of the classical tradition . . . I believe the classical writers would have used . . . [behavioral technology] had it been available to them.' In believing that, however, Eulau is denying the classical approach's firm distinction between scholarship and technical or scientific expertise.

In sum, there are points of difference and points of agreement between behaviouralists and traditionalists. If, on the one hand, we stress the points of difference, we get a profound contrast between behaviouralism and traditionalism. The two approaches can be seen to hold categorically different conceptions of the world—ontology—and fundamentally different ideas of the best way to gain knowledge of the world—epistemology (see web links 11.01 and 11.02). On the other hand, if we stress the points of agreement, the two approaches are 'different ends of a continuum of scholarship rather than completely different games . . . Each type of effort can inform and enrich the other and can as well act as a check on the excesses endemic in each approach' (Finnegan 1972: 64). When the battle rages, the contenders tend to draw up their positions very sharply, emphasizing points of difference. When the smoke clears, more moderate voices on both sides often emphasize areas of agreement. As we shall see, the methodological debate in IR illustrates both positions.

Positivist Methodology in IR

Positivism is an important methodology in IR (see web links 11.05 and 11.09). A lot of research is being done using methodologies based on positivist principles. Journals such as *International Studies Quarterly*, *Journal of Conflict Resolution* and *American Political Science Review* publish many articles based on positivist methodology. There are several versions of positivism; we cannot discuss all of them. The conception of positivism presented here is that of 'moderate positivism' (Nicholson 1996a).

Positivist methodology in political science, including IR, is a legacy of behaviouralism: it employs most behaviouralist assumptions and attitudes although usually in a more sophisticated way. It views the social and political world, including the international world, as having regularities and patterns that can be explained if the correct methodology is properly applied. It is based on the same assumption of the unity of all the sciences including the social sciences. The social scientist is no different from any other scientist in this regard. It argues that observation and experience are keys to constructing and judging scientific theories. It holds that there can be an objective knowledge of the world—or at least 'a great deal of intersubjective agreement' (Nicholson 1996a: 131). It emphasizes the centrality of empirical propositions: i.e. the reasons for accepting hypotheses are evident from careful observation of reality. 'We observe events and on the basis of these observations hope to predict the consequences of actions carried out now or in the future' (Nicholson 1996a: 132).

The leading philosophy of science criteria for a good scientific (positivist) theory are summarized in Box 11.5, which is based on Vasquez (1995: 230). According to that conception, IR theories should consist of empirical propositions that are logically related and can be tested against evidence so that 'the theory as a whole is confirmed or refuted by observations' of data (Nicholson 1996a: 132).

The theory is precise: positivist theories are limited and specific. The theory is non-relativist: it holds everywhere that the specified conditions (independent variables) obtain. The kernel of positivism is its epistemology which asserts that scholars can make generalizations about the social world, including international relations, which are verifiable. That is based on empirical theories whose propositions are (or are striving to be) related in a logical way: 'some propositions imply other propositions' (Nicholson 1996a: 129). The theory is consistent with well-established knowledge in related fields of inquiry. That recollects the behaviouralist unity of the natural and social sciences. Finally, its basic

---

BOX 11.5   **Seven criteria of a good empirical theory**

1. Accurate and limited.
2. Non-relativist (universal).
3. Verifiable or falsifiable.
4. Powerful in its explanations.
5. Amenable to improvement.
6. Consistent with well-established knowledge.
7. Parsimonious.

Source: Vasquez (1995: 230)

BOX 11.6   **Is that an empirical theory? Waltz's test**

1. State the theory being tested.
2. Infer hypotheses from it.
3. Subject the hypotheses to experimental or observational tests.
4. In taking steps 2 and 3, use the definitions of terms found in the theory being tested.
5. Eliminate or control perturbing variables not included in the theory under test.
6. Devise a number of distinct and demanding tests.
7. If a test is not passed, ask whether the theory flunks completely, needs repair and restatement, or requires a narrowing of the scope of its explanatory claims.

Source: Waltz (1979: 13)

---

propositions are parsimonious: they are capable of statement in a spare and lucid fashion; the simplest theory is often the best.

Positivist approaches do not usually present themselves by waving a flag called 'positivism'. So how can we tell if a theory is scientific in positivist terms? According to Kenneth Waltz (1979: 13) whether or not an IR theory is an empirical theory—i.e. positivist—can be determined by a test involving the questions raised in Box 11.6. The test gives an indication of the most important conditions that theories in IR should be able to meet to count as scientific or empirical. Waltz recognizes that the steps in Box 11.6 are rigorous and 'laboratory-like'; therefore, they may be difficult to carry out in practice. For example, it may be difficult to eliminate non-relevant, perturbing variables in carrying out the test; after all, the real world is not a laboratory where variables can be excluded or controlled. As a second-best procedure, Waltz suggests a less rigorous procedure, summarized in Box 11.7.

Kaplan's systems theory outlined above was not only criticized by Waltz but it also inspired Waltz (1979) to furnish a theory of international politics of his own that could meet the test of Box 11.6: Waltzian neorealism. The substance of neorealism was reviewed in Chapter 3.

Waltz constructs his theory in such a way that if we can accept its assumptions, concepts and logic, certain expectations and predictions follow about behaviour and outcomes in international politics. For example, it can be predicted from the theory that states 'will engage in balancing behavior' and that such behaviour has 'a strong tendency towards balance in the system' (Waltz 1979: 128). It can be predicted, further, that 'bipolar systems' have a stronger tendency towards stability and order than 'multipolar systems'. According to Waltz's structural theory, it is not that states are motivated to create and preserve order among themselves; the independent variable is not behavioural: it is not a consequence of foreign policy. Rather, it is structural: the structure of international anarchy produces that effect. The international structure pushes states towards acting in certain ways that can be predicted by theory.

Neorealism and positivism are often equated in IR. But that equation is too narrow: positivism is broader than neorealism. According to Nicholson (1996b), there are basically two general research programmes of contemporary positivism in IR: (1) a programme of quantitative research, one important strand of which is associated with peace research; and (2) a programme of rational choice analysis, such as game theory (see web links 11.05, 11.06 and 11.07). Because positivists are seeking to establish verifiable empirical generalizations and ultimately to build empirical theory, they are inclined towards quantification, including the use of mathematical models. 'Quantification comes into play when one is trying to test theories' (Nicholson 1996b: 136). A programme of quantitative research involves explanatory analysis. The criteria and test outlined in Boxes 11.5 and 11.6 are applicable to theories based on quantitative research. A programme of rational choice is logical, rather than strictly quantitative, and has features of economic analysis: it rests on certain assumptions (actors are rational, actors seek to optimize, etc.) and logical analysis (if x then y; if demand increases, and supply remains the same, prices increase). (See Chapter 9 for a brief discussion of rational choice theory in foreign policy.)

Post-Positivist Methodology in IR

Positivism provoked a reaction in the form of several post-positivist methodologies, including critical theory, postmodernism and normative theory, all of which repudiated the scientific methods of positivism. Instead, in various ways, all these methodologies presupposed methods distinctive to human beings as creatures who must live in society with each other in order to live a human life. Post-positivist methodology rests on the proposition that people conceive, construct and constitute the worlds in which they live, including the international world, which is an entirely human arrangement. Social science is a different methodology from that of natural science. There are several versions of *post*-positivism. We can only discuss some of the most widely-adopted methodologies.

Critical Theory

This methodological approach is mainly a development of Marxist thought and could be described as neo-Marxism (see web link 11.13). It was developed by a small group of German scholars many of whom were living in exile in the United States. They were known collectively as 'the Frankfurt School' (see web links 11.14 and 11.15). In IR, critical theory is closely linked to Marxist IPE (see Chapter 7). Two leading IR critical theorists are Robert Cox (1981; 1996) and Andrew Linklater (1990; 1996). Critical theorists reject three basic postulates of positivism: an objective external reality; the subject/object distinction; and value-free social science. According to critical theorists, there is no world politics or global economics which operates in accordance with immutable social laws. The social world is a construction of time and place: the international system is a specific construction of the most powerful states. Everything that is social, including international relations, is changeable and thus historical. Since world politics are constructed rather than discovered, there is no fundamental distinction between subject (the analyst) and object (the focus of analysis).

For critical theorists, knowledge is not and cannot be neutral, either morally or politically or ideologically. All knowledge reflects the interests of the observer. Knowledge is always biased because it is produced from the social perspective of the analyst. Knowledge thus discloses an inclination—conscious or unconscious—towards certain interests, values, groups, parties, classes, nations and so on. All IR theories are biased too. Robert Cox (1981) expressed that view in a frequently quoted remark: 'Theory is always for someone and for some purpose.' Cox draws a distinction between positivist or 'problem-solving' knowledge

---

BOX 11.8   **Robert Cox on critical theory as historical utopianism**

Critical theory allows for a normative choice in favor of a social and political order different from the prevailing order, but it limits the range of choice to alternative orders which are feasible transformations of the existing world . . . Critical theory thus contains an element of utopianism in the sense that it can represent a coherent picture of an alternative order, but its utopianism is constrained by its comprehension of historical processes. It must reject improbable alternatives just as it rejects the permanency of the existing order.

Cox (1996: 90)

and critical or 'emancipatory' knowledge. Problem-solving knowledge is conservative: it seeks to know that which exists at present. It is biased towards the international status quo which is based on inequality of power and excludes many people. It cannot lead to knowledge of human progress and emancipation, which is the knowledge that critical theorists seek to provide. According to Robert Cox (1996), critical theory contains an element of historical utopianism.

Critical theory is not confined to an examination of states and the state system but focuses more widely on power and domination in the world generally. Critical theorists seek knowledge for a political purpose: to liberate humanity from the 'oppressive' structures of world politics and world economics which are controlled by hegemonic powers, particularly the capitalist United States. They seek to unmask the global domination of the rich North over the poor South. Critical theorists in this regard are almost indistinguishable from Marxist IPE scholars. Their orientation towards progressive change and their desire to use theory to help bring about such change is also reminiscent of idealism. Critical theorists are openly political: they advocate and promote their progressive (usually socialist) ideology of emancipation believing that conservative scholars and liberal scholars are defending and promoting their political values. Critical theorists thus believe that theoretical debates are basically political debates. Like the interwar idealists, critical theorists are trying to bring about the social and political revolution that their ideology proclaims. The difference is: critical theorists reject the possibility of academic detachment and objectivity, whereas the idealists were blissfully unaware of it.

Their view of knowledge as inherently political separates critical theorists from behaviouralists, from those positivists who disdain using scientific knowledge for political purposes, and from classical theorists. According to critical theorists, IR scholars cannot be detached from the subject matter they are studying because they are connected with it in many subtle and some not so subtle ways. They are part of the human world they are studying. They are involved in that world. Whether they realize it or not social scientists and social science are instruments of power. Critical theorists seek to identify the political interests that different IR theories and theorists serve. But even more than that, they seek to use their knowledge to advance what they believe is the ultimate end of all knowledge: the great goal of human emancipation from global social structures which until now have privileged a relatively small minority of the world's population at the expense of the majority. Critical IR theory can thus be understood as explicitly and avowedly revolutionary: it seeks to overthrow the existing world political and economic system.

The main problem with this outlook is the problem it poses for academic independence and the integrity of scholarly and scientific research. If 'theory is always for someone and for some purpose' how can anyone decide whether it is a good theory in purely academic terms? The value of any theory would be based on political values: does it promote my political or ideological beliefs? It would not be based on academic values: does it shed light on the world, increase our knowledge of it, and ultimately demystify it? If IR theory is really political rather than scientific or scholarly there is no neutral way to decide which theory is the best academically. If that is so there can be no truly academic disagreements and controversies. Academic debates would really be political debates in disguise. But if IR theories and all other social science theories really are political how can we justify them as academic subjects? Why should critical theory or any IR theory be taken as a statement of knowledge if it is really a statement of politics? If theory is always an expression of political interests rather than academic curiosity, political science is neither science nor scholarship: it is politics. All of that may of course be true. But if it is true it is hard to justify IR scholarship (including this book) in purely academic terms.

A moderate version of critical theory is: no knowledge is completely value-free but even when that is the case there is a difference between pure partisan politics and intellectual understanding and scientific knowledge sought by progressive IR theorists. That academic enterprise does not take place in complete isolation from or ignorance of politics, but it does attempt to come up with systematic and detached analysis. Robert Cox's work is an example of how critical theorists struggle with finding their place between these views. While he is a political advocate for radical change, he is also the author of scholarly works that are widely recognized in the academic study of IR.

Postmodernism

Postmodernism is a social theory that originated among a group of post-war French philosophers who rejected the philosophy of existentialism which was prevalent in France in the late 1940s and early 1950s. Postmodernism did not enter IR until the 1980s, however. A leading postmodern theorist in IR is Richard Ashley (1996). Like critical theorists, postmodernists seek to make scholars aware of their conceptual prisons (Vasquez 1995). The most important conceptual prison is that of modernity itself and the whole idea that modernization leads to progress and a better life for all (for this idea, see Chapter 4). Postmodernists cast doubt on the modern belief that there can be objective knowledge of social phenomena. They are critical of classical liberals who believe in 'enlightenment': e.g. Kant. They are also critical of contemporary positivists who believe in 'science': e.g. Waltz. Both Kant and Waltz are wedded to a belief in the advancement of human knowledge which postmodernists regard as erroneous and unfounded. Postmodernists see neorealism as the epitome of intellectual error and academic arrogance. Neorealism is the prime example of an intellectual prison that postmodernists see themselves breaking out of.

Postmodern IR theorists reject the notion of objective truth. They dispute the idea that there is or can be ever-expanding knowledge of the human world. Such beliefs are intellectual illusions—i.e. they are subjective beliefs, like a religious faith. The neorealists may think that they have found the truth about IR, but they are mistaken. Postmodernists pour cold water on the belief that knowledge can expand and improve, thus giving humans increasing mastery over not only the natural world but also the social world including the international system. They are deeply sceptical of the idea that institutions can be fashioned that are fair and just for all of humankind: men and women everywhere. They debunk the notion of universal human progress.

Postmodernism has been defined as 'incredulity towards metanarratives' (Lyotard 1984: xxiv). Metanarratives are accounts such as neorealism or neoliberalism that claim to have discovered the truth about the social world. Postmodernists consider such claims to be far-fetched and lacking in credibility. The great theoretical constructions of IR such as realism or liberalism are houses of cards that will fall down with the first breeze of deconstructive criticism. Postmodernists argue, for example, that neorealist claims about the unchanging anarchical structure of international politics cannot be sustained because there are no independent and impartial grounds for judging them. There are no such grounds because social science is not neutral; rather, it is historical, it is cultural, it is political and therefore biased. Every theory, including neorealism, decides for itself what counts as 'facts'. There is no neutral or impartial or independent standpoint to decide between rival empirical claims. Empirical theory is myth. In other words, there is no objective reality; everything involving human beings is subjective. Knowledge and power are intimately related; knowledge is not at all 'immune from the workings of power' (Smith 1997: 181); see Box 11.9.

Postmodernists are deconstructivists who speak of theories as 'narratives' or 'meta-narratives'. Narratives or meta-narratives are always constructed by a theorist and they are thus always contaminated by his or her standpoint and prejudices. They can thus be decon-structed: i.e. taken apart to disclose their arbitrary elements and biased intentions. The main target of postmodernist deconstruction in IR is neorealism. Here is a theory which claims that only a few elements of information about sovereign states in an anarchical international system can tell us most of the big and important things we need to know about international relations. And the theory even claims to validly explain international politics 'through all the centuries we can contemplate' (Waltz 1993: 75).

Postmodernist critiques of neorealism target the anarchical structure and ahistorical bias of the theory (Ashley 1986: 289; Walker 1993: 123). Because the theory is ahistorical it leads to a form of reification in which historically produced social structures are presented as unchangeable constraints given by nature. Emphasis is on 'continuity and repetition' (Walker 1995: 309). Individual actors are 'reduced in the last analysis to mere objects who must participate in reproducing the whole or . . . fall by the wayside of history' (Ashley 1986: 291). It follows that neorealism has big difficulties in confronting change in interna-tional relations. This discloses a poverty of theoretical imagination. Any thought about

---

BOX 11.9   Postmodernist view of knowledge and power

All power requires knowledge and all knowledge relies on and reinforces existing power relations. Thus there is no such thing as 'truth', existing outside of power. To paraphrase Foucault, how can history have a truth if truth has a history? Truth is not something external to social settings, but is instead part of them . . .

Postmodern international theorists have used this insight to examine the 'truths' of interna-tional relations to see how the concepts and knowledge-claims that dominate the discipline in fact are highly contingent on specific power relations.

Smith (1997: 181)

alternative futures remains frozen between the stark alternatives of either domestic sovereign statehood and international anarchy or the (unlikely) abolition of sovereign statehood and the creation of world government.

What is the contribution of postmodernist IR methodology? One benefit is the deflation of academic egos and conceits: scholars typically claim too much for their theories. Neorealism is a good example of that: it does not really live up to its billing; it provides less knowledge of IR than it claims to provide. Another benefit is the scepticism that postmodernism attaches to the notion of universal truths that are said to be valid for all times and places. That is typical of realism and also of much liberal idealism. Pouring cold water on academic or scientific pretensions can be a good thing.

But there is also a negative side. Why should we accept the analysis of the postmodernists if theory is always biased in some way? Why should the deconstruction be believed any more than the original construction? If every account of the social world is arbitrary and biased, then postmodernism cannot be spared: its critique can be turned upon itself. Postmodernist Richard Ashley says there is no 'positionality'—i.e. there are no stable platforms or certitudes—upon which social speech, writing, and action can be based. Yet, ironically, what makes postmodernism intelligible, including the work of Ashley, is its conformity to the basic conventions of intellectual and academic inquiry which are the foundations of all knowledge, including social knowledge. His own writing conforms to the conventions of English grammar and vocabulary, and no doubt he lives his own life as we live our lives within the compass of interpersonal standards of time, space and so on which are marked and measured by calendars, clocks, miles, kilometres, etc. There are similar conventions of international law, politics and economics. These measures and standards are some of the most fundamental elements of the modern world.

A more worrying problem is that postmodernism can deteriorate into nihilism—i.e. negativism for its own sake (see web link 11.18). Criticism can be made merely for the sake of criticism. Narratives can be taken apart with nothing to take their place. Ultimately, postmodernists can become estranged from the social and political world that they seek to understand. A world exclusively of contingency and chance (Ashley 1996), rather than choice and reason, may cease to be either intelligible or meaningful. In short, there is something about postmodernism which may appeal to nihilists. But nihilism cannot provide any foundations of knowledge because it rejects the possibility and the value of knowledge.

There is a moderate postmodernism that is premised on the notion that our ideas and theories about the world always contain elements of both subjectivity and objectivity. The subjective element is tied to our adherence to different values and concepts and the inescapable fact that each and every one of us looks out upon the world from his or her personal standpoint. The objective element is tied to the fact that we can actually agree about very substantial insights about what the real world is like. We speak the same language. We calculate in the same units of weights and measures. All that is solid does not melt into air. At the core of this middle ground is the notion of intersubjectively transmissible knowledge (Brecht 1963: 113–16). Such knowledge is bound by standards of documentation and clarity of exposition; put differently, such knowledge is compelled to demonstrate that it is not the result of wishful thinking, guesswork or fantasy; it must contain more than purely subjective valuations. Moderate postmodernism approaches the position of the constructivists, which is based on the concept of intersubjectivity.

Normative Theory

Normative IR theory is not really post-positivist; it is pre-positivist (see web links 11.24 and 11.25). Indeed, it is both modern and pre-modern: it is part of the history of political thought and it can be traced back as far as European antiquity, for example in the writings of Thucydides. Leading contemporary normative theories of IR are provided by Chris Brown (1992), Mervyn Frost (1996), Terry Nardin (1983), and Brown, Nardin and Rengger (2002). Chris Brown (1992: 3) defines the approach succinctly: 'by normative international relations theory is meant that body of work which addresses the moral dimension of international relations and the wider questions of meaning and interpretation generated by the discipline. At its most basic it addresses the ethical nature of the relations between communities/states.' International politics involves some of the most fundamental normative issues that human beings ever encounter in their lives: issues of order, of war and peace, of justice and injustice, of human rights, of intervention in state sovereignty, of environmental protection and similar ethical questions of a fundamental kind.

In many respects, though not all respects, normative theory is synonymous with the classical approach, except that it reaches farther into political theory and moral philosophy and it draws heavily on recent developments in these fields. 'Normative theory' is really another name for the political theory or the moral philosophy of international relations.

Most positivist IR scholars draw a basic distinction between empirical theory and normative theory. They see the latter as exclusively *prescriptive*. In other words, (positivist) empirical theory is a theory of facts, of what actually happens, whereas normative theory is a theory of values, of an ideal world that does not exist as such. Most normative theorists would reject that distinction as misleading. As normative theorists see it, normative theory is about both facts and values. The 'facts' of normative theory are the *existential rules*, institutions and practices which have normative content, for example, rules about the conduct of war, or about human rights. Normative theory is primarily concerned with giving a theoretical account of rules, institutions and practices which can be located in the state system at the present time or in the past. The theorist seeks to make explicit the normative issues, conflicts and dilemmas involved in the conduct of foreign policy and other international activities (see web link 11.26). In other words, normative theory is empirical in its own way. Furthermore, normative theorists point out that so-called non-normative theories are also value-based. The authors of those theories merely fail to be explicit about their normative premises and values.

Normative theorists attempt to clarify the basic moral issues of international relations. One noteworthy attempt is that of Chris Brown (1992) who summarizes the main normative controversies of world politics in terms of two rival moral outlooks which are captured by the terms 'cosmopolitanism' and 'communitarianism' (these normative problems are also taken up by International Society theory, see Chapter 5). Cosmopolitanism is a normative doctrine which focuses on individual human beings and on the whole community of humankind as the basic right- and duty-bearing units of world politics. Communitarianism is a contrasting normative doctrine which focuses on political communities, particularly nation-states, as the fundamental normative units of world politics whose rights, duties and legitimate interests have priority over all other normative categories and agencies. For Brown, a big part of contemporary normative theory is concerned with assessing these rival moral doctrines. One of the tasks of normative theory is determining which of these two important doctrines has priority and which ought to have priority. The questions are complex. Which rights do states have? Should they be allowed to possess weapons of mass destruction which are a threat to humankind? Which rights do individuals have? Do individual rights come before state rights perhaps by being inherent in human nature? Are individuals and their rights formed by states—i.e. subjects, citizens? There are no simple answers. Many theorists are content to live with the proposition that the normative conflict between cosmopolitanism and communitarianism cannot be resolved once and for all; it can merely be understood and hopefully managed in an enlightened fashion.

Brown presents what is perhaps the most widespread view of normative theory in IR at the present time. A less widespread but in some ways more fundamental attempt to interrogate the morality of individuals and the morality of political communities is set forth by Mervyn Frost (1996):

> normative theory should be directed in the first place to the question: What should I, as citizen (or we the government, or we the nation, or we the community of states) do? But finding an answer to this kind of question usually depends on finding an answer to a prior question which is quite different. This prior and more important question is about the ethical standing of the institutions within which we find ourselves (and the ethical standing of the institutions within which others find themselves).

According to Frost, if we find that states are more important than other institutions, we might conclude that in certain circumstances it is a duty of citizens to risk their lives to safeguard their state. The aim of normative theory is to sort out 'the ethical standing of institutions' in relation to each other (Frost 1996: 4).

A third approach to normative theory is linked to the International Society school (see Chapter 5) and focuses on the ethics of international law (Nardin 1983) and the ethics of statecraft (Jackson 2000). This approach addresses questions such as the following: Which groups of people qualify for recognition as sovereign states? Are the international responsibilities of all states the same or do some states have special responsibilities? Are there any conceivable circumstances under which a sovereign state's right of self-defence could be legitimately infringed? Is there any valid normative basis for denying admission to the nuclear club? Is international society responsible for providing personal security or is that an exclusively domestic responsibility of sovereign states? Is international society responsible for governing independent countries whose governments have for all intents and purposes ceased to exist? Must 'ethnic cleansing' always be condemned? Does the goal of defending or developing democracy justify military intervention and occupation of a country? Can international society reasonably expect national leaders to put their own soldiers in danger to protect human rights in foreign countries? Is there any normative basis for justifying the use of force to change international boundaries? Are there any conceivable circumstances under which global environmental protection could justifiably interfere with state sovereignty?

This third approach attempts to *theorize* the normative *practices* of states and state leaders. It emphasizes that international ethics, at the core, concern the moral choices of statespeople. Thus the answers to international normative questions, such as those listed above, are provided in the first instance by the practitioners involved. The main task of normative theory is to interrogate those answers with the aim of spelling out, clarifying and scrutinizing the framework of justification disclosed by them. This approach emphasizes that international ethics, just like ethics in any other sphere of human activity, develops within the activity itself—in this case the activity of statecraft—and is adapted to the characteristics and limits of human conduct in that sphere (Jackson 2000). According to this third approach to normative theory, scholars must assess the conduct of statespeople by the standards which are generally accepted by those same statespeople. Otherwise theory not only misjudges practices and loses touch with reality but it also misunderstands and misrepresents the moral world in which state leaders must operate and must be judged.

Normative theory rejects positivism as a flawed methodology that cannot address what normative theorists consider to be the most fundamental issues of international relations: moral decisions and dilemmas. Yet normative theory also parts company with those post-positivists who repudiate the classical tradition of political theory and moral philosophy. However, that also means that normative theory, like constructivism, is exposed to attack from both sides: it is exposed to the positivist critique that it fails to explain anything in scientific terms; and it is exposed to the postmodernist critique that it is dealing in the myths, delusions and deceptions of supposedly antiquated classical values. Normative theorists and constructivists share a common approach in focusing on intersubjective ideas and beliefs (see web links 11.21 and 11.26). But most constructivists are hoping to create a proper social science (see Chapter 6), whereas most normative theorists are content to preserve, transmit and augment the classical political theory of international relations (Brown et al. 2002; Jackson 2005).

Explaining IR versus Understanding IR

The basic methodological divide in IR concerns the nature of the social world (ontology) and the relation of our knowledge to that world (epistemology). The ontology issue is raised by the following question: is there an *objective* reality 'out there' or is the world one of experience only, i.e. a *subjective* creation of people (Oakeshott 1966)? The extreme objectivist position is purely naturalist and materialist: i.e. international relations is basically a thing, an object, out there. The extreme subjectivist position is purely idealist: i.e. international relations is basically an idea or concept that people share about how they should organize themselves and relate to each other politically; it is constituted exclusively by language, ideas and concepts.

The epistemology issue is raised by the following question: in what way can we obtain knowledge about the world? At one extreme is the notion of scientifically *explaining* the world. The task is to build a valid social science on a foundation of verifiable empirical propositions. At the other extreme is the notion of *understanding* the world. This latter task is to comprehend and interpret the substantive topic under study. According to this view, historical, legal or moral problems of world politics cannot be translated into the terms of science without misunderstanding them.

We have indicated several times above that there is both a 'confrontationist' and a 'cooperative' view of the ontological divide between objectivism and subjectivism and the epistemological divide between explaining and understanding. One extreme position is taken up by behaviouralists and some positivists who strive for scientific theory based on a view of the world as an objective reality. Another extreme position is taken up by postmodernists for whom reality is a subjective creation of people. As regards epistemology, some postmodernists find that a satisfactory interpretation of the social and political world is possible, but other postmodernists reject even that (see the remarks above, about a nihilistic tendency in postmodernism). According to some scholars, only the extreme positions are intellectually coherent. A choice has to be made between 'positivist' and 'post-positivist' methodology. The two cannot be combined, because they have 'mutually exclusive assumptions' (Smith 1997: 186) about the world of international relations.

However, other IR scholars strive to avoid the extreme positions in the methodological debate. They seek out a middle ground which avoids the stark choice between either objectivism or subjectivism, either pure explaining or pure understanding. The desire for the middle ground is contained already in Max Weber's (1964: 88) definition of 'sociology' as 'a science which attempts the *interpretive* understanding of social action in order thereby to arrive at a causal *explanation* of its course and effects'. Weber is saying that it is true that scholars must understand the world in order to carry out their research into social phenomena. He is also saying, however, that that does not prevent scholars from proceeding to frame hypotheses to test empirical theories that seek to explain social phenomena. On that view (Sørensen 1998), IR is not compelled to a cruel choice between extreme versions of positivism or post-positivism. It can proceed on a methodological middle ground between subjectivism and objectivism, and between explaining and understanding. In other words, there is not an insurmountable gulf between positivist and post-positivist methodological extremes. Instead of an 'either/or' it is a 'both/and': rather than having to choose between extremes on the two dimensions we have discussed (subjectivity versus objectivity and explaining versus understanding), it is a question of finding a place somewhere on the continuum between the extremes.

Box 11.10 gives an indication of the appropriate position of the different methodological approaches on the two dimensions. The question mark behind postmodernism reflects our doubts as regards the position of that approach on the explaining/understanding axis.

| BOX 11.10 | The methodological debate: a summary |

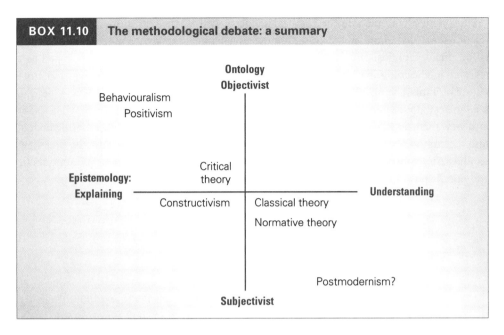

Postmodernism is 'understanding' in its critique of established theories, but it also contains a nihilistic tendency, as noted above. That creates doubts as to where the approach belongs on this axis. Nihilism is neither explaining nor understanding but, rather, is a different category. Some methodological approaches—e.g. constructivism and critical theory as well as the classical and normative approaches—are oriented more towards the middle ground than the extremes. It is noteworthy that some of the major debates within the established theoretical traditions in IR concern precisely this issue of the proper combination. The issue is at the heart of debates, for example, between classical realists and neorealists (see Chapter 3); between different currents of the International Society school (see Chapter 5); and between various schools within liberalism (see Chapter 4). This chapter has shown how the debate continues within and between the different post-positivist approaches. However we choose to view this question, there can be little doubt but that it is the most fundamental methodological issue in IR.

Conclusion

Many scholars are sceptical that international relations really lend themselves to strictly scientific inquiry. They take issue with Waltz's claim that the complex world of international relations can be squeezed into a few law-like statements about the structure of the international system and the balance of power. They would also be very concerned if rational choice theory were a basis of foreign policy (see Chapter 9) because important subjective questions that call for judgement and interpretation are left out of account.

Such critics, who include the classical scholars, believe that the study of international relations requires a humanistic kind of knowledge which emphasizes judgement, interpretation, history, philosophy and law. Other critics say that positivism is handicapped as a research methodology because it cannot come to terms with the complex and contradictory nature of human beings. There are two different ways of approaching this debate. One is to see the positions as completely incompatible, 'like two ships passing in the night'. The other is to view them as different versions of what is basically the same project of gathering insight into the complex world of international relations. Many post-positivists take the first view, emphasizing opposition instead of connection. But there are also examples of a moderate and middle position.

KEY POINTS

- Some of the most important IR questions are methodological in nature. Such issues became prominent with the 'behavioural revolution' in the 1950s and 1960s. Since the end of the Cold War, methodological issues have returned to centre-stage in a debate between positivist and post-positivist methodologies.

- The behaviouralist approach: a concern with explanatory rather than normative theory; a concern with recurring patterns rather than the single case; a concern with operational concepts that have measurable empirical reference rather than reified concepts; a concern with conceptual frameworks; a concern with techniques of precise data gathering, measurement and presentation.

- The traditional, or classical, approach: a sceptical approach that derives from philosophy, history and law, and is characterized by explicit reliance upon the exercise of discernment and judgement. Knowledge of any human subject is derived from a scientifically imperfect process of perception and intuition; generalizations about international relations are, at best, always tentative, temporary and incomplete.

- Post-positivist approaches include: critical theory; postmodernism; and normative theory. Critical theory is a development of Marxist thought; it seeks to unmask the global domination of the rich North over the poor South. Critical theory views knowledge as inherently political; social scientists and social science are instruments of power.

- Postmodernism disputes the notions of reality, of truth, of the idea that there is or can be ever-expanding knowledge of the human world. Narratives, including meta-narratives, are always constructed by a theorist and they are thus always contaminated by his or her standpoint and prejudices. Narratives can thus be deconstructed: i.e. taken apart to disclose their arbitrary elements and biased intentions.

- Normative theory attempts to clarify the basic moral issues of international relations. The main normative outlooks are cosmopolitanism and communitarianism. The questions raised by these outlooks are complex. Which rights do states have? Which rights do individuals have? Do individual rights come before state rights? International ethics also concern the moral choices of statespeople. Even more fundamentally, normative theory addresses philosophical questions concerning what are 'rights', how are 'individual rights' similar to or different from 'state rights', and so forth.

- The two basic methodological dimensions of IR are the nature of the social world (ontology) and the relation of our knowledge to that world (epistemology). The ontological dimension concerns the nature of social reality: is it an objective reality 'out there' or is it a subjective creation of people? The epistemological dimension concerns the ways in which we can obtain knowledge about the world. Can we scientifically explain it or must we instead interpretively understand it?

- There is a 'confrontationist' and a 'cooperative' view of the methodological divide. The confrontationist view sees an insurmountable gulf between positivist and post-positivist methodology. The cooperative view sees a middle ground between different approaches.

QUESTIONS

- Pick a concrete issue, such as for example the distribution of power in the world at the end of the Cold War. What are the differences between a behaviouralist and a traditional approach to that issue?

- What is the methodological difference between scientifically explaining an international phenomenon and historically interpreting an international event or episode?

- Compare the IR methodologies of Kaplan and Waltz. Which is more satisfactory?

- Summarize the main issues in the debate between positivists and post-positivists. Which side in the debate do you favour? Why?

- Identify at least two major post-positivist approaches. What are the most significant methodological similarities and differences between the approaches identified?

- What is the better way of looking at IR methodologies: as categorically different or as conceptually overlapping?

- Outline the methodological outlooks of the classical approach and normative theory. Are there any significant differences between them or are they basically the same approach?

GUIDE TO FURTHER READING

Brown, C., Nardin, T. and Rengger, N. (2002). 'Introduction', in C. Brown, T. Nardin and N. Rengger (eds), *International Relations in Political Thought*. Cambridge: Cambridge University Press.

Bull, H. (1969). 'International Theory: The Case for a Classical Approach', in K. Knorr and J. N. Rosenau (eds), *Contending Approaches to International Politics*. Princeton: Princeton University Press.

Jackson, R. (2005). *Classical and Modern Thought on International Relations: From Anarchy to Cosmopolis*. New York: Palgrave Macmillan.

Kaplan, M. (1964). *System and Process in International Politics*. New York: Wiley.

Nicholson, M. (1996a). 'The Continued Significance of Positivism?', in S. Smith, K. Booth, and M. Zalevski (1996). *International Theory: Positivism and Beyond*. Cambridge: Cambridge University Press, 128–49.

Nicholson, M. (1996b). *Causes and Consequences in International Relations*. London: Pinter.

Smith, S. (1997). 'New Approaches to International Theory', in J. Baylis and S. Smith (eds), *The Globalization of World Politics*. Oxford: Oxford University Press, 165–90.

Smith, S., Booth, K. and Zalewski, M. (eds) (1996). *International Theory: Positivism and Beyond*. Cambridge: Cambridge University Press.

WEB LINKS

Web links mentioned in the chapter plus additional links can be found on the Online Resource Centre that accompanies this book.
www.oxfordtextbooks.co.uk/orc/jackson_sorensen3e/

GLOSSARY

'anarchical society' A term used by Hedley Bull to describe the worldwide order of independent states who share common interests and values, and subject themselves to a common set of rules and institutions in dealing with each other. The concept of 'anarchical society' combines the realist claim that no world 'government' rules over sovereign states, with idealism's emphasis on the common concerns, values, rules, institutions and organizations of the international system.

behaviouralism An approach that seeks increasing precision, parsimony, and predictive and explanatory power of IR theory. Behaviouralists believe in the unity of science: that social science is not fundamentally different from natural science; that the same analytical methods—including quantitative methods—can be applied in both areas. The behaviouralists also believe in interdisciplinary studies among the social sciences.

Bretton Woods The system of international economic management, setting the rules for commercial exchange between the world's major industrial states. Allied states set up the system in the New Hampshire resort town of Bretton Woods in July 1944.

bureaucratic structures and processes approach to foreign policy A strongly empirical (evidence-based) sociological approach to foreign policy that focuses primarily on the organizational (or bureaucratic) context in which decision-making takes place. The 'bureaucratic' approach is seen by supporters to be superior to other approaches by virtue of its empirical analysis of the relationship between decision-making and organizational structure. This approach therefore emphasizes specific context over the inherent rationality of any foreign policy decision; it seeks to clarify the context-based reasons for individual foreign policies, but does not have a strong normative, prescriptive component.

classical realism A theory of IR associated with thinkers such as Thucydides, Niccolò Machiavelli and Thomas Hobbes, and with the neoclassical realist

Hans Morgenthau. They believe that the goal, the means and the uses of power are a central preoccupation of international relations, which is an arena of continuous rivalry and potential or actual conflict between states that are obliged to pursue the goals of security and survival. In comparison with neorealism, which largely ignores moral and ethical considerations in IR, classical realism has a strong normative doctrine.

cognitive approach Unlike the 'bureaucratic' and other sociological approaches, this approach focuses on the individual decision-maker, with particular attention to the psychological aspects of decision-making. Robert Jervis has studied misperception, and the construction of erroneous 'images' of others, as it pertains to these state leaders. Margaret Herman studied the personalities of dozens of government leaders, arguing that such factors as experience, political style and world-view affect the ways leaders conduct their foreign policies.

communitarianism A normative doctrine that focuses on political communities, especially nation-states, which are seen as fundamental agents and referents in world politics. According to this position, states' interests come before those of individuals or that of humanity in general.

comparative approach to foreign policy A form of policy analysis inspired by the behaviouralist movement in political science. Unlike the traditional approach to foreign-policy analysis, in which information is sought about a single country's policy, the comparative approach amasses substantial data about the content and context of many countries' foreign policies. Rather than merely prescribe action for a specific country in a specific context, the goal of the comparative approach is to develop systematic theories and explanations of the foreign-policy process in general.

cosmopolitanism A normative doctrine that focuses on individual human beings and the whole of humanity, seen as fundamental agents and referents in world politics, whose needs should come before the interests of states.

critical theory A post-positivist approach to IR influenced by Marxist thought advanced by the 'Frankfurt School'. Critical theory rejects three basic postulates of positivism: an objective external reality, the subject/object distinction and value-free social science. Critical theorists emphasize the fundamentally political nature of knowledge. They seek to liberate humanity from the conservative forces and 'oppressive' structures of hegemonic (US-dominated) world politics and global economics. Critical theorists are similar to idealists in their support for progressive change and their employment of theory to help bring about that change.

'defensive realism' According to Kenneth Waltz's theory, a 'defensive realist' recognizes that states seek power for security and survival, but striving for excessive power is counterproductive because it provokes hostile alliances by other states.

dependency theory Draws on classical Marxist analysis, but is different from classical Marxism in a basic respect. Unlike Marx, dependency theorists do not expect capitalist development to take root and unfold in the Third World in the same way that capitalism first took place in Western Europe and North America. The main aim of dependency theory is to critique the dependency form that capitalist development is seen to take in the Third World. In short, dependency theory is an attack on late capitalism. It is an effort to provide the theoretical tools by which Third World countries can defend themselves against globalizing capitalism.

economic liberalism Adam Smith (1723–90), the father of economic liberalism, believed that markets tend to expand spontaneously for the satisfaction of human needs—provided that governments do not interfere. He builds on the body of liberal ideas that are summarized in Chapter 4. These core ideas include the rational individual actor, a belief in progress and an assumption of mutual gain from free exchange. But Smith also adds some elements of his own to liberal thinking, including the key notion that the economic marketplace is the main source of progress, cooperation and prosperity. Political interference and state regulation, by contrast, is uneconomical, retrogressive and can lead to conflict.

'ecoradicals' Those who believe that environmental problems are highly serious. Dramatic changes of lifestyles plus population control are necessary in order to promote sustainable development.

emancipatory theory Seeking to counter realism, emancipatory theorists, such as Ken Booth and Andrew Linklater, argue that IR should seek to understand how men and women are prisoners of the existing state system, and how they can be liberated from the state and from the other oppressive structures of contemporary world politics, which can be reconstructed along universal solidarist lines.

'empirical' statehood Part of the external basis of a state's sovereignty; the extent to which a state fulfils its role as a substantial political-economic organization. A successful state in terms of empirical statehood has developed efficient political institutions, a solid economic basis and a substantial degree of national unity (internal popular support for the state).

epistemology The philosophical study of how one comes to 'know' something, and what is ultimately 'knowable'. One position is that the world can be 'explained', from outside, by a social-scientific test of empirical propositions. That view is particularly widespread among American IR scholars. The opposite position holds that the world can only be 'discerned', 'comprehended' and 'interpreted', from inside, by historical, legal and philosophical analysis. That view is gaining ground in the United States but is still more likely to be found among British and continental European IR scholars.

ethics of statecraft Ensuring national security and state survival is the fundamental responsibility of statecraft and the core normative doctrine of classical realism. The state is considered to be essential for the good life of its citizens. The state is thus seen as a protector of its territory, of the population, and of their distinctive and valued way of life. The national interest is the final arbiter in judging foreign policy.

'failed states' Weak states incapable of creating domestic order. State failure is a case of extreme weakness involving a more-or-less complete breakdown of domestic order. Examples are Somalia, Rwanda, Liberia and Sudan.

foreign policy The manner in which states interact with each other states, international organizations and foreign non-governmental actors (such as NGOs, corporations and terrorist organizations). Foreign policy thus includes all competitive and cooperative strategies, measures, goals, guidelines, directives, understandings, agreements, etc., through which a state conducts its international relations. By virtue of their separate international existence, all states are obliged to develop and execute foreign policy towards these other states and international organizations. Normally the key policymakers are leading government officials, namely presidents, prime ministers, foreign ministers, defence ministers, etc. Dealing with everything from the conduct of war to the regulation of imported goods, policymaking tends to involve means–end and cost–benefit analyses of realistic goals and available means to achieve them.

foreign-policy analysis Involves scrutinizing foreign policies and placing them in a broader context of academic knowledge. There are many approaches to the analysis of foreign policy, with each having different descriptive and prescriptive goals and paying attention to various dimensions (sociological, psychological, historical context, etc.) of the decision-making process. Foreign-policy analysis often involves instrumental analysis, studying the best means to reach an advisable goal; it may also include a prescriptive component, that is, making recommendations for the best course to follow.

functionalist theory of integration A theory coined by David Mitrany. He argued that greater interdependence in the form of transnational ties between countries could lead to peace. Mitrany believed, perhaps somewhat naïvely, that cooperation should be arranged by technical experts, not by politicians. The experts would devise solutions to common problems in various functional areas: transport, communication, finance, etc. Technical and economic collaboration would expand when the participants discovered the mutual benefits that could be obtained from it. When citizens saw the welfare improvements that resulted from efficient collaboration in international organizations, they would transfer their loyalty from the state to international organizations.

gender issues The starting-point for introducing gender to IR is often the debate about basic inequalities between men and women and the consequences of such inequalities for world politics. Compared with men, women are a disadvantaged group in the world. Women own about 1 per cent of the world's property and make up less than 5 per cent of the heads of state and cabinet ministers. Women put in about 60 per cent of all working hours, but they take home only 10 per cent of all income. Women also account for 60 per cent of all illiterates and about (together with their children) 80 per cent of all refugees.

globalization Globalization is the spread and intensification of economic, social and cultural relations across international borders.

'hard' revolutionism A version of revolutionism that seeks the violent destruction of the system or society of sovereign states and its replacement by a new global order based on an exclusive universalist ideology. Lenin is an example of a hard revolutionist.

hegemonic stability theory A hegemon, a dominant military and economic power, is necessary for the creation and full development of a liberal world market economy, because in the absence of such a power, liberal rules cannot be enforced around the world. That, in its simplest form, is the theory of hegemonic stability which is indebted to mercantilist thinking about politics being in charge of economics.

hegemony In IR, a concept referring to a state's power relative to that of other states. A state may be considered a hegemon if it is so powerful economically and militarily that it is a dominant influence on the domestic and foreign policies of other states. Depending on its level of power, a state may be a regional hegemon (e.g., Germany immediately prior to and during the Second World War) or a global hegemon (e.g., many agree, the United States in the late twentieth and early twenty-first centuries).

ideational view In the ideational view held by social constructivists ideas always matter. The material world is indeterminate; it needs to be interpreted. Without ideas there can be no larger context of meaning. Ideas define the meaning of material power.

imperialism The projection of power by a political entity for the purpose of territorial expansion and political and economic influence beyond its formal borders. Much of history has been marked by the expansion and demise of empires: the Roman Empire, the Mongol Empire, the British Empire and the

Ottoman Empire, to name but a few. After the Second World War, the last of the great empires (with the possible exception of the Chinese) were dissolved.

institutional liberalism This strand of liberalism picks up on earlier liberal thought about the beneficial effects of international institutions. The earlier liberal vision was one of transforming international relations from a 'jungle' of chaotic power politics to a 'zoo' of regulated and peaceful intercourse. This transformation was to be achieved through the building of international organizations, most importantly the League of Nations. Present-day institutional liberals are less optimistic than their more idealist predecessors. They do agree that international institutions can make cooperation easier and far more likely, but they do not claim that such institutions can by themselves guarantee a qualitative transformation of international relations, from a 'jungle' to a 'zoo'. Powerful states will not easily be completely constrained. However, institutional liberals do not agree with the realist view that international institutions are mere 'scraps of paper', that they are at the complete mercy of powerful states. They are of independent importance, and they can promote cooperation between states.

interdependence liberalism A branch of liberal thinking which argues that a high division of labour in the international economy increases interdependence between states, and that discourages and reduces violent conflict between states. There still remains a risk that modern states will slide back to the military option and once again enter into arms races and violent confrontations. But that is not a likely prospect. It is in the less developed countries that war now occurs, because at lower levels of economic development land continues to be the dominant factor of production, and modernization and interdependence are far weaker.

international justice Along with international order, a fundamental normative value of the International Society tradition. This approach discerns tendencies towards both communicative justice (as in diplomatic practices) and distributive justice (as in the provision of development aid) in international relations.

international order An order between states in a system or society of states. Along with international justice, international order is a fundamental normative value of the International Society tradition. Hedley

Bull identifies four goals necessary for international order: preserving international society; upholding the independence of member states; maintaining peace; and adhering to norms governing war, diplomacy and sovereignty. Responsibility for the pursuit and preservation of international order lies with the great powers, whose fundamental duty, according to Bull, is to maintain the 'balance of power'.

International Political Economy (IPE) IPE is about international wealth and international poverty; about who gets what in the international system. If economics is about the pursuit of wealth and politics about the pursuit of power, the two interact in puzzling and complicated ways. It is this complex interplay in the international context between politics and economics, between states and markets, which is the core of IPE.

international relations (IR) IR is the shorthand name for the subject of international relations. The traditional core of IR concerns the development and change of sovereign statehood in the context of the larger system or society of states. Contemporary IR not only concerns political relations between states but a host of other subjects: economic interdependence, human rights, transnational corporations, international organizations, the environment, gender, inequalities, development, terrorism and so forth.

International Society School This approach to IR emphasizes the simultaneous presence in international society of both realist and liberal elements. There is conflict and there is cooperation; there are states and there are individuals. These different elements cannot be simplified and abstracted into a single theory that emphasizes only one aspect—e.g. power. International Society theorists argue for an approach that recognizes the simultaneous presence of all these elements.

international state of nature This is a permanent condition of actual or potential war between sovereign states. War is necessary, as a last resort, for resolving disputes between states that cannot agree and will not acquiesce. Human society and morality is confined to the state and does not extend into international relations, which is a political arena of considerable turmoil, discord and conflict between states in which the great powers dominate everybody else.

'juridical' statehood Part of the external basis of a state's sovereignty. A state must be viewed as a formal or legal institution by other states—hence the fact that, for example, Quebec will never be a sovereign state unless Canada, the United States and others recognize it as such. In addition to sovereignty itself, this dimension of statehood includes the right to membership in international organizations and the possession of various international rights and responsibilities.

laissez-faire The idea of the freedom of the market from all kinds of political restriction and regulation, supported by early economic liberals. Yet even these liberals were aware of the need for a politically constructed legal framework as a basis for the market. Laissez-faire does not mean the absence of any political regulation whatsoever; it means that the state shall only set up those minimal underpinnings that are necessary for the market to function properly. This is the classical version of economic liberalism. At the present time this view is also put forward under labels such as 'conservatism' or 'neoliberalism'; the content is basically the same, however. The 'conservative/neoliberal' economic policies of Margaret Thatcher in Britain and of Ronald Reagan in the Unites States were both based on classical laissez-faire doctrines.

'level-of-analysis' approach Foreign-policy theories analysed at three different levels initially conceptualized by Kenneth Waltz: the systemic level involving the distribution of power among states; the nation-state level involving the type of government, the relations between the state and groups in society, and the bureaucratic make-up of the state apparatus; and the level of the individual decision-maker, involving his or her way of thinking, basic beliefs, personal priorities and so forth.

liberal approach Foreign-policy theorists concerned with multilateral questions are likely to take a liberal approach, emphasizing international institutions—such as the United Nations or the World Trade Organization—as means of reducing international conflict and promoting mutual understanding and common interests.

liberalism The liberal tradition in IR emphasizes the great potential for human progress in modern civil society and the capitalist economy, both of which can flourish in states which guarantee individual liberty.

The modern liberal state invokes a political and economic system that will bring peace and prosperity. Relations between liberal states will be collaborative and cooperative.

Marxism The political economy of the nineteenth-century German philosopher and economist Karl Marx in many ways represents a fundamental critique of economic liberalism. Economic liberals view the economy as a positive-sum game with benefits for all. Marx rejected that view. Instead, he saw the economy as a site of human exploitation and class inequality. Marx thus takes the zero-sum argument of mercantilism and applies it to relations of classes instead of relations of states. Marxists agree with mercantilists that politics and economics are closely intertwined; both reject the liberal view of an economic sphere operating under its own laws. But where mercantilists see economics as a tool of politics, Marxists put economics first and politics second. For Marxists, the capitalist economy is based on two antagonistic social classes: one class, the bourgeoisie, owns the means of production; the other class, the proletariat, owns only its labour power which it must sell to the bourgeoisie. But labour puts in more work than it gets back in pay; there is a surplus value appropriated by the bourgeoisie. That is capitalist profit and it is derived from labour exploitation.

materialist view According to the materialist view, power and national interest are the driving forces in international politics. Power is ultimately military capability, supported by economic and other resources. National interest is the self-regarding desire by states for power, security or wealth. Power and interest are seen as 'material' factors; they are objective entities in the sense that because of anarchy states are compelled to be preoccupied with power and interest. In this view, ideas matter little; they can be used to rationalize actions dictated by material interest.

mercantilism The world-view of political elites that were at the forefront of building the modern state. They took the approach that economic activity is and should be subordinated to the primary goal of building a strong state. In other words, economics is a tool of politics, a basis for political power. That is a defining feature of mercantilist thinking. Mercantilists see the international economy as an arena of conflict between opposing national interests, rather than an area of cooperation and mutual gain. In brief, economic competition between states is a 'zero-sum game' where one state's gain is another state's loss.

'modernists' Those who believe that environmental challenges are not a serious challenge to advanced societies. Progress in knowledge and technology will enable us to protect the environment.

modernization theory A liberal theory of development; the basic idea is that Third World countries should be expected to follow the same developmental path taken earlier by the developed countries in the West: a progressive journey from a traditional, pre-industrial, agrarian society towards a modern, industrial, mass-consumption society. Development means overcoming barriers of pre-industrial production, backward institutions and parochial value systems which impede the process of growth and modernization.

national security The policies employed and the actions undertaken by a state to counter real or potential internal and external threats and to ensure the safety of its citizens. This is one of the fundamental responsibilities of the state to its people, and *the* fundamental state responsibility according to the realist view of IR. Before the advent of the state and the state system, security was provided by family, clan, warlord or another locally based entity; this responsibility, among others, was gradually transferred to the state.

neoliberalism A renewed liberal approach which seeks to avoid the utopianism of earlier liberalist theory. Neoliberals share classical liberal ideas about the possibility of progress and change, but they repudiate idealism. They also strive to formulate theories and apply new methods which are scientific.

neorealism This theory developed by Kenneth Waltz analyses how the decentralized and anarchical structure of the state system, in particular the relative distribution of power of states, is the central focus. Structures more or less determine actions. International change occurs when great powers rise and fall and the balance of power shifts accordingly. A typical means of such change is great-power war. Actors are less important because structures compel them to act in certain ways. An ethics of statecraft is thus unnecessary.

normative theory Can be viewed as the political theory or moral philosophy that underlies IR. Normative theory is primarily concerned to understand fundamental values of international life, the moral dimensions of international relations and the place of ethics in statecraft. Although it focuses on values, rules, practices and the like, normative theory is not necessarily a prescriptive approach to IR.

North Atlantic Treaty Organization (NATO) An international defence organization established in 1949 to provide the assured concerted defence of each of its member states. NATO (whose primary member was and is the United States) and the signatories of the Warsaw Pact (whose primary member was the Soviet Union) were the two rivals (though fundamentally the United States and the Soviet Union) in the Cold War and the bipolar world order. NATO outlived the Warsaw Pact and recently accepted seven new members, including six former Warsaw Pact countries, in 2004.

'offensive realism' A theory developed by John Mearsheimer, in contrast with 'defensive realism'. Great powers, according to this theory, are perpetually seeking ways to gain power over their rivals, towards the ultimate goal of hegemony.

ontology The philosophical study of the nature (reality) of the world and its components. Methodological divisions and debates in IR often reflect differing and even contradictory ontologies: e.g. whether an 'objective' world exists outside human experience, or only a 'subjective' world constructed by human experience. The claim that international relations is an external 'thing' or 'object' or 'reality' is associated with behaviouralist and positivist approaches, such as neorealism. The alternative claim that international relations consists of shared human understandings expressed via language, ideas and concepts is associated with International Society, normative theory, constructivism and postmodernism.

pluralism Along with solidarism, one of two International Society approaches to the potential conflict between state sovereignty and respect for human rights. A pluralist view of the state system emphasizes the primacy of state sovereignty: a policy of non-intervention must be maintained even when another state is experiencing (or complicit in) a humanitarian crisis within its borders. Civil rights (within states) take precedence over human rights (between states).

positivism A methodology in IR that employs most of the attitudes and assumptions of behaviouralism but does so in a more sophisticated way. Positivism is a fundamentally scientific approach. Its advocates and adherents believe that there can be objective knowledge of the social and political dimensions of the world, and that this knowledge is obtainable through the careful development and testing of empirical propositions. The social scientist is no different from any other scientist in this regard.

postmodern states States with high levels of cross-border integration. The economy is globalized rather than 'national'. The polity is characterized by multi-level governance at the supranational, national and subnational level. Collective loyalties are increasingly projected away from the state.

postmodernism A post-positivist approach to IR that rejects the modern, enlightenment idea that ever-expanding human knowledge will lead to an improved understanding and mastery of the international system. A distinctive feature of postmodernist discourse in IR is an inclination toward scepticism, debunking and deconstruction of 'universal truths'—such as those advanced by Kant or Marx or Waltz—that are supposed to be valid for all times and places.

post-positivism A methodology developed largely in reaction to positivist claims. Post-positivism presupposes methods that acknowledge the distinctiveness of human beings as such: i.e. creatures that must live with and among each other in order to live a human life. Post-positivist methodology rests on the proposition that people conceive, construct and constitute the worlds in which they live, including the international world, which is an entirely human arrangement and nothing else. Social science is a different methodology from that of natural science.

post-positivist approaches This is a cluster of different approaches to IR. They include critical theory, postmodernism and normative theory. These approaches are sceptical of the behaviouralist view that the world can be scientifically explained; they are also sceptical of regarding international relations as an 'objective reality out there'. International relations is sooner a subjective creation of people.

public goods Such goods are characterized by non-excludability; others cannot be denied access to them.

The air that we breathe is an example of such a good. A lighthouse is another example of a public good; so is a road or a pavement. The elements of a liberal world economy, such as a currency system for international payments, or the possibility to trade in a free market, are other examples of public goods. Once created, they are there for the benefit of all.

quasi-state A state that possesses juridical statehood but is severely deficient in empirical statehood. A large number of states in the Third World can be defined this way: they are recognized as states and participate in the state system, but they have weak or corrupt political institutions, underdeveloped economies and little or no national unity.

RAM (Rational Actor Model) An approach to foreign-policy analysis at the systemic level that views the sovereign state as a unitary actor driven by a motivation to advance its national interests, and that assumes that decisions made by the state are based on rational choice.

rational choice theory Neoclassical economics present a simple model of individuals and their basic behaviour. That model—called rational choice theory—is relevant, so the economists claim, not merely for economics, but for every other sphere of human behaviour. Rational choice begins with individuals. Whatever happens in the social world, including in international relations, can be explained by individual choices. What a state or any other organization does can be explained by choices made by individuals as well. This view is called methodological individualism. Furthermore, individual actors are rational and self-interested. They want to make themselves better off. This is true for everybody; not merely for sellers and buyers in economic markets, but also for bureaucrats and politicians. Finally, when individuals act in a rational and self-interested way, the overall result or outcome for states or systems will be the best possible. Just as 'the invisible hand' in liberal economics leads from individual greed to the best possible economic result for all, so the individual actions by bureaucrats and politicians lead to the best possible outcome. So if we want to understand what governments do, our first priority must be to understand the preferences, that is the goals, of public officials. They will be looking for private benefits: re-election, promotion, prestige and so on. Once we understand how these preferences condition their behaviour, we are in a position to understand how state policies are affected. That is a basic claim of rational choice theory.

rationalism One of three interacting philosophies (along with realism and revolutionism) whose dialogue, according to Martin Wight, is essential to an adequate understanding of IR. Rationalists, such as Hugo Grotius, are more optimistic in their view of human nature than are realists. Rationalism conceives of states as legal organizations that operate in accordance with international law and diplomatic practice; international relations are therefore norm-governed policies and activities based on the mutually recognized authority of sovereign states.

realism The realist tradition in IR is based on: (1) a pessimistic view of human nature; humans are self-interested and egoistic; (2) a conviction that international relations are conflictual and can always lead to war; (3) a high regard for the values of national security and state survival; and (4) a basic scepticism that there can be progress in international politics.

republican liberalism This strand of liberalism is built on the claim that liberal democracies are more peaceful and law-abiding than are other political systems. The argument is not that democracies never go to war; democracies have gone to war as often as have non-democracies. But the argument is that democracies do not fight each other. This observation was first articulated by Immanuel Kant in the late eighteenth century in reference to republican states rather than democracies. It was resurrected by Dean Babst in 1964 and it has been advanced in numerous studies since then.

revolutionism One of three interacting philosophies (along with realism and rationalism) whose dialogue, according to Wight, is essential to an adequate understanding of IR. Revolutionists, such as Kant and Marx, are solidarists who believe in the 'moral unity' of humankind beyond the state. They hold in common a progressive aim of changing (even eliminating) the international state system in the expectation of creating a better world. Revolutionists are more optimistic than rationalists and realists about human nature: they believe in the achievability of human perfection.

'security dilemma' An important paradox inherent in the state system. A fundamental reason for the existence of states is to provide their citizens with security from internal and external threats; however, the existence of these armed states threatens the very security they are expected to maintain.

social constructivism Constructivists argue that the most important aspect of international relations is social, not material. Furthermore, they argue that this social reality is not objective, or external, to the observer of international affairs. The social and political world, including the world of international relations, is not a physical entity or material object that is outside human consciousness. Consequently, the study of international relations must focus on the ideas and beliefs that inform the actors on the international scene as well as the shared understandings between them.

social constructivist approach A theory of foreign policymaking as an intersubjective world, whose ideas and discourse can be scrutinized in order to arrive at a better understanding of the process. The discourse of actors is seen to shape policymaking, since policies are conveyed by speech and writing. Some constructivists claim that identity, rooted in ideas and discourse, is the basis for a definition of interests and thus lies behind any foreign policy.

sociological liberalism A branch of liberal thinking which stresses that IR is not only about state–state relations; it is also about transnational relations, i.e. relations between people, groups and organizations belonging to different countries. The emphasis on society as well as the state, on many different types of actor and not just national governments, has led some to identify liberal thought by the term 'pluralism'.

soft power Also termed 'co-optive power', soft power is, according to Joseph Nye, the ability to structure a situation so that other nations develop preferences or define their interests in ways consistent with one's own nation.

'soft' revolutionism A version of revolutionism that seeks the abandonment of the existent state system by a peaceful revolution of ideas. Immanuel Kant and Mohandas Gandhi, as well as Christian pacifists and secular humanists more generally, are examples of soft revolutionists.

solidarism Along with pluralism, one of two International Society approaches to the potential conflict between recognition of state sovereignty and respect for human rights. A solidarist view stresses individuals, not states, as the ultimate members of international society; there exist both the right and the duty of states to intervene in foreign countries for humanitarian reasons.

sovereignty/sovereign state As applied to a state, sovereignty includes both ultimate internal authority and external recognition. Internally, a state is sovereign when it exercises supreme authority over the affairs and people within its territory; externally, a state is sovereign when it is recognized as such by the international community, i.e., its territorial integrity and *internal* sovereignty are respected and upheld. Presently, the greatest threat to sovereignty is the rise in prominence of IGOs, NGOs and the global economy (and globalization in general), all of which increase state interdependence and accountability.

state The main actor in IR, sometimes referred to as a 'country' or a 'nation-state'. The term is used in reference to both the populated territory of the state and the political body that governs that territory. The state is a territory-based sociopolitical organization entrusted with the responsibility of defending basic social conditions and values, including security, freedom, order, justice and welfare. Because of their role as protectors of security, states have a monopoly on the authority and power to engage in war. Though states differ in their level of success in defending the aforementioned values, the state is understood to have legal jurisdiction (sovereignty) over its own affairs and population. In popular view, the Peace of Westphalia (1648), following the Thirty Years War, marked the formal beginning of the modern sovereign state and modern international relations.

'state of nature' Thomas Hobbes' famous description of the original, pre-civil existence of humankind, a state in which life is 'solitary, poor, nasty, brutish, and short'. In their natural condition, all people are endangered by everyone else, and nobody is able to ensure his or her security or survival. This mutual fear and insecurity is, according to Hobbes, the driving force behind the creation of the sovereign state.

state system An organization of independent states wherein mutual sovereignty is recognized; relations are subject to international law and diplomatic practices;

and a balance of power exists among states. Historically, the geopolitical outcome of the Peace of Westphalia was the first (albeit only European) state system in the modern sense. We now speak of a global state system, as the world's inhabitable land is covered entirely by states and their territories. With the dissolution of the Soviet Union, the break-up of both Czechoslovakia and Yugoslavia, and the end of the Cold War, there are now nearly 200 states in the state system.

strategic realism This theory developed by Thomas Schelling analyses how a state can employ power to get a rival to do what the state desires, i.e. through coercion instead of brute force, which is always dangerous and inefficient. Unlike classical and neoclassical realism, strategic realism does not make normative claims; values are taken as given and not weighed during analysis. Rather, the theory seeks to provide analytical tools for diplomacy and foreign policy, which are seen to be instrumental activities that can be best understood via game theoretical analysis.

'strong liberals' Liberal theorists who maintain that qualitative change has taken place. Today's economic interdependence ties countries much closer together; economies are globalized; production and consumption take place in a worldwide marketplace. It would be extremely costly in welfare terms for countries to opt out of that system. Today there is also a group of consolidated liberal democracies for whom reversion to authoritarianism is next to unthinkable, because all major groups in society support democracy. These countries conduct their mutual international relations in new and more cooperative ways.

structural violence The oppression and hardship that people suffer from political and economic structures that subject them to unequal positions. Johan Galtung invented the concept in order to identify types of violence different from direct violence.

structuration A concept suggested by Anthony Giddens as a way of analysing the relationship between structures and actors. Structures (i.e. the rules and conditions that guide social action) do not determine what actors do in any mechanical way, an impression one might get from the neorealist view of how the structure of anarchy constrains state actors. The relationship between structures and actors involves intersubjective understanding and meaning. Structures do constrain actors, but actors can also transform structures by thinking about them and acting on them in new ways. The notion of structuration therefore leads to a less rigid and more dynamic view of the relationship between structure and actors. IR constructivists use this as a starting-point for suggesting a less rigid view of anarchy.

terrorism The unlawful use or threatened use of violence against civilians, often to achieve political, religious or similar objectives. International terrorism involves the territory or the citizens of more than one country. Terrorism is nothing new; it has probably existed ever since human societies began to regulate the use of violence. It is the unusual scale and intensity of the 11 September 2001 attacks in New York and Washington, and later attacks in Ankara, Madrid, London and elsewhere that has put the issue of international terrorism high on the agenda.

'think tanks' Private research organizations that disseminate useful information and provide expert advice with the aim of influencing government policies. They were initially developed in the United States by philanthropists and public intellectuals who recognized the importance of addressing, debating and (hopefully) solving troublesome issues of American foreign policy, particularly war. They have subsequently been developed in many other countries. American 'think tanks' are differentiated from their foreign counterparts by the degree to which politicians in the United States actively seek advice from these organizations.

traditional approach to foreign policy Proponents include Niccolò Machiavelli, Hugo Grotius and Henry Kissinger. The traditional approach, with its attention to the specific historical foreign policies of a particular country, analyses the substance of foreign policy as practised, as opposed to the systematic theories and explanations advanced by more analytical and scientific approaches to foreign policy.

'verstehen' Max Weber emphasized that the social world (i.e. the world of human interaction) is fundamentally different from the natural world of physical phenomena. Human beings rely on 'understanding' of each other's actions and assigning 'meaning' to them. In order to comprehend human interaction, we cannot merely describe it in the way we describe physical phenomena, such as a boulder falling off a cliff; we need a different kind of interpretive understanding, or 'verstehen'. Is the pat of another person's face a punishment or a caress? We cannot know until we assign meaning to the act. Weber concluded that 'subjective understanding is the specific characteristic of sociological knowledge'. Constructivists rely on such insights to emphasize the importance of 'meaning' and 'understanding'.

'weak liberals' Liberal theorists who accept a great deal of the realist critique of liberal theory, especially that anarchy persists and there is no escape from self-help and the security dilemma.

world system analysis An approach developed by Immanuel Wallerstein. A world system is characterized by a certain economic and a certain political structure with the one depending on the other. In human history, there have been two basic varieties of world systems: world-empires and world-economies. In world-empires, such as the Roman Empire, political and economic control is concentrated in a unified centre. World-economies, in contrast, are tied together economically in a single division of labour, but politically, authority is decentralized, residing in multiple polities, in a system of states. Wallerstein's key focus is the analysis of the modern world-economy, characterized by capitalism.

REFERENCES

Adler, E. (2001). 'Constructivism and International Relations', in W. Carlsnaes, T. Risse and B. A. Simmons (eds), *Handbook of International Relations*. London: Sage, 95–118.

Adler, E. and Barnett, M. N. (1996). 'Governing Anarchy: A Research Agenda for the Study of Security Communities', *Ethics and International Affairs*, 10/1: 63–98.

—— (eds) (1998). *Security Communities*. Cambridge: Cambridge University Press.

Allison, G. (1971). *Essence of Decision: Explaining the Cuban Missile Crisis*. New York: HarperCollins.

—— (2004). *Nuclear Terrorism: The Ultimate Preventable Catastrophe*. New York: Times Books.

Allison, G. and Zelikow, P. (1999). *Essence of Decision: Explaining the Cuban Missile Crisis*, 2nd edn. New York: Longman.

Amin, S. (1975). 'Toward a Structural Crisis of World Capitalism', *Socialist Revolution*, 5/1: 1–25.

—— (1976). *Unequal Development*. Sussex: Harvester Press.

—— (1990). *Delinking: Towards a Polycentric World*. London: Zed.

Amsden, A. (1989). *Asia's Next Giant: South Korea and Late Industrialization*. New York: Oxford University Press.

Amsden, A. and Chu, W. (2003). *Beyond Late Development: Taiwan's Upgrading Policies*. Cambridge, Mass.: MIT Press.

Angell, N. (1909). *The Great Illusion*. London: Weidenfeld & Nicolson.

Ashley, R. K. (1986). 'The Poverty of Neorealism', in R. O. Keohane (ed.), *Neo-Realism and Its Critics*. New York: Columbia University Press, 255–301.

—— (1996). 'The Achievements of Post-Structuralism', in S. Smith, K. Booth and M. Zalewski (eds), *International Theory: Positivism and Beyond*. Cambridge: Cambridge University Press, 240–53.

Axelrod, R. (1984). *The Evolution of Cooperation*. New York: Basic Books.

Bain, W. (2003). *Between Anarchy and Society*. Oxford: Oxford University Press.

Baldwin, D. A. (ed.) (1993). *Neorealism and Neoliberalism: The Contemporary Debate*. New York: Columbia University Press.

Ball, C. (1998). 'Nattering NATO Negativism? Reasons Why Expansion May Be a Good Thing', *Review of International Studies*, 24 (Jan.): 43–68.

Barber, P. (1979). *Diplomacy: The World of the Honest Spy*. London: The British Library.

Barrett, M. (1980). *Women's Oppression Today: Problems in Marxist Feminist Analysis*. London: Verso.

Baun, M. J. (1996). *An Imperfect Union: The Maastricht Treaty and the New Politics of European Integration*. Boulder: Westview Press.

Beck, U. (1992). *Risk Society*. London: Sage.

Bellamy, A. J. (ed.) (2005). *International Society and its Critics*. Oxford: Oxford University Press.

Bendor, J. and Hammond, T. H. (1992). 'Rethinking Allison's Models', *American Political Science Review*, 86 (June): 301–22.

Berlin, I. (1969). *Four Essays on Liberty*. Oxford: Oxford University Press.

Biersteker, T. J. and Weber, C. (eds) (1996). *State Sovereignty as a Social Construct*. Cambridge: Cambridge University Press.

Birnie, P. (1992). 'International Environmental Law: Its Adequacy for Present and Future Needs', in A. Hurrell and B. Kingsbury (1992: 51–84).

Blumenthal, M. W. (Chief Executive Officer of the Unisys Company) (1988). 'The World Economy and Technological Change', *Foreign Affairs*, 66: 537–8.

Boggs, C. (2005). *Imperial Delusions: American Militarism and Endless War*. Lanham: Rowman & Littlefield.

Booth, K. (1991). 'Security and Emancipation', *Review of International Studies*, 17 (Oct.): 313–26.

—— (1995). 'Human Wrongs and International Relations', *International Affairs*, 71: 103–26.

Botcheva, L. and Martin, L. (2001). 'Institutional Effects on State Behaviour: Convergence and Divergence', *International Studies Quarterly*, 45/1: 1–26.

Boulding, K. (1962). *Conflict and Defense: A General Theory*. New York: Harper & Row.

—— (1979). *Stable Peace*. Austin: University of Texas Press.

Brecht, A. (1963). *Man and His Government*. New York: Harcourt, Brace.

Bridges, R. et al. (eds) (1969). *Nations and Empires*. London: Macmillan.

Brierly, J. L. (1938). *The Law of Nations*, 2nd edn. Oxford: Oxford University Press.

Brown, C. (1992). *International Relations Theory: New Normative Approaches*. New York: Harvester Press.

—— (1997). *Understanding International Relations*. London: Macmillan.

Brown, C., Nardin, T. and Rengger, N. (eds) (2002). *International Relations in Political Thought*. Cambridge: Cambridge University Press.

Brown, L. (1989). 'Reexamining the World Food Prospect', in L. Brown (ed.), *State of the World 1989*. Washington, DC: Worldwatch Institute, 41–58.

Brown, S. (1994). *The Causes and Prevention of War*, 2nd edn. New York: St Martin's Press.

Brownlie, I. (1979). *Principles of Public International Law*, 3rd edn. Oxford: Clarendon Press.

Bull, H. (1969). 'International Theory: The Case for a Classical Approach', in K. Knorr and J. N. Rosenau (eds), *Contending Approaches to International Politics*. Princeton: Princeton University Press, 20–38.

—— (1972). 'International Relations as an Academic Pursuit', *Australian Outlook*, 26: 251–62.

—— (1975). 'New Directions in the Theory of International Relations', *International Studies*, 14: 280–90.

—— (1979). 'Recapturing the Just War for Political Theory', *World Politics*, 32: 590–9.

—— (1984). 'The Great Irresponsibles? The United States, the Soviet Union, and World Order', in R. O. Matthews, A. G. Rubinoff and J. C. Stein (eds), *International Conflict and Conflict Management*. Scarborough: Prentice-Hall Canada.

—— (1985). *Justice in International Relations* (The Hagey Lectures). Waterloo: University of Waterloo Press.

—— (1990). 'The Importance of Grotius in the Study of International Relations', in H. Bull et al. (1990: 65–93).

—— (1995). *The Anarchical Society: A Study of Order in World Politics*, 2nd edn. London: Macmillan.

Bull, H., Kingsbury, B. and Roberts, A. (eds) (1990). *Hugo Grotius and International Relations*. Oxford: Clarendon Press.

Bull, H. and Watson, A. (eds) (1984). *The Expansion of International Society*. Oxford: Clarendon Press.

Burchill, S. et al. (2001). *Theories of International Relations*. Basingstoke: Palgrave Macmillan.

Burton, J. (1972). *World Society*. Cambridge: Cambridge University Press.

Butterfield, H. (1953). *Christianity, Diplomacy and War*. London: Epworth.

—— (1973). *The Whig Interpretation of History*. Harmondsworth: Penguin.

Buzan, B. (2004). *From International to World Society?* Cambridge: Cambridge University Press.

Buzan, B., Jones, C. and Little, R. (1993). *The Logic of Anarchy: Neorealism to Structural Realism*. New York: Columbia University Press.

Camilleri, J. A. and Falk, J. (1992). *The End of Sovereignty? The Politics of a Shrinking and Fragmenting World*. Aldershot: Elgar.

Campbell, D. (1998). *National Deconstruction: Violence, Identity, and Justice in Bosnia*. Minneapolis: University of Minnesota Press.

Caporaso, J. A. (1993). 'Global Political Economy', in A. W. Finifter (ed.), *Political Science: The State of the Discipline*, ii. Washington, DC: American Political Science Association, 451–83.

Cardoso, F. H. (1972). 'Notas sobre el estado actual de los estudios sobre dependencia', *Revista Latinamericana de Ciencias Sociales*, 4: 3–31.

Cardoso, F. H. and Faletto, E. (1979). *Dependency and Development in Latin America*. Berkeley: University of California Press.

Carlsnaes, W. (2002). 'Foreign Policy', in W. Carlsnaes, T. Risse and B. Simmons (eds), *Handbook of International Relations*. London: Sage, 331–49.

Carlson, L. J. (2002). 'Game Theory: International Trade, Conflict and Cooperation', in R. Palan (ed.), *Global Political Economy: Contemporary Theories*. London: Routledge, 117–30.

Carnoy, M. (1984). *The State and Political Theory*. Princeton: Princeton University Press.

Carr, E. H. (1964 [1939]). *The Twenty Years' Crisis*. New York: Harper & Row.

Carter, A. (1993). 'Towards a Green Political Theory', in A. Dobson and P. Lucardie (eds), *The Politics of Nature: Explorations in Green Political Theory*. London: Routledge.

Castells, M. (1998). *The Power of Identity*. Oxford: Blackwell.

Cerny, P. G. (1990). *The Changing Architecture of Politics: Structure, Agency and the Future of the State*. London: Sage.

—— (1993). 'Plurilateralism: Structural Differentiation and Functional Conflict in the Post-Cold War World Order', *Millennium: Journal of International Studies*, 22/1: 27–51.

Christensen, T. J. (1996). *Useful Adversaries: Grand Strategy, Domestic Mobilization, and Sino-American Conflict 1947–1958*. Princeton: Princeton University Press.

Cipolla, C. M. (1977). 'Introduction', in C. M. Cipolla (ed.), *The Fontana Economic History of Europe*. Glasgow: Fontana/Collins, 7–8.

Clark, G. (1960). *Early Modern Europe: From about 1450 to about 1720*. Oxford: Oxford University Press.

Claude, I. (1971). *Swords into Ploughshares*, 4th edn. New York: Random House.

Coates, A. J. (1997). *The Ethics of War*. Manchester: Manchester University Press.

Cobden, R. (1903). *Political Writings*, 2 vols. London: Fisher Unwin.

Collingwood, R. G. (1946). *The Idea of History*. Oxford: Clarendon Press.

Commission on Global Governance (1995). *Our Global Neighbourhood*. New York: Oxford University Press.

Cooper, R. (1996). *The Post-Modern State and the World Order*. London: Demos.

—— (2002). 'The New Liberal Imperialism', *Observer*, 7 April.

Copeland, D. (2000). 'The Constructivist Challenge to Structural Realism', *International Security*, 25/2, 187–212.

Cox, M. (ed.) (2002). 'The World Crisis and the Origins of International Relations', *International Relations*, 16/1, April (issue on the origins of the IR discipline).

Cox, R. W. (1981). 'Social Forces, States and World Orders', *Millennium*, 10: 126–55.

Cox, R. W. (1987). *Production, Power and World Order: Social Forces in the Making of History*. New York: Columbia University Press.

—— (1992). 'Towards a Post-Hegemonic Conceptualization of World Order: Reflections on the Relevancy of Ibn Khaldun', in J. N. Rosenau and E.-O. Czempiel (eds), *Governance without Government: Order and Change in World Politics*. Cambridge: Cambridge University Press, 132–59.

—— (1994). 'Global Restructuring: Making Sense of the Changing International Political Economy', in R. Stubbs and G. R. D. Underhill (eds), *Political Economy and the Changing Global Order*. London: Macmillan, 45–60.

—— with Sinclair, T. J. (1996). *Approaches to World Order*. Cambridge: Cambridge University Press.

—— (2002). 'Reflections and Transitions', in R. W. Cox with M. G. Schechter, *The Political Economy of a Plural World: Critical Reflections on Power, Morals, and Civilization*. London: Routledge, 26–44.

Daly, M. (1979). *Gyn/Ecology: The Metaethics of Radical Feminism*. London: Women's Press.

Der Derian, J. (1987). *On Diplomacy*. Oxford: Blackwell.

Dessler, D. (2000). 'Review of Alexander Wendt: Social Theory of International Politics', *American Political Science Review*, 94/4: 1002–3.

Deudney, D. (1996). 'E Pluribus Unum: The Problem of Liberal Identity and Community in Pluralistic Security Community Theory', paper for ISA Annual Meeting, 17–21 Apr., San Diego.

Deudney, D. and Ikenberry, G. J. (1999). 'The Nature and Sources of Liberal International Order', *Review of International Studies*, 25/2: 179–96.

Deutsch, K. W. et al. (1957). *Political Community and the North Atlantic Area*. Princeton: Princeton University Press.

Dicken, P. (2003). *Global Shift: Reshaping the Global Economic Map in the 21st Century*. London: Sage.

Diehl, P. F. and Gleditsch, N. P. (eds) (2000). *Environmental Conflict. An Anthology*. Boulder: Westview Press.

Donnelly, J. (1992). 'Twentieth-Century Realism', in T. Nardin and D. Mapel (eds) (1992: 85–111).

Dougherty, J. E. and Pfaltzgraff, R. L. (1971). *Contending Theories of International Relations*. New York: Lippincott.

Doyle, M. W. (1983). 'Kant, Liberal Legacies and Foreign Affairs', pts. 1 and 2, *Philosophy and Public Affairs*, 12/3: 205–35 and 12/4: 323–54.

——(1986). 'Liberalism and World Politics'. *American Political Science Review*, 80/4: 1151–69.

Dunn, J. (1984). *Locke*. Oxford: Oxford University Press.

Eagly, A. H. and Chaiken, S. (1993). *The Psychology of Attitudes*. Dallas: Harcourt Brace.

Easton, D. (1961). 'An Approach to the Analysis of Political Systems', in S. S. Ulmer (ed.), *Introductory Readings in Political Behavior*. Chicago: Rand McNally, 136–57.

——(1965). *A Framework for Political Analysis*. Englewood Cliffs: Prentice-Hall.

——(1971). *The Political System*, 2nd edn. New York: Knopf.

Ebenstein, W. (1951). *Great Political Thinkers: Plato to the Present*. New York: Holt, Rinehart, Winston.

Eckersly, R. (1992). *Environmentalism and Political Theory: Towards an Ecocentric Approach*. London: UCL Press.

——(2004). *The Green State: Rethinking Democracy and Sovereignty*. Cambridge, Mass.: MIT Press.

The Economist, (1997). 'Policing for Profit', 19–25 Apr.: 21–3.

Ehlstain, J. B. (1987). *Women and War*. New York: Basic Books.

Eisenstein, H. (1983). *Contemporary Feminist Thought*. London: Hall.

Elkins, D. J. (1995). *Beyond Sovereignty: Territory and Political Economy in the Twenty-First Century*. Toronto: Toronto University Press.

Elman, M. (ed.) (1997). *Paths to Peace: Is Democracy the Answer?* Cambridge, Mass.: MIT Press.

Enloe, C. (1990). *Bananas, Beaches, and Bases: Making Feminist Sense of International Relations*. Berkeley: University of California Press.

——(1994). *The Morning After: Sexual Politics at the End of the Cold War*. Berkeley: University of California Press.

——(2004). *The Curious Feminist: Searching for Women in a New Age of Empire*. Berkeley: University of California Press.

Escobar, A. (1995). *Encountering Development*. Princeton: Princeton University Press.

Eulau, H. (1963). *The Behavioral Persuasion in Politics*. New York: Random House.

Evans, G. and Newnham, J. (1992). *The Dictionary of World Politics*. London: Harvester Wheatsheaf.

Evans, P. B. (1989). 'Predatory, Developmental, and Other Apparatuses: A Comparative Political Economy Perspective on the Third World State', *Sociological Forum*, 4/4: 561–88.

Evers, T. and Wogau, P. von (1973). ' "Dependencia": Lateinamerikanische Beiträge zur Theorie der Unterentwicklung', *Das Argument*, 79/4–6: 414–48.

Falk, R. (1985). 'A New Paradigm for International Legal Studies', in R. Falk, F. Kratochwil and S. H. Mendlovitz (eds), *International Law: A Contemporary Perspective*. Boulder: Westview Press.

Fallows, J. (1994). *Looking at the Sun*. New York: Pantheon.

Fann, K. T. and Hodges, D. C. (eds) (1971). *Readings in US Imperialism*. Boston: Porter Sargent.

Fierke, K. M. (2001). 'Critical Methodology and Constructivism', in K. M. Fierke and K. E. Jørgensen (eds) (2001: 115–35).

Fierke, K. and Jørgensen, K. E. (2001) (eds). *Constructing International Relations: The Next Generation*. London: M. E. Sharpe.

Finley, M. I. (1983). *Politics in the Ancient World*. New York: Cambridge University Press.

Finnegan, R. B. (1972). 'International Relations: The Disputed Search for Method', *Review of Politics*, 34: 40–66.

Finnemore, M. (1996). *National Interests in International Society*. Ithaca and London: Cornell University Press.

——(2003). *The Purpose of Intervention: Changing Beliefs about the Use of Force*. Ithaca and London: Cornell University Press.

Finnemore, M. and K. Sikkink (2001). 'Taking Stock: The Constructivist Research Program in International Relations and Comparative Politics', *Annual Reviews of Political Science*, 4: 391–416.

Foot, R., Gaddis, J. L. and Hurrell, A. (eds) (2003). *Order and Justice in International Relations*. Oxford: Oxford University Press.

Forde, S. (1992). 'Classical Realism', in T. Nardin and D. Mapel (eds) (1992: 62–84).

Fortes, M. and **Evans-Pritchard, E. E.** (eds) (1940). *African Political Systems*. London: Oxford University Press.

Frank, A. G. (1967). *Capitalism and Underdevelopment in Latin America*. New York: Monthly Review Press.

—— (1969). *Latin America: Underdevelopment or Revolution?* New York: Monthly Review Press.

—— (1971). 'On the Mechanisms of Imperialism: The Case of Brazil', in K. Fann and D. Hodges (eds) (1971: 237–8).

—— (1977). 'Dependence is Dead, Long Live Dependence and the Class Struggle: An Answer to Critics', *World Development*, 5/4: 355–70.

—— (1980). *Crisis: In the World Economy*. London: Heinemann.

—— (1997). *Freedom Review*, 28/1: 15.

Friedman, M. (1962). *Capitalism and Freedom*. Chicago: University of Chicago Press.

—— (1993). 'Cooperation, Competition Go Hand in Hand', *Nikkei Weekly*, 15 November: 1–23.

Frost, M. (1996). *Ethics in International Relations*. Cambridge: Cambridge University Press.

Fukuyama, F. (1989). 'The End of History?', *National Interest*, 16: 3–18.

—— (1992). *The End of History and the Last Man*. New York: Avon.

Gaddis, J. (1987). *The Long Peace: Inquiries into the History of the Cold War*. New York: Oxford University Press.

Gadzey, A. T.-K. (1994). *The Political Economy of Power: Hegemony and Economic Liberalism*. New York: St Martin's Press.

Gallie, W. B. (1978). *Philosophers of Peace and War: Kant, Clausewitz, Marx, Engels and Tolstoy*. Cambridge: Cambridge University Press.

Gatens, M. (1989). *Feminism and Philosophy: Perspectives on Equality and Difference*. London: Routledge.

George, A. (1972). 'The Case for Multiple Advocacy in Making Foreign Policy', *American Political Science Review*, 66: 751–95.

—— (1980). *Presidential Decisionmaking in Foreign Policy: The Effective Use of Information and Advice*. Boulder: Westview Press.

—— (1993). *Bridging the Gap: Theory and Practice in Foreign Policy*. Washington, DC: United States Institute of Peace.

George, J. (1994). *Discourses of Global Politics: A Critical (Re)Introduction to International Relations*. Boulder: Lynne Rienner.

Giddens, A. (1984). *The Constitution of Society*. Berkeley: University of California Press.

Gilbert, M. (1995). *The First World War*. London: HarperCollins.

Gill, S. (1994). 'Knowledge, Politics, and Neo-Liberal Political Economy', in R. Stubbs and G. R. D. Underhill (eds), *Political Economy and the Changing Global Order*. London: Macmillan, 75–89.

Gilpin, R. (1981). *War and Change in World Politics*. Cambridge: Cambridge University Press.

—— (1984). 'The Richness of the Tradition of Political Realism', *International Organization*, 38/2 (Spring): 287–305.

—— (1987). *The Political Economy of International Relations*. Princeton: Princeton University Press.

—— (2001). *Global Political Economy: Understanding the International Economic Order*. Princeton: Princeton University Press.

Gleick, P. H. (1993). 'Water and Conflict: Fresh Water Resources and International Security', *International Security*, 18/1: 79–112.

Goldgeier, J. (1997). 'Psychology and Security', *Security Studies*, 6: 137–66.

Goldgeier, J. and **McFaul, M.** (1992). 'A Tale of Two Worlds: Core and Periphery in the Post-Cold War Era', *International Organization*, 46/1: 467–92.

Goldhagen, D. J. (1996). *Hitler's Willing Executioners: Ordinary Germans and the Holocaust*. New York: Knopf.

Goldstein, J. and **Keohane, R. O.** (eds) (1993). *Ideas and Foreign Policy: Beliefs, Institutional and Political Change*. Ithaca: Cornell University Press.

Gong, G. W. (1984). *The Standard of 'Civilization' in International Society*. Oxford: Clarendon Press.

Goodin, R. (1990). 'International Ethics and the Environment Crisis', *Ethics and International Affairs*, 4: 93–110.

—— (1992). *Green Political Theory*. Cambridge: Polity.

Gowa, J. (1999). *Ballots and Bullets: The Elusive Democratic Peace*. Princeton: Princeton University Press.

Gray, C. (2002). 'World Politics as Usual after September 11: Realism Vindicated', in K. Booth and T. Dunne (eds), *Worlds in Collision: Terror and the Future of Global Order*. London: Palgrave Macmillan, 235–45.

Grieco, J. M. (1997). 'Realist International Theory and the Study of World Politics', in M. W. Doyle and G. J. Ikenberry (eds), *New Thinking in International Relations*. Boulder: Westview Press, 163–202.

—— (1993). 'Anarchy and the Limits of Cooperation: A Realist Critique of the Newest Liberal Institutionalism', in D. A. Baldwin (ed.), *Neorealism and Neoliberalism: The Contemporary Debate*. New York: Columbia University Press, 116–43.

Gurr, T. R. and Harff, B. (1994). *Ethnic Conflict in World Politics*. Boulder: Westview Press.

Gutkind, P. and Wallerstein, I. (eds) (1976). *The Political Economy of Contemporary Africa*. Beverly Hills: Sage.

Haas, E. B. (1958). *The Uniting of Europe: Political, Social and Economic Forces 1950–1957*. Stanford: Stanford University Press.

—— (1975). *The Obsolescence of Regional Integration Theory*. Berkeley: Institute of International Studies.

—— (1976). 'Turbulent Fields and the Theory of Regional Integration', *International Organization*, 30/2: 173–212.

Haas, P. M. et al. (eds) (1993). *Institutions for the Earth*. Cambridge, Mass.: MIT Press.

Hacking, I. (1999). *The Social Construction of What?* Cambridge: Harvard University Press.

Haftendorn, H., Keohane, R. O. and Wallander, C. (eds) (1999). *Security Institutions over Time and Space*. New York: Oxford University Press.

Halliday, F. (1994). *Rethinking International Relations*. Vancouver: UBC Press.

Hardin, D. (1982). *Collective Action*. Baltimore: Johns Hopkins University Press.

Hardt, M. and A. Negri (2000). *Empire*. Cambridge Mass.: Harvard University Press.

Hart, P., Stern, E. K. and Sundelius, B. (eds) (1997). *Beyond Groupthink: Political Dynamics and Foreign Policy-making*. Ann Arbor: University of Michigan Press.

Helman, G. B. and Ratner, S. R. (1992–3). 'Saving Failed States', *Foreign Affairs*, 89: 3–21.

Herman, M. (1951). *Political Realism and Political Idealism*. Chicago: University of Chicago Press.

—— (1984). 'Personality and Foreign Policy Decision Making: A Study of 54 Heads of Government', in S. Chan and D. Sylvan (eds), *Foreign Policy Decision Making*, New York: Praeger.

Herz, J. (1950). 'Idealist Internationalism and the Security Dilemma', *World Politics*, II/2: 157–81.

Hettne, B. (1995). *Development Theory and the Three Worlds*. Harlow: Longman.

—— (1996). *Internationella relationer*. Lund: Studentlitteratur.

Heurlin, B. (1996). *Verden 2000: Teorier og tendenser i international politik*. Copenhagen: Gyldendal.

Hirst, P. and Thompson, G. (1992). 'The Problem of "Globalization": International Economic Relations, National Economic Management and the Formation of Trading Blocs', *Economy and Society*, 21/4: 357–94.

Hobbes, T. (1946). *Leviathan*. Oxford: Blackwell.

Hoffmann, S. (1977). 'An American Social Science: International Relations', *Daedalus*, 106: 41–61.

—— (1990). 'International Society', in J. D. B. Miller and R. J. Vincent (eds), *Order and Violence: Hedley Bull and International Relations*. Oxford: Clarendon Press, 13–17.

—— (1991). 'Ethics and Rules of the Game Between the Superpowers', in L. Henkin (ed.), *Right v. Might: International Law and the Use of Force*. New York: Council on Foreign Relations Press.

Holbraad, C. (1990). 'Hedley Bull and International Relations', in J. D. B. Miller and R. J. Vincent (eds), *Order and Violence: Hedley Bull and International Relations*. Oxford: Clarendon Press, 186–204.

Hollis, M., and Smith, S. (1990). *Explaining and Understanding International Relations*. Oxford: Clarendon Press.

Holm, H.-H., and Sørensen, G. (eds) (1995). *Whose World Order? Uneven Globalization and the End of the Cold War*. Boulder: Westview Press.

Holsti, K. J. (1988). *International Politics: A Framework for Analysis*. Englewood Cliffs: Prentice Hall.

—— (1991). *Peace and War: Armed Conflicts and International Order 1648–1989*. Cambridge: Cambridge University Press.

—— (1996). *The State, War, and the State of War*. Cambridge: Cambridge University Press.

Holsti, O. (1967). 'Cognitive Dynamics and Images of the Enemy: Dulles and Russia', in J. C. Farrell and

A. P. Smith (eds), *Image and Reality in World Politics*. New York: Columbia University Press, 16–39.

—— (2004). 'Theories of International Relations', www.duke.edu/-p.feaver/holsti.

Holsti, O. and Rosenau, J. N. (1984). *American Leadership in World Affairs: Vietnam and the Breakdown of Consensus*. Boston: Allen Unwin.

Homer-Dixon, T. F. (1995). 'Environmental Scarcities and Violent Conflict', in S. M. Lynn-Jones and S. Miller (eds), *Global Dangers: Changing Dimensions of International Security*. Cambridge, Mass.: MIT Press, 144–79.

Hopf, T. (1998). 'The Promise of Constructivism in International Relations Theory', *International Security*, 23/1: 171–200.

—— (2002). *Social Construction of International Politics*. Ithaca and London: Cornell University Press.

Howard, M. (1976). *War in European History*. Oxford: Oxford University Press.

Hughes, B. B. (1991). *Continuity and Change in World Politics: The Clash of Perspectives*. Englewood Cliffs: Prentice Hall.

Hurrell, A. (1995). 'International Political Theory and the Global Environment', in K. Booth and S. Smith (eds), *International Relations Today*. University Park: Pennsylvania State University Press, 129–53.

Hurrell, A. and Kingsbury, B. (eds) (1992). *The International Politics of the Environment*. Oxford: Clarendon Press.

IISS (2004). 'Combating Transnational Terrorism', *IISS Strategic Comments*, 10: 10.

Ikenberry, G. J. (ed.) (2001b). *American Foreign Policy: Theoretical Essays*, 4th edn. Boston: Scott Foresman.

—— (2001a). *After Victory: Institutions, Strategic Restraint and the Rebuilding of Order after Major Wars*. Princeton: Princeton University Press.

—— (2002). 'America's Imperial Ambition', *Foreign Affairs*, 81/5: 49–60.

Iyad, A. (1983). *Without a Homeland*. Tel Aviv: Mifras.

Jackson, R. (1990). *Quasi-States: Sovereignty, International Relations and the Third World*. Cambridge: Cambridge University Press.

—— (1992). 'Dialectical Justice in the Gulf War', *Review of International Studies*, 18: 335–54.

—— (1993). 'Armed Humanitarianism', *International Journal* 48 (Autumn): 579–606.

—— (1995). 'The Political Theory of International Society', in K. Booth and S. Smith (eds), *International Relations Today*. University Park: Pennsylvania State University Press, 110–28.

—— (1996a). 'Can International Society be Green?', in R. Fawn and J. Larkins (eds), *International Society after the Cold War*. London: Macmillan, 172–92.

—— (1996b). 'Is There a Classical International Theory?' in S. Smith et al. (1996: 203–18).

—— (ed.) (1999). 'Sovereignty at the Millennium', *Political Studies*, Special Issue, 47/3: 423–30.

—— (2000). *The Global Covenant: Human Conduct in a World of States*. Oxford: Oxford University Press.

—— (2005). *Classical and Modern Thought on International Relations: From Anarchy to Cosmopolis*. New York: Palgrave Macmillan.

James, A. (1986). *Sovereign Statehood: The Basis of International Society*. London: Allen & Unwin.

Janis, I. L. (1982). *Groupthink: Psychological Studies of Policy Decisions and Fiascos*, 2nd edn. Boston: Houghton Mifflin.

Jervis, R. (1968). 'Hypotheses on Misperception', *World Politics*, 20: 454–79.

—— (1976). *Perception and Misperception in International Politics*. Princeton: Princeton University Press.

—— (1998). 'Realism in the Study of World Politics', *International Organization*, 52/4: 971–91.

Johnston, A. I. (1996). 'Cultural Realism and Strategy in Maoist China', in P. Katzenstein (ed.), (1996a: 216–51).

Jones, E. L. (1981). *The European Miracle: Environments, Economies and Geopolitics in the History of Europe and Asia*. Cambridge: Cambridge University Press.

Kacowicz, A. M. (1995). 'Pluralistic Security Communities in the Third World? The Intriguing Cases of South America and West Africa', paper for ISA Annual Meeting, 22–5 Feb., Chicago.

Kagan, R. (2003). *Paradise and Power: America and Europe in the New World Order*. New York: Atlantic Books.

Kahler, M. (1997) 'Inventing International Relations: International Relations Theory after 1945', in M. Doyle and G. J. Ikenberry (eds), *New Thinking in International Relations Theory*. Boulder: Westview, 20–54.

Kant, I. (1795). 'Perpetual Peace', repr. in H. Reiss (ed.), *Kant's Political Writing*. Cambridge: Cambridge University Press (1992), 93–131.

Kaplan, M. (1964). *System and Process in International Politics*. New York: Wiley.

Kapstein, E. B. (1993). 'Territoriality and Who is "US"?', *International Organization*, 47/3: 501–3.

Katzenstein, P. (1996a) (ed.). *The Culture of National Security: Norms and Identity in World Politics*. New York: Columbia University Press.

—— (1996b). *Cultural Norms and National Security*. Ithaca and London: Cornell University Press.

Kay, C. (1989). *Latin American Theories of Development and Underdevelopment*. London: Routledge.

Keene, E. (2002). *Beyond the Anarchical Society*. Cambridge: Cambridge University Press.

Kegley, C. W., Jr. and Wittkopf, E. R. (1991). *American Foreign Policy*, 4th edn. New York: St Martin's Press.

Kennan, G. (1954). *Realities of American Foreign Policy*. Princeton: Princeton University Press.

Kennedy, P. (1993). *Preparing for the Twenty-First Century*. New York: Vintage.

Keohane, R. O. (1984). *After Hegemony: Cooperation and Discord in the World Political Economy*. Princeton: Princeton University Press.

—— (ed.) (1986). *Neo-Realism and Its Critics*. New York: Columbia University Press.

—— (1989a). *International Institutions and State Power: Essays in International Relations Theory*. Boulder: Westview Press.

—— (1989b). 'International Relations Theory: Contributions of a Feminist Standpoint', *Millennium: Journal of International Studies*, 18/2: 245–55.

—— (1993). 'Institutional Theory and the Realist Challenge after the Cold War', in D. A. Baldwin, *Neorealism and Neoliberalism: The Contemporary Debate*. New York: Columbia University Press, 269–301.

—— (1995). 'Hobbes's Dilemma and Institutional Change in World Politics: Sovereignty in International Society', in H.-H. Holm and G. Sørensen (eds), *Whose World Order? Uneven Globalization and the End of the Cold War*. Boulder: Westview Press, 165–87.

Keohane, R. O. and Hoffmann, S. (eds) (1991). *The New European Community: Decisionmaking and Institutional Change*. Boulder: Westview Press.

Keohane, R. O. and Martin, L. L. (1995). 'The Promise of Institutionalist Theory', *International Security*, 20/1: 39–51.

Keohane, R. O. and Milner, H. V. (eds) (1996). *Internationalization and Domestic Politics*. New York: Cambridge University Press.

Keohane, R. O. and Nye, J. S. (eds) (1971). *Transnational Relations and World Politics*. Cambridge, Mass.: Harvard University Press.

—— (1975). 'International Interdependence and Integration', in F. Greenstein and N. Polsby (eds), *Handbook of Political Science*, viii: *International Politics*. Reading, Mass.: Addison-Wesley, 363–414.

—— (1977). *Power and Interdependence: World Politics in Transition*. Boston: Little, Brown.

—— (1987). 'Power and Interdependence Revisited', *International Organization*, 41/4: 725–53.

—— (1993). 'Introduction: The End of the Cold War in Europe', in R. O. Keohane, J. S. Nye and S. Hoffmann (eds) (1993: 1–23).

Keohane, R. O., Nye, J. S. and Hoffmann, S. (eds) (1993). *After the Cold War: International Institutions and State Strategies in Europe, 1989–1991*. Cambridge, Mass.: Harvard University Press.

Keynes, J. M. (1963). *Essays in Persuasion*. New York: Norton.

Kindleberger, C. (1973). *The World in Depression, 1929–1939*. Berkeley: University of California Press.

Kiras, J. D. (2005). 'Terrorism and Globalization', in J. Bayliss and S. Smith (eds), *The Globalization of World Politics*. Oxford and New York: Oxford University Press, 480–97.

Kissinger, H. (1994). *Diplomacy*. New York: Simon & Schuster.

Klarevas, L. (2004). 'Political Realism: A Culprit for the 9/11 Attacks', *Harvard International Review*, Fall: 18–22.

Knutsen, T. L. (1997). *A History of International Relations Theory*. Manchester: Manchester University Press.

Kozak, D. C. (1988). 'The Bureaucratic Politics Approach: The Evolution of the Paradigm', in D. C. Kozak and J. Keagle (eds) (1988: 3–15).

Kozak, D. C. and Keagle, J. (eds) (1988). *Bureaucratic Politics and National Security: Theory and Practice*. Boulder: Lynne Rienner.

Krasner, S. D. (ed.) (1983). *International Regimes*. Ithaca: Cornell University Press.

Krasner, S. D. (1988). 'Sovereignty: Institutional Perspective', *Comparative Political Studies*, 21: 66–94.

—— (1992). 'Realism, Imperialism, and Democracy: A Response to Gilbert', *Political Theory*, 20/1: 38–52.

—— (1993). 'Westphalia and All That', in J. Goldstein and R. O. Keohane (eds), *Ideas and Foreign Policy: Beliefs, Institutional and Political Change*. Ithaca: Cornell University Press, 235–65.

—— (1994). 'International Political Economy: Abiding Discord', *Review of International Political Economy*, 1/1: 13–19.

—— (1999). *Sovereignty: Organized Hypocrisy*. Princeton: Princeton University Press.

Kratochwil, F. (1989). *Rules, Norms and Decisions*. Cambridge: Cambridge University Press.

Krauthammer, C. (2004). 'Democratic Realism: An American Foreign Policy for a Unipolar World', Washington: Irving Kristol Lecture.

Kuhn, T. S. (1970). *The Structure of Scientific Revolutions*. Chicago: University of Chicago Press.

Lake, D. A. (1992). 'Powerful Pacifists: Democratic States and War', *American Political Science Review*, 86/1: 24–37.

—— (2001). 'Beyond Anarchy: The Importance of Security Institutions', *International Security*, 26/1: 129–60.

Lal, D. (1983). *The Poverty of 'Development Economics'*. London: Institute of Economic Affairs.

Landry, D. and Maclean, G. (1993). *Materialist Feminism*. Oxford: Blackwell.

Lapidoth, R. (1992). 'Sovereignty in Transition', *Journal of International Affairs*, 45/2: 325–47.

Larsen, H. (1997). *Foreign Policy and Discourse Analysis: France, Britain, and Europe*. London: Routledge.

Lasswell, H. (1958). *Politics: Who Gets What, When, How*. New York: World Publishing.

Layne, C. (1993). 'The Unipolar Illusion: Why New Great Powers Will Rise', *International Security*, 17: 5–51.

—— (1994). 'Kant or Cant: The Myth of the Democratic Peace', *International Security*, 19/2: 5–49.

Lee, K. (1993). 'To De-Industrialize: Is It so Irrational?', in A. Dobson and P. Lucardie (eds), *The Politics of Nature: Explorations in Green Political Theory*. London: Routledge.

Leite, N. (1951). *The Operational Code of the Politburo*. New York: McGraw Hill.

Lenin, V. I. (1939). *Imperialism: The Highest Stage of Capitalism*. New York: International Publishers.

Levy, M. A., Young, O. R. and Zürn, M. (1995). 'The Study of International Regimes', *European Journal of International Relations*, 1/3: 267–330.

Lewis, W. A. (1970). *Theory of Economic Growth*. New York: Harper & Row.

Liberal International (1997). 'The Liberal Agenda for the 21st Century: The Quality of Liberty in Open Civic Societies', Oxford: Congress of Liberal International.

Lijphart, A. (1994). *Electoral Systems and Party Systems*. Oxford: Oxford University Press.

Lindberg, T. (2005). 'The Atlanticist Community', in T. Lindberg (ed.), *Beyond Paradise and Power*. Oxon: Routledge, 215–35.

Linklater, A. (1989). *Beyond Realism and Marxism*. New York: St Martin's Press.

—— (1990). *Beyond Realism and Marxism: Critical Theory and International Relations*. Basingstoke: Macmillan.

—— (1996). 'The Achievements of Critical Theory', in S. Smith et al. (eds) (1996: 279–98).

—— (1998). *The Transformation of Political Community: Ethical Foundations of the Post-Westphalian Era*. Columbia: University of South Carolina Press.

Lipson, C. (1984). 'International Cooperation in Economic and Security Affairs', *World Politics*, 37 (Oct.): 1–23.

—— (2003). *Reliable Partners: How Democracies Have Made a Separate Peace*. Princeton: Princeton University Press.

List, F. (1966). *The National System of Political Economy*. New York: Kelley.

Little, R. (1996). 'The Growing Relevance of Pluralism?', in S. Smith et al. (eds) (1996: 66–86).

Lodge, J. (ed.) (1993). *The European Community and the Challenge of the Future*. New York: St Martin's Press.

Lomborg, B. (2001). *The Sceptical Environmentalist*. Cambridge: Cambridge University Press.

Lowi, M. R. (1993). 'Bridging the Divide: Transboundary Resource Disputes and the Case of West Bank Water', *International Security*, 18/1: 113–38.

Ludde-Neurath, R. (1985). 'State Intervention and Export-Oriented Development in South Korea', in G. White and R. Wade (eds), *Developmental States in East Asia*. Brighton: IDS Research Reports No. 16, 62–126.

Lyotard, J.-F. (1984). *The Postmodern Condition: A Report on Knowledge*. Manchester: Manchester University Press.

McGlen, N. and Sarkess, M. (1993). *Women in Foreign Policy: The Insiders*. New York: Routledge.

McGwire, M. (1998). 'NATO expansion: "A Policy Error of Historic Importance"', *Review of International Studies*, 24 (Jan.): 23–42.

Machiavelli, N. (1961). *The Prince*, trans. G. Bull. Harmondsworth: Penguin.

—— (1984). *The Prince*, trans. P. Bondanella and M. Musa. New York: Oxford University Press.

Mann, M. (2003). *Incoherent Empire*. London: Verso.

Maoz, Z. and Russett, B. (1993). 'Normative and Structural Causes of Democratic Peace, 1946–86'. *American Political Science Review*, 87/3: 624–38.

Martinussen, J. (1997). *State, Society and Market: A Guide to Competing Theories of Development*. New York: St Martin's Press.

Marx, K. and Engels, F. (1955). *The Communist Manifesto*, ed. S. Beer. New York: Appleton-Century-Crofts.

Mayall, J. (1989). *Nationalism and International Society*. Cambridge: Cambridge University Press.

—— (1996). *The New Interventionism: 1991–1994*. Cambridge: Cambridge University Press.

Mearsheimer, J. (1993). 'Back to the Future: Instability in Europe after the Cold War', in S. Lynn-Jones (ed.), *The Cold War and After: Prospects for Peace*. Cambridge, Mass.: MIT Press, 141–92.

—— (1995a). 'A Realist Reply', *International Security*, 20/1: 82–93.

—— (1995b). 'The False Promise of International Institutions', in M. E. Brown et al. (eds), *The Perils of Anarchy: Contemporary Realism and International Security*. Cambridge, Mass.: MIT Press, 332–77.

—— (2001). *The Tragedy of Great Power Politics*, New York: W. W. Norton.

Meinecke, F. (1957). *Machiavellism: The Doctrine of Raison d'Etat and Its Place in Modern History*. New Haven: Yale University Press.

Mill, J. S. (1963). 'A Few Words on Non-Intervention', in G. Himmelfarb (eds), *Essays on Politics and Culture: John Stuart Mill*. New York: Anchor.

Milner, Helen (1991). 'The Assumption of Anarchy in International Relations Theory: A Critique', *Review of International Studies*, 17: 67–85.

Mitchell, J. (1977). *Women's Estate*. Harmondsworth: Penguin.

Mitrany, D. (1966). *A Working Peace System*, repr. with introd. by H. J. Morgenthau. Chicago: Quadrangle.

Moravcsik, A. (1991). 'Negotiating the Single European Act: National Interests and Conventional Statecraft in the European Community', *International Organization*, 45: 19–56.

—— (1997). 'Taking Preferences Seriously: A Liberal Theory of International Politics', *International Organization*, 51/4: 513–53.

Morgenthau, H. J. (1960). *Politics among Nations: The Struggle for Power and Peace*, 3rd edn. New York: Knopf.

—— (1965). *Scientific Man versus Power Politics*. Chicago: Phoenix Books.

—— (1985). *Politics among Nations: The Struggle for Power and Peace*, 6th edn. New York: Knopf.

Morrison, K. (1995). *Marx, Durkheim, Weber*. London: Sage.

Mueller, J. (1990). *Retreat from Doomsday: The Obsolescence of Major War*. New York: Basic Books.

—— (1995). *Quiet Cataclysm: Reflections on the Recent Transformation of World Politics*. New York: HarperCollins.

—— (2004). *The Remnants of War*, Ithaca: Cornell University Press.

Münkler, H. (2005). *Imperien*, Berlin: Rohwolt.

Myers, N. and Simon, J. L. (1994). *Scarcity or Abundance? A Debate on the Environment*. New York: Norton.

Myrdal, G. (1957). *Economic Theory and Underdeveloped Regions*. London: Duckworth.

Naisbitt, J. (1994). *Global Paradox*. New York: Avon.

Nardin, T. (1983). *Law, Morality and the Relations of States*. Princeton: Princeton University Press.

Nardin, T. and Mapel, D. (eds) (1992). *Traditions of International Ethics*. Cambridge: Cambridge University Press.

Navari, C. (1989). 'The Great Illusion Revisited: The International Theory of Norman Angell', *Review of International Studies*, 15: 341–58.

Nederveen Pieterse, J. (2000). 'Trends in Development Theory', in R. Palan (ed.), *Global Political Economy: Contemporary Theories*. London: Routledge, 197–215.

Neibuhr, R. (1932). *Moral Man and Immoral Society*. New York: Scribner's.

Nicholls, D. (1974). *Three Varieties of Pluralism*. London: Macmillan.

Nicholson, M. (1996a). 'The Continued Significance of Positivism?', in S. Smith et al. (eds) (1996: 128–49).

—— (1996b). *Causes and Consequences in International Relations*. London: Pinter.

Nixson, F. (1988). 'The Political Economy of Bargaining with Transnational Corporations: Some Preliminary Observations', *Manchester Papers on Development*, 4/3: 377–90.

NSS (2002). *The National Security Strategy of the United States of America*. Washington, DC: Office of the President.

Nunn, E. (1996). 'The Rational Choice Approach to IPE', in D. N. Balaam and M. Veseth, *Introduction to International Political Economy*. Upper Saddle River: Prentice Hall, 77–99.

Nye, J. S., Jr. (1988). 'Neorealism and Neoliberalism', *World Politics*, 40/2: 235–51.

—— (1990). *Bound to Lead: The Changing Nature of American Power*. New York: Basic.

—— (1993). *Understanding International Conflicts*. New York: HarperCollins.

—— (2002). *The Paradox of American Power*. New York: Oxford University Press.

—— (2003). 'US Power and Strategy after Iraq', *Foreign Affairs*, 82/4: 60–73.

—— (2004). *Understanding International Conflicts: An Introduction to Theory and History*. Harlow: Pearson Higher Education/Longman—with foreword by Stanley Hoffmann.

Oakeshott, M. (1966). *Experience and its Modes*. Cambridge: Cambridge University Press.

—— (1975). *Hobbes on Civil Association*. Oxford: Blackwell.

OECD (Organization for the Economic Cooperation and Development) (1993). *Trade Policy Issues*. Paris: OECD.

Ohmae, K. (1993). 'The Rise of the Region State', *Foreign Affairs*, 72/2: 78–87.

Onuf, N. (1989). *A World of Our Making*. Columbia: University of South Carolina Press.

—— (1995). 'Intervention for the Common Good', in G. Lyons and M. Mastanduno (eds), *Beyond Westphalia?* Baltimore: Johns Hopkins University Press, 43–58.

Osiander, A. (1994). *The States System of Europe, 1640–1990*. Oxford: Clarendon Press.

Oye, K. A. (ed.) (1986). *Cooperation under Anarchy*. Princeton: Princeton University Press.

Palan, R. (2002). 'New Trends in Global Political Economy', in R. Palan (ed.), *Global Political Economy: Contemporary Theories*. London: Routledge, 1–19.

Parish, R. and Peceny, M. (2002). 'Kantian Liberalism and the Collective Defense of Democracy in Latin America', *Journal of Peace Research*, 39/2: 229–50.

Parry, J. H. (1966). *Europe and a Wider World: 1415–1715*, 3rd edn. London: Hutchinson.

Paterson, M. (1996). 'Green Politics', in S. Burchill and A. Linklater (eds), *Theories of International Relations*. London: Macmillan, 252–75.

Payne, A. (2005). *The Global Politics of Unequal Development*. Basingstoke: Palgrave Macmillan.

Pearlstein, R. M. (2004). *Fatal Future? Transnational Terrorism and the New Global Disorder*. Austin: University of Texas Press.

Peterson, M. J. (1992). 'Transnational Activity, International Society and World Politics', *Millennium*, 21: 371–88.

Peterson, V. S. and Runyan, A. S. (1993). *Global Gender Issues*. Boulder: Westview Press.

Plato (1974). *The Republic*. Indianapolis: Hackett.

Polanyi, K. (1957). *The Great Transformation: The Political and Economic Origins of Our Time*. New York: Farrar Rinehart.

Pollack, M.A. (2005). 'Theorizing the European Union: International Organization, Domestic Polity, or Experiment in New Governance?', *Annual Review of Political Science*: 357–98.

Pollard, S. (1971). *The Idea of Progress: History and Society*. Harmondsworth: Penguin.

Pompa, L. (1982). *Vico: Selected Writings*. Cambridge: Cambridge University Press.

Porter, G., Brown, J. and Chasek, P. (2000). *Global Environmental Politics*. Boulder: Westview Press.

Prebisch, R. (1950). *The Economic Development of Latin America and Its Principal Problems.* New York: United Nations.

Price, R. and Reus-Smit, C. (1998). 'Dangerous Liaisons? Critical International Theory and Constructivism', *European Journal of International Relations,* 4/3: 259–94.

Rapaport, A. (1960). *Fights, Games, Debates.* Ann Arbor: University of Michigan Press.

Ravenhill, J. (ed.) (2005). *Global Political Economy.* Oxford: Oxford University Press.

Reich, R. (1992). *The Work of Nations: Preparing Ourselves for 21st-Century Capitalism.* New York: Vintage.

Reus-Smit, C. (1997). 'The Constitutional Structure of International Society and the Nature of Fundamental Institutions', *International Organization,* 51/4: 555–89.

Rhodes, E. (2003). 'American Grand Strategy: The Imperial Logic of Bush's Liberal Agenda', *Policy,* Summer: 1–14.

Ricardo, D. (1973). *The Principles of Political Economy and Taxation.* London: Dent.

Richardson, J. (1990). 'The Academic Study of International Relations', in J. D. B. Miller and R. J. Vincent (eds), *Order and Violence: Hedley Bull and International Relations.* Oxford: Clarendon Press, 140–85.

Risse, T., Ropp, S. C. and Sikkink, K. (eds), (1999). *The Power of Human Rights: International Norms and Domestic Change.* Cambridge: Cambridge University Press.

Risse-Kappen, T. (ed.) (1995). *Bringing Transnational Relations Back In.* Cambridge: Cambridge University Press.

Rittberger, V. (ed.) (1993). *Regime Theory and International Relations.* Oxford: Clarendon Press.

Rodrik, D. (1997). *Has Globalization Gone Too Far?* Washington DC: Institute for International Economics.

Rosati, J. A. (2000). 'The Power of Human Cognition in the Study of World Politics', *International Studies Review,* 2/3: 45–79.

Rosato, S. (2003). 'The Flawed Logic of Democratic Peace Theory', *American Political Science Review,* 97 (November): 585–602.

Rose, G. (1998). 'Neoclassical Realism and Theories of Foreign Policy', *World Politics,* 15/1: 144–72.

Rosecrance, R. (1986). *The Rise of the Trading State: Commerce and Conquest in the Modern World.* New York: Basic Books.

—— (1995). 'The Obsolescence of Territory', *New Perspectives Quarterly,* 12/1: 44–50.

—— (1999). *The Rise of the Virtual State.* New York: Basic Books.

Rosenau, J. N. (1966). 'Pre-theories and Theories and Foreign Policy', in R. B. Farrell (ed.), *Approaches to Comparative and International Politics.* Evanston: Northwestern University Press.

—— (1967). 'Games International Relations Scholars Play', *Journal of International Affairs,* 21: 293–303.

—— (1980). *The Study of Global Interdependence: Essays on the Transnationalisation of World Affairs.* New York: Nichols.

—— (1990). *Turbulence in World Politics: A Theory of Change and Continuity.* Princeton: Princeton University Press.

—— (1992). 'Citizenship in a Changing Global Order', in J. N. Rosenau and E.-O. Czempiel (eds), *Governance Without Government: Order and Change in World Politics.* Cambridge: Cambridge University Press, 272–94.

—— (2003). *Distant Proximities: Dynamics Beyond Globalization:* Princeton: Princeton University Press.

Rosenblum, N. L. (1978). *Bentham's Theory of the Modern State.* Cambridge, Mass.: Harvard University Press.

Rostow, W. W. (1960). *The Stages of Economic Growth: A Non-Communist Manifesto.* Cambridge: Cambridge University Press.

—— (1978). *The World Economy: History and Prospect.* Austin: University of Texas Press.

Rousseau, J.-J. (1964). 'Que l'état de guerre nait de l'état social', in *Œuvres Complètes,* iii. Paris: Pléiade.

Ruggie, J. G. (1998). *Constructing the World Polity: Essays on International Institutionalization.* London: Routledge.

Russett, B. M. (1985). 'The Mysterious Case of Vanishing Hegemony, or, Is Mark Twain Really Dead?' *International Organization,* 36/2: 207–34.

—— (1989). 'Democracy and Peace', in B. Russett et al. (eds), *Choices in World Politics: Sovereignty and Interdependence.* New York: Freeman, 245–61.

—— (1993). *Grasping the Democratic Peace: Principles for a Post-Cold War World*. Princeton: Princeton University Press.

Sachs, W. (ed.) (1992). *The Development Dictionary*. London: Zed.

—— (ed.) (1993). *Global Ecology: A New Arena of Political Conflict*. London: Zed.

Samuelson, P. A. (1967). *Economics: An Introductory Analysis*, 7th edn. New York: McGraw Hill.

Schelling, T. (1980). *The Strategy of Conflict*. Cambridge, Mass: Harvard University Press.

—— (1996). 'The Diplomacy of Violence', in R. Art and R. Jervis (eds), *International Politics*, 4th edn. New York: HarperCollins, 168–82.

Schmid, A. P. (2005). 'Terrorism and Human Rights: A Perspective from the United Nations', *Terrorism and Political Violence*, 17: 25–35.

Schmidt, B. C. (1998). *The Political Discourse of Anarchy: A Disciplinary History of International Relations*. Albany: SUNY Press.

Schneider, G. (1995). 'Integration and Conflict: The Empirical Relevance of Security Communities', paper for 2nd Pan-European Conference on International Relations. 13–16 Sept., Paris.

Scholte, J. A. (2005). *Globalization: A Critical Introduction*, 2nd edn. London: Macmillan.

Schwartz, H. (2000). *States versus Markets: The Emergence of a Global Economy*, 2nd edn. London: Macmillan.

Schweller, R. L. (1992). 'Domestic Structure and Preventive War: Are Democracies More Pacific?', *World Politics*, 44/2: 235–69.

—— (1998). *Deadly Imbalances: Tripolarity and Hitler's Strategy of World Conquest*. New York: Columbia University Press.

Senghaas, D. (1989). 'The Development Problematic: A Macro-Micro Perspective', *Journal of Peace Research*, 26/1: 57–69.

Shaw, M. (1992). 'Global Society and Global Responsibility', *Millennium*, 21: 421–34.

Simon, J. and Kahn, H. (eds) (1984). *The Resourceful Earth*. Oxford: Blackwell.

Singer, H. and Wildavsky, A. (1993). *The Real World Order: Zones of Peace, Zones of Turmoil*. Chatham, NJ: Chatham House.

Singer, J. D. (1961). 'The Level-of-Analysis Problem in International Relations', *World Politics*, 145/1: 77–92.

Smith, M. J. (1992). 'Liberalism and International Reform', in T. Nardin and D. Mapel (eds) (1992: 201–24).

Smith, S. (1995). 'The Self-Images of a Discipline', in K. Booth and S. Smith (eds), *International Relations Theory Today*. University Park: Pennsylvania State University Press; Cambridge Polity, 24–5.

—— (1997). 'New Approaches to International Theory', in J. Baylis and S. Smith (eds), *The Globalization of World Politics*. Oxford: Oxford University Press, 165–90.

Smith, S., Booth, K. and Zalewski, M. (eds) (1996). *International Theory: Positivism and Beyond*. Cambridge: Cambridge University Press.

Sørensen, G. (1983). *Transnational Corporations in Peripheral Societies: Contributions Towards Self-Centered Development?* Aalborg: Aalborg University Press.

—— (1992). 'Kant and Processes of Democratization: Consequences for Neorealist Thought', *Journal of Peace Research*, 29/4: 397–414.

—— (1993a). *Democracy and Democratization: Processes and Prospects in a Changing World*. Boulder: Westview Press.

—— (1993b). 'Democracy, Authoritarianism and State Strength', *European Journal of Development Research*, 5/1: 6–34.

—— (1997). 'International Conflict and Cooperation: Toward an Analysis of Contemporary Statehood', *Review of International Studies*, 23/3 (July): 253–69.

—— (1998). 'IR Theory After the Cold War', *Review of International Studies*, 24/5: 83–100.

—— (1999). 'Sovereignty: Change and Continuity in a Fundamental Institution', *Political Studies*, 47: 590–604.

—— (2001). *Changes in Statehood: The Transformation of International Relations*. London and New York: Palgrave.

—— (2004). *The Transformation of the State: Beyond the Myth of Retreat*. London and New York: Palgrave Macmillan.

Spegele, R. (1996). *Political Realism in International Theory*. Cambridge: Cambridge University Press.

Spero, J. E. (1985). *The Politics of International Economic Relations*. London: Allen & Unwin.

Spruyt, H. (2002). 'New Institutionalism and International Relations', in R. Palan (ed.), *Global*

Political Economy: Contemporary Theories. London: Routledge, 130–43.

Steans, J. (1998). *Gender and International Relations: An Introduction*. Cambridge: Polity.

Stein, A. A. (1990). *Why Nations Cooperate: Circumstance and Choice in International Relations*. Ithaca: Cornell University Press.

Steinbrunner, J. (1974). *The Cybernetic Theory of Decision*. Princeton: Princeton University Press.

Stent, A. E. (2005). 'Review of Ted Hopf: Social Construction of International Politics', *Journal of Cold War Studies*, 7/1: 184–86.

Stoessinger, J. G. (1993). *Why Nations Go to War*. New York: St Martin's Press.

Stohl, M. and G. A. Lopez (eds) (1984). *The State as Terrorist: The Dynamics of Governmental Violence and Repression*. Westport, Conn.: Greenwich Press.

Strange, S. (1970). 'International Economics and International Relations: A Case of Mutual Neglect', *International Affairs*, 46/2: 304–15.

—— (1987). 'The Persistent Myth of Lost Hegemony', *International Organization*, 41: 551–74.

—— (1988). *States and Markets: An Introduction to International Political Economy*. London: Pinter.

—— (1995). 'Theoretical Underpinnings: Conflicts between International Relations and International Political Economy', paper for the British International Studies Association Annual Meeting, Dec., Southampton.

Streeten, P. P. (1979). 'Multinationals Revisited', *Finance and Development*, 16/2: 39–43.

Stubbs, R. and Underhill, G. R. D. (2000). *Political Economy and the Changing Global Order*. Oxford: Oxford University Press.

Swerdlow, A. (1990). 'Motherhood and the Subversion of the Military State: Women Strike for Peace Confronts the House Committee on Un-American Activities', in J.-B. Elshtain and S. Tobias (eds) (1990), *Women, Militarism, and War: Essays in Politics, History, and Social Theory*. Savage, MD: Rowman & Littlefield.

Sylvester, C. (1994). *Feminist Theory and International Relations in a Postmodern Era*. Cambridge: Cambridge University Press.

Tannenwald, N. (2005). 'Ideas and Explanation: Advancing the Theoretical Agenda', *Journal of Cold War Studies*, 7/2: 13–42.

Taylor, A. J. P. (1957). *The Trouble Makers: Dissent over Foreign Policy 1792–1939*. London: Panther.

Tetreault, M. A. (1992). 'Women and Revolution: A Framework for Analysis', in V. S. Peterson (ed.), *Gendered States: Feminist (Re) Visions of International Relations Theory*. Boulder: Lynne Rienner.

Thompson, J. E. and Krasner, S. D. (1989). 'Global Transactions and the Consolidation of Sovereignty', in E.-O. Czempiel and J. N. Rosenau (eds), *Global Changes and Theoretical Challenges: Approaches to World Politics for the 1990s*. Lexington, Mass.: Lexington Books, 195–221.

Thompson, K. W. (1980). *Masters of International Thought: Major Twentieth-Century Theorists and the World Crisis*. Baton Rouge: Louisiana State University Press.

Thompson, W. R. (1996). 'Democracy and Peace: Putting the Cart Before the Horse?', *International Organization*, 50/1: 141–75.

Thucydides (1972). *History of the Peloponnesian War*, trans. R. Warner. London: Penguin.

—— (1980). *The Peloponnesian War*. Harmondsworth: Penguin.

Tickner, J. A. (1992). *Gender in International Relations*. New York: Columbia University Press.

Tilly, C. (1992). *Coercion, Capital and European States*. Oxford: Blackwell.

Tong, R. (1989). *Feminist Thought: A Comprehensive Introduction*. London: Unwin Hyman.

Toye, J. (1987). *Dilemmas of Development: Reflections on the Counterrevolution in Development Theory*. Oxford: Blackwell.

Tranholm-Mikkelsen, J. (1991). 'Neofunctionalism: Obstinate or Obsolete? A Reappraisal in Light of the New Dynamism of the EC', *Millennium*, 20: 1–22.

True, J. (1996). 'Feminism', in S. Burchill and A. Linklater (eds), *Theories of International Relations*. London: Macmillan, 210–51.

Tucker, R. W. (1977). *The Inequality of Nations*. New York: Basic Books.

Twing, S. (1998). *Myths, Models, and US Foreign Policy: The Cultural Shaping of Three Cold Warriors*. Boulder: Lynne Rienner.

Underdal, A. (1992). 'The Concept of Regime "Effectiveness" ', *Cooperation and Conflict*, 27/3: 227–40.

UN (United Nations), *Statistical Yearbook*, annual edns. New York: UN.

—— (1997a). *World Economic and Social Survey 1997*. New York: UN.

—— (1997b). *World Investment Report 1997*. New York: UN.

UNDP (United Nations Development Programme) (Annually). *Human Development Report*. New York: Oxford University Press.

UN General Assembly (1970). *Declaration on Principles of International Law*, Resolution 2625.

Vasquez, J. (1995). 'The Post-Positivist Debate', in K. Booth and S. Smith (eds), *International Relations Theory Today*. Cambridge: Polity, 217–40.

—— (1996). *Classics of International Relations*, 3rd edn. Upper Saddle River, NJ: Prentice-Hall.

Vincent, R. J. (1986). *Human Rights and International Relations*. Cambridge: Cambridge University Press.

—— (1990). 'Grotius, Human Rights, and Intervention', in H. Bull et al. (1990: 241–56).

Vincent, R. J. and **Wilson, P.** (1993). 'Beyond Non-Intervention', in I. Forbes and M. Hoffmann (eds), *Political Theory, International Relations, and the Ethics of Intervention*. London: Macmillan.

Viner, J. (1958). *The Long View and the Short: Studies in Economic Theory and Policy*. New York: Free Press.

Wade, R. (1985). 'State Intervention in Development: Neoclassical Theory and Taiwanese Practice', in G. White and R. Wade (eds), *Developmental States in East Asia*. Brighton: IDS Research Reports No. 16: 23–62.

Waldron, J. (2003). 'Security and Liberty: The Image of Balance', *The Journal of Political Philosophy*, 11/2: 191–210.

Walker, R. B. J. (1993). *Inside/Outside: International Relations as Political Theory*. Cambridge: Cambridge University Press.

—— (1995). 'International Relations and the Concept of the Political', in K. Booth and S. Smith (eds), *International Relations Theory Today*. University Park: Pennsylvania State University Press, 306–28.

Wallerstein, I. (1974). *The Modern World System*, i. New York: Academic Press.

—— (1979). *The Capitalist World-Economy: Essays*. Cambridge: Cambridge University Press.

—— (1983). *Historical Capitalism*. London: Verso.

—— (1984). *The Politics of the World-Economy: The States, Movements, and Civilizations: Essays*. Cambridge: Cambridge University Press.

—— (1991). *Unthinking Social Science: The Limits of Nineteenth-Century Paradigms*. Cambridge: Polity.

—— (2004). *World-Systems Analysis: An Introduction*. Durham: Duke University Press.

Walt, S. M. (1998). 'International Relations: One World, Many Theories', *Foreign Policy* (Spring): 29–46.

Waltz, K. N. (1959). *Man, the State and War: A Theoretical Analysis*. New York: Columbia University Press.

—— (1979). *Theory of International Politics*. New York: McGraw-Hill; Reading: Addison-Wesley.

—— (1986). 'Reflections on "Theory of International Politics": A Response to My Critics', in R. O. Keohane (ed.), *Neorealism and Its Critics*. New York: Columbia University Press, 322–47.

—— (1993). 'The Emerging Structure of International Politics', *International Security*, 18/2: 44–79.

—— (2002). 'Structural Realism after the Cold War', in G. J. Ikenberry (ed.), *America Unrivaled: The Future of the Balance of Power*. Ithaca and London: Cornell University Press, 29–68.

Watson, A. (1982). *Diplomacy: The Dialogue between States*. London: Methuen.

—— (1992). *The Evolution of International Society*. London: Routledge.

Webber, M. (1995). 'Changing Places in East Asia', in G. I. Clark and W. B. Kim (eds), *Asian NIEs and the Global Economy*. Baltimore: Johns Hopkins University Press.

Weber, M. (1964). *The Theory of Social and Economic Organization*. New York: Free Press.

—— (1977). *Critique of Stammler* (trans. Guy Oakes). New York: Free Press.

Weiss, J. (1988). *Industry in Developing Countries: Theory, Policy and Evidence*. London: Croom Helm.

Weiss, L. (1998). *The Myth of the Powerless State*. New York: Cornell University Press.

Weiss, T. G. and **Collins, C.** (1996). *Humanitarian Challenges and Intervention*. Boulder: Westview Press.

Weller, M. (ed.) (1993). *Iraq and Kuwait: The Hostilities and Their Aftermath*. Cambridge: Grotius Publications.

Welsh, J. M. (1995). *Edmund Burke and International Relations*. London: Macmillan.

Wendt, A. (1987). 'The Agent–Structure Problem in International Relations Theory', *International Organization*, 41: 335–70.

—— (1992), 'Anarchy is What States Make of It', *International Organization*, 46: 394–419.

—— (1994). 'Collective Identity Formation and the International State', *American Political Science Review*, 88: 384–96.

—— (1995). 'Constructing International Politics', *International Security*, 20/1: 71–81.

—— (1999). *Social Theory of International Politics*. Cambridge: Cambridge University Press.

Wheeler, N. (1996). 'Guardian Angel or Global Gangster: A Review of the Ethical Claims of International Society', *Political Studies*, 44: 123–35.

White, G. (1984). 'Developmental States and Socialist Industrialisation in the Third World', *Journal of Development Studies*, 21/1: 97–120.

Wight, M. (1966). 'Why is There No International Theory?', in H. Butterfield and M. Wight (eds), *Diplomatic Investigations*. London: Allen & Unwin, 12–33.

—— (1977). *Systems of States*. Leicester: Leicester University Press.

—— (1986). *Power Politics*, 2nd edn. Harmondsworth: Penguin.

—— (1987). 'An Anatomy of International Thought', *Review of International Studies*, 13: 221–7.

—— (1991). *International Theory: The Three Traditions*, ed. G. Wight and B. Porter. Leicester: Leicester University Press.

Williams, J. and Little, R. (2006). *Anarchical Society in a Globalized World*. New York: Palgrave Macmillan.

World Bank (1994). *World Tables 1994*. Washington, DC: World Bank.

—— (1996). *World Development Report 1997*. New York: Oxford University Press.

World Commission on Environment and Development (1987). *Our Common Future* (The Brundtland Report). New York: Oxford University Press.

Yetiv, S. A. (2004). *Explaining Foreign Policy: US Decision Making and the Persian Gulf War*. Baltimore: John Hopkins University Press.

Young, O. R. (1986). 'International Regimes: Toward a New Theory of Institutions', *World Politics*, 39/1: 104–22.

—— (1989). *International Cooperation: Building Regimes for Natural Resources and the Environment*. Ithaca: Cornell University Press.

Zacher, M. W. (1992). 'The Decaying Pillars of the Westphalian Temple', in J. N. Rosenau and E.-O. Czempiel (eds), *Governance Without Government: Order and Change in World Politics*. Cambridge: Cambridge University Press, 58–102.

Zacher, M. W. and Matthew, R. A. (1995). 'Liberal International Theory: Common Threads, Divergent Strands', in C. W. Kegley, Jr., *Controversies in International Relations: Realism and the Neoliberal Challenge*. New York: St Martin's Press, 107–50.

Zakaria, F. (1998). *From Wealth to Power: The Unusual Origins of America's World Role*. Princeton: Princeton University Press.

Zalewski, M. (1993). 'Feminist Standpoint Theory Meets International Relations Theory: A Feminist Version of David and Goliath?', *Fletcher Forum*, 17: 13–32.

Zartman, W. I. (1995). *Collapsed States: The Disintegration and Restoration of Legitimate Authority*. Boulder: Lynne Rienner.

Zehfuss, M. (2002). *Constructivism in International Relations: The Politics of Reality*. Cambridge: Cambridge University Press.

Zürn, M. (1995). 'The Challenge of Globalization and Individualization: A View from Europe', in H.-H. Holm and G. Sørensen (eds), *Whose World Order? Uneven Globalization and the End of the Cold War*. Boulder: Westview Press, 137–65.

INDEX

Page numbers followed by a star (*) refer to items in the glossary